D1063809

The Greek Imperative Mood
in the New Testament

Studies in Biblical Greek

D. A. Carson
General Editor

Vol. 12

PETER LANG
New York • Washington, D.C./Baltimore • Bern
Frankfurt • Berlin • Brussels • Vienna • Oxford

Joseph D. Fantin

The Greek Imperative Mood in the New Testament

A Cognitive and Communicative Approach

PETER LANG
New York • Washington, D.C./Baltimore • Bern
Frankfurt • Berlin • Brussels • Vienna • Oxford

Library of Congress Cataloging-in-Publication Data

Fantin, Joseph D.
The Greek imperative mood in the New Testament: a cognitive
and communicative approach / Joseph D. Fantin.
p. cm. — (Studies in biblical Greek; v. 12)
Includes bibliographical references and index.
1. Greek language, Biblical—Imperative. 2. Greek language—Imperative.
3. Bible. N.T.—Language, style. 4. Bible. N.T. Greek—
Criticism, Textual. I. Title.
PA344.I3F36   487'.4—dc22   2009044510
ISBN 978-0-8204-7487-8
ISSN 0897-7828

Bibliographic information published by **Die Deutsche Nationalbibliothek**.
Die Deutsche Nationalbibliothek lists this publication in the "Deutsche
Nationalbibliografie"; detailed bibliographic data is available
on the Internet at http://dnb.d-nb.de/.

The paper in this book meets the guidelines for permanence and durability
of the Committee on Production Guidelines for Book Longevity
of the Council of Library Resources.

Printed in Germany

To Robin

Contents

Illustrations

Abbreviations

ASV   American Standard Version

BAGD Bauer, W., W. F. Arndt, F. W. Gingrich, and F. W. Danker. *A Greek English-Lexicon of the New Testament and Other Early Christian Literature*. 2d ed. Chicago, 1979

BDAG Bauer, W., F. W. Danker, W. F. Arndt, and F. W. Gingrich. *A Greek English-Lexicon of the New Testament and Other Early Christian Literature*. 3d ed. Chicago, 2000

BDF   Blass, F., A. Debrunner, and R. Funk. *A Greek Grammar of the New Testament*. Chicago, 1961

KJV   King James Version

LACUS Linguistic Association of Canada and The United States

LSJ   Liddell, H. G., R. Scott, H. S. Jones, and R. McKenzie. *A Greek-English Lexicon*. 9th ed. with a revised supplement, 1996. Oxford, 1940

MM   Moulton, J. H., and G. Milligan. *The Vocabulary of the Greek Testament Illustrated from the Papyri and Other Non-Literary Sources*. London, 1930

NA[26]   *Novum Testamentum Graece*. 26th rev. ed.

NA[27]   *Novum Testamentum Graece*. 27th rev. ed.

NASB New American Standard Bible

NCSL Neuro-cognitive stratificational linguistics

NET   New English Translation (NET Bible)

NIV   New International Version

NKJV   New King James Version

NRSV   New Revised Standard Version

PHI   Packard Humanities Institute. 2 CDs: CD-ROM #7, *PHI Greek Documentary Texts*; CD-ROM 5.3, Latin texts and Bible versions. [In this work only CD-ROM #7 was used].

P.Oxy   Oxyrhynchus Papyri

RSV   Revised Standard Version

RT   Relevance theory

SAT   Speech Act theory

TLG   *Thesaurus Lingua Graecae* (CD E)

UBS[4]   *The Greek New Testament*. 4th rev. ed.

In addition, traditional grammatical abbreviations (e.g., 2 sg; impv; etc.) and symbols representing manuscripts (from the above critical editions of the New Testament) are used.

Acknowledgments

It is impossible to acknowledge all the people who have influenced this work both formally and informally. In its original form as a PhD dissertation for Dallas Theological Seminary, the helpful and insightful comments of the readers, Buist Fanning, Daniel Wallace, and Richard Taylor, provided important direction without which this project would not have been possible. Additionally, credit must be given to the New Testament Department at Dallas Theological Seminary and especially Dr. Daniel Wallace from whom I took all my formal New Testament Greek courses. The input from the department's well planned exegetical training program and especially Dr. Wallace's personal knowledge and influence cannot be underestimated on the grammarian they helped to produce (and by extension, this book). Also I wish to thank D. A. Carson, the editor of the Studies in Biblical Greek series, for his kind words about the original dissertation and for inviting me to include my book in a series for which I have great respect. The patience of the staff at Peter Lang was appreciated as this project continually was delayed for various reasons. Jackie Pavlovic, my final production contact at Peter Lang, was especially helpful as I needed her input when I was finally able to devote significant time to complete the project. The completion of the book occurred on a semester sabbatical granted to me by Dallas Theological Seminary. I thank the administration for this generous opportunity to focus on projects such as this. I have been fortunate to have a number of quality interns who have helped with the tedious job of proof reading. I express my thanks to John Pullium, Matt Jones, Luke Tsai, and John Frawley. Finally, my wife Robin, daughter Jillian, and son David all helped in the creation of the index. A tedious task made more manageable by their help. Of course, a project such as this demands that one leave the nest and attempt to fly on his own. Thus, deficiencies are the responsibility of the author.

I also express appreciation to the Gramcord Institute for both its search engine and the Greek and Hebrew fonts used in this volume (greek parse and hebrew parse).

On a personal level, sincere thanks must be given to my wife Robin. She has endured the PhD process and the writing of this book. During this time she has worked hard as a RN, we had our daughter, Jillian, moved to the UK, had our son, David, and returned to Dallas Theological Seminary. My appreciation for her patience and sacrifice cannot be adequately expressed in a short acknowledgment. Like the original dissertation, it is to her that this work is dedicated.

Most importantly, I express my deepest gratitude to Christ himself without whom this project would not have been completed nor would it have had a purpose.

Soli Deo gloria

Joe Fantin

Prologue

The study of a *language* is a complicated endeavor. The belief that a language or an aspect of a language may be tidily isolated and analyzed like a child's puzzle or even a car engine is at best naïve and misleading. Puzzles and engines have self-contained contexts each with simple functions for themselves and their components. In all cases, the boundaries are well defined. In contrast, language, although a unique system in itself, is an important element of *communication*. Communication may use language and/or other means of transmitting a message from one party to its intended destination. Both language and communication are also elements of *human behavior*. However, unlike puzzles and engines, there are no clear boundaries between language and other means of communication; nor are there clear boundaries between language, communication, and other types of human behavior. Rather, there is interaction between language, context, nonverbal actions, etc., at many levels. Each is informed by the others to varying degrees. Each is related as if they have long branches which reach deep into the others that cannot be dislodged without destroying all the constituents involved.

The study of language cannot be divorced from a number of fields of study. Especially important are sociology, psychology, anthropology, and even philosophy. The communication process is significantly informed by these disciplines. Few areas of (morphological/syntactical) language analysis result in greater interaction between theoretical linguistics and sociology than the imperative mood. The interpretation of an imperative in a communication situation is often determined by sociological considerations such as politeness, etc. Therefore, although this study will primarily be linguistic, it must also consider (specifically) many nonlinguistic elements of communication and (generally) human behavior. I am not suggesting that others have failed to study the Greek imperative mood and other grammatical issues with an interest in the more general areas of communication and human behavior. Every appeal to context and issues related to the force of the imperative are concerned with broader matters. Nevertheless, to faithfully cover this topic, a more explicit emphasis on these areas must be made.

The psychological issues related to the imperative must also be explored. This is necessarily related to the communicative emphasis within a sociological framework. Although little is known about the brain and/or mind, consideration of what is known about this area must be incorporated when pursuing a linguistic topic even if observations are minimal or not always as conclusive as one would wish. Such work can be expanded as further knowledge is discovered. Cognitive questions must be asked. They will help keep conclusions psychologically plausible.

This book is titled, *The Greek Imperative Mood in the New Testament: A Cognitive and Communicative Approach*. Although a *cognitive* approach is essentially an aspect (though not so limited) of a *communicative* approach, it is nevertheless made explicit in the title because this area is often overlooked in analysis. This work will attempt to answer two questions. First, what does the imperative mood contribute to the communication situation? And second, what does the communication situation contribute to the imperative mood? The first question is concerned with the *meaning* of the imperative mood. The second is concerned with the context-dependent *usages* of the mood.

As I complete this work I am not unaware of a number of areas which may have been incorporated and which may have been of additional help to readers. My approach has been necessarily theoretical. This is because sound practical application must be based on solid theoretical grounds. Therefore, the reader may have wished to see more exegetical interaction than is presented. I have not attempted to avoid exegesis. I have included what I have felt to be the most important and/or difficult passages in order to demonstrate that a new paradigm is needed and how the paradigm presented here helps solve various problems. Nevertheless, in-depth interaction with major interpreters is restricted to select problem passages. To have dealt in any depth with a number of passages (even in as limited manner as with Acts 2:38 and Eph 4:26), would have resulted in a work too large for the present project.

As a scholar attempting to contribute both to the academic and ecclesiastical communities, I share the goal that academic work must ultimately contribute to the understanding (and applying) of the biblical text (exegesis and exposition). It is my hope that this work will contribute to this goal in some way. If it does not help the church universal, it may ultimately have been a wasted effort. Printer ink, trees for paper, and the reader's time could have been spared and I could have been sitting on the beach enjoying God's creation.

While acknowledging the need for more exegetical application of my theory, I make no apologies for the theoretical nature of this work. This project may be viewed as part one of two. If I receive positive feedback on the paradigm presented here, it may be worthwhile to apply it more thoroughly to exegetical concerns and possibly even attempt to apply it in detail to the entire New Testament. In addition, much of the philosophy and method presented in chapter 1 may be adapted for other types of grammatical work.

Finally, a word needs to be said about works and discussions of the imperative mood which preceded this work. I note in chapter 1 that one reason for this study is that the imperative mood has generally been neglected by Greek grammarians. This statement is accurate. For example, the generally recognized most important Greek grammar available during work on this project devoted approximately one column (about half a page) to its main discussion of the mood.[1] Another important work, although devoting an entire chapter to the optative, deals with the imperative only within its discussions of tenses and other moods.[2] However, the situation is not quite as bleak as it seems. A number of grammarians have made important observations (albeit unsystematic) about the imperative (e.g., the importance of rank, problems with the conditional classification, etc.) that are developed more fully in this study.[3] It is hoped that this work will present a systematic means of dealing with the mood which will aid in understanding the imperative more adequately.

---

[1]BDF, 195-96.

[2]Nigel Turner, *Syntax*, vol 3, *A Grammar of New Testament Greek*, ed. James Hope Moulton (Edinburgh: T. & T. Clark, 1963), 74-78, 85-86, 93-98, 102, 303. When the imperative is discussed in the context of other moods, the topic of discussion is often concerning the other moods which may function in a similar manner to the imperative.

[3]See for example James L. Boyer, "A Classification of Imperatives: A Statistical Study," *Grace Theological Journal* 8 (1987): 35-54; Daniel B. Wallace, *Greek Grammar beyond the Basics: An Exegetical Syntax of the New Testament* (Grand Rapids: Zondervan Publishing House, 1996), 485-93; Stanley E. Porter, *Idioms of the Greek New Testament*, 2d ed., Biblical Languages: Greek, vol. 2 (Sheffield: JSOT Press, 1994), 50-61.

Chapter 1

Introduction

The Greek imperative mood has been generally neglected by grammarians and exegetes in the study of the New Testament. It has been neglected, but not ignored. All Greek grammars and relevant exegetical studies deal with the imperative. However, with one exception (with reference to the tenses used with the mood–to be described in chapter 2), it seems that little new ground has been broken in this area over the last hundred or more years.[1] There have been a number of studies involving the imperative either directly or indirectly. However, these studies have been highly selective. Most prominently, the imperative has been analyzed with reference to the relationship between the tenses used with the mood, namely, the aorist and present.[2] Thus, the emphasis has not been on the meaning of the mood itself nor on a comprehensive analysis of its usage but rather on the use of the tenses in commands and prohibitions. In this book it will be argued that the imperative mood has been discussed in an

---

[1]Compare the treatments of the imperative mood in G. B. Winer, *A Treatise on the Grammar of New Testament Greek*, trans. W. F. Moulton, 3d rev. ed. (Edinburgh: T. & T. Clark, 1882; reprint, Eugene, OR: Wipf and Stock Publishers, 1997), 390-99, and A. T. Robertson, *A Grammar of the Greek New Testament in the Light of Historical Research*, 4th ed. (Nashville: Broadman Press, 1934), 941-50, with Richard A. Young, *Intermediate New Testament Greek: A Linguistic and Exegetical Approach* (Nashville: Broadman and Holman Publishers, 1994), 141-45, and Daniel B. Wallace, *Greek Grammar beyond the Basics: An Exegetical Syntax of the New Testament* (Grand Rapids: Zondervan Publishing House, 1996), 485-93. With the exception of the treatment of the tenses with the imperative (see below), these studies differ in only minor ways. There is no significant dissimilarity between the earlier and later works regarding the general treatment of the mood itself.

[2]See for example the following important studies: K. L. McKay, "Aspect in Imperatival Constructions in New Testament Greek," *Novum Testamentum* 27 (1985): 201-26; Buist M. Fanning, *Verbal Aspect in New Testament Greek*, Oxford Theological Monographs, ed. J. Barton et al. (Oxford: Clarendon Press, 1990), 325-88; Stanley E. Porter, *Verbal Aspect in the Greek of the New Testament, with Reference to Tense and Mood*, Studies in Biblical Greek, ed. D. A. Carson, vol. 1 (New York: Peter Lang, 1989), 335-61. This emphasis seems to have begun with McKay; however, Louw discussed this issue even earlier. See Johannes P. Louw, "On Greek Prohibitions," *Acta Classica* 2 (1959): 43-57. This development will be discussed in detail in chapter 2.

insufficient manner. Despite progress in specific areas of imperative research, studies of the mood as a whole as reflected in traditional approaches fails to provide a comprehensive and systematic account of the mood's meaning and usage. This work will attempt to fill this gap. It will suggest a meaning for the mood in general and will describe usage in a more complex manner than has heretofore been undertaken.

In this chapter, the thesis of this book will be introduced, essential terminology will be defined, some of this work's presuppositions will be exposed (and defended as necessary), preliminary methodological considerations will be discussed, limitations will be made explicit, and the study will be summarized.

The Need for this Study

There are at least four reasons that this study should be pursued. First, the imperative mood has a significant presence in the New Testament. Of approximately 19,167 finite verb occurrences, about 8.5% (1633) are imperatives.

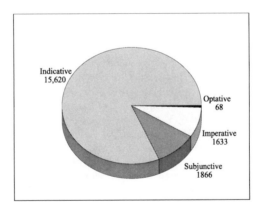

Figure 1: Moods in the Greek New Testament.[3]

---

[3]This count is based on the UBS[4] Greek text and the morphological tagged text by The Gramcord Institute, (*GRAMCORD Greek New Testament for Windows 2.3bm with Database 5.3*, [Vancouver, WA: The Gramcord Institute, 1998]). These numbers reflect a twenty-occurrence discrepancy. There are 19,167 finite verbs in the New Testament; however, the individual moods

The proportion of imperatives is even higher in some books such as James (55 of 263 finite verbs, 21%) and Titus (14 of 61 finite verbs, 23%). Given its considerable presence, the mood demands significant attention.

Second, as mentioned above, there has been a general neglect among Greek scholars concerning the meaning and usage of the imperative mood.[4] The focus

in this chart add up to 19,187. This is due to certain forms which may be parsed in more than one manner. This chart reflects the larger number but this does not affect the proportions it is attempting to reflect.

[4]Some grammars have given only minimum space to the imperative. For example, one recent grammar devotes over two chapters to mood, one for the indicative and subjunctive (27 pages) and the another for the optative (16 pages); Nigel Turner, *Syntax*, vol. 3, *A Grammar of New Testament Greek*, ed. James Hope Moulton (Edinburgh: T. & T. Clark, 1963), 90-133. The imperative is not given a separate chapter but is handled throughout the volume (see especially, 74-78, 85, 93-98).

Concerning the neglect of biblical languages in general, in the early 1960s H. A. Gleason Jr. lamented over the state of Hebrew and Greek language teaching in the seminaries and their use among graduates. By his observation, the preparation of teachers and students was so poor that unless things improved, it would be best to stop teaching the biblical languages entirely. However, he states, "to drop our Greek and Hebrew would be simply to acknowledge defeat and reconcile ourselves to perpetual mediocrity in Biblical studies" (H. A. Gleason Jr., "Some Contributions of Linguistics to Biblical Studies," *The Hartford Quarterly* 4 [1963]: 54). This sad state of affairs was repeated a decade later with reference to Greek grammar studies in general. At the *Fifth International Congress on Biblical Studies* held in Oxford (1973), Lars Rydbeck charged the New Testament scholarly community with neglecting the study of Greek grammar. Rydbeck suggested three reasons for this neglect: theologians today are lacking a classical education, an "artificial antithesis between theological and grammatical interpretation" with a principal focus upon the latter, and the "false assumption" that with Bauer's lexicon and Blass-Debrunner's grammar, all necessary work in this area has been completed ("What Happened to Greek Grammar after Albert Debrunner?," *New Testament Studies* 21 [1974–1975]: 424). These areas still contribute to the neglect of grammar; however, with a number of recent works emphasizing grammatical subjects, the future seems promising. The series in which the present volume is a part is ongoing and has recently published volumes 14 and 15: Daniel B. Wallace, *Granville Sharp's Canon and Its Kin: Semantics and Significance*, Studies in Biblical Greek, ed. D. A. Carson, vol. 14 (New York: Peter Lang, 2009) and Constantine R. Campbell, *Verbal Aspect and Non-Indicative Verbs: Further Soundings in the Greek New Testament*, Studies in Biblical Greek, ed. D. A. Carson, vol. 15 (New York: Peter Lang, 2008). Other important volumes in this series include, Porter, *Verbal Aspect* and K. L. McKay, *A New Syntax of the Verb in New Testament Greek: An Aspectual Approach*, Studies in Biblical Greek, ed. D. A. Carson, vol. 5 (New York: Peter Lang, 1994). Other important books on grammar include, Fanning, *Verbal Aspect*; Denny Burk, *Articular Infinitives in the Greek of the New Testament: On the Exegetical Benefit of Grammatical Precision*. New Testament Monographs, ed. Stanley E. Porter, vol. 14 (Sheffield: Sheffield Phoenix Press, 2006); etc. Also, Bauer's lexicon has been significantly revised (BDAG, 2000) and Blass-Debrunner is currently being revised (completion and final release date for this is unknown; for a brief history of the Blass-Debrunner revision, see Wallace, *Granville Sharp's Canon*, 1-2, n. 6, 7. Nevertheless, these issues (generally) and others listed in this section (specifically) have contributed to a lack of progress in the study of the imperative

of recent scholarship has been on the meaning of the tenses used with the mood. The neglect of the mood in a broad sense may have developed for a number of reasons. The term *imperative* seems to be self-explanatory. It suggests that the mood is used for commands and prohibitions. This is certainly true. However, the imperative is not the exclusive mood for commands and prohibitions nor is it limited to these functions. It is misleading to assume that the imperative is so defined. It is possible that in light of more (relatively speaking) elusive moods such as the subjunctive and optative, a mood named *imperative* already communicates something to the learner of Greek and because one's first impression about this mood is partially accurate, further in-depth study is not immediately pursued.[5]

This leads to the third reason that this study is needed. There seems to be confusion between the imperative as a morphological mood and the imperative as a semantic command or prohibition.[6] This does not necessarily mean that

---

mood.

[5]This statement is probably most accurate in relation to students. When a new student is confronted with a number of new categories, the appearance of the existence of a mood which seems familiar is welcomed. However, this may also lead advanced students and experts to look elsewhere for research projects. Also, the accuracy of this statement may vary with reference to students whose first language is not of Indo-European origin.

[6]A distinction must be made between *imperative* as a mood and *imperative* as a sentence type. The latter is in contrast to declarative and interrogative. The former in Greek is in contrast to the indicative, subjunctive, and optative. It is only the imperative mood which is identified by morphology that this work is concerned. The use of the same term for both distinct (though related) linguistic concepts has contributed to the confusion over the study of the imperative. For an example of the imprecise use of this term in a New Testament grammar, see Alexander Buttmann, *A Grammar of the New Testament Greek* (Andover, MA: Warren F. Draper, 1873), 257. John Lyons makes a further distinction between *mood* (as described here), *sentences* (as described here), and *utterances* (statements, questions, and mands [his term, borrowed from Skinner, to cover commands, advice, etc.]); *Semantics*, 2 vols. (Cambridge: Cambridge University Press, 1977), 633-35, 745-46 and idem, *Linguistic Semantics: An Introduction* (Cambridge: Cambridge University Press, 1995), 32-40 (in the later work Lyons' three way distinction is *word* (lexical) meaning, *sentence* meaning, and *utterance* meaning. However, the comparison with grammar is clear (see p. 181 concerning the use of common mood names for sentence types). Lyons believes that the *utterance/sentence* distinction must be postulated because not all declaratives are statements (e.g., an interrogative may include an embedded declarative or a declarative sentence such as "it is cold" may actually be a command or request [mand] for someone to turn up the heat; Lyons, *Semantics*, 635 and idem, *Linguistic Semantics*, 181-82; see also the discussion of indirect speech acts in chapter 2 below). For a critique and use of Lyons' distinction, see F. R. Palmer, *Mood and Modality*, Cambridge Textbooks in Linguistics (Cambridge: University Press, 1986), 23-26.

Unfortunately, most secondary literature deals with the imperative sentence type, not the grammatical imperative mood. Although this does not make these studies useless, it does demand

scholars have failed to recognize this distinction; however, the study of the semantic (or as will be proposed later, *sememic*[7]) command/prohibition has seemed to eclipse the meaning of the mood.[8] In fact, many studies of *imperativeness* of various languages begin with the sememic level and attempt to answer the question: how does a speaker/writer communicate a command or prohibition (imperative)?[9] This is a valuable study; however, it seems premature with reference to the imperative mood. The structural mood must first be defined and its usages explained. Once this is completed for all of the moods, the question of how to form a sememic command can be pursued with reliable foundational analysis.[10] In Greek, a number of structures (most commonly the imperative, indicative, and subjunctive) may be used for this purpose.[11] This

---

they be used with care. See for example, Martin Huntley, "The Semantics of English Imperatives," *Linguistics and Philosophy* 7 (1984): 103-33.

[7]The term *sememic* will be explained further below. A technical use for the term *semantic* will also be introduced. Therefore, at this stage, in order to keep the terminology consistent, *sememic* will be used here in a context where some would use the term *semantic*.

[8]This may be because the study of commands and prohibitions seems to have important practical consequences with reference to the New Testament. However, as will be demonstrated below, the important study of commands and prohibitions needs to be built upon solid morphological grounds.

[9]See for example C. L. Hamblin, *Imperatives* (Oxford: Basil Blackwell, 1987).

[10]This process may of course be pursued in a spiralic manner (by analogy, similar to the hermeneutic spiral). As each linguistic area is analyzed, it informs and refines the student's understanding of the other. Nevertheless, an initial priority to structure must be granted. It is the structure that provides the data (it is what one actually *has* to analyze); the semantics (sememics) must be determined from the structure. This is especially critical with languages which are no longer in use for the purpose of spontaneous communication. No native speakers exist for such languages with whom conceptual issues can be verified.

[11]For example, the future indicative is used for commands and prohibitions: ἔσεσθε οὖν ὑμεῖς τέλειοι, "therefore, be perfect" (Matt 5:48) and οὐκ ἐπιθυμήσεις "do not lust" (Rom 7:7). This use of the future indicative is often in Old Testament quotations; however, it is also used elsewhere (see Matt 6:5 [note the variant reading, the singular, here is also future tense]). The aorist subjunctive is also used to express prohibitions: Μὴ νομίσητε ὅτι ἦλθον καταλῦσαι τὸν νόμον ἢ τοὺς προφήτας·, "Do not think that I have come to destroy the law or the prophets" (Matt 5:17). Also, there is a rare use of the aorist subjunctive in a (structural) subordinate clause following an *imperatival* ἵνα where the subjunctive functions as a command (e.g., Mark 5:23 and Eph 5:33). These passages are structurally dependent upon a subjunctive main verb; however, they function independently (Wallace, *Exegetical Syntax*, 476-77). Also, it is interesting to compare Matt 19:18 with the parallel passages Mark 10:19 and Luke 18:20. In the Matthew passage, the future indicative is used as a prohibition; however, in Mark 10:19 and Luke 18:20 the negated aorist subjunctive is used. In addition to the indicative and subjunctive, commands and prohibitions can be communicated through infinitives (e.g., Rom 12:15) and participles (e.g., 1 Pet 2:18); see Wallace, *Exegetical Syntax*, 608, 650-51 and Robertson, (*Grammar*, 942-46) who also sees an example of an optative used as a command (Mark 11:14);

work will explore this at an introductory level;[12] however, a full discussion of sememic commands must await further development. It is hoped that this work can be an important resource for such a study.

Fourth, the time is right for a fresh study of the imperative mood. New advances in biblical studies and linguistics are providing opportunities for analysis that did not exist in the past. For example, computer databases and search engines such as *Gramcord*,[13] *Thesaurus Lingua Graecae*,[14] and *PHI: Greek Documentary Texts*[15] are now readily accessible to perform searches of both the New Testament and wider Greek literature. Ten years ago it may have taken hundreds of hours to search painstakingly through the New Testament to produce a list of imperative verbs for analysis. Today such a search takes only seconds with *Gramcord*. The results with *Gramcord* are also much more accurate because it is working with a set database that has been revised over the years as errors in tagging have been discovered. Also, the use of *Gramcord*

---

however, Wallace classifies this passage as a *voluntative optative* and considers it one of three examples of an imprecatory prayer in the New Testament (*Exegetical Syntax*, 481-83).

Although not an identical situation, the imperative vs. command/prohibition, morphological/structure vs. semantics relationship can be compared to the grammatical category of the sentence type *interrogative* vs. the semantic meaning category of *question* (see Rodney Huddleston, "The Contrast Between Interrogatives and Questions," *Journal of Linguistics* 30 [1994]: 425-31).

[12]Issues such as why a writer chooses one mood or another to communicate a particular command in a context with various participants must be introduced. However, this study cannot go much beyond the range of the morphological imperative mood.

[13]*Gramcord* (*GRAMCORD Greek New Testament for Windows 2.3bm [later 2.4cb] with Database 5.3*, [Vancouver, WA: The Gramcord Institute, 1998]) is a software program which searches a morphologically tagged Greek New Testament (UBS[4]) and yields results based upon selected morphological characteristics. Searches can be simple, comprised of only one word, or complex, including complicated strings of grammatical and lexical detail. *Gramcord* was programmed by Paul Miller and initially tagged by James Boyer. There are other software packages available which perform the same functions.

[14]*Thesaurus Lingua Graecae* CD-ROM E (Los Altos, CA: Packard Humanities Institute,1999) is a CD-ROM containing Greek texts from Homer to 1453 CE. This CD may be searched for various words and phrases. This tool makes available to this work Hellenistic, classical and other Greek literature which may provide insight into imperative usage. This database, further expanded, is now also available on-line (by subscription) at www.tlg.uci.edu. As will be discussed, the approach of this work will be primarily synchronic, not diachronic. Nevertheless, the non-Hellenistic literature can provide valuable insight where little Hellenistic data is available.

[15]*PHI Greek Documentary Texts* CD-ROM #7 (Los Altos, CA: Packard Humanities Institute, 1991–1996) is one of two searchable CD-ROMs from the Packard Humanities Institute. This CD contains inscriptions and papyri. The second [CD-ROM #5.3, 1991] includes Latin texts and Bible versions.

avoids errors which result from human searching such as missing forms due to a lack of knowledge, fatigue, etc. Beyond this, other searches can be made specifying the grammatical and lexical context even further (e.g., what imperatives are followed by an accusative noun). It is possible that in the past a study might include one or two such searches; however, the difficulty and time-consumption of such an endeavor would make this rare. Today, the possibilities of such searches can be done very quickly allowing the student to do as many searches as deemed necessary for this study.[16] Also, although a tool such as *Thesaurus Lingua Graecae* cannot produce as powerful searches as *Gramcord* because it is not morphologically tagged, it can search for specific lexemes throughout Greek literature. Thus, the student can produce a list of occurrences of one word such as ἰδού in a vast corpus of Greek literature.[17]

Another development making a fresh study of the imperative mood prudent at this time is the multitude of modern linguistic theories[18] which are providing new ways to analyze biblical texts.[19] Various linguistic theories are providing

---

[16]It is acknowledged that the nature of *Gramcord* as a morphological search tool may demand that the student set up a search which yields more examples than fit the desired search criteria. Thus, analysis is always demanded of the produced database. For example, a search of the imperative followed by an accusative will need to allow words to come between the verb and noun. In all cases (whether the object directly follows the imperative or has words intervening), it must be confirmed that the accusative is the object of (or in some way related to) the imperative and not another verb in the context. Nevertheless, this is a small price to pay for such a powerful tool.

[17]With wildcard characters more complex searches can be accomplished.

[18]It is generally considered that *modern linguistics* began with the posthumous publication of the class notes of Ferdinand de Saussure, *Cours de linguistique générale*, ed. Charles Bally, Albert Sechehaye, and Albert Reidlinger (Lausanne: Librairie Payot and Cⁱᵉ, 1916); third edition, 1949; English translation: *Course in General Linguistics*, ed. Charles Bally, Albert Sechehaye, and Albert Reidlinger, trans. Wade Baskin (New York: McGraw-Hill Book Company, 1959); all citations in this work are from the third French edition unless otherwise noted. Prior to Saussure, linguistics was primarily concerned with diachronic and historical matters (philology). Space does not permit a discussion of the developments since Saussure; however, see appendix 1 for a brief and select history of the subject.

[19]The use of linguistics as a tool for biblical studies is not new. Influential works such as James Barr, *Semantics of Biblical Language* (Oxford: Oxford University Press, 1961) and G. B. Caird, *The Language and Imagery of the Bible* (Philadelphia: Westminster Press, 1980) utilized linguistic insights. Since the publication of these works and not necessarily influenced by them, there have been a number a works written specifically on the use of linguistics for biblical studies. Generally (although there are exceptions) these works are written by linguists. It seems that the modern New Testament scholar wishing to contribute in the area of Greek must at least have a basic familiarity with this field. As early as 1960, H. A. Gleason Jr., in his inaugural address as professor of linguistics at Hartford Seminary stated, "Certainly for anyone who is to

New Testament scholars with valuable insights into the text which were not available to previous generations.[20] It must be emphasized that new developments in linguistics do not minimize the importance of the work of previous generations;[21] rather, with the work of the past as a foundation, one must use the new tools to evaluate, refine, and further develop an understanding of the Greek of the New Testament. Many scholars working in Greek were (and still are) classical philologists. Most scholars focused on Greek and/or Latin to the exclusion of other languages. One practical reason for this emphasis is the incredible amount of work involved in order to master these languages and their literature.[22] It was natural for western scholars, many of whose vernaculars were

---

concentrate on Biblical studies, instruction in linguistics would seem today to be essential. I would venture to suggest that for all seminary students it could be most helpful" ("Linguistics in the Service of the Church," *Hartford Quarterly* 1 [1960]: 16-17). A thorough survey of linguistic works by New Testament scholars and linguistic contributions to New Testament studies is beyond the scope of this work. Nevertheless, a brief survey is included in appendix 1.

[20]Unfortunately, the rapid rise of linguistic theories which were not necessarily developed to analyze ancient languages (nor exegesis) has caused a number of problems for New Testament scholars. These problems include terminology differences, methodological questions, and expected problems arising from applying a field not originally developed for exegetical purposes. I am not convinced that these problems have been addressed adequately nor am I convinced that many using modern linguistic tools are even aware of the seriousness or even the existence of such problems. There are so many theories imposing their view of language upon New Testament scholarship that serious division must develop as they have within the field of linguistics itself. In appendix 1, I will support and further develop some concerns over the present use of linguistics in New Testament studies and provide suggestions for future research. I am not suggesting that linguistics should not be used by New Testament scholars. It seems that linguistics has contributed to the progress being made in New Testament grammatical studies; however, I am concerned with compatibility and the plethora of linguistic theories being used.

Having made the above cautious statement about the use of linguistic theories within New Testament studies, I must confess that I fear that this work will only add to the many diverse linguistic voices attempting to be heard and place a further burden on the reader to superficially familiarize himself with yet other areas of method and study. Nevertheless, it is hoped that the present study will be able to make a sustained contribution to the understanding of the imperative mood despite further developments within the young field of linguistics.

[21]The modern Greek scholar must be thankful for the rich heritage of which he is an heir (see the possibly overly enthusiastic comments of Robert S. P. Beekes, "The Historical Grammar of Greek: A Case Study in the Results of Comparative Linguistics," in *Linguistic Change and Reconstruction Methodology*, ed. Philip Baldi [Berlin: Mouton de Gruyter, 1990], 305-09). The use of modern advances should be seen as continuing the grand tradition of Greek studies, not an abandonment of what has preceded.

[22]Another possible reason for the neglect of other languages (especially languages not spoken by powerful nations) was the illusion that languages such as Latin and Greek were somehow superior to other (sometimes called *primitive*) languages. However, modern descriptive linguistic studies of languages in various cultures have demonstrated that this is not the case. All

descended from Latin, to view Greek (and other languages) through Latin.[23] The full impact of Latin on the understanding of Greek is only now being recognized.[24] Works on verbal aspect including those cited above have exposed the reliance on the Latin tense system for modern scholarship's understanding of Greek.[25] If Latin has shaped the present understanding of Greek, it is also true that the language of instruction often shapes its presentation. For example, the teaching of the Greek tense system to English speakers is often little more than translation. To some extent this is to be expected. However, after initial learning, the Greek language in general and, in the present example, the Greek verbal system in particular, must be understood in relationship to itself. When the Greek student encounters an aorist verb, he should not immediately think

---

languages have extensive vocabularies and complicated structures which enable their speakers to communicate extremely complex ideas. Thus, languages of so-called "primitive cultures" are not inferior to Greek, Latin, or other languages of the "civilized" world. (Eugene A. Nida, *Customs and Cultures: Anthropology for Christian Missions* [New York: Harper and Row, Publishers, 1954], 204-205; also, with reference to a comparison of Latin with English, see Margaret Berry, *An Introduction to Systemic Linguistics: 1. Structures and Systems* [New York: St. Martin's Press, 1975], 10.) This misunderstanding is also illustrated in an entertaining manner by Nida in *Linguistic Interludes* (Glendale, CA: Summer Institute of Linguistics, 1947), 1-88; see especially, 62-88.

[23]John Hewson suggests four reasons why Latin is the best known of the ancient Indo-European languages: (1) Latin was the Roman Empire's official language and thus Medieval Europe's *lingua franca*; (2) it has a tradition of grammatical analysis going back 2,000 years; (3) the medieval grammatical tradition was exclusively in Latin; (4) Western European languages borrowed the Latin alphabet and thus the study of Latin demanded no further alphabet to be learned (and until fairly recently Latin was required for university entrance since many texts were written in Latin) (John Hewson and Vit Bubenik, *Tense and Aspect in Indo-European Languages: Theory, Typology, Diachrony*, Series 4 – Current Issues in Linguistic Theory, ed. E. F. Konrad Koerner, vol. 145 [Amsterdam: John Benjamins Publishing Company, 1997], 189). Thus it is not surprising that western scholars have had the tendency to see languages through *Latin–colored lenses*.

One example where the influence of Latin is evident involves the labeling of grammatical forms. These labels are often descriptive in one language and become abstract technical terms in another. For example, the label *accusative* for the substantival case which often is used to grammaticalize the verbal goal (direct objects, etc.) is the result of a mistranslation from the Greek αἰτιακὴ πτῶσις, "the case pertaining to what is effected" (or "indicating the thing caused by the verb," LSJ) through the derived verb αἰτιάομαι ("accuse, censure," LSJ) to the Latin, *accusativus*, derived from *accuso* ("I accuse") (Leonard Bloomfield, *Language* [New York: Holt, Rinehart and Winston, 1933; reprint, Chicago: University of Chicago Press, 1984], 457-58). It is the confusing term *accusative* that has become fixed when a label such as *objective* would be preferred. See also Robertson, *Grammar*, 466.

[24]The influence of the vernacular languages themselves (e.g.,German, English, French, etc.) must be noted.

[25]See especially, Fanning, *Verbal Aspect*, 9, 16.

of the English simple past but should understand the aorist in relation to other Greek tenses, especially in this case, the present. Modern linguistics emphasize the structure of language in a systematic manner.[26] It is not enough to discuss particular grammatical minutia in isolation.[27] Rather, the analysis of all aspects of a language must be brought together in order to understand the language. A language is not a collection of grammatical observations but rather a system of related linguistic elements which cannot stand alone.

Among the important contributions the field of linguistics brings to the discussion of Greek is its experience with and observations gleaned from many languages.[28] Exposure to numerous languages both from within the Indo-European family and from without will open up options for the New Testament scholar that familiarity with Greek alone might not provide.[29] However, such familiarity does not guarantee value in all areas.[30] Thus, the modern New Testament Greek scholar must also be equipped to deal with and incorporate valuable insights from linguistics while maintaining a mastery of *Koine* Greek.[31]

---

[26]Stanley E. Porter, "Studying Ancient Languages from a Modern LinguisticPerspective: Essential Terms and Terminology," *Filología Neotestamentaria* 2 (1989): 152.

[27]Elementary classical grammars are often guilty of this (ibid.).

[28]Walter R. Bodine, "Discourse Analysis of Biblical Literature: What It Is and What It Offers," in *Discourse Analysis of Biblical Literature: What It Is and What It Offers*, ed. Walter R. Bodine (Atlanta: Scholars Press, 1995), 10.

[29]The study of other languages in the history of Greek verbal aspect studies has been important (Fanning, *Verbal Aspect*, 16-17). Also, note the discussion of Greek aspect within a volume on verbal aspect in general (Hewson and Bubenik, *Tense and Aspect*, 24-45).

[30]Fanning, *Verbal Aspect*, 17.

[31]The study of the Greek language and the field of linguistics are entirely distinct disciplines with different (to some extent) methods and goals. One field cannot fully function primarily as a handmaiden of the other. If this is the case, the subjugated field will become static and no longer be able to contribute to the other. Greek scholars will be able to contribute to linguistics with in-depth insights which the linguist is unable to explore fully (the linguist must have this relationship with many who have mastered different individual languages). At the same time, the linguist will be able to provide valuable insights into language in general which may be applicable to Greek. With reference to verbal aspect, the former emphasizing Greek includes works such as Porter, *Verbal Aspect*, Fanning, *Verbal Aspect*, and McKay, *New Syntax*, and the latter with a general linguistic perspective include works such as Bernard Comrie, *Aspect*, Cambridge Textbooks in Linguistics, ed. B. Comrie et al. (Cambridge: Cambridge University Press, 1976) and Hewson and Bubenik, *Tense and Aspect*. These two types of studies must make use of one another in order to maximize their value. It is very difficult to wear both hats. Of course, one may be a *Greek linguist*. However, this is not as simple as it may seem. There are many different schools of linguistics and few have mastered the theories of many of these (see appendix 1). Also, there is much the linguist needs to do which is not directly applicable to Greek. Therefore, although true *Greek linguists* may exist, it is preferable to see two distinct

Thus the words of Richard Erickson are convicting: "We are poor stewards if we make so little use of the vast amount of knowledge now pouring forth from the disciplines of structural linguistics and semantics."[32] Unfortunately, thus far many New Testament scholars have not utilized the results of linguistics in their study of the New Testament.[33]

One area which suggests that a fresh study of the imperative mood is needed is the inability of works to date to present a fully convincing explanation for the existence and use of the third person imperative.[34] One purpose of this study will be to demonstrate how this form fits into the imperative scheme.

---

types of scholars, the linguist who concentrates his efforts in Greek (and possibly related languages and/or various time periods in Greek) and the (Hellenistic) Greek scholar who utilizes a linguistic theory (or theories) to help him understand the language.

[32]Richard J. Erickson, "Linguistics and Biblical Language: A Wide-Open Field," *Journal of the Evangelical Theological Society* 26 (1983): 263. Erickson's statement should be broadened to include more than just *structural* linguistics.

[33]Daryl Schmidt suggests two factors contributing to the lack of interest of New Testament scholars in Chomskyan linguistics (see appendix 1 for explanation of this label): first, new traditions are usually only applied to the study of New Testament grammar only after such traditions are established (of which many theories of linguistics are not); second, the domination by the historico-critical method in New Testament studies ("The Study of Hellenistic Greek Grammar in Light of Contemporary Linguistics," *Perspectives in Religious Studies* 11 [1984]: 32-33). Schmidt's critique is true of use of linguistics in general. However, to some extent this is changing, as has been demonstrated by the works cited above (and in appendix 1).

[34]This statement may be too strong. It is not that the third person imperative is not accounted for. Most grammars discuss it. For example, both Young and Wallace note that the *permissive* idea often communicated through the English translation, "let him ..." does not accurately represent the Greek meaning. Young merely raises the issue in context of brief a discussion of Acts 2:38. He wonders whether the change from second to third person of the imperative verbs has "any significance on the soteriological necessity of the two actions." By raising the issue, Young seems to be suggesting that this may be the case (*Intermediate*, 143). Wallace suggests that the translation "he must" or periphrastically, "I command him to" better communicates the meaning of the form. He warns expositors that they are "responsible to explain the underlying Greek form" (*Exegetical Syntax*, 486). In other words, Wallace reminds the reader that this is an imperative form. Porter also rejects the *permissive* sense and affirms the *imperative* force of this form: "The third person Greek imperative is as strongly directive as the second person" (Stanley E. Porter, *Idioms of the Greek New Testament*, 2d ed., Biblical Languages: Greek, vol. 2 [Sheffield: JSOT Press, 1994], 55). In all three cases these discussions are very short. Issues such as the roles of the participants, reasons for the choice of third person, and other unique questions about the form are not explored in detail. This opens the door for further study of this form and its relationship to the imperative mood as a whole.

Linguistics and Communication

Two distinct but related areas of study are language and the communication process. Language is a tool by which human beings communicate.[35] Communication is a sociological event where two or more individuals or groups interact and exchange some type of information. Language is essentially a means of communication.[36] However, communication is not limited to language. Beyond this simple distinction, little more is agreed upon concerning the nature of communication and language.[37] Because little discussion of these areas occurs within biblical studies, it seems helpful to include such a section in this work. Most language-related works within New Testament studies include a number of assumptions which are not usually made explicit. This may be unintentional; however, these assumptions directly influence this work's conclusions. Where these assumptions differ, often the conclusions will have irreconcilable disagreements. This may seem rather harsh and somewhat unwarranted in light of the present use of linguistics by Greek grammarians. However, as within the field of linguistics itself presently, these assumptions (and related methodological issues) *will* be a source of conflict within the field. Much of this conflict will take form in discussions about exegetical conclusions. But division will actually be deeply rooted within the assumptions of the different linguistic approaches to the biblical text. For this reason, I wish to both explain and defend my assumptions.[38] This will be developed as the work

---

[35]A discussion of whether or not non-humans have *language* (verbal, non-verbal, or both) is beyond the scope of this work. For purposes of this work, only human language and communication are under consideration.

[36]Although it seems that language may be used for non-communicative purposes (e.g., an opera singer breaking a glass with her voice—assuming of course that she is singing a word or other linguistic element), such uses are clearly the exception.

[37]This may be an overstatement. Certainly there is much in common between theories. However, there are significant differences concerning very important components of language and communication.

[38]I am not attempting to play the role of a prophet here. I am merely attempting to point out that differences in linguistic theory are significant and in some cases the theories are incompatible. This is not usually acknowledged by New Testament scholars working with linguistics. Often there is simply a challenge to the field to utilize the tool of linguistics in their research. I suspect that there are at least two reasons for this. First, the use of linguistics is rather new and thus discovery eclipses any potential problems. Second, most significant exegetical conclusions using the tool of linguistics are by *biblical* scholars whose linguistic training is minimal. Therefore, they are not fully aware of the potential problems with and incompatibilities among the theories. In addition, the number of biblical scholars using linguistics is still minimal

proceeds.

Linguistics is the study of language.[39] Such a field should naturally contribute to the study of ancient texts such as those used in the New Testament. It is the premise of this work that it does. However, the field of linguistics is quite broad and contains a number of sub-disciplines. There is *theoretical* or *general linguistics* which attempts to answer basic questions about language: What is language? How does it work? Etc. This is often what first comes to mind when one thinks of linguistics. Among the various sub-disciplines there are *historical linguistics* which is concerned with the history and development of particular languages, *sociolinguistics* which is concerned with the relationship between society/culture and language, and *psycholinguistics* which is concerned with the relationship between psychology and language.[40] *Theoretical linguistics* can be contrasted with *applied linguistics* which uses the insights gained from theoretical linguistics and applies them in various areas such as language-teaching. Of particular importance for this work is *descriptive linguistics*. In contrast to *theoretical linguistics* which is concerned with the question: What is language?, *descriptive linguistics* is concerned with describing particular languages. These two fields are closely related but are distinct.

The preceding paragraph made use of the common word *language*. However, when the linguist begins to consider the various uses of the word, he

---

and there is still a general "us *versus* them" attitude between scholars using linguistics and scholars using more traditional methodology. However, when more formal linguists begin to venture into scholarly exegetical work, differences in theory should begin to become more evident. This point will be explored more fully in appendix 1.

[39]The terms *linguistics* and *linguist* are ambiguous to many. When one hears that a person is a *linguist*, the common assumption is that this person knows many languages. This may or may not be true. However, this is not what determines that an individual is a linguist. One can know a number of languages and not be a linguist (although the term is sometimes used to describe such people). The linguist (proper) studies *language in general*. Naturally, specific languages are essential objects of inquiry; however, such languages serve as data to be analyzed in the pursuit of understanding language in general (although the goal of understanding a specific language may also be involved). As will be discussed shortly, the field of linguistics can contribute significantly to the study of specific languages. For further discussion of what linguistics is not, see Porter, "Studying Ancient Languages," 159-68.

[40]In the case of psycholinguistics and sociolinguistics it is difficult to determine whether these should be categorized as sub-disciplines of linguistics or of psychology and sociology respectively. Or are they separate fields which incorporate insights from and inform the various disciplines? Whatever the case, there is considerable cross-disciplinary work taking place.

realizes that he must be more precise.[41] Consider the following six uses of the word language cited by Lamb:

1. language as a set of utterances or a set of sentences or a set of texts
2. language as an organized collection of linguistic units (such as phonemes and words) of which texts are composed
3. language as a skill: "*Only humans have language*"
4. language as a process
5. language as a system capable of producing and understanding utterances or sentences
6. language as a propensity and ability to learn how to speak (something which all normal children have).[42]

Therefore, it is necessary to be more precise in one's terminology. Not all of the above areas are matters of concern in this work. However, three distinct areas must be distinguished at this point in order to clarify how the word *language* will be used here. First, the abstract *system* which actually produces written texts and verbal utterances will be called the *linguistic system*. The *linguistic system* is neither the concept communicated nor the actual utterance/text. Second, the actual utterances/texts themselves will be called the *linguistic extension*. Finally, the process of producing and understanding will be called the

---

[41]The definition of *language* is complex. The discussion here cannot do justice to all of the issues involved in the debate. The term *language* itself is ambiguous which contributes to the problem. How one answers the question of which specific usage of the term *language* (as listed below in the text) is to be defined will result in different answers. The ambiguity of the word *language* led to Saussure's terms *langage* (human speech), *langue* (a language such as English), and *parole* (the actual utterances produced by a speaker, or *use* of language); Saussure, *Cours*, 25, 30. Johannes P. Louw ("Linguistics and Hermeneutics," *Neotestamentica* 4 [1970]: 11-12) states, "This threefold distinction . . . accounts for the insight that *langue* and *parole* are manifestations of *langage* as a total phenomenon." See also John Lyons, *Introduction to Theoretical Linguistics* (Cambridge: Cambridge University Press, 1968), 51-52.

The purpose of the discussion here is not to define *language* in a manner acceptable to all or even the majority of linguists and grammarians. Rather, it is merely to clarify the usage of terms used in this work. For further discussion of the difficulty of definition, see John Lyons, *Language and Linguistics: An Introduction* (Cambridge: Cambridge University Press, 1981), 1-8.

[42]Sydney Lamb, "Language, Thought, and Mind: An Invitation toNeuro-Cognitive Linguistics" (Unpublished course book: Rice University, 1996), 1.7 (some modification was made for display purposes).

linguistic process.[43] The New Testament text itself is a *linguistic extension* which is the observable evidence of a *linguistic system*. In this volume the New Testament text will be studied in order to understand the underlying *linguistic system*. It is within the context of the *linguistic system* that the imperative mood is to be discussed. For purposes of this work, the term *language* will only refer to the *linguistic system*.[44]

Modern linguistics has provided an important tool for the study of the New Testament. Although there are a number of theories available with differing world views, methods, and goals, the field of linguistics as a whole has contributed to the study of Greek and other languages. Such contributions include the priority of synchronic over diachronic analysis and the priority of a descriptive over prescriptive analysis. These contributions and others will be discussed below.

In addition to the general contribution of the field of linguistics, specific theories have the potential to contribute in unique ways. There are a number of modern linguistic theories (and variations on those theories) which could be used for the analysis of the Greek imperative mood in the New Testament (some of these will be discussed in appendix 1). To some extent this work will be eclectic, utilizing insights from many theories; however, two theories will be adopted as the primary theoretical basis for the analysis. First, *neuro-cognitive stratificational linguistics* (NCSL) as developed by Sydney Lamb[45] will be used

---

[43]Ibid., 1.9. See also Louis Hjelmslev's influential distinction between *form*, *substance*, and *purport* (*A Prolegomena to a Theory of Language*, 2d ed., trans. Francis J. Whitfield [Madison, WI: University of Wisconsin Press, 1961]). Hjelmslev's work was a crucial influence upon Lamb (see *Outline of Stratificational Grammar* [Washington D.C.: Georgetown University Press, 1966], 2). Similar linguistic distinctions (but less influential than Hjelmslev in the present work) include Saussure's *langage*, *langue*, and *parole* (*Cours*, 25, 30) and Chomsky's *competence* (language knowledge) and *performance* (language use); Noam Chomsky, *Aspects of the Theory of Syntax* (Cambridge, MA: MIT Press, 1965), 4, 8-14. See also Andrew Radford, *Transformational Syntax* (Cambridge: Cambridge University Press, 1981), 2-3. However, although there are similarities, important differences exist among each of these sets of distinctions probably due to goals and methods of each approach. For the difference between Saussure's *langue* and *parole* and Chomsky's *competence* and *performance* distinction, see Lyons, *Language*, 9-10.

[44]David Lockwood (*Introduction to Stratificational Linguistics* [New York: Harcourt Brace Jovanovich, 1972], 3) uses the two labels synonymously.

[45]Neuro-cognitive stratificational linguistics (NCSL) was developed by Sydney Lamb in the late 1950s and early 1960s. It appears that in the 1990s Lamb began to use only the label "neuro-cognitive" linguistics; the term "stratificational" is added here to maintain an explicit tie to Lamb's earlier work of which NCLS is a development (and present forms developed by others).

to understand the *linguistic system* itself, including its structure. Second, *relevance theory* (RT) developed by Dan Sperber and Deirdre Wilson will provide the structure for understanding the communication process.[46] As

---

Extensive development of this theory is not necessary here. The principles used from this theory will be developed below. Appendix 1 includes further discussion of NCSL.

[46]Relevance theory (RT) was developed by Dan Sperber and Deirdre Wilson. Their foundational work is *Relevance: Communication and Cognition* (Cambridge, MA: Harvard University Press, 1986). A second edition appeared in 1995 which made only a few modifications based on further work in the area. In some places they added material to clear up possible misunderstandings and they added a chapter with some minor modifications and clarifications concerning the theory (*Relevance: Communication and Cognition*, 2d ed. [Oxford: Blackwell, 1995]); all citation will be from the second edition. Important principles from RT will be developed somewhat inductively throughout this chapter. However, appendix 1 includes further information about RT which is not relevant for the present argument.

This is not the first scholarly work utilizing RT in New Testament studies. See Stephen Pattemore, *The People of God in the Apocalypse: Discourse, Structure, and Exegesis*, Society of New Testament Studies Monograph Series 128 (Cambridge: Cambridge University Press, 2004). This volume uses RT as its methodological foundation (the title of the Ph.D. thesis on which it is based is, "The People of God in the Apocalypse: A Relevance-Theoretic Study" [University of Otago, 2000]). Its inclusion in this important series suggests RT is a valid methodological basis for New Testament work. Two articles by biblical scholars using RT have recently appeared in a biblical studies journal, Karen H. Jobes, "Relevance Theory and the Translation of Scripture," *Journal of the Evangelical Theological Society* 50 (2007): 773-97 and Gene L. Green, "Lexical Pragmatics and Biblical Interpretation," *Journal of the Evangelical Theological Society* 50 (2007): 799-812. For a number of years now there has been a group meeting at the International Society of Biblical Literature devoted to RT and biblical studies, "Relevance Theory and Biblical Interpretation." Participants include scholars from the fields of biblical studies and Bible translation. I have also used RT for a non-grammatical purpose in a Ph.D. thesis for the University of Sheffield under the supervision of Loveday Alexander ("The Lord of the Entire World: *Lord Jesus*, a Challenge to *Lord Caesar*?" [Ph.D. Thesis, 2007; to be published under the same title by Phoenix Press, Sheffield]). In addition it is worth noting the translation-focused thesis: Kevin Gary Smith, "Bible Translation and Relevance Theory: The Translation of Titus" (D.Litt. diss., University of Stellenbosch, South Africa, 2000); and the recent second edition of a Summer Institute of Linguistics translator's book (based on a University College of London 1987 Ph.D. thesis): Ernst-August Gutt, *Translation and Relevance: Cognition and Context*, 2d ed. (Manchester, UK: St. Jerome, 2000; first edition published in 1991). See also, Raymond C. Van Leeuwen, "Bible Translation and Hermeneutics," in *After Pentecost: Language and Biblical Interpretation*, Scripture and Hermeneutics Series, vol. 2, ed. Craig, Bartholomew, Colin Green, and Karl Möller (Grand Rapids: Zondervan Publishing House, 2001), 284-311. Additionally, a recent article applied RT to biblical hermeneutics: Tim Meadowcroft, "Relevance as a Mediating Category in the Reading of Biblical Texts: Venturing beyond the Hermeneutic Circle," *Journal of the Evangelical Theological Society* 45 (2002): 611-27. Another study of hermeneutics uses observations from RT without fully utilizing the theory, See Kevin J. Vanhoozer, "From Speech Acts to Scripture Acts: The Covenant of Discourse and the Discourse of Covenant," in *After Pentecost: Language and Biblical Interpretation*, Scripture and Hermeneutics Series, vol. 2, ed. Craig, Bartholomew, Colin Green, and Karl Möller (Grand Rapids: Zondervan Publishing House, 2001), 13-15. Finally, although not a complete RT approach, the theory figures prominently in

discussed above, the rapidly developing (and thus somewhat unstable) state of linguistics demands a cautious approach when adopting a theory for use. The theory certainly will undergo further development and refinement. Acceptance of these theories does not demand that every aspect of them endure the test of time. In practice, what is occurring in this work is the utilization of important insights about language and communication gleaned from these theories. These insights will all be developed within this work.[47]

The use of these two theories does not suggest that other models would not be beneficial for the analysis of the imperative mood.[48] For example, Halliday's systemic model has been used with value by Porter[49] and Reed.[50] However, I believe that NCSL and RT will prove to be most helpful for this project.[51] One persuasive reason for this conclusion is the explicit emphasis each of these theories has on the cognitive aspects of language.[52] It seems difficult to conceive of language and communication analysis without at least keeping this area in

---

Jeannine K. Brown's *Scripture as Communication: Introducing Biblical Hermeneutics* (Grand Rapids: Baker Book House, 2007).

[47]This approach explains why so much space is devoted to introductory matters in this chapter. The purpose here is to defend specific proposals and insights from these theories (not the entire theories, although it is believed given the present understanding of language that these theories are sound). Therefore, it is hoped that the use of aspects of these theories will be defensible despite developments and criticisms of the theories themselves. These linguistic theories were not developed for either exegesis nor analysis of dead languages (for the goals and purposes of various linguistic theories, see appendix 1). Nevertheless, it is believed the insights gleaned from these theories will prove theoretically viable and helpful in this project.

[48]For a discussion of Halliday's view on competing linguistic theories, see also Christopher Butler, *Systemic Linguistics: Theory and Applications* (London: Batsford Academic and Educational, 1985), 226-27.

[49]Porter, *Verbal Aspect*.

[50] Jeffrey T. Reed, *A Discourse Analysis of Philippians: Method and Rhetoric in the Debate Over Literary Integrity*, Journal for the Study of the New Testament Supplement Series, ed. Stanley E. Porter, vol. 136 (Sheffield: Sheffield Academic Press, 1997).

[51]Concerning NCSL (especially as developed by Fleming), Walter Bodine, after considering the available theoretical models, seems to concur, "If I had to make a choice at this time, I would probably work within the stratificational model" ("How Linguists Study Syntax," in *Linguistics and Biblical Hebrew*, ed. Walter R. Bodine [Winona Lake, IN: Eisenbrauns, 1992], 102).

[52]These are not the only theories which attempt to consider this area in their research. However, especially in NCSL, neuro-cognitive goals are explicit. NCSL analyzes language to understand how the brain works and to understand what language is (Lamb, "Language, Thought, and Mind," I.3). To my knowledge, this is the only theory which used both direct data from languages and physiology in its application.

mind when approaching a spoken utterance or written text.[53] It serves as a constraint to help keep the theory and analysis as psychologically real as possible. In other words, if a theory of language seems entirely artificial or unable to be explained by what is known to be true of the mind, it should be abandoned. Present scientific understanding of the brain and mind is minimal. Therefore, one must be careful to avoid imposing one's own understanding of the function of the mind on the analysis. Nevertheless, although one cannot directly observe the mind, one can observe what the mind produces (e.g., language).[54] NCSL even attempts to give an account of slips of the tongue and unintended puns from a neurological perspective.[55] The reader need not be concerned here that this work is going beyond the topic of the imperative mood in the New Testament. This discussion has been undertaken solely to establish sound reasons for using the theories mentioned above. Of course, it is hoped that the analysis presented in this study can contribute to an understanding of the mind. However, such a project must await development elsewhere.

Synchronic Analysis

One important contribution that modern linguistics has to offer the study of Greek is its emphasis on synchronic analysis. Since the New Testament was written within a rather short period of time, it is wise to concentrate primarily on this period of time to understand the language. In contrast, diachronic analysis often focuses upon language change over the years. This is a helpful study in itself. However, for the purpose of understanding the meaning of a

---

[53]Another reason for the use of these theories is that they are those which I am most familiar. However, study of these theories has been motivated by the belief that they would be most beneficial.

[54]Lamb, "Language, Thought, and Mind," VII.4-6.

[55]See Peter A. Reich, "Evidence for a Stratal Boundary from Slips of the Tongue," *Forum Linguisticum* 2 (1977): 119-32; Gary S. Dell and Peter A. Reich, "Slips of the Tongue: The Facts and a Stratificational Model," in *Rice University Studies: Papers in Cognitive-Stratificational Linguistics,* ed. James E. Copeland and Philip W. Davis, vol 66, no. 2 (Houston: William Marsh Rice University, 1980), 19-34; and Peter A. Reich, "Unintended Puns," in *The Eleventh LACUS Forum 1984,* ed. Robert A. Hall Jr. (Columbia, SC: Hornbeam Press, Incorporated, 1985), 314-322. See also Lamb ("Language, Thought, and Mind," X.2-8) who makes explicit cognitive statements based on Reich's work. An evaluation of the degree to which these writers are successful in their thesis is beyond the scope of this work.

given text at a specific time, such development is less helpful than a synchronic analysis.

Saussure uses illustrations of a plant stem and a chess game in progress to demonstrate the differences in the two types of approaches. A traversal cut of a plant stem or one single board layout of a chess game (the entire board at a specific time) provide a different view of each than if one examines a lengthwise cut plant stem or studies an entire game of chess. In the former, the analysis focused upon all the specific areas of the item being studied at one specific time (or in the case of the plant, one specific cross-section of the stem). In the latter, the change over time is emphasized (or in the case of the plant stem, the entire length of the stem). The chess example has the added aspect of illustrating individual changes. Each board change is the result of just one move. Each consecutive board is analogous to a different synchronic state. Language is similar.[56] At any one time a language displays a number of specific characteristics. However, over time something changes (e.g., a vowel shift) and the result is that the language is slightly different. In many ways it is the same (as the chess board is after one move); however, it is now distinctive. As time proceeds language continues to change. An early stage might look very different from a later stage. The study of this change is a diachronic or historical study. The study of the intricacies of a specific time-period is a synchronic analysis.

Both synchronic and diachronic analyses are important.[57] However, synchronic analysis must be given priority for the study of the New Testament. Diachronic analysis can be helpful when one is able to demonstrate the relevance of an earlier change for the time period of the New Testament. This principle is not often followed and exegetical errors result. Such errors are most

---

[56]Saussure, *Cours*, 124-27. See also Lyons, *Theoretical Linguistics*, 45-50 and Porter, "Studying Ancient Languages," 153. Wallace prefers an analogy of a football game in process because it recognizes the necessity of previous developments which are essential to make sense of the present state of the game thus acknowledging the importance of diachronics albeit subordinate in importance to synchronics (*Exegetical Syntax*, 4). Lyons (*Language*, 56-57) suggests that the chess analogy breaks down because each chess game is governed by specific rules and has a specific beginning and an end. This is not true of language. Lyons' comments are also applicable to Wallace's football analogy. Nevertheless, these analogies are helpful to understand the basic distinction between synchronic and diachronic analysis but should not be pressed too far.

[57]Porter ("Studying Ancient Languages," 153) correctly states, "Synchronic analysis is dependent upon continuous and ongoing development of the language."

easily observed with reference to the use of words.[58]

In addition to the specific temporal focus of synchrony, it is also important to consider the local area of the language under analysis. It is not uncommon for differences to occur in a language that is used during the same time but in different areas (or even different subcultures within the same area). The English spoken in Southern Australia is different from that spoken in London or New York. The English spoken in Boston differs from that spoken in Atlanta, etc.[59] These different but understandable expressions of language are often called *dialects*. The initial extant evidence for Greek reveals a number of different dialects (these include in the pre-Hellenistic period [800–330 BCE]: Aeolic, Attic, Doric, and Ionic). Therefore, the student of a language must be concerned with both time and locality.

This study is fortunate because the influence of Alexander the Great resulted in a general uniformity of Greek throughout much of the Mediterranean world. It was the main means of communication for the Eastern Roman Empire during the time the books of the New Testament were composed. Hellenistic Greek was not completely homogenous;[60] however, because it was used to communicate throughout a large area, the differences are relatively minimal.[61]

---

[58]For example, it is not helpful for someone to note a classical meaning of κεφαλή as *origin* or *source* for the word's meaning in 1 Cor 11:2-16, since it appears that it was not used this way in New Testament times. Past word or grammatical development is of minimal value for New Testament interpretation (although see below in this note) unless it can be proven that the New Testament writer (or the average language-user of that period) understood the history (and intended this history to inform the usage). See D. A. Carson, *Exegetical Fallacies*, 2d ed. (Grand Rapids: Baker Book House, 1996), 35-37. However, diachronic analysis takes on a much more significant role for the interpreter when he is faced with minimal synchronic data. Nevertheless, the difficulties posed by diachronic analysis demand the interpreter even in these circumstances acknowledge potential uncertainty due to the nature of his data.

[59]Even within minimal distance, the language usage may differ. Differences in language are often reflective of differences in culture.

[60]See Wallace, *Exegetical Syntax*, 20-30.

[61]There are other factors which also contribute to differences in a language among its users. These include whether or not the language is the speaker's first, the influence of other languages, education, social status, etc. No person's use of language is exactly like another's (everyone has his own *idiolect*); however, these differences are usually minimal and can be assumed under the topic of *style* (see also the discussion in Rydbeck, "What Happened to Greek Grammar," 425-27).

Descriptive Approach

Another important contribution of modern linguistics to the study of various languages is an emphasis on the description of language in contrast to a prescriptive approach.[62] The descriptive linguist approaches his task by observing a particular language and analyzing it as it occurs/occurred.[63] The results are a description of the language.[64] No attempt is made to determine *correct* usage or grammar. A poor analogy can be drawn with astronomy. The astronomer observes the stars and tracks their movements. There is no attempt to determine which astronomical movements are best, purest, or correct. Neither is there an attempt to label movements which do not fit the common pattern as *incorrect*.[65] In contrast, a prescriptive approach does maintain (with varying levels of strictness) a standard of *correctness*, Stanley Porter states:

---

[62]Berry, *Introduction 1*, 3-4; Charles Carpenter Fries, *The Structure of English: An Introduction to the Construction of English Sentences* (New York: Harcourt, Brace and World, 1952), 3-8 (particularly with reference to English); H. A. Gleason Jr., *An Introduction to Descriptive Linguistics*, rev. ed. (New York: Holt, Rinehart and Winston, 1961), 11, 210-11; Lyons, *Theoretical Linguistics*, 42-44; Porter, "Studying Ancient Languages," 153-55. Charles Hockett correctly associates descriptive linguistics with synchronics in contrast to a diachronic historical approach (*A Course in Modern Linguistics* [New York: Macmillan Company, 1958], 303). For a helpful illustration of this debate, see Nida (*Linguistic Interludes*, 40-61).

The label *prescriptive* here refers to pre-linguistic models of language study where learning often involved the learning and application of rules for correctness. Although Chomskyan linguistics are often considered *generative*, they are not what is being argued against here.

[63]It was mentioned above that descriptive linguistics is a rather recent development; however, this is not entirely accurate. Bloomfield (*Language*, 11) mentions a Hindu grammar dated at 350 to 250 BCE which accurately described the language based upon observation, not theory. Nevertheless, until recently the descriptive approach was not generally followed.

[64]Porter ("Studying Ancient Languages," 151) states, "modern linguistics is empirically based and explicit. This means that linguistics does not rely upon data which is not accessible to every investigator, and its conclusions are stated in terminology open for examination."

[65]Some may object to this analogy by noting that there are significant differences between the constellations and grammar. Granted, no analogy is perfect. However, both subjects are working phenomena which observers must analyze from outside without control over their development (the universe exists and is sustained and grammar is an essential component of communication). Additionally, there are conscious attempts made by some to standardize their language (e.g., Germany). In such cases there results *correct* and *incorrect* language expression. However, this is entirely different than what I am concerned with here. In these cases, a group of insiders are working to standardize language for a consistent present and future use. What they are attempting to do may be a legitimate social or political exercise (although this may be questioned); however, it is an artificial activity not part of the language process itself. I am concerned with looking at a language long since used in order to understand it on its own terms. I have neither the interest (nor the right) to standardize it.

Prescriptive grammars reflect the view of language often repeated by purists, who insist that language must be used in a certain way in order to be correct. In fact many books–disguised as short guides on style–have been written to instruct in proper usage. Some nations even have linguistic societies which vote to approve or disprove inclusion of certain lexical items on the basis of conformity to some arbitrary standard."[66]

A problem associated with the prescriptive approach is the failure of rules to keep up with the actual change in a language.[67] Most are familiar with (and some have had experience with) the stereotypical elderly English teacher who sternly corrects poor students who might utter "it is *me*" instead of "it is *I*."[68] Why is the latter presumed preferable to the former? The reason usually suggested is that "I" is the subject of the copulative verb ("is") and therefore the first person pronoun should be nominative. This is understandable. However, is not English syntax generally determined by a relatively fixed word order? Is it not just as logical to assume "me" instead of "I" because it *follows* the verb? This is probably the reason so many actually use "me" in common speech. The clause "it is I" may have been standard when such rules were constructed but should they be binding today? If one insists that they should, why stop there? Would it not be more logical to return to the middle English Chaucerian form, "it am I" (late fourteenth- century).[69] This would seem preferable because this explicitly maintains the concord between the first person pronoun and the verb. Is it possible that the grammatical number in such clauses changed from "am" to "is" because of the importance of word order in usage (third person subject based on its position in the sentence)? This seem likely.[70] Nevertheless, why stop here? One could go back even further to the old English (Anglo-Saxon)

---

[66]"Studying Ancient Languages," 154.

[67]It is important to note that modern descriptive linguists who have brought the importance of synchronic linguistics to the forefront also are sensitive to the importance of diachronics.

[68]A similar problem arises with the use of who/whom in "I do not know *who* the boy went to see" instead of "I do not know *whom* the boy went to see."

[69]See for example "The Knight's Tale," line 878 and "The Miller's Prologue and Tale," line 663 in Geoffrey Chaucer, *The Canterbury Tales: Nine Tales and the General Prologue*, ed. V. A. Kolve and Glending Olsen (New York: W. W. Norton and Company, 1989), 44, 91 (respectively).

[70]Charles Carpenter Fries, *American English Grammar: The Grammatical Structure of Present-Day American English with Especial Reference to Social Differences of Class Dialects* (New York: Appleton-Century-Crofts, 1940), 91.

usage.[71] In Matthew 14:27 and John 6:20 the Latin *ego cum*[72] is translated by *"Ic hyt eom"*[73] ("I it am"). The form, "it is I" appears as early as the fifteenth-century in English Mystery[74] plays.[75] The form appears in Shakespeare (early seventeenth-century).[76] It is likely that it was the influence of word order[77] which caused the grammatical person change in the verb.[78] It would seem only natural that this trend continue and that the pressure of word order lead to the objective "me" for the clause final first person singular pronoun in this clause.

---

[71]The dating of the old English period begins with the earliest extant documents from the eighth-century until the end of the eleventh-century. G. L. Brook, *A History of the English Language* (London: Andre Deutsch, 1958), 41.

[72]The underlying Greek here is ἐγώ εἰμι; however, it is likely that the Anglo- Saxon translation was based on the Vulgate.

[73]John M. Kemble and Charles Hardwick, eds., *The Gospel According to Saint Matthew in Anglo-Saxon and Northumbrian Versions, Synoptically Arranged: With Collations of the Best Manuscripts* (Cambridge: Cambridge University Press, 1858), 118; [Walter W. Skeat, ed.], *The Gospel According to Saint John in Anglo-Saxon and Northumbrian Versions, Synoptically Arranged, with Collations Exhibiting All the Readings of All MSS* (Cambridge: Cambridge University Press, 1878), 56. The Anglo-Saxon manuscripts represented range in date from the beginning of the eleventh-century to the mid to late twelfth-century. Also, an alternate spelling for *"hyt"* is *"hit."*

[74]English mystery plays are also called *miracle* plays. These are religious plays including Bible stories.

[75]See for example "The Flight into Egypt" (2) in the Towneley cycle (Peter Happé, ed., *English Mystery Plays: A Selection* [Harmondsworth, Middlesex, England: Penguin Books, 1975], 312 [for the dating of the Towneley cycle, see page 12]). See also the following sections in the first Passion Play of the *Ludus Coventriae* (1468 CE, see p. 14): "The Last Supper" (170, p. 450) and "The Betrayal" (210, p. 460) for the forms "it is not I" and "it was I" respectively. [N.B. The dating presented here is of the manuscripts, thus the plays may be dated slightly earlier (see H. C. Schweikert, *Early English Plays* [New York: Harcourt, Brace and Company, 1928], 22-28)].

[76]See for example "Measure for Measure," A.D. 1605 (words of the deputy Angelo in act 2, scene 2) "Cymbeline" A.D. 1609 (words of Posthumus Leonatus in act 5, scene 5); William Shakespeare, *The Complete Works of William Shakespeare* (New York: Avenel Books, 1975), 107, 914.

[77]English is a Germanic language; however, old English in many ways was closer to German than middle and to a greater extent modern English. Two important characteristics which old English shared with German were a freer word order and case inflection for substantives. It was through the Norman influence (beginning in 1066 and including the conquest of England) that French began to exert a strong influence on English. This contributed to the loss of most case endings and a stronger fixed word order in middle (and thus modern) English (Brook, *History*, 51; see also Stuart Robertson and Frederic G. Cassidy, *The Development of Modern English*, 2d ed. [Englewood Cliffs, NJ: Prentice-Hall, 1954], 111-19, 281, 285-97). Generally, it is the Norman influence which native English-speaking Ph.D. students (and others) curse when attempting to learn German but learn to love when they attempt French.

[78]Fries, *American English Grammar*, 91.

However, the construction of a rule has prevented this from wide- scale acceptance until recently.[79]

The notion of *correctness* exposes another underlying fallacy of prescriptivism. Communication can take place effectively with different grammars. Communication is the goal and purpose which grammar must serve. Given a number of different grammars which communicate effectively, which should be deemed *correct*? And on what grounds should such a decision be made? In the case of English, why does the grammar represented in many college handbooks resemble that which is spoken in portions of the northeast? Does it communicate more effectively than a southern or an African American dialect? Clearly the answer is "no." Is it not likely that the reason for the precedence of the dialect which is assumed *correct* is due to the power and influence of the speakers of that dialect when it became established as *correct*?[80] There is nothing ontologically better about one form of English than another.[81]

---

[79]For further information on this specific issue as well as a discussion of the who/whom debate in sentences such as "**who/whom** will the man visit," see Fries, *American English Grammar*, 91-96. With reference to English, Harry R. Warfel suggests that focusing attention on a few such examples, the descriptivists "have hooted at 'prescriptive' grammars and have created in educational circles a thoroughly rebellious attitude toward all formal study of the English language" (*Who Killed Grammar?* [Gainesville, FL: University of Florida Press, 1952], 18). If the issue were merely a few examples, Warfel would be correct. However, the issue is deeper and goes to the core of the difference in approaches (description vs. prescription). Also, Warfel is wrong in his characterization of descriptivists and their goals. A more accurate depiction of the descriptive approach will be discussed below.

[80]Nida, *Linguistic Interludes*, 43-48. Also, one must acknowledge the contribution of literature to the development of *correctness*. Although literature represents a rather small portion of English texts and utterances, it has a disproportionate influence on the development of *correct* grammar. This is unfortunate because literature survives over time. As has been pointed out above, knowledge of diachronics is important but the focus on a grammar for a specific time period (such as the New Testament period) must be synchronic. Generally, it is unwise to impose previous grammar upon present usage.

[81]This should not be taken to infer that some type of linguistic free-for-all is acceptable. Certainly, there must be some standards in a given place at a given time. However, three cautions must be noted lest a return to a prescriptive linguistic tyranny occur. First, given a diverse society, any standards must be rather general. To assume a dialect of one group should be more acceptable within a sphere of many influences could result in elitism. Mass media to some extent has seemed to provide some leveling out of diversity; however, this phenomenon is more complex than it would at first seem. Media has brought many diverse types of speech to a wider audience. Although this certainly has contributed to the way people speak, it seems it has contributed more to the understanding of language between various groups. In other words, different groups understand each other better due to media exposure. Also, although media contributes to standardization, this standardization is broader than any single dialect. This might be due to the sensitivity to various dialects demanded by media. Second, there is no reason to

Rather, the development of a belief in a *better* English is based on sociology, not language.[82]

The descriptive linguist determines the grammar of a language by observing data for a specific time (and to some extent even in a specific area). He must account for all language occurrences ranging from that which is spoken by the masses to that which is written by the specialists (and all those in between). This is probably an overstatement. There certainly are utterances (including mistakes) which need not be accounted for. Language in practice is simply not a clean and perfect endeavor. Some *waste* is inevitable. This is not a concession to prescriptivism. Nevertheless, the descriptive principle which demands an attempt to account for as much language utterance as possible is important. Further discussion will continue to nuance the position of this work.

Some have reacted strongly to a descriptive approach to language.[83] One reason for this may be the manner in which the position is represented.[84] Some believe that the descriptive approach will result in an "anything goes"

---

demand that a standard must mean only one way of stating things. It seems that a standard could be rather flexible allowing for more than one way of communicating the same concept. This is the case with lexemes. One often has a number of words at one's disposal to identify an object (car, auto, etc.). Although not a perfect analogy (and acknowledging contextual/genre influence upon word choice), a (limited) variety of acceptable grammatical constructions would be acceptable. In this way the standard would be more representative of the population as a whole. Third, and admittedly very difficult, one should attempt to reject the link between language usage and social position. This link with the prescriptive notions of the past has made it difficult for some to achieve their potential. The person not schooled in the *preferred* dialect not only has the negative label associated with his speech but also must attempt to learn an entirely new dialect to be accepted. In the past, the standards of language could be more precise (i.e., local groups would have their dialects with less sociological implications). The wider and more diverse society becomes, the more need there will be for a wider standard.

[82]Once this is realized, it should make the analogy with astronomy above more understandable.

[83]See for example Warfel, *Who Killed Grammar?* Although in no way extreme nor a defense of a traditional prescriptive approach (thus I do not wish to imply a similar approach to that of Warfel), see Wallace's interaction with Young on Rev 1:4 (*Exegetical Syntax*, 63, notes 96 and 97 with Young, *Intermediate*, 13; Wallace's comments should be read in light of his discussion on pp. 6-7).

[84]Warfel mentions a caption in an article printed in the Detroit *Free Press* based on an interview with the descriptivist and English professor at the University of Michigan, Charles Fries (Warfel does not include a date; however, it seems likely based on the context that the year was 1951), "Grammar? It Ain't Gotta Be Perfect, U-M Prof Defends Us as Says, 'It's Me,' 'None Are,' 'Lay Down.'" Fries wrote an objection to the portrayal of his views but Warfel assumes that this is the logical conclusion of Fries' work (Warfel, *Who Killed Grammar?*, 6).

grammatical chaos.[85] This is not the case. A balanced approach to description should quell such fears. However, the descriptivist's approach may cause a loss of *certainty* for the grammarian entrenched in *rules* and *standards*. Old established rules may need to be reevaluated in light of common usage. In the midst of the description vs. prescription controversy, the polemical nature of the debate seems to have distorted both positions in some contexts. The descriptivist does not deny the notion of standard or appropriate context-bound usages,[86] nor does the prescriptive grammarian deny the reality of language change[87] or different types of usage in various contexts.[88] Communities at specific times develop standards that are generally followed. They facilitate communication by keeping a general norm for the community. These standards evolve without prescriptive direction and may change over time.[89] These are not rules which if departed from result in *incorrectness*. Rather, they are standards that come and go as the language is used to meet the needs of the community. Departing from a standard at a specific time may in fact have the added communicative effect of *emphasis* in one form or another (e.g., shock). Using a standard which long since has been abandoned may serve to allude to a previous time or event associated with that time. However, this should not minimize the distinction that remains. Standards for one community of language-users (in a specific time and place) must not be imposed on other communities using the same language (in the form of rules).[90] The descriptivist is interested in observation and description in contrast to the prescriptive

---

[85]Such seems to be implied by Warfel's title, *Who Killed Grammar?*

[86]Berry, *Introduction 1*, 7-8. See also the quotation from John Lyons below.

[87]Warfel, *Who Killed Grammar?*, 30. To be fair, at times prescriptivists may be portrayed in a less than accurate manner. Even Nida's portrayal of the prescriptivist, Dr. Zilch, in *Linguistic Interludes* is probably stereotypical. Nevertheless, the arguments for prescriptive grammar in this book have probably all been argued elsewhere. See the preface of *Linguistic Interludes*, 3-4.

[88]The ninth edition of the *Harbrace College Handbook* clearly makes a distinction between formal and informal language (albeit primarily with reference to certain words); John C. Hodges and Mary E. Whitten, *Harbrace College Handbook*, 9th ed. (New York: Harcourt Brace Jovanovich, 1982), 219-22, 225. Nevertheless, even here there are certain rules determining usages in appropriate contexts.

[89]When language is viewed at a specific time and place, certain norms are present; however, an earlier or later view of the same language (as well as in different areas) may or may not have the same standards.

[90]Nevertheless, it is acknowledged that many aspects of any language remain uniform through many periods of a language's existence.

emphasis to regulate language usage.[91] A well balanced approach to descriptive linguistics will undergird this work. Such an approach is presented succinctly by John Lyons:

> It should be stressed that in distinguishing between description and prescription, the linguist is not saying that there is no place for prescriptive studies of language. It is not being denied that there might be valid cultural, social or political reasons for promoting the wider acceptance of some particular language or dialect at the expense of others. In particular, there are obvious administrative and educational advantages in having a relatively unified literary standard. It is important, however, to realize two things: first, that the literary standard is itself subject to change; and second, that from the point of view of its origin the literary standard is based generally upon the speech of one socially or regionally determined class of people and, as such, is no more 'correct', no 'purer' (in any sense that the linguist can attach to these terms) than the speech of any other class or region. If the literary standard has a richer vocabulary (that is to say, if those who do a good deal of reading and writing have a larger vocabulary) this is because, through literature, one may enter vicariously into the lives of many societies, including those of the past, and share in their diverse experiences.
>
> In condemning the literary bias of traditional grammar, the linguist is merely asserting that language is used for many purposes and that its use in relation to these functions should not be judged by criteria which are applicable, only or primarily, to the literary language. The linguist is not denying that there is a place in our schools and universities for the study of the literary purposes to which language is put. Still less is he claiming to enter the field of literary criticism. This point has often been misunderstood by critics of linguistics.[92]

The reason that this issue is important for this study and for New Testament Greek studies in general is that if taken to logical extreme, the prescriptive

---

[91]Generally, prescriptive linguists focus primarily on written (literary) text and descriptive linguists on spoken language. This may account for some of the underlying differences of the two approaches. The prescriptive grammarian looks at texts which exhibit *standard* usage. The descriptive linguist often focuses on spoken texts (in some cases he is working in cultures with no written standard). However, neither group ignores the other manner of communication. Nevertheless, a notion which suggests that written communication is somehow superior to spoken language is unsustainable (see Berry, *Introduction 1*, 11-12).

[92]Lyons, *Theoretical Linguistics*, 43-4. This approach should satisfy the criticism of Wallace (*Exegetical Syntax*, 6, n. 27). Wallace's observation that expressions such as "ungrammatical" or "non-Greek" (based on the "linguists perception what can occur ...") betray a subtle from of presciptivism among descriptive linguists is astute. As far as this work is concerned, the New Testament was produced by ancient communicators who were using the language of the day. One must trust that they were better equipped for the communication task in Greek (whether native Greek speakers or not) than us and I will not cast a negative judgment over their use of the language. Some may wish to compare and contrast the Greek in the New Testament with classical; however, such comparisons should not involve value judgments. The phrases mentioned by Wallace will not be used when evaluating New Testament Greek usage.

approach would demand a *correct* Greek based on classical usage.[93] As a result, the common language of the New Testament would be continually compared to classical Greek and its *apparent* shortcomings would be listed and subjected to appropriate criticism. Such an approach overlooks the nature of *Koine* Greek and any Semitic influence that may exist.[94] With reference to the imperative mood, the goal of this work is to describe its meaning and usage as it occurs in a particular body of literature which was produced at a particular time in history in a relatively limited area. It is not concerned with demonstrating rules for usage. This is self-evident when studying a *linguistic system* that is no longer active. There is no need to produce new texts or utterances (*linguistic extension*); rather, the goal is to understand the meaning of the text. This is accomplished by observing the form in context and determining its meaning and usage.[95]

---

[93]The history of the Greek language has been plagued by this problem. For example, see Geoffrey Horrocks, *Greek: A History of the Language and Its Speakers*, Longman Linguistic Library, ed. R. H. Robins, G. Horrocks, and D. Denison (London: Longman, 1997), 51.

[94]Even if one acknowledges a relative uniqueness to *Koine* Greek and its independence from classical, it is likely that the prescriptivist would still use classical as the yardstick for discussion of Greek. Although it is unlikely that James Hope Moulton would have considered himself a "prescriptivist," his work nevertheless continually compares the Greek of the New Testament and papyri with classical Greek. He even goes beyond mere comparison and uses classical as the measure for "correct" Greek (albeit he seems to acknowledge the relative nature of his measure [see 65-66]). Moulton states about the article, "since in all essentials its use is in agreement with Attic. It might indeed be asserted that the NT is in this respect remarkably 'correct' when compared with the papyri" (*Prolegomena*, 3d ed., vol. 1, *A Grammar of New Testament Greek* [Edinburgh: T. & T. Clark, 1908], 80-81).

[95]Descriptive linguistics has been contrasted here with a prescriptive approach. However, the term *descriptive* may also serve as a label for the linguistic period from Saussure to Chomsky which emphasized data. Chomsky began a new period which focuses on rules and can be labeled *generative*. Lockwood (*Introduction*, 12) suggests a third period with a new focus called *cognitive*. Although influenced by both previous periods, the cognitive period is concerned with "relationships representing the information in the speaker's brain." Lockwood views stratificational linguistics (NCSL) in the forefront of this development. However, although the present work is highly influenced by NCSL, it is inaccurate to suggest that a new period has dawned. The most influential linguistic school is still generative. Lamb himself admits that *cognitive linguistics* has not advanced very far ("Language, Thought, and Mind," 2). Also, some stratificational models do not emphasize the cognitive aspect to the extent of Lamb (see Ilah Fleming, *Communication Analysis: A Stratificational Approach*, 2 vols. [Dallas: Summer Institute of Linguistics, 1988-1990]; Pamela Cope, *Introductory Grammar: A Stratificational Approach* [Dallas: Summer Institute of Linguistics, 1994]). Although the cognitive goal is emphasized by Lamb ("Language, Thought, and Mind") and others (e.g., Lockwood, *Introduction*), their number is small.

Structural Approach

The modern linguistic approach which has been adopted emphasizes description and synchrony. The object of the investigation (the New Testament) is an extant finite piece of written literature. Therefore, it is demanded that the approach in this work begin with structure before proceeding to meaning.[96] Thus, conclusions here are based on empirical evidence as is the case with other sciences.[97]

A Greek Perspective

In the section above entitled *The Need for This Study* it was argued that the developments in linguistics provided a renewed opportunity to understand Greek on its own merit apart from the influences of Latin and the vernaculars of the student. To some extent the influence of one's own language knowledge and experience will influence one's understanding of Greek. However, a synchronic and descriptive approach to language makes it more likely that Greek will be understood on its own terms. Although this goal is not entirely achievable and is made more difficult by the absence of native speakers, it will be a conscious objective of this work.[98] The Greek in which the New Testament was written was the common idiom of the day, *Koine* Greek. This was used roughly between 330 BCE–330 CE.[99]

---

[96]Wallace, *Exegetical Syntax*, 5-7. There is a place for studies which attempt to determine what structures realize a specific meaning (e.g., in what way may a command be communicated). However, as will be defended below, such studies can only be successfully undertaken with sufficient knowledge about the particular structures involved.

[97]Lyons, *Theoretical Linguistics*, 51.

[98]Porter ("Studying Ancient Languages," 152) warns of the danger of teaching Greek in a manner which is only understandable in terms of the student's native language. His solution is to present the material in a systematic manner which enables the student to grasp the structure of the system instead of learning it in small (what seems to be) unrelated segments. Thus, for example, the larger structure of the verbal system should be presented in addition to discussion of the individual tenses.

[99]For a detailed discussion of ancient Greek (up to and including *Koine*) and its evolution, see Geoffrey Horrocks, *Greek*, 1-127. For a discussion of the Indo-European Family of languages in general, see Gleason, *Introduction*, 457-63. For a comparison of Greek imperative morphology with other languages, including Latin, but especially Sanscrit, see Joseph Wright, *Comparative Grammar of the Greek Language* (London: Henry Frowde, 1912), 330-34.

The Linguistic System as a Relational Network

This work will proceed from the assumption that the *linguistic system* should be viewed as a system of relationships between various linguistic strata. The rationale for such an assumption will be presented after a brief description of the network itself.[100] The *linguistic system* is composed of a number of individual stratal systems which handle specific linguistic phenomena involving a particular minimal unit.[101] Each stratum is *related* to other strata and the entire stratal system is related in a network. The individual minimal unit of a stratum is *emic* and indicated by the suffix *-eme*.[102] For example, the minimal unit of the

---

[100]The NCSL description of the strata within the network of a *language system* will generally follow that proposed by Lamb (*Outline*), further developed by Lockwood (*Introduction*) with later adjustments to better account for the neuro-cognitive emphasis of the theory (Lamb, "Language, Thought, and Mind"). This unpublished work has recently been published in a revised form as *Pathways of the Brain: The Neurocognitive Basis of Language*, Amsterdam Studies in the Theory and History of Linguistic Science: Series IV – Current Issues in Linguistic Theory, ed. E. F. Konrad Koerner. (Amsterdam: John Benjamins Publishing Company, 1999). However, in two significant areas the influence of Fleming will be evident. First, within each stratum, Fleming (*Communication Analysis*, 2:6, 7) concentrates on one (*emic*, below); however, Lockwood (*Introduction*, 14-29, especially, 22-23) discusses further sub-units which seems to result in slightly different, although more precise, terminology. Such modification seems unnecessary for the purposes of this work. Second, Fleming does not include a lexemic stratum. As will become evident below, for much of this work, the direct *sememic* and *morphological* relationship will be primary. Thus, although it is maintained here that an intervening stratum occurs, direct contact between the sememic and morphemic strata is assumed. Except where necessary (e.g., a discussion of lexemic meaning as a pragmatic influence), there will be no discussion of the intervening stratum between the sememic and morphemic. A more detailed discussion of the various strata will occur below.

[101]Fleming, *Communication Analysis*, 2:6.

[102]Ibid., 2:xxvi, 6, 26. An *emic* unit is a contrastive unit within a system determined through analysis (i.e., two *emic* units must be essentially different and thus each contribute differently to the construction of meaning). This is in contrast to the *etic* unit which is nonessential and not necessarily contrastive. *Etic* units are the basic pre-analyzed units which the linguist first encounters when approaching a language. Analysis determines which *etic* structures are contrastive, *emic* (see Fleming, *Communication Analysis*, 2:xxvi, 27). For example, there is one Greek plural morpheme (ᵐ/plural/) in contrast to a singular morpheme (ᵐ/singular/). A discussion of symbolism will occur below. The plural morpheme is the *emic* unit while there are a number of etic expressions of the plural that one notices when approaching the text (e.g., -οι, -αι, -ων, etc.). Fleming seems to have borrowed the *emic/etic* distinction from tagmemics. These terms were coined by Kenneth L. Pike in 1954 in *Language in Relation to a Unified Theory of the Structure of Human Behavior* (Part 1), Preliminary ed. (Glendale, CA: Summer Institute of Linguistics, 1954), 8. See also Walter A. Cook, *Introduction to Tagmemic Analysis* (New York: Holt, Rinehart and Winston, 1969), 19; Pike, *Linguistic Concepts: An Introduction to Tagmemics* (Lincoln, NE: University of Nebraska Press, 1982), xii, 44-47, 73-74; idem, *Talk, Thought, and*

phonological stratum is the *phoneme*, the minimal unit for the morphological stratum is the *morpheme*, and so on. The combination or relationship of *emes* on a single stratum form the *tactic pattern* or *tactics* of that stratum.[103] For example, the phonotactics[104] include combinations of phonemes which occur in a given language. This combination is language-specific and determined through doing *phonology*. Thus, the results of phonology for a language would include a list of specific phonemes, the order in which the phonemes may occur,[105] and their corresponding environmentally-bound (called *realization*, see below) phonetic sound.[106] The tactic pattern of a *linguistic system* may be viewed horizontally in contrast to the relationship between strata which will be discussed presently.

The number of strata for individual languages will vary. Lamb originally proposed that various languages could have as few as four and as many as six strata.[107] However, later it was determined that this was probably an

---

Thing: The Emic Road Toward Conscious Knowledge (Dallas: Summer Institute of Linguistics, 1993), 15-22; and Thomas N. Headland, Kenneth L. Pike, and Marvin Harris, eds., *Emics and Etics: The Insider/Outsider Debate*, Frontiers of Anthropology, vol. 7 (Newbury Park, CA: Sage Publications, 1990).

[103]Lockwood, *Introduction*, 6, 15; Fleming, *Communication Analysis*, 2: 16-19; idem, "Communication Analysis: A Stratificational Approach," vol. 1 (n.p.: Summer Institute of Linguistics, 1990), 32-34 [unpublished].

[104]As with *eme*, the term *tactic* can be joined with a particular stratal name to label a particular stratum's ordering/pattern (e.g., morphotactics, semotactics, etc.). In this terminology, the lexotactics (the arrangement of lexemes) would be similar to what is traditionally labeled *syntax*. It has been observed that the arrangement of linguistic units is not limited to the relationship between words (lexotactics, syntax) but similar ordering occurs throughout the *language system*. For example, such relationships can be seen within words (morphotactics; e.g., in Greek, the case morpheme always occurs word finally) and among phonemes (phonotactics; e.g., in ancient Greek there is no option to begin a word with γμ; however, these two letters may occur as an intervocalic sequence, the former closing and the latter opening a syllable: πρᾶγμα). NCSL makes this pattern among stratal systems explicit.

[105]Not all tactics are ordered. For morphology and phonology, ordering is demanded by the (linear) expression of the language. However, semology is highly unordered, not being constrained by speaking and/or writing.

[106]Thus, the morphological study of a language should produce a list of morphemes, their ordering within a word if necessary, and their corresponding phonemic representation. This procedure occurs for all strata. Although there are significant differences between languages, some similarities do emerge. For example, most languages would have a rather limited list of phonemes but a large number of morphemes and lexemes.

[107]Lamb, *Outline*, 1.

overstatement.[108] Lockwood suggests the minimum for any language is three.[109] The three major components of the system are semology, grammar, and phonology, each of which may have two strata.[110] A simple representation of this can be illustrated as follows:

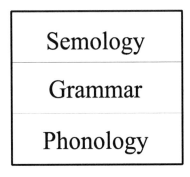

Figure 2: Simple linguistic system

As has been noted, the *language system* as illustrated in figure 1, is the intermediary between a concept and the *linguistic expression*. A basic overview of the relationships in the *linguistic system* may be described as follows: The semology provides the linguistic sememic information of the concept. The grammar then (among other things) places this information in a linear pattern which can be expressible. The phonology provides principles of acceptable expression which can yield an actual acceptable and understandable utterance.

This simple illustration needs to be refined to reflect the observations made above concerning the precise nature of the *linguistic system* and its relationship to other conceptual and linguistic phenomena. It seems appropriate to postulate a four-strata *linguistic system* for many languages including Greek.[111] Each stratum handles specific phenomena particular to itself. First, the phonemic stratum is where minimal sounds (phones) are analyzed and distinct phonemes

---

[108]Lockwood, *Introduction*, 7.
[109]Ibid.
[110]Lamb, *Outline*, 1.
[111]Languages such as Chinese which do not seem to have the extensive distinction between a lexology and a morphology may be better analyzed with a three-strata model.

are determined.[112] Next, the morphological stratum is where minimal meaningful units (morphemes) are considered. Simply speaking, roots, suffixes (e.g., tense, mood, number), and function-morphemes[113] are handled here. The morphotactics describe the arrangement of these morphemes within a word. The morphological stratum is related to the lexemic stratum which contains words and phrases expressed by one or more morphemes. Lexology handles word, phrase, and clause issues. Also, the arrangement of lexemes (traditional syntax) is described appropriately here in the tactic pattern (lexotactics).[114] Finally, semology handles semantic or semological phenomena; here meaning is tied directly to *the linguistic system*. Individual units on this stratum are labeled sememes.[115] The actual *concept* to be communicated is outside the range of the *linguistic system* but interacts with the semology. The *expression* (spoken words or written texts, the *linguistic extension*) is also outside of the *linguistic system* but is the output produced by the system. A hierarchy of abstraction is evident. The most concrete aspect of verbal communication is the utterance/text and the most abstract is the actual concept. Thus, in an encoding process, the abstract

---

[112]There are differences of opinion concerning the definition of *phoneme*. It may roughly be compared to a letter in a writing system. There are a limited number of letters in every language but many different sounds. Not all differences in sounds are significant. This analogy is very poor (although it is more applicable if the comparison is made to Spanish which has a writing system that is closer to actual speech than English); however, identification of phonemes is irrelevant to this work and thus no further discussion is necessary. For various approaches to phonology and the definition of the phoneme, see Lyons, *Theoretical Linguistics*, 112-32; Gleason, *Introduction*, 257-85; and Robert E. Callary, "Phonology," in *Language: Introductory Readings*, ed. Virginia P. Clark, Paul A. Eschholz, and Alfred F. Rosa (New York: St. Martin's Press, 1981), 279-80, 294-305.

[113]A *function morpheme* is a word which has a grammatical meaning, not necessarily a lexical meaning (e.g., articles, some particles, etc.).

[114]Although a four-strata *linguistic system* has been postulated, it is evident that there is a close relationship between the lexemic and morphemic strata. Fleming (*Communication Analysis*, 2:3-13, 241-95) and Cope (*Introductory Grammar*, 3-6; 23-91) handles both lexemic and morphological phenomena on one stratum, the *morphemic stratum*. Also, one writer discussing modern Greek notes the close relationship between morphology and syntax both from a language-specific and language-universal perspective (Angela Ralli, "On the Morphological Status of Inflectional Features: Evidence from Modern Greek," in *Themes in Greek Linguistics II*, ed. Brian D. Joseph, Geoffrey C. Horrocks and Irene Philippaki-Warburton [Amsterdam: John Benjamins Publishing Company, 1998], 60-71).

[115]The term *sememes* is patterned after other major units on their respective strata (i.e., phonemes, morphemes, and lexemes). Some may wish to use the term *semantic* here; however, in order to avoid confusion, in this study the term *semantic* will be avoided with reference to this stratum because it will be used in a specific manner below.

concept goes through successively less abstract linguistic strata until it is finally expressed in a concrete utterance or text. This relationship between strata is called *realization*. The abstract concept is realized by certain sememes which is realized by certain lexemes which is realized by various morphemes and finally realized in the phonology by phonemes. The phonemes are then realized into various phonetic patterns (sounds) determined in the phonology.[116]

The realizational relationship is bi-directional. As introduced above, it is helpful to view these strata as hierarchal. The higher the stratum, the more abstract. For example, the phonemic stratum is closer to the actual expression or surface structure (and thus more concrete) than the sememic stratum which is closer to the abstract concept. The higher strata are *realized by* the lower strata. The lower *realize* the higher strata.[117] A more complex description of the *linguistic system* and its relationship to the *concept* and *expression* is as follows:

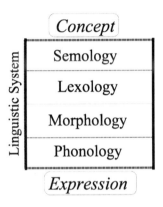

Figure 3: A stratified view of a linguistic system
in relation to other aspects of communication

---

[116]Phones really only refer to speech. Written text might be better discussed through *graphology* (graphemes, graphs, etc.). However, although there are particular nuances to graphemics, in principle it is similar to phonology. Therefore, to avoid further introduction of difficult terminology, *phonology* will be used to refer to that which realizes both speech and text (as is done by many).

[117]See Lamb, *Outline*, 5-7; Lockwood, *Introduction*, 27; and Fleming, *Communication Analysis*, 2:19-21.

What is the rationale for such strata? Why does one not just take a concept and speak or write it? Why so much detail? The above discussion should have convinced the reader that such an approach is necessary to accurately analyze a language. However, one further illustration will be presented.

If one wishes to communicate to another the concept {cat} why not just say [kʰat]?[118] Unfortunately, language is not so simple. If a one-to-one correspondence could be achieved between concept and expression there would be no need for strata. One does not merely think of a *cat* and then express it. There are many types of cats. Is the intended concept one particular type of *cat* or the entire group? Let it be assumed that one wishes to communicate the concept {tiger}. The semology will need to contain sememes which describe *tiger*. These sememes include ˢ/cat/, ˢ/large/, ˢ/striped/, etc.[119] If ˢ/striped/ is not included, it is possible that the referent is a lion. One task of semology is to provide the sememic components of the concept. The lexology will provide the correct term for the concept {tiger} (i.e., the picture in the communicator's mind of a large furry striped feline) or ˢ/large + striped + cat/. The lexeme is ˡ/tiger/. Notice that one lexeme realizes a number of sememes. The morphology of this is simple since it is comprised of only one morpheme.[120] However, if the

---

[118]Minimal linguistic symbols will be employed in this work. However, in this section it will be necessary to use symbols to distinguish between concepts, expression, and the various strata. Elsewhere this work will primarily be dealing with the morphological and semological strata which will be obvious from context and symbols will not be necessary. The reason it is used in this section is to help defend the need for a stratified view of language. Once this is accomplished, little appeal will need to be made to other strata. *Concepts* will be represented in curly brackets { } and phonetic symbols are represented by square brackets [ ]. The units of the various strata in the *linguistic system* will be represented by forward slashes / /. If no superscript precedes the first it refers to phonemes. Other strata -emes will include the superscript representing the first letter of that stratum's name. Thus, ˢ/cat/ is the sememe "cat," ˡ/cat/ is the lexeme "cat," ᵐ/cat/ is the morpheme "cat," and /cat/ represent the three phonemes "c," "a," and "t." The abstract concept "cat" is represented by {cat} and the actual phonetic expression of "cat" is represented by [kʰat]. (N.B., the phonetic symbols [consonants, vowels, and diacritics] adopted here are those of the International Phonetic Association, [IPA]; see Geoffrey K. Pullum and William A. Ladusaw, *Phonetic Symbol Guide*, 2d ed. [Chicago: University of Chicago Press, 1996]). It is important to note that the use of the letters "c," "a," and "t" in representing the concept, sememe, lexeme, and morpheme, does not mean that these items are dividable. For example, {cat} represents the concept of a four legged feline mammal, not the label "cat."

[119]This example is simplified for the purpose of brevity.

[120]One might argue that this complicated exercise is unnecessary. When one wishes to express the concept {tiger} he need only say *tiger*. However, this approach is insufficient in at least two fatal ways. First, it fails to observe that {tiger} is complex and includes various sememic traits such as ˢ/cat/, ˢ/large/, etc. Second, it fails to demonstrate the patterns and

concept was a pair of tigers, a second morpheme would be necessary, namely, ᵐ/plural/. This seems simple, ᵐ/tiger + plural/ will realize ˡ/tigers/. However, what if the lexeme to be made plural is ᵐ/ox/? The morphology and phonology would provide the realization environments[121] to assure the correct expression is *oxen* instead of *oxes* or *oxs*. Among the issues handled in phonology is to assure the correct "t" is expressed. Word initial "t" in English is aspirated [tʰ] not unaspirated [t].[122]

The above illustration demonstrates the need for a stratified view of language. There is no one-to-one relationship between concept and expression. This process is further complicated because there is not necessarily a one-to-one correspondence between strata. In some cases a one-to-one correspondence exists (as with ˡ/tiger/ being realized by ᵐ/tiger/). However, this is not that common. The *linguistic system* is much more complex.[123]

Thus, individual strata provide an opportunity to deal with various linguistic phenomena in an organized manner. Whenever a one-to-one correspondence between strata does not exist, an *interstratal discrepancy* occurs. There are a number of such discrepancies; however, for this work only two need to be discussed.[124] First, one element in an upper stratum can be realized by more than

---

similarities among complex concepts. It is natural to group concepts that share traits. There even may be evidence that similar linguistic elements are closely related (even closely connected) in the brain (see Lamb, "Language, Thought, and Mind," 16.12-15). Additionally, simply stated, a term (lexeme) is not intrinsically related to a concept. A term is simply a symbol representing the concept (again I am being overly simple here especially in light of the previous discussion on the *linguistic system*—I am merely illustrating a point). This is easily demonstrated in three ways. First, considering different languages, different labels can have the same referent. The labels "cat" in English and "gato" in Spanish refer to the same animal. Second, also considering different languages, one term can mean completely different things. "Gift" in English and German refer to quite different things (German: "poison"). Finally, even in the same language one term can have multiple uses ("fly" as an insect and as a verb; also, compare the middle English and modern use of "nice").

[121]An *environment* is the immediate context of the phenomena. In this case (oversimplified), the environment is the determiner of which plural ending to use.

[122]The English speaker is usually unaware that he has two different types of "t" in his speech. In most environments including word initial and word final, it includes aspiration. However, in some environments, such as following a word initial "s," there is no aspiration. Compare the "t" in the English words, *tack* and *stack*. The phonology deals with these issues.

[123]Further justification for a stratified and relational approach could be presented. What is discussed above should provide sufficient grounds upon which the work may proceed. For further discussion consult the NCSL works mentioned above.

[124]For a complete treatment of *interstratal discrepancies*, see Lockwood, *Introduction*, 27-28.

one element on a lower stratum. This is called *diversification*. Second, more than one element in an upper-level stratum can be realized by a single element in a lower stratum. This is called *syncretization*.[125]

This work will focus upon two strata, the morphemic and the sememic. This linguistic discussion is important because it provides sound linguistic theory for why a single sememe such as ˢ/command/ can be realized (diversification) by at least two morphological forms (the imperative and subjunctive) and more importantly, why a single morphological form (e.g., the imperative) can be the realization (syncretization) of two or more sememes (e.g., ˢ/command/, ˢ/request/, ˢ/permission/, etc.). A stratified view of the *linguistic system* provides a means for dealing with different phenomena in a systematic manner. It provides the basis for limiting this work to the morphological imperative without embarking on a study of ˢ/command/ in general. In fact with the precedence of structure already established, this view of language seems to support the notion that before an adequate treatment of ˢ/command/ can be undertaken, study of each morphological mood should be completed.

Therefore, this study will proceed by analyzing the morphological imperative mood. It will attempt to determine which sememes are realized by this mood.[126] It begins with morphology because this most closely resembles what is actually found when one approaches the text. Semology is not seen, one encounters a *linguistic extension* (expression) which through analysis makes evident its morphology.[127]

The discussion thus far has revealed, for the purpose of this work, two

---

[125]Originally the term used for this discrepancy was *neutralization* (Lamb, *Outline*, 17-18; Lockwood, *Introduction*, 27). However, Lockwood felt that this was ambiguous and changed the term to *syncretization* (Verbal Class Lecture Notes Transcribed by the Author, LIN 831 [East Lansing, MI: Michigan State University, M.A. Program, Winter Term 1988]). This change is reflected in David G. Lockwood, "Introduction to Stratificational Linguistics, rev. [unpublished] ed." (East Lansing, MI: Michigan State University, 1987), 2:19.

[126]For a similar discussion concerning the interaction between sememic and grammatical case, see David G. Lockwood, "On Lexemic and Morphemic Case," in *Rice University Studies: Papers in Cognitive-Stratificational Linguistics,* vol. 66, no. 2, ed. James E. Copeland and Philip W. Davis (Houston: William Marsh Rice University, 1980), 35-58.

[127]The analysis of Greek to determine its morphology (especially its morphotactics) and phonology has been completed. All introductory Greek textbooks devote a significant portion of the student's time to learning various noun, verb, adjective, etc. forms. There are also volumes devoted to this area. See the "stimulating" volume by James Hope Moulton and Wilbert Francis Howard, *Accidence and Word-Formation*, vol. 2, *A Grammar of New Testament Greek* (Edinburgh: T. & T. Clark, 1929).

distinct strata which interact with one another. This study will attempt to determine any inherent semantic meaning resulting from the choice of the imperative mood. It has also been noted that various sememes from the semological stratum are realized by the morphological imperative mood. Such sememes are not the inherent meaning; rather, they result from an interaction of the inherent meaning with various other features. To this point the discussion has only assumed the presence of such sememes but has not accounted for their existence. Nor has any means been suggested that for determining which sememe is realized by the imperative mood in a specific context. It is not sufficient merely to posit the existence of these sememes. Nor should it be assumed that any specific sememe can occur in any context thus making the meaning of the imperative nothing more than random selection. If this is the case, one cannot view the imperative mood in a cohesive matter.

The discussion thus far might seem to suggest that there are a number of related but distinct meanings which can be realized by imperative morphology. However, the goal of this work is to go beyond this surface level of analysis and accomplish two goals. First, this work will attempt to determine the primary inherent or core meaning of the mood (i.e., what meaning does the imperative mood bring to the sentence, discourse, etc.?). Second, this work will attempt to identify the various sememes the mood realizes in various contexts and to determine which contextual features determine individual usages. Acknowledging that an imperative form can realize a number of sememes (^{s}/command/, ^{s}/request/, ^{s}/permission/, etc.) is of little value unless some means of determining when a specific sememe occurs can be established (at least to some degree). In order to accomplish this goal it is important to go beyond the *linguistic system* itself and analyze the communication process. Only such an analysis will provide this work with a means of discussing various contextual features which may not be directly linked systematically to the *linguistic system*. In short, a discussion of pragmatics is necessary. NCSL has provided a basis for the micro-analysis of the *linguistic system*. However, it does not seem capable to account for the entire communication system within its neurological framework.[128] It is this discussion to which we now turns.

---

[128]NCSL has not ignored the communication situation. This is a major focus of the work of Fleming (see *Communication Analysis*, 2:2-23) and those following her (e.g., Cope, *Introductory Grammar*, 3-6). However, this approach is based exclusively on a *code* model of communication which seems unable to account for communication in an accurate and economical manner (see

The Nature of Communication

Before proceeding further into issues of method, a brief discussion of the communication process must be undertaken.[129] "In linguistics language is not *in itself* communication, it merely *serves to* communicate."[130] The predominant model of communication both within linguistics and more generally is called the *code* model. Essentially, this model attempts to account for the manner in which a concept (thought or message) is transferred from one person to another (or from one person's mind to another's) to enable the receiver to reconstruct (understand) the original concept. Language is viewed as a code consisting of symbols and rules shared by both parties in the communication process. Thus, communication takes place when a concept (or message) is transferred from the speaker/writer to another so that the latter understands the original utterance/text.[131]

---

below). In short, a code model assumes all aspects of communication (verbal and non-verbal) as well as other factors which inform communication (e.g., culture, social setting, etc.) are encoded and decoded in the communication process. This makes for an incredibly complex view of communication. This does not make this theory incorrect; however, it is the position of this paper that there is a more accurate manner in which to account for communication. Therefore, this work will utilize a quite different linguistic insight for this purpose.

[129]The purpose of this seemingly obvious or irrelevant topic is to further ground this study not only in sound linguistic analysis but also in a accurate view of real world phenomena. Any study of language must also be prepared to demonstrate that it is valid beyond the narrow scope of the study. It has been my observation that some theoretical linguistic studies have become so focused on the analysis of data and the development of theory that a psychologically realistic basis is lost.

[130]Louw, "Linguistics and Hermeneutics," 11.

[131]Sperber and Wilson (*Relevance*, 2) state that "From Aristotle through to modern semiotics, all theories of communication were based on a single model, which we will call the *code model*" (italics in the original). Aristotle (*de Interpretatione* 1) for example states: "Now spoken sounds are symbols of affections in the soul, and written marks symbols of spoken words. And just as written marks are not the same for all men, neither are spoken sounds. But what these are in the first place signs of— affections of the soul—are the same for all; and what these affections are likenesses of—actual things—are also the same." For a basis of the modern *code* approach, see Saussure, *Cours*, 23-35, especially, 32-35. The study of code or signs is called *sémiologie* (semiology) by Saussure (*Cours*, 32-35) or *semiotics* by others (e.g., see Lyons, *Language*, 17-24). For a non-linguistic example of a code model, see Sandra A. Cericola, "Communication Skills: The Art of Listening," *Plastic Surgical Nursing* 19 (1999): 41-42. The nature of this article is instructional and thus emphasizes aspects of communication such as listening, hearing ability and attention. The focus is on the receiver of the communication and the listening process which is viewed as having four steps: sensing, interpreting, evaluating, and responding. Although the term *code* does not occur in the article, words like *stimulus* and especially *signal* reveal the influence of the code model; however, it is unknown whether the author was ever exposed to a

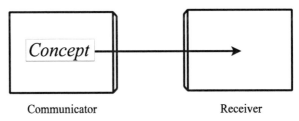

Communicator   Receiver
Figure 4: Basic communication (code model)

This model can be expanded to include more detail. The communicator wishing to communicate a concept (from his mind) which itself cannot be transferred directly, encodes the thought through some type of encoder/transmitter (the *linguistic system*) and sends it in the form of a code through a channel (the linguistic extension; i.e., utterance, text, etc.), which is then received and decoded resulting in a reconstructed message in the mind of the receiver. This can be illustrated as follows:[132]

---

formal description of the model. This seems to support the notion that this model is prevalent in society. To the author's credit, some emphases (e.g., *sensing*, *interpreting*, and *evaluating* instead of *decoding* [see below]) point toward the model which will be suggested in this work.

The following discussion of the code model in this work is necessarily simplistic and not nuanced. This is done in order to highlight basic weaknesses and avoid unnecessary and excessive details of the model and its many forms.

[132]The following type of diagram illustrating communication seems to go back to one presented by Warren Weaver in Claude E. Shannon and Warren Weaver, *The Mathematical Theory of Communication* (Urbana, IL: University of Illinois Press, 1949), 7. The diagram presented here is significantly different in detail but the process is similar. See also Roman Jakobson, "Closing Statement: Linguistics and Poetics," in *Style in Language*, ed. Thomas A. Sebeok (Cambridge, MA: MIT Press, 1960), 353 and Sperber and Wilson, *Relevance*, 4-5. For a more detailed description of this diagram (although slightly different but in essence the same) than is presented here, see Lyons, *Semantics*, 36-41. Lyons views the model as "highly idealized" but nevertheless "not without value" (39).

The model originally seems to have been based on a mechanical communication situation (e.g., telegraphy, telecommunications, radio, etc.). Here the model is modified to account for the distinction made above between the *language system* and *language extension*. This modification makes the nature of the code more explicit. The original made no such distinction and the *channel* in that version of the model was the actual *area* in which the encoded message traveled (e.g., air, wire, etc.). Since such area is a given and not analyzable and since the distinction between the *language system* and the *language extension* is important for this work, in order to avoid further complicating the diagram, the *channel* will only refer the *linguistic extension* itself, not the actual *area* in which the message is transmitted. This does not mean that the area of transmission is unimportant or nonexistent; however, given the *system* and *extension* distinction, the observable *language extension* (the code) is explicitly illustrated here as the channel in which the non-directly observable *language system* travels. Thus, the channel in the model presented here takes

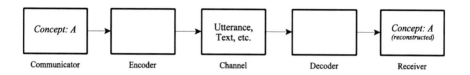

Figure 5: Code model of communication

On the surface this model seems adequate to explain the communication process. A simple and inadequate analogy can be made with communication over a telephone or through a television (leaving aside the communicative process of the *linguistic system*, speaking, etc. and just focusing on the mechanics of the communication act). For example, a person may pick up a phone to call another. The former speaks a message into the phone which transforms the spoken message into some type of electrical current in order that it might be able to travel through the phone lines. The receiver hears the message only after the electrical current is changed back into audible sounds.

This model does seem able to handle some communication. For example, the following sentence seems to be easily explained in this manner: "The Apostle Paul preached in Athens, Greece." The writer's thought is encoded and expressed in these symbols (words). The reader decodes the message (sharing a similar *linguistic system*) and understands the utterance.

Unfortunately, communication is not so simple.[133] The following statement also seems to be explained in this way: "I ate chicken for dinner yesterday." The encoding and decoding seem clear again. However, this sentence can be used by different people at different times and in different places. In each case the referent of the pronoun "I" and the specific day "yesterday" could differ. To fully decode this utterance and receive the intended meaning of the sentence, it is important that one knows these details.[134] Thus, it has been proposed to

---

on added linguistic importance.

[133]Even at the basic level discussed above, it must be questioned whether any two people will have the same encoding and decoding mechanisms which would result in the *exact* reconstruction of a speaker's message in the hearer's mind of anything beyond the most simple exchanges.

[134]This may seem like a trivial matter; however, the meaning of the sentence would differ depending on the referents. Interpretation without referents is incomplete.

establish another level in the *linguistic system* to handle such issues using rules. Rules include, "the pronoun 'I' always refers to the speaker" and "the deictic marker 'yesterday' refers to a day previous to the day the utterance occurred." These may be termed *pragmatic rules* and are used to input non-linguistic information into the encoding and decoding aspects of the communication process. For this process to work, each participant must have access to the same set of rules. This could become complicated.

With terms like "I" and "yesterday" this process seems possible.[135] However, with the use of the third person the situation becomes more complicated. The utterance "he ate chicken for dinner" cannot so simply be explained. No shared rule among all communicators could be established to identify "he" in all cases.[136] However, for the moment let it be conceded that such a system can be constructed.

The code model can only work as long as communication consists of straightforward direct linguistic material with explicit intentions and clear referents. Unfortunately, not all communication takes place in this way. For example, note the following brief exchange:

Bill: Mary, your new hair style looks nice.
Mary: Thanks.

Based on the code model this exchange seems simple enough to understand. Bill, wishing to communicate to Mary that he likes her new hair style, states, "Mary, your new hair style looks nice." Mary, appreciative of Bill's recognition and comment, replies, "Thanks." However, not in all dialogues are the intentions of the communicator so straightforward. This analysis assumes a straightforward motive on the part of Bill, namely, that he wishes to compliment Mary on her hair. The code model provides no other option. However, let it be assumed that Bill is interested in asking Mary out on a date and needs an opening line. It is easy to conceive that Bill may or may not be interested in

---

[135]Those acquainted with the discussion concerning Romans 7 realize that even a simple rule identifying the pronoun "I" with the speaker can be much more complicated than one would initially expect.

[136]Even the original sentence here is not always interpretable with rules. If this sentence was found on an undated and unsigned piece of paper, the reader would not know who was eating nor when eating took place. He merely could conclude that someone ate chicken the day before that person wrote the sentence.

CHAPTER 1: INTRODUCTION   47

complimenting Mary's hair but needs an indirect way to lead into his primary purpose. If Mary's response is cold, he may just end the conversation immediately:

> Bill: Mary, your new hair style look nice.
> Mary (sarcastically and cold): Thanks.
> Bill: Bye.

From the linguistic data alone, this looks like a normal conversation. However, by noting Bill's primary intention of asking Mary out and the emotional response of Mary, one could conclude that Bill will give up his attempt for now and may or may not try again.[137] However, if she looks flattered he may take the dialogue further:

> Bill: Mary, your new hair style looks nice.
> Mary (with a big smile): Thanks.
> Bill: Now you look like you are ready for a night on the town.

Bill's intentions are still hidden in some respects. He may be cautious, not wishing to endanger a friendly relationship that he enjoys with Mary. A straight-out rejection of his desire by Mary could be awkward for both involved. However, at this stage it is likely that Mary senses Bill's unspoken intention. Mary's next response may lead to a more direct question:

> Bill: Mary, your new hair style looks nice.
> Mary (with a big smile): Thanks.
> Bill: Now you look like you are ready for a night on the town.
> Mary: Yes, too bad I have no one to go with.

Bill cannot yet be entirely certain that Mary will not reject his offer of a date. However, at this point he will probably sense that by Mary's last comment she may desire to go out (most likely with him) and thus ask her out. This illustration could continue and take many different directions; however, it will be considered only once more. Bill may have exposed his intentions earlier if

---

[137]In this case, the intention of Bill does not necessarily need to be understood by Mary.

Mary's initial response would have been more straightforward:

> Bill: Mary, your new hair style looks nice.
> Mary (with a big smile): Thanks. I just wish I had somewhere to go.

It would not be difficult for Bill to interpret Mary's reply to be an invitation for him to ask her out and thus he would expose to his intention even earlier.

This simple illustration demonstrates that there is much more taking place in a communication situation than merely the straightforward encoding and decoding of a message. The code model cannot account for intentions; therefore, only in the first dialogue could it provide the means for an accurate interpretation. Based on the code model, the interpretation which just about every American adult who witnessed this exchange would assume should not be possible.[138] There was nothing in the linguistic data that could point to the intentions of Bill (and Mary). On this model Mary's reply, "Thanks. I just wish I had somewhere to go," only communicates that Mary wants to go somewhere. Nothing is explicitly stated that she would wish to go out with Bill. Thus in such cases the code model seems inadequate, or more strongly, artificial.

Thus, the notion of *communicative intention* is an important non-linguistic aspect of communication. This point will be developed further both below and within later chapters.

One more illustration will be presented which should lead the reader to a better and more complete understanding of the communication process:

> Bill (sees Mary working behind her desk): How was your hiking trip last weekend?
> Mary (points to her leg under her desk in a cast)
> Bill: It looks like you had a lot of fun!

It may be argued that some of the communication in the earlier illustration may be accounted for within the code model given the existence of a complex mechanism which permits contextual information to inform the linguistic code.

---

[138]Or at least not likely without an extremely complex code system which takes into account non-linguistic communication. This is not impossible; however, the complexity demanded by such a model makes one suspicious of its plausibility. Thus, a model of communication not based solely on code is desirable. It is this consideration which will be explored further below.

Whether this is the best means of accounting for this is questionable. Nevertheless, one could conceive of a complex code model which may explain the exchange. However, the present illustration cannot adequately be accounted for because the reply portion of the communication does **not** include any linguistic code. Thus, communication can occur without code. How then is communication taking place? Let the illustration be analyzed further.

Bill immediately recognizes that Mary had some type of accident and that in answer to his inquiry, her gesture meant that she had a lousy time. Why is this so clear? Bill did not understand this because he decoded some type of linguistic code. Even if the code model could be stretched to include non-verbal activity, this decoding process would only yield a meaning such as "my leg is broken." It would not necessarily communicate "I had a lousy time."[139]

A breakthrough in communication theory occurred in 1957 in an article by Paul Grice simply entitled, "Meaning."[140] In this article Grice attempts to clarify the meaning of *mean* by demonstrating that there are different usages of the term. Specifically he discusses one usage of the term *meaning* which he labels "meaning$_{NN}$."[141] Grice suggests that to say that "someone meant$_{NN}$ something by (the utterance) *x*" is basically to say that "someone intended *x* to produce an effect in his hearers through their recognition of the intention of the speaker."[142] This initial work served as a foundation for a theory of meaning which Grice continued to develop throughout his life. It also has provided the groundwork for a theory of communication.[143] In 1967, Grice gave a series of papers at

---

[139]Some may argue that the decoding process would indeed yield this interpretation; however, for this to be the case many assumptions are taken for granted which are not explicit to the code. The code must include an extremely complex mechanism including various pragmatic systems which seem cognitively difficult to justify.

[140]H. Paul Grice, "Meaning," *Philosophical Review* 66 (1957): 377-88. A collection of Grice's articles was published entitled, *Studies in the Way of Words* (Cambridge, MA: Harvard University Press, 1989). This work includes all Grice's articles mentioned in this book. However, unless otherwise specified, all references to Grice's works in this volume will be to the original articles.

[141]Grice, "Meaning", 379.

[142]Ibid., 384-86.

[143]Sperber and Wilson, *Relevance*, 21. The term *groundwork* may be most accurate here. It may be stating too much to say that Grice himself proposed, and through this and later work, developed a theory of communication. It may be more accurate to view Grice's work as a theory of utterance interpretation (Deirdre Wilson and Dan Sperber, "On Grice's Theory of Conversation," in *Conversation and Discourse: Structure and Interpretation*, ed. Paul Werth [New York: St. Martin's Press, 1981], 175-76, n.1).

Harvard's William James Lectures[144] where he developed his ideas further and presented a theory of utterance interpretation. In short, Grice suggested that communication as presented in the two previous illustrations above was based on *inference*.[145] Grice introduced the phrase *conversational implicature* to label the resulting inferred meaning in a particular context.[146] In other words, a theory of pragmatics is necessary to understand an utterance in context.

It does not seem to be difficult to acknowledge that an inferential model of communication is superior to the code model. In fact it seems commonsensical.[147] However, without further development one's theory would only be a step beyond the code model. A given statement or action can communicate (infer) different things. This work has been critical of the code model for its inability to effectively deal with anything except straightforward dialogue. However, just because it is recognized that communication (both verbal and non-verbal) is inferential, there is no guarantee that one will receive the correct inference from a statement or action. In the previous illustration, the revealing of a cast on a leg could mean a number of things. Bill never wonders why Mary is showing him her cast. He does not even consider the possibility that she is showing him how well the bright white cast goes with her shirt nor does he take out his pen and begin signing the cast as might be appropriate in a different context. Also, why does Bill not ask himself, "how did Mary break her leg"? He does not wonder if Mary broke it falling down stairs, skiing, mud wrestling, or in any other manner. Despite the fact that there could be many reasons why one person would show another a cast and that there are a number

---

[144]The entire lecture series is printed in Grice, *Words*, 3-143.

[145]H. Paul Grice, "Logic and Conversation," in *Syntax and Semantics*, vol. 3, *Speech Acts*, ed. P. Cole and J. Morgan (New York: Academic Press, 1975), 41; Sperber and Wilson, *Relevance*, 21-24.

[146]Grice, "Logic," 43-45. The notion of *conversational implicatures* is more complex than is described here. It will be further developed in the next section. Grice also discusses *conventional implicatures* which are more closely related to the semantics than *conversational implicatures* (ibid., 50). See also Stephen C. Levinson, *Pragmatics*, Cambridge Textbooks in Linguistics (Cambridge: University Press, 1983), 127-32 and Mari Broman Olsen, *A Semantic and Pragmatic Model of Lexical and Grammatical Aspect* (New York and London: Garland Publishing, 1997), 23, n.12. Unless otherwise noted, *implicature* will refer to *conversational implicature*.

[147]Although coding is present (as in the examples above), inference can override coding and thus is more basic to the communication process. Ernst-August Gutt, *Relevance Theory: A Guide to Successful Communication in Translation* (Dallas and New York: Summer Institute of Linguistics and United Bible Societies, 1992), 13.

ways one might break one's leg, Bill knows that Mary is replying negatively to his inquiry about her hiking trip on which she broke her leg.[148]

Grice did not merely raise issues such as intention and inference. Nor did he merely propose the pragmatic notion of conversational implicatures. He also provided a means of determining what was specifically implied by a communicative action. Grice assumes a *cooperative principle* as adhered to by all participants in a communication situation. This principle states, "Make your conversational contribution such as is required, at the stage at which it occurs, by the accepted purpose or direction of the talk exchange in which you are engaged."[149] With this principle Grice developed four categories which are further divided into a number of maxims and sub-maxims "which will, in general, yield results in accordance with the Cooperative Principle"[150]:

Quantity (the size of your contribution)
> 1. Make your contribution as informative as is required.
> 2. Do not make your contribution more informative than is necessary.

Quality (supermaxim: try to make your contribution true)
> 1. Do not say what you believe to be false.
> 2. Do not say that for which you lack adequate evidence.

Relation
> 1. Be relevant.

Manner (relating to *how* something is said, not *what* as the previous three)
> 1. Avoid obscurity of expression
> 2. Avoid ambiguity
> 3. Be brief
> 4. Be orderly[151]

---

[148]With this simple example, it may be argued that context supplies the information to guarantee the correct interpretation. This is accurate but the point here is that the code model is *unable* to account for context. The purpose here will be to explore important issues and suggest a model which is powerful enough to responsibly handle context.

[149]Grice, "Logic," 45.

[150]Ibid.

[151]Ibid., 45-46.

Although they are not without value, this work will ultimately reject Grice's maxims; nevertheless, they are explicitly stated here because of their influential nature. There is discussion and development of Grice's theory and maxims (thus some have modified the view to various degrees). Nevertheless, they are generally considered foundational to the study of pragmatics.[152] It is important to note that Grice does not believe that all of these maxims are always followed in practice nor that there are not other maxims (e.g., be polite); rather, these are what would be present in an ideal situation.[153]

Despite the influence of Grice, not all have been entirely satisfied with his approach. Some scholars working in the field of pragmatics have pointed out problems with Grice's framework and made modifications which seem to demand radical revision of the system. His work has not been (entirely) rejected; rather, it has been developed.[154] First, the maxims themselves seem to be problematic, leaving many questions unanswered.[155] What do they actually mean?[156] What does it mean to be "as informative as required"? Do speaker's really abide by the first maxim of quality, "do not say what you believe to be false" (or be truthful)?[157] How were these maxims decided upon? Are these the

---

[152]See Levinson, *Pragmatics*, 100-166.

[153]Grice, "Logic," 47.

[154]Rejection and development of Grice's theory exists in various degrees. See below for the reaction of RT. No matter how extreme a theory has responded/reacted to Grice, it must be acknowledged that his work was highly influential on the new theories.

[155]This paragraph is based on the work of Deirdre Wilson and Dan Sperber ("An Outline of Relevance Theory," *Notes on Linguistics* 39 [1987]: 10) and Diane Blakemore (*Understanding Utterances: An Introduction to Pragmatics* [Oxford: Blackwell Publishers, 1992], 26). For a more detailed critique of Grice, see Diane Blakemore, *Semantic Constraints on Relevance* (Oxford: Basil Blackwell, 1987), 21-27; Wilson and Sperber, "On Grice's Theory," 155-79; and idem, *Relevance*, 31-38.

[156]For example, what is relevance? Even Grice acknowledges the difficulty of this maxim (Grice, "Logic," 46). See also Sperber and Wilson, *Relevance*, 36 and Paul Werth, "The Concept of 'Relevance' in Conversational Analysis," in *Conversation and Discourse: Structure and Interpretation*, ed. Paul Werth (New York: St. Martin's Press, 1981), 130.

[157]This assumption of truthfulness in communication is problematic and should be abandoned. It fails to acknowledge that a correspondence between reality and language does not necessarily exist (Wallace, *Exegetical Syntax*, 10-11). When one makes a statement, there is no guarantee or principle which demands that the speaker must (or even should) say something he believes. If this were the case, no one could quote or repeat information which is not believed. Of course, there may be social values and institutional situations which may dictate behavior in certain contexts; however, this is not the domain of linguistic analysis but the study of social institutions and culture. Also, the presence of these institutional and cultural controls do not guarantee that they will be obeyed. This error has been propagated in the study of the Greek indicative mood which is sometimes explained as the mood of truthfulness or a "simple question

only maxims? As discussed above, Grice himself acknowledged that these need not all be present at once for effective communication to occur nor are they the only possible maxims. Therefore, since all maxims do not always need to be present for effective communication, could one add the maxim *be polite*?[158] One wonders whether *be polite* is not more important than *be brief*?[159] It seems difficult to maintain a theory with so many variables. Second, what is the origin of these maxims?[160] Are they universal? Or do they differ across cultures? Has sufficient work been done to verify answers to these questions?

These problems have led to developments of Grice's approach. Such developments maintain as foundational the crucial observation that communication is inferential and the identification of (pragmatic) implicatures (in contrast to semantic or inherent meaning). At the heart of the problem of Grice's work is the cooperative principle and the maxims. Is there a better way of comprehensively explaining the communicative action? Sperber and Wilson, building upon Grice, generally reject the cooperative principle and maxims and in their place postulate a principle,[161] namely, *relevance*.[162] They then developed this notion beyond Grice and made it the basis for a communication theory.[163] Generally, in order for something to be *relevant* it must somehow interact with one's present understanding and assumptions about the world. It should also contribute some new information to the communication situation.[164] The result of Sperber and Wilson's work is a theory of pragmatics (and to some extent

---

of fact" (Ernest DeWitt Burton, *Syntax of Moods and Tenses in New Testament Greek*, 3d ed. [Edinburgh: T. & T. Clark, 1898], 73). It may be that Burton's description is just too imprecise. For a corrective view see Wallace, *Exegetical Syntax*, 444 (see also 690-96 for a discussion of a similar problem with conditionals). This will be discussed further in chapter 2.

[158]Grice ("Logic," 47) discusses this possible maxim.

[159]The length of this chapter may suggest to the reader that for me, the writer, the maxim *be brief* is unimportant (or at least less important) than *be polite*.

[160]Wilson and Sperber, "Outline," 10.

[161]Actually, the original single principle has been expanded into two for clarity (see below).

[162]Wilson and Sperber, "On Grice's Theory," 164-75. Grice's maxim and RT's principle(s) are not identical, see below.

[163]As mentioned above, a comprehensive explanation of *relevance theory* appeared in 1986 with a minimally revised second edition published in 1995 (Sperber and Wilson, *Relevance: Communication and Cognition*, 2d ed. [Oxford: Blackwell, 1995]). See also Blakemore, *Understanding Utterances*, 27.

[164]Wilson and Sperber, "Outline," 11. New informational material may add completely new information, serve to strengthen an existing interpretation(s) and/or assumption(s), or contradict an existing interpretation(s) and/or assumption(s) (ibid., 11-12).

communication) called *relevance theory* (RT).[165]

Sperber and Wilson further place their communication theory within the cognitive framework by attempting to incorporate psychological observations.[166] Is an utterance really primarily constrained by the various maxims such as *be brief* or *avoid ambiguity*? In some senses these are important considerations in communication, but many examples can be immediately brought to mind where they do not apply. Common communication is not concerned with these maxims. Some people purposely talk endlessly, not necessarily because they have information to contribute but because of other more selfish motives. Special communication situations such as teaching might demand excessive repetition. Also, ambiguity may be intentionally used to conceal important information or protect another person. Again, Grice did not believe all maxims are adhered to always. All of Grice's maxims are important observations about communication; however, they are not necessarily the best way to describe and account for the communication process.[167]

Relevance theory rejects Grice's cooperative principle and maxims and instead postulates a principle called *relevance*. RT's *principle of relevance*,[168] although sharing similarities with Grice's maxim of the same name, should not be confused with it nor should it be assumed that RT is merely using *relevance* to sum up Grice's theory. The two are distinct theories.[169] In their second edition, Sperber and Wilson's original single *principle of relevance* has been

---

[165]Although related, there are significant differences between Grice's theory and Relevance Theory. There is no need to fully explore these differences here. This book is primarily utilizing the latter. Nevertheless, appendix 1 contains some information about the differences of these theories.

[166]For RT, communication is not necessarily transferring a thought from one person to another; rather, it is "a matter of enlarging mutual cognitive environments" (Sperber and Wilson, *Relevance*, 193). This position is partially due to the observation that there are thoughts that two people are unable to share. Sperber and Wilson do have a point; however, it may be overstated. There does seem to be an attempt at thought transference at some level in some (but not necessarily all) communication. It seems preferable to acknowledge that an attempt may be made to transfer thoughts even though perfect transference may be unattainable in some (or even many) cases.

[167]For a detailed process of dealing with and demonstrating the insufficiency of the individual maxims, see Wilson and Sperber, "On Grice's Theory," 164-75.

[168]Sperber and Wilson, *Relevance*, 155-63.

[169]Ibid.,161-63.

revised and restated as two *principles of relevance*.[170] The first is concerned with cognition and the second is concerned with communication:

1. Human cognition tends to be geared to the maximization of relevance.
2. Every act of ostensive communication [communication which comes with a communicative intention] communicates a presumption of its own optimal relevance.

Thus, instead of a number of maxims, the notion of *relevance* drives communication. The participants in the communication process contribute to the communication situation with input that is relevant for the situation. Under these principles, brevity, clarity, etc. (some of Grice's maxims) are assumed. However, with *relevance* as the driving factor, these secondary notions are not always necessary. Thus, if the communicative intention involves concealing the identity of a person for some reason, the most relevant utterance (or other stimulus) is ambiguous. In this way, there is no maxim–*avoid ambiguity*–to be violated. Instead ambiguity is being used to further the purpose of the communicative intent. The first principle assumes that in a given communicative act, a communicative contribution will be relevant enough to be worth processing by the hearer. It will not include extraneous information that does not add to the conversation which is either irrelevant or already assumed by another means (e.g., context, background knowledge, etc.). Thus, to be relevant, a communicative act must build on previous utterances within a conversation and/or begin new a topic of conversation and be tied to background beliefs or the larger context in some way.[171]

It now is worth considering seemingly non-relevant utterances such as redundant utterances or regressions. Neither of these types of utterances violates this principle. Redundancy may contribute to relevance by adding the notion of *importance* (or another strengthening notion). Regression may serve to add

---

[170]This was developed in the added postscript of the 1995 edition (Sperber and Wilson, *Relevance*, 260-66). In the first edition of this work, only the second principle listed below was explicitly called the *principle of relevance*. The double principle (or division into two principles) was the result of further consideration and clarification by the authors.

[171]Gutt, *Relevance Theory*, 21-24. Concerning background beliefs, see also Diane Brockway, "Semantic Constraints on Relevance," in *Possibilities and Limitations of Pragmatics: Proceedings of the Conference on Pragmatics, Urbino, July 8-14, 1979*, ed. Herman Parret, Marina Sbisà, and Jef Verschueren (Amsterdam: John Benjamins, 1981), 57-62.

additional background information, add a relevant side issue for consideration, or even serve as a corrective mechanism if the communication situation is in danger of breaking down.[172]

In an inferential model of communication driven by the *principles of relevance*, all communicative actions, whether verbal or non-verbal, code or non-code, serve as *evidence* to be interpreted.[173] Relevance constrains the possible interpretations of an utterance. The previous illustration is worth returning to:

Bill (sees Mary working behind her desk): How was your hiking trip last weekend?
Mary (points to her leg under her desk in a cast)
Bill: It looks like you had a lot of fun!

With the *principles of relevance* dictating this analysis of communication, Mary's action of pointing to her leg cast clearly is a communicative action meant to answer Bill's specific question.[174] Bill will not pull out his pen to sign the cast, an action that he might do in a different context in response to the same action. Nor will Bill wonder how Mary broke her leg. Relevance suggests Mary's action is answering Bill's question.

There is one other aspect of this illustration that has not yet been discussed. Bill's response to Mary's sorry state is "It looks like you had a lot of fun!" This response does not make sense within a code model of communication (unless of course Mary is masochistic and Bill is aware of this, an option unlikely here[175]). Irony and other figurative language are difficult to understand within

---

[172]These are just a few ways the *principle of relevance* can be demonstrated (or adhered to) in these types of utterances. What is important is that these utterances are considered relevant and as such they are not rejected as *useless*.

[173]Sperber and Wilson, *Relevance*, 170; Gutt, *Relevance Theory*, 12.

[174]The reader may be unimpressed here with the analysis noting that clearly such an interpretation is meant by the action. However, it must be remembered that such an intuitive assumption cannot be assumed in a purely semiotic approach. Non-linguistic elements clearly are entailed in this interpretation. Appeals to context are correct; however, such appeals have not been based on a systematic theory. The *principles of relevance* are meant to give a theoretical basis to the notion and use of context.

[175]Of course this is not impossible. Further information on Bill might cause one to conclude that this is indeed the intention of Bill's statement. However, given a standard cultural situation, without other information to cause one to think otherwise, irony is the most likely interpretation.

most attempts at explaining communication. It seems to be minimized or discussed only within a special context for figurative language. Such a practice gives priority to *literal* over *figurative* uses of language. This view of language usage fails to observe that figurative language is very common and in no way *non-normal*. An adequate description of language must be able to account for figurative language within its description of common language usage. An overemphasis upon literal at the expense of figurative may result in a skewed view of communication which may overlook figurative language in all but the most obvious instances.[176] However, a *relevance* model acknowledges that this common (normal) use of language functions naturally within the communication process.[177] Both figurative language and non-figurative language are *normal* communication.[178] From the perspective of RT (and I maintain the perspective of an adequate communication model proven through empirical study[179] of language), "there is no reason to think that the optimally relevant interpretive expression of a thought is always the most literal one. The speaker is presumed to aim at optimal relevance, not literal truth."[180] Bill's comment to Mary about "fun" is not insensitive or mere nonsense, it is ironic

---

[176]This error is often propagated in basic Bible study guides and elementary hermeneutic texts. For example, the interpretive principle that states, 'interpret literally unless there is something explicit (nonsense, contradiction, etc.)' has been suggested as a guide to instruct the interpreter when to look for figurative language (see J. Robertson McQuilkin, *Understanding and Applying the Bible* [Chicago: Moody Press, 1983], 140-41). Such an approach to any literature fails to appreciate the richness of human language.

[177]E. W. Bullinger, whose view of figures includes minor form differences and thus is broader than that which is common, states, "A figure is simply a word or a sentence thrown into a peculiar *form*, different from its original or simplest meaning or use. These forms are constantly used by every speaker and writer. It is impossible to hold the simplest conversation, or to write a few sentences without, it may be unconsciously, making use of figures" (*Figures of Speech Used in the Bible, Explained and Illustrated* [London: Eyre and Spottiswoode, 1898; reprint, Grand Rapids: Baker Book House, 1968], xv; italics are in the original). Although phrases like "original or simplest meaning or use" are insufficient (although no more insufficient than this work's use of *normal* or *literal*), Bullinger's point is important: figurative language is common.

[178]Concerning metaphor and metonymy, see Nam Sun Song, "Metaphor and Metonymy," in *Relevance Theory: Applications and Implications*, ed. Robyn Carston and Seiji Uchida (Amsterdam: John Benjamins Publishing Company, 1998), 87-104.

[179]The empirical evidence is the observable occurrences of figurative language in communication.

[180]Sperber and Wilson, *Relevance*, 233. Whether or not RT is the most effective communication model, the prominence of figurative language within common communication suggests that figurative language cannot be treated as secondary. RT treats it in manner demanded by its usage.

and adds humor to the situation. This is more colorful than merely acknowledging Mary's injury and/or her disastrous weekend. Figurative language is not merely a *literal* meaning couched in associative wording. Rather, it adds to the communication situation by including aspects of color, allusions to the collective aspects of the culture, etc.[181]

Therefore, the model of communication adopted here is inferential. The communicator uses various stimuli as evidence which is intended to be interpreted by the receiver in order to communicate the intended message. Failure of communication may occur for a number of reasons.[182] It may be due to insufficient evidence being presented or the evidence may be misinterpreted. Misinterpretation may be due to poor presentation of the evidence, faulty reasoning, a lack of a shared cognitive environment which both people can draw upon for interpreting the world, or just a simple mistake in interpretation.[183] The role of evidence in communication also suggests that various levels of certainty occur in the interpretation process. Thus, some communication events may be stronger than others. Weak communication may be reinforced with further evidence. For example, if Mary sees that Bill has some chocolates and desires to have one, she may first purposefully look at the chocolates in a manner which

---

[181]*Relevance* also helps to explain which association(s) of a metaphor or simile (or other figurative language) is implied by the figure. While eating dinner if one sees a person (Jim) eating a lot, he might say, "Jim is a pig." Most immediately interpret this as a statement concerning Jim's eating habits, specifically that he eats too much. No one assumes that the speaker believes Jim has a curly tail or would make a good ham sandwich if so processed. The cultural belief that pigs eat a lot (whether true or not) is what would be the assumed meaning of the utterance. However, in a different context, the intention of the same metaphor has a different meaning. If one visits Jim in his home and notices that there are clothes all over the floor, one might conclude, "Jim is a pig." The cultural belief that pigs are filthy (again, whether true or not) is what would be the assumed meaning of the utterance. The interpretations of these utterances occur naturally for the American. Why does one not assume that in the second instance, Jim's eating habits are being discussed? *Relevance.*

Accounting for figurative language has been a major focus of relevance theory. See for example Sperber and Wilson, *Relevance*, 217-24, 241-43; Blakemore, *Understanding Utterances*, 155-79; Gutt, *Relevance Theory*, 46-60; Song, "Metaphor and Metonymy," 87-104; and three articles from a symposium on irony held in Osaka Japan (1993) by Ken-Ichi Seto, Hideki Hamamoto, Masa-aki Yamanashi plus a response from Sperber and Wilson published in Robyn Carston and Seiji Uchida, eds., *Relevance Theory: Applications and Implications* (Amsterdam: John Benjamins Publishing Company, 1998), 239-93.

[182]I am sure that further consideration will reveal additional reasons for mis- communication.

[183]The interpretation of utterances in and inferential model always includes an element of risk (Wilson and Sperber, "Outline," 9). It is maintained that the *principle(s) of relevance* is the most satisfactory way to minimize this risk.

she hopes her intentions will be interpreted by Bill. If Bill is unsure of this intention or misses it altogether, he may ignore Mary's glance. Mary may reinforce this evidence by an indirect statement about hunger or more forcefully she may directly ask for a chocolate.[184]

The previous discussion does not mean that there is no use in communication for the notion of *code*. As discussed in the previous section, the *linguistic system* is relational and code is an important aspect of this network. Also, there are some utterances which seem to be interpreted in this manner (as with the first example in this section). However, code alone is not the basis of communication. Rather, it serves as a piece of evidence in the communication process. Communication works both by code and inference.

At this stage the reader may ask, "How does this extended discussion of communication contribute to this work?" This will be discussed presently. Because communication is *inferential* and because code serves as *evidence* to contribute to interpretation, it becomes evident that the explicit *literal* meaning of sentences themselves may not accurately yield the intended meaning of an utterance. An author assumes background knowledge, includes contextual information, and uses (in the case of the New Testament) other linguistic means to communicate his intention. The *principles of relevance* constrain possible interpretations to those which are relevant within a specific context. A distinction will be made between the contextless (straightforward) meaning and the meaning dependent upon contextual input. The former will be called *semantic meaning* and the later, *pragmatic meaning*. These terms will be defined and further developed in the next subsection. Thus, within a communication situation raw linguistic information with input from contextual features is used to communicate a message from one party to another. The varied contextual information will contribute significantly to the intended meaning of a communicative act. A distinction will be made in this work between the semantic meaning of an utterance (or grammatical form) and its specific pragmatic meaning in context. Although code models of communication do incorporate a notion of pragmatics, it only seems to be in the form of rules as mentioned above. The inferential model of communication

---

[184]This exchange could be analyzed much more thoroughly and would result in further important observations concerning intentions, evidence, interpretation, and communication. Also, looking at reasons for using specific evidence would be beneficial. However, such further discussion is beyond the scope of this work.

provides a basis for linguistic code with semantic meaning to have many potential context-dependent meanings (these are the sememes introduced above; e.g., ˢ/command/, ˢ/request/, ˢ/permission/, etc.[185]). The interpreter must determine what pragmatic or contextual meaning is most probable. It has been this chapter's conclusion that the *principle(s) of relevance* provides the basis for such an interpretive process.[186] In the next section this work will define and develop the semantic and pragmatic distinction and demonstrate how it will apply to the analysis of a grammatical form.

Semantic and Pragmatic Distinction[187]

The preceding subsection has explored the communication situation and observed that communication primarily occurs through an inferential process. Although code is an important aspect of communication, it serves as evidence to be interpreted. This understanding of the communication process has surfaced an important issue needing further development. It has become evident that an isolated utterance may contain meaning.[188] However, an isolated utterance may be interpreted differently (and thus have a different meaning) in different contexts. The utterance itself is evidence which the receiver of the communication must interpret in the most relevant manner in order to understand the utterance. The isolated meaning (which may not naturally occur)

---

[185]In chapter 4 the traditional labels noted here will be abandoned. However, although the classification system there will be more complex, it will be possible to still use these labels to varying degrees.

[186]Grice's work will also be very helpful despite the proposed development assumed in this work.

[187]This subsection continues the discussion of communication begun in the previous subsection. However, because of the importance of this issue for the methodology of this paper (next section), it will be discussed separately.

[188]It may be argued that a *linguistic extension* cannot exist in isolation and therefore meaning only occurs in a context. This seems to be similar to the philosophical question, "if a tree falls in the woods and no one is present to hear it (and thus it goes unheard), did the tree falling actually make a sound?" The answer to such a question may depend on whether one wishes to see the event from the perspective of the tree falling or the potential hearer who can attest to the event. This is similar (although not identical) to the issue at hand. An either/or choice is not necessary. A grammatical form, lexeme, phrase, or longer utterance does have meaning. If it did not, it would not add to a discourse. However, this meaning interacts with other linguistic meaning and context for its meaning in a specific context.

is inherent in the form. The meaning of the utterance in a specific communication situation is the result of the interaction between the inherent meaning and contextual features. This resultant meaning will differ as the context changes.

At the simplest level, the referent of a word may differ in various contexts. The sentence, "I purchased a cowboy today" will have a different meaning (albeit in the domain of reference) depending upon the identity of the speaker. The natural interpretation of this sentence is that a person is buying a toy cowboy. It could refer to a father who has purchased the toy for his son. Or the child himself could have purchased it for his own use. Each context contributes to the intended meaning. However, this same utterance may have an entirely different meaning if the referent of "I" is Jerry Jones, the owner of the Dallas Cowboys football team. If Mr. Jones appeared on the news and made this statement, no one would wonder why he was on television announcing the purchase of a toy. The viewers would be interested in which player the Dallas Cowboys had acquired and how he would contribute to the success of the team. This illustration and the preceding have demonstrated the existence of two distinct types of meaning.

The difference in meanings can be attributed to different contextual information interacting with the semantics inherent in the statement. The latter is purely linguistic knowledge. The former meaning is derived from contextual or non-linguistic background knowledge. For the purpose of this work direct,[189] purely linguistic meaning will be labeled *semantics* and indirect linguistic meaning and non-linguistic meaning will be called *pragmatics*. The notion of *directness* and *indirectness* is simply whether the linguistic information under consideration is the direct language code being considered or language code from the context having bearing on the language code under consideration. For example, a polite word such as "please" although linguistic will impact the pragmatic implicature(s) of a subsequent word in the imperative mood. Also, when describing the pragmatics of a grammatical form or structure, lexical meaning of a specific occurrence of a verb in the grammatical form/structure must be classified as indirect since it really is not part of the grammatical form/structure. If the lexeme itself was the element of analysis, this meaning would be semantic and considered in the domain of *lexical semantics*. However,

---

[189]The term "direct" and its opposite "indirect" will be explained below.

it is a contextual features as far as the form/structure is concerned.[190]

Thus, one may summarize and define the important terms as follows: *semantic meaning* is the inherent linguistic meaning encoded and expressed by the *linguistic system* in an utterance without reference to non-linguistic factors such as beliefs, social considerations, etc., or other contextual linguistic elements. It is the linguistic meaning directly involved in the linguistic element under discussion.[191] *Pragmatics* is indirect linguistic (contextual) meaning and non-linguistic meaning including factors such as beliefs, social considerations, etc., and its relationship to the communicators. *Pragmatic implicature* is the resultant meaning of any non-linguistic factors such as beliefs, social considerations, etc., and indirect contextual linguistic meaning interacting with

---

[190]I needed to introduce the notions of *direct* and *indirect* linguistic code because the simple linguistic/non-linguistic distinction to define semantics and pragmatics is insufficient for the purposes here.

[191]This definition is my own but is based on the work of many others: Blakemore, *Understanding Utterances*, 40; Julia S. Falk, "Semantics," in *Language: Introductory Readings*, ed. Virginia P. Clark, Paul A. Eschholz, and Alfred F. Rosa (New York: St. Martin's Press, 1981), 399; Sperber and Wilson, *Relevance*, 9-10; Adrian Akmajian, Richard A. Demers and Robert M. Harnish, *Linguistics: An Introduction to Language and Communication*, 2d ed. (Cambridge, MA: MIT Press, 1984), 529; John G. Cook, *The Structure and Persuasive Power of Mark: A Linguistic Approach*, The Society of Biblical Literature Semeia Studies (Atlanta: Scholars Press, 1995), 4. Also, important to this definition is the notion of *inherent meaning*. This is meaning that the linguistic expression brings to the utterance unrelated to any contextual effects. See Stephen H. Levinsohn (*Discourse Features of New Testament Greek: A Coursebook*, 2d ed. [Dallas: Summer Institute of Linguistics, 2000], ix) and Lyons who suggests that a structure's "inherent meaning is determined by its characteristic use" (*Language*, 167-68). This seems too simplistic for the purposes in this work and will be further developed. Inherent semantic meaning is similar to (and in this work influenced by) Wallace's (*Exegetical Syntax*, 2-3) *unaffected* or *ontological meaning*. Note Wallace's (ibid., 2, n. 8) clarification of the term *ontological* (see also Lyons, *Linguistic Semantics*, 323-25). However, despite the influence of others, any deficiency in the proposed definition is my own. For a discussion of the history semantic studies (including some discussion of definition), see Leo Pap, "Semantics–Syntactics–Pragmatics: A New Look at an Old Distinction," in *The Eleventh LACUS Forum 1984*, ed. Robert A. Hall (Columbia, SC: Hornbeam Press, 1985), 304-309.

It is not uncommon to include within a discussion (and definition) of semantics the study of reference, denotation, and sense (although reference may be handled in pragmatics). These are important areas of study; however, these seem primarily limited to the specific sub-field of semantics, namely, *lexical semantics*. For a specific discussion of this sub-field (see Falk, "Semantics," 400-404 and Lyons, *Linguistic Semantics*, 46-130). Lexical semantics has also been discussed within biblical studies (see Darrell L. Bock, "New Testament Word Analysis," in *Introducing New Testament Interpretation*, ed. Scot McKnight [Grand Rapids: Baker Book House, 1989], 101-4; Johannes P. Louw, *Semantics of New Testament Greek* [Atlanta: Scholars Press, 1982], 1-66; Moisés Silva, *Biblical Words and Their Meaning: An Introduction to Lexical Semantics* [Grand Rapids: Zondervan Publishing House, 1983]).

the semantic meaning.[192] Any communication situation includes both semantic and pragmatic meaning. In the study of linguistics, these areas are rather new.[193]

---

[192]As with the definition of *semantics*, the definitions of *pragmatics* and *pragmatic implicature* are my own but are based on the work of many others: Blakemore, *Semantic Restraints*, 1; Idem, *Understanding Utterances*, 40; Sperber and Wilson, *Relevance*, 10; Akmajian, Demers, and Harnish, *Linguistics*, 527; Radford, *Transformational Syntax*, 3; Cook, *Structure and Persuasive Power*, 4. Pragmatic implicature is similar (and here influenced by) Wallace's (*Exegetical Syntax*, 2-3) *affected* or *phenomenological meaning*. However, within RT (including some influences listed here), development of this concept goes beyond the definition used here which remains firmly Gricean (see the brief comments about this in appendix 1) and despite the influence of others, any deficiency in the proposed definition is my own. Defining pragmatics is much more difficult than is presented here. In fact some descriptions seem to be defining entirely different concepts. Compare for example the definitions of Egger (*How to Read the New Testament: An Introduction to Linguistic and Historical-Critical Methodology*, ed. Hendrikus Boers [Peabody, MA: Hendrickson Publishers, 1996], 125), Olsen (*Semantic and Pragmatic Model*, 17; who seems to use *pragmatics* and *pragmatic implicatures* synonymously), and Cook (*Structure and Persuasive Power*, 4). It is difficult to understand how all these definitions are explaining the same linguistic term. For a detailed discussion of issues of definition, see Levinson, *Pragmatics*, 5-35.

It seems like the variation in definitions is dependent upon the context of the discussion and the purpose in which the concept is being used. Thus, it may not be accurate to propose that these definitions or even this work's definition is *the* definition of *pragmatics*; rather, it seems like the term *pragmatic* is used to label the aspect of meaning which includes external features and influences that are not explicit in the linguistic form or item. This is contrasted with *semantic* which is the linguistic meaning of the form or item. If one is making this contrast in a discussion of spoken utterances, written discourse, or a grammatical form, the definition will vary accordingly. In order to avoid this confusion, it may be preferable in grammatical works such as this and Olsen's work on verbal aspect (discussed briefly below) to use Wallace's (*Exegetical Syntax*, 2-3) terms, *affected* for pragmatics and *unaffected* for semantics; however, this terminology is not common nor does it communicate the more universal notion of pragmatics and semantics which seem to apply at many levels of the communication process. These areas do share some properties (as the definition here suggests) and this relationship is lost with other terminology. Therefore, these terms will be maintained in this work despite their problematic history.

[193]There has always been an acknowledgment of the importance of semantics and pragmatics. However, as a primary focus of study, serious attention has been more recent. Early focus on the *linguistic system* in modern linguistic theories primarily included phonology, morphology, and especially syntax. See for example the emphasis in Bloomfield, *Language*; Noam Chomsky, *Syntactic Structures* (The Hague: Mouton, 1957); idem, *Aspects*; Gleason, *Introduction*; and Hockett, *Course*. These works do not ignore semantics and pragmatics but treat them in a relatively unsystematic way. Lyons who devotes more space to semantics than most of the others who proceeded him (1968) states, "Many of the more influential books on linguistics that have appeared in the last thirty years devote little or no attention to semantics" (*Theoretical Linguistics*, 400). Since then some major works (e.g., Lyons, *Semantics*; idem, *Linguistic Semantics*; Levinson, *Pragmatics*; Jacob L. Mey, *Pragmatics: An Introduction* [Oxford: Blackwell Publishers, 1993]) and many minor works and articles have appeared in these areas; however, compared with phonology and grammar (morphology and syntax), these fields have

This may contribute to the lack of consensus on terminology discussed above. Most linguists acknowledge a distinction between semantic and pragmatic meaning, but where the domain of one ends and the other begins is less certain. Such a discussion is rather involved and will not be pursued here.[194]

Thus far the discussion here of semantic and pragmatic meaning has been confined to utterances and texts no smaller than the clause. The present work is an analysis of a single grammatical element, the imperative mood. Can the semantic and pragmatic distinction be meaningful at this level? It is the assumption of this work that it is and that it provides the basic framework within which the imperative mood will be analyzed and classified. One successful example of an application of semantic and pragmatic insights applied to a grammatical category is found in Mari Olsen's Northwestern University dissertation on verbal aspect.[195] In this work, Olsen uses this distinction to identify obligatory features which constitute the semantic meaning and non-obligatory pragmatic implicatures.[196] A similar use of this distinction will be incorporated here.[197]

---

much ground to make up.

[194]For example, Lyons defines semantics much broader than most linguists (*Linguistic Semantics*, xii-xiii, 1-45). Simply stated it is the "study of meaning" (ibid., xii). Thus, for Lyons, semantics includes much of what others (including this work) consider the domain of pragmatics. See also Pap, "Semantics–Syntactics–Pragmatics," 310 and the close association between semantics and pragmatics in A. Sophia S. Marmaridou, "Semantic and Pragmatic Parameters of Meaning," *Journal of Pragmatics* 11 (1987): 721-36. Concerning this distinction specific languages, see Flor Aarts, "Imperative Sentences in English: Semantics and Pragmatics," *Studia Linguistica* 43 (1989): 119-134 and Villy Rouchota, "The Subjunctive in Modern Greek: Dividing the Labor between Semantics and Pragmatics," *Journal of Modern Greek Studies* 12 (1994): 185-201. This articles has similarities with the approach taken in this work. A semantic meaning is postulated and then pragmatic usages are described. Also, it is based on an RT approach to the issue. For a brief discussion of three approaches to the boundaries of semantics and pragmatics, see Geoffrey N. Leech, *Principles of Pragmatics* (London: Longman, 1983), 5-7. Leech briefly describes theories that emphasize semantics (and thus pragmatics is understood within this framework), pragmatics (semantics are understood within this framework), and a mediating position to which he claims to hold.

[195]This dissertation was published as *A Semantic and Pragmatic Model of Lexical and Grammatical Aspect* (New York and London: Garland Publishing, 1997).

[196]Ibid., 17-22. The nature of Olsen's distinction will be discussed below. See chapter 3 and especially appendix 3.

[197]N.B.: the present work is not purely a pragmatic analysis. Thus far the semantic/pragmatic distinction has been discussed primarily at a clausal (and larger) level. It is only a model (analogy) for analysis of specific grammatical points. The distinction between semantic meaning and pragmatic effects is necessary to explain how the communicators are able to understand an utterance which seems unrelated to the linguistic form in which it is presented. More importantly,

It is not sufficient to observe a semantic/pragmatic distinction without reference to how these meanings will be determined. This work will discuss the possibility of identifying *the* semantic meaning of the imperative mood and will propose a theory which seems to best account for the data. The solution will be to propose *inherent semantic meaning* for the mood. This meaning may be eclipsed to some extent by pragmatic factors but should remain present in the form. An exception to this will be some idiomatic expression which over time may have lost all connection to the imperative mood. Next various factors which interact with the semantics and thus yield pragmatic implicatures will be considered. These pragmatic implicatures are the sememes realized by the imperative mood in context (e.g., ˢ/command/, ˢ/request/, ˢ/permission/, etc.). The task will be twofold: to identify the various sememes and to determine what contextual features present in a context result in the specific sememe's realization.

Preliminary Methodological Considerations

Much consideration of method has already been presented. Also, more detailed methodological discussion will occur in chapters 3 (semantics) and 4 (pragmatics) prior to dealing with the specific content of those chapters. This section will review and propose general methodological principles for the work. Thus far it has been suggested that the approach of this book will be descriptive and primarily synchronic. There will be a priority given to structure and this work is concerned only with the morphological imperative mood. This study will attempt to keep structure and meaning in their proper place and maintain a consistent relationship between them.[198] This will occur in the following

---

it is necessary to explain how one form can have different meanings in different contexts. This work is using the principle of this distinction to separate and analyze the inherent meaning of the form from the meaning resulting from the interaction of the semantics with contextual features. This also can be argued with reference to Olsen's work. In both approaches, some linguistic information (albeit contextual) is involved in the pragmatic analysis.

[198]It is hoped that this will avoid the error of those (including Colwell) who apply Colwell's rule (and its *supposed* converse) to the anarthrous pre-verbal predicate nominative construction. Colwell in his discussion of definite anarthrous predicate nominatives began his study of a structural element (the anarthrous noun in a specific word order context) with a database limited by a predetermined semantic identification (definite). This approach has value for disciplines such as textual criticism; however, it is irrelevant for grammar because it seems to put the cart

manner. The search for the semantic meaning will begin by looking at the
structure (in a broad manner, the imperative mood contrasted to other moods).
The search for pragmatic usages will begin by looking at structural clues and
the environments in which the mood occurs. Where a certain pragmatic usage
is found in a specific contextual environment, this will be noted. Predetermined
meaning will not be imposed on structure.

A distinction between semantics and pragmatics is assumed. Nevertheless,
an important element of the method here will be an interaction between the
search for semantic meaning and an analysis of the pragmatic implicature. To
some extent these studies must inform one another. Thus, after initial work on
semantics, both semantics and pragmatics will be developed together (with a
priority given to structural considerations). Nevertheless, initial priority must
be given to semantics because conclusions here will inform usage (and
implicature). In other words, without a sound general understanding of the raw
imperative mood, a focused discussion of pragmatics will be impossible.

Limitations

There are a number of limitations inherent in this work that must be
presented at the onset. In the preface to this work, I noted a few limitations that
the choice of the project demanded. In this section, I will emphasize the
limitation within the project itself that must be adhered to in order to avoid this
project from becoming too cumbersome.

The first limitation regards the state of linguistics. There are a number of
schools of linguistics available. Some of these can supplement one another
while others are incompatible. Also, theories continue to evolve, some schools
break off for their own specific needs, while others fade away. Even the
linguistic scholar may not have a grasp over the entire field. For one such as
myself whose focus is New Testament studies, a comprehensive understanding
of the entire field is not possible. Nevertheless, it seems possible to adequately

---

before the horse. The starting point must be structure because that is what is found when one first
approaches the text. Semantic conclusions follow (see E. C. Colwell, "A Definite Rule for the
Use of the Article in the Greek New Testament," *Journal of Biblical Literature* 52 [1933]: 12-21
and Wallace's evaluation of Colwell [*Exegetical Syntax*, 5-6, 256-62]).

utilize two theories with benefit for the purposes here.[199]

Second, the primary purpose of this work is to determine the meaning and usage of the imperative mood. It is not a study on the way in which commands and prohibitions can be formed in the Greek. The Greek *command* and *prohibition* will be discussed in appropriate places; however, this is a study which needs sound morphological analysis before a full analysis can be pursued.

Third, the issue of tenses of the imperative will not be discussed beyond an introductory summary of recent work and where they directly contribute to this work's analysis. This is the area in which most work has been done recently and there is no need to revisit the issue at length here.

Fourth, the notion of *imperativeness* is also an important topic within philosophy. However, the analysis here is necessarily linguistic. It is linguistic evidence that this work is attempting to explain. Linguistics and philosophy overlap significantly and this study will not be able to avoid some discussion of philosophy. However, adequate treatment of this rich area is beyond the scope of this work. This is partially due to the morphological focus of this paper. Philosophy's interest in this area is primarily upon the command/prohibition function and is not restricted by morphology.[200]

Fifth, in some areas this work will limit itself to representative portions of the New Testament. Imperatives from all authors and literary genres will be considered. Concerning Paul, imperatives from each major epistolary groups will be analyzed.[201] Not every imperative (over 1600) will be examined. The

---

[199]See however my reservations discussed in appendix 1.

[200]For a discussion of the distinction between the linguistic and philosophical approaches (maintaining a value in both), see Arthur Merin, "Imperatives: Linguistics vs. Philosophy," *Linguistics* 29 (1991): 669-702. For a treatment of imperatives from a philosophical standpoint, see Hamblin, *Imperatives*. This study seems to be the most comprehensive of its kind and will be utilized in this work. However, its philosophical nature must be noted which diminishes its value for this project. In an article on the imperative, Flor Aarts ignores Hamblin because Hamblin's *imperative* is broader than his study and "does not contribute anything new to the linguistic issues with which it is concerned" ("Imperative Sentences," 123). On the other hand, Dominique Boulonnais seems to prefer those areas of Hamblin's work which are less focused on linguistic issues (review of *Imperatives*, by C. L. Hamblin, *Journal of Pragmatics* 16 [1991]: 286-87). See also the treatment of *commands* from a (philosophical) logic perspective by Nicholas Rescher, *The Logic of Commands* (London: Routledge, 1966).

[201]I am assuming four groups of Paul's epistles which can be divided by both chronology and content. These are: second missionary journey epistles: 1 and 2 Thessalonians; major epistles: Romans, Galatians, 1 and 2 Corinthians; prison epistles: Ephesians, Colossians, Philippians, and

basic database from which we will draw imperatives (although not all will be analyzed) is as follows with the number of imperatives in parentheses (idioms as described in chapter 3 are not factored in these figures): Matt 1-5, 10-13 (71); Mark 13-16 (47); Luke 1-5, 13 (37); John 1-4, 15-17, 20-21 (51); Acts 1-5, 15-20, 23-28 (53[202]); Rom (62); 1 Cor 1-7, 12-16 (75);[203] Phil (21); 1 Thess (19); 1 Tim 2, 4, 6 (24); Phlm (4); Heb (29); Jas 1, 3, 5 (31); 1 Pet 1, 3, 5 (20); 2 Peter (7); 1 John (10); 2 John (3); 3 John (2); Jude (5); Rev 1-9, 21-22 (55). In addition, where a peculiar feature is isolated (e.g., synoptic parallels, third person, etc.) all applicable New Testament examples will be discussed.

Since the focus here is upon as varied a database as possible, the list may seem proportionally lopsided (in relationship to all imperatives) in favor of smaller works such as James, Peter, etc. However, this approach seems best because it should reduce redundancy that may occur if an exact proportion of

---

Philemon; pastoral epistles: 1 and 2 Timothy, Titus. I am aware of two potential problems raised by my classification scheme. First, a number of these epistles are held to be inauthentic by many (and in some cases a majority of) scholars. I will assume Pauline authorship here without defense. For a detailed discussion and support of my position, see the appropriate books such as Donald Guthrie, *New Testament Introduction*, 4th ed. (Downers Grove, IL: InterVarsity Press, 1990). Second, the dating of Galatians is by no means certain. Many in recent years, especially in America and Britain have embraced an early date of this epistle, viewing it as Paul's first. This is by no means certain. Again, there is no need for a defense of my position since it has little if any impact on my analysis. The fourfold group is merely a guide to be certain that I cover as wide a variety of passages as possible.

[202]In addition to omitted idioms, ἔγειρε (Acts 3:6) is omitted in the database here which is included in brackets in NA[27]. The verb is included in A, C, E, 33, 1739, and the many manuscripts represented by gothic M (among others). However, the shorter and preferred reading is supported by the Greek manuscripts, ℵ, B, D (and the Sahidic version).

[203]In light of the desire for a diverse database, one might question the inclusion of so many imperatives from 1 Corinthians especially since the entire book of Romans is also used. First Corinthians contains 100 imperatives of which 75 are part of the database. The reason for its inclusion is its unique status among the Pauline corpus. First Corinthians represents a portion of a correspondence between Paul and a church of which his authority should have been unquestioned; however, it was quite strained. Additionally, the third person is used quite frequently in this book. There are more occurrences here than in any other book (although in terms of the number of occurrences against words in a book, 1 Corinthians places third with 6.9 per 1000 words–only the small books: James (8.6/1000) and 1 Timothy (8.2/1000) have more. Twenty percent of all third person imperatives occur in 1 Corinthians (47 of 234; 39 of which fall within the sample). Over 7% (17) occur within chapter 7 alone. The contextual information is important and it will be suggested that the relationship between author and recipient may influence the use of the third person. Additionally, Romans is unique in that it is the only major epistle written by Paul in which he had little if any history with the original intended readers of the epistle.

imperatives throughout the New Testament was chosen.[204]

This database is most applicable to chapter 4 where a new paradigm will be suggested and defended. Chapter 3 will generally utilize the database but the points argued there demand different types of data. The first major section is straightforward and demands a significant variety of contexts to make its point but it does not demand examination of the entire database. The other major section must account for all "parallel" verbs in the synoptics (see the chapter for the uses of "parallel" here).

Finally, I am certain that there are areas concerning the imperative which some readers would have wished to have seen pursued more thoroughly. Unfortunately, time and space do not permit this project to explore the many interesting issues related to the imperative. For example, more time could have been devoted to the use of the negative with the imperative, application to further texts,[205] etc., Nevertheless, it is hoped most interests of readers may be touched on here.

Summary and Overview

Using established insights from modern linguistics in general[206] and further specific insights from neuro-cognitive stratificational linguistics and relevance theory, this work has established a sound linguistic basis for the proposed study of the Greek imperative mood. The priority of both synchronic and descriptive analysis have been demonstrated. It has been determined that one must attempt to understand the New Testament through a *Koine* Greek lens. It has been demonstrated that the *linguistic system* is composed of a number of interrelated subsystems or strata which handle different phenomena at each level. This work

---

[204]This would result in a database of almost two-thirds of the imperatives being from the gospels and Acts. This may reflect the proportion of both the imperatives and the literature of the New Testament; however, accuracy demands as varied a database as possible. In addition, the chapter choices still maintain a significant narrative presence while exploiting the variety of literature within the gospels and Acts themselves.

[205]The preface noted my desire to see this work applied more fully in exegesis. As noted there, I am not avoiding exegesis and there should be sufficient examples within to demonstrate the exegetical value of this work.

[206]In some cases these insights have been used in previous traditional approaches to the New Testament; however, here this work is providing a linguistic basis for the insights.

will be primarily concerned with the imperative mood (expressed on the morphological stratum) and the meaning(s) which it realizes. Also, this chapter has attempted to place this study within its larger contexts both cognitively and within the communication situation. These areas will both provide a theoretical basis for the study and maintain a control to prevent analysis which cannot be cognitively nor communicatively probable. Communication primarily operates through inference where linguistic code may serve as evidence to be interpreted by the one receiving the communicative act. A distinction is made within the communication situation between inherent semantic meaning which includes linguistic information and pragmatic implicature which results from the contextual contributions of the communicative participants' world. Finally, this communicative principle was discussed and it was suggested that it can be applied in a narrow study such as a grammatical form.

It is hoped that this study will result in determining the mood's range of meaning and its usage in the New Testament. Chapter 2 will provide further introductory material. Specifically, it will focus on how the imperative mood has been viewed within New Testament Greek studies and modern linguistics. This chapter will deal with Speech Act Theory in some detail. The reason for this is twofold. First, it is a natural theory in which to apply an analysis of imperatives. Second, this book will glean a few principles from the theory while ultimately rejecting the theory itself. The rejection will demand a rather detailed defense because of its importance within *command* studies generally.

Chapter 3 will attempt to discover the semantic meaning of the imperative mood. It will try to answer the question, "what does the imperative mood mean?" in order to answer further questions such as "what does the use or choice of the imperative mood by an author bring to the communication situation?" and "why use the imperative mood?" In other words, the inherent (semantic) meaning of the mood will be determined. This will be done in a number of ways. The chapter will analyze the imperative mood in various contexts, compare the imperative to other moods, and consider suggestions for the meaning of the mood as this process is undertaken. For further refinement and development of semantic analysis, see chapter 3.

Chapter 4 will analyze a number of factors which interact with the semantic meaning and result in pragmatic implicatures. There are proposals concerning how to determine implicatures.[207] This work will consider certain contextual features which seem to affect the meaning of the imperative in context. Areas of analysis will include: social status, social distance, politeness, rank, lexical nuances, additional contextual words, grammatical person, and the position of the imperative within an event sequence. These will not necessarily all be looked at separately (many of the social elements may be looked at together). Finally, this book will consider the notion of *benefaction* and its relationship to the imperative.[208] Each of these areas will be considered as the mood is analyzed. If these features can predict the meaning of the mood in context, this will be noted. Also, within this chapter, special attention will be given to the third person imperative and the so-called "conditional" imperative.

In some ways this approach does not differ significantly from the approach found in traditional grammars where the imperative mood is defined and various usages are suggested.[209] However, our approach will result in a significantly different paradigm for explaining the mood. It is hoped that this approach will lead to more certain conclusions and to a measure of predictability concerning usages when these forms are encountered in a specific context. The traditional approach tends to depend on intuition to determine what usage is probable.[210] This approach will utilize insights from contextual features to better predict when a specific pragmatic meaning (usage) is present.

---

[207]Grice discusses five such features. Implicatures are *cancelable* (the implicature may be canceled by additional information), *nondetachable* (inference is based on the semantic meaning, not the form of the utterance), *calculability* (its presence can be demonstrated from the utterance), *non-conventional* (not explicit from the semantic meaning), and the potential of different implicatures of an utterance based on context (Grice, "Logic," 57-58 and Levinson, *Pragmatics*, 114-18). These are further developed in H. Paul Grice, "Further Notes on Logic and Conversation," in *Syntax and Semantics, vol. 9: Pragmatics*, ed. P. Cole (New York: Academic Press, 1978), 114-16. See also Lyons, *Linguistic Semantics*, 286-90. Olsen (*Semantic and Pragmatic Model*, 17-18) emphasizes one of these features, *cancelability* (or as Levinson, *Pragmatics*, 114 labels it, *defeasiblity*) as the basis for her distinction between semantic meaning and (conversational) pragmatic implicatures.

[208]Grice's five implicature features are not the basis of this study. Each of these points may be challenged (Levinson, *Pragmatics*, 118-22). Olsen's dependence upon *cancelability* works well as a basis for the explanation of her data; however, I am not certain that there can be *uncancelable* meaning (see appendix 3).

[209]See for example Wallace, *Exegetical Syntax*, 485-93.

[210]This is a broad generalization. Some have used important contextual features to determine usage. See for example Wallace who discusses structural features in which the *conditional* imperative is found (*Exegetical Syntax*, 489-90). However, a thorough study of a number of potential features has not yet been undertaken on the imperative mood in *Koine* Greek.

Chapter 2

The Imperative Mood in New Testament and Linguistic Studies

Introduction

In the previous chapter the theoretical and methodological foundation was laid for an analysis of the Greek imperative mood. However, before this discussion may commence, a number of further preliminary matters must be undertaken. A brief survey of work on the Greek imperative mood will be presented with a focus on its treatment by New Testament grammarians. This will be followed by a discussion of some select linguistic approaches to the imperative mood.[1]

The Imperative in New Testament Greek Studies

This section will briefly survey approaches to the imperative mood found in New Testament grammars. First the meaning of the mood itself will be examined. This will be followed by a discussion of the proposed usages of the imperative. Finally, a discussion of the recent study of the tenses used with the mood will be undertaken.[2]

The Meaning of the Greek Imperative Mood[3]

Although there are some differences among New Testament scholars with

---

[1]For a brief discussion of mood in general, see appendix 2.

[2]A survey of ancient Greek studies is beyond the scope of this work. Observations will be made only as necessary.

[3]This section is merely a survey. Development of this subject will occur in chapter 3.

reference to the meaning of the imperative mood, generally, there is little disagreement concerning its essence. In his intermediate grammar, Daniel B. Wallace describes the imperative as the "mood of *intention*, ... the mood furthest removed from certainty, ... [the mood which] moves in the realm of *volition* ... and *possibility*."[4] The imperative portrays *intention* in the sense that it merely presents a potential and intended state of the verbal idea. As the imperative is produced it is only potentially realized. *Actuality* depends on the response of the addressee(s).[5] Thus, *actuality* is not portrayed linguistically in the imperative mood. Only an *intention* is explicit. This is why the imperative is "furthest removed from certainty" in its portrayal of the verbal idea.[6] The imperative is in contrast to the indicative which is most certain, the subjunctive which is probable or desirable, and the optative which is merely possible.[7] Finally, the imperative "moves in the realm of volition." In other words, it expresses the will of the speaker.[8] As demonstrated in chapter 1, communication involves inference and intention. Therefore, although the imperative grammatically may be the mood of volition, real language use may include and use other means for communicating volition. Nevertheless, this basic distinction is helpful when one remembers the complexity and relative nature of the communication situation.

Although most other descriptions of the mood are less detailed and less satisfactory, most agree with Wallace. Some are not as clear about the portrayal nature of language but nevertheless, assuming this notion, they seem to describe

---

[4]*Greek Grammar beyond the Basics: An Exegetical Syntax of the New Testament* (Grand Rapids: Zondervan Publishing House, 1996), 485.

[5]The imperative is "to be realized by another" (Maximilian Zerwick, *Biblical Greek Illustrated by Examples*, trans. Joseph Smith, Scripta Pontificii Instituti Bibilici, vol. 114 [Rome: Editrice Pontificio Istituto Biblici, 1963], 100).

[6]Other terminology for *actuality* and *certainty* include *reality* and *factuality* (see respectively James A. Brooks and Carlton L. Winbery, *Syntax of New Testament Greek* (Lanham, MD: University Press of America, 1979), 103 and Richard A. Young, *Intermediate New Testament Greek: A Linguistic and Exegetical Approach* [Nashville: Broadman and Holman Publishers, 1994], 136). Whatever terminology is adopted, it is important to remember that language only *portrays* or *presents* reality, certainty, or factuality. There is no necessary correspondence between grammar and the real world. This was briefly discussed above in chapter 1.

[7]See Wallace, *Exegetical Syntax*, 446. Wallace classifies the indicative as the only mood of actuality, and the subjunctive, optative, and imperative with decreasing levels (respectively) of potentiality.

[8]This comprehensive definition implies that the imperative by its very nature points to future action (see the classical grammar by Herbert Weir Smyth, *Greek Grammar*, rev. G. M. Messing [Cambridge, MA: Harvard University Press, 1956], 409).

the mood in compatible (albeit too simplistic) terms with Wallace's more comprehensive definition.[9] Others do not really define the imperative but merely describe its range of meaning (command, prohibition, request, etc.).[10]

In light of the complex nature of the imperative, it is unwise to label it simply as the mood of command.[11] This point was argued in chapter 1.

---

[9]David Alan Black, *It's Still Greek to Me: An Easy-to-Understand Guide to Intermediate Greek* (Grand Rapids: Baker Books, 1998), 97, 100; Brooks and Winbery, *Syntax*, 115; H. E. Dana and Julius R. Mantey, *A Manual Grammar of the Greek New Testament* (New York: Macmillan Publishing Co., 1927), 166, 174; Wesley J. Perschbacher, *New Testament Greek Syntax: An Illustrated Manual* (Chicago: Moody Press, 1995), 345. Porter maintains that the imperative is used to direct someone's action (*Idioms of the Greek New Testament*, 2d ed., Biblical Languages: Greek, vol. 2 [Sheffield: JSOT, 1994], 53). The classical grammarians Raphael Kühner and Bernhard Gerth state: "Er ist der Modus der unmittelbaren Willensäusserung des Redenden, ..." (*Ausführliche Grammatik der griechischen Sprache*, 4th ed., vol. 1 [Leverkusen: Gottschalksche, 1955], 236).

[10]BDF, 195; Friedrich Blass and Albert Debrunner, *Grammatik des neutestamentlichen Griechisch*, ed. Friedrich Rehkopf, 17th ed. (Göttingen: Vandenhoeck and Ruprecht, 1976), 313; Ernest DeWitt Burton, *Syntax of Moods and Tenses in New Testament Greek*, 3d ed. (Edinburgh: T. & T. Clark, 1898), 80-81; Robert W. Funk, *A Beginning-Intermediate Grammar of Hellenistic Greek*, vol. 2, *Syntax*, 2d ed. (Missoula MT: Society of Biblical Literature, 1973), 637; S. G. Green, *Handbook to the Grammar of the Greek Testament*, rev. ed. (London: Religious Tract Society, 1907), 309; Ernst G. Hoffmann and Heinrich von Siebenthal, *Griechische Grammatik zum Neuen Testament* (Riehen: Immanuel-Verlag, 1985), 361; K. L. McKay, *A New Syntax of the Verb in New Testament Greek: An Aspectual Approach*, Studies in Biblical Greek, ed. D. A. Carson, vol. 5 (New York: Peter Lang, 1994), 53; G. B. Winer, *A Treatise on the Grammar of New Testament Greek*, trans. W. F. Moulton, 3d rev. ed. (Edinburgh: T. & T. Clark, 1882; reprint, Eugene, OR: Wipf and Stock Publishers, 1997), 391; however, Winer describes the indicative, conjunctive (subjunctive) and optative as follows: "The indicative denotes the *actual*, the conjunctive and optative that which is merely *possible*" (ibid., 351). Except for the omission of the imperative, this is very similar to approaches to the moods that were described above. Interestingly, concerning classical Greek which has significant similarities with Greek of the New Testament, Smyth says only that "The imperative is used in commands and prohibitions" (*Greek Grammar*, 409). William Goodwin initially states that "The imperative is used to express commands and prohibitions" but then expands the command category to include exhortations and entreaties (*An Elementary Greek Grammar*, rev. and enl. ed. [Boston: Ginn and Company, 1879], 258, 290).

[11]Wallace, *Exegetical Syntax*, 485. Nevertheless, some do label this the mood of *command and prohibition*; however, most acknowledge that *command* is broadly defined to include less forceful utterances such as requests, permission, etc.

The Range of Usage of the Greek Imperative Mood[12]

Most New Testament grammars acknowledge a range of force for the imperative. At one end of the spectrum is a (strong) *command* and at the other is a weak forced *permissive* or *tolerative* usage. The permissive usage is rare and not necessarily positive. It may merely reflect that the speaker resigns himself to the possibility that an action may occur. This is why some scholars such as Wallace clarify this with other labels such as *toleration* or *allowance*.[13] Although this usage is not so restricted, it is often expressed with a third person imperative.[14] The usage of *request* falls in between *command* and *permission*. Also, with the negative particle μή (and in rare cases with the negative conjunction, μηδέ),[15] the imperative is used for *prohibitions*. It is common for present imperatives to be negated; however, prohibitions in the aorist are much more commonly expressed with μή (and in rare cases with the negative conjunction, μηδέ[16]) and the aorist subjunctive.[17]

These four usages are generally acknowledged.[18] Some note that the

---

[12]This section is merely a survey. Development of this subject will occur in chapter 4. Nevertheless, limited evaluation will take place concerning questionable usage suggestions.

[13]*Exegetical Syntax*, 488.

[14]Also, a third person imperative is not restricted to this usage.

[15]There are nine occurrences of imperative prohibitions negated by μηδέ: Mark 13:15 (the only aorist); Luke 3:14 (in a construction with the negative conjunction, aorist subjunctive, καί and the present imperative); John 14:27; Rom 6:13; 1 Cor 10:7, 10; Eph 4:27; 2 Thess 3:10; Heb 12:5.

[16]There are seven occurrences of the negative conjunction μηδέ with the aorist subjunctive used as a prohibition: Matt 7:6; 23:10; Luke 3:14; 17:23; Col 2:21 (2x); 1 Pet 3:14.

[17]Most negative imperatives are present tense (approximately 140). Only eight negative aorist imperatives occur in the New Testament and all are in the third person: Matt 6:3; 24:17, 18; Mark 13:15 (2x; the second aorist imperative occurrence is negated by μηδέ); Luke 17:13 (2x). In all cases, Jesus is the speaker of the prohibition imperative. These rare examples will be discussed briefly in a subsection of chapter 4.

[18]These usages are covered in Black, *It's Still Greek to Me*, 100 (he mentions only these four "main usages"); BDF, 195 (they list three categories: command, request, concessive, the later includes permissive, conditional, and concessive usages); Blass, Debrunner, and Rehkopf, *Grammatik*, 313 (this is similar to the English translation, BDF, [Befehl, Bitte, Zugeständnis]; however, the German edition acknowledges that the imperative may be used [I assume as sub-uses of Zugeständnis] as Kondizional oder Konzessivsatz); Brooks and Winbery, *Syntax*, 115-17; James L. Boyer, "A Classification of Imperatives: A Statistical Study," *Grace Theological Journal* 8 (1987): 36-37; Burton, *Syntax*, 80-81 (permission is grouped with conditional and concessive and described as the mood which is "used to express consent, or merely propose an hypothesis"); William Douglas Chamberlain, *An Exegetical Grammar of the Greek New Testament* (New York: Macmillan, 1941; reprint, Grand Rapids: Baker Book House, 1979), 86;

difference in force between *command* and *request* involves the social rank of the participants.[19] A request is used when an inferior addresses a superior. However, there is no systematic development of this important observation. It follows that when the imperative is used in prayers, it is being used as a *request*.[20]

Command:[21]

Matt 2:20   ἐγερθεὶς **παράλαβε** τὸ παιδίον καὶ τὴν μητέρα αὐτοῦ ...
                Get up and **take** the child and his mother ...[22]

John 5:11   **ἆρον** τὸν κράβαττόν σου καὶ **περιπάτει**.
                Take up your stretcher and **walk**

Dana and Mantey, *Manual Grammar*, 175-76; Green, *Handbook*, 309; Hoffmann und von Siebenthal, *Griechische Grammatik*, 361; McKay, *New Syntax*, 53; Perschbacher, *Greek Syntax*, 345-48 (although Perschbacher lists more but narrower usages that others include within these categories; e.g., exhortation, invitation, demand); A. T. Robertson, *A Grammar of the Greek New Testament in Light of Historical Research*, 4th ed. (Nashville: Broadman Press, 1934), 946-948; A. T. Robertson and W. H. Davis, *A New Short Grammar of the Greek Testament for Students Familiar with the Elements of Greek*, 10th ed. (New York: Harpers, 1931; reprint, Grand Rapids: Baker, 1977), 312-13; Wallace, *Exegetical Syntax*, 485-89; Winer, *Treatise*, 390-91 ("The imperative mood regularly expresses a summons or command, sometimes however merely a permission, ... a consent or acquiescence"); Young, *Intermediate*, 141-45. Not every grammar uses the examples given below for the respective category. For a slightly different approach to classification, see David W. King, "Jesus' Use of the Imperative" (Th.D. diss., Southwestern Baptist Theological Seminary, 1963).

[19]Boyer, "Imperatives," 53-54; Brooks and Winbery, *Syntax*, 116; Perschbacher, *Greek Syntax*, 345; Wallace, *Exegetical Syntax*, 487; Young, *Intermediate*, 144-45.

[20]However, J. H. Greenlee has an additional category labeled *prayers (A Concise Exegetical Grammar of New Testament Greek*, 5th rev. ed. [Grand Rapids: William B. Eerdmans Publishing Company, 1986], 46). This does not seem necessary given the description of the *request* category. Boyer maintains a single category but makes the use of this imperative in prayers explicit by labeling this usage *requests and prayers* ("Imperatives," 36).

[21]Robertson labels this *command or exhortation* (*Grammar*, 946). Some have a separate category called *exhortation* or *hortatory* (Chamberlain, *Exegetical Grammar*, 86; Perschbacher, *Greek Syntax*, 346; Hoffmann und von Siebenthal, *Griechische Grammatik*, 361 [Zuspruch]; however, no examples are listed and it is uncertain whether its listing of usages are separate categories or a loose range of meaning).

[22]All quotations in this work of the Greek text are from NA[27]. All translations are my own.

Request/Entreaty:[23]

Matt 6:9b-13   Πάτερ ἡμῶν ὁ ἐν τοῖς οὐρανοῖς· **ἁγιασθήτω** τὸ ὄνομά
                  σου· 10 **ἐλθέτω** ἡ βασιλεία σου· **γενηθήτω** τὸ θέλημά
                  ... 11   τὸν ἄρτον ἡμῶν τὸν ἐπιούσιον **δὸς** ἡμῖν
                  σήμερον· 12 καὶ **ἄφες** ἡμῖν τὰ ὀφειλήματα ἡμῶν, ὡς
                  καὶ ἡμεῖς ἀφήκαμεν τοῖς ὀφειλέταις ἡμῶν· 13 καὶ μὴ
                  εἰσενέγκῃς ἡμᾶς εἰς πειρασμόν, ἀλλὰ **ῥῦσαι** ἡμᾶς ἀπὸ
                  τοῦ πονηροῦ
                  Our Father who is in heaven, **let** your name be **set apart**, [10] **let**
                  your kingdom **come**, **let** your will/desire be **done**, ..., [11] **give**
                  to us today our daily bread, [12] and **forgive** us our sins as we
                  forgive those who have offended us, [13] and do not lead us into
                  temptation but **deliver** us from evil

Luke 11:1   κύριε, **δίδαξον** ἡμᾶς προσεύχεσθαι
                  Lord, **teach** us to pray

Permission/Toleration:

Matt 8:32[24]   [Demons ask Jesus to allow them to be cast into a herd of pigs]
                  καὶ εἶπεν αὐτοῖς· **ὑπάγετε**
                  ... and he said to them, "**go**"

1 Cor 7:36   [Paul is instructing his readers about singleness and marriage
                  and states concerning those with strong passions] **γαμείτωσαν**
                  ... **let him marry**

---

[23]Wallace also calls this a *polite command* (*Exegetical Syntax*, 487).

[24]Wallace points out that in the context of casting out demons, this has a double nuance of
command and *permission* (Ibid., 489).

Prohibition:

Rom 6:12   **Μὴ** οὖν **βασιλευέτω** ἡ ἁμαρτία ἐν τῷ θνητῷ ὑμῶν
σώματι
Therefore, **do not allow** sin **to rule** in your mortal body

Eph 5:18   **μὴ μεθύσκεσθε** οἴνῳ
Do not get drunk with wine

1 John 4:1   **μὴ** παντὶ πνεύματι **πιστεύετε**
Do not believe every spirit

There are a number of other usages of the imperative mood which are not as obvious as the above. Most New Testament grammarians acknowledge a *conditional* usage.[25] Wallace has demonstrated that this usage seems to occur in a specific structural environment. All undisputed examples have the conditional imperative in the protasis and a future indicative in the apodosis (separated by καί). In an imperative + καί + imperative construction, probable and possible conditional imperatives in the protasis are followed by an imperative which has the force of a future indicative in the apodosis.[26] Also, the

---

[25]BDF, 195 (within a broader usage labeled *concessive*); Boyer, "Imperatives," 38-40; Brooks and Winbery, *Syntax*, 117; Wallace, *Exegetical Syntax*, 489-92; Young, *Intermediate*, 145. Most classical grammars consulted did not include a *conditional* usage (see William Watson Goodwin, *Syntax of the Moods and Tenses of the Greek Verb* [Boston: Ginn and Company, 1890], 86-89 [however, he does note that the imperative may be used to "express a mere assumption," 87, this is close to a conditional in meaning]; Smyth, *Greek Grammar*, 409-11; John A. Thompson, *A Greek Grammar: Accidence and Syntax. For Schools and Colleges* [London: John Murray, 1902], 327-28). However, the grammars by Schwyzer-Debrunner and Rijksbaron are exceptions (the latter seems to include the conditional with "concession or supposition") (*Griechische Grammatik, ii. Syntax und syntaktische Stilistik* [Munich: C. H. Beck, 1950], 344; *The Syntax and Semantics of the Verb in Classical Greek: An Introduction* [Amsterdam: J. C. Gieben, 1984], 42).
[26]Daniel B. Wallace, "Ὀργίζεσθε in Ephesians 4:26: Command or Condition?" *Criswell Theological Review* 3 (1989): 367-71. Winer suggests that the first imperative in an imperative + καί + imperative construction may be conditional but does not further discuss the relationship (in meaning) between the imperatives except to say, "When two imperatives are connected by καί, the first sometimes contains the condition (supposition) upon which the action indicated by the second will take place, or the second expresses a result which will certainly ensue" (*Treatise*, 391); see also Boyer who suggests that the labeling of a conditional imperatives falls within one of two groups: first, the imperative + καί + future indicative structure which is discussed here and

imperative retains its imperatival force.[27]

Matt 7:7   Αἰτεῖτε καὶ δοθήσεται ὑμῖν
                If you ask, you will be given to you (**ask** and it will be given
                to you)

John 1:46   ἔρχου καὶ ἴδε
                If you come, <u>you will see</u> (come and see)

A few grammarians have a category called *concession*.[28] However, most include this within the conditional usage.[29] Brooks and Winbery question its existence but suggest that there are two possible examples in the New Testament, John 7:52 and Ephesians 4:26. In both cases, this classification is questionable. See chapter 4.

There are a number of less common usages which are often suggested. These include *pronouncement*,[30] *greeting*,[31] and *warning*.[32] An imperative is classified a *pronouncement* in a statement which itself performs an action.[33] It is a passive voice imperative and the recipient is not in a position to obey the imperative. Some of these types of statements are considered speech acts.[34]

---

second, it is sometimes so labeled to explain a difficult passage ("Imperatives," 38-40). Wallace's work refines that of Boyer.

[27]Wallace, "Ephesians 4:26," 368-69. This is brought out when one adds the phrase "and I want you to" to the protasis. Thus, for the second example below: "If you come (and I want you to), you will see."

Possibly the most controversial passage that has been suggested as a *conditional* is Eph 4:26. This passage contains two imperatives separated by the conjunction: ὀργίζεσθε καὶ μὴ ἁμαρτάνετε. Some grammarians classify this as *conditional* (e.g., Robertson, *Grammar*, 949; Winer, *Treatise*, 391) and others classify it as *concessive* (e.g., Brooks and Winbery, *Syntax*, 118 [this possible usage will be discussed next].

[28]Brooks and Winbery, *Syntax*, 118.

[29]Robertson, *Grammar*, 948-49; Wallace, "Ephesians 4:26," 356-57. Some group the three categories, permission, concession, and conditional together (see BDF, 195).

[30]Wallace, *Exegetical Syntax*, 492-93. See also the observations concerning the passive imperative below.

[31]Ibid., 493; Young, *Intermediate*, 145.

[32]Hoffmann und von Siebenthal, *Griechische Grammatik*, 361 (Mahnung); Young, *Intermediate*, 145.

[33]Of course there are other factors involved beside the words themselves (e.g., the qualifications of the speaker, etc.). This was not discussed in Wallace's brief treatment but is discussed below in the section entitled, *Speech Act Theory*.

[34]Speech acts and the theory bearing its name will be discussed in detail below.

Mark 1:41   καθαρίσθητι
              Be cleansed!

Imperatives used as a *greeting* seem to be idiomatic expressions which have lost any real imperative force. Imperatives such as ἔρρωσθε ("farewell," Acts 15:29) and χαῖρε ("hail," Matt 26:49; 27:29; Mark 15:18; Luke 1:28; John 19:3) serve as greetings.[35] However, in the case of plural χαίρετε, the idiomatic usage does not seem to occur in the New Testament. It seems to retain its imperative force, "rejoice."[36]

It has been suggested that an imperative may be used as a *warning*.[37] This usage only occurs with two words, βλέπετε and προσέχετε (*look out, beware, take care*; βλέπετε: Mark 8:15; 12:38; Acts 13:40; Phil 3:2 [3x]; Col 2:8; προσέχετε: Luke 20:46). The warning nuance is natural for these words; therefore, it seems more likely that this is not a separate usage but rather a *command* using specific lexemes.[38]

A number of other classifications are suggested. However, these are questionable. Wallace mentions a *potential* imperative which may occur in the

---

[35]These are the only occurrences of these forms in the New Testament.

[36]The plural imperative occurs ten times: Matt 5:12; 28:9; Luke 6:23 (aorist, χάρητε); 10:20; 2 Cor 13:11; Phil 2:18; 3:1; 4:4; 1 Thess 5:16; 1 Pet 4:13. Wallace lists 2 Cor 13:11 as an example of a greeting but acknowledges it may be a command (*Exegetical Syntax*, 493). He leans toward a greeting based on "well-worn usage in Hellenistic literature as a term of greeting." Wallace is in good company (ASV, NIV, KJV, NKJV, RSV, and NRSV are among those who see this as a greeting). However, no examples from Hellenistic Greek are given. Nevertheless, it seem likely that it is so used (LSJ). Wallace also maintains that it is unlikely that Phil 3:1 is a greeting (ibid., 493 n. 114). This would leave 2 Cor 13:11 as the only example of the plural used as a greeting in the New Testament. In light of New Testament usage, it seems preferable to avoid classifying χαίρετε as greeting without imperative force unless there is good reason to conclude otherwise. However, it must be noted that this usage cannot be ruled out based soley on only nine other occurrences. It seems that this form may be a greeting in some contexts outside the New Testament. The infinitives of this verb seem to be used both as a greeting (Acts 15:23; 23:26; Jas 1:1) and otherwise (Luke 15:32; Rom 12:15; 2 Cor 2:3; 7:7 2 Jn 10, 11). However, in the New Testament, the burden of proof lies with those who maintain that this imperative is a greeting.

[37]Perschbacher, *Greek Syntax*, 348-49 (labeled *warning or caution*); Young, *Intermediate*, 145. All examples cited by these authors are listed here.

[38]Of the twenty-three occurrences of βλέπετε as an imperative (this is also the form for the indicative), two do not seem to be warnings (1 Cor 10:18; 16:10) and another is possible but unlikely (Heb 12:25). *Gramcord* suggests an imperative option for its indicative parsing in Acts 2:33; however, the indicative is likely in this context. Other occurrences of the imperative are Matt 24:4; Mark 4:24; 13:5, 9, 23, 33; Luke 8:18; 21:8; 1 Cor 8:9; Gal 5:15; Eph 5:15; Heb 3:12; 2 Jn 8.

apodosis of an (conditional) imperative + καί + imperative construction.[39] However, as discussed above, in such cases, this imperative seems to have the force of a future indicative. This category is disputed.[40] There are a number of other categories suggested for the imperative. However, in most cases these have few examples.[41]

The imperative mood primarily occurs in the second person. However, unlike languages such as English, it also has a third person. The majority of occurrences are second person (1397, 86%); however, the third person has a significant presence (234, 14%).

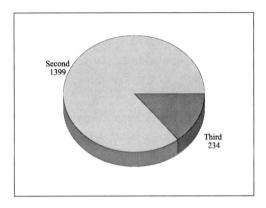

Figure 6: Second and Third Person Imperatives

Because the third person imperative form does not occur in English, it is difficult to translate. It is often translated with "let" which may conceal its force

---

[39]Wallace, *Exegetical Syntax*, 492. Concerning this construction in the papyri, see Basil G. Mandilaras, *The Verb in the Greek Non-Literary Papyri* (Athens: Hellenic Ministry of Culture and Sciences, 1973), 306-7.

[40]Wallace, *Exegetical Syntax*, 492.

[41]In addition to those already mentioned, other sub-usages include *challenge to understanding* (Boyer, "Imperatives," 38), *exclamation* (Perschbacher, *Greek Syntax*, 346; Boyer, "Imperatives," 37-38), *invitation* (Perschbacher, *Greek Syntax*, 346), *Einladung* (Hoffmann und von Siebenthal, *Griechische Grammatik*, 361). Perschbacher is especially precise in his usage categorization. In addition to those already credited to him, he includes a *demand* imperative (much stronger than request) and a *challenge or dare* imperative (*Greek Syntax*, 347-48). However, it seem like he ignores important similarities between usages and postulates categories with few examples. Many of these usages may be better viewed within larger categories noting the intrusion of lexical meaning. Boyer's ("Imperatives," 35-40) classification may be the most thorough for the New Testament and acknowledges that some occurrences are not easily classified (40).

and suggest a *permissive* nuance. The third person is used with such a nuance. For example, εἰ δὲ ὁ ἄπιστος χωρίζεται, **χωριζέσθω·** (1 Cor 7:15, If an unbeliever leaves, **let him leave**). However, the third person is not always used in this manner. In James 1:5, it is used for a command, Εἰ δέ τις ὑμῶν λείπεται σοφίας, αἰτείτω παρὰ τοῦ ... θεοῦ (If any of you lack wisdom, **let him ask** of God ...). Because the reader is accustomed to imperatives in the second person, the translation seems to obscure the command nature of this passage. Nevertheless, the third person imperative is a legitimate imperative and it must be so considered in analysis. It will be demonstrated that the factor of person will have a bearing on the force of the imperative. However, at this stage the imperative is simply being discussed within current New Testament studies. In order to maintain the imperative nature of the third person, Wallace suggests translations such as "he must" or "I command him" to be used as demanded.[42]

Boyer classifies the third person imperative into four categories.[43] First, indirect commands to *you*. These are general commands that are aimed at the hearer (thus, similar to the second person).[44] Second there are third person imperatives which are used as actual commands to a third party. These two categories are the most common. The remaining two occur infrequently. Third, the form may be used to communicate what is required of a third party. Fourth, a third person may be used as a promise or warning of something that will be.

The nature of the passive demands special treatment. It seems unnatural for an imperative to be directed to someone who is not the doer of the verbal action.[45] The passive is the least common voice for the imperative used in the New Testament. Less than 10% of imperatives (156 of 1631) are passive.[46]

---

[42]*Exegetical Syntax*, 486. See also Porter who states, "The third person Greek imperative is as strongly directive as the second person" (*Idioms*, 55).

[43]Boyer, "Imperatives," 47-48. The description of Boyer will be brief here. It will be discussed further (with examples) in chapter 4.

[44]Boyer divides this category into four. These will be mentioned in chapter 4.

[45]This description of the passive is too simplistic. However, it is suggested here because this is the manner it which it is often understood.

[46]This is slightly less than this voice's occurrence among finite verbs and all verbal forms. There are 19,167 finite verb: 14,442 are active, 2349 are middle and 2382 are passive (about 12.5%). Due to double parsing in *Gramcord*, the statistics for individual voices include six finite forms counted twice. When all verbal forms are considered, the percentage is slightly higher: 28,114 total verb forms, 20,696 are active, 3519 are middle, and 3918 are passive (about 14%). Due to double parsing in Gramcord, the statistics for individual voices include about nineteen forms counted twice. The slight differences do not affect the percentages. It is interesting to note that unlike the broader statistical context of finite verbs and all verbal forms, the imperative has

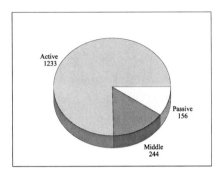

Figure 7: The Voices of the Imperative Mood[47]

Boyer categorizes passives in two distinct groups.[48] First, there are those which carry a *permissive* meaning such as "allow it to happen," "receive it," or "accept it." Such passives demand no personal action from the one to whom it is directed.[49] An example of this group is καθαρίσθητι (Be cleansed!; Mark 1:41). Members of this group are also classified as *pronouncement* imperatives (see above). Second, there are passives where the one to whom the verb is directed is still responsible for the action. Translations such as "see to it," or "get it done" bring out this meaning. Thus, they simply state the same thing as the active statement in a different manner. An example of this group is μεταμορφοῦσθε τῇ ἀνακαινώσει τοῦ νοός ... (be transformed by the renewing of your mind; Romans 12:2).[50]

---

a significantly greater amount of middles than passives. See chart 3.

[47]Although viewing the middle voice as primary, *Gramcord* parses ἐνδύσασθε in Col 3:12 as both middle and passive and is counted with both when the individual voices are searched. Here it is only counted as middle. Some imperatives (e.g., the present middle and passive) have the same form. Unless made explicit otherwise, the classification of each form follows *Gramcord*.

[48]Boyer, "Imperatives," 49-50. See also Young, *Intermediate*, 143. Young is using Boyer's work.

[49]Boyer, "Imperatives," 49.

[50]Ibid. Boyer also makes three further observations about the passive imperative. First, passive deponent verbs occur in the imperative (e.g., πορεύθητι in Matt 8:9). Second, some passives seem to be passive transforms with the same meaning as the corresponding active statement (e.g., compare the active imperatives in Mark 15:13-14 [σταύρωσον] with the passives in the parallel passage in Matt 27:22-23 [σταυρωθήτω]). Third, with some verbs which have active forms with a causative nuance, in the passive, they express the state or condition resulting from the verbal action (e.g., πείθω: the active indicative means *to persuade*, the passive means *to be convinced, to be confident* [ibid., 49-50]). These observations are interesting but not helpful

There does not seem to be significant differences between classical and *Koine* usage of the imperative mood. This similarity must not be overstated. The important Greek grammar, BDF, is primarily a discussion of differences between the New Testament (an example of *Koine*) and classical Greek.

In the late second-century the rhetorician Hermogenes stated that "... the imperative is most of all a harsh form" (or "the harshest form").[51] Also, according to Aristotle, a fifth-century sophist Protagoras apparently criticized Homer for using an imperative to address the goddess at the beginning of the *Iliad* (1), "sing (ἄειδε) of the wrath, Goddess, ..." Aristotle suggests that Protagoras is incorrectly applying a rhetorical rule to poetry, "What fault can one see in Homer's 'Sing of the wrath, Goddess'?–which Protagoras has criticized as being a command where a prayer was meant, since to bid one do or not do, he tells us is a command. Let us pass over this, then, as appertaining to another art, and not to that of poetry."[52]

Early grammarians were much more sober in their discussion of the imperative mood. In a number of places in his *Syntax*, Apollonius Dyscolus mentions the imperative mood.[53] However, his most developed discussion

---

for the purposes here. First, deponent verbs do not have active forms in some tenses; therefore, the passive must be used. Second, the passive transform is a questionable reality (see the discussion of deep structure and related issues in the following subsection below entitled, *Various Theoretical Linguistic Approaches*). Also, there may be redaction or discourse reasons for the difference in voice from one passage to another. Third, these observations are concerning the passive voice, not the imperative mood.

One study focuses upon the passive and classifies it into eight categories: non-passive, stative, lexical, third person view of the author, performative, passive of faith, permissive, and result passive of indirect commands (Scot R. Douglass, "The Passive Imperative and Its Significance in Romans 12:1-2" [Th.M. thesis, Dallas Theological Seminary, 1988], 10-37). This classification system includes structural and meaning (both usage and lexical) based categories and does not clearly distinguish issues of voice and mood. This method is not entirely compatible with that which was proposed in chapter 1 in this work. This work is an attempt to understand the semantic meaning and pragmatic usages of the mood. Features such as lexical nuances and context will be utilized for the latter goal. Lexical nuances themselves are not usages. They contribute to usage but are not considered a separate category. This observation can be made about other classifications.

[51]Σχήματα δὲ τραχέα μάλιστα μὲν τὰ προστακτικά (*Concerning Types of Style* [περὶ ἰδεῶν]; 1.7.100 [also called, *Concerning Issues*]). Source TLG CD E.

[52]*Poetics*, 18.

[53]See for example Book III. 19, 31, 72, 90, 141, Book IV. 48. Book numbers follow Householder, *Apollonius Dyscolus*. Concerning Apollonius' view on the imperative, see also Peter Matthews, "Greek and Latin Linguistics," in *History of Linguistics*, vol. 2, *Classical and Medieval Linguistics*, ed. Guilio Lepschy (London and New York: Longman, 1994), 88.

occurs in Book III sections 101-122. No grand claims are made for the mood. In these section, Apollonius discusses (among other issues) the tenses and person used with the mood. He seems to view *time* as an element of the form (101) but also notes the durative nature of the present (102). He rejects first person imperatives (104-110), observes social rank is involved in the use of the imperative (105),[54] and notes a connection between the vocative and the imperative (116-119).[55]

The New Testament grammarian James Hope Moulton draws a distinction between the imperative "in the age of the papyri" and in the New Testament. In the former, "Imperatives are normal in royal edicts, in letters to inferiors, and among equals when the tone is urgent, or the writer indisposed to multiple words: they are conspicuously few in petitions."[56] In the latter, "we find a very different state of things. The prophet is not accustomed to conciliate his hearers with carefully softened commands; and in the imperial edicts of Him who 'taught with authority' and ethical exhortations of men who spoke in His name, we find naturally a large proportion of imperatives."[57]

In general, there is little if any difference between New Testament usage, other Greek of the time, and earlier classical literature.[58] Even if it may be granted that there is a difference of usage in the literary classical works, such a distinction does not carry through to the non-literary papyri. The mood was used to communicate everything from the "strictest order to the humblest prayer."[59] The imperative is common in the non-literary papyri. This may be due to its nature. It often is unsophisticated and requests are made in the

---

[54]As mentioned above, Apollonius incorrectly notes that the speaker is always the superior.

[55]Book III. 116, "We mentioned above . . . that many [second person dual and plural imperative] forms are homophonous with indicative forms, . . . And since vocatives plurals are homophonous with nominatives, and indicatives go with nominatives and vocatives go with imperatives, then *dianoeisthe anthrōpoi* is two-ways ambiguous." Bracketed words are those of the editor (Householder) and italics are in the original. This distinction cannot be maintained. A connection between the vocative and imperative is explored by others. One authors notes significant differences between the vocative and imperative subject in English (Eirlys E. Davies, *The English Imperative* [Kent, England: Croom Helm, 1986], 137-44).

[56]James Hope Moulton, *Prolegomena*, 3d ed., vol. 1, *A Grammar of New Testament Greek*, (Edinburgh: T. & T. Clark, 1908), 172-73.

[57]Ibid., 173.

[58]BDF, 195. The classical grammar by Smyth (*Greek Grammar*, 409) presents a range of usages similar to that presented in New Testament grammar (however, as mentioned above some classical grammarians, including Smyth, omit mention of a conditional imperative.

[59]Mandilaras, *Verb*, 296.

simplest form.[60]

Concerning classical and other non-biblical uses of the imperative, there are a number of points which can be inferred from these observations. First, in some contexts the imperative is viewed as harsh or strong. Second, the force of the imperative may be determined by lexical consideration.[61] Third, participants of certain social rank may have more flexibility in using (harsh) imperatives Fourth, there was a means of communicating a prayer (probably the optative) other than with the imperative (within a rhetorical setting). Fifth, some believed (as Protagoras) that the manner in which the imperative was used in rhetoric should be used in broader contexts.[62] Sixth, with respect to the force of the imperative, other than in formal rhetoric, it was used in a broad manner, similar to the New Testament.

This brief survey has demonstrated a relatively uniform understanding of the usages of the imperative mood. Most imperatives are classified by New Testament grammarians as *commands, requests, permissive,* and *prohibitions.*[63] Scholars of other ancient Greek literature also see this variety of force in the usage of the imperative. Also, there are less common usages in the New Testament such as *conditional, pronouncement,* and *greeting.* Although some have suggested possible usages such as *concessive* and *potential,* in general these are not widely accepted.

Although these usages have been identified, little work has been done to determine when and where these occur. Wallace's structural observations concerning the *conditional* imperative are rare in a field which seems dominated by intuitive labeling. Intuition and context are factors in this study; however, it seems preferable to attempt to put in place a more reliable system to help

---

[60]Ibid.

[61]The usage of the term "force" here will need to be more clearly defined. It will be noted that it can be used in more than one way. The primary usage in this work for the classification of imperatives will differ from the usage here. This development will occur later in chapter 4.

[62]Protagoras' comments are directed only toward poetry in the context of Aristotle's discussion of rhetoric. It may be that Protagoras believed that the imperative should be used uniformly in all Greek. However, it would be unwise to apply his statement beyond its explicit intent. The context in which this statement was made is not available. This is important in view of the apparent usage in less formal writing. Also, since Homer was considered a *literary work,* if one wishes to broaden the application of this statement, although still uncertain, one may be able to maintain that it refers to literary use. For possible explanations of Protagoras' meaning, see Miller, "Limitation of the Imperative," 433-34.

[63]*Permission* is rare and *request* is not common. However, they are more common than others not listed here.

determine usage. It would be preferable to utilize a system based not on individual (isolated) usages but one which may be more comprehensive incorporating various usages as part of a larger and complete system. Such a system must consider the participants, verb meaning, and other contextual (pragmatic) elements. This is a primary goal of this work and will be the subject of chapter 4.

The Tenses Used with the Imperative

In the New Testament the imperative mood appears in three tenses: present, aorist, and perfect. The perfect is rare and will be discussed first. The remainder of this section will be devoted to the present and aorist. A summary of the tenses used with the imperative in the New Testament can be charted as follows,

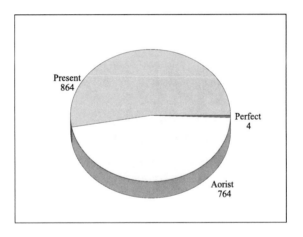

Figure 8: Tenses of the Imperative Mood[64]

The perfect imperative is rare in the New Testament. The form clearly

[64]Although viewing the present tense as primary, *Gramcord* parses ἐκχέετε in Rev 16:1 as both present and aorist and is counted with both when the individual tenses are searched. Here it is only counted as present.

occurs in Mark 4:39 (πεφίμωσο) and Acts 15:29 (ἔρρωσθε).[65] Also, the form
ἴστε which can be either indicative or imperative occurs in Eph 5:5, Heb 12:17,
and Jas 1:19. Ephesians 5:5 is probably imperative. James 1:19 could be either
but is likely imperative. Hebrews 12:17 is probably indicative.[66] The form
ἔρρωσθε is the only occurrence of this word (ῥώννυμι) in the New Testament.
It is an idiom often used at the end of letters to express a final greeting such as
good bye or *farewell*. It does not really carry any imperative force.[67] The form
ἴστε is from οἶδα which only occurs in the perfect and pluperfect in the New
Testament. Its force is the same as the present and aorist tenses respectively.
Therefore, its meaning here has the force of the present tense. This leaves only
πεφίμωσο as a potential perfect (force) imperative in the New Testament.
However, it is difficult to determine any significance based on one occurrence.

---

[65]Also in Acts 23:30 there are some witnesses which add one of two perfect variants at the
end of the verse. First, ἔρρωσο occurs in ℵ E Ψ 1739. The form translated into Latin occurs in
the Vulgate text, *Editio Clementina* (vg[cl]) and in the Syriac versions. Second, ἔρρωσθε occurs
in P and 1241. There is confusion in NA[27] concerning the majority of Greek witnesses (the
Byzantine texts and the non-Byzantine minuscules). The first option has listed in support the
manuscripts represented by gothic M which include the majority of these texts. However, the
second option is supported by the manuscripts represented by the symbol *pm* which represents
a split in the majority (those manuscripts represented by gothic M). In the system proposed by
the editors, gothic M and *pm* should not be opposing options (p. 56*). In this system either gothic
M may support one reading or the majority may be presented as split and thus *pm* will occur with
more than one option (but not against gothic M). This seems to be an error in the apparatus of
NA[27]. It seems probable that gothic M is incorrect for the first variant and should instead be *pm*.
This solution is supported by the split in Byzantine witness in UBS[4] (both options are represented
by *Byz*[pt] [part of the Byzantine witnesses] in the apparatus). Although gothic M of NA[27] is broader
than *Byz* of UBS[4], the significance of the Byzantine witness within gothic M supports this
conclusion that *pm* should be with both options in NA[27]. Therefore, the majority is split between
the two variants.
    Nevertheless, although the first variant has impressive witnesses, neither is persuasive. The
text adopted by the editors (which omits the perfect) has equal or slightly stronger external
evidence (A B 33; the Latin manuscript, gig, and the Vulgate text, *Vulgata Stuttgartiensis* [vg[s]];
and the all extant copies in Coptic) Internal evidence also favors the omission. It was a common
conclusion to a letter (as Acts 15:29) and thus it could naturally be added. However, it is difficult
to understand why it would be omitted. It is also the shorter reading. All these arguments
considered, the omission is to be preferred.
    [66]Porter maintains that there are only four perfect imperatives (Mark 4:39; Acts 15:29; Eph
5:5; Jas 1:19). However, he suggests that Jas 1:19 may be indicative and he considers Heb 12:17
indicative (*Verbal Aspect*, 362).
    [67]The Acts 15:29 occurrence is at the end of a recorded letter written by James at the
Jerusalem council. This word is common in the conclusions of the letters of Ignatius (see
Ephesians 21:2, *Magnesians* 15, *Philadelphians* 11:2, and *to Polycarp* 8:3). See also the
occurrences in the Septuagint listed below.

The verb, φιμόω occurs only seven times in the New Testament. Three are imperatives, the perfect in Mark 4:39 and the aorist in Mark 1:25 and Luke 4:35.[68] It is not possible to make firm conclusions based on the limited data but it may be that the present middle/passive imperative form was not an option for New Testament writers.[69]

The perfect imperative is rare in the Septuagint, occurring only nineteen times.[70] Also, the perfect imperative is restricted in ancient Greek generally.[71]

---

[68]Other occurrences of φιμόω are Matt 22:12, 34; 1 Tim 5:18; 1 Pet 2:15.

[69]This verb is rather rare. It seems to have been non-literary and may even be slang (MM). In addition to its seven New Testament occurrences, it only occurs three times in the Septuagint (Deut 25:4; 4 Macc 1:35; Sus 1:60). A Search of the entire TLG CD-ROM E and PHI CD-ROM #7 for any middle/passive imperative of φιμόω was made. The search was constructed to locate the following forms (assuming the potential regular forms [no lexicon (LSJ, BAGD, BDAG, MM) suggested an irregular form]): φιμου [2sg], φιμουσθω [3sg], φιμουσθε [2pl], φιμουσθων/φιμουσθωσαν [3pl]; (N.B. accents not included for searching purposes). This search yielded eight late Christian occurrences: φιμοῦ (2x in Olmpiodorus Diaconus [AD VI]); φιμούσθω (Athanasius [AD IV], Cyrillus [AD IV], Nicephorus [AD VIII–IX]; 2x in Doctrina Patrum [AD VII–VIII] φιμούσθωσαν (Epiphanius [AD IV]). Additionally, ". . . φιμου" occurs in P.Oxy 2195 col. 2, line 6. However, this is a genitive noun; it is either the full noun or the ending only. The perfect form which is found in the New Testament (πεφίμωσο) occurs 42 other times. However, most of these usages occur in fourth-century religious works and most seem to refer to the event recorded in Mark 4 (John Chrysostom [14x]; Cyrillus [6x]; Concilia Oecumenica [4]; Gregory of Nyssa [3x]; Basil of Caesarea [5x]; Theodorus [2x];Athanasius; Didymus Caecus; Eusebius; Epiphanius; Theodoretus; Gregoranius Nazianzenus; Psellus; and Catena in Joannem). However, Winer maintains significance for the perfect form, "The perfect imperative is used when an action, completed in itself is to endure in its effects; e.g., Mk. iv. 39, in Christ's address to the troubled sea, πεφίμωσο, be (and remain) still" (Treatise, 395-96; italics original).

[70]Over half of these occurrences can be attributed to three verbs: ἔρρωσθε (5x: 2 Macc 9:20; 11:21, 28, 33; 3 Macc 7:9) πεποιθέτω/πεποίθατε (3x: Job 12:6/Jer 7:4; 9:3); κέκραξον (3x: Jer 22:20; 31:20; 40:3). The other eight occurrences are ἴσθι (Tob 4:14), ἀπολελύσθωσαν (1 Macc 10:43), εἰήσθω (2 Macc 6:17), δεδηλώσθω δεδηλώσθω (2 Macc 7:42), οἴδατε (Job 27:12), παρείσθυσαν (Zeph 3:16), κεκλήσθω (Isa 4:1), and κεκραγέτωσαν (Isa 14:31).

[71]J. E. Harry, "The Perfect Subjunctive, Optative and Imperative in Greek," *Classical Review* 19 (1905): 348, 355-56; E. A. Sonnenschein, "The Perfect Subjunctive, Optative, and Imperative in Greek–A Reply," *Classical Review* 19 (1905): 440. These two articles are the first of four which evaluate an aspect of Sonnenschein's previously published grammar (and secondarily, the grammars of others). In the first article, Harry accuses the grammarian of giving too little attention to the perfect in the non-indicative moods (Harry, "Perfect Subjunctive," 347-54). In the second, Sonnenschein responds by noting the importance of brevity and feels that little used forms are not worth the student's time (Sonnenschein, "Perfect Subjunctive–A Reply," 439-40). This discussion also involves the meaning of the perfect and is concluded the following year (see J. E. Harry, "The Perfect Subjunctive, Optative and Imperative in Greek Again," *Classical Review* 20 [1906]: 100-103 and E. A. Sonnenschein, "The Perfect Subjunctive, Optative, and Imperative in Greek," *Classical Review* 20 [1906]: 155-56).

The major focus of imperative work in recent years has been devoted to the meaning of the present and aorist tenses as used in commands and prohibitions. This is primarily due to a recent emphasis in verbal aspect and the correction of a misunderstanding concerning prohibitions. The latter will be discussed first.

Winer's comments on the aorist and present imperatives are representative of the understanding of these forms in the nineteenth-century,

> The aorist imperative ... is used in reference either to an action which rapidly passes and should take place at once, or at any rate to an action which is undertaken once only ... The present imperative is used in reference to an action which is already commenced and is to be continued, or which is lasting and frequently repeated. Hence it is commonly employed in the measured and unimpassioned language of laws and moral precepts ... [72]

Although these comments need to be refined in light of recent work in verbal aspect, they seem to account for much of the New Testament data. The descriptions are quite broad allowing for some flexibility in interpretation.

However, in the twentieth-century, many grammarians and exegetes maintained a view of prohibitions which claimed that the present tense form was used to stop an ongoing process (*stop doing*) and the aorist was used to prohibit an action from beginning (*do not start*).[73]

Early in the twentieth-century a number of articles appeared in *The Classical Review* devoted to the meaning of prohibitions.[74] The issue at hand was introduced briefly by W. Headlam in 1903 at the conclusion of an article.[75]

Some perfect forms are more infrequent than others (e.g., the second person perfect middle and passive [Harry, "Perfect Subjunctive," 354]).

[72]*Treatise*, 393-94.

[73]Although many discuss this in relation to both commands and prohibition, it is really within the context of prohibitions where this is applied. Also, this section is devoted to sememic prohibitions and is not restricted to imperative morphology as is this work. However, this is an important historical study and is significant for the imperative mood.

[74]I am indebted to Daniel B. Wallace for much of this chronology (i.e., pointing out many of the articles and helping make sense of some of them; "The Article with Multiple Substantives Connected by Καί in the New Testament: Semantics and Significance" [Ph.D. diss., Dallas Theological Seminary, 1995], 11-12 (recently revised and published as *Granville Sharp's Canon and Its Kin: Semantics and Significance*, Studies in Biblical Greek, ed. D. A. Carson, vol. 14 [New York: Peter Lang, 2009], 11-12) ; idem, *Exegetical Syntax*, 714-17). See also Boyer, "Imperatives," 42-45 and Stanley E. Porter, *Verbal Aspect in the Greek of the New Testament, with Reference to Tense and Mood*, Studies in Biblical Greek, ed. D. A. Carson, vol. 1 (New York: Peter Lang, 1989), 344-46.

[75]"Some Passages of Aeschylus and Others," *Classical Review* 17 (1903): 286-95.

Headlam contrasts an aorist subjunctive (μὴ τοῦτο ποιήσῃς) and (the similar meaning) future indicative (ὅπως μὴ ποιήσεις) meaning "see to it that you do not do this" with the present imperative (μὴ τοῦτο ποίει) meaning "do not do as you are doing," "do not continue doing so," or "*cease* to do so."[76] In other words, the aorist is used to prohibit one from beginning an action and the present commands the ceasing of an action already in process. In a footnote, Headlam gives credit for this observation to Dr. Henry Jackson, noting that he probably got it from [Richard] Shilleto who probably derived it from Gottfried Hermann.[77] In a brief response, Jackson corrects Headlam and acknowledges that it was from Thomas Davidson that he got this usage. Jackson states,

> Davidson told me that, when he was learning modern Greek, he had been puzzled about the distinction, until he heard a Greek friend use the present imperative to a dog which was barking. This gave him the clue. He turned to Plato's *Apology*, and immediately stumbled upon the excellent instances 20 E μὴ θορυβήσητε, before clamour begins, and 21 A μὴ θορυβεῖτε, when it has begun. Ever since Davidson explained the distinction to me, I have kept a watch upon instances of particular prohibitions, and I am convinced that the rule holds.[78]

In response to both Headlam and Jackson, H. Darnley Naylor argued that

---

[76]Ibid., 295. The similarity in form between the aorist subjunctive and future contributes to the conclusion about the meaning of the aorist.

[77]Ibid., 295, n. 1. Hermann's distinction was made early in the nineteenth- century and soon after appeared in volume 1 of his *Opuscula* in 1827 in piece called "de praeceptis quibusdam atticistarum dissertatio." After examining the aorist and present imperatives in a number of Greek works (e.g., Sophocles, Homer), Hermann states,

> Iam igitur sic erit de omni ista vetandi ratione statuendum: μὴ cum imperativo praesentis proprie de omittendo eo, quod quis iam faciat, intelligi, sed saepius tamen etiam ad ea trahi, quae quis nondum facere aggressus sit; aoristi autem imperativum tantummodo de non incipiendo usurpari, in quo quidem genere coniunctivum aoristi Graecos praetulisse; idque Atticis maxime, ut dubitantius loqui amantibus, ita placuisse, ut apud hos rarissime imperativus aoristi inveniatur (Godofredi Hermanni, *Opuscula*, vol. 1 [Leipzig: Apud Gerhardum Fleischerum], 1827; reprint, Gottfried Hermann, *Opuscula*, vol. 1 [Hildesheim: Georg Olms Verlag, 1970], 275).

[78]Henry Jackson, "Prohibitions in Greek," *Classical Review* 18 (1904): 263. Jackson also mentions that he was unaware of Hermann's statement until he read Headlam's article. Also, although this distinction was based on a modern Greek example, it does not seem to be considered a canon in modern Greek (it is not mentioned); see for example Douglas Q. Adams, *Essential Modern Greek Grammar* (Mineola, NY: Dover Publications, 1987), 67-69; Albert Thumb, *Handbook of the Modern Greek Vernacular: Grammar, Texts, Glossary*, trans. S. Angus (Edinburgh: T. & T. Clark, 1912), 127-29, 199-200.

although the distinction drawn by these scholars is valid in some cases, it is merely one of a number of possible distinctions.[79] Naylor attacks the tense distinction in a number of ways. He points out that the positive imperatives (commands) have no such distinction; therefore, it is unlikely to occur in prohibitions.[80] Naylor also cites a number of examples where the prohibitions in both tenses violate the canon. He even questions Jackson's interpretation of μὴ θορυβεῖτε in Plato's *Apology*.[81]

On the page which Naylor's article ends, Headlam begins a defense of his canon.[82] Claiming to have read "almost the whole of Greek literature,"[83] he concludes confidently "that the distinction is true in the vast majority of cases."[84] The remainder of the article is devoted to examples from classical literature to support his case.[85] Headlam does not deny that Naylor has produced texts which do not follow the rule. However, his examples are considered exceptions to the general rule.[86]

A year later Naylor responded to Headlam with more examples in a brief one-page article.[87] In this article Naylor emphasizes only the present tense prohibitions. He believes that Headlam has a strong case for the meaning of the aorist.[88] He cites examples where the present prohibition does not mean *cease*

---

[79]H. Darnley Naylor, "Prohibitions in Greek," *Classical Review* 19 (1905): 26- 30. Naylor states, "the distinction drawn by Hermann [and Headlam and Jackson] undoubtedly occurs, *but it is not the only distinction*" (ibid., 30).

[80]Ibid., 27.

[81]Ibid., 30.

[82]"Greek Prohibitions," *Classical Review* 19 (1905): 30-36. In an issue later that year, a brief comment appeared which referred to both Naylor and Headlam's articles (by date, not name) and applies Headlam's canon for the present tense to John 20:17 (H. J. Roby, "The Imperative in St. John 20:17," *Classical Review* 19 [1905]: 229). However, Naylor's objections are not noted.

[83]Headlam, "Greek Prohibitions," 31.

[84]Ibid., 31.

[85]Ibid., 32-36.

[86]Ibid., 36.

[87]H. Darnley Naylor, "More Prohibitions in Greek," *Classical Review* 20 (1906): 348.

[88]Ibid., 348. In his previous work, he acknowledged that the future nuance of the aorist subjunctive prohibition was somewhat expected by the forward looking nature of commands and prohibitions; however all imperatives have a future perspective whether they are is prohibiting a future act or ceasing an act in process (Naylor, "Prohibitions," 27). Smyth states that "all [the imperative's] tenses refer to the future" (Smyth, *Greek Grammar*, 409). Nevertheless, in that article Naylor concluded that the aorist is not limited to the *do not start* nuance (Naylor, "Prohibitions," 27, 30). It seems like in the later article, Naylor may have conceded the aorist; he does not make reference to his previous discussion. He states in this article, "I am still only half-convinced: that is, I feel that Dr. Headlam has a strong case only so far as the aorist *e.g.* μὴ

what you are doing. He argues that his examples should not be considered in isolation. He points out that in "the vast majority of cases ... it is impossible to decide whether, *e.g.* μὴ ποίει must necessarily mean 'cease doing.'"[89] This is an important point of method. When a number of nuances are possible, one meaning should not be pressed merely because it adheres to a canon. Language is simply too flexible for such an approach. Instead, one needs to continually ask which meaning is most probable in a given context. A possible meaning should not be accepted merely because it is part of a canon.[90]

Finally, in another article in *Classical Review* during the same year, R. C. Seaton reiterates that the aorist subjunctive prohibition forbids a future act. He also is convinced that Naylor is correct concerning the present imperative prohibition. It cannot be maintained that this form involves both a reference to the past and future.[91] Seaton, however, points out that some (not all) of Naylor's examples of the present may not fit the canon because of the lexical meaning of the verb.[92] This is another important methodological point.

While this debate was occurring in *Classical Review*,[93] James Hope Moulton introduced the canon to students of the New Testament in his *Prolegomena* in 1906.[94] However, he acknowledged that it was not without exceptions.[95] Nevertheless, the canon was maintained and has been followed by

---

ποιήσῃς is concerned" (Naylor, "More Prohibitions," 348).

[89]Ibid., 348.

[90]Nevertheless, patterns can be observed which may suggest a specific nuance is more probable. However, slavish adherence to a canon should not occur. The more a pattern is observed, the stronger its ability to predict a usage becomes. This method must initially focus on the text to discover usages in context without a predetermined template with which to view the text. It also must initially focus on examples which meanings are as clear as possible. However, Headlam's (and other's) canon under discussion here has not been proven by extensive analysis.

[91]R. C. Seaton, "Prohibition in Greek," *Classical Review* 20 (1906): 438. In other words, the present does not necessarily demand the ceasing of an action in process.

[92]Ibid., 438.

[93]Not all have followed this canon closely. In his brief survey of classical Greek, Rijksbaron discusses the present in the same manner as the canon demands; however, no mention of the debate or canon is made and he states that this distinction is only one "among others" (*Syntax and Semantics*, 43-44).

[94]James Hope Moulton, *Prolegomena*, vol. 1, *A Grammar of New Testament Greek Based on W. F. Moulton's Edition of G. B. Winer's Grammar* (Edinburgh: T. & T. Clark, 1906), 122-26. With the exception of this and the following footnote, All other references to this work will be to the third edition of 1908 previously cited.

[95]Moulton, *Prolegomena*, 1st ed., 125-26.

many others.[96]

Although there were precursors,[97] the decisive blow to this canon occurred

---

[96]See Brooks and Winbery, *Syntax*, 116; Dana and Mantey, *Manual Grammar*, 301-302 (acknowledging exceptions); William Heidt, "Translating New Testament Imperatives," *Catholic Biblical Quarterly* 13 (1951): 254-56 (present only). One Bible translator accepts the rule and strongly encourages fellow translators to apply it (and insights discussed about questions) to their work. He states,

> ... I feel that it would be worth our while to take another look at our own translations, examining them carefully and comparing them with the Greek original to see whether we could incorporate such grammatical insights into our work, thus transforming a less perfect translation into a more perfect one. I feel strongly that these insights, although we tend to play them down, do play a vital role in the work of translation by communicating to it a living reality (A. P. Fernando, "Translation of Questions and Prohibitions in Greek," *The Bible Translator* 27 [1976]: 140-41).

This rule is common (to various degrees) in beginning Greek text books. See James M. Efird, *A Grammar for New Testament Greek* (Nashville: Abingdon Press, 1990), 121; Eugene Van Ness Goetchius, *The Language of the New Testament* (New York: Charles Scribner's Sons, 1965), 263 (acknowledges exceptions); James W. Voelz, *Fundamental Greek Grammar* (St. Louis, MO: Concordia Publishing House, 1986), 189, 216; Bernard Guy and Jacques Marcoux, *Grec du nouveau testament* (n.p.: Editions Béthel, 1985), 209 (for the present only, not the aorist subjunctive; it is not certain whether the rule as described here was the influence [directly or indirectly] upon these writers' conclusion). For a more accurate description of the tenses of the imperative in a basic grammar, see William D. Mounce, *Basics of Biblical Greek: Grammar* (Grand Rapids: Zondervan Publishing House, 1993), 309-10.

[97]Johannes P. Louw in an article as early as 1959 challenged this canon by appealing to Apollonius Dyscolus. It was concluded that the tenses in both positive commands and negative prohibitions should generally be similar ("On Greek Prohibitions," *Acta Classica* 2 [1959]: 43-57). I can only speculate concerning the reason this article's influence was minor. New Testament scholars may have overlooked it because its focus was not on biblical Greek. Nevertheless, Louw's treatment is not as satisfactory as McKay's (see below) which makes use of insights gleaned from aspect theory. Shortly after Louw, Willem Frederik Bakker published a monograph on aspectual differences with the imperative (*The Greek Imperative: An Investigation into the Aspectual Differences between the Present and Aorist Imperatives in Greek Prayer from Homer up to the Present Day* [Amsterdam: Uitgeverij Adolf M. Hakkert, 1966]). However, with reference to later developments, in retrospect, although Bakker's work contains much that is helpful, it was a step backward since it maintained a notion of time in the distinction between the tenses with the imperative (e.g., see his discussion on p. 64). Bakker has been followed (and developed) by James Voelz who views *connection* between the addressees and action as the essential difference between the tenses. The present involves this connection but the aorist does not ("The Use of the Present and Aorist Imperatives and Prohibitions in the New Testament" [Ph.D. diss., University of Cambridge, 1977]). For an interaction with both Louw and Bakker, see K. L. McKay, "Aspects of the Imperative in Ancient Greek," *Antichthon* 20 (1986): 41-58. McKay goes beyond these approaches and incorporates insights from aspect studies as the explanation for the tense choice. This will be discussed presently.

It may also be noted that aspect studies were making great advances in other (especially

in 1985 with the publication of K. L. McKay's article, "Aspect in Imperatival Constructions in New Testament Greek."[98] In this article McKay placed the imperative within verbal aspect theory and thus redefined the essence of the tenses as used with the imperative. The aorist form is used to urge (or prohibit) action as an activity as a whole while the present form is used to urge (or prohibit) activity as an ongoing process.[99] This more general and accurate understanding of the tense form places the canon of Headlam and others in its correct perspective. The *cease doing* nuance is one of many possible meanings for the present tense imperative. The *do not start doing* nuance is one of a number of possible meanings for the aorist. This seems to be what Naylor was attempting to say (although without the theoretical background) as he explained these nuances as one option respectively among many[100] and that the *cease doing* nuance for the present was unprovable in the majority of cases.[101]

Two other observation about the tenses with commands and prohibitions are necessary to consider. First, it has long been suggested that the aorist tense form is often used for *specific commands* and the present tense form for *general precepts*.[102] Second, the aorist is more likely to be used if *urgency* is

---

Slavic) languages. In such areas, enough advancement had been made that some were proposing different (rival) theories of verbal aspect for a specific language. See for example Steven P. Hassman's proposal for Russian, "Aspect Use in the Imperative: An Alternate View," *Russian Language Journal* 40 (1986): 25-32. It was inevitable that such work would begin to impact Greek studies.

[98]*Novum Testamentum* 27 (1985): 201-26. This article includes all forms used for commands and is not limited to the imperative mood.

[99]Ibid., 206-7. Although there are some differences between stative and non- stative action verbs, McKay maintains that "in many realizations the difference between action and stative verbs in the imperative is not obvious (207).

Other major works on verbal aspect have utilized McKay's insights (see Buist M. Fanning, *Verbal Aspect in New Testament Greek*, Oxford Theological Monographs, ed. J. Barton et al. [Oxford: Clarendon Press, 1990], 325-88 and Porter, *Verbal Aspect*, 335-61). Little can be added to the thoroughness of these works in this area. New Testament grammars are beginning to reflect this observation (see Wallace, *Exegetical Syntax*, 715-17; Young, *Intermediate*, 144).

[100]Naylor, "Prohibitions," 30

[101]Naylor, "More Prohibitions," 348.

[102]As suggested by the traditional approaches of BDF, 172; Funk, *Beginning-Intermediate Grammar*, 640; W. G. Morrice, "Translating the Greek Imperative," *The Bible Translator* 24 (1973): 129-30; F. W. Mozley, "Notes on the Biblical Use of the Present and Aorist Imperative," *Journal of Theological Studies* 4 (1903): 279; Zerwick, *Biblical Greek*, 79.

demanded.[103] Although lexical and other considerations may cause exceptions to this observation, developments in aspect theory generally support these notions.[104] Nevertheless, there are exceptions to this pattern and thus it is unwise to elevate these observations to the status of rules.[105] It is one thing to observe a pattern of usage but it is quite another to demand that it be applied in a prescriptive manner.[106] The distinction between the aorist and present tense in the imperative mood (as with the subjunctive and optative) is one of aspect, not time.[107]

---

[103]As proposed by Chamberlain, *Exegetical Grammar*, 86-87; Heidt, "Translating," 254; Moulton, *Prolegomena*, 173. It has also been observed that the aorist is more common in prayers than the present. This seems to first have been observed by Mozley in his study of biblical Greek ("Notes," 279-82). Others followed Mozley with reference to other types of Greek. See for example the study by E. Kieckers who observes this pattern in a number of ancient Greek authors ("Zum Gebrauch des Imperativus Aoristi und Praesentis," *Indogermanische Forschunger* 24 [1909]: 10-17). See also Porter, *Verbal Aspect*, 347-50 and Fanning, *Verbal Aspect*, 380-82.

[104]Fanning, *Verbal Aspect*, 325-88 and Constantine R. Campbell, *Verbal Aspect and Non-Indicative Verbs: Further Soundings in the Greek New Testament*, Studies in Biblical Greek, ed. D. A. Carson, vol. 15 (New York: Peter Lang, 2008), 81-100. Concerning urgency, the aorist may be used this way but it is not demanded (Fanning, *Verbal Aspect*, 369-70).

[105]Fanning, *Verbal Aspect*, 340-79; Campbell, *Verbal Aspect and Non-Indicative Verbs*, 81-100. Also, Young suggests the distinction between general precepts and specific commands as well as the nuance of urgency with the aorist are based on context, not the verb itself (*Intermediate*, 142-43). Concerning the general-specific distinction, Young is correct to note exceptions to the general rule (see the chart in Fanning, *Verbal Aspect*, 332); however, exceptions do not make this observation invalid. In every case, context (as well as lexical nuances) must be considered and its contribution may demand a different interpretation. It seems that these are descriptive observations about common usages of these forms. This is meant to be general, not applicable in every instance. Few aspects of any language are without exception. This is also followed by Black (*It's Still Greek to Me*, 101) and Perschbacher (*Greek Syntax*, 357). Also, Young's concern about urgency must be taken seriously. Context may contribute to the nuance of urgency. Boyer ("Imperatives," 45-46) argues against viewing the aorist as *more urgent* and suggests students may over emphasize the importance of this tense because there is no such tense in English (making it seem special). He also points out that the notion *more urgent* is rather vague. Boyer's arguments have merit. Nevertheless, the nature of the aorist aspect make it the likely choice (all things being equal) when the nuance of urgency is needed.

[106]See the section entitled *Descriptive Approach* in chapter 1.

[107]Fanning, *Verbal Aspect*, 325; Older works often saw this distinction as one of *Aktionsart* (sometimes called aspect; however, this term was not precisely defined in biblical studies until recently). See Walter C. Barrett, "The Use of Tense in the Imperative Mood in First Corinthians" (Th.M. thesis, Dallas Theological Seminary, 1973), 18, 59; Funk, *Beginning-Intermediate Grammar*, 640-46 (aspect); Goetchius, *Language of the New Testament*, 226 (called *aspect*); Mandilaras, *Verb*, 296 (aspect); Moulton, *Prolegomena*, 173-74; Mozley, "Notes," 279 (sees both time and *Aktionsart* as factors for the present imperative). After surveying a number of grammars and concluding that the distinction between the tenses in one of *Aktionsart*, Barrett states, "It is evident, when the grammarians are examined, that the use of tense in the imperative is not fully

For the present tense (imperfective aspect), a focus upon the internal nature of an action lends itself to universal, customary, or progressive senses demanded by general precepts. This is in contrast to specific commands which are narrow in focus and dependent upon the immediate circumstances.[108] For example, Paul states in Rom 12:14, **εὐλογεῖτε** τοὺς διώκοντας [ὑμᾶς], **εὐλογεῖτε** καὶ **μὴ καταρᾶσθε** (**Bless** those who persecute [you], **bless** and **do not curse**"). These are common in epistles which are often didactic in nature.

The aorist tense (perfective aspect) presents the verbal action in its entirety without reference to its internal make up. This can effectively be used to communicate specific commands. For example, in Acts 2:22, Peter addresses the Jewish pilgrims gathered in Jerusalem, **ἀκούσατε** τοὺς λόγους τούτους (**listen** to these words).[109] These are common in narrative which is often descriptive in nature.[110]

In this section recent work on the imperative mood in Greek studies has been surveyed. We have presented both meanings and usages of the mood as understood by the major works on the subject. This has provided a starting point on which this work will be able to build as it attempts to present a more comprehensive treatment of the mood.

---

understood" ("Use of Tense," 18). With the recent insights from verbal aspect theory, it would seem that the challenge implicit in these words has been met. C. F. D. Moule's distinction between the present and aorist (although based on *Aktionsart*) is as close as the older grammarians came to that which is proposed here, "In general the Present Imperative commands (or, with μή, prohibits) *continued* or *habitual* action, the Aorist as *specific* action" (italics in the original); *An Idiom Book of New Testament Greek*, 2d ed. (Cambridge: Cambridge University Press, 1959), 135. Moule acknowledges that this rule is "extremely fluid" (ibid., 135).

[108]A general precept may be described as "a moral regulation which is broadly applicable; a rule for conduct to be applied in multiple situations; a command or prohibition to be followed by an individual or a group not only in the immediate situation in which it is given, but also in subsequent (repeated or continuing) circumstances in which the precept is appropriate" (Fanning, *Verbal Aspect*, 327-28). A specific command can be described as "an order or request for action to be done in a particular instance. The speaker commands or prohibits some attitude or action, but does so only in reference to the immediate circumstances and hearers involved: he does not intend to regulate conduct in broader terms" (ibid., 328).

[109]For further examples of this distinction with both commands and prohibitions (see ibid., 332-35, 337-39).

[110]The observation that the present tense form occurs commonly in epistles and the aorist tense form occur commonly in narrative is very general. Both types of tenses are found in both types of literature (see the table in Fanning [ibid., 330]). For a (pre-modern aspect studies) discussion of the tenses in the imperative in the gospel of John see Edwin A. Abbott, *Johannine Grammar* (London: Adam and Charles Black, 1906), 318-22.

The Imperative in General Linguistic Studies

The imperative has been studied in a number of languages and from various linguistic perspectives.[111] Many such studies are of little value for this work except where they uncover universal imperative characteristics which can apply to this study. As discussed in chapter 1, it seems like more effort has been spent on the sememic notions of command/prohibition than on the meaning of a morphological imperative mood. In this section, a few such approaches will be examined and important contributions gleaned where evident.

Speech Act Theory

When considering language use and specifically language use as often reflected by the imperative mood, one's linguistic intuition may immediately lead to *speech act theory*. It has been observed that language can be used in ways other than merely communicating thoughts, facts, etc. Other functions are apparent when one considers the following sentences:

A. I baptize you in the name of the Father, Son, and Holy Spirit.
B. I promise I will give you my paper this Friday.

In sentence A, the presence of the utterance itself is demanded for a baptism to

---

[111]Studies surveyed concerning meaning and/or form of the imperative in various languages include: L. O. Adéwolé, "The Yorùbá Imperative," *African Languages and Cultures* 4 (1991): 130-12; S. Agesthialingom, "Imperative in Old Tamil," *Indian Linguistics: Journal of the Linguistic Society of India* 41 (1980): 102-15; Flor M. Bango de la Campa, "Aportaciones para un estudio del imperativo en francés moderno," *Verba* 11 (1984): 293-306; Christina Y. Bethin, "Syllable Structure and the Polish Imperative Desinence," *Slavic and East European Journal* 31 (1987): 76-89; A. Bogusławski, "The Problem of the Negated Imperative in Perfective Verbs Revisited," *Russian Linguistics* 9 (1985): 225-39 (on Russian); Mark J. Elson, "Present Tense and Imperative Innovation in Ukranian Conjugation," *Slavic and East European Journal* 32 (1988): 265-82; Joseph F. Eska, "The Third Person Imperative Desinences in Old Irish," *Historische Sprachforschung* 105 (1992): 257-63; Ilya Gershevitch, "The Ossetic 3rd Plural Imperative," *Transactions of the Philological Society* 89 (1991): 221-234; Steven P. Hassman, "Aspect Use in the Imperative," 25-32 (on Russian); Anthony Mattina, "Imperative Formations in Colville-Okanagan and in the Other Interior Salishan Languages," *Glossa* 14 (1980): 213-32; Oscar E. Swan, "The Morphophonemics of the Russian Imperative," *Russian Linguistics* 8 (1984): 39-47. Other can certainly be listed.

actually be accomplished. An immersion of a person into water is not enough. These words uttered by a qualified person must accompany the immersion (sprinkling, etc.) of an individual (not the speaker) for baptism to take place.[112] In sentence B, the one uttering this statement does more than inform the hearer that his paper will be given to him on Friday. The speaker commits himself to this end.[113] The recognition that utterances themselves can actually accomplish acts and function in ways other than exclusively communicating information has led to the study of such uses of language. A significant linguistic and philosophical attempt to study and account for this phenomenon is called *speech act theory* (SAT).[114]

Speech act theory has been a major focus in the recent study of pragmatics. This is because speech acts demonstrate a functional use of language heretofore not explicitly considered. Levinson includes speech acts with presupposition and implicature as the central phenomena to be accounted for in pragmatic

---

[112]In such instances a number of conditions must be met for these acts to be accomplished. Neither the words, water, ritual, or qualified person alone will result in the act. All of these features must be executed at a specific time, in a specific place, and in a specific manner for the act to be accomplished. For a detailed discussion of specific types of (felicity) conditions (propositional content, preparatory, sincerity, and essential), see J. L. Austin, *How to Do Things with Words* (Cambridge, MA: Harvard University Press, 1962), 44-45 and J. R. Searle, *Speech Acts: An Essay in the Philosophy of Language* (London: Cambridge University Press, 1969), 57-67. See also Stephen C. Levinson, *Pragmatics*, Cambridge Textbooks in Linguistics (Cambridge: University Press, 1983), 229, 237-40, 244-46 and John Lyons, *Semantics* (Cambridge: Cambridge University Press, 1977), 733-35.

[113]Various levels of commitment may be involved depending upon the context in which such a statement is made. For example, the level of commitment may differ depending upon the relationship between the speaker and hearer as well as the circumstances which prompted the utterance. If the speaker is a social equal or peer, the commitment may be lower than if the hearer is a superior (e.g., teacher, professor, etc.) to whom a paper must be given to fulfill some requirement (e.g., for a class). Also, the shorter utterance, "I will give you my paper on Friday" may also commit the speaker to fulfilling the statement (note, it could also be a prediction); however, the addition of *I promise* seems to impose a higher level commitment upon the speaker.

[114]It is necessary to make a distinction between speech acts themselves and SAT. The former is the use of language to accomplish acts. The evidence for such a use of language is clearly demonstrated by the examples above. SAT has arisen to attempt to account for this within language usage in general. This approach views all utterances as *acts* in some sense, even if the act is merely informative. Thus, SAT is a broader than merely accounting for usages such as those cited above (and may even include nonverbal communication). Lyons states concerning the work of the theory's founder, "What Austin offers then is, in principle, a unified theory of the meaning of utterances within the framework of a general theory of social activity" (Lyons, *Semantics*, 735). To what extent this theory is sufficient to accomplish this goal will be discussed briefly below. However, with or without SAT, one's theory of communication must be able to account for speech acts.

theory.[115] By its very nature, this theory would seem to be a natural candidate for use in analyzing the imperative mood.

The two foundational proponents of this theory are J. L. Austin and J. R. Searle. The philosopher John Austin laid the groundwork for the theory; however, it is the theory's development by John Searle which has commonly been followed. Searle utilized (and reworked) Grice's insights concerning intention in his theory.[116] It will be this approach which will briefly be discussed here.[117]

---

[115]Levinson, *Pragmatics*, 226. Also, one writer seems to view pragmatics as primarily a study of speech acts (Madelon E. Heatherington, "Pragmatics," in *Language: Introductory Readings*, ed. Virginia P. Clark, Paul A. Eschholz and Alfred F. Rosa [New York: St. Martin's Press, 1981], 418-24). Another maintains that "a theory of speech acts is needed as part of a(ny) theory of utterance meaning" (Gerald Gadazar, "Speech Act Assignment," in *Elements of Discourse Understanding*, ed. A. K. Joshi, B. L. Webber, and I. A. Sag [Cambridge: Cambridge University Press, 1981], 65).

[116]Searle, *Speech Acts*, 44-50.

[117]The literature on SAT is considerable and within this literature there are differences. Even the label *speech act* is ambiguous (Levinson, *Pragmatics*, 242-243). A thorough discussion of this theory (and its variations) is beyond the scope of this work. An application of SAT to the Greek imperative mood within the context of the entire verbal system may be fruitful. However, for reasons stated below in the text, it will be clear why it is believed that this theory will not be most beneficial for the purposes here. For a brief overview of SAT (see ibid., 226-283 and Lyons, *Semantics*, 725-45).

There have been applications of SAT to the New Testament. See for example Takashi Manabe, "Speech Act Theory Based Interpretation Model for Written Texts" (Ph.D. diss., University of Texas at Arlington, 1984), 318-62; Richard A. Young, "A Classification of Conditional Sentences Based on Speech Act Theory," *Grace Theological Journal* 10 (1989): 29-49; and Karl J. Franklin, "Speech Act Verbs and the Words of Jesus," in *Language in Context: Essays for Robert Longacre*, ed. Shin Ja J. Hwang and William R. Merrifield (Dallas: Summer Institute of Linguistics and University of Texas at Arlington, 1992), 241-261. Young also mentions SAT in a discussion about pragmatics in a section of his grammar devoted to discourse analysis (Young, *Intermediate*, 265). However, in this work he does not demonstrate the value of the theory for biblical studies (as he does for conditionals in his 1989 article). An issue of *Semeia* entitled, *Speech Act Theory and Biblical Criticism*, was devoted to SAT and included theoretical, practical, responsive, and bibliographic items (Hugh C. White, [ed.], *Semeia* 41 [1988]: 1-178). Anthony Thiselton used a form of SAT in his massive commentary on 1 Corinthians (*The First Epistle to the Corinthians: A Commentary on the Greek Text*, New International Greek Testament Commentary [Grand Rapids: William B. Eerdmans Publishing Company, 2000], see 41-52 and its use throughout). A volume dedicated to Thiselton includes a number of articles using the theory (Craig Bartholomew, Colin Green, and Karl Möller [eds.], *After Pentecost: Language and Biblical Interpretation*, Scripture and Hermeneutics Series, vol. 2 [Grand Rapids: Zondervan Publishing House, 2001]). More recently, David A. Montgomery has proposed an interpretive method from a SAT perspective to understand directives using John 1:38 as an example ("Directives in the New Testament: A Case Study of John 1:38," *Journal of the Evangelical Theological Society* [2007]: 275-88; although related, his term "directive" differs

Searle followed up his initial work[118] on speech acts with an article on speech act taxonomy.[119] In this work Searle identifies five types of speech acts.

---

from that used later in this work) and Kit Barker has argued for using SAT at the genre and canonical levels to understand Psalm 137 ("Divine Illocutions in Psalm 137," *Tyndale Bulletin* 60 [2009]: 1-14).

Although it is Searle's development of the theory which has generally been the basis of further development, a brief word on Austin's work is in order. In the 1955 William James Lectures at Harvard University (this is the same series where twelve years later Paul Grice discussed his insights on *intention* in language, see chapter 1), Austin delivered a series of lectures on the functions of speech. These lectures are published in Austin, *How to Do Things with Words* (Cambridge, MA: Harvard University Press, 1962). Most generally, Austin distinguished between *constatives* (saying) and *performatives* (doing); ibid., 3, 47, 54-55. (Austin prefers *constative* to *descriptive* because "not all true or false statements are descriptive," ibid., 3). Austin makes a distinction between *explicit performatives* (as in the initial example), "I promise I will give you my paper on Friday" and *primary utterances*, "I will give you my paper on Friday" (ibid., 69). The latter utterance may or may not have the same meaning as the former (e.g., the latter could be a promise [of varying degrees] or a prediction). Unsatisfied with (and rejecting) the *constative/performative* contrast as the basis for his model (ibid., 90-94), Austin moved to a distinction between a *locutionary act* (similar to stating a certain sentence with a certain sense and reference—traditional meaning; e.g., *he said that*), an *illocutionary act* (utterances with a certain force; e.g., ordering, informing, warning, undertaking, etc.; e.g., *he argued that*), and a *perlocutionary act* (what is achieved by the utterance, the effects; e.g., persuading, convincing, deterring, surprising, and misleading; e.g., *he convinced me that* [ibid., 98-109; especially 102, 108]). See also Levinson, *Pragmatics*, 235-36.

Austin departed from the constative/performative distinction to a *theory of speech acts* by suggesting preliminary classifications of types of *illocutionary acts*. Levinson notes that it is *illocutionary acts* with which SAT is exclusively concerned (*Pragmatics*, 236). Austin lists five types of speech acts: *verdictives* (a judicial act consisting of delivering an official or unofficial finding; e.g., verbs include: acquit, convict, etc.), *exercitives* (a decision, not judgment, that something is to be; e.g., appoint, demote, name, order, etc.), *commissives* (commits the speaker to a specific course of action; e.g., promise, covenant, etc.), *behabitives* (reactions to other's actions, attitudes, etc.; e.g., apologize, thank, etc.), and *expositives* (explaining of views, making arguments, clarifying, exposition; e.g., testify, state, remark, explain, etc.); Austin, *How to Do Things with Words*, 147-63. See these pages for further examples of the various types of speech acts. Austin makes it clear throughout this section that his classifications are preliminary. This judgment seems to be confirmed as it is Searle's development which has been followed. For a discussion of the weaknesses of Austin's classification scheme, see J. R. Searle, *Expression and Meaning: Studies in the Theory of Speech Acts* (Cambridge: Cambridge University Press, 1979), 8-12.

[118]Searle, *Speech Acts.*

[119]J. R. Searle, "A Taxonomy of Illocutionary Acts," in *Language Mind and Knowledge*, ed. K. Gunderson (Minneapolis: University of Minnesota Press, 1975), 344-69. This article is reprinted with minor adjustment in Searle, *Expression and Meaning*, 1-29. Unless stated otherwise, all references made to this article will be from the later edition.

1. *Assertives*,[120] commits the speaker to some (varying) extent to the truth of a proposition (e.g., verbs include: assert, conclude, deduce, etc.).
2. *Directives*, the speaker attempts (in varying degrees) to get the hearer to do something (e.g., order, command, request, ask, pray, etc.).
3. *Commissives*, commits the speaker to some (varying) extent to a future action (e.g., shall, intend, favor, threat, promise, etc.).
4. *Expressives*, the speaker expresses some type of psychological state with his words (e.g., welcome, apologize, thank, etc.).
5. *Declarations*, the speaker uses words to bring about something at that moment (e.g., resign, baptize, declare war, etc.).[121]

Therefore, much of SAT involves (but is not limited to[122]) classifying utterances into these categories.

An imperative is normally classified as a single directive (or a specific type of directive such as request, command, etc.[123] However, one author has developed and applied SAT to the imperative mood more rigorously than it has often been treated. At the beginning of an article exploring speech acts in a few modern languages, Per Durst-Andersen suggests that in contrast to traditional mono-layered structure approaches to the imperative, "any imperative necessarily involves three speech acts and therefore must have a multi-layered structure."[124] In other words, Durst-Andersen has noticed that a specific imperative utterance such as "go ahead" may function both as *advice* and *permission*. There is no need to choose a single speech act.[125] This modification

---

[120]Searle, ("Taxonomy," 354-55) in 1975 originally used the term *representative* but later (in the republished work) he changed it to *assertive* because he thought the former was too broad. He states, "any speech act with a propositional content is in some sense a representation" Searle, *Expression and Meaning*, viii, n.1).

[121]Ibid., 12-20. See also Levinson, *Pragmatics*, 240.

[122]Again, it should be emphasized that the discussion of SAT here is extremely minimal. For a more complete account of the theory, see the sources mentioned above.

[123]Lyons, *Semantics*, 745.

[124]Per Durst-Andersen, "Imperative Frames and Modality: Direct vs. Indirect Speech Acts in Russian, Danish, and English," *Linguistics and Philosophy* 18 (1995): 613.

[125]Ibid. Durst-Andersen develops the idea of *imperative frames*, each of which consists of three speech acts. The first applies to the hearer and has ethical implications (permission, obligation; negated: prohibition, non-obligation). The second speech act is the actual request (speech act of the same name). The final speech act applies to the speaker and carries with it what

to the theory may result in it being more accurate for describing actual communication. However, as will be developed below, it seems that SAT itself is theoretically and methodologically questionable and although it may yield important insights, it will not be used as a theoretical basis for this work.

Recognizing that the imperative mood is strongly *functional* and that the act of *doing something* is emphasized in imperative communication, it seems logical that this system would be fruitful for inquiry into the imperative mood. However, given the linguistic foundation of this work in NCSL and RT, the benefits of SAT would be minimal in this work for a number of reasons.

First, although SAT rightly attempts to account for a use of language which has been previously ignored, this functional nature of language (utterances for *doing*) accounts for a small percentage of actual utterances.[126] This is especially true for written communication which is highly informative.[127] Therefore, to create a grid for looking at language usage based on a minority of utterances seems unwise.[128] A better method would be to account for such functional uses of language *within* a structure based primarily on more common usages of language.[129]

Second, speech act theory's potential contribution to this work is minimal given the linguistic foundation already established in chapter 1. Despite the elaborate classification of speech acts, the important linguistic insight that communication is accomplished primarily by inference still needs to be accounted within this system. If SAT could provide and alternate means of

---

the speaker expects and the force of the utterance (advice, suggestion, order, etc.); ibid., 613-14.

[126]This is referring to the types of action represented by the examples given above (which are the type often discussed in such studies). However, in some sense, all utterances in some way are *doing* something, even if the *doing* is merely informing (thus such *information only* utterances have an illocutionary force of *statement*). This is understood by SAT proponents and incorporated into their system. The concern here is with the emphasis placed on the minority of functional or "action" type words. These seem to be the driving force behind the system.

[127]However, see the application of SAT to written texts in Manabe, "Speech Act Theory," 232-365.

[128]Although, due to the nature of the imperative, it is acknowledged that SAT may be more beneficial for this mood than the indicative. The imperative is among the "minority of utterances" which drove the development of the theory. Nevertheless, a theory is less attractive that is not maximally beneficial for the entire mood system.

[129]This may be the way in which the theory is used by some (i.e, within a larger theory of pragmatics). This seems to be the way Levinson (*Pragmatics*, 226) views the theory.

explaining communication, its consideration would be more attractive.[130] However, it does not. In fact it seems lacking in its ability to account for the communication situation. The theory may account for certain verbal acts; however, it does not seem to be able to account for *interaction* in the communication process.[131] Indeed, Searle incorporates Grice's notion of inference in his theory.[132] However, this development seems to be in the background while the emphasis is on types of functions.[133] Nevertheless, granting an understanding of the communication process similar to that proposed in chapter 1 (albeit in the background), it must be determined whether SAT provides a more complete basis for the analysis of the imperative mood than is presented in the method section of chapter 1. It does not seem so. There is some overlap between the approaches and some insights from SAT will be incorporated in chapter 3 (see discussion below). However, for reasons discussed below, there is nothing of significant value which should cause this project to use SAT as a basis for analysis. In fact the opposite will be proven true. There are reasons why SAT will not be the most effective means of analysis for this work.

Third, there is a methodological difference between this work and SAT. Speech act theory is concerned with higher level discourse matters than morphology. In other words, it is concerned with classifying various utterances according to their function. In the present work, the concern is to understand the

---

[130]Of course if this was the case, the next step would be to determine which system was most beneficial. However, based on the development of the theory thus far, such a further step is not possible.

[131]Dorothea Franck, "Seven Sins of Pragmatics: Theses about Speech Act Theory, Conversational Analysis, Linguistics and Rhetoric," in *Possibilities and Limitations of Pragmatics: Proceedings of the Conference on Pragmatics, Urbino, July 8–14, 1979,* ed. Herman Parret, Marina Sbisà, and Jef Verschueren (Amsterdam: John Benjamins, 1981), 226-27. Franck also points out that communication is dynamic and speech act theory's presentation of communication is static. She notes that breaking up a conversation into speech acts fails to capture "the internal 'logic' of the conversation" (ibid., 229).

[132]Searle, *Speech Acts*, 44-50. However, Franck remarks that "The notion of context [in SAT] is a marginal one with a primarily remedial function" ("Seven Sins of Pragmatics," 230). Also, on the related notion of *intentionality* in SAT, see also J. R. Searle, *Intentionality: An Essay in the Philosophy of Mind* (Cambridge: Cambridge University Press, 1983) and Manabe, "Speech Act Theory," 20-97.

[133]K. Bach and R. M. Harnish, criticize Searle's approach because it "fails to do justice" to three important factors in communication: content, context, and communication intention. Their work attempts place SAT more solidly within a theory of communication (*Linguistic Communication and Speech Acts* [Cambridge, MA: MIT Press, 1979], xi).

imperative mood itself. As discussed in chapter 1, the focus of this work is upon the meaning and usage of the Greek imperative mood, not on commands and prohibition. The two overlap but are not the same. SAT is concerned with higher functions (analogous to commands and prohibitions) and not with the meaning of a specific mood. Although the theory may be compatible with theories of semantics,[134] SAT is essentially concerned with pragmatics. The present work begins with structure and works toward semantics and then finally pragmatics (with some overlap) within an inferential model of communication. SAT begins with function and then determines where various structures are to be classified. It begins with pragmatics. The approaches are directly opposite. This methodological difference cannot be understated.

Also, SAT is not specific enough for the needs of this work. It is not enough to know that certain imperatives are *directives*. It must also be determined what strength the *directive* carries[135] (request, command, etc.).[136]

Fourth, there are serious problems with SAT itself. Some of the more obvious will be listed here.[137] First, related to the previous point, SAT is

---

[134]See Paul Gochet, "How to Combine Speech Act Theory with Formal Semantics: A New Account of Searle's Concept of Proposition," in *Possibilities and Limitations of Pragmatics: Proceedings of the Conference on Pragmatics, Urbino, July 8–14, 1979*, ed. Herman Parret, Marina Sbisà, and Jef Verschueren (Amsterdam: John Benjamins, 1981), 251-61.

[135]Speech Act theorists do acknowledge this. See the list of speech acts above with the more specific descriptive words in parenthesis. This seems to be what Franklin is attempting to do with the *speaking* verbs in the gospels (e.g., say, answer, tell, etc.); "Speech Act Verbs," 241-61.

[136]In some ways, SAT would be more suited for study of *mood* in general rather than *a* mood in particular (although even here it is questionable whether it would be best even for this purpose). Lyons views SAT as providing "a general framework . . . for the discussion of the syntactic and semantic distinctions that linguists have traditionally described in terms of mood and modality" (*Semantics*, 725). Nevertheless, it will be pointed out below that SAT is valuable for understanding the semantic meaning of the imperative. It will be considered in chapter 3. However, the theory itself cannot be the basis for the analysis because (among other reasons) the goal of this work is to account for both the semantics and pragmatics of the mood.

[137]Up to this point the discussion has been concerned with why SAT is less adequate as a basis for this study than what has been proposed in chapter 1. With few exceptions, the weakness of the theory itself has not been discussed. This point will address essential inadequacies in the theory. Because a thorough exposition of the theory was not presented, a thorough criticism is also unwarranted and due to the many diverse expressions of the theory, such a comprehensive task is far beyond the scope of this small section. Here only select inadequacies will be discussed. For a more comprehensive critique of the theory, see Stephen C. Levinson, "The Essential Inadequacies of Speech Act Models of Dialogue," in *Possibilities and Limitations of Pragmatics: Proceedings of the Conference on Pragmatics, Urbino, July 8-14, 1979*, ed. Herman Parret, Marina Sbisà, and Jef Verschueren (Amsterdam: John Benjamins, 1981), 473-92; Levinson, *Pragmatics*, 251-76, 278-83; Franck, "Seven Sins of Pragmatics," 225-36.

concerned with classifying function. However, both Austin and Searle's taxonomy examples involve classifying actual verbs.[138] Classifying verbs by their function as speech acts is different than classifying verbs by their procedural characteristics as stative, accomplishment, etc.[139] The latter classifies verbs by an inherent (lexical) semantic characteristic which is pure only in a contextless environment. The procedural characteristic must interact with other grammatical (e.g., aspect) and contextual information (e.g., adverbs). This interaction results in a specific use (meaning) in a specific context. The former classifies the verb in the way it functions in a specific context. Although Searle classifies the verb *promise* as a *commissive* because of its use in sentences like, "I promise I will be there." It can also be used as a *directive*, "promise me you will be there."[140] It should be noted that the verb form used in the taxonomies are usually the first person singular present verbs with the pronoun "I."[141] This gives the examples a unified appearance and seems to result in the most straight forward literal (and contextless) meaning[142] of the verb. Thus, it may be that the objection raised here is merely one over terminology, proponents being ultimately concerned with an underlying deep structure.[143] Nevertheless, the focus is placed on the verbs themselves (albeit as deep-structured semantic entities) which seems to suggest a less than adequate means of classification.

This problem can be easily overcome by simply classifying the use of the utterance and not the verb itself. This seems to be what Levinson does when he presents the taxonomy.[144] His examples are not lists of verbs but rather lists of functions. For example, after introducing commissives, he describes the

---

[138]This is demonstrated when both give examples using the first person (e.g., *I conclude*); see for example Austin, *How to Do Things with Words*, 151 and Searle, *Expression and Meaning*, 17. This is briefly discussed further below. It is also explicitly stated by these writers that they are classifying *verbs* (see Austin, *How to Do Things with Words*, 83-90 [although the model was developed beyond this], 149-50 and Searle, *Expression and Meaning*, 14, "Verbs denoting members of this class are . . ."; see also Lyons, *Semantics*, 736-38).

[139]See Fanning, *Verbal Aspect*, 127-163.

[140]It must be granted that the goal of this directive is to elicit the commissive, "I promise . . ."

[141]For an explanation of the use of this form, see Austin, *How to Do Things with Words*, 67-68. See also Searle's discussion and examples (*Expression and Meaning*, 20-27).

[142]This description is problematic but must suffice for lack of a more satisfactory term.

[143]See Searle, *Expression and Meaning*, 20-21. See also the discussion of the verb *say* in Austin, *How to Do Things with Words*, 92-93 and Lyons, *Semantics*, 740-42.

[144]Also, Franklin does seem to make a distinction between Speech Acts and speech act verbs ("Speech Act Verbs," 241-42). However, this article focuses on the verbs.

examples of this speech act as "paradigm cases: promising, threatening, offering." Thus the statement above, "promise me you will be there" is not classified as a *commissive* based on its verb but as a *directive* since it attempting to get the hearer to do something. Searle seems to be able to handle these cases when his discussion of Grice's contribution is presented;[145] nevertheless, Searle's (and Austin's) taxonomy is a taxonomy of verbs.

Second, the previous criticism focused upon the classification of verbs. Even if in general SAT primarily concerned with classifying function,[146] there still seems to be a desire to correlate syntactic structure with speech acts. Searle seems to maintain that the three major sentence types in English (declarative, imperative, and interrogative[147]) generally have the forces of stating, ordering (or requesting), questioning.[148] This makes the error of assuming a literal force for these sentence types and disregards rhetorical questions, questions used as polite requests, irony, etc.[149] This is complicated further when one considers such *indirect* statements[150] as "could you open the window?" used as a request, "go ahead and break the vase" used an ironical imperative, and "should we continue in sin that grace might increase?" (Rom 6:1) used as a rhetorical question.[151] Thus, its seems unlikely that a "correlation between syntactic sentence types and generic speech acts can be maintained unless a whole range of utterance types [such as the previous three examples] are excluded as 'insincere' or 'defective', or the traditional typology of speech act types is abandoned."[152]

The only manner in which one may account for these types of (less than straight forward types of) language usage is through some type of an inferential

---

[145]Searle, *Speech Acts*, 43-50. This will be briefly revisited below.

[146]This may be accomplished by noting that the verb taxonomies are based on the deep structure meanings of utterances and not surface structure verb occurrences or by specifically classifying functions.

[147]As has been discussed in chapter 1, this terminology is confusing. These terms are not equivalent to *moods* (indicative, imperative, etc.).

[148]Searle, *Expression and Meaning*, 20-27.

[149]Levinson, "Essential Inadequacies," 476-78; Gadazar, "Speech Act Assignment," 64-83.

[150]Speech acts associated with these types of statements may be labeled *indirect speech acts*.

[151]See Levinson, *Pragmatics*, 263-76 and Dan Sperber and Deirdre Wilson, *Relevance: Communication and Cognition*, 2d ed. (Oxford: Blackwell, 1995), 247. For a discussion of direct and indirect forms of the speech acts, *request* and *threat*, see Peter Gingiss, "Indirect Threats," *Word* 37 (1986): 153-58.

[152]Sperber and Wilson, *Relevance*, 247. See also Gadazar, "Speech Act Assignment," 76-79.

component within the theory. A number of such models have been suggested[153] and inference is included in Searle's own model which incorporates the work of Grice.[154] However, once inference as a primary factor in communication is granted, one is back to determining the best explanation for the communication. It has been demonstrated in chapter 1 that *Relevance Theory* provides what seems to be a more cognitively sound model for this purpose.[155]

A third problem associated with SAT involves both its theory and method. Speech Act theorists emphasize determining what speech acts exist and how these acts should be classified. They also seem to assume that recognition and classification of a speech act is required by both the speaker and hearer for communication and comprehension to take place.[156] This of course is important in some cases (e.g., marrying, adult baptizing, promising, thanking, etc.),[157] but it cannot be assumed true for all communication.[158] For example, utterances such as "I will meet Jim at school today" used by the speaker as a prediction

---

[153]See Levinson, *Pragmatics*, 268-76. See also the model presented by Bach and Harnish (*Linguistic Communication*) which takes an "intention-and-inference" approach to speech acts while claiming to be at odds with both Austin and Searle in significant ways (ibid., xvi).

[154]Searle, *Speech Acts*, 43-50. The issue of indirect speech acts was also explored in J. R. Searle, "Indirect Speech Acts," in *Syntax and Semantics,* vol. 3: *Speech Acts*, ed. P. Cole and J. Morgan (New York: Academic Press, 1975, 59-82. This article is reprinted in Searle, *Expression and Meaning*, 30-57. Unless stated otherwise, all references made to this article will be from the later work. In this article Searle confirms the need to determine and classify the speech acts of the implicatures of an utterance.

[155]For a discussion of how *RT* accounts for speech acts, see Sperber and Wilson, *Relevance*, 243-54. For an RT approach to *speech act conditionals* (in contrast to a SAT approach), see Eu-Ju Noh, "A Relevance-Theoretical Account of Metarepresentative Uses in Conditionals," in *Current Issues in Relevance Theory*, ed. Villy Rouchota and Andreas H. Jucker (Amsterdam: John Benjamins Publishing Company, 1998), 287-300.

[156]See for example Searle's foundational discussion of *meaning* (*Speech Acts*, 48-50). Searle modifies the analysis of meaning proposed by Grice and concludes that a hearer must understand the intention of the speaker to understand the meaning the speaker intended. He argues his point by demonstrating that in the utterance "Hello," the intention of *greeting* must be understood in order for a greeting to take place. See also Searle's discussion of communicating a promise (ibid., 57-61). Searle's select examples fit his system; however, this principle cannot be applied in all circumstances. This will be discussed forthwith.

[157]For example, with an utterance such as "I now pronounce you husband and wife" all essential participants (e.g., minister, bride, groom) must be aware of the speech act being performed in order for the act to succeed. Sperber and Wilson consider such speech acts to be institutional acts and thus belong to the study of institutions, not verbal communication (*Relevance*, 244-45).

[158]Diane Blakemore, *Understanding Utterances: An Introduction to Pragmatics* (Oxford: Blackwell Publishers, 1992), 92-94; Sperber and Wilson, *Relevance*, 244-46. The following discussion is based on these works.

does not demand cognitive recognition of the prediction for effective communication to occur.[159] Whether or not the speaker or hearer (in this case, not Jim) realizes that this is predictive does not nullify the fact that it is a prediction; thus, the speech act is performed. In other words, it is *not* essential to communication that the hearer realize the predictive intention for this utterance. In this case, as far as the hearer is concerned, only the information that the speaker will meet Jim today is relevant.[160] Sperber and Wilson use an analogy of a tennis player to illustrate this. It is important for a player to know the different types of tennis strokes; however, one does not need to know how to classify a stroke in order to perform it.[161]

Therefore, due to serious problems with SAT, it will not be the basis for this work. It would be unwise to base this project on a theory which is neither compatible in method with the goals of this work nor has an adequate linguistic (and philosophical) basis as a theory of communication. Indeed, it is questionable whether this theory will be feasible when further work is done in this area.[162]

Although SAT has been rejected as a theoretical basis for this study, it is not without value for this work. Since the theory has primarily been concerned with the function of language and since the imperative mood is highly functional, some insights can be gained.[163] Specifically, some of the work done on *directives* seems to contribute to the discussion of the semantic meaning of the mood.[164] This work will not be as concerned with the various *directive* verbs;

---

[159]This does not suggest that the predictive (or other) intention is not important to communicate in certain contexts.

[160]See ibid., 245. Blakemore gives an example of a warning, "the path is slippery here," and demonstrates that the relevance for the hearer is the slippery state of the path whether or not the hearer understands that this is a warning (*Understanding Utterances*, 93-94).

[161]Sperber and Wilson, *Relevance*, 244. There are also some utterances which do not seem to be either institutional or cognitively incognizant (e.g., those of *saying*, *telling*, and *asking* [ibid., 246]).

[162]Levinson is "skeptical" concerning whether or not the theory(s) "will be viable in the long run" (*Pragmatics*, 278). He believes it is even now being "superseded" by more complex approaches to pragmatics (ibid., 278-83).

[163]Speech act theory was criticized above for emphasizing a minimal percentage of utterances. However, since usages of the imperative mood will often be among this small percentage, work in this area will be informative for the purposes of this work. It would be unwise to ignore the extensive work done in non-declarative moods using SAT.

[164]Although in this work's final analysis, the usage of the word *directive* will not be identical to that used in SAT.

rather, the functional meaning of *directive* will be utilized in the determination of the semantic meaning of the imperative mood.

Various Theoretical Linguistic Approaches

Many linguistic theories have been applied to the imperative mood. Most commonly, it is discussed within the larger context of language in general or as part of the *linguistic system* of a specific language. In this section a sampling of approaches to the mood will be presented. No attempt will be made to draw conclusions concerning the meaning of the imperative mood in Greek. This will be the focus of the next chapter. However, critiques of the approaches will be undertaken in a concise manner.

First, there are approaches which attempt to explain the imperative in relation to the indicative through a deep structure–surface structure relationship. In such cases there is an underlying deep structure, usually a declarative or indicative, which undergoes some type of imperative transformation. Thus, a deep structure such as "you will open the door" when undergoing an imperative transformation would result in "open the door."[165] Although it is most common for the deep structure to be assumed declarative, an imperative deep structure undergoing a transformation to produce a declarative surface structure has been postulated.[166]

---

[165] Adrian Akmajian and Frank Heny, *An Introduction to the Principles of Transformation Syntax* (Cambridge, MA: MIT Press, 1975), 233-36. Noam Chomsky suggests that imperative statements are forms of elliptical sentences where the subject (noun phrase) and auxiliary verb are dropped (*The Logical Structure of Linguistic Theory* [New York and London: Plenum Press, 1975], 553-54). Concerning deep structure and transformations, see also Noam Chomsky, *Aspects of the Theory of Syntax* (Cambridge, MA: MIT Press, 1965), 16-18, 64-106; Andrew Radford, *Transformational Syntax* (Cambridge: Cambridge University Press, 1981), 14-211. It has also been suggested that an actual imperative component may be embedded at the deep structure level. However, such a proposal's validity is questioned (Akmajian and Heny, *Transformational Syntax*, 233-36). In general (although with some unique aspects) this approach is also followed by Richard Zuber in his attempt to account for all non-declarative sentences (*Non-Declarative Sentences*, Pragmatics and Beyond 4:2 ed. Hubert Cuyckens, Herman Parret, and Jef Verschueren [Amsterdam: John Benjamins Publishing Company, 1983]).

[166] This seems to be the belief of Bertrand Russell, *An Inquiry into Meaning and Truth* (London: George Allen and Unwin, 1940), 26-29 (another relevant series of lectures delivered at Harvard's William James Lecture series [1940]).

By noting that second person imperatives in some languages (e.g., Latin and English) have no added inflection for tense and person (e.g., *go*), one may conclude that the imperative is a

This approach has the advantage of making explicit any connection between an imperative and its similarly worded indicative. However, to assume that this relationship is one of derivation is problematic. In the main view that the imperative comes from the indicative, is it certain that the indicative is the most basic mood? (The opposite can also be asked). Even if this could be proven, to suggest that the imperative is derived from the indicative and that an imperative transformation is responsible for this seems difficult to sustain. Language seems to be learned through patterning,[167] not the acquisition[168] and execution of transformations.[169]

---

more basic linguistic form. As Lyons states concerning this approach (although not committed to it), "the imperative, as the principal mood of will and desire, is ontologically more basic than the indicative, the mood of statement" (Lyons, *Semantics*, 747). Such a view of language may be based on an evolutionary model where utterances first appeared to provide simple instructions to others. A child often uses a higher proportion of imperatives because it is in his interest to make his needs known in a manner which will result in the fulfillment of his desire. This model is highly problematic. First, it is impossible to know how language first developed. Second, the lack of tense and person inflections are not universal (e.g., Greek). Third, in languages which lack such inflection, others explanations are possible. The lack of a person does not hinder communication because the direction of the imperative is usually obvious. The short form also is possible due to linguistic economy. It seems expedient for languages in some cases to have short forms for imperatives which may need to be spoken quickly for the good of the participants (e.g., if a rock is falling toward a person, a short imperative *move* is the quickest and most effective way to get the hearer to get out of the rock's way). These suggestions cannot be proven as the reason for the short form. They are only mentioned to demonstrate that the short form can be explained by means other than by *evolution*. Also, this does not mean that no evolution occurs in language. Evolution does take place. However, it is questionable whether imperatives evolved into statements.

On the other hand, although Robertson and Davis do not discuss a deep structure, they suggest that the Greek imperative was a late development (*New Short Grammar*, 306-7). The ideas which it expressed were communicated by other means (e.g., subjunctive, future indicative, etc.) many of which were still being used during the first- century.

It has been suggested that the imperative is an unmarked form of a *directive*. This is also based on the observation that the imperative in languages such as English and Latin is not inflected for its mood (although it may be for person, Latin: "Dic!" second person singular, "Speak!" and "Dicite!" second person plural, "Speak!"); F. R. Palmer, *Mood and Modality*, Cambridge Textbooks in Linguistics (Cambridge: Cambridge University Press, 1986), 29, 108.

[167]One area where patterning is evident is the common mistakes made by early language learners. For example, it is not uncommon for such individuals to incorrectly use words patterned from regular verbs when an irregular verbs is appropriate (e.g., "he comed" or "she goed" instead of "he came" or "she went").

[168]The question of whether transformations are innate or learned is irrelevant for this project.

[169]That a relationship exists between similarly worded indicatives and imperatives is obvious by the wording of the statements themselves. A common deep structure need not be postulated for this purpose.

For a detailed discussion and critique of approaches mentioned above, see C. L. Hamblin,

Second, Shi Zhang produced a dissertation which explored the state of the imperative within linguistic theory.[170] Although a number of languages were considered, the primary focus of the project was English. In this study, Zhang, acknowledging the neglect of the imperative within generative grammar,[171] looked at how the imperative was treated by a select number of linguistic theories. Zhang's view of the imperative includes four characteristics. The first three are structural. Imperatives are restricted to second person or third person indefinite (e.g., *you/somebody/everybody goes*), they do not have tense inflection, and they utilize *do* for the purpose of negation (*do not go*).[172] The fourth is semantic.[173] Imperatives are intentional and the action, state, or event of the imperative is unrealized at the time of its production. Because English is the basis for the study, these characteristics are not significantly helpful. The Greek imperative is richer with its tense system and has an unrestricted third person.

Zhang also makes a distinction between *strong* and *weak* imperatives. Strong imperatives are those which meet the four characteristics and are a direct command.[174] For English, the semantic requirements for analysis correspond with the structural form.[175] Strong imperatives are the only concern of his work. However, for Greek it seems like this is too restrictive. Also, the method for this project demands structure as the only criterion for eligibility in this study.

Zhang's study focuses primarily on two (Chomskyan) linguistic theories, *government and binding* and *extended categorical grammar*. *Government and binding* treats imperatives and non-imperatives as derivable from a deep structure.[176] Thus, this approach would be classified with the approach first discussed in this subsection which Hamblin considers "reductionist."[177] It is

---

Imperatives (Oxford: Basil Blackwell, 1987), 97-136. Hamblin labels such approaches, "Reductionist Theories."

[170]"The Status of Imperatives in Theories of Grammar" (Ph.D. diss., University of Arizona, 1990). A comprehensive review and critique cannot be undertaken here. Only the most relevant portions of this work will be discussed.

[171]Ibid., 43, 177.

[172]Ibid., 13.

[173]Ibid.

[174]Ibid., 12.

[175]Although this does not take into consideration the rich communication situation discussed in chapter 1 of our study..

[176]Ibid., 43-120.

[177]*Imperatives*, 97-136.

related to the theory considered above. It is a later development. In order to maintain a derivational approach, Zhang postulates an imperative element in the deep structure[178] and other theoretical assumptions in order that it may be applied to the English imperative.[179] He realizes that there is something distinct about the imperative but *government and binding* only implicitly acknowledges this.[180]

The treatment of *extended categorical grammar* departs from postulating an underlying deep structure of a common clause for both imperatives and non-imperatives.[181] It does not have a transformational component but is based on categorical lexicon and rules for grammar. The lexicon associates words with syntactic categories (a word may be associated with a number of categories) and the rules provide the syntactic constructions.[182] Possibly the most illuminating aspect of this theory is the appeal to pragmatic information to determine the use of the imperative.[183] For example, the use of *please* in a sentence seems to demand the imperative be a request rather than a command.[184] This bears a striking resemblance to the approach suggested in chapter 1 of this work. However, Zhang has not developed it beyond a cursory level.

Although Zhang's study has a different purpose and a different theoretical and methodological basis, it makes important contributions to the study of the imperative mood. First, it is acknowledged that the imperative has been neglected in generative grammars. It has been maintained in this work that it has been neglected by Greek grammarians. Second, although derivation is not rejected, Zhang clearly acknowledges the distinctiveness of the imperative mood. Third, he acknowledges a pragmatic element in the analysis of the imperative. Fourth, Zhang's study is an example of an analysis of the imperative

---

[178]Zhang, "Status of Imperatives," 67. This was mentioned briefly above and again this work concurs that such a theoretical element is impossible to prove (Akmajian and Heny, *Transformation Syntax*, 233-36). Other analysis seems preferable; however, Zhang's emphasis on a distinct imperative is commendable from within a transformational perspective.

[179]See "Status of Imperatives," 92 for a summary of these assumptions. For another *government and binding* study devoted to the English imperative, see Frits Beukema and Peter Coopmans, "A Government-Binding Perspective on the Imperative in English," *Journal of Linguistics* 25 (1989): 417-36. Much of this article is devoted to the (grammatical) subject of the imperative verb; therefore, this study does not contribute to the present project.

[180]Zhang, "Status of Imperatives," 119-20.

[181]Ibid., 92-120.

[182]Ibid., 93-94.

[183]Ibid., 114-19.

[184]Ibid.

which is not dependent upon SAT.[185] The present volume is also such a work.

Third, although the imperative has been discussed by non-Chomskyan (descriptive) theories, to my knowledge a major work on the imperative such as Zhang's for any language has not been produced. Rather, it has usually been handled within a more general discussion of mood, the verb, or the *linguistic system*.[186] One study which devotes itself to the imperative is Gloria Anzilotti's paper given at the fifteenth LACUS Forum held at Michigan State University in 1988.[187] This study attempts to break away from the grammatical imperative and understands it as a social process.[188] This study again focuses on the sememic command and attempts to demonstrate the imperative force in many types of sentences. For example, in addition to the obvious content, the exclamation "Fire!" may include the imperative intention *run*[189] and the greeting, "Hello" may actually be intending an implicit "talk to me."[190]

Although Anzilotti is focusing on the sememic command, she makes important observations that apply to both the imperative mood and the communication process. She understands the importance of *intention* in communication and especially concerning the imperative situation.[191] She also places the study within the bounds of pragmatics. Anzilotti states,

---

[185]Zhang states that one reason the imperative should be studied within grammatical theories is that "it is claimed that a study of imperatives should be within the realm of speech acts rather than syntax and that (English) imperatives are subsumed under other tenseless clauses; thus imperatives do not play a role in syntactic analysis" (ibid., 178).

[186]These are of little value for this study because they really do not focus on the imperative but rather deal with it briefly within a specific linguistic framework. Only minimal attention is paid to the mood. See for example Christopher S. Butler, *Systemic Linguistics: Theory and Applications* (London: Batsford Academic and Educational, 1985), 44-45, 56-57, 171-72; Walter A. Cook, *Introduction to Tagmemic Analysis* (New York: Holt, Rinehart and Winston, 1969), 50, 52-53; Benjamin Elson and Velma Pickett, *Beginning Morphology and Syntax* (Dallas: Summer Institute of Linguistics, 1983), 110-11; M. A. K. Halliday, *An Introduction to Functional Grammar*, 2d ed. (London: Edward Arnold, 1994), 87-88; Kenneth L. Pike and Evelyn G. Pike, *Grammatical Analysis*, 2d ed. (Dallas: Summer Institute of Linguistics and the University of Texas at Arlington, 1982), 127 (within the context of a chart on Mazatec clauses). As has been the case thus far, in some of these works, there are often two separate discussions taking place at the same time, (i.e., the imperative as a mood and the imperative as a sentence type).

[187]"The Imperative—An Octopus Network," in *The Fifteenth LACUS Forum 1988*, ed. Ruth M. Brend and David G. Lockwood (Lake Bluff, IL: Linguistic Association of Canada and the United States, 1989), 153-67.

[188]Ibid., 153.

[189]Ibid.

[190]Ibid., 154.

[191]Ibid., 153-59.

"Furthermore, if pragmatics is a description of language intentionally used, then imperative modality is intimately bound with pragmatics, for purposeful writing will typically spring from some level of desire to produce further action."[192] As has been discussed in chapter 1, these insights are foundational for this work.

Fourth, relevance theory, the communication or pragmatic theory discussed previously in this book at some length has produced some studies in imperatives (sememic command/prohibition) and related areas. Important for RT are the notions of *potential* and *desirable* worlds.[193] If an imperative sentence is viewed by the hearer as desirable for the speaker, it will be interpreted as an order, request, or plea. If the hearer interprets the imperative as desirable for himself, it will be interpreted as advice, instruction, or permission.[194] A more precise interpretation is gained through the pragmatic context in which an imperative is given. For example, the manner (or force) in which an utterance will be understood (e.g., order, request, plea, etc.) is somewhat limited by a number of factors including the social position of the speaker in relation to the hearer and whether or not the hearer is able to actually perform (or accomplish) the imperative.[195] For example, the imperative "open the window" may be interpreted as an order from a boss to a employee or as a request among friends. If a friend asks, "give me a cookie," this may be a request; however, if the cookie is greatly desired, it may be interpreted as pleading or even begging. Since this theory is foundational for this work, much will be helpful here. However, to my knowledge there has been no similar study of the ancient Greek imperative. In addition, this work will ultimately understand the role of social

---

[192]Ibid., 158. Although Anzilotti's *imperative* is the sememic command, it certainly includes the grammatical mood.

[193]Deirdre Wilson and Dan Sperber, "Mood and the Analysis of Non-Declarative Sentences," in *Human Agency: Language, Duty and Value*, ed. J. Dancy, J. Moravcsik and C. Taylor (Stanford, CA: Stanford University Press, 1988), 79-91; Diane Blakemore, *Understanding Utterances: An Introduction to Pragmatics* (Oxford: Blackwell Publishers, 1992), 112-13; Billy Clark, "Relevance and 'Pseudo-Imperatives'," *Linguistics and Philosophy* 16 (1993): 79-92.

[194]Blakemore, *Understanding Utterances*, 112-13. RT acknowledges that audienceless cases do exist such as "please do not rain" or to a automobile, "start." Of course, these examples treat an inanimate object as hearer (unless these are considered prayers). Also, there may be predetermined cases where the speaker hopes something has already taken place. For example, if someone anticipates making an uncomfortable visit, he may say (to himself concerning the other party in a form which is directed to the other party), "please be out" (Wilson and Sperber, "Mood," 81; Blakemore, *Understanding Utterances*, 113). In such cases, there is really no hearer and the event is beyond anyone's control.

[195]Ibid., 110-14. See also Wilson and Sperber, "Mood," 79-91.

rank slightly differently (see chapter 4).

Fifth, there is a rather comprehensive treatment of *imperativeness* which was not written by a linguist. Charles L. Hamblin's *Imperatives*[196] is a philosophical treatment of the subject. There are two characteristics of Hamblin's work which make this study less helpful for the purposes of this project. First, it is not limited by a specific grammatical form.[197] Second, it is primarily concerned with English.[198] These two features are associated because English has no distinguishing morphological inflection for the imperative. Nevertheless, the study is very helpful, especially to provide options for pragmatic usages. The first chapter is devoted to describing and classifying the many types of imperatives such as commands, requests, etc.[199] Hamblin's classification is helpful and in many ways resembles the usages in New Testament studies.

1. Imperatives proper:
    (a) Wilful, non-accountable: COMMANDS, REQUESTS, DEMANDS;
    (b) Non-wilful, accountable: ADVICE, INSTRUCTIONS, SUGGESTIONS, RECIPES (or under 3b?), WARNING(?);
    (c) Straddling (a) and (b): INVITATIONS;
    (d) Stragglers: FORMAL or RHETORICAL, WISHES, MALEDICTIONS, EXHORTATIONS. IMMEDIATE imperatives, *Let's* (connections with 3(a));
    (e) Imperative in effect(?): APPOINTMENTS, VOTINGS, and DECREES.
2. Permissives: COMMAND-PERMISSIVES, REQUEST-PERMISSIVES etc., AUTHORIZATIONS (sometimes like le).
3. Para-imperatives (3(a)-(c) all with *to*-contents or *that-someone*-contents
    (a) First-person: UNDERTAKINGS, PROMISES, VOWS (Subdivisible as COMMAND-UNDERTAKINGS, etc.?);
    (b) Forceless: PLANS, SCHEMES, PLOTS;

---

[196]C. L. Hamblin, *Imperatives* (Oxford: Basil Blackwell, 1987).
[197]Ibid., 3.
[198]Ibid., 46.
[199]Ibid., 1-45.

    (c) Mental act and state: INTENTIONS, DECISIONS, WANTS;

    (d) Getting-to: PERSUASIONS, INCITINGS.[200]

Of interest is a distinction between willful imperatives (e.g., commands, request, etc.) and non-willful imperatives (e.g., advice, instruction, etc.)[201] which in some ways resembles the *desirability* notion of RT above. However, Hamblin's account is more speaker focused.[202]

    Hamblin is reluctant to define *imperative* but views the concept broadly.[203] It seems to be both grammatical and functional. Hamblin's focus on English results in many structural imperatives. Like Zhang, third person imperatives may exist with indefinite subjects. However, unlike Zhang, Hamblin acknowledges the existence of a first person plural imperative (*let's* or *do/don't let us*).[204]

Summary

    This chapter has briefly surveyed the meaning and usage of the imperative mood in Greek among New Testament scholars and the imperative in more general (primarily linguistic) fields of study. It seems evident that a more precise instrument is needed for classifying the mood than has been applied in New Testament studies. A commonly accepted method for analyzing functional language, speech act theory, was found to be lacking due to internal deficiencies in the system. Most studies have gone beyond a limited study of a morphological mood and have been concerned with broader issues such as the construction of commands. In the next two chapters, a fresh linguistic approach to the imperative mood will be presented. It is hoped that the result of this study

---

[200]Ibid., 44-45 (emphasis [all capitals] is in the original). As mentioned above, Hamblin is classifying the sememic imperative. For the purpose of this study, all morphological imperatives are *real* or *proper* imperatives.

[201]Ibid., 10.

[202]Ultimately, it will be maintained that a volitional element throughout this work's view of the imperative. Hamblin's distinction will be dealt within the notion of *benefit*. See chapter 4.

[203]Ibid., 3.

[204]Ibid., 35, 58-61. The first person singular imperative also seems to exist in at least one language. See for example Kenneth Shields' article attempting to explain the origin of this form in Hittite ("The Hittite First Person Singular Imperative Suffix *-lu*," Journal of *Indo-European Studies* 11 [1983]: 365-72).

will be twofold. First, it will clarify the mood in New Testament studies. Second, it will contribute solid data to the study of commands and prohibitions.

Chapter 3

Semantic Analysis

Introduction

In chapters 1 and 2 of this work, a number of preliminary and foundational matters were introduced, surveyed, and/or developed. The nature of the communication process was discussed in detail and it was demonstrated that language often functions as evidence to be interpreted within a communication situation. No utterance occurs in a vacuum. Every *linguistic extension* exists in a context. The language code itself brings important information to the communication situation; however, factors of context, both linguistic and non-linguistic, affect the meaning of the author's intended communicative offering. This chapter will focus upon what the imperative brings to the communication situation. Two related questions will be pursued: 1. What is the meaning of the imperative mood? and 2. Why did the author use the imperative in a particular instance? The latter question assumes an available choice for the communicator. For New Testament authors, this choice was one of grammatical mood: indicative, subjunctive, optative, or imperative.[1] In other words, this work will

---

[1]Of course as with many grammatical categories, all four options may not be available for a specific lexeme (in this case a verb). Reasons for reduction of choices may include particular historical developments such as an evolution or overlap of usages between moods or a preference for one mood in usage until another drops out being eclipsed by the prominent mood. This process seems to have been occurring for the optative (for all verbs) in New Testament times (see briefly below). Because language develops in an often untidy and unpredictable manner, it is impossible to assume crisp distinctions allowing for clear choices in all cases. It will be helpful to clarify the usage of the term *choice* here and throughout this work. The choice of language forms is not necessarily a conscious choice where the mind considers a number of surface structure options (i.e., should I choose A, B, or C?). Such a procedure seems to minimize a stratified understanding of language by seeing the communicator as merely choosing a mood. Rather, the choice takes place at the conceptual level by means of committing to a certain line of communication. It is unlikely that in most situations the communicator consciously considers the choices before him. He uses what is familiar. Indeed, most native speakers do not normally realize that a mood choice is available (i.e., they are not consciously making a choice). They merely attempt to communicate with the most appropriate language code which through

attempt to define the imperative in terms of its *ontological, unaffected, inherent,* or as was defined previously in the context of this work, its *semantic* meaning.[2] In order to answer these questions a number of issues must be pursued. First, terminology must be refined and it must be determined whether a *semantic* meaning actually exists; and if so, what is the likelihood of discovering it through the method proposed. Second, specific methodology for our task must be described. Third, this work must isolate idioms which have morphological imperative form but may not function as such. These idiomatic lexemes have developed over time and may have originally had an imperative semology; however, they have become fixed and may no longer retain this function. Therefore, they must be omitted from consideration in the analysis of this work. Finally, this work must attempt to analyze the text in order to determine (to the best of our ability) the semantic meaning of the imperative.

Definition and Existence

The discussion thus far suggests that the *semantic* meaning of the imperative mood is the raw, naked imperative. It is the imperative mood at its essence. It is the meaning which is unaffected by either context or lexical contribution. If the imperative could exist without any lexical verbal meaning and in isolation from any context, what would remain would be the semantic meaning, the meaning of the *imperative*. No more, no less.

In light of the what has been said thus far about semantic meaning, three questions must be raised and answered. Does such a linguistic notion exist? If it does, can it be discovered? And if so, can such an abstract concept be of any real value for the analysis of the New Testament? The answer to the first question seems to be *yes*, a semantic meaning does exist. If the mood brought no meaning on its own to a communication situation, there would be no reason

---

experience has communicated effectively in similar situations in the past. In this way there is a choice taking place but not in a calculated manner: imperative vs. indicative vs. subjunctive vs. optative). To some extent this will be discussed in further detail later in this chapter.

[2]It must again be reiterated that the literature includes a number of definitions for the term *semantic*. Although there are similarities between these, there are also significant differences. The usage of the term here is not entirely unique; nevertheless, its emphases may not be compatible with all usages of the term.

to use it.[3] A verbal system of four moods suggests each has something to offer and there is a reason for the choice of a specific mood by the communicator. Simply speaking, this meaning is *why* the imperative mood was chosen by the author.

A strong word of caution must be presented before continuing. As has already been noted, a language changes over time. A form begins to take on functions which it may not have had previously. Conversely, a form may lose functions that may have been common in the past. Although this is more acute for pragmatic interpretation, function sheds light on the meaning of the form. At the time of the composition of the New Testament, for example, the optative mood was losing much of its presence as its functions begin to be taken over by other forms.[4] As the history of the Greek language is considered, the analysis

---

[3]Communication cannot occur without some meaning related to form.

[4]In *Koine* Greek many of the functions of the optative were taken over by the subjunctive. See Daniel B. Wallace, *Greek Grammar beyond the Basics: An Exegetical Syntax of the New Testament* (Grand Rapids: Zondervan Publishing House, 1996), 480; Stanley E. Porter, *Idioms of the Greek New Testament*, 2d ed., Biblical Languages: Greek, vol. 2 (Sheffield: JSOT Press, 1994), 59; and Geoffrey Horrocks, *Greek: A History of the Language and Its Speakers*, Longman Linguistic Library (London: Longman, 1997), 53-54. Although the mood is not rare during the first-century of the common era, apart from its use in idiomatic expressions, it does not seem to have been an "integral part of the verbal system" (J. A. L. Lee, "Some Features of the Speech of Jesus in Mark's Gospel," *Novum Testamentum* 27 [1985]: 13). One author commenting about the period just after the Hellenistic (and thus demonstrates preceding developments) notes the blurring of use between the subjunctive and optative suggests a very close relationship between the moods and states, "we consider the subjunctive and optative as variations of the same mood" (Frederick Walter Augustine Dickinson, *The Use of the Optative Mood in the Works of John Chrysostom*, Catholic University of America Patristic Studies, vol. 11 [Washington DC: Catholic University of America, 1926], 8). The reasons for the shift in use are many and include the normal processes of language change to facilitate the communication process. Henry Harmon's suggestion that the lack of the optative in Hebrew and Aramaic is the reason for its general disuse among Jewish writers of Greek may have some merit; however, his suggestion that the intellectual decline of the Greeks (especially in Athens) resulted in the decline of the optative because the subtle "thought" was no longer expressed cannot be sustained in light of the previous discussion of language presented in the first chapter of this work (Henry M. Harmon, "The Optative Mode in Hellenistic Greek," *Journal of the Society of Biblical Literature and Exegesis* 6 [1886]: 11-12).

There may also be a tendency in *Koine* toward using the imperative in certain cases where the optative would be used in classical (BDF, 194). McKay suggests that the use of the imperative λαβέτω in Acts 1:20 in place of the Septuagint's λάβοι in the quotation of Psalm 108:8 (Hebrew [109:8]: יִקַּח, qal imperfect from לקח) may be an example of the decline of the optative. However, he later suggests that this may have been a purposeful change in Acts in order to apply it more directly to the audience of Acts, a purpose more suited to the imperative than to the optative (*A New Syntax of the Verb in New Testament Greek: An Aspectual Approach*, Studies

in this chapter is taking a sample linguistic slice from a language in the midst of an evolving process. To complicate matters further, the different authors may be at slightly different points in this process. This work's attempt at discovering the semantic meaning of the imperative is limited to this specific window of time. The meaning may or may not apply at other periods. Nevertheless, although imperfect, a culture's notion and use of a mood should be rather uniform during a period of time in order to facilitate communication. Fortunately, a mood such as the imperative seems to have a rather consistent meaning across time, culture, and even languages.[5] Nevertheless, these observations demand that this work proceed with caution.[6]

Even if one may concede the existence of a semantic meaning as defined above, the impossibility of isolating the form from both context and lexical content makes any attempt at a concrete or authoritative statement about this meaning questionable. This skepticism is well placed and the answer to the second question of whether or not the semantic meaning can be discovered is far less certain than the first. However, even if a definitive statement cannot be made, the existence of a semantic meaning demands that one at least attempt to discover it. The use of the imperative form as well as the choice of other forms in specific contexts can shed light on this meaning (see the method section

---

in Biblical Greek, ed. D. A. Carson, vol. 5 [New York: Peter Lang, 1994], 54, 85).

[5]See for example the treatments of the imperative across a wide range of time: compare the classical grammar of Herbert Weir Smyth, *Greek Grammar*, rev. G. M. Messing (Cambridge, MA: Harvard University Press, 1956), 409-11 with the New Testament grammar of BDF, 195-96. See also modern Greek treatments such as David A. Hardy, *Greek: Language and People. A BBC Television Course in Modern Greek for Beginners*, ed. Terry Doyle (London: BBC Books, 1983), 274-75 (most modern grammars consulted had little beyond a brief statement about the command usage for the imperative; e.g., Douglas Q. Adams, *Essential Modern Greek Grammar* [New York: Dover Publications, 1987], 67-69; George Thomson, *A Manual of Modern Greek* [London: Collet's (Publishers) , 1967], 17 [only discussed in a sentence in the section "The Verb;" the imperative was not mentioned in the section entitled "The Moods," ibid., 28-9]). Willem Bakker's study of aspectual differences of the imperative through Greek history demonstrates that the situations in which the present and aorist were used differed at times from one period to another. However, the general use of the imperative mood continued to be used for similar functions despite the aspectual fluctuation (*The Greek Imperative: An Investigation Into the Aspectual Differences Between the Present and Aorist Imperatives in Greek Prayer From Homer Up to the Present Day* [Amsterdam: Uitgeverij Adolf M. Hakkert, 1966]).

[6]It may further be noted that the wide area represented by the authors of the New Testament, the proficiency of Greek among the individual authors, and the knowledge of other languages (including whether or not Greek was the first and/or primary language of a specific author) also complicate matters.

below). Nevertheless, because any statement made about the semantic meaning of the imperative cannot be verified with absolute certainty, the results of the analysis will not be *the* semantic meaning but tentative conclusions *toward a semantic meaning*. Because of human limitations, which include one's inability to go outside of the language system to observe language[7] and the inability to isolate a grammatical form from its context and the lexical meaning of its constituents, it is unlikely that complete and absolute statements will ever be made about this meaning. However, as language helps one to observe the workings of the mind (see chapter 1), the use of a particular mood permits one to observe the semantic meaning of that mood. In other words, one can observe and to some extent analyze the inaccessible through the product of its function.[8] Nevertheless, the picture will be blurry.

The attempt to discover the semantic meaning of the mood is not merely the *boiling-down* of the usages to the least common denominator.[9] Although attempting to determine what characteristics are shared by all realizations of the mood does provide important data for the analysis in this work, this is only one aspect of this project. It will also be necessary to contrast the mood's occurrence

---

[7]Also, the degree to which language itself influences the thought process and conceptual world of a culture is not a settled matter.

[8]The philosophical notion that suggests that what is not observable does not exist cannot be maintained. Whether or not anyone hears a tree fall in the forest, there is one less tree standing than before it fell. Also, mankind continually learns about the universe by attempting to discover that which cannot be directly observed. Despite powerful telescopes, there are many hypotheses about space. Some hypotheses are proven through more observation and study, others are disproved. Some beliefs about the world are strongly maintained despite no direct observation. Did atoms exist before they were discovered? Was the world round prior to this being proven? There are realities which exist whether or not one ever considers them or even if one is wrong concerning them.

[9]The semantic meaning must also be distinguished from the "root" meaning of the mood. The root meaning is the original meaning of the mood. Some consistency is expected over time. However, assuming language change, some alteration will occur. Because in most cases the oldest utterances of a language are lost, this meaning cannot be determined with certainty. Moulton, acknowledging the impossibility of determining this for most moods, says of the imperative, "The Imperative is tolerably clear: it represented command—prohibition was not originally associated with it, and in Greek only partially elbowed its way in, to be elbowed out again in the latest developments of the language" (*Prolegomena*, 3d ed., vol. 1, *A Grammar of New Testament Greek* [Edinburgh: T. & T. Clark, 1908], 164). The synchronic priority of this work is intended to avoid this fallacy.

with the others to determine its uniqueness.[10] Some fundamental aspects of meaning may even be eclipsed by contextual features.[11] Such meaning should not be rejected merely because of its omission in certain realizations (as a boiling-down approach would demand). Rather, such aspects will become clear when the analysis is broadened beyond the imperative to the mood system in its entirety. Thus, semantic analysis is both internally focused on the imperative and externally focused on its role among the other moods. In this manner one avoids missing important aspects of meaning which may not be evident in a *boiling-down* of usage approach.

Finally, the third question can be answered. Given the abstract nature, lack of absolute certain conclusions, and problems related to the study of semantic meaning, should this analysis even proceed? There are at least three reasons to answer this affirmatively. First, if this work is correct and there is an abstract semantic meaning, its very existence demands that it be pursued. Second, a major focus of this work will be on the pragmatic usages of the imperative. However, it is unwise to pursue this study without a serious attempt to determine the meaning of the mood itself. Usages in context must follow from the meaning of the mood itself. Semantic and pragmatic analysis must both proceed together. Each analysis informs and refines the other.[12] Third, as Wallace has pointed out, the postulation of an unaffected (semantic) meaning avoids the potential problem of applying an affected (pragmatic) usage within a specific context to other occurrences of the grammatical category to which it

---

[10]This is much more complex than it is stated here. It is not always possible to determine why a specific mood is used. A number of factors may be involved in this choice which are not dependent upon a contrast with another mood. Such factors include style, the author's proficiency in the language (thus limited choices), etc. This will be discussed below in the section devoted to method.

[11]In the case of idiomatic lexemes, this eclipse may be total. However, the analysis must permit a certain amount of eclipsing of meaning because total isolation of form is impossible. Also, an idiom often takes on added and sometimes completely unrelated meaning. This is not involved here.

[12]It is often stated that meaning does not exist apart from context. This is true in some respects: especially when it means that accurate meaning about a form, an utterance, etc., cannot be determined (interpreted) outside of its context. However, this statement can be misleading or even incorrect if it is understood to mean that form does not have any meaning at all. First, as stated above, if form did not bring meaning to the table, why use a particular form? Second, meaning can exist apart from context; however, it may not be the intended meaning of the communicator. Thus, a form does evoke a field of meaning in itself. Contextual features narrow this meaning.

may not apply.[13]

Having presented a description of the semantic meaning which will be pursued in this chapter, two further areas must considered in order to refine and clarify the understanding of the use of the term in this work.[14] First, some consider the semantic meaning of a word to be the dictionary meaning.[15] This description may be somewhat compatible with ours if a dictionary presents a meaning for an entry which is meant to be general and not necessarily usage-specific.[16] However, many dictionaries simply list usages without including a more general universal meaning.[17] Also, it is important to make a distinction between lexical semantics and the semantic meaning of a grammatical form. The former usually involves notions of *sense* and *reference*.[18] These are not

---

[13]Wallace, *Exegetical Syntax*, 2-3. Rich Erickson (review of *Greek Grammar Beyond the Basics*, by Daniel B. Wallace, *Journal of the Evangelical Theological Society* 42 [1999]: 129) questions why Wallace includes a discussion of the *unaffected* meaning for grammatical categories in his grammar. He notes the minimal space given to this notion and the lack of future appeal to this meaning. However, it seems Wallace's approach justly handles the relationship between unaffected (semantic) and affected (pragmatic) meaning. He introduces the category and briefly describes its meaning. Then, in a more detailed discussion, usages are explored. Despite Erickson's criticism, the unaffected meaning is generally a common thread throughout the usages. For a description of Wallace's approach (which is very similar to the approach used in this work), see *Exegetical Syntax*, 2-3.

See also the discussion of conjoiners by Jakob K. Heckert, *Discourse Functions of Conjoiners in the Pastoral Epistles* (Dallas: Summer Institute of Linguistics, 1996). In this study, although not using the same terminology as used here, Heckert seems to attempt a similar task. He concludes the conjoiners in the Pastoral epistles each have one basic function with varying usages.

[14]These have been discussed in some manner above. However, they are discussed specifically here in order to avoid confusion because these concepts are quite common.

[15]See Samos Grammenidis, "The Verbs Πηγαινω and Ερχομαι in Modern Greek," in *Themes in Greek Linguistics: Papers from the First International Conference on Greek Linguistics, Reading, September 1993*, ed. Irene Philippaki-Warburton, Katerina Nicolaidis and Maria Sifianou (Amsterdam: John Benjamins Publishing Company, 1994), 193.

[16]See for example LSJ's entry for λύω which includes the gloss "loosen" and then is followed by a number of meanings dependent on contextual considerations. However, this format is not consistent within the lexicon. In some cases, the glosses are merely a list of possible meanings of a word (see LSJ's entry for καπηλεία).

[17]See for example BAGD and BDAG (compare with LSJ's entry for λύω).

[18]Lexical semantics were briefly introduced in chapter 1. See Darrell L. Bock, "New Testament Word Analysis," in *Introducing New Testament Interpretation*, ed. Scot McKnight (Grand Rapids: Baker Book House, 1989), 101-102; Johannes P. Louw, *Semantics of New Testament Greek* (Atlanta: Scholars Press, 1982), 47-54 (the word *sense* is not used); Moisés Silva, *Biblical Words and Their Meaning: An Introduction to Lexical Semantics* (Grand Rapids: Zondervan Publishing House, 1983), 102-103.

aspects of grammatical semantics.[19] Nevertheless, although this terminology is imprecise, when a dictionary definition is presented for an entry without reference to context, an imperfect analogy to the semantic concept described in this work can be made.[20]

Second, it is not uncommon to associate *semantic* meaning with grammatical or linguistic meaning and contrast this with non-linguistic *pragmatic* meaning or use.[21] This is not entirely incompatible with the use here. Both approaches focus upon linguistic meaning. However, for at least two reasons this contrast is misleading with reference to the usage of the terms in this work. First, the distinction between linguistic and non-linguistic communicative actions is too imprecise. Although it is acknowledged that the line between semantics and pragmatics may be blurred at times, the criteria of the presence or absence of linguistic code for the distinction does not consider various aspects of the communicative situation where linguistic information may be used in uncharacteristic ways. Second, in this work pragmatics is much more powerful than this simple distinction maintains. Pragmatics may include

---

[19]*Grammatical semantics*, the semantics of a grammatical form, should not be confused with what some term *grammatical meaning* (Bock, "Word Analysis," 101; and especially Louw, *Semantics*, 57-58) which includes the grammatical function a word may have (e.g., the type of dative; this is similar to the usages of pragmatic meanings this will be explored in chapter 4) and the semantic role (e.g., subject, object, etc.) which is the manner in which a word functions in relation to other words. In both cases, these meanings are based on the analysis of a specific lexeme and thus are really part of lexical semantics (albeit the former makes use of the pragmatic analysis described later in this work).

[20]Some descriptions of the preposition system of Greek provide a good analogy. Some grammarians attempt to present the entire preposition system in the form of a chart (or in a number of charts). In such cases, each preposition can be viewed in its relationship to the entire system and a general function can be seen for each (by using a similar chart for each preposition, this is still observable). In this way the reader can visualize the function of the preposition without reference to a specific translation. Thus a more general unaffected meaning may be observed. See for example Porter, *Idioms*, 142-80; Wallace, *Exegetical Syntax*, 358-59; and the "Tale of 12 Mice" chart in David Alan Black, *It's Still Greek to Me: An Easy-to-Understand Guide to Intermediate Greek* (Grand Rapids: Baker Books, 1998), 85. Wallace seems to have modified the chart presented by Dana and Mantey (*A Manual Grammar of the Greek New Testament* [New York: Macmillan Publishing Co., 1927], 113).

[21]This distinction is not usually exact since pragmatics is not viewed as being completely void of linguistic content or form. Rather the field of pragmatics includes an account of how non-linguistic elements interact or influence meaning (including *intent*). See Richard A. Young, *Intermediate New Testament Greek: A Linguistic and Exegetical Approach* (Nashville: Broadman and Holman Publishers, 1994), 7 (who views semantics as including pragmatics) and John G. Cook, *The Structure and Persuasive Power of Mark: A Linguistic Approach*, The Society of Biblical Literature Semeia Studies (Atlanta: Scholars Press, 1995), 4.

linguistic elements and are the result the semantic meaning interacting with context (both linguistic and non-linguistic). Therefore, although this distinction may have similarities with the use of the terms here, as a rule, the linguistic/non-linguistic determination must be rejected.

In conclusion, for the imperative mood, the semantic meaning is the meaning which a grammatical form brings to the communication process unaffected by context or lexical content. Although isolation of a form from these factors is impossible and thus not directly observable, it is reasonable to pursue a study of the semantic meaning of the imperative mood at the time of the writing of the New Testament. Nevertheless, the conclusions here must bear these limitations in mind.

Method

The general method for this section has been briefly outlined above in chapter 1. In order to determine the semantic meaning of the mood, this work must analyze relevant texts from two perspectives. First, the mood must be considered in various contexts to roughly determine its range of meaning. In order to avoid introducing unnecessary controversy at this stage, this will begin by looking exclusively at passages classified by other grammars without (generally) questioning such classifications. Passages which are categorized differently by the grammars will not be considered.[22] All qualifying examples in major categories (see below) will be mentioned with the exception of the *conditional* and *prohibition*.[23] In this way this work will be able to determine

---

[22]This approach is far from perfect but will avoid peculiar classifications which may undermine the credibility of the analysis. Ideally, it would be preferable for all the grammars consulted to discuss the same passages; however, this is not the case. Where more than one grammar classifies an imperative in a certain way, this will carry most weight (multiple attestation). However, this is not the case with most passages in which this work must be content with the classification of only one grammarian.

[23]The reason not all conditionals will be mentioned here is that the category is somewhat controversial and no uniform agreement exists over exactly what determines a conditional imperative. The conditional imperative will be looked at in detail in chapter 4 where more examples will be discussed in detail. In this chapter only a few *common* conditional imperatives will be presented to demonstrate the point in the section. There are two reasons not all *prohibitions* will be presented below. First, as mentioned above and will be developed below, this category is somewhat misleading. The new paradigm will avoid a specific category devoted to prohibition. Second, practically, in the database there are far more imperatives in this category

what characteristics are *shared* by the mood in various contexts. Next, this work will briefly note observations with some passages from the *limitation* section of chapter 1. The individual usages will not be refined here. Such development awaits chapter 4.

Second, this chapter will compare and contrast the imperative with other moods. Analysis of parallel statements in similar contexts by the same author where the only difference in the statements is the mood of the same verb (e.g., subjunctive and imperative) would be ideal. Unfortunately, the database used here will not allow for such simplicity. Therefore, an examination of how a specific author uses the moods (especially the imperative and subjunctive) will be in order. Also, it may be helpful to compare parallel statements in the gospels where one author uses one mood and another author uses the another mood. In this way, the uniqueness of the mood should be able to be highlighted.

Again it will be helpful to present some cautious words before proceeding. First, it must be reiterated that the semantic meaning cannot necessarily be limited to the *shared characteristics* of its various usages (the *boiling-down* of meaning discussed above). Second, it is impossible to know with certainty why an author chooses a specific mood in context. Even where the same word is used with different moods in parallel passages by two authors (e.g., Matthew and Mark), although the difference may be semantic, it also may merely be stylistic. One cannot get into the minds of the authors.[24] Third, the development of language results in a shift of grammatical function. Some moods begin to take on characteristics of others.[25] Some moods begin to fade out of use while

---

than is needed for the discussion here. Additional prohibition imperatives from the select database will be mentioned only in a footnote.

[24] The complexities of analyzing a dead language are numerous. If a native speaker could be produced, issues of style and choice could be determined much more accurately. Access to the originator of a specific communication act would be ideal (e.g., Luke, Paul, etc.). For further information on the importance of native speakers (with caution) for understanding a language (here specifically for translation work but applicable for the issue discussed here), see Katharine Barnwell, "Training of Mother-Tongue Translators," *Notes on Translation* 78 (1980): 26-29; John Beekman, "Missionary Translators, Committees, and Nationals," *Notes on Translation* 22 (1966): 17-18; Ellis W. Deibler, Jr., "National Involvement and Translation Checking," *Notes on Translation* 71 (1978): 2-16; Naomi Glock, "The Native Author—An Unexpected Goldmine," *Notes on Translation* 59 (1976): 33-34; Jerome Hugs, "Relationship Between Naivete Checker and Translation Consultant: A Native Perspective," *Notes on Translation* 111 (1986): 22-24; Kenneth Williams, "Extending the Usefulness of Informants," *Notes on Translation* 22 (1966): 18.

[25] See the discussion above concerning the subjunctive in *Koine* taking on optative functions.

functions are shifted elsewhere. These developmental processes are ongoing and the change from one function to another cannot be pinpointed. This results in considerable overlap among the meanings of the mood.

This twofold method seems to be the most appropriate for the task. With the lack of a contextless environment, the presence of the select textual corpus within a process of language change, and the indirect nature of this work's analysis, proceeding with caution is the only option available. The conclusions will have to be presented in a manner that reflects a level of uncertainty.[26]

Identifiable Idiomatic Expressions (Idiomatic Lexemes)

An *idiom* is a word, phrase, or statement used figuratively which over time loses association with its non-figurative meaning and becomes a fixed expression.[27] The process of idiomization is continually occurring with various forms in various stages of the process. When an expression reaches true idiomization, the link to its original meaning is broken and the history of the expression becomes of little or no value for contemporary usage.[28] When an expression or word becomes a true fixed idiom is uncertain,[29] and various attempts to identify true idioms have been undertaken.[30] The subject of idiom formation and identification is beyond the scope of this work. Only a few comments need to be made in this regard. The important issue for this work is the disassociation of the idiom from its non-figurative meaning. Therefore, the process of idiomization may result in the loss of original meaning. This is not

---

[26]A recent dissertation on verbal aspect by Mari Olsen has made a similar distinction between semantic and pragmatic to that which is followed here. However, certain significant differences are apparent and it will not be adopted for the purposes here. This work was published as *A Semantic and Pragmatic Model of Lexical and Grammatical Aspect* (New York and London: Garland Publishing, 1997). A brief discussion and critique (i.e., reasons it will not be used for the analysis here) of Olsen's theory is presented in appendix 3.

[27]See Richard A. Spears, *NTC's American Idioms Dictionary*, 2d ed. (Lincolnwood, IL: National Textbook Company, 1994), x.

[28]The history of a specific idiom is an interesting study; however, since this history cannot be assumed to be in the mind of the communicator, it cannot be used to inform the meaning of the utterance.

[29]Nevertheless, the distinction between figures of speech and idioms is assumed (John Beekman, "Idiomatic Versus Literal Translations," *Notes on Translation* 18 [1965]: 6).

[30]See the discussion in A. P. Cowie, "Phraseology," in *The Encyclopedia of Languages and Linguistics*, ed. R. E Asher and J. M. Y. Simpson, vol. 6 (Oxford: Pergamon Press, 1994), 3174.

always the case (as will become evident); however, these idioms must not be allowed to inform this work's analysis. Although in some cases the imperative semantics may exist, it will be methodologically preferable to avoid such lexemes because the amount of influence from the idiomization process cannot be determined.

It is not uncommon for an idiom to be a phrase which once frozen into an idiom functions as a unit (i.e., a single lexeme [e.g., "kick the bucket" meaning "death"]).[31] The individual words and their non-figurative meanings are irrelevant to the meaning of the lexeme. Also, idioms may be a single word used in a non-figurative manner. It is not uncommon for native speakers to use idiomatic words and phrases without considering the idiomatic nature of the lexeme.

Therefore, imperatives which function as idioms and within idiomatic phrases must be identified and removed from this analysis. The New Testament contains a number of such lexemes. It is often the case that when an imperative form is used in/as an idiom, it functions as a greeting or an exclamation. For the purpose of this study the following forms will not be considered in the analysis:[32] ἄγε,[33] ἔρρωσθε,[34] δεῦρο/δεῦτε,[35] ἰδού,[36] ἴδε,[37]

---

[31]Traugott and Pratt call this "semantic unity" (*Linguistics for Students of Literature* [New York: Harcourt Brace Jovanovich, 1980], 96).

[32]See also Buist M. Fanning, *Verbal Aspect in New Testament Greek*, Oxford Theological Monographs, ed. J. Barton et al. (Oxford: Clarendon Press, 1990), 330.

[33]Two of the three occurrences of ἄγε occur in the exclamatory phrase, ἄγε νῦν (Jas 4:13; 5:1; only the latter falls within the sample but will be excluded from the database because of its idiomatic nature). The final occurrence (2 Tim 4:11) is an imperative but will be omitted from the analysis as a caution (due to its idiomatic nature elsewhere) and because the database is sufficient without it (also, 2 Timothy is not part of the limited sample).

[34]This form is commonly used to conclude letters (BDAG: ῥώννυμι). In the New Testament it occurs only at the conclusion of the Jerusalem Church's letter to Gentile Christians (Acts 15:29). Although this verse occurs in the sample, it will be omitted from the analysis.

[35]The twenty occurrences of δεῦρο/δεῦτε are usually considered adverbs (see BDAG).

[36]There are 200 occurrences of ἰδού in the New Testament. This form appears to be aorist middle of εἶδον (ὁράω). However, these forms are accented differently. The exclamation is pointed with the acute accent (ἰδού) and the non-idiom is accented with the circumflex accent (ἰδοῦ); see BDAG. The latter does not occur in the New Testament. For a different view of this and the following word (ἴδε), see Wallace, *Exegetical Syntax*, 60, n. 88.

[37]This form is aorist active of εἶδον (ὁράω). Although there do seem to be a few full imperatival usages of this form in *imperative [...]* + καί + ἴδε constructions (John 1:46; 7:52; 11:34; 20:27), the majority of the thirty-four occurrences are interjections or exclamations (Matt 25:20, 22, 25; 26:65; Mark 2:24; 3:34; 11:21; 13:1, 21 [2x]; 15:4, 35; 16:6; John 1:29, 36, 47; 3:26; 5:14; 7:26; 11:3, 36; 12:19; 16:29; 18:21; 19:4, 14, 26, 27; Rom 11:22 [Gramcord classifies

χαῖρε/χαίρετε/χάρητε.[38]

Toward a Semantic Meaning of the Imperative Mood

In the preceding chapter, Wallace's "description" of the imperative mood was cited. Wallace's words and the brief comments concerning his description are worth repeating: the imperative is the "mood of *intention*, ... the mood furthest removed from certainty, ... [the mood which] moves in the realm of *volition ...* and *possibility.*"[39] The imperative portrays *intention* in the sense that it merely presents a potential and intended state of the verbal idea. As the imperative is produced, it is only potentially realized. *Actuality* depends on the response of the addressee(s).[40] Thus, *actuality* is not portrayed linguistically in the imperative mood. Only an *intention* is explicit. This is why the imperative is "furthest removed from certainty" in its portrayal of the verbal idea.[41] The imperative is in contrast to the indicative which is most certain, the subjunctive

---

this as an imperative]; Gal 5:2). The imperatival force is not lacking in any of these usages. However, they seem to be fixed expressions and therefore withheld from the analysis.

[38]All five occurrences of the singular are idioms (Matt 26:49; 27:29 ‖ Mark 15:18; Luke 1:28; John 19:3). There is one certain occurrence of the plural χαίετε (out of eleven) which as an idiomatic greeting (Matt 28:9). The other ten occurrences (Matt 5:12; Luke 10:20 [2x]; 2 Cor 13:11; Phil 2:18; 3:1; 4:4 [2x]; 1 Thess 5:16; 1 Pet 4:13) and the one occurrence of the aorist passive, χάρητε (Luke 6:23) all seem to maintain an imperative force ("rejoice"). Nevertheless, all examples in the database will be omitted for two reasons. First, there is a tendency for these words to be used in potential fixed expressions (χαίρετε ἐν κυρίῳ, Phil 3:1; 4:4; χάρητε ἐν ἐκείνῃ τῇ ἡμέρα, Luke 6:23). Second, as with ἄγε, the database is sufficient for analysis without the seventeen imperative occurrences of this verb.

[39]*Exegetical Syntax*, 485.

[40]The imperative is "to be realized by another" (Maximilian Zerwick, *Biblical Greek Illustrated by Examples*, trans. Joseph Smith, Scripta Pontificii Instituti Bibilici, vol. 114 [Rome: Editrice Pontificio Istituto Biblici, 1963], 100).

[41]Other terminology for *actuality* and *certainty* include *reality* and *factuality* (see respectively James A. Brooks and Carlton L. Winbery, *Syntax of New Testament Greek* (Lanham, MD: University Press of America, 1979), 103 and Young, *Intermediate*, 136). Whatever terminology is adopted it is important to remember that language only *portrays* or *presents* reality, certainty, or factuality. There is no correspondence between grammar and the real world. This was briefly discussed above in chapter 1 in the subsection entitled "Communication".

which is probable or desirable, and the optative which is merely possible.[42] Finally, the imperative "moves in the realm of volition." In other words, it expresses the will of the speaker.[43] As has been noted in chapter 1, communication involves inference and intention. Therefore, although the imperative grammatically may be the mood of volition, real language use may include and use other means for communicating volition. Nevertheless, this basic distinction is helpful when one remembers the complexity and relative nature of the communication situation.

Wallace cautions the reader after describing the mood and states, "There are many exceptions" to his description of the imperative.[44] A significant issue faced in this work is to determine what is communicated by the imperative. The description needs to account for a significant portion of the data. In cases where the usages do not seem to fit the description, this chapter will need to inquire whether there is a reason for such departures.

This work's working theory of the meaning of the imperative will focus upon the description Wallace has provided. The imperative mood is *volitional*. It expresses the *intention* of the communicator. And the realization of the verbal idea is not within the verb phrase itself; rather, its fulfillment is only *possible*. To modify this description into a more linguistic semantic meaning and using the language of speech act theory, the imperative mood is a *volitional directive*.[45] Thus, this study will proceed with this assumption and will attempt to demonstrate this meaning from within the text. Some discussion will necessarily begin to explore pragmatic issues related to usage; however, this

---

[42]See Wallace, *Exegetical Syntax*, 446. Wallace classifies the indicative as the only mood of presentation of actuality/certainty, and the subjunctive, optative, and imperative with decreasing levels (respectively) of potentiality.

[43]This comprehensive definition implies that the imperative by its very nature points to future action (see Smyth, *Greek Grammar*, 409).

[44]Wallace does acknowledge that "in almost every instance the *rhetorical* power of the imperative is still felt" (*Exegetical Syntax*, 485).

[45]Lyons, discussing the imperative mood generally, states, "if a language has a grammatical mood which is used distinctly and characteristically for the purpose of imposing one's will on others for the purpose of issuing directives, that mood is traditionally described as the **imperative** (*Linguistic Semantics: An Introduction* [Cambridge: Cambridge University Press, 1995], 256). Lyons' description may be too restrictive for this works's purposes but nevertheless provides support for the label here. In addition, Shi Zhang, who is concerned with the broader notion of *imperative* (i.e., sentence type), uses the term "directive" as one of three uses of the term imperative ("The Status of Imperatives in Theories of Grammar" [Ph.D. dissertation, University of Arizona, 1990], 11).

will only be sketchy. Further development will await chapter 4.

Now it will be worth looking more closely at this work's initial description of the semantic meaning. This will be refined and supplemented. Then this chapter will briefly contrast the imperative with other moods. Finally, this work will bring together these studies and describe the *volitional directive* more precisely.

Imperative Semantics 1: Internal Considerations

In chapter 2 Greek and linguistic approaches to the imperative mood were surveyed. Although some treatments were primarily focused upon the sememic command, in general the volitional force of the imperative is recognized.[46] In this section selected passages from the New Testament will be analyzed in order to confirm this meaning. As was described previously, as a starting point, this work will be using the classifications of verbs by a number of grammarians. For the sake of this exercise, usages for the mood have been assumed.[47] Occurrences

---

[46]In discussions of *modality*, one would classify the imperative as *deontic* (involving an element of the will) in contrast to *epistemic* (involving knowledge, beliefs, etc.). See F. R. Palmer, *Mood and Modality*, Cambridge Textbooks in Linguistics, ed. B. Comrie et al. (Cambridge: Cambridge University Press, 1986), 18-19 and from an RT approach, Anna Papafragou, "Modality and Semantic Underdeterminacy," in *Current Issues in Relevance Theory*, ed. Villy Rouchota and Andreas H. Jucker (Amsterdam: John Benjamins Publishing Company, 1998), 237-38. The latter work does not deal with imperatives directly but is mentioned for its relationship to the subject at hand. However, Papafragou ties modality closer to truth commitment which seem to violate the principle that language does not necessarily reflect reality but is a portrayal of reality. Also, modality as discussed in these works is more complex than this work's twofold contrast may indicate.

[47]In other words, this work is building upon the work of others. This does not mean the method uncritically accepts such findings (as will be reflected in some footnotes). Ultimately, a different paradigm for imperative usage will be proposed. In order to avoid the use of excessive footnotes, each example will be followed by a brief code(s) in parentheses identifying the grammar(s) which classify the imperative as recorded here. Unfortunately, many treatments of the imperative do not give classifications of moods in an organized manner (this is not necessarily a fault but not useful for the purpose here) (e.g., Zerwick, *Biblical Greek*; Nigel Turner, *Syntax*, vol. 3, *A Grammar of New Testament Greek*, ed. James Hope Moulton [Edinburgh: T. & T. Clark, 1963]). The works and codes used for the examples are as follows: (B) BDF, 195-96; (Bo) James L. Boyer, "A Classification of Imperatives: A Statistical Study," *Grace Theological Journal* 8 (1987), 36-39; (Bu) Ernest DeWitt Burton, *Syntax of Moods and Tenses in New Testament Greek*, 3d ed. (Edinburgh: T. & T. Clark, 1898), 80-81; (M) Moulton, *Prolegomena*, 172; (R) A. T. Robertson, *A Grammar of the Greek New Testament in the Light of Historical Research*, 4th ed. (Nashville: Broadman Press, 1934), 446-49; (W) Wallace, *Exegetical Syntax*, 486-93; (Y) Young,

are categorized according to these usages and labeled *command* imperative, *request/entreaty* imperative, *permissive/toleration* imperative, *conditional* imperative, and *prohibition* (imperative).[48] An attempt to determine the semantic meaning of the mood based on the distribution of usages in these passages will be made. In addition the analysis will be broadened by noting other examples from the New Testament as set out in the limitations section of chapter 1. Chapter 4 will be devoted to usage; however, one can utilize the preliminary work in this area by choosing passages variously categorized in order to demonstrate the volitional nature of the mood itself.[49]

Probably the most common and straightforward of imperative usages are those simply labeled *command*:[50]

Matt 5:12   χαίρετε[51] καὶ ἀγαλλιᾶσθε (Bo)
               rejoice and **be glad**

Matt 5:42   τῷ αἰτοῦντί σε **δός** ... (Bu)
               give to the one who asks of you ...

Intermediate, 141-45. Further grammars could be consulted; however, this is sufficient for this work's purposes. Also, as mentioned above, only passages without classification disagreement among works consulted will be presented here to avoid issues of classification.

[48]Terminology differs between grammars. Terminology differences were mentioned in chapter 2 (subsection: "The Range of Usage of the Imperative"). In some cases, grammars included multiple categories as classified here under one heading (see BDF). Where more specificity could be reasonably deduced, it has been so classified here. Where verses are noted with further classification ambiguity within a grammar, decisions will be noted in footnotes.

In addition, this section will only be concerned with the major categories of the imperative. Some minor usages (often peculiar to one grammarian) will be mentioned briefly without significant discussion. This is not because such usages are not of value. The purpose here is to get a general meaning of the imperative. Some peculiar categories will be discussed; however, in many cases, these are issues related to pragmatics and will be incorporated into the discussion of chapter 4.

[49]The purpose here is not to refine the usage categories. Rather, well known examples of differing usages of the imperative are used to demonstrate the volitional nature of the mood.

[50]Throughout this section (all the classifications listed below), the translation will be rather literal. Nevertheless, the translation here will highlight the classification to the extent accuracy (in translation) permits.

[51]As noted above in the discussion of idioms, χαίρετε is considered an idiom (albeit here retaining imperative force as mentioned) and will not be considered in the analysis for reasons discussed; nevertheless, it is included here for illustrative purposes as it meets the proposed requirements for discussion (i.e., mentioned by a grammarians without contradiction).

Matt 5:44   **ἀγαπᾶτε** τοὺς ἐχθροὺς ὑμῶν καὶ **προσεύχεσθε** ὑπὲρ τῶν
διωκόντων ὑμᾶς (R)
love your enemies and **pray** for those who persecute you

Matt 8:9   καὶ γὰρ ἐγὼ ἄνθρωπός εἰμι ὑπὸ ἐξουσίαν, ἔχων ὑπ᾽
ἐμαυτὸν στρατιώτας, καὶ λέγω τούτῳ· **πορεύθητι**, καὶ
πορεύεται, καὶ ἄλλῳ· **ἔρχου**, καὶ ἔρχεται, καὶ τῷ δούλῳ
μου· **ποίησον** τοῦτο, καὶ ποιεῖ (Bo)
for I also am a man under authority, having soldiers under me,
and I say to this one, "**Go**," and he goes, and to another,
"**Come**," and he comes, and to my servant, "**Do** this," and he
does [it]

Mark 2:14   Καὶ παράγων εἶδεν Λευὶν τὸν τοῦ᾽ Ἀλφαίου καθήμενον
ἐπὶ τὸ τελώνιον, καὶ λέγει αὐτῷ· **ἀκολούθει** μοι ... (W)
And while passing by he saw Levi the son of Alphaeus siting
in the tax office and he said to him, "**Follow** me" ...

Mark 6:10   καὶ ἔλεγεν αὐτοῖς· ὅπου ἐὰν εἰσέλθητε εἰς οἰκίαν, ἐκεῖ
μένετε ἕως ἂν ἐξέλθητε ἐκεῖθεν (W)
and he said to them, "Whenever you enter into a house,
remain there until you leave from there"

Mark 6:37   ὁ δὲ ἀποκριθεὶς εἶπεν αὐτοῖς· **δότε** αὐτοῖς ὑμεῖς
φαγεῖν (W)
but answering he said to them, "You **give** them [something] to
eat"

Luke 12:19   καὶ ἐρῶ τῇ ψυχῇ μου, ψυχή, ἔχεις πολλὰ ἀγαθὰ κείμενα
εἰς ἔτη πολλά· **ἀναπαύου, φάγε, πίε, εὐφραίνου** (W)
and I will say to my soul, "Soul, you have many good things
stored for many years, **relax, eat, drink, be glad**"[52]

---

[52]Although Luke 12:19 is best classified as a *command* imperative, the nuance in this internal
dialogue seems to involve less *command* meaning than other examples in this section. This seems
to point to deficiencies in the present system which will be addressed in chapter 4.

John 2:5
λέγει ἡ μήτηρ αὐτοῦ τοῖς διακόνοις· ὅ τι ἂν λέγῃ ὑμῖν **ποιήσατε** (W)
his mother said to the servants, "Whatever he says to you, **do**"

John 2:16
ἄρατε ταῦτα ἐντεῦθεν, μὴ ποιεῖτε[53] τὸν οἶκον τοῦ πατρός μου οἶκον ἐμπορίου (W)
remove these things from here, stop making my Father's house a market house (place)

John 5:11
ἆρον τὸν κράβαττόν σου καὶ **περιπάτει** (W)
take up your bed and **walk**

Acts 5:8
ἀπεκρίθη δὲ πρὸς αὐτὴν Πέτρος· **εἰπέ** μοι … (W)
and Peter answered and said to her, "**Tell** me …"

Rom 6:13
μηδὲ **παριστάνετε**[54] τὰ μέλη ὑμῶν ὅπλα ἀδικίας τῇ ἁμαρτίᾳ, ἀλλὰ **παραστήσατε** ἑαυτοὺς τῷ θεῷ … (W)
and do not go on presenting your members as tools of unrighteousness, but **present** yourself to God …

1 Cor 1:31
ὁ καυχώμενος ἐν κυρίῳ **καυχάσθω** (W)
let the one who boasts, **boast** in the Lord

2 Cor 10:7
εἴ τις πέποιθεν ἑαυτῷ Χριστοῦ εἶναι, τοῦτο λογιζέσθω πάλιν (W)
if anyone is confident in himself that he is Christ's [lit. to be of Christ], **let** him **consider** this again

2 Cor 13:5
Ἑαυτοὺς **πειράζετε** εἰ ἐστὲ ἐν τῇ πίστει (W)
Test yourselves [to determine] if you are in the faith

---

[53]Although this imperative is very similar to the preceding imperative (*command*), in traditional grammar, it is often not classified as the former which obscures the similarities between the two. Rather, with all negative imperatives despite force, it is merely classified *prohibition*.
[54]See note on John 2:16 above.

Gal 6:1 ... **καταρτίζετε** τὸν τοιοῦτον ἐν πνεύματι πραΰτητος (W)

... **restore** such a one in a spirit of humility

1 Thess 5:16 Πάντοτε **χαίρετε**[55] (R)

Rejoice always

2 Tim 1:14 τὴν καλὴν παραθήκην **φύλαξον** διὰ πνεύματος ἁγίου τοῦ ἐνοικοῦντος ἐν ἡμῖν (W)

guard the previous things entrusted to you through the Holy Spirit who lives in you

Heb 12:14 Εἰρήνην **διώκετε** μετὰ πάντων (W)

Pursue peace with everyone

Heb 13:17 **Πείθεσθε** τοῖς ἡγουμένοις ὑμῶν καὶ **ὑπείκετε** (W[56])

Obey those who lead you and **submit**

James 1:5-6 Εἰ δέ τις ὑμῶν λείπεται σοφίας, **αἰτείτω** ... 6 **αἰτείτω** δὲ ἐν πίστει μηδὲν διακρινόμενος (Y, W [v.#5 only])

But if anyone lacks wisdom, **let** him **ask** ... but **let** him **ask** in faith without doubting (or, he **must ask**)

Jude 21 ἑαυτοὺς ἐν ἀγάπῃ θεοῦ **τηρήσατε** (W)

keep yourselves in the love of God

Rev 1:19 **γράψον** οὖν α εἶδες ... (W)

therefore, **write** the things which you have seen ...

---

[55]See the note on χαίρετε in Matt 5:12 in the section on *commands* above. That discussion also applies here.

[56]Wallace only classifies the first imperative.

Rev 19:10   ὅρα μή·[57] σύνδουλός σού εἰμι ... τῷ θεῷ **προσκύνησον**
                ... (W)
                do not do that, I am a fellow servant ... **worship** God ...

In each of these examples (with a few concerns noted) the speaker is attempting to elicit a certain response from the party to whom the imperative sentence is directed. The communicator desires the recipient to do something (volition). The speaker presents the imperative in a manner which seems to suggest that the hearer will or strongly should fulfill the imperative. The directed party can be the reader as is the case in all epistolary literature. However, in narrative the directed party may be a character within the story itself as is the case with the passages from the gospels and Acts. Although the primary recipient of the imperative in narrative is within the story, it seems likely that the reader is also an intended recipient of the imperative in some cases (Matt 5:42).[58] It can be further stated that the directive is rather forceful in these examples.[59] In other words, the intention of the communicator is to strongly direct the recipient toward the intended action. Thus, the classification *command* is a natural label.

This classification clearly demonstrates the volitional and directive force of the imperative. The *command* strength makes these most prominent within this classification system.

---

[57]The imperative ὅρα with μή is an idiom meaning "don't do that" (BDAG). This certainly retains command (or prohibition) force. However, it is uncertain whether both this and the later imperative are classified by Wallace as *command* since this passage is merely listed and not quoted. I am assuming here that only the latter is meant by Wallace. However, this does not necessarily mean that he would not classify this as command.

[58]Of course many passages are far too context-specific to apply to the reader (e.g., John 5:11, ἆρον τὸν κράβαττόν σου καὶ περιπάτει). Nevertheless, in literature such as the New Testament (as well as literature with possible moral intention such as Plutarch's *Lives*), there is certainly an implied imperative aimed at the reader. Such direction may not be explicit and its purpose may be aimed at behavior and/or belief modification (or confirmation). This fascinating area of study is far beyond the scope of this linguistic work. Nevertheless, some of the material developed in this project (especially the discussion of the communication process, including *relevance*) should be helpful in utilizing context-specific information (background material) and exegesis to help determine the intention of narrative units for its implied and intended readers. This work's communication insights should also be helpful for taking this a step further and applying these texts to readers in vastly different contexts from the original (including the twenty-first-century reader).

[59]What has been mentioned thus far in this paragraph could apply to all imperatives. However, this statement and those following are more focused on this classification.

There are other examples where imperatives have an identical nuance (volitional and directive); however, the force of the *command* is weakened. These usages include a weak or polite command (often labeled *request*):

Matt 6:9b-13   Πάτερ ἡμῶν ὁ ἐν τοῖς οὐρανοῖς· **ἁγιασθήτω** τὸ ὄνομά σου· 10 **ἐλθέτω** ἡ βασιλεία σου· **γενηθήτω** τὸ θέλημά σου, ὡς ἐν οὐρανῷ καὶ ἐπὶ γῆς· 11 τὸν ἄρτον ἡμῶν τὸν ἐπιούσιον **δὸς** ἡμῖν σήμερον· 12 καὶ **ἄφες** ἡμῖν τὰ ὀφειλήματα ἡμῶν, ὡς καὶ ἡμεῖς ἀφήκαμεν τοῖς ὀφειλέταις ἡμῶν· 13 καὶ μὴ εἰσενέγκῃς ἡμᾶς εἰς πειρασμόν, ἀλλὰ **ῥῦσαι** ἡμᾶς ἀπὸ τοῦ πονηροῦ (Y, W [9-11])

Our Father who is in heaven, **let** your name be **set apart**, [10] **let** your kingdom **come**, **let** your will/desire be **done**, ..., [11] **give** to us today our daily bread, [12] and **forgive** us our sins as we forgive those who have offended us, [13] and do not lead us into temptation but **deliver** us from evil

Matt 8:31-32   οἱ δὲ δαίμονες παρεκάλουν αὐτὸν λέγοντες· εἰ ἐκβάλλεις ἡμᾶς, **ἀπόστειλον** ἡμᾶς εἰς τὴν ἀγέλην τῶν χοίρων. 32 καὶ εἶπεν αὐτοῖς· ὑπάγετε (Bu, R, W)[60]

The demons were asking him, "If you cast us out, **send** us into the herd of swine" and he said to them, "Go"

Matt 26:39   πάτερ μου, εἰ δυνατόν ἐστιν, **παρελθάτω** ἀπ᾽ ἐμοῦ τὸ ποτήριον τοῦτο (W)

My Father, if it is possible, **let** this cup **pass by** me

---

[60]There are two imperatives in this passage. The second (ὑπάγετε) is classified as *permission* (see below). Robertson makes this explicit. Wallace and Burton also list this passage (Matt 8:31-32) in their category equivalent to the *permission/toleration*. In Wallace's case it is clear (by bold font) that only the second imperative should be so classified. Burton does not specify which imperative is intended; however, it is likely verse 31 is merely providing context to help illustrate the classification.

Matt 26:42   πάτερ μου, εἰ οὐ δύναται τοῦτο παρελθεῖν ἐὰν μὴ αὐτὸ
               πίω, **γενηθήτω** τὸ θέλημά σου (W)[61]
               My Father, if this is unable to pass unless I drink it, **let** your
               will **be done**

Mark 9:22   ἀλλ' εἴ τι δύνῃ, **βοήθησον** ἡμῖν σπλαγχνισθεὶς ἐφ' ἡμᾶς
               (Bu, R, W)
               but if you are able to do anything, **help** us and have pity on us

Luke 7:6-7   κύριε, **μὴ σκύλλου**,[62] ... ἀλλὰ **εἰπὲ** λόγῳ, καὶ **ἰαθήτω**
               ὁ παῖς μου (W)
               Lord, **do not be troubled** ... but **say** the word and **let** my
               servant **be healed**

Luke 11:1   κύριε, **δίδαξον** ἡμᾶς προσεύχεσθαι (W)
               Lord, **teach** us to pray

Luke 15:6   **συγχάρητέ** μοι (W)
               Rejoice with me

Luke 17:5   Καὶ εἶπαν οἱ ἀπόστολοι τῷ κυρίῳ· **πρόσθες** ἡμῖν πίστιν
               (Bu, R, W)
               And the apostles said to the lord, **increase** our faith

John 4:7   λέγει αὐτῇ ὁ Ἰησοῦς· **δός** μοι πεῖν (W)
               Jesus said to her [the Samaritan woman], "**Give** me something
               to drink"

---

[61]The *request* nuance in Matt 26:42 is very minimal if present at all. Jesus here seems to be using this imperative to express his willingness to go along with God's plan. Therefore, it may be classified as *permission*.

[62]Wallace (*Exegetical Syntax*, 488) acknowledges the negative (μὴ) but nevertheless classifies this as *request*. Here is an example of someone classifying a negative imperative by its force, not by the presence of the negative marker.

John 4:31   Ἐν τῷ μεταξὺ ἠρώτων αὐτὸν οἱ μαθηταὶ λέγοντες·
ῥαββί, **φάγε** (W)
In the meantime, the disciples were asking him, saying,
"Rabbi, **eat**"

John 17:11   πάτερ ἅγιε, **τήρησον** αὐτοὺς ἐν τῷ ὀνόματί σου (Bu, R,
W)
holy Father, **keep** them in your word

John 11:34   καὶ εἶπεν· ποῦ τεθείκατε αὐτόν; λέγουσιν αὐτῷ· κύριο,
ἔρχου καὶ **ἴδε** (Y)
and he said "Where have you laid him?" They said to him,
"Lord, **come** and **see**"

John 19:21   ἔλεγον οὖν τῷ Πιλάτῳ οἱ ἀρχιερεῖς τῶν Ἰουδαίων· **μὴ
γράφε**·[63] ὁ βασιλεὺς τῶν Ἰουδαίων (W)
therefore, the high priests of the Jews were saying to Pilate,
"**do not write** [or, you should not write], 'the king of the
Jews'"

Acts 1:24   καὶ προσευξάμενοι εἶπαν· σὺ κύριο καρδιογνῶστα
πάντων, **ἀνάδειξον** ον ἐξελέξω ἐκ τούτων τῶν δύο ἕνα
(W)
and they prayed and said, "You, Lord, the one knowing hearts
of all, **show** which one from these two you chose

2 Cor 5:20   δεόμεθα ὑπὲρ Χριστοῦ, **καταλλάγητε** τῷ θεῷ (W)
We ask (or, beg) on behalf of Christ, **be reconciled** to God

2 Cor 12:13 **χαρίσασθέ** μοι τὴν ἀδικίαν ταύτην (W)
forgive me this injustice

---

[63]See note on Luke 7:6-7 above.

Phlm 18   εἰ δέ τι ἠδίκησέν σε ἢ ὀφείλει, τοῦτο ἐμοὶ **ἐλλόγα**. (W)
            but if he wronged you or owes you anything, **charge** this to me

Rev 22:17   Καὶ τὸ πνεῦμα καὶ ἡ νύμφη λέγουσιν· **ἔρχου**. καὶ ὁ
            ἀκούων **εἰπάτω**· **ἔρχου**. καὶ ὁ διψῶν **ἐρχέσθω**, ὁ θέλων
            λαβέτω ὕδωρ ζωῆς δωρεάν (Y)
            And the Spirit and the bride say, "**Come**," and **let** the one who
            hears **say**, "**Come**" and **let** the one who is thirsty **come**, **let** the
            one who desires **take** the gift of living water

Rev 22:20   Λέγει ὁ μαρτυρῶν ταῦτα· ναί, ἔρχομαι ταχύ.᾽Αμήν,
            ἔρχου κύριο᾽Ιησοῦ (W)
            The one who testifies to these things says, "Yes, I am coming
            quickly." Amen, **Come** Lord Jesus

These examples further demonstrate the volitional and directive nuances of
the imperative mood. In every case the speaker desires some response from the
hearer. The communication initiator wishes to direct the recipient in some
manner. However, unlike the set of examples labeled *command*, the response
of the hearer seems less certain and more dependent upon the will of the hearer.
In other words the passages as presented seem to demand an interpretation
which views the imperative communicated with less confidence than the
command examples.[64] Thus the imperative comes across *weaker*. This
interpretation of course is context-dependent.[65] When these verses are compared
with those labeled *command* in the example above, a number of observations
become visible which seem to contribute to the weakened force as translated in
these examples.[66] First, there is the issue of rank. Often when an imperative is

---

[64]As has been reiterated throughout this project, this is only the *means* in which the
imperatives are presented. This may or may not have any correlation with reality (i.e., that which
the communicator actually believes). There may be many reasons the communicator wishes to
present the imperative in this manner. Some of these will be discussed immediately.

[65]Context may include structural clues (e.g., words which suggest this weakened force; e.g.,
παρεκάλουν, Matt 8:31–although other factors may also be involved) or cultural practices and/or
belief (e.g., John 4:31; it would not seem appropriate for followers of a Rabbi to *command* their
master to eat!).

[66]A number of grammarians acknowledge various features which contribute to the
weakening force of an imperative; see for example Boyer, "Imperatives," 36; Moulton,
Prolegomena, 172-73; Wallace, *Exegetical Syntax*, 487; Young, *Intermediate*, 144-45. However,

used by one from an inferior social status toward a superior; the pragmatic force of the mood seems to be weakened (e.g., Matt 8:31; Luke 11:1; 17:5; John 4:31; 19:21; Rev 22:20). However, there may be other contextual features which cause a communicator to speak with greater or lesser force. These factors may even seem to override or reverse the force associated with the standard social rank observation made above (e.g., John 4:7; 2 Cor 5:20). The issue of rank will be discussed in detail in chapter 4. At this stage this work only wishes to observe that often when lower-ranked parties address higher-ranked parties, there seems to be a weakened force. Whether this is due to rank itself and/or to other features awaits further analysis. It is not surprising that this is the category in which many imperatives in prayers are classified (e.g., Matt 6:9b-13; 26:39, 42; John 17:11; Acts 1:24). Prayers are in essence low rank individuals appealing to the one of highest rank, namely God.[67]

Before proceeding it will be helpful to mention a methodological issue which may be considered by readers of this work at this point. Thus far, it has been suggested that a specific mood form has weaker force in some places than it does in others. In fact, it is possible for exact word forms to be classified with different forces (compare δός in Matt 5:42 and Matt 6:11 above). How can this be justified? Is not our cultural understanding of a situation being forced upon the text at this point? After all, with the exception of examples with certain introductory words such as παρεκάλουν in Matt 8:31, no structural factors have [yet] been identified to distinguish force. Is it really correct to assume that individuals in the New Testament (especially Jesus, the Son of God) did not approach the Father in prayer with the same force as he would communicate to his disciples? When one looks at the Psalms, it is rather shocking to see the boldness in which the Psalmists approach God. In other words, is one of the principles set forth in chapter 1 being violated, namely, that the text must be approached from a Greek, not English, perspective?

This is a valid concern especially for those passages without any explicit means of identifying a weakened force (such as a word of *asking*). In chapter 4 this work will attempt to present a more accurate (less intuitive) approach to force. However, for now, this charge may be responded to in a number of ways

---

to my knowledge there has been no significant analysis and description of these factors.

[67]Prayers are usually in the aorist tense; however, there are exceptions (e.g., Luke 11:3 (δίδου); 22:42 (γινέσθω). It is interesting to note the respective parallels to these present tense prayer verbs are in the aorist: Matt 6:11 (δός); 26:42: (γενηθήτω).

(however, I am somewhat sympathetic to the concern here). First, it must acknowledge the potential danger here and admit that one cannot completely overcome cultural biases. This is a weakness compounded when one studies a language which is no longer in use. One cannot do anthropological studies to determine such cultural factors and how they are expressed in language.[68]

Second, one must remember that the interpretation of the text and the communication situation are larger than language code. The New Testament student who believes a mastery of Greek alone is sufficient for understanding scripture is hopelessly deluded. An immersion into the time period, including its history, literature, lifestyle, etc., is a vital and a never-ending pursuit in an attempt to understand the text. In other words, one must attempt to get into the cultural and thought-world of the writers and recipients of the Bible. The result of such a study is a growing understanding of non-linguistic information which impacts the interpretation of scripture. Such information will be helpful to understand issues such as the force of the imperative.

Third, all humanity is part of a continuing story. Although every culture has significant differences, all people share much in common. This seems to be the case even with language and culture; specifically, in areas of social interaction (including politeness, etc.). This work will be drawing on some insights from this field as it constructs a new paradigm for the imperative mood.[69] I am not suggesting that all cultures have identical or even necessarily similar means of expressing aspects of social situations such as politeness. Nor am I suggesting that all cultures place a similar emphasis on such issues. This is not the case. However, all cultures seem to include these factors to varying degrees. Although degrees and importance may vary, I am unaware of any culture whose

---

[68]This seems to be a somewhat unavoidable weakness of all grammars of ancient Greek. To some extent, classification schemes (whether for the genitive case, present tense, etc.) are explicit attempts to present usages that correspond to the target language's understanding of the world. This is not intended to be a criticism of grammars, especially of those which acknowledge this weakness. In fact, this seems to be the best approach for beginning (first two years) students. This provides a methodologically manageable manner of tackling new and difficult data. In other words, the student can learn step by step and build on previous learning in a structured manner which maximizes the student's time. However, the problem is real and an unavoidable weakness which can only be minimized through continual textual and cultural familiarity with the ancient community whose writings are being studied.

[69]In chapter 4, the work of Penelope Brown and Stephen C. Levinson will be extensively utilized (*Politeness: Some Universals in Language Usage* [Cambridge: Cambridge University Press, 1987]).

imperative force is opposite to or significantly different from our own.[70] It is clear that issues such as honor, shame, politeness, etc. play more of a role in some cultures than in others. In the case of the communities of New Testament, it is likely that these issues were more central and contributed more non-verbal controlling features to the communication situation than in the present western culture.[71] Therefore, not to acknowledge the potential impact such features may have on the imperative mood would be negligence. In fact, in light of New Testament cultural studies, there may be more significance in this area then one is readily able to discern from one's own cultural perspective which results in an insufficient emphasis given to such issues.[72]

Finally, chapter 4 will analyze the data and suggest explicit structural elements which will respond to this objection directly. In this way, the concern about rank here can be avoided.

In conclusion, despite a lack of structural evidence at this stage, the uncertainty of cultural interpretation of an ancient society, and the danger of contemporary bias, it seems worthwhile to note force changes where context seems demand such differences. The reasons for these force changes will be addressed in the next chapter.

Although rare, there are examples where the force of the imperative is very weak at best. These are often labeled *permissive* or *toleration* imperatives:

---

[70]In other words, I am unaware of any societies which demonstrate in a different manner (e.g., a command having weaker force than a request, a inferior addressing a superior involves more force than the opposite, etc.).

[71]See chapter 4 for further discussion on issues such as honor and shame and politeness.

[72]This does not mean that use of such material is not without difficulties. There is a measure of uncertainty introduced in the interpretive process. Also, eisegesis needs to be carefully avoided (often this can be done by acknowledging one's ignorance). However, to ignore such evidence and its contribution to the communication situation would result in an uninformed and ultimately faulty exegesis of the text.

Matt 8:31-32   οἱ δὲ δαίμονες παρεκάλουν αὐτὸν λέγοντες· εἰ ἐκβάλλεις ἡμᾶς, ἀπόστειλον ἡμᾶς εἰς τὴν ἀγέλην τῶν χοίρων. 32 καὶ εἶπεν αὐτοῖς· **ὑπάγετε** (B,[73] Bu,[74] M, R, W, Y)[75]

The demons were asking him, "If you cast us out, send us into the herd of swine" and he said to them, "**Go**"

Matt 10:13   καὶ ἐὰν μὲν ᾖ ἡ οἰκία ἀξία, **ἐλθάτω** ἡ εἰρήνη ὑμῶν ἐπ᾽ αὐτήν, ἐὰν δὲ μὴ ᾖ ἀξία, ἡ εἰρήνη ὑμῶν πρὸς ὑμᾶς **ἐπιστραφήτω** (R)

and if the house is worthy, **let** your peace **come** upon it, but if it is not worthy, **let** your peace **return** to you

Matt 23:32   καὶ ὑμεῖς **πληρώσατε** τὸ μέτρον τῶν πατέρων ὑμῶν (R, W)

complete then the measure [of guilt, sin] of your fathers

Luke 7:40   καὶ ἀποκριθεὶς ὁ᾽ Ἰησοῦς εἶπεν πρὸς αὐτόν· Σίμων, ἔχω σοί τι εἰπεῖν. ὁ δέ· διδάσκαλε, **εἰπέ**, φησίν (Bo)

and Jesus answered and said to him, "Simon, I have something to say to you." And he said, "Teacher, **speak**"

---

[73]BDF is not as clear as one would like; however, it seems that this fits into its broad category called *concession* which includes the permission nuance.

[74]Burton groups and discusses usages "to express consent" and "to propose a hypothesis" together. These correspond to the *permission/tolerance* and *conditional* usages. In this discussion he has four examples. It is clear from his discussion that he considers Matt 8:31-32 and 1 Cor 7:36 to be "consent" (*permission/tolerance*) and Luke 6:37 and John 2:19 to be "hypothetical" (*conditional*).

[75]Actually only verse 32 is applicable here (as is only mentioned in B, M, Y). However, verse 31 is included to provide context to make clear the classification. See also the note on this passage in the discussion of the previous category.

John 19:6   Ὅτε οὖν εἶδον αὐτὸν οἱ ἀρχιερεῖς καὶ οἱ ὑπηρέται ἐκραύγασαν λέγοντες· σταύρωσον σταύρωσον. λέγει αὐτοῖς ὁ Πιλᾶτος· **λάβετε** αὐτὸν ὑμεῖς καὶ **σταυρώσατε** ... (Bo)

Therefore, when the high priests and attendants saw him, they shouted, "Crucify! Crucify!" Pilate replied, "You **take** and **crucify** him ..."

1 Cor 7:15   εἰ δὲ ὁ ἄπιστος χωρίζεται, **χωριζέσθω** (Bo, M, W)

but if the unbelieving one departs, **let** him **depart**

1 Cor 7:36   Εἰ δέ τις ἀσχημονεῖν ἐπὶ τὴν παρθένον αὐτοῦ νομίζει, ἐὰν ᾖ ὑπέρακμος καὶ οὕτως ὀφείλει γίνεσθαι, ὁ θέλει **ποιείτω**, οὐχ ἁμαρτάνει, **γαμείτωσαν** (Bu,[76] W, Y)

But if anyone thinks he is acting improperly toward his virgin, if she be of age and it must be thus, **let** him **do** what he wants he does not sin, **let** them **marry**

2 Cor 12:16   [15 ... ἧσσον ἀγαπῶμαι;] 16 **Ἔστω** δέ (R, W[77])

[15 ... am I to be loved less?] 16 then **let** it **be**

These examples are not be classified as either *commands* or *requests*. Labels such as *permission*, *toleration*, etc. suggest a minimal force. This observation seems accurate. The reasons for this will be explored in chapter 4. Nevertheless, the *directive* force and *volitional* element are still apparent. If one associated this work's semantic notion of volition with the *actual* desire of the communicator, then this notion would have to be abandoned. However, language cannot be assumed to represent the actual desires of the communicators without specific signals suggesting this is the case (and this is not necessarily a guarantee).[78] The analyst only has access to what the

---

[76]See note above for Burton on Matt 8:31-32.

[77]Wallace lists 2 Cor 12:16 as "possible."

[78]For example, if one uses language to basically say, "I desire x" meaning, "What I really desire is x, and only x, with no other pretenses, and this truly represents my desire, etc." However, even in such a case, truthfulness cannot be guaranteed. In addition there is the added complication that a person may not really understand his own desires and motives.

communicator wishes to portray as his desire through the communication act. Language is a tool one uses to communicate something. Reality and actual desires must be determined by a number of factors. The meaning of the imperative which is being labeled *volitional*, does not necessarily mean that it is the speaker's desire. Rather, the imperative presents the language code in a way which portrays a specific manner for the action/event/belief/etc. to be carried out. It is in this way that it is volitional. The decision to use the imperative is the decision to present the verbal action in a manner desired by the speaker. In reality the speaker may not truly desire this or may have other non-verbal goals behind the imperative. In addition, This may seem like mere permission in some contexts. However, permission, toleration, etc. are forms of volition. They communicate to the hearer that the action may continue. Whether the speaker likes the action is not relevant. He chooses to present the proposed action in manner that expresses his will for the action to proceed (or not proceed in the case of negated imperatives).

The difficulty with the evidence of volition despite the discussion above further demonstrates the observation about the importance of *force* with the imperative. If a *command* has the most force of all imperatives, *permission/toleration* has the weakest force of examples thus far. A number of elements may contribute to the complexity of this usage. See chapter 4.

In addition to the three categories already discussed, there seems to be a number of examples of *conditional* imperatives in the New Testament. This is a debated category and the nuance of condition seem to be clearly a product of context. Specifically, the relationship between the imperative clause and its subsequent clause is determinative. Therefore, clause level analysis is demanded for this usage. This issue is somewhat beyond the scope of this analysis; however, because of its importance and its assumed usage as parallel with others by some,[79] it will be discussed in chapter 4. For the purpose here, only a few main examples will be presented.

---

[79]In other words, an imperative is classified *either* as command *or* as a request *or* as a conditional, etc.

Matt 7:7   Αἰτεῖτε καὶ δοθήσεται ὑμῖν, ζητεῖτε καὶ εὑρήσετε, κρούετε καὶ ἀνοιγήσεται ὑμῖν (W)
Ask and it will be given to you, **seek** and you will find, **knock** and it will be opened to you (**If you ask** [and do so], it will be given to you, **if you seek** [and do so], you will find, **if you knock** [and do so], it will be opened to you)

Matt 8:8   καὶ ἀποκριθεὶς ὁ ἑκατόνταρχος ἔφη· κύριε, οὐκ εἰμὶ ἱκανὸς ἵνα μου ὑπὸ τὴν στέγην εἰσέλθῃς, ἀλλὰ μόνον εἰπὲ λόγῳ, καὶ ἰαθήσεται ὁ παῖς μου (W)
And the centurion answered [and] said, "Lord, I am not worthy that you might enter my home [lit. under my roof], but only **say** the word, and my servant will be healed (... , but **if you would** only **say** the word [and do so] ...)

John 1:39   ... ἔρχεσθε καὶ ὄψεσθε (W)
"... **come** and you will see" (**if you come** [and do so], ...)

Eph 5:14   ἔγειρε, ὁ καθεύδων, καὶ ἀνάστα ἐκ τῶν νεκρῶν, καὶ ἐπιφαύσει σοι ὁ Χριστός (R, W)
Arise, one who sleeps, and **awaken** from the dead and Christ will shine on you (**If you arise** [and do so], sleeper, and **[if you] awaken** [and do so] from the dead, Christ will shine on you)

Jas 4:7b   ἀντίστητε δὲ τῷ διαβόλῳ καὶ φεύξεται ἀφ' ὑμῶν
but **resist** the devil and **he will run away** from you (but **if you resist** the devil [and do so] ...)

Jas 4:8   ἐγγίσατε τῷ θεῷ καὶ ἐγγιεῖ ὑμῖν
draw near to God and **he will draw near to you** (**if you draw near** to God [and do so] ...)

Jas 4:10   ταπεινώθητε ἐνώπιον κυρίου καὶ ὑψώσει ὑμᾶς
be humble before the Lord and he will exalt you (**if you are humble** before the Lord [and be so] ...)

If the temptation to look at the relationship between clauses is avoided and this study is limited to the imperative clause, it seems clear that the verb form maintains its *directive* and *volitional* nuances. These are true imperatives.[80] In each case the speakers use these imperative clauses to direct action (e.g., Matt 7:7, Jesus instructs his hearers to ask, seek, and knock; Matt 8:8; instructions in James, etc.). The language presents the action as something the speaker desires the hearer(s) to perform, as something he wants (or does not want) the hearers to do. The following clause gives the result of the action if the imperative is followed.[81] This of course will inform the interpretation of the imperative clause; however, this occurs on a higher level (stratum) of the language system. In addition, it can be observed that different forces seem to be associated with different imperatives (e.g., compare Matt 7:7 with Matt 8:8). Force has been a factor in classification elsewhere (e.g., *command* vs. *request*). Therefore, unless a reason for doing otherwise is suggested, a difference in force should be considered here as a factor contributing to different classifications as well.

Finally, there is a category labeled *prohibition*. Structurally, this is an imperative negated by the particle μή (or related particles).[82]

Matt 6:3   σοῦ δὲ ποιοῦντος ἐλεημοσύνην **μὴ γνώτω** ἡ ἀριστερά
               σου τί ποιεῖ ἡ δεξιά σου[83] (W)
               when you are giving to the needy, **do not allow** your right
               hand know what you left hand is doing

John 6:20   ὁ δὲ λέγει αὐτοῖς· ἐγώ εἰμι· **μὴ φοβεῖσθε** (R)
               but he said to them, "It is me, **do not be afraid**"

---

[80]Stanley E. Porter, *Verbal Aspect in the Greek of the New Testament, with Reference to Tense and Mood*, Studies in Biblical Greek, ed. D. A. Carson, vol. 1 (New York: Peter Lang, 1989), 352-53; see also Wallace, *Exegetical Syntax*, 490.

[81]Porter (*Verbal Aspect*, 353) uses the terms "pragmatic" and "contextual" to account for the conditional nuance. This is what is being suggested by noting contributions toward interpretation beyond the word/mood itself. This is beyond morphological analysis but nevertheless will be discussed in chapter 4.

[82]As previously suggested, there are many examples in the representative grammars of this usage. This section will provide enough examples to demonstrate the point. For a detailed list of examples for this category, see Wallace, *Exegetical Syntax*, 487.

[83]This is one of the few examples of an aorist imperative with μή in the New Testament (in addition it is third person). It is the only one included in the list of representative examples. It is meant to provide as wide a range of examples as possible. See further discussion on this below and in chapter 4.

Acts 10:15   καὶ φωνὴ πάλιν ἐκ δευτέρου πρὸς αὐτόν· ἅ ὁ θεὸς
               ἐκαθάρισεν, σὺ μὴ κοίνου (W)
               and a voice again [came] to him a second time, "What God has
               made clean, **do not make unclean**"

Rom 12:2a   καὶ **μὴ συσχηματίζεσθε** τῷ αἰῶνι τούτῳ (Y)
               and **do not be conformed** to this age

1 Cor 6:9   Ἢ οὐκ οἴδατε ὅτι ἄδικοι θεοῦ βασιλείαν οὐ
               κληρονομήσουσιν; **μὴ πλανᾶσθε·** οὔτε πόρνοι οὔτε
               εἰδωλολάτραι ... (R)
               Do you not know that the unrighteous will not inherit the
               kingdom of God? **Do not be deceived**, neither fornicators, nor
               idolaters ...

1 Jn 2:15   **Μὴ ἀγαπᾶτε** τὸν κόσμον μηδὲ τὰ ἐν τῷ κόσμῳ (W)
               Do not love the world, nor the things in the world

Rev 5:5   καὶ εἷς ἐκ τῶν πρεσβυτέρων λέγει μοι· **μὴ κλαῖε** (W)
               and one of the elders said to me, "**Do not cry** ..."

The representative examples cited above clearly demonstrate the volitional and directive nuance of the imperative mood. Whether instruction (Matt 6:3; Acts 10:15; Rom 12:2a; 1 John 2:15), rhetorical exhortation (1 Cor 6:9), or comfort (John 6:20; Rev 5:5)[84] the negative imperative in each case is used to present the communicator's directive to avoid doing, feeling, or believing something. Also, these *prohibitions* are presented in a manner that suggests that the communicator desires (for whatever reason) for the negative imperative to be heeded.

The category of *prohibition* is somewhat confusing when superficially viewed in the traditional paradigm. It is usually defined as a negative *command*. This seems straightforward enough; it is a negative *command* in contrast to negative *request, permission*, etc. However, within the traditional paradigm, it

---

[84]These labels are intentionally broad (and overlap) and are not intended to be subclassifications of this category. Some of these verses could be described by more than one label.

often seems more general, merely a negative imperative. This perception may be due to the minimal space often devoted to the imperative, the fluidity of the term *command* in grammatical discussion, and often the omission of (or lack of emphasis) on any negatives in other categories (e.g., *request*).[85] The result is that one may read the grammars with the misunderstanding that μή and the imperative should merely be interpreted as *prohibition*. There are some who clearly suggest the former by noting its specific relationship to the *command* category and by including negatives in other categories.[86]

In addition, considering the similarities between the categories of *command* and *prohibition* and the possibility of negatives in other categories, it seems a separate category of *prohibition* may be misleading. It elevates the negative in strong-forced imperatives to the level of a specific category and minimizes its use in other classifications. This seems unwise if one wishes to maintain a balanced paradigm. Because of potential confusion and the concerns just noted, it seems best to dispose of the *prohibition* category and see negation as an additional feature that may be added to an imperative. This will be briefly developed in chapter 4.

The negative imperative is almost always in the present tense. The negative particle μή with the aorist subjunctive is used for aorist negative directives.[87] The few cases of a negative aorist imperative in the New Testament are all in

---

[85]See for example Young, *Intermediate*, 145-47; however, to be fair, this is probably more due to presentation (as described here) than any actual incorrect classification. In addition, although not exclusively writing about *Koine* Greek, Jannaris' description of prohibition could be faulted with this error. However, he is not using "prohibition" as a label in contrast to a command, request, etc., but as a concept: "Prohibition being nothing else than a negative command . . . or exhortation (deprecation)" A. N. Jannaris, *An Historical Greek Grammar Chiefly of the Attic Dialect* (London: Macmillan, 1897), 449.

[86]See for example Wallace, *Exegetical Syntax*, 487-88 (this includes the classification of Luke 7:6 and John 19:21 as negative *requests*); Boyer, "Imperatives," 36-37. Burton (*Syntax*, 80-81) does not really classify imperatives in his very brief treatment. Therefore, he does not include a category for *prohibitions*; however, he includes 1 Thess 5:19 with "commands and exhortations" and suggests that Luke 6:37 is an hypothesis (i.e., *conditional*) here.

[87]P.Oxy 744.4 (1 BC) has a negative present subjunctive μὴ ἀγωνιᾷς (do not worry/keep from worrying). Although common in modern Greek, this is rare for this period. This letter, probably from a soldier to his wife, cannot be made to represent standard usage. However, it may represent the flexibility of Greek during the period as spoken (and sometimes written) by the masses.

the third person and are recorded words of Jesus.[88] The reason the negated imperative is not generally used in the aorist is uncertain.[89] As far as the meaning of the negative directives in New Testament times is concerned, there does not seem to be any significant reason for the subjunctive to be used for aorist prohibition and present for imperative.[90]

These examples seem to represent the primary usages found in the New Testament. Most grammar seem to agree with these usages. There are a few minor usages often classified. However, some of these seem to be idiomatic in nature[91] and all seem to involve the directional and volitional nuances in some manner.[92]

---

[88]The total number of occurrences of third person aorist negative imperatives is eight: Matt 6:3; 24:17, 18; Mark 13:15 (2x; the second aorist imperative occurrence is negated by μήδέ); Luke 17:31 (2x). Actually, this number is misleading. These passages will briefly be discussed in a subsection of chapter 4.

[89]C. F. D. Moule, *An Idiom Book of New Testament Greek*, 2d ed. (Cambridge: Cambridge University Press, 1959), 21.

[90]Nevertheless, there may be a diachronic reason for the use of the rare second person negative aorist imperative in Greek literature (not in the New Testament). This will be discussed briefly in the next section. Other languages display similar restrictions on the negative imperative. Hebrew, for example, does not permit negative imperatives. These are all realized with a jussive form. Such usage cannot account for the New Testament usage since this is the general pattern in *Koine* and classical Greek also.

[91]This seems to be the case with the *greeting* imperative (see Wallace, *Exegetical Syntax*, 493).

[92]As noted in the previous chapter, many other usages have been suggested. Wallace mentions a debatable category labeled *potential* imperative (ibid., 492). These are imperatives which occur in an apodosis of a conditional statement with another imperative (a conditional imperative) in the protasis. In this case, the imperative seems to have a meaning similar to the future indicative. This will need to be addressed further when conditional imperatives are discussed. Wallace also mentions certain passive imperatives in which the addressee is neither able to obey or fulfill. These he labels *pronouncement* imperatives and suggests they are in imperative form for rhetorical effect. They are statements fulfilled at the moment of speaking (see Mark 1:41, καθαρίσθητι, be cleansed; ibid., 492). These statements are proper speech acts (see chapter 2). The volitional nature of such statements is clear: a recipient is either not present or not capable of fulfilling the desire of speaker. As has been seen, a number of conditions must be met for a proper speech act to exist. Most of these (e.g., authority of the speaker) are pragmatic contextual features. These must be in place for the speech act to achieve its purpose. In addition to these contextual features, certain grammatical elements must also be present, most importantly the passive voice. It does not seem that these speech acts depart from this work's definition of an imperative. The speech act expresses the desire of the speaker and the fulfillment of the action is directive; however, no addressee can fulfill the action; rather, the addressee may be the recipient (if one exists). It is the voice and context which give these imperatives their functional use. Also, it must be noted that these expressions function both on the (verb) phrase and clausal level. This seems to also be the case with conditionals. In order to analyze these imperatives more

This work's larger database confirms the usages described here. The vast majority of passages should be classified as *command*.[93] In all cases, there seems to be a volitional and directive nuance.

The analysis thus far has confirmed this work's thesis that the imperative mood is directional and volitional. It can thus be tentatively concluded that the difference between imperatives is not one of essence but rather force (or at least this is one distinguishing factor). As the mood is looked at more closely in chapter 4, other distinguishing factors among imperatives will be discovered. However, it seems that force is the most important among these. Some imperatives are used as strong directive commands. Others are used with very light force.

Thus far this study has restricted its analysis to imperatives themselves. In order to refine and verify the semantic meaning already mentioned, this study must briefly look beyond imperative in order to determine why it may be used instead of another mood.

Imperative Semantics 2: External Comparisons

In the previous section the imperative mood has been observed in an internal manner. In other words, the mood itself was considered and this study attempted to determine its meaning. This section will approach the question of meaning from a different angle. By comparing the imperative with other moods, this work will attempt to further understand its essence. The best way to proceed

---

fully, they must be considered with their discourse contribution. Because of the unique element of the passive, the analysis will primarily focus on non-passives. Nevertheless, once the particular nature of these imperatives is accounted for, they should fit within the analysis. Also, not all passives are so used, in some cases, the recipient does need to contribute to the fulfillment of the action (e.g., 2 Cor 5:20, . . . καταλλάγητε τῷ θεῷ; . . . be reconciled to God). Birger Bergh demonstrates the existence of real passive imperatives (he is proving the command nature of the imperative in such constructions). Although his primary focus is Latin, his work applies more broadly. Bergh observes two types of passive imperatives. First, logical imperatives which follow a previous imperative ("do come and be looked after"). Second, the type discussed above (speech acts) where the words themselves seem to perform the action ("On Passive Imperatives," *Lingua Posnaniensis* 32-33 [1991]: 31-38).

[93]See for example, Matt 2:13 (3x); 10:27; Mark 14:38 (2x); Luke 5:23; Acts 3:19 (2x); 1 Cor 14:1; Phlm 22; Heb 10:32; Rev 1:11; etc. Further classification will avoided here since the point of this section is to present examples of rather certain traditional classification. The classification here will necessarily be influenced by the classification system being proposed in chapter 4.

is to compare the imperative with constructions that function in a similar manner in an attempt to determine the differences between these constructions and the imperative.[94] There are a number of constructions which seem to mirror imperative usage.[95] Most obvious is the future indicative.[96] The imperative is a mood which looks to the future; therefore, the use of the future indicative for a similar meaning is natural. The aorist subjunctive also plays a prominent role in imperative type constructions. This is especially true for negative directives in the aorist. It is a general rule that aorist negative directives are almost exclusively realized by the aorist subjunctive (see below).

Most grammars discuss constructions which may be used as imperative type clauses (i.e., usually commands).[97] The normal pattern for discussion involves

---

[94]Although defining mood as a sentence type (not grammatically), Donald Davidson's statement is illustrative of this work's purpose, "A satisfactory theory of [sentence level] mood … must assign an element of meaning to utterances in a given mood that is not present in utterances in other moods" ("Moods and Performances," in *In Meaning and Use: Papers Presented at the Second Jerusalem Philosophical Encounter April 1976*, ed. Avishai Margalit [Dordrecht, Holland: D. Reidel Publishing Company, 1979], 14-15). See also the use of Davidson in Deirdre Wilson and Dan Sperber, "Mood and the Analysis of Non-Declarative Sentences," in *Human Agency: Language, Duty and Value*, ed. J. Dancy, J. Moravcsik and C. Taylor (Stanford, CA: Stanford University Press, 1988), 78-79.

[95]One classical grammar lists eight "equivalents" to the imperative with minimal discussion (subjunctive, future, ὅπως with the future, optative with ἄν, infinitive [primarily in poetry and legal language], optative, impatient or passionate questions, δεῖ, χρή, ἄξιον, and δέομαι ὑμῶν with the infinitive (Basil Lanneau Gildersleeve, *Syntax of Classical Greek, from Homer to Demosthenes* [New York: 1900-1911; reprint, New York: American Book Company, 1980], 166-167). This seems to imply that these are interchangeable with the imperative. This study seems to demand a different conclusion.

[96]E.g., Matt 4:10; 1 Pet 1:16. Possibly the most dramatic use of the (negated) future in this way occurs in the recording of the decalogue (LXX: Exod 20:3-17; Deut 5:7-21). This of course reflects the Hebrew imperfects.

[97]Because this work's approach is somewhat different, it is worthwhile to point the reader to a number of such treatments: BDF, 172-74; Boyer, "Imperatives," 46-47, 50-53; Helena Kurzová, *Zur syntaktischen Struktur des Griechoschen /Infinitiv und Nebensatz/* (Prague: Academia Verlag der Tschechoslowakischen Akademie der Wissenschaften, 1968), 52-54; Moulton, *Prolegomena*, 176-83; Porter, *Idioms*, 56-59; Robertson, *Grammar*. 942-46; A. T. Robertson and W. H. Davis, *A New Short Grammar of the Greek Testament for Students Familiar with the Elements of Greek*, 10th ed. (New York: Harper, 1931; reprint, Grand Rapids: Baker Book House, 1977), 306-7; Turner, *Syntax*, 76-78, 93-98; Wallace, *Exegetical Syntax*, 714-24; G. B. Winer, *A Treatise on the Grammar of New Testament Greek*, trans. W. F. Moulton, 3d rev. ed. (Edinburgh: T. & T. Clark: 1882; reprint, Eugene, OR: Wipf and Stock Publishers, 1997), 396-99. These are helpful treatments of the subject. Their existence permits this work to avoid duplication of this approach. However, in some cases sources may be mentioned on specific constructions. In addition see more detailed treatments on specific constructions such as A. P. Salom, "The Imperatival Use of the Participle in the New Testament," *Australian Biblical Review*

a list of various types of constructions which can function in a similar fashion to the imperative. Although this may be helpful for a full treatment of directives in Greek, it does little to shed light on the imperative mood. In this section similar statements will be compared which occur both with imperatives and with other constructions. This should help in determining its uniqueness. Ideally, it would be helpful to have a considerable number of sets of utterances by single individuals that are identical in all matters except for the mood of the verb (e.g., speaker 1: you may eat the fish; eat the fish, you eat the fish; speaker 2: you may leave; leave; you leave; etc). Unfortunately, the database here does not provide such simplicity. Therefore, parallel passages in the synoptic gospels will be looked at where the authors used different moods and attempt to determine the significance of the chosen mood.

The following symbols will be used to indicate parallel and contrasting moods between verses (in parallel sections) respectively, ‖ and ∦. The term "parallel" refers to verbs having the same *mood* in a parallel statement in a parallel section (the same pericope recorded in different gospels). In other words, each grouping of verses is considered parallel (part of parallel pericopes) and within these groups, the verbs may be parallel (represented by ‖) or contrasting (represented by ∦). Therefore, when "parallel" (and "contrasting") are mentioned, the verbs are being discussed. The passages are assumed parallel by their inclusion in the discussion. For the purpose of this work, not every word or phrase in the parallel passage[98] must necessarily be exact. However, it must be clear that the clause in which the verb(s) occurs is conceptually parallel (compare the exact parallels in Mark 1:3 ‖ Matt 3:3 ‖ Luke 3:4[99] with conceptual parallels [with significantly different wording] in Mark 1:15 ‖ Matt 4:17).[100] A different lexeme may occur among the parallel verbs on occasion. In the discussion below, for the sake for thoroughness, lexeme differences will be noted. However, a different lexical choice using the same mood does not contribute to the morphological analysis. In other words, the only concerned is

---

11 (1963), 41-49.

[98]The term "parallel" will also retain its common usage when discussing parallel pericopes.

[99]However, note the slight difference at the end of these verses (αὐτοῦ) with Isa 40:3 (LXX) from which this is a quotation: τοῦ θεοῦ ἡμῶν.

[100]The imperative is the same. Note Mark has an additional unparalleled imperative; however, it is related to the paralleled imperative by καί.

with mood choice, not lexeme choice.[101] Parallels with identical moods are *not* important for the purposes here since little can be determined from them beyond observing that all appropriate authors felt this mood was best suited for the communicative purpose or that one author or more felt comfortable with the expression of the source used.[102] In addition, although noted on occasion, imperatives which have no parallel statements despite very similar surroundings will generally not be discussed.[103] It would be nice to postulate reasons for omissions or additions; however, this seems to involve too much speculation.

Before proceeding, a few cautions are in order; some previously mentioned and reiterated here, others new. It is not entirely possible to know why a specific author uses a specific mood. The reason could be a significant meaning change or it could simply be style or authorial preference. Therefore, as this work proceeds, it is important to keep this limitation in mind. Markan priority will be

---

[101]Further work could be done to determine the relationship between lexeme choice and mood. In cases where certain verbs cannot be realized in certain moods, mood choice is limited. However, it may be worthwhile to pursue this further and look at verb distribution among moods. Results of such a study could add to this project; however, the number of verbs without the imperative or subjunctive options seems to be minimal (tense limitations are more common). Further discussion is beyond the scope of this project.

[102]This section could not have been undertaken without Kurt Aland, ed., *Synopsis of the Four Gospels: Greek-English Edition of the Synopsis Quattuor Evangeliorum*, 10th ed. (Stuttgart: German Bible Society, 1993). However, some passages presented as parallel (in the sense of pericopes, not verbs) by Aland were not so considered here. If the content of Aland's parallels clearly demonstrates that there was no literary dependence nor a common source, it was not treated as parallel. This is clearly the case with the infancy narratives and genealogies in Matthew (chapters 1–2) and Luke (chapters 1–2; 3:23-38) which are printed in parallel columns in Aland. However, if there was even a remote chance of a relationship, the passages are considered parallel (e.g., the Sermons in Matthew 5–7 and roughly Luke 6). In most cases, when the parallel is remote, little conceptual parallels with verbs (as defined above) occur. See the following note for further information on this type of parallel.

[103]In other words, passages will usually not be discussed which are near identical (within a recorded utterance) but one or more gospel has a short imperative clause which does not occur in the other(s). See for example the imperative in Luke 20:2 without parallel in Mark 11:28 ‖ Matt 21:23 (also, Matt 22:17). Luke's two word phrase seems to have been added by him. Passages where extended sections of recorded utterances do not appear or where the entire (or most of the) utterance involves the imperative clause are not in view in this statement. Although in both types the omission or addition may be due to higher discourse features (including story)–not issues of mood, the later types seem more probable. If it could be proven that the small additions/omissions such as Luke 20:2 contrast the imperative with zero mood (instead of subjunctive, etc.) this could be of value; however, at this time I am not certain how one could do this effectively and convincingly or if such a contrast exists at all (thus all may be contrasts at a discourse level). Therefore, all will generally be treated the same and will not factor into the analysis.

assumed for this work's analysis.[104] Therefore, where differences occur, this work will assume Matthew and/or Luke have changed Mark. Where Luke and Matthew differ (without a Markan parallel), the picture is not as simple. A common lost source(s) will be assumed[105] and where good reason exists to postulate whether one has changed the original, it will be done. Otherwise, lack of any independent evidence for such a source makes firm statements in this matter impossible. In any event, the evangelists will be assumed to have actively written their works; therefore, they are individually responsible for the mood used (whether directly from the source or for having changed it).[106]

The imperative mood occurs regularly in the synoptic gospels. There are 720 occurrences in 522 verses.[107] A number of these occurrences are parallel[108] and many imperatives occur in parallel passages where one or more gospel does not include the detail of another. These are the same pericopes recorded in

---

[104]See among others: Robert H. Stein, *The Synoptic Problem: An Introduction* (Grand Rapids: Baker Book House, 1987).

[105]It may be helpful to label this source Q; however, the associations of this label may make it less desirable. Whether or not a source of sayings existed as some have postulated as Q seems uncertain. Nevertheless, if Q merely refers to shared material between Luke and Matthew, it would apply here. See the cautious words (although going further than this work's position) of Stein on the subject (ibid., 109-12).

[106]I am not unaware of problems with Markan priority. W. R. Farmer, although not changing the overall consensus, has reopened the debate in this area (*The Synoptic Problem: A Critical Analysis* [New York: Macmillan, 1964]). What was considered a certain conclusion of New Testament scholarship from the end of the nineteenth-century until recently, now is approached with more caution. See the discussion of the impact of Farmer on the theory of Markan priority in Stephen Neill and Tom Wright, *The Interpretation of the New Testament: 1861–1986*, 2d ed. (Oxford: Oxford University Press, 1988), 360. In addition, I am not completely comfortable with some pillars of Markan priority such as a primitive (or poor) Markan grammar being changed or corrected by the others (see David Alan Black, "Discourse Analysis, Synoptic Criticism, and Markan Grammar: Some Methodological Considerations," in *Linguistics and New Testament Interpretation*, ed. David Alan Black, Katharine Barnwell, and Stephen Levinsohn [Nashville: Broadman Press, 1992], 90-98). Nevertheless, it seems to be the best solution at this time (and it does seem to handle even the grammatical data from the aforementioned argument better than other approaches). Therefore, due to a lack of a better solution and in light of the state of general New Testament scholarship in this matter, the presupposition of Markan priority seems prudent. Nevertheless, since the gospel writers are assumed to be conscious participants in the writing of their works, they are responsible for the words and structures used, whether they maintained or changed their original.

[107]Matthew: 286 occurrences in 209 verses; Mark: 150 in 107; Luke: 284 in 206. Many of these occur in unique pericopes to the individual gospels. Unparalleled imperatives will not be discussed in this section nor listed in a footnote.

[108]These parallels are not important for the analysis and therefore are not included here. A list of all parallels is included in appendix 4.

different gospels but for some reason one or more gospel does not include a parallel clause to the other(s) with the imperative (using the term "parallel" as mentioned above). For example, see the parallel statement in the temptation narrative recorded in Matt 4:3 ‖ Luke 4:3 and Matt 4:6 ‖ Luke 4:9. The parallel pericope recorded in Mark 1:12-13 does not record any of the detail mentioned in the other two synoptics and therefore does not present an opportunity for parallel statements.[109] This section is concerned only with those relationships where there is disagreement. However, there are occasions where two gospels will be parallel against another.[110]

The synoptic data reveal that the various forms often noted as additional means of communicating imperative meaning contrast with the imperative mood in similar and/or parallel contexts. Subjunctives, future indicatives, other indicatives, infinitives, and participles all realize similar propositions. However, this cannot suggest that these are merely interchangeable. In most cases, a

---

[109]A similar situation where this type of omitted parallel exists is when one or more gospel includes an imperative in direct speech where its parallel(s) does not include the direct speech (e.g., Mark 4:39 [2 impvs] against Matt 8:26 ‖ Luke 8:24; Matt 17:7 [2 impvs] a statement not in the parallel pericopes: Mark 9:2-10 ‖ Luke 9:28-36; Mark 9:25 [1 impv] against Matt 17:18 ‖ Luke 9:42). In most cases these situations are also unimportant because they are single occurrences and no verbal (i.e., the verb) parallel exists. This is true for the examples cited here (it is also likely that the Luke and Matthew temptation narratives have no dependence on Mark–except possibly for chronological placement). The omission of the detail apparently does not fit the purpose of the author (a decision based on higher level discourse considerations). However, when only a little content is omitted (such as just the phrase with the imperative, not merely the entire direct speech or narrative section) it may be worth pursuing further to attempt to determine if the imperative itself may be the reason for the omission. In most cases, the omission seems to be unrelated to the imperative but rather the phrase, clause, or larger section is simply not deemed to contribute to author's purpose and thus omitted (see Matt 11:4 which is not included in Luke's parallel passage [7:24-35] and the imperative clause in Mark 14:6 which is not found in Matt 26:10 ‖ Luke 7:44; if no dependence is assumed, the additional information is irrelevant to the author without it–thus, omission in this case is an inapplicable term). There are many parallel pericopes between two synoptics where the portion including the imperative in one is not present in the other without any significant reason evident (for the purposes here). These will not be listed here (and thus considered independent). Also, when all three gospels share a common pericope and only two demonstrate a parallel verbal clause, if they are parallel in mood, they are listed in appendix 4 (and occasionally in footnotes here) with the two parallel passages only (if mentioning the third seems appropriate, this will be done in parentheses; this is the case with the temptation narrative–it was only considered a parallel between Matt and Luke); if there is a difference in mood, this will be discussed in the text.

[110]It is only the non-parallel relationships with which this work is interested. However, the parallel relationships are mentioned here to get a fuller picture in cases where one disagrees with two.

reason for the difference may be noted. I am not suggesting that there can never be interchangeable forms. Language is simply too complex for such a statement. Nevertheless, differences can often be noted when one author uses an imperative where another uses a different form.

Every parallel which meets the requirements described above will be discussed. In addition to the division of examples by form, those examples will be marked with an asterisk (*) where a direct quotation is contrasted with a description in narrative. The reason for this is twofold: first, it keeps all the similar forms together; second, the use of the asterisk here will simplify the discussion of this phenomenon later in this section.[111]

One of the most significant mood interchanges occurs between the subjunctive and the imperative. There are two types of interchange found in the examples between these moods. First, when an author chooses to use a negative prohibition in the aorist, the normal realization is the subjunctive (in contrast to a present imperative)[112]:

Matt 5:40   **ἄφες** αὐτῷ καὶ τὸ ἱμάτιον
                 allow (give to) him also your coat

Luke 6:29   καὶ τὸν χιτῶνα <u>μὴ κωλύσῃς</u>
                 and <u>do not withhold</u> your shirt

Matt 6:31, 34   <u>μὴ</u> οὖν <u>μεριμνήσητε</u> λέγοντες· τί φάγωμεν; ἤ· τί πίωμεν;
                 ἤ· τί περιβαλώμεθα; ... [34] <u>μὴ</u> οὖν <u>μεριμνήσητε</u> εἰς τὴν
                 αὔριον
                 therefore, <u>do not be anxious</u> saying, "what should we eat?" or
                 "what should we drink?" or "with what should we be clothed?"
                 ... [34] therefore, <u>do not be anxious</u> concerning tomorrow

---

[111]This will provide easy access to these examples without the need to restate them.

[112]See chapter 2 for a discussion of the importance of the contrast in verbal aspect between the aorist and present.

Luke 12:29, 32   καὶ ὑμεῖς **μὴ ζητεῖτε** τί φάγητε καὶ τί πίητε καὶ μὴ μετεωρίζεσθε (second imperative not paralleled–thus, not in bold) ... [32] **Μὴ φοβοῦ**, ...

and **do not seek** what you should eat and what you should drink and do not worry ... [32] **Do not be afraid**, ...

Matt 10:28   καὶ **μὴ φοβεῖσθε** ἀπὸ τῶν ἀποκτεννόντων τὸ σῶμα ...

and **do not fear** those who kill the body ...

Luke 12:4   <u>μὴ φοβηθῆτε</u> ἀπὸ τῶν ἀποκτεινόντων τὸ σῶμα ...

<u>do not fear</u> those who kill the body ...[113]

Matt 10:9-10a   <u>Μὴ κτήσησθε</u> (aorist subjunctive) χρυσὸν μηδὲ ἄργυρον μηδὲ χαλκὸν εἰς τὰς ζώνας ὑμῶν, μὴ πήραν εἰς ὁδὸν ...

<u>Do not take</u> gold nor silver nor copper in your belts, no bag for a trip ...

Luke 10:4   **μὴ βαστάζετε** (present imperative) βαλλάντιον, μὴ πήραν, μὴ ὑποδήματα ...

do not carry a purse, nor bag, nor sandals ...[114]

---

[113]In the case of the Matt 10:28 ∥ Luke 12:4 example, it is likely that the aspectual character is desired. Within this context, the same verb is paralleled two more times. In the first instance (10:28 ∥ 12:5) Matthew uses the present imperative (without negation) and Luke uses the aorist imperative (without negation) thus each maintains the aspect of the previous negated directive (imperative and subjunctive respectively; note, at the end of the clause, Luke repeats the exact aorist imperative, this seems to emphasize or reinforce the directive). In the second parallel, both authors use the negated present imperative (identical to Matthew's first form in 10:28). It is possible that Luke changes aspect here to emphasize the more general nature of the directive which Matthew has maintained throughout. However, the difference between Matthew and Luke may be insignificant in light of the meaning of the entire pericope which is basically identical. No certain statements speculating the reason for the aspect shift can be put forth.

[114]This parallel is questionable: Matthew's account is about the sending of the twelve and Luke's account is about the sending of the seventy. However, it is possible that similar instruction was given to both groups (most likely in Aramaic). Also, there is no reason that these instructions could not have appeared in the other context (assuming the authors [or their source] wanted a specific aspect here demanding the choice of mood).

Mark 13:7 (||[115] Matt 24:6[116])   ὅταν δὲ ἀκούσητε πολέμους καὶ ἀκοὰς
πολέμων, **μὴ θροεῖσθε**
but when you hear of wars and news of wars,
do not be alarmed

Luke 21:9   ὅταν δὲ ἀκούσητε πολέμους καὶ ἀκαταστασίας, <u>μὴ</u>
<u>πτοηθῆτε</u>
when you hear of wars and disturbances, <u>do not be terrified</u>

This type of interchange is of little value since it is impossible to know whether the use of the aorist subjunctive is due to the author's desire for a certain aspectual quality or the modal quality. However, although certainty cannot be achieved in every instance,[117] it would not be unwise to maintain that it is the aspectual quality primarily desired for the following reason: the normal means of communicating a negative directive in the aorist is the negative aorist subjunctive.[118] The normal present negative directive is the imperative. Thus, if present (imperfective) aspect is desired, the negative imperative is used. If the aorist (perfective) aspect is appropriate, the negated aorist subjunctive is used. The function of the aorist subjunctive when used as a negative directive seems to be consistent with what one would expect from a negative aorist imperative (if it was commonly used for such a purpose).[119] The negated aorist subjunctive

---

[115]Where parallels exist, usually only the first mentioned is quoted directly. Unless significant differences exist in the parallel, only differences in the verb itself (e.g., lexeme, person, etc) will be noted.

[116]Matthew has an additional imperative (ὁρᾶτε) preceding the negative imperative here.

[117]In other words, one cannot know for certain what mood the author would have used if the verb was present or not negated.

[118]E.g., Matt 5:17; 2 Thess 3:13. The negated second person aorist imperative is very rare in ancient Greek literature (however, see Homer *Iliad* 4.410; 18.134; *Odyssey* 24.248) and does not occur in the New Testament. The negated third person imperative is also rare but does occur in the New Testament (8x; see chapter 4). The negated third person aorist subjunctive does occur in the New Testament as a prohibition (1 Cor 16:11; 2 Thess 2:3) although not exclusively as such (Mark 10:15; Luke 7:23; Rom 4:8; it is much more common not functioning as a directive). Nevertheless, the negated third person aorist imperatives cannot be explained due to a lack of a subjunctive option.

[119]There does not seem to be any identifiable synchronic reason for the use of the aorist subjunctive in negative prohibitions. It functions as an imperative would. Schwyzer–Debrunner simply see the negative aorist subjunctive as the proper form ("Teils alt, teils jünger ist μή Imper. Aor., regelrecht dagegen μή mit Imper. Präs" Eduard Schwyzer, *Griechische Grammatik, ii. Syntax und syntaktische Stilistik*, ed. Albert Debrunner [Munich: C. H. Beck, 1950], 343).

is not used exclusively for this purpose.[120] Nevertheless, in light of the parallels it seems probable that the imperative would be used in these cases.[121] Therefore, these are not *real* examples of mood differences in parallel.[122]

The second type of interchange occurs when one synoptic includes a subjunctive in a clause introduced by a word such as ἐάν, ἕως, ἵνα, or ὅταν[123] which demands a subjunctive verb. Whether it is the conjunction which governs the choice of the mood or the mood which demands the specific conjunction is

---

However, there may be an historical explanation for the rare use of the second person negated aorist imperative. Laurence Stephens, analyzing the negative second person aorists directives in Homer (only thirteen total: ten subjunctive [*Iliad* 5.684; 9.33; 9.552; 15.115; 23.407; 24.568; 24.779; *Odyssey* 3.55; 11.251; 15.263]; three imperative [Iliad 4.410; 18.134; *Odyssey* 24.248]) suggests that the aorist imperatives are remains of negative aorist injunctives which were used late into the oral epic period (late into the oral epic tradition), "The Origins of Homeric Peculiarity: MH Plus Aorist Imperative," *Transactions of the American Philological Association* 113 (1983): 69-78. If this is the case, second person negated aorist imperatives may have less in common with the negative present imperative than the negative aorist subjunctive. However, although interesting, this is unhelpful for study since there are no second person negative aorist imperatives in the New Testament. Also, although third person negative aorist imperatives do occur in the New Testament, they are not part of Stephen's study nor does this seem like a better explanation for its presence than what will be suggested in chapter 4. In addition, Stephen's study was with a very minimal amount of data (it is actually quite shocking that only thirteen negative aorist directives occur in Homer) and demands quite a leap in time from the late oral epic period to the time of Homer (not to mention to the time of the New Testament).

[120]For example: Jas 2:16; in dependent clauses: Matt 6:18; Heb 12:3; 1 John 2:1; 2 John 8; Rev 18:4; with ἐαν μή: Rev 2:5; 3:3; with οὐ μή: Matt 5:20, 26; Gal 5:16; 2 Pet 2:10. As mentioned above, the most common use of the third person negative aorist subjunctive is *not* directive.

[121]M. W. Humphreys suggests that the aorist subjunctive may be used instead of the imperative in negative commands for politeness reasons ("On Negative Commands in Greek," *Transactions of the American Philological Association* 7 [1876]: 46-49). He maintains that the negative imperative may be too strong of a prohibition in some cases. However, this explanation does not really account for the data. First, as noted above, there does not seem to be any difference in force with the subjective than what one would see with an imperative. Second, the difference between present and aorist is best accounted for by their aspectual differences, not politeness. Third, Humphreys' suggestion really does not account for why the aorist is not used in a negative imperative construction. Why not retain both? The subjunctive could be used when a more polite directive is necessary for both present and aorist. In this manner, the aspectual differences could be maintained.

[122]Another example of imperative and aorist subjunctive prohibitions in the synoptics is: Mark 13:21 (impv) ∥ Matt 24:23 ∥ Luke 17:23 (subj).

[123]There are other conjunctions, etc. that govern the subjunctive. However, these are the only ones which appear in the examples.

uncertain.[124] Because of the conjunction, the subjunctive clause must be a subordinate clause. There is no example of a contrast between an imperative and a subjunctive where both are in independent clauses. This seems significant and will be discussed briefly below. Nevertheless, because one cannot be certain whether it was the desire for a subordinate clause or a desire for the subjunctive mood that caused the mood choice, the use of individual passages from this type of data will be somewhat minimalistic (noting cautions already stated). Nevertheless, the contrast between the imperative in the main clause and the subjunctive in a subordinate clause suggest a significant purpose for the imperative. This purpose is somewhat explained by the directive and volitional natures of the mood. Relatively speaking, these are highlighted verbs. They stand out in the discourse. Not much can be said about the specifics, but one can note this general observation revealed by this contrast.

Mark 5:23   ἵνα ἐλθὼν ἐπιθῇς τὰς χεῖρας αὐτῇ
                  that you may come and lay your hand on her

Matt 9:18   ἀλλὰ ἐλθὼν ἐπίθες τὴν χεῖρά σου ἐπ' αὐτήν
                  but come and lay your hand upon her

Mark 6:10 (‖Matt 10:11)   ἐκεῖ μένετε (Matt: μείνατε) ἕως ἂν ἐξέλθητε
                           ἐκεῖθεν
                           remain there until you depart from there

Luke 9:4   ἐκεῖ μένετε καὶ ἐκεῖθεν ἐξέρχεσθε.
                  Remain there and depart from there

Mark 6:25   ᾐτήσατο λέγουσα· θέλω ἵνα ἐξαυτῆς δῷς μοι ἐπὶ πίνακι
                  τὴν κεφαλὴν Ἰωάννου τοῦ βαπτιστοῦ
                  She said, "I desire that at once you give me on a platter the
                  head of John the Baptist

---

[124]This is unfortunate because if one could demonstrate the clause structure is dictated by the mood choice, these contrastive pairs would be even more valuable. Nevertheless, these are helpful contrasts which shed light on the use of the imperative mood.

Matt 14:7   **δός** μοι, φησίν, ὧδε ἐπὶ πίνακι τὴν κεφαλὴν Ἰωάννου
              τοῦ βαπτιστοῦ
              "**Give** to me," she said, "here, upon a platter, the head of John
              the baptist"

Mark 11:22   καὶ ἀποκριθεὶς ὁ Ἰησοῦς λέγει αὐτοῖς· **ἔχετε** πίστιν
              θεοῦ
              and answering Jesus said to them, "**Have** faith in God"

Matt 21:21a   ἀποκριθεὶς δὲ ὁ Ἰησοῦς εἶπεν αὐτοῖς· ἀμὴν λέγω ὑμῖν,
              <u>ἐὰν</u> <u>ἔχητε</u> πίστιν καὶ μὴ διακριθῆτε ...
              and answering Jesus said to them, "Truly, I say to you, <u>if</u> you
              <u>have</u> faith and do not doubt ..."

Mark 11:25   Καὶ ὅταν στήκετε προσευχόμενοι, **ἀφίετε** εἴ τι ἔχετε
              κατά τινος
              And whenever you stand praying, **forgive**, if you have
              anything against anyone

Matt 6:14   <u>Ἐὰν</u> γὰρ <u>ἀφῆτε</u> τοῖς ἀνθρώποις τὰ παραπτώματα αὐτῶν
              ...
              For <u>if</u> you <u>forgive</u> men [or, others] their trespasses ...[125]

---

[125]The contexts of these two passages make this a difficult parallel event; however, as elsewhere the wording and thought of the passages themselves are very close and thus might go back to a parallel source/event (or sayings which may have been repeated during Jesus ministry).

Mark 11:29   ὁ δὲ' Ἰησοῦς εἶπεν αὐτοῖς· ἐπερωτήσω ὑμᾶς ἕνα λόγον,
καὶ **ἀποκρίθητέ** μοι καὶ ἐρῶ ὑμῖν ἐν ποίᾳ ἐξουσίᾳ
ταῦτα ποιῶ
and Jesus said to them, "I will ask you one thing, and **answer**
me and I will tell you by what authority I do these things"[126]

Matt 21:24   ἀποκριθεὶς δὲ ὁ' Ἰησοῦς εἶπεν αὐτοῖς· ἐρωτήσω ὑμᾶς
κἀγὼ λόγον ἕνα, ὃν <u>ἐὰν εἴπητέ</u> μοι κἀγὼ ὑμῖν ἐρῶ ἐν
ποίᾳ ἐξουσίᾳ ταῦτα ποιῶ
and Jesus said to them, "I also will ask you one thing, which <u>if</u>
you <u>might answer</u> me, I also will tell you by what authority I
do these things"

Luke 20:3   ἀποκριθεὶς δὲ εἶπεν πρὸς αὐτούς· ἐρωτήσω ὑμᾶς κἀγὼ
λόγον, καὶ **εἴπατέ** μοι
and answering, he said to them, "I also will ask you a thing and
tell me"

Matt 26:63 (∥ Mark 14:61[127])   ἐξορκίζω σε κατὰ τοῦ θεοῦ τοῦ ζῶντος
<u>ἵνα</u> ἡμῖν <u>εἴπῃς</u> εἰ σὺ εἶ ὁ χριστὸς ὁ
υἱὸς τοῦ θεοῦ
I put you under oath in the name of[128] the
living God, <u>that</u> you <u>should tell</u> us whether
you are the Christ, the Son of God

Luke 22:67   εἰ σὺ εἶ ὁ χριστός, **εἰπὸν** ἡμῖν
if you are the Christ, **tell** us

---

[126]Mark 11:30 includes an identical imperative (ἀποκρίθητέ μοι); however, this is
unparalleled in the other synoptics. Also, Luke 20:2 includes an imperative phrase (εἰπὸν ἡμῖν)
unparalleled in either Mark or Matthew. Luke's addition may serve to heighten the boldness of
his opponents.

[127]The parallel passage in Mark 14:61 also has a mood contrast with the imperative;
however, Mark has an indicative and will be listed also in that section.

[128]Or "by the living God;" however, the expression seems idiomatic as reflected in the
translation.

Matt 6:9   οὕτως οὖν **προσεύχεσθε** ὑμεῖς …
                 Pray then like this …

Luke 11:1   <u>ὅταν</u> <u>προσεύχησθε</u> **λέγετε** …
                 <u>When</u> you <u>pray</u>, **say** …

There is a need for an imperative in the introduction to this prayer. Luke's choice to use the more mundane λέγετε may be due to his desire to place the emphasis upon the imperatives within the prayer itself. This may also be accomplished through the temporal subordinate subjunctive clause. In either case, the use of the subordinate clause seems to demand that a little more emphasis be placed upon the prayer as opposed to the teaching event. This observation is similar to what will be noted about an author's use of the participle and indicative in some cases. What seems to be emerging is a tendency for some to use the imperative in a more forefronted manner. This would seem rather natural considering the directive nature of the mood. This really needs much further verification and such a study falls outside the scope of this project.[129] Nevertheless, at minimum this observation serves to strengthen the conclusion about the directive nature of the mood.

The final three examples (in undisputed parallel passages) of the conjunction with subjunctive and imperative contrast reflect a pattern which will be encountered much more frequently with other forms. The imperative is used in direct discourse while other moods (or forms) are used in narrative describing the event. In the first example, the imperative occurs in direct discourse while the parallels in Matthew and Mark (indicative and subjunctive) and Matthew (indicative, subjunctive, and subjunctive) are explanatory of the event recorded in Luke.

---

[129]A thorough study of the various moods at a discourse level is needed to follow through with this observation.

*Mark 15:11   οἱ δὲ ἀρχιερεῖς ἀνέσεισαν[130] τὸν ὄχλον ἵνα μᾶλλον τὸν Βαραββᾶν ἀπολύσῃ αὐτοῖς
               but the chief priests incited the crowd that he might release Barabbas instead

*Matt 27:20   Οἱ δὲ ἀρχιερεῖς καὶ οἱ πρεσβύτεροι ἔπεισαν τοὺς ὄχλους ἵνα αἰτήσωνται τὸν Βαραββᾶν, τὸν δὲ' Ἰησοῦν ἀπολέσωσιν
               But the chief priests and the elders persuaded the crowds that they might release Barabbas and might kill Jesus

*Luke 23:18   'Ανέκραγον δὲ παμπληθεὶ λέγοντες· **αῖρε** τοῦτον, **ἀπόλυσον** δὲ ἡμῖν τὸν Βαραββᾶν
               But they cried out together saying, "**Take away** this man and **release** to us Barabbas

It seems likely that only one verb is parallel (Mark: ἀπολύσῃ; Matthew: αἰτήσωνται; and Luke: **ἀπόλυσον**); however, what is of primary interest is the manner in which the different authors chose to include the event.[131] Luke gives the reader an up-close and personal use of the imperative as the event is recorded. It is likely that this was a conscious choice on the part of Luke to change his source. The other passages seem a little more distant and serve to explain what happen (not show the reader).

The two other examples for imperative and subjunctive interchange also involve direct discourse and narrative description. However, these parallels are not as pure as the previous. In these examples, the subjunctive also occurs in a subordinate clause with an appropriate particle.[132] In the first example, Luke

---

[130]The parallel indicatives (in Mark, ἀνέσεισαν [incited] and in Matthew, ἔπεισαν [persuaded]) are unparalleled in Luke who does not inform the reader of the behind the scenes persuasive activity of the leaders.

[131]A question of sources here is not really relevant because, as mentioned above, it is being maintained that an author *chose* to describe the event in the way he penned it. It seems like Matthew merely used Mark with little change; however, Luke departed from this and used discourse. One cannot know if Luke had an additional source or changed his material. Nor is one able to discern whether Matthew consciously thought of (and rejected) the more direct option chosen by Luke.

[132]They are included here rather than above because the distinction of discourse and narrative will become more important as this work proceeds.

gives one an up close and personal look at the event while Mark merely describes it. In the second, it is Mark providing the reader with close perspective and it is Matthew who describes it.

*Mark 6:8   ἵνα μηδὲν <u>αἴρωσιν</u> εἰς ὁδόν
              <u>that</u> they <u>should take</u> nothing for the journey

*Luke 9:3   μηδὲν **αἴρετε** εἰς τὴν ὁδόν
              take nothing for the journey

*Mark 6:22   εἶπεν ὁ βασιλεὺς τῷ κορασίῳ· **αἴτησόν** με ὅ ἐὰν θέλῃς,
              καὶ δώσω σοι
              the king said to the girl, "**Ask** me whatever you wish and I will
              give it [to] you"

*Matt 14:7   ὅθεν μεθ᾽ ὅρκου ὡμολόγησεν αὐτῇ δοῦναι ὅ <u>ἐὰν</u>
              <u>αἰτήσηται</u>
              therefore, with an oath he promised to give to her <u>whatever</u> she
              <u>asked</u>

Now this work will return to an interesting observation about the use of the subjunctive in subjunctive/imperative contrasts. With the exception of the negative aorist subjunctive, all subjunctives in synoptic parallels with imperatives occur in subordinate clauses. This may suggest that authors using the imperatives desire to stress the directive in these cases. There is no evidence that one author prefers the imperative to the subjunctive in the examples.[133] When (especially) Matthew and Luke change Mark, the examples show both changes to the imperative and to the subjunctive.

In addition to the subjunctive, there is significant interchange with the

---

[133]Since the analysis thus far has been comparative, one cannot rule out that the subjunctive functions as a rather milder form of command (R. W. Moore, *Comparative Greek and Latin Syntax* [London: G. Bell and Sons, 1934], 85; Moore acknowledges that this is the case "especially in Latin;" although he does not limit it to Latin). However, one finds no evidence of this based on the comparative analysis of parallel passages. Also, since the imperative may have different forces, such a conclusion seem less probable for the Greek of the New Testament. See chapter 4.

indicative mood.[134] There are a number of different patterns. First, there is the contrast between the future indicative and the imperative.[135]

Matt 8:8   καὶ ἰαθήσεται ὁ παῖς μου
                and my servant <u>will be healed</u>

Luke 7:7   καὶ ἰαθήτω ὁ παῖς μου
                and **let** my servant **be healed**[136]

Matt 10:27   ὃ λέγω ὑμῖν ἐν τῇ σκοτίᾳ **εἴπατε** ἐν τῷ φωτί, καὶ ὃ εἰς
                τὸ οὖς ἀκούετε **κηρύξατε** ἐπὶ τῶν δωμάτων
                What I speak to you in the darkness, **speak** in the light, and
                what you hear whispered in your ear, **proclaim** upon the roofs

---

[134]Although the optative certainly can exhibit imperative-type meaning (see Moulton, *Prolegomena*, 179; Porter, *Idioms*, 222-23), there are no examples of this contrast in the synoptics.

[135]David S. New argues that the future indicative (with and without the negative) which often occurs in Old Testament quotations is not a Hebraism but an real imperative-like command. However it is not identical to the imperative mood. Rather, the future portrays the action as fact ("The Injunctive Future and Existential Injunction in the New Testament." *Journal for the Study of the New Testament* 44 [1991]: 125–26). See also on the future indicative as a command: Basil G. Mandilaras, *The Verb in the Greek Non-Literary Papyri* (Athens: Hellenic Ministry of Culture and Sciences, 1973), 188-90, 303-4. For a discussion of the future as a prohibition, see R. Whitelaw, "On Μή Prohibitive with Future Indicative," *Classical Review* 2 (1888): 322-23.

[136]Many important manuscripts have the future indicative (as Matthew): א, A, C, D, etc. and the manuscripts represented by gothic M in NA[27]. However, the imperative also has strong external support including P[75] and B. Internal evidence would seem to favor the imperative because it is difficult to explain why one would change from the less volitional future to the imperative directed at Jesus and at the same time differ from Matthew. The tendency would seem to be to harmonize to Matthew and use a less direct form spoken to Jesus. Although this work will suggest a possible reason to favor the future in chapter 4, it seems best to maintain the imperative here (and ultimately there). The harmonization of imperative to future seems to occur occasionally. See also the discussion of Luke 21:19 (imperative) ⫽ Mark 13:13 ‖ Matt 24:13 (future) below.

Luke 12:2   ἀνθ᾽ ὧν ὅσα ἐν τῇ σκοτίᾳ εἴπατε ἐν τῷ φωτὶ
<u>ἀκουσθήσεται</u>, καὶ ὅ πρὸς τὸ οὖς ἐλαλήσατε ἐν τοῖς
ταμείοις <u>κηρυχθήσεται</u> ἐπὶ τῶν δωμάτων
Therefore, as much as you said in the light, it <u>will be heard</u> in
the light, and whatever you whispered in private rooms, it <u>will
be proclaimed</u> upon the roofs

Although the first part of Luke 12:2 is not identical to Matt 10:27, the imperative clause in Matthew (with εἴπατε) does seem parallel to the passive future indicative in Luke.[137] This example enlightens the difference between the imperative and future indicative. In the former the outcome is not guaranteed. It is dependent upon the hearers' response to the directive. In the latter the outcome seems more certain.[138] This difference is further emphasized by the use of the third person and passive in Luke which removes the focus from the hearers.

Matt 25:21-23   ἔφη αὐτῷ ὁ κύριος αὐτοῦ· εὖ, δοῦλε ἀγαθὲ καὶ πιστέ,
ἐπὶ ὀλίγα ἧς πιστός, ἐπὶ πολλῶν σε <u>καταστήσω</u>· εἴσελθε
εἰς τὴν χαρὰν τοῦ κυρίου σου. ... 23 ἔφη αὐτῷ ὁ κύριος
αὐτοῦ· εὖ, δοῦλε ἀγαθὲ καὶ πιστέ, ἐπὶ ὀλίγα ἧς πιστός,
ἐπὶ πολλῶν σε <u>καταστήσω</u>· εἴσελθε εἰς τὴν χαρὰν τοῦ
κυρίου σου
his lord said to him, "Well done good and faithful slave, you
are faithful with few [things], I <u>will put</u> you in charge of many;
enter into the joy of your lord ..." his lord said to him [another
slave], "Well done good and faithful slave, you are faithful
with few [things], I <u>will put</u> you in charge of many; enter into
the joy of your lord"

---

[137]The form εἴπατε also occurs in the Luke passage. However, this is not parallel with the imperative with the same form in Matthew (the context makes clear that the form in Matthew is imperative and the form in Luke is indicative). The aorist indicative εἴπατε in Luke is better viewed as parallel with the similar word, λέγω.

[138]This analysis is supported by that of David New mentioned previously.

Luke 19:17-19 καὶ εἶπεν αὐτῷ· εὖγε, ἀγαθὲ δοῦλε, ὅτι ἐν ἐλαχίστῳ
πιστὸς ἐγένου, **ἴσθι** ἐξουσίαν ἔχων ἐπάνω δέκα πόλεων.
... 19 εἶπεν δὲ καὶ τούτῳ· καὶ σὺ ἐπάνω **γίνου** πέντε
πόλεων
and he said to him, "Well done, good slave; because you were
faithful in the insignificant, **be** in authority over ten cities ..."
and he said to him [another slave] "also, and you **be** over five
cities"

Although the accounts in Matt 25:14-30 and Luke 19:11-27 are very similar, there are significant differences. Even the verses quoted here are quite different. Matthew's verses 25:21 and 25:23 are identical and many details of the passage differ.[139] This may cause one to question wether the two accounts are parallel at all. However, the imperatives in Matt 25:28 and Luke 19:24 seem clearly parallel and despite differences in detail, there are significant similarities. Therefore, it seems probable that these are parallel and it was Luke who probably made the changes to an original.[140] This then is a probable example of a future indicative being changed into an imperative.

The use of the future does give the passage a different sense. The focus seems to be on the *resolve* of the speaker. In the imperative passage, the speaker is bestowing the privileges on his servants. Given the social status of the parties involved (servant and master), the future may demonstrate the foregone nature of the action commanded in the parallel. It is unlikely that the imperatives would not be realized. A similar social distinction seems to be in place between teacher and disciple. However, this time it seems likely that Luke changed from the imperative of Mark (followed by Matthew) to the future. Two further examples seem to confirm the *resolve* nuance for the future:

---

[139]Concerning imperatives, the repeated imperative phrase in Matthew (**εἴσελθε** εἰς τὴν χαρὰν τοῦ κυρίου σου) is unparalleled in Luke. Also, considering the entire pericope, Luke 19:13 includes an imperative in an unparalleled saying. Also, The final verses of this pericope each contain imperatives (Matt 1; Luke 2x). However, Matt 25:30 and Luke 19:27 contain no parallel material.

[140]If parallel, the repetition in Matthew 25:21 and 25:23 would seem to suggest that if a common source underlie both accounts, Luke was more likely to have changed the original. It is unlikely that Matthew would change a unique (relatively speaking) saying to simply duplicate the previous. However, although not assumed here, it also fits the data to maintain that Matthew was Luke's original.

Mark 14:14 (‖ Matt 26:18b)   εἴπατε τῷ οἰκοδεσπότῃ (Matt: αὐτῷ)
                                Say to the house owner (Matt "him")

Luke 22:10   καὶ <u>ἐρεῖτε</u> τῷ οἰκοδεσπότῃ τῆς οἰκίας
                  and <u>you will say</u> to owner of the house

Mark 11:3   καὶ ἐάν τις ὑμῖν εἴπῃ· τί ποιεῖτε τοῦτο; **εἴπατε·** ὁ
                  κύριος αὐτοῦ χρείαν ἔχει, καὶ εὐθὺς αὐτὸν ἀποστέλλει
                  πάλιν ὧδε
                  and if anyone says to you, "Why are you doing this?" **Say,**
                  "The lord has need of it ..."

Luke 19:31 (‖ Matt 21:3 with minor differences)   καὶ ἐάν τις ὑμᾶς
                                                     ἐρωτᾷ· διὰ τί λύετε;
                                                     οὕτως <u>ἐρεῖτε</u>· ὅτι ὁ
                                                     κύριος αὐτοῦ χρείαν
                                                     ἔχει
                                                     and if anyone asks you,
                                                     "Why are you untying
                                                     [it]?" You <u>will say,</u> "The
                                                     Lord has need of it"

Finally, one further example is worth noting. Although there is a textual problem, it seem likely that this example best fits in this section.

Mark 13:13 (‖ Matt 24:13)   ὁ δὲ ὑπομείνας εἰς τέλος οὗτος <u>σωθήσεται</u>
                            but the one enduring to the end <u>will be saved</u>

Luke 21:19   ἐν τῇ ὑπομονῇ ὑμῶν **κτήσασθε** τὰς ψυχὰς ὑμῶν
                  in your endurance, **acquire** [or: you will acquire] your life

In the Luke passage, NA[27] (following the text established in NA[26]) includes the aorist imperative which has strong external evidence (including ℵ, D, L, W, f^1, and vast majority of manuscripts represented by gothic M). However, there is equally strong evidence in support of the future indicative (κτησεσθε) which was included in the 25th edition of Nestle-Aland's text (support includes A, B, Θ, f^{13}, and 33). Fitzmyer suggests that whichever reading is correct, a translation in English like the future indicative is demanded.[141]

Although the internal evidence also seems rather closely divided, it seems like the aorist imperative is definitely the more difficult reading. This is especially true if one attempts to maintain the imperative meaning as has been developed in this chapter. If Fitzmyer is correct, this is an example of an imperative functioning as a future indicative. However, although the imperative does function in a similar manner to the future, the future does not seem to include the directive feature as part of its semantic (unaffected) meaning. The imperative, however, seems to retain this force. Therefore, this observation may seem to shift the internal evidence slightly in favor of the future. Although the imperative is a more difficult reading, assuming Fitzmyer's translation observation is correct, the burden of proof seems to be to on those wishing to prove the imperative is used this way. The imperative does not seem to be used as Fitzmyer suggests elsewhere in the New Testament. Thus, Fitzmyer may be incorrect about the meaning of the imperative if the aorist imperative is original. Before concluding that the future is original, one must give a reasonable explanation of how the imperative arose (and why it has such strong support) in light of the difficulty of the reading. It seems like the only sustainable reason for the existence of the imperative is an early unintentional error. The imperative retaining its directive force is not overly problematic. First, if imperative, Luke would seem to have deliberately changed Mark. Luke has changed the lexeme, and it is not uncommon for mood to be sustained despite such changes (see appendix 4). If this is the case, the best reason for the mood change would be to utilize the directive force of the imperative. Also, the later change to a future is easily explained by the difficulty of the aorist imperative.

---

[141] Joseph A. Fitzmyer, *The Gospel According to Luke (X-XXIV)*, Anchor Bible, ed. William Foxwell Albright and David Noel Freedman, vol. 28A (Garden City, NY: Doubleday and Company, 1985), 2.1341. Most translations (e.g., NASB, NIV, NRSV; however, see KJV and NKJV) seem to reflect the future indicative. It is difficult to determine whether this is a conscious effort to translate the imperative as future (after text critical work has been done) or these versions are following the 25th edition of Nestle-Aland's text (or other modern editions which have the future: Westcott-Hort, Merk, and Bover). It seems probable that these translations are merely following the text they used. However, it is possible that the NRSV translators did the text critical work since the NA[26] was available when this translation was published (unless they were following the RSV here).

Second, Luke omits Mark's eschatological phrase, εἰς τέλος. This may be due to Luke's theological emphasis[142] and/or Luke may simply desire to emphasize the present with the directive here. Although the future seems to be demanded by context, this may be too narrow of a view of Lukan theology and the use of the directive imperative. This imperative could be an exhortation and thus the entire verse should be so interpreted. The tendency would be to harmonize the gospel accounts. Considering these issues and given the impressive external evidence for the imperative, it seems like the imperative here has slightly stronger support as the original reading.[143]

A second imperative and indicative contrast occurs where one author uses an interrogative clause demanding an indicative in contrast to the imperative in another.

Mark 14:61 (‖Matt 26:63[144])　σὺ εἶ ὁ χριστὸς ὁ υἱὸς τοῦ εὐλογητοῦ;
　　　　　　　　　　　　　　are you the Christ, the son of the blessed one?

Luke 22:67　εἰ σὺ εἶ ὁ χριστός, εἰπὸν ἡμῖν
　　　　　　if you are the Christ, tell us

Mark 5:35　τί ἔτι σκύλλεις τὸν διδάσκαλον;
　　　　　　why do you trouble the teacher anymore?

Luke 8:49　μηκέτι σκύλλε τὸν διδάσκαλον
　　　　　　Do not trouble the teacher anymore

Matt 21:6　καὶ εἶπαν αὐτῷ· ἀκούεις τί οὗτοι λέγουσιν;
　　　　　　and they said to him, "Do you hear what they are saying?"

---

[142]Ibid.

[143]Unfortunately, this conclusion results in a further problem, namely, the two passages seem to have quite different meanings. It is beyond the scope of this study to delve into redactional and interpretive issues at this point. This tension must be left for later resolution.

[144]The parallel passage in Matt 26:63 also has a mood contrast with the imperative; however, Matthew passage has a subjunctive and was listed in that section.

Luke 19:39   καί τινες τῶν Φαρισαίων ἀπὸ τοῦ ὄχλου εἶπαν πρὸς
              αὐτόν διδάσκαλε, **ἐπιτίμησον** τοῖς μαθηταῖς σου
              And some of the Pharisees from the crowd said to him,
              "Teacher, **rebuke** your disciples"

In each of the above examples, Luke uses the imperative. In the first two, it seems that Luke changed Mark's interrogative into an imperative clause. Based on this observation, it is likely that if Matthew and Luke used the same source in the third example, the original is reflected in Matthew and Luke changed the interrogative again. However, in each case, the imperatives are rather weak and it is possible that the interrogatives were used originally because of the social status of the parties involved. Luke may have decided to add some explicit vividness to the account by using imperatives. This addition seems to make explicit the directive nuance reflected only implicitly in the interrogatives.

In the next example Luke is again changing Mark's interrogative. In this case, the sentence structure, not the verb form changes. The Matthew passage also includes an imperative; however, the parallel here may be somewhat stretched. Nevertheless, in the Mark passage, Jesus seems very polite, an attitude which seems unwarranted based on the unsympathetic response of the crowd. Luke's negative imperative is not overly harsh but nevertheless provides a directive nuance. Matthew goes even further and seems to confront hypocrisy directly.

Mark 5:39   τί θορυβεῖσθε καὶ <u>κλαίετε</u>;
              why are you worried and <u>weep</u>?

Luke 8:52   **μὴ κλαίετε**, οὐ γὰρ ἀπέθανεν ἀλλὰ καθεύδει
              Do not weep, for she is not dead but asleep

Matt 9:24   **ἀναχωρεῖτε**, οὐ γὰρ ἀπέθανεν τὸ κοράσιον ἀλλὰ
              καθεύδει
              Go away, for the girl is not dead but asleep

In the last example of interrogative and imperative contrast,[145] again Mark is using an interrogative; however, this time only Matthew uses an imperative. Luke uses a declarative. This is the introduction of Jesus' explanation of the parable of the sower. Both Matthew and Luke get right to the interpretation, *directing* the hearers (and readers) to the interpretation. Mark uses the transition as a didactic opportunity for the disciples.

Matt 13:18   ὑμεῖς οὖν **ἀκούσατε** τὴν παραβολὴν τοῦ σπείραντος
                 Therefore, **hear** the parable of the sower

Mark 4:13   Καὶ λέγει αὐτοῖς· <u>οὐκ οἴδατε</u> τὴν παραβολὴν ταύτην,[146]
                 καὶ πῶς πάσας τὰς παραβολὰς γνώσεσθε;
                 And he said to them, "<u>Do you not understand</u> this parable? And
                 how will you understand all the parables?"

Luke 8:11   <u>Ἔστιν</u> δὲ αὕτη ἡ παραβολή ...
                 Now the parable <u>is</u> this ...

The final type of indicative and imperative contrast (non discourse/narrative) occurs when both clauses appear to be parallel without any other external features (i.e., interrogative) and the indicative is not future tense. Interestingly enough, outside of a direct discourse/narrative contrast, there are no certain verbal contrasts. First, there is an imperative parallel with a non-verbal clause where the indicative (θέλεις) is implied by ellipsis.

Mark 14:36   ἀλλ' οὐ τί ἐγὼ θέλω ἀλλὰ τί σύ
                 but not what I desire but what you [desire]

---

[145]There may be one further parallel: Mark 14:41 ‖ Matt 26:45 (καθεύδετε and ἀναπαύεσθε). However, both the indicative and imperative can be realized by these forms. Gramcord parses these in Mark as imperative (primary) with the indicative as an option. If indicative, these would be part of an interrogative sentence (as in Matthew). Because the interpretation of Mark could go either way and the forms are identical, these will not be viewed as a contrast in mood.

[146]Although the punctuation here is not a question mark (;), this clause, as the following, is a certainly a question. The sentence-final question mark may apply to both clauses.

Matt 26:39   πλὴν οὐχ ὡς ἐγὼ θέλω ἀλλ' ὡς σύ
              not as I desire but as you [desire]

Luke 22:42   πλὴν μὴ τὸ θέλημά μου ἀλλὰ τὸ σὸν **γινέσθω**
              still not my desire but **let** yours **be done**[147]

In addition, there are two questionable parallels which are worth noting.[148] However, considering their difficulty and the lack of other similar type parallels, they must contribute little beyond mere observation.

Matt 18:15   ἐάν σου ἀκούσῃ, <u>ἐκέρδησας</u> τὸν ἀδελφόν σου
              if he listens to you, you have <u>won over</u> your brother

Luke 17:3   καὶ ἐὰν μετανοήσῃ **ἄφες** αὐτῷ
              And if he repents, **forgive** him

It is questionable whether Matt 18:15-18 is parallel with Luke 17:3 and its wider context (particularly verse 4); however, the similarities of the sections are striking. If these can be viewed as parallel, the reason for the different mood is probably due to issues related to plot and context rather than grammar (this would account for the drastic differences).[149] Luke's passage is shorter and within a larger section about forgiveness. Matthew continues to discuss issues related to the relationship between the one being confronted and the one confronting. Luke's instruction uses the imperative to make clear the response demanded by the later. There is no discussion about what to do if the individual does not repent.

---

[147]It is possible that Luke's imperative is parallel to the exact form in Matt 26:42. However, Matthew explicitly states this is Jesus' second of three prayers (Mark 14:39 merely mentions that Jesus prays but does not give the words). Luke's account does not give any indication of more than one prayer setting. The Nestle-Aland *Synopsis* is being followed here which parallels the verses as listed here and leaves Matt 26:42 as unparalleled in Luke.

[148]There is also a possible [very] weak parallel between Matt 23:32 (imperative clause, καὶ ὑμεῖς πληρώσατε τὸ μέτρον τῶν πατέρων ὑμῶν [complete the measure of you fathers] which is paralleled by an indicative statement in Luke 11:48. However, the content is so different (both verbally and conceptually) that if there was a common source (probably more clearly reflected in Matthew due to its difficulty), there is little evidence of this now.

[149]In other words, Luke's primary purpose for making the change is not to change the mood but for higher level reasons, the mood change is secondary and thus not the focus of his redaction.

Finally, the following, although quite different, could possibly be parallel.[150] This is Jesus' response to one who approaches him about the most important commandments.

Mark 12:34   οὐ μακρὰν <u>εἶ</u> ἀπὸ τῆς βασιλείας τοῦ θεοῦ
               "You <u>are</u> not far from the kingdom of God"

Luke 10:28   τοῦτο **ποίει** καὶ ζήσῃ
               "**Do** this and you will live"

It is possible that Luke did change this from Mark's original. However, The change may have more to do with redactional issues than grammar (again this would account for the drastic differences). Luke is not adverse to using the phrase ἡ βασιλεία τοῦ θεοῦ. it is quite common (see in this chapter, 10:9, 11). His use of τοῦτο **ποίει** καὶ ζήσῃ must be seen as quite deliberate. The verb ζήσῃ is significant. It is used to replace the entire phrase ἀπὸ τῆς βασιλείας τοῦ θεοῦ. Nevertheless, in this work's entire database and outside of a discourse/narrative contrast (see below), this is the example with the most potential to be an explicit non-future non-interrogative indicative/imperative contrast.[151]

There are many imperative and (non-future) indicative contrasts where the imperative is in direct speech and indicative is in narrative[152]

*Mark 5:13 (‖ Luke 8:32)   καὶ <u>ἐπέτρεψεν</u> αὐτοῖς
                             And he <u>gave leave</u> to them

*Matt 8:32   καὶ εἶπεν αὐτοῖς· **ὑπάγετε**
               And he said to them, "**Go**"[153]

---

[150]In addition to the difference in wording, the Markan pericope includes a scribe as the one who approaches Jesus. Luke (and Matthew although no parallel to this statement exists) states it was a lawyer who approaches Jesus. However, it seems that the lawyer who would be interested in the Mosaic law would also be considered a scribe (see Matt 22:34-35).

[151]Nevertheless, it is acknowledged that this is a problematic example.

[152]Mark 6:31 (imperative in direct discourse) and Matt 14:13 (indicative in narrative) are close but not quite conceptual parallels.

[153]Luke also omits the previous direct speech recorded in Mark 5:12 and Matt 8:31. However, Luke does not narrate the content of the saying here.

*Mark 10:49   καὶ στὰς ὁ'Ιησοῦς εἶπεν· **φωνήσατε** αὐτόν
                and stopping, Jesus said, "**call** him"

*Matt 20:32   καὶ στὰς ὁ'Ιησοῦς <u>ἐφώνησεν</u> αὐτοὺς καὶ εἶπεν ...
                And stopping, Jesus <u>called</u> them and said ...

*Luke 18:40   σταθεὶς δὲ ὁ'Ιησοῦς <u>ἐκέλευσεν</u> αὐτὸν ἀχθῆναι πρὸς
                αὐτόν
                And stopping, Jesus <u>ordered</u> him to be brought to him

*Mark 6:39   καὶ <u>ἐπέταξεν</u> αὐτοῖς ἀνακλῖναι πάντας συμπόσια
                συμπόσια ἐπὶ τῷ χλωρῷ χόρτῳ
                And he <u>commanded</u> them to all sit in groups on the green grass

*Matt 14:18   ὁ δὲ εἶπεν· **φέρετέ** μοι ὧδε αὐτούς
                Then he said, "**Bring** them here to me"

*Luke 9:14   εἶπεν δὲ πρὸς τοὺς μαθητὰς αὐτοῦ· **κατακλίνατε** αὐτοὺς
                κλισίας [ὡσεὶ] ἀνὰ πεντήκοντα
                Then he said to his disciples, "**Make** them sit in groups of
                [about] fifty each"

*Mark 14:23   καὶ <u>ἔπιον</u> ἐξ αὐτοῦ πάντες
                and they all <u>drank</u> from it

*Matt 26:27   **πίετε** ἐξ αὐτοῦ πάντες
                Drink from it, all of you[154]

*Mark 7:17   <u>ἐπηρώτων</u> αὐτὸν οἱ μαθηταὶ αὐτοῦ τὴν παραβολήν
                his disciples <u>were asking</u> him about the parable

---

[154]The parallel pericope in Luke 22:15-20 does not include this or a parallel phrase (v. 20).

*Matt 15:15   Ἀποκριθεὶς δὲ ὁ Πέτρος εἶπεν αὐτῷ· **φράσον** ἡμῖν τὴν παραβολὴν [ταύτην]

And Peter answered and said to him, "**Explain** the parable to us"

*Mark 7:26   ἡ δὲ γυνὴ ἦν Ἑλληνίς, Συροφοινίκισσα τῷ γένει· καὶ <u>ἠρώτα</u> αὐτὸν ἵνα τὸ δαιμόνιον ἐκβάλῃ ἐκ τῆς θυγατρὸς αὐτῆς

Now the woman was a Gentile, Syrophoenician by race, and she <u>was asking</u> him to cast out (or that he might cast out) the demon from her daughter

*Matt 15:25   ἡ δὲ ἐλθοῦσα προσεκύνει αὐτῷ λέγουσα· κύριε, **βοήθει** μοι

But she came and knelt before him saying, "lord, **help** me"[155]

*Mark 13:4   **εἰπὸν** ἡμῖν ... (Matthew has **εἰπὲ** ἡμῖν [same parsing: 2 sg aor act impv])

Tell us ...

*Luke 21:7   Ἐπηρώτησαν δὲ αὐτὸν <u>λέγοντες</u>[156] ...

And they <u>asked</u> him <u>saying</u> ...

---

[155]In the earlier part of this pericope (Mark 7:25 and Matt 15:22-24), Matthew includes two imperatives in direct speech unparalleled in Mark. Also, later, Mark 7:27 includes an imperative in a speech clause not found in Matthew.

[156]Despite the participle, this example is included here with the indicatives. The participle is common in this type of statement. The indicative is the main verb.

*Matt 10:14   καὶ ὃς ἂν μὴ δέξηται ὑμᾶς μηδὲ ἀκούσῃ τοὺς λόγους ὑμῶν, ἐξερχόμενοι ἔξω τῆς οἰκίας ἢ τῆς πόλεως ἐκείνης **ἐκτινάξατε** τὸν κονιορτὸν τῶν ποδῶν ὑμῶν
And whoever does not receive you nor listen to your words, while going outside of that house or city, **shake off** the dust from your feet

*Luke 10:10-11a   εἰς ἣν δ' ἂν πόλιν εἰσέλθητε καὶ μὴ δέχωνται ὑμᾶς ἐξελθόντες εἰς τὰς πλατείας αὐτῆς **εἴπατε**· 11 καὶ τὸν κονιορτὸν τὸν κολληθέντα ἡμῖν ἐκ τῆς πόλεως ὑμῶν εἰς τοὺς πόδας <u>ἀπομασσόμεθα</u> ὑμῖν
now whichever city you enter and they do not receive you, go into its streets and **say**, "Even the dust sticking to our feet from your city, we <u>wipe off</u> against you"[157]

All imperatives occur in direct speech quotations while indicatives occur in descriptions of the event in which the imperatives had taken place. In many cases the indicative explains what is happening. When Mark parallels Matthew or Mark parallels Matthew and Luke, Mark is usually indicative (exceptions: Mark 10:49 [impv] ‖ Matt 20:32 and (‖) Luke 18:40 [ind]), Matthew is usually discourse (see previous exception), and Luke agrees with Matthew twice (once with the indicative [see again the exception mentioned above]; and once with the imperative [discourse]: Matt 14:18 ‖ Luke 9:14 ‖ Mark 6:69 [ind]). In an additional parallel, Luke agrees with Mark against Matthew and has an indicative. (Mark 5:13 ‖ Lule 8:32 ‖ Matt 8:32). Finally, in the only parallel between Mark and Luke (without a Matthew parallel), it is Mark who uses the imperative in discourse (Mark 13:4 ‖ Luke 21:7). When only Matthew and Luke are parallel, Matthew has the imperative and Luke, the indicative (Matt 10:14

---

[157]The imperative is parallel with the indicative here. The preceding imperative in Luke introduced within direct speech what the listeners should say (as direct speech). It is possible that the change to first person within the second level of direct speech accounts for the indicative (there is no first person imperative). However, if this was the case one might expect a subjunctive. More likely, the structure of the speech demands the indicative. First, the direct speech is embedded within direct speech and thus the speech itself is what is *directed*. In Matthew, the action is commanded. The Lukan saying does not command action but speech. The speech (and imperative in Matthew) does not command the hearers to do anything. Rather, the speech explains their action.

∥ Luke 10:10-11b). The Matthean discourse against Mark's descriptions is to be expected since the stress on the former is often speech while the latter is fast-paced narrative.

The imperative also contrasts with the infinitive.[158] Above, in Matt 6:9 ∥ Luke 11:1 it has been observed that the imperative in Matthew was a subjunctive in Luke. An additional word (not found in Matthew) realizes the directive force (through the imperative). This can be observed in a similar situation with the infinitive.

Matt 7:13   **Εἰσέλθατε** διὰ τῆς στενῆς πύλης ...
               Enter through the narrow gate ...

Luke 13:24   **ἀγωνίζεσθε** εἰσελθεῖν διὰ τῆς στενῆς θύρας ...
               Struggle to enter through the narrow door ...

However, unlike the discussion above, where the Lukan imperative was using a common lexeme and thus seemed to shift emphasis upon the forthcoming imperatives in the prayer, here the different imperatives seem to emphasis different aspects of Jesus' teaching. The Matthew passage places the emphasis upon *entering* where the Lukan passage emphasizes the *struggle* involved in following Jesus. Thus, the imperative verb in each case involves the emphasis.

There also are examples of the imperative/infinitive contrast where the lexical roots are the same.

---

[158]The so-called *imperatival* infinitive is rare in the New Testament. It functions as an independent verb. Wallace (*Exegetical Syntax*, 608) notes only two examples (Rom 12:15 and Phil 3:16). Turner and Moulton (*Syntax*, 78) mention that it is "frequent in the papyri" and BDF (196) states that it is "extremely old and is especially common in Homer." However, it appears to be rare in classical Greek (Kurzová, *syntaktischen Struktur*, 52); for a detailed study of the imperatival infinitive in classical Greek, see Schwyzer-Debrunner, *Griechische Grammatik*, 380-83; for the imperatival infinitive in classical Greek poetry see Victor Bers, *Greek Poetic Syntax in the Classical Age* (New Haven, CT: Yale University Press, 1984), 166. For further information on this infinitive usage in the New Testament see Moulton, *Prolegomena*, 179-80 and James L. Boyer, "The Classification of Infinitives: A Statistical Study," *Grace Theological Journal* 6 (1985): 14-15 with the corrective discussion in Wallace (*Exegetical Syntax*, 608). The synoptic contrasts all involve subordinate clauses, they are not classified as *imperatival* imperatives, nor do they involve the directive force of the *imperatival*.

Mark 10:43 (‖Matt 20:26 with some minor differences)

> οὐχ οὕτως δέ ἐστιν ἐν ὑμῖν, ἀλλ' ὅς ἂν θέλῃ μέγας
> <u>γενέσθαι</u> ἐν ὑμῖν ἔσται ὑμῶν διάκονοος
> but it is (or "shall") not be so among you, but whoever wishes
> <u>to be</u> great among you, he will be the servant of all

Luke 22:26   ὑμεῖς δὲ οὐχ οὕτως, ἀλλ' ὁ μείζων ἐν ὑμῖν γινέσθω ὡς
               ὁ νεώτερος καὶ ὁ ἡγούμενος ὡς ὁ διακονῶν
               but for you not so, but **let** the greatest among you **become** as
               the youngest and the leader [become] as the servant

Mark 15:31 (‖ Matt 27:42a)   ὁμοίως καὶ οἱ ἀρχιερεῖς ἐμπαίζοντες
                               πρὸς ἀλλήλουςμετὰ τῶν γραμματέων
                               ἔλεγον· ἄλλους ἔσωσεν, ἐαυτὸν οὐ
                               δύναται <u>σῶσαι</u>
                               Likewise also the chief priests with the scribes
                               were ridiculing [him] among themselves, they
                               were saying, "he saved others, he is unable <u>to</u>
                               <u>save</u> himself"

Luke 23:35   Καὶ εἱστήκει ὁ λαὸς θεωρῶν. ἐξεμυκτήριζον δὲ καὶ οἱ
               ἄρχοντες λέγοντες· ἄλλους ἔσωσεν, **σωσάτω** ἐαυτόν ...
               And the people stood watching and even the leaders were
               ridiculing [him] saying, "He saved others, **let** him **save** himself
               ..."

In these examples, a definite shift in emphasis can be observed between the
passages. The passages with the imperative have a strong emphasis upon the
verbal content of imperative. It is the focus of the sentence. It seems like Luke
is taking a simple aspect of the Markan passage and raising it to a level of
significance with the imperative. This is not a surprise because with few
exceptions, the infinitive cannot be the main verb of a sentence. Additionally,

in the second example, there are a number of interesting features.[159] However, here we are only concerned with the imperative and infinitive contrast. Nevertheless, I hesitate to make significant statements about this example within the analysis because there may be more going here than mood choice (as stated in the previous footnote).

In addition there are a number of infinitives in narrative contrasting with imperatives in discourse.

*Mark 5:8   ἔλεγεν γὰρ αὐτῷ· **ἔξελθε** τὸ πνεῦμα τὸ ἀκάθαρτον ἐκ τοῦ ἀνθρώπου

For he was saying to him, "Unclean spirit, **come out** of the man"

*Luke 8:29   παρήγγειλεν γὰρ τῷ πνεύματι τῷ ἀκαθάρτῳ <u>ἐξελθεῖν</u> ἀπὸ τοῦ ἀνθρώπου

For he was commanding the unclean spirit <u>to come out</u> from the man

*Mark 15:14   οἱ δὲ περισσῶς ἔκραξαν· **σταύρωσον** αὐτόν

but all the more they cried out, "**Crucify** him!"

---

[159]Such interesting issues include identical verb roots with different moods and person throughout the larger section (Mark 15:29-32; Matt 27:39-43; Luke 23:35 [Luke condenses the section]). Luke's use of the third person imperative σωσάτω seems to parallel the infinitive (σῶσαι) in Matthew and Mark since all are introduced by ἔσωσεν. However, Both Matthew and Mark use a third person imperative in the following clause (καταβάτω). Since Luke does not include this phrase one may wonder whether he wanted to retain the third person imperative and thus changed Mark's (followed by Matthew) σῶσαι for this purpose. Thus, it may be somewhat parallel to both, the lexeme of the infinitive but the person and mood of the imperative verb. Mark and Matthew are primarily interested in the challenge to Jesus to come down from the cross (see Mark 15:30 and Matt 27:40 quoted above). This is not Luke's main interest at this point in the discourse. Matthew and Mark have already recorded an imperative from the crowd directed at Jesus to save himself (σῶσον σεαυτόν; Matt 27:40; Mark 15:30). Luke will record the same clause two times after the third person usage (23:37, 30). Further work in this passage could result in some interesting insights into the synoptic problem and especially concerning Luke's redaction. This is beyond the scope of this work. See chapter 4 for some additional discussion of these passages.

*Matt 27:23   οἱ δὲ περισσῶς ἔκραζον λέγοντες· **σταυρωθήτω**
but all the more they were crying out saying, "**Let** him **be crucified!**"

*Luke 23:23   οἱ δὲ ἐπέκειντο φωναῖς μεγάλαις αἰτούμενοι αὐτὸν σταυρωθῆναι
but the crowds [were] asking with loud voices [that] he <u>be crucified</u>

*Matt 10:7-8   πορευόμενοι δὲ **κηρύσσετε** ... ἀσθενοῦντας **θεραπεύετε** ...
and go and **preach** ... **heal** the sick

*Luke 9:2   καὶ ἀπέστειλεν αὐτοὺς <u>κηρύσσειν</u> τὴν βασιλείαν τοῦ θεοῦ καὶ <u>ἰᾶσθαι</u>
And he sent them <u>to preach</u> the kingdom of God and <u>to heal</u>

*Matt 22:3   καὶ ἀπέστειλεν τοὺς δούλους αὐτοῦ <u>καλέσαι</u> τοὺς κεκλημένους εἰς τοὺς γάμους ...
And he sent his servants <u>to call</u> those invited to the wedding ...

*Luke 14:17   καὶ ἀπέστειλεν τὸν δοῦλον αὐτοῦ τῇ ὥρᾳ τοῦ δείπνου εἰπεῖν τοῖς κεκλημένοις· **ἔρχεσθε**, ὅτι ἤδη ἕτοιμά ἐστιν
And he sent his servants at the time of the banquet to say to those invited, "**Come**, everything is now ready"[160]

*Mark 12:1 (‖ Luke 20:9 with minor differences)
Καὶ ἤρξατο αὐτοῖς ἐν παραβολαῖς <u>λαλεῖν</u>
And he began <u>to speak</u> to them in parables

---

[160]Also, imperatives in quoted speech in Luke 14:18-19 seem to be paralleled by a simple statement in Matt 22:5 (with the indicative). However, unlike the examples in this section, the imperative clause seems to give more developed information than can be deduced from the declarative statement.

*Matt 21:33   Ἄλλην παραβολὴν ἀκούσατε
"**Listen** to another parable"

There are only five examples in this category so no patterns of usage by the evangelists can be identified with any authority. Nevertheless, Matthew still tends to have more imperatives (three of four passages cited). Mark also has more imperatives than infinitives (two of three). Luke, who reflects more closely a literary style of Greek, has one imperative and four infinitives.

Participles are somewhat similar to infinitives as they both are non-finite verbs which have many specific usages. As expected, contrasts of participles are found with the imperative mood.

First: Mark 2:9-11; Matt 9:5-6; Luke 5:23-24. In order to observe the relationship among these passages, only the significant verbs and appropriate conjunctions will be reproduced here (without translation).[161] The context, the healing of the paralytic, is well known.

Mark 2:9
ἔγειρε καὶ ἆρον ... καὶ περιπάτει; ... ἔγειρε ἆρον ... καὶ ὕπαγε

Matt 9:5
ἔγειρε καὶ περιπάτει; ... ἐγερθεὶς ἆρόν ... καὶ ὕπαγε

Luke 5:23
ἔγειρε καὶ περιπάτει; ... ἔγειρε καὶ ἄρας ... πορεύου

Both Matthew and Luke use a participle where Mark uses an imperative (although the actual lexemes are reversed). Nevertheless, these participles seem to focus the emphasis upon the imperatives. Luke is especially helpful. As in Matthew, Luke omits the first occurrence of ἆρον and includes the imperative form in the second part of the passage, Luke subordinates the participle to the following imperative. It is possible that for Mark and Matthew the act of lifting the pallet may have Sabbath breaking implications– important themes in their works (although there is no mention on which day this occurs), Luke is

---

[161]There is no parallel verb to Matthew's introductory imperative θάρσει ("Cheer up," "Courage," etc.). This imperative seems to function as a greeting although its directive force is not to be ignored.

primarily concerned with the *rising* and *going* of the paralytic which vindicates Jesus to his critics.[162]

Mark 14:13a (‖ Matt 26:18a)   καὶ ἀποστέλλει δύο τῶν μαθητῶν αὐτοῦ καὶ λέγει αὐτοῖς· **ὑπάγετε** εἰς τὴν πόλιν
…
And he sent two of his disciples and said to them, "**Go** into the city …"

Luke 22:8   καὶ ἀπέστειλεν Πέτρον καὶ Ἰωάννην εἰπών· <u>πορευθέντες</u> ἑτοιμάσατε[163] ἡμῖν τὸ πάσχα ἵνα φάγωμεν
and he sent Peter and John saying, "<u>Go</u> and prepare the Passover for us that we may eat"

Mark 14:38 (‖ Matt 26:41)   **γρηγορεῖτε** καὶ προσεύχεσθε[164]
watch and pray

Luke 22:46   <u>ἀναστάντες</u> προσεύχεσθε
<u>rise</u> and pray

Mark 16:7   ἀλλὰ **ὑπάγετε εἴπατε** τοῖς μαθηταῖς αὐτοῦ καὶ τῷ Πέτρῳ …
but **go, tell** his disciples and Peter …

Matt 28:7   καὶ ταχὺ <u>πορευθεῖσαι</u> **εἴπατε** τοῖς μαθηταῖς αὐτοῦ …
and quickly <u>go</u> and **tell** his disciples …

---

[162]Vindication is also the main point of Matthew and Mark. However, Sabbath breaking is also a theme of these books and although not the primary purpose of these passages, it nevertheless contributes to this theme.

[163]The imperative (ἑτοιμάσατε) in Luke 22:8 is unparalleled in Mark 14:13 and Matt 26:18.

[164]This imperative (προσεύχεσθε) is paralleled in all three gospels.

Mark 15:30   σῶσον σεαυτὸν <u>καταβὰς</u> ἀπὸ τοῦ σταυρο
                save yourself by coming down from the cross

Matt 27:40   σῶσον σεαυτόν, εἰ υἱὸς εἶ τοῦ θεοῦ, [καὶ] κατάβηθι ἀπὸ
                τοῦ σταυροῦ
                save yourself, if you are the Son of God, [and] **come down**
                from the cross

The participle in Mark 15:30 supports the main focus of the verse from
Mark's perspective. The participle communicates the means by which the main
imperative (σῶσον; paralleled in Matthew) is to be accomplished.[165] Although
saving himself and *coming down from the cross* are probably related in Matthew
also, he seems to associate *coming down from the cross* with proof of Jesus'
divine sonship.

Finally, there is only one example of a participle in narrative and an
imperative in discourse.

Mark 1:44 (|| Matt 8:4)   καὶ λέγει αὐτῷ· **ὅρα** μηδενὶ μηδὲν εἴπῃς,
                            ἀλλὰ **ὕπαγε** σεαυτὸν **δεῖξον** τῷ ἱερεῖ καὶ
                            προσένεγκε (Matt has alternate form [same
                            parsing]: **προσένεγκον**) περὶ τοῦ καθαρισμοῦ
                            σου ἃ προσέταξεν Μωϋσῆς, εἰς μαρτύριον
                            αὐτοῖς
                            And he said to him, "**see** that you say nothing to
                            no one, but **go**, **show** yourself to the priest and
                            offer for your cleansing what Moses commanded
                            for a testimony to them"

---

[165]It seems best to interpret this participle as *means*. This category is common and this
example fits most if not all the observed characteristics noted by Wallace (ibid., 628-29).
Nevertheless, all translations consulted (NASB, NIV, NRSV, RSV, KJV, NKJV, and the recent
version of the NET Bible) seem to interpret this as imperative by adding "and" and translating
this as an imperative: "save yourself and come down from the cross." The imperatival use of the
participle is rare. It seems wise to avoid labeling this imperatival when another explanation seems
preferable. It must be noted that these translations may be translating this passage in this manner
for stylistic reasons. However, the participle's interpretation is ambiguous and the imperatival
participle is an option.

Luke 5:14   καὶ αὐτὸς <u>παρήγγειλεν</u> αὐτῷ μηδενὶ εἰπεῖν, ἀλλὰ
               <u>ἀπελθὼν</u> **δεῖξον** σεαυτὸν τῷ ἱερεῖ καὶ **προσένεγκε** περὶ
               τοῦ καθαρισμοῦ σου καθὼς προσέταξεν Μωϋσῆς, εἰς
               μαρτύριον αὐτοῖς
               And he <u>ordered</u> him to tell no one, but <u>go</u> and **show** yourself to
               the priest and **offer** for your cleansing as Moses commanded
               for a testimony to them

In this example Luke retains the main imperatives (δεῖξον and προσένεγκε)
but changes the other two. First, Luke uses a different lexeme (παρήγγειλεν)
in the indicative in place of Jesus' initial imperative (ὅρα). Also, Luke's
indicative is part of the narration describing what the others make explicit in
Jesus' words. Second, a lexeme change also occurs when Luke replaces Jesus'
imperative (ὕπαγε) with a (circumstantial) participle.

Again, although the examples are minimal, they highlight one aspect of this
work's analysis that has only marginally been evident thus far. In many cases
(especially with non-finite contrasts), when a change is made from imperative
to a non-imperative, it is often Luke making the switch.[166] In the previous set of
examples, every Lukan example uses the participle[167] where Mark (and in some
cases Matthew) uses the imperative.

Luke's more liberal use of infinitives and participles may be attributed to
his Greek style which is more polished than either Matthew or Mark. More
stylistic Greek includes more subordinate clauses and a more liberal use of non-
finite verb forms. In essence Luke's Greek is a little more sophisticated.[168]

Before concluding this section, one further possible parallel between the
imperative and an idiomatic expression will be discussed. In Luke 5:10 the
negated imperative μὴ φοβοῦ corresponds to the dubious parallel δεῦτε ὀπίσω
μου. (Mark 1:17 ‖ Matt 4:17). The latter includes an idiomatic adverb (or
interjection) with imperative morphology. Although the pericopes in all three

---

[166]This does not mean that Luke prefers not to use the imperative. He uses the mood
throughout his works. What is merely being stated that if a change is made, it will usually be by
Luke.

[167]The first participial example is rather complex but still generally supports this claim.

[168]This statement may seem to be close to violating our principle of description over
prescription. This is not intended. What is merely being pointed out is that Luke's work
represents a more literary *Koine* than the other synoptic writers. Uses of terms such as "polished"
and "sophisticated" are not intended to be value judgments.

synoptics are very close, the Lukan phrase here seems to be so significantly different that it causes one to wonder whether a completely different tradition underlies this saying of Jesus. Therefore, it would be unwise to speculate on the reasons for Luke's use of the imperative here.

This section has observed a number of characteristics which set the imperative apart from other moods and forms. The imperative is primarily used as a main verb, it is the verbal focus of the sentence. Its contrast with the subjunctive in dependent clauses and its exclusive use in direct speech (against narrative) demonstrate a strong and almost emphatic (relatively speaking) nuance compared with other moods in similar contexts. That is, it may best be described as a *directive*. The imperative's use in direct speech is similar to its use in the epistles which are essentially a direct discourse[169] from writer to reader. The directive force seems clear although it is not exclusive to the imperative. However, the imperative always is directive. Again, its use in synoptic parallels where the parallel form is a different mood, participle, or infinitive often seemed to suggest that the imperative used was more prominent than the other mood in the parallels (especially when participles, infinitives, and dependent clause subjunctives contrast with an imperative in a synoptic parallel passage). Also, the distribution observed (speech, epistolary) suggests a volitional element is also apparent. This will be developed further below.

The Distribution of the Imperative

Before describing more explicitly what is meant by *volitional-directive*, one further area may contribute to an understanding of the semantic meaning of the mood, namely, its distribution within the epistles. New Testament epistles often include a strong persuasive purpose and in such cases, it is worthwhile observing how the imperative mood is used within these books at the level of discourse. It seems that the role of the imperative mood should be important to a persuasive genre of literature. Based on this assumption its distribution will be considered within epistolary literature.

It has been observed in classical Greek rhetoric (specifically, Attic

---

[169]The similarity of the terms "directive" and "direct" describing speech and discourse is incidental.

oration[170]), with the exception of some verbs, that the imperative has usually been viewed as having a strong tone and thus often does not appear until the final section(s) of the speech. It was not normally used in the introductory proem (or prooemium) which served to gain the audience's favor.[171] The nature of the speech and the length of the proem seem to determine the initial occurrence(s) of the imperatives. The important observation to be gleaned here is that the imperative does not appear (relatively) early in the speech.[172] Strong (force) imperatives are reserved for the epilogue.[173] Thus, it seems safe to postulate a principle that imperatives generally appear late in such speeches.

Although Miller asserts that letters may display a variety of patterns,[174] in many of the New Testament epistles Miller's principle seems to be followed. The use of significant imperatives does not occur until late in many of the letters. In the first eleven chapters of Romans, only thirteen of its sixty-two imperatives occur. The first is in Rom 3:4 and the next in 6:11. However, in the final four chapters there are forty-nine imperatives (although seventeen are in the conclusion of which sixteen are ἀσπάσαθε). Second Corinthians demonstrates a similar pattern. There are twenty-two total: eight in chapters 1-8, fourteen in chapters 9-13; the first does not occur until 5:20. Galatians has twenty-one imperatives: three in chapters 1-3, eighteen in chapters 4-6; of the three in the first half, two appear early in the rebuke in 1:8-9 which has a tone demanding imperatives. The book of Ephesians has forty-one. Only one occurs in the first three chapters, 2:11. Colossians has thirty imperatives of which only four occur in chapters 1-2 with the first occurring in 2:6. In 1 Thessalonians the first of twenty imperatives occurs in the last verse of chapter 4; the remaining

---

[170]This is limited to Attic oration because the forthcoming observations are based upon the study of this genre (C. W. E. Miller, "The Limitation of the Imperative in the Attic Orators," *American Journal of Philology* 13 [1892]: 399-436). The classical orators whose works were analyzed in this study included Aeschines, Andocides, Antiphon, Demosthenes, Dinarchus, Isaeus, Isocrates, Lycurgus, and Lysias (general dates: V–III BC)

[171]Ibid., 426-32. There are exceptions to this principle (ibid., 432). There may be occasions, such as a in a speech given by an important figure or when urgency is necessary that the imperative may occur in this section of the speech (ibid., 428).

[172]"Yet it must be remembered that the important point is that the imperative must be kept as far as possible from the beginning of the speech. The longer the prooemium, the more liable we should be to find the imperative. On the other hand, when the matter is urgent and the time allotted for the speech is short, the prooemium is shortened or omitted altogether, and the almost inevitable imperative comes nearer to the beginning of the speech, . . ." (ibid., 432).

[173]Ibid., 433-36.
[174]Ibid., 428-29.

are all in the final chapter, chapter 5. In 2 Thessalonians all seven occur in the second half of the book, beginning at 2:15. First Timothy has forty-three imperatives. Four in the first three chapters of which the first occurs in 2:11. Titus has fourteen, ten of which occur in 2:15-3:15, the last sixteen verses of the book. In Philemon all four imperatives occur in the last nine verses. Although in Hebrews the first of twenty nine imperatives occurs in 1:6, twenty occur in the final two chapters. First Peter has thirty-five and although the first occurs in 1:13, twenty four occur in the second half of the book, 3:10-5:14). In 2 Peter there are seven and although the first occurs early in the book, 1:5, five occur in the final chapter. In 2 John and 3 John (three and two respectively), all occur in the second half of these short letters. In the book of Jude all nine occur in the last nine verses, 17-25.[175]

There are a few New Testament epistles which do not seem to follow the rhetoric pattern.[176] Although 1 John follows the pattern by not beginning with an imperative (the first does not occur until 2:15), most of its ten imperatives occur in the middle of the book and only one in the final chapter. First Corinthians, Philippians, 2 Timothy, and James have imperatives throughout their contents. The cases of 1 Corinthians, Philippians, and 2 Timothy may reflect their personal tone; however, even personal letters such as 2 Corinthians and Philemon followed the proposed pattern.[177] James is a unique case. It has fifty-five imperatives and they seem to be most evenly distributed of any of the letters.[178] Of the epistles, only 1 Corinthians and Romans have more. James has the highest proportion of imperatives in the New Testament (31.5 per 1000 words). Its structure is loose. Thus, it might be reasonable to not expect it to

---

[175]Although commonly discussed in the context of Pauline theology, the *indicative-imperative* structure seems like a common strategy for presenting one's case (if grammar can be a guide); see George Eldon Ladd, *A Theology of the New Testament*, ed. Donald A. Hagner, rev. ed. (Grand Rapids: William B. Eerdmans Publishing Company, 1993), 568-96.

[176]It is important to keep in mind that rhetorical strategies like many other descriptive observations about literature are not absolute essentials for composition. Authors have the freedom to use whatever they feel most benefits their goals for writing their work.

[177]The imperative distribution in 1 Corinthians may be explained by its nature. It has more imperatives than any other epistle (100) and in light of the problems being addressed, one might expect Paul to use any rhetorical device at his disposal to get the church to listen to him. However, the nature of the letter is a continual process of raising and answering questions. Thus, it is not structured like other letters such as Romans or Ephesians.

[178]The five chapters of James have 12, 11, 4, 12, and 16 imperatives respectively.

follow other literary conventions. Some question whether it is an epistle at all.[179] However, even if considered a letter, it is not a typical example of the genre.[180]

The observation of the distribution of the imperative within the New Testament epistles supports the notion that the imperative is a *volitional-directive*. Its use primarily at the end of the letters seems to suggest that it is used within a careful strategy of persuasion. Fulfillment of the imperatives by the addressees is essential to the success of the work. Therefore, significant time is spent leading up the imperative section in order to gain the confidence of the reader before expressing the volitional-directives. This suggests the imperatives are rather strong and have the potential to be rejected if not expressed at the right time and in an appropriate manner.

The Imperative as a Volitional-Directive

This chapter's analysis has confirmed the thesis that the imperative mood is *directional* and *volitional*. Force and contextual features have been seen that factor into differences but in all cases the directional volitional characteristics remain. Directives themselves can be simply seen as attempts to get someone to do something.[181] Most moods can be used for this purpose. It seems that there are two things which set the imperative apart from other moods. First, it is always a directive. Other moods can be used to direct[182] but the non-imperatives can also be used for other purposes. Second, it seems to include a volitional element. Kühner's statement over 150 years ago summarizes the balanced approach attempted in this work, "The Imp. is the mode which expresses desire;

---

[179]See Werner Georg Kümmel, *Introduction to the New Testament*, trans. Howard Clark Kee, rev. and enl. ed. (Nashville: Abingdon Press, 1975), 408.

[180]See D. A. Carson and Douglas J. Moo who view James as a "literary letter" which contains or a "homily" or "homilies," (*An Introduction to the New Testament*, 2d ed. [Grand Rapids: Zondervan Publishing House, 2005], 629-30).

[181]J. R. Searle, *Expression and Meaning: Studies in the Theory of Speech Acts* (Cambridge: Cambridge University Press, 1979), 13. This also explains what has been observed by some as the *simple* or *basic* nature of the imperative mood. This is vividly seen in the papyri in which the imperative is common. One prominent grammarian of the papyri suggests that this may be due to the papyri's rather unsophisticated nature. He sees the imperative as a simple way of asking for something (Mandilaras, *Verb*, 296).

[182]For example, a person may state to another either directly or indirectly: "I like black coffee," "I might enjoy a cup of black coffee.," "is the coffee ready?" etc., and will communicate to the sensitive listener, "[please] give me a cup of coffee."

it denotes that which the speaker conceives and represents as something desired, whether it an be an actual objective reality or not."[183] This explicit encoding of *direction* and *volition* suggests this mood is more likely to evoke a response from the addressee. Indeed, the mood demands some response. Therefore, it seems stronger than the other moods and has more potential to offend. Its use in synoptic parallels where a parallel form is a different mood, participle, or infinitive often seemed to suggest that the imperative used was more prominent within the sentence than the other moods in the parallels. Therefore, it is suggested that the speaker's choice of the imperative is significant and will not be used in carefully composed communication actions without reason.

To reiterate what has been said elsewhere, the notion of volition may seem rather minimal in places. But it seems this way only when language is being consider as corresponding to reality. As a portrayal of reality, this work is suggesting that a volitional element exists. This may partially be evident in the observation that the imperative only occurs in direct speech or epistolary literature. Volition is a personal characteristic. Although it can be evident in other moods, it usually is *described* (e.g., "Jim *wants* the ball) or expressed with volitional verbs (e.g., I *desire/want*). The imperative *expresses* volition despite lexeme choice (e.g., *give* me the ball; *throw* the fish back). It is not insignificant that generally the imperative mood is used only in imperative sentence-types.[184]

Summary

It has been determined that although absolute certainty cannot be achieved it is worthwhile to attempt to establish the semantic meaning of the imperative mood. By analyzing the mood itself and by comparing it with other moods it has been concluded that the imperative mood is essentially a *volitional-directive*. By nature, this definition suggests that the imperative is a rather strong mood, being

---

[183]Raphael Kühner, *Grammar of the Greek Language: For the Use of High Schools and Colleges*, trans. B. B. Edwards and S. H. Taylor (Boston: B. B. Mussey and Co., 1849), 347.

[184]Maria Luisa Rivero and Arhonto Terzi, "Imperatives, V-Movement and Logical Mood," *Journal of Linguistics* 31, (1995): 305. One may argue that there may be idiomatic uses of the grammatical imperative that are not in imperative sentences. This can be granted but the idiomatic expression demands special consideration and the actual statement in another context could be an imperative statement. Also, the opposite is not true. Imperative sentence types can have verbs in various moods.

used in contexts where a speaker wishes (*volition*) to get another (or others) to do something (*directive*). This meaning will interact with contextual features and thus realize related but different meanings (usage) in various contexts. This is the subject of the next chapter.

Chapter 4

Pragmatic Analysis

Introduction

Chapter 3 demonstrated that the essence of the imperative mood was directive, specifically, *volitional-directive*. A definition was nuanced noting that *volitional* did not necessarily correspond to "real-world" willful desire. Rather, it was a portrayal of reality. Acknowledging that the semantic meaning is volitional-directive helps but serves as only half of the concern here. Mood, like all language, does not occur in a vacuum. Our volitional-directive may be tempered, enhanced, etc., by its context. Analysis of the contextual (both linguistic and non-linguistic) features and the resultant meaning is, for the purposes here, called *pragmatic analysis*. Chapter 1 introduced the following distinctions important for this work. *Semantic meaning* is the inherent linguistic meaning encoded and expressed by the *linguistic system* in an utterance without reference to non-linguistic factors such as beliefs, social considerations, etc., or other contextual linguistic elements. It is the linguistic meaning directly involved in the linguistic element under discussion. *Pragmatics* is indirect linguistic (contextual) meaning and non-linguistic meaning including factors such as beliefs, social considerations, etc., and its relationship to the communicators. *Pragmatic implicature* is the resultant meaning of any non-linguistic factors such as beliefs, social considerations, etc., and indirect contextual linguistic meaning interacting with the semantic meaning.[1]

---

[1]As noted when these definitions were first introduced, although they were influenced by others, they ultimately are my own. Pragmatics as a field of study is highly influenced by the works of Grice and Speech Act theory. Relevance theory (a communication theory) is essentially a theory of pragmatics. For a detailed treatment of pragmatics from the more traditional perspective (i.e., Grice and Speech Act Theory [often critical of RT]), see Stephen C. Levinson, *Pragmatics*, Cambridge Textbooks in Linguistics, ed. B. Comrie et al. (Cambridge: University Press, 1983). For an application of the more traditional pragmatic approach to ancient Greek (not New Testament), see N. E. Collinge, "Thoughts on the Pragmatics of Ancient Greek," *Proceedings of the Cambridge Philological Society* 214 [n.s. 34] (1988): 1-13.

This chapter will discuss various pragmatic features which interact with the semantic meaning and determine the *pragmatic implicatures* or resulting usages based on the analysis. Actually, this is not new. Traditional analysis which labels types of imperatives as *command, request,* etc., is doing a type of pragmatic analysis. However, this has been rather simplistic and primarily based on the subjective judgment of the grammarian.[2] One simply looks at an imperative and attempts to decide in which usage category it should be classified. There is little attempt to determine why or what factors contribute to this.[3]

It is the contention here that the traditional analysis with its resulting paradigm insufficiently accounts for the imperative mood. Problems exposed already include:[4] 1. No real consensus has formed on how many usages of the imperative exist.[5] 2. Apart from the *command* category, no real consensus exists on the labels that should be given to even the most common usages (*permission* or *toleration*? etc.) 3. The traditional paradigm has somewhat different types of categories. For example, is *prohibition* a separate category simply because it is negated? Does the *conditional* label really describe a category parallel to *command* and *request*? 4. Related to the former problem, the traditional paradigm is one-dimensional. When the exegete consults a grammar for the use of a specific imperative mood, he is usually given a choice of mutually exclusive categories in which he must choose the most appropriate one for his verb of concern. Sometimes a passage fails to fit into a main category. This

---

[2]No one can escape subjectivity in any grammatical work. Nevertheless, one must strive to continually expose one's biases and take steps to minimize their impact on one's conclusions. I am not suggesting that complete objectivity can be obtained here. However, the traditional analysis does little to minimize subjectivity by identifying factors which may contribute to usage. This is what this work hopes to advance here.

[3]Wallace does more than most, especially when he attempts to discern structural characteristics of the "conditional" imperative ("Ὀργίζεσθε in Ephesians 4:26: Command or Condition?" *Criswell Theological Review* 3 [1989]: 353-72; idem, *Greek Grammar beyond the Basics: An Exegetical Syntax of the New Testament* [Grand Rapids: Zondervan Publishing House, 1996], 489-92).

[4]Since chapters 1 and 2 were primarily descriptive, not every one of these points may have been identified as a problem. However, the problematic status of these points (to greater and lesser extent) all seems self-evident if ones' goal is a unified account and paradigm of the imperative mood.

[5]Compare for example the minimal categories presented by BDF (195-96) with the many described by Perschbacher (*New Testament Greek Syntax: An Illustrated Manual* [Chicago: Moody Press, 1995], 345-49).

results in the proliferation of "minor" usages. For example, should the three occurrences of the verb βλέπετε in Phil 3:2 be classified as *command* or *warning*? If one makes a choice at this level, it may minimize important nuances of the label not chosen. However, if one claims both should be applied, the usefulness of the paradigm may be weakened.[6] The mutually exclusive choice is not the case with all grammarians;[7] however, the very manner of presentation of the usages suggests one must choose among options. This selection process is almost purely based on intuition and its resulting experience. 5. The traditional paradigm fails to explicitly recognize important features of the imperative situation such as who *benefits* from the fulfillment of the verbal action?[8]

This chapter will focus on a number of pragmatic elements and present a new paradigm for the classification of imperative usage. Specifically, contextual elements such as social status/rank, politeness, event-sequence, person, and lexical will be considered to determine new criteria for force. This work's notion of *force* will be rather simple. It will merely be describing directness relative to the lexemic meaning of the verb. An imperative will be considered strong-forced unless there is a contextual reason to view it as weak.[9] As for the relative nature of force, an illustration may be helpful. The raw imperatives "tap" and "hit" will be considered to have identical force even though "hitting" is much more forceful than "tapping." Force is relative to its own lexemic content.[10] In addition this work will analyze the direction in which *benefit* is

---

[6]This charge can be somewhat avoided if more than one label is used sparingly and very carefully. However, what will be suggested below is that there is a better way to classify the verbs.

[7]See, for example, Wallace's comments on Matt 8:31-32 (*Exegetical Syntax*, 489).

[8]The only way this can be avoided is to resort to the undesirable practice of creating more and more categories.

[9]This is not a random decision. As has been demonstrated, the choice of the imperative involves the choice of a (relatively) stronger forced mood. This will become even clearer as this work progresses.

[10]In addition, the notion of *force* used here should not be confused with concepts like "illocutionary force" which are often mentioned in discussions of directives (see the comments on Austin's work in chapter 2). For further discussion of mood and illocutionary force, see Deirdre Wilson and Dan Sperber, "Mood and the Analysis of Non-Declarative Sentences," in *Human Agency: Language, Duty and Value*, ed. J. Dancy, J. Moravcsik, and C. Taylor (Stanford, CA: Stanford University Press, 1988), 77-79. For a discussion of speaker commitment and force, see Hidemitsu Takahashi, "English Imperatives and Speaker Commitment," *Language Sciences* 16 (1994): 371-85. Takahashi's study considers spoken English and is of little benefit for the analysis of a fixed ancient text.

projected by fulfillment of the imperative to add an additional element to an understanding of imperative usage. The new classification paradigm will be multidimensional to account for the complexity of the mood's usage. It will account for factors of *force* and *benefit*. In addition, although important for the factor of force, the *event time* in which an imperative occurs will be considered. The three factors of the new paradigm will be discussed in further detail below. In addition, the role of negation in the paradigm will briefly be mentioned. Finally, the third person and the existence of so-called "conditional" imperatives will be discussed.

Definition and Method

Much has already been stated concerning the definition of *pragmatics* and *pragmatic implicatures* in this work. The field of pragmatics involves indirect contextual linguistic meaning (both lexical and other words in context).[11] Non-linguistic meaning and *pragmatic implicatures* are the resultant meanings of the interaction between the semantic meaning and pragmatic features. With reference to this study, this is the meaning of the imperative in context, namely, what traditional grammars label "usages."

When considering the semantic meaning of the imperative mood, a number of preliminary questions needed to be answered such as: does a semantic meaning exist? If so, can it be discovered? And finally, is it worth pursuing? It was concluded that an inherent, unaffected, semantic meaning does exist; however, a thorough identification or understanding of it is unlikely. Nevertheless, since this work is dealing with a document as important as the New Testament, it was worthwhile to pursue. An attempt to understand the essence of the mood was an important step in the process of understanding the meaning in specific contexts.

Fortunately, questions of existence and relevance are not an issue with the

---

[11]As explained in some detail in chapter 1, indirect linguistic meaning involves two types of linguistic information: other words in the context and lexical nuances of the verb itself which is unrelated to the mood. The latter stresses the pragmatic meaning when discussing the mood (or other grammatical features). If one was discussing the lexeme's meaning, such information would belong to what is often labeled *lexical semantics*. The concern here is the pragmatics of the meaning of the imperative mood without specific reference to the individual lexical items. Therefore, lexical information is *indirect* linguistic information for this work's purposes.

pragmatics of the mood. The mood is used in various contexts and has various nuances depending upon the information provided by those contexts. Unfortunately, I have not discovered any sustained pragmatic treatment of the morphological imperative mood in any language. Therefore, discussion of secondary literature on the subject will necessarily be drawn from discussion of the imperative as a sentence type; that is, the imperative (or better: command/prohibition) in contrast to the declarative and interrogative. Nevertheless, acknowledging the distinction in approaches between these and ours, such studies can contribute to this work's understanding of the imperative mood in Greek.

The importance of pragmatics for this study cannot be overstated. In fact, some see a pragmatic theory alone as able to account for the imperative concept.[12] This overstates the case for this study's needs as chapter 3 has demonstrated. Nevertheless, despite the apparent, self-evident usefulness of pragmatics, formulating and using a method to accomplish the goals of pragmatic analysis present no easy task.[13] Further complications arise when using a "dead" language as the focus of analysis.[14] In general, theories of pragmatics describe living languages. In addition, oral communication situations seem prominent. This is easily explained because such situations most easily provide data for analysis. These analyses usually have direct access to the participants for further questioning. Most often the people doing the analysis share much of the same cognitive environment with those creating the data. In these cases, determining pragmatic elements important for analysis is easily revealed and utilized.

In order to overcome the problems with a pragmatic analysis of a dead language, this work will need to appeal to more universal linguistic and social elements and to continually remember the cognitive aspect of its method as a

---

[12]William Downes, "The Imperative and Pragmatics," *Journal of Linguistics* 13 (1977): 77.

[13]Werner Kummer, "Formal Pragmatics," in *Pragmatik: Handbuch pragmatischen Denkens*, ed. Herbert Stachowiak (Hamburg: Felix Meiner Verlag, 1993), 120.

[14]However, note the significant work on Latin (Rodie Risselada, *Imperatives and Other Directive Expressions in Latin: A Study in the Pragmatics of a Dead Language*, Amsterdam Studies in Classical Philology, ed. Albert Rijksbaron, Irene J. F. de Jong, and Harm Pinkster, vol. 2 [Amsterdam: J. C. Gieben, 1993]). Risselada's approach depends much more upon speech act theory than this study does.

restraint (see chapter 1).[15] In addition, the approach to pragmatics here seems to encroach upon other fields of study such as sociolinguistics. Therefore, although one needs to always be concerned about anachronism, one can glean important principles from this field.[16]

In the introduction to this chapter, it was suggested that the traditional paradigm of usages for the imperative mood was simplistic and thus limited in its application. Grammarians do not necessarily suggest that the interpreter approaching a specific imperative mood in context must choose a single usage classification such as command, request, permission, conditional, prohibition, etc.; however, the presentation often implies it. This one-dimensional approach fails to capture the complexity of the imperative mood and it often seems to mix unrelated items as choice options. It makes sense that one might need to classify an imperative as either *command* or *request* based on the force of the verb. Or, one may need to choose between *command* and *prohibition* whether or not a strong-forced imperative is negated. However, one questions whether someone must choose between *command* or *conditional*. Such classifications describe different phenomena. The latter depends upon higher level discourse (sentence) considerations.

This chapter will propose a more complex classification theory which should account for the data in the New Testament. This approach which is multidimensional improves upon the traditional approach. Specifically, each imperative will be considered in three categories. First, the *force*, whether strong or weak, will be considered. Second, who *benefits* by fulfillment of the action will be noted. Finally, where the imperative falls within the sequence of an event or action (*event-sequence*) will be noted. To some extent all of these are related and may contribute to the others. *Event-sequence* is especially important for the determination of *force*. Nevertheless, an adequate account of the imperative mood needs to take into account all three individually.

Although I suspect other classification systems may be devised and utilized

---

[15]Klaus-Uwe Panther and Linda Thornburg challenge various theories such as RT, Gricean approaches, and Speech Act Theory to utilize a cognitive approach to discourse analysis ("A Cognitive Approach to Inferencing in Conversation," *Journal of Pragmatics* 30 [1998]: 755-69). The authors' interests are quite different than ours; however, their insight for the need of a cognitive approach is also assumed in this work's approach.

[16]Levinson, *Pragmatics*, 374-75. Levinson also mentions psycholinguistics which can roughly include an emphasis on the cognitive. Pragmatics is a field which may add much to many different fields (ibid., 376-78).

with various measures of success, given the evident problems of the traditional approach, the analysis of the data, and secondary literature, this system seems worthwhile to pursue. It seems to solve the problems associated with the traditional approach and account for the data. It does not solve all problems and may introduce some unforeseen issues at this time. Nevertheless, this work will proceed confidently for two reasons. First, the approach taken here handles the data fairly well. Second, no attempt to describe a significant aspect of a system of language with any specificity can provide an absolute, exceptionless account of the linguistic phenomenon. Language is simply too elastic for this. Given language change over time, differences within contemporary usage, the diversity and unpredictability of both community and individual needs and usage for language, the traditional approach can only make such goals unpractically idealistic. Therefore, this work will proceed not because it will solve every problem but because it offers to further the understanding of the imperative mood.

The vast majority of imperatives are classified traditionally as *commands*. Boyer's figures strongly suggest this. He counts 1357 imperatives (83%) which would be classified as either *command* or *prohibition*.[17] Using the terminology which will be developed below, this work's analysis suggests that the most common imperative is strongly-forced, addressee-benefitting, and event-initiating. Although this observation is important, it will be imperatives that vary from this which will be most important for the analysis here. This work will consider the most common imperative characteristics *unmarked*. Where imperatives differ, this work will need to question why and develop a means of predicting this difference.

The method used here will look at each of the three factors of a new multidimensional paradigm individually. The element of *force* will demand the most attention. This element involves the most factors and will be discussed first. The predetermined database will be utilized and an attempt to determine what factors contribute to a weakening of force. Structural considerations (e.g., person, honor terms) and sociological theories (e.g., rank, politeness) will be

---

[17]James L. Boyer, "A Classification of Imperatives: A Statistical Study," *Grace Theological Journal* 8 (1987): 36. Boyer also notes that there are 28 other imperatives that are "given alternate identification as command" (ibid., n. 2). Of course, lumping both commands and prohibitions together may not be ideal for this work's purposes. However, the main reason for citing this statistic is to demonstrate that the overwhelming classification of imperative usage is *command*.

examined. The notion of *benefit* is more subjective. However, in many cases, it will be clear when the fulfillment of an imperative benefits the speaker or the hearer. It will be important to determine who benefits from the action. The difference between an *order*[18] and a *warning* is not related to *force* but one of *benefit*. When classifying an imperative, both *force* and *benefit* must be determined. Finally, where an imperative fits within an *event-sequence* will be important. Most imperatives function to begin an event or action. However, occasionally they are responsive or reactive. In these cases the *force* of the imperative is significantly weakened. In addition to the impact on *force*, the notion of *event-sequence* is important in its own right. In addition to *force* and *benefit*, *event-sequence* will add color to the imperative mood profile.

Therefore, this work will proceed as follows: using the suggested database, each imperative will be examined and identify issues relating to force, benefit, and event-sequence. In cases where imperatives differ from an unmarked imperative, a reason will be postulated. Then this work will pursue these reasons with the database established in chapter 1 and throughout the entire New Testament if necessary.

Factors Contributing to the Force of an Imperative

The limited sample of passages in the first section of analysis (internal considerations) in chapter 3 used to determine and illustrate the semantics of the imperative mood was taken from the conclusions of other grammarians. It seems clear that the majority of uses of the mood would be classified as *command*.[19] In this group, a number of contextual characteristics can be identified. After briefly noting these characteristics, the larger control group will be considered. First, the one using the imperative would be considered of higher social-rank than the hearer.[20] This may not always be the case (e.g., there were no examples of equally-ranked participants). However, there was one possible exception to the observation concerning higher-ranked imperative users,

---

[18]Labels such as *order* will be more specifically described below.

[19]These findings are in agreement with Boyer's findings mentioned above.

[20]Again Boyer's observation is revealing: 1416 (87%) were spoken by higher-ranking individuals to lower. Of these 1310 are *command* and 53 are *request* (ibid., 54). This will be explored more thoroughly with this work's data.

namely, Wallace's example of John 2:16:[21]

ἄρατε ταῦτα ἐντεῦθεν, μὴ ποιεῖτε[22] τὸν οἶκον τοῦ πατρός μου
οἶκον ἐμπορίου
remove these things from here, stop making my Father's house a market
house (place)

It is questionable whether Jesus would be viewed as being of "higher" social-rank than the businessmen (and possibly also those who permitted their activities, i.e., the temple officials). Three points may be made in response. First, John's portrayal of Jesus (from the very beginning of the gospel) indicated superiority to all others in the book (with the exception of the Father).[23] Second, Jesus was at this time considered a "teacher" and although not all would see him as of higher-rank, certainly some would, especially his followers (including the author John). Third, Jesus acted not on his own authority but as the prophets of the Old Testament; he acted on God's behalf.[24]

Therefore, it is best to consider this verse as fitting the higher to lower-rank observation. It does, however, raise the question of how one views social-rank within literature. This will be explored briefly in the next section.

Another factor that reveals itself is the use of the third person. In the limited control group, only 4 of 37 (just over 10%) *command* examples (two are within the same passage) are third person (1 Cor 1:31; 2 Cor 10:7; Jas 1:5-6).

---

[21]Wallace, *Exegetical Syntax*, 486.

[22]Although this imperative is very similar to the preceding (*command*), in traditional grammar, it is often not classified as the former which obscures the similarities between the two. Rather, with all negative imperatives despite force, it is merely classified *prohibition*.

[23]Some may object to my appeal to the book's author and not emphasize Jesus's historical words themselves. I believe this concern will be satisfied below. Nevertheless, it is worth noting that it is unlikely (although not impossible) that Jesus used Greek in this context and that it is not possible to know whether these are the exact words (translated or not) of Jesus (*ipsissima verba*) or the "voice" of Jesus (*ipsissima vox*). Therefore, an appeal here to the one who records the words is acceptable.

[24]It seems probable that he was fulfilling an Old Testament messianic prophecy here (Zech 14:21; see C. H. Dodd *Interpreting the Fourth Gospel* [Cambridge: Cambridge University Press, 1953], 300). Also D. A. Carson notes John may be alluding to Mal 3:1, 3 (*The Gospel According to John*, Pillar New Testament Commentary, ed. D. A. Carson [Grand Rapids: William B. Eerdmans Publishing Company, 1991], 179). This is supported by the response of his opponents who request a sign for a claim implicit in his action (2:18-20). For a discussion of the prophetic role of Jesus throughout this pericope (with a focus on 2:19–the destruction of the temple saying), see E. P. Sanders, *Jesus and Judaism* (London: SCM Press, 1985), 72-76.

However, the weaker-force *request* examples are better represented with 8 of 29 (27.6%) being third person (Matt 6:9b-13 [3x]; 26:39, 42; Rev 22:17 [3x]; note that six of these occur within two passages). Finally, of the examples with the weakest force imperative, those labeled *permission/toleration*, have 50% (5 of 10) third person imperatives (Matt 10:13 [2x]; 1 Cor 7:15, 36; 2 Cor 12:16). Because the database is rather limited, these figures can prove little. However, they suggest one possible insight into the cause of force, namely person. It seems the third person imperatives tend to be associated with less force than second person imperative. This will be explored in further detail.

One further characteristic is worth noting before proceeding. Chapter 3 considered some imperatives which appeared to have very little if any force. Traditional grammars label these as imperatives of *permission*, *allowance*, *toleration*, etc. These will be examined more closely and a further contextual element will be discovered that both contribute to *force* and are worth adding as a separate element to this work's paradigm of features for understanding the usage of the mood.

Politeness and the Imperative

Entire volumes could be written on the impact of culture upon the imperative mood. This is especially true of the cultural notions related to interaction between peoples and groups of various social-ranks and the means and tactics by which they relate and attempt to maintain a positive sense of being in their own eyes and those of the community. This includes areas such as honorifics, honor/shame, and politeness. However, detailed development cannot be pursued here.[25] Nevertheless, the importance of this issue demands that it be addressed. Indeed, it will be maintained that such issues are essential for understanding the concept of force with the imperative mood.

A rather new area of New Testament studies, a social-scientific approach,

---

[25]I suspect a number of research projects could be undertaken in this area. For example, politeness strategy and mood usage, politeness and discourse in the gospels, etc. Although not exclusively about politeness, David A. Montgomery has recently written an article from a SAT perspective that considers issues of politeness and other factors in biblical interpretation ("Directives in the New Testament: A Case Study of John 1:38," *Journal of the Evangelical Theological Society* [2007]: 275-88).

is interested in *honor* and *shame*.[26] This area is controversial but nevertheless seems to have contributed to an understanding of some aspects of the New Testament. I suspect that in the future this area may contribute to an understanding of the imperative; however, because of its recent development (and uncertain results) and its controversial aspect,[27] it will be utilized here only minimally and without any type of systematic application. It will primarily be used to support the direction as described below.

The notion of politeness appears to be a universal trait among cultures.[28] This is clearly suggested by the title of an important book on the subject, *Politeness: Some Universals in Language Usage*.[29] Theories of politeness[30] assume that interaction among communicators is not simply one of stating propositions to one another. Rather, there are complex interactions between participants in which these participants use various strategies to communicate their message in a way in which it will be received and responded to in a desired manner. This will ideally be done in the most efficient way known by the communicator.[31] The existence of politeness strategies is a universal cultural

---

[26]Influential scholars in this area include Bruce Malina and Jerome Neyrey. For a concise introduction to the issues involved, see Jerome H. Neyrey, *Honor and Shame in the Gospel of Matthew* (Louisville, KY: Westminster John Knox Press, 1998), 1-10. For a general introduction to honor and shame within the larger cultural picture, see Bruce J. Malina, *The New Testament World: Insights From Cultural Anthropology*, 3d ed. (Louisville, KY: Westminster John Knox Press, 2001), 27-57.

[27]Major proponents have been criticized for claiming too much from this approach. This has contributed to the controversy surrounding the theory. However, excesses do not necessarily mean the theory is without value. David deSilva takes this approach and uses the theory to analyze the book of Hebrews. His work on Hebrews, originally a Ph.D. dissertation, contains a helpful summary of the theory, problems associated with claims made by the major proponents, and a defense for its use despite these claims based on the essential value of the theory (*Despising Shame: Honor Discourse and Community Maintenance in the Epistle to the Hebrews*, Society of Biblical Literature Dissertation Series, ed. Pheme Perkins, vol. 152 [Atlanta: Scholars Press, 1995], 11-23).

[28]Politeness is not unrelated to honor and shame; however, the emphasis here will be placed upon politeness.

[29]Penelope Brown and Stephen C. Levinson, *Politeness: Some Universals in Language Usage* (Cambridge: Cambridge University Press, 1987).

[30]In addition to Brown and Levinson, see especially Geoffrey N. Leech, *Principles of Pragmatics* (London: Longman, 1983), 78-84, 107-14, 169-71.

[31]See Dan Sperber and Deirdre Wilson, *Relevance: Communication and Cognition*, 2d ed. (Oxford: Blackwell, 1995), 46-49.

trait; however, the specifics of these theories may differ among cultures.[32]

Brown and Levinson note three important factors about participants which will influence what types of strategies will be used to accomplish their communicative goal(s).[33] First, the *social distance* between participants will provide some restraint on the communication process.[34] This is a relative category. For example, two Texans of different backgrounds may seem quite distant and possibly not pay notice to each other while passing on a Dallas street. However, if they see each other in Beijing China, they might immediately associate with one another. This is because their social distance is quite close compared to the native Chinese all around them. Communicators close in social distance will communicate differently than those who are distant. Second, the *relative power* of communicators will impact the strategies of the participants. This also may be relative. The obvious boss-to-employer relationship has a relatively fixed power structure while in the employment situation. However, people may assume different levels of power in different situations. Take for example two people, a mechanic and a New Testament scholar, in two situations, a Bible study and a repair shop. In the former circumstance, the notion of power is with the New Testament scholar; however, in the latter situation, power is with the mechanic. Third, *absolute rank* is the culturally established fixed rank.

Brown and Levinson's discussion of these elements is much more complex than presented here. These factors are then further developed in a number of ways and applied in various situations. Essentially, participants within a communication situation wish to maintain *face*. The notion of *face*, the public image each individual wants to claim for himself,[35] is viewed as a driving factor

---

[32]John Lyons, *Linguistic Semantics: An Introduction* (Cambridge: Cambridge University Press, 1995), 279.

[33]Brown and Levinson, *Politeness*, 74-83.

[34]Although not entirely unrelated, I am not here concerned with larger communication situations among various types of social groups in which significant differences in social status result in different types of communication between groups of different status. See James C. Scott, *Domination and the Arts of Resistance: Hidden Transcripts* (New Haven, CN: Yale University Press, 1990) and various applications of Scott's theory to New Testament studies in Richard A. Horsley, *Hidden Transcripts and the Arts of Resistance: Applying the Work of James C. Scott to Jesus and Paul*. Semeia Studies 48 (Atlanta: Society of Biblical Literature, 2004). Implications of Scott's theory may provide insight into the use of imperatives; however, its focus tends to be on higher level discourse functions and thus is not taken into account here.

[35]For a more detailed description of *face*, see ibid., 61-64.

in communication (this is similar to/related to honor and shame). Depending upon where participants rank within the three factors, they will use different strategies to maintain *face*, effectively communicate (to achieve their purpose), and do so with the effort demanded by the communication situation.

Actions which threaten *face* in normal communication situations are approached with care. This is especially true in lower- to higher-ranked communication situations. Various strategies to maintain mutual *face* may be employed.[36] It will be demonstrated that this is the case in such communication situations recorded in the New Testament. Additionally, this chapter will observe that even in higher to lower-ranked situations, politeness strategies will be used for the purpose of encouraging imperatives to be obeyed.

Politeness strategies are employed throughout communication. Their use with sentences in the imperative mood accounts for only a small part of such strategies. In fact, in a general communication situation, a prominent politeness strategy often includes avoiding the imperative except where absolutely necessary. It also may involve placing the imperative in well-positioned places within the discourse (e.g., at the end).[37]

---

[36]Ibid., 68-84.

[37]In chapter 3 it was noted that in many letters imperatives came at the end. This observation supported the notion that the imperative was a *volitional-directive*. Politeness was not mentioned at that stage of the project because the purpose there was semantic analysis. Andrew Wilson used a theory of politeness in an analysis of Philemon with helpful results ("The Pragmatics of Politeness and Pauline Epistolography: A Case Study of the Letter to Philemon," *Journal for the Study of the New Testament* 48 [1992]: 107-19). Wilson noted that in light of the cultural conventions concerning runaway slaves, Paul's somewhat vague request to Philemon on behalf of Onesimus would have been quite difficult for Philemon (significant loss of *face*). Therefore, Paul uses politeness strategies throughout the letter. Paul does not begin his letter with his characteristic self-designation "apostle" (this is only omitted elsewhere in Paul's very personal epistle Philippians and his two earliest letters, 1 and 2 Thessalonians). Paul, although Philemon's spiritual superior, does not say so directly in the beginning. Rather, they are brothers (ἀδελφοί). Paul is quite indirect about his main request about Onesimus, avoiding the imperative until verses 17-18. The imperative is first used in the apodosis of a conditional sentence: εἰ οὖν με ἔχεις κοινωνόν, **προσλαβοῦ** αὐτὸν ὡς ἐμέ. (Therefore, if you have me [as a] partner, accept him as [you would] me). Paul associates his relationship with Philemon with the master's relationship to the slave. The imperative in verse 18 is used as a gracious offer to Philemon minimizing any damages owed the master by the slave. This removes one obstacle for reconciliation between master and slave. In verse 20, the third person imperative is used (... **ἀνάπαυσόν** μου τὰ σπλάγχνα ἐν Χριστῷ; refresh my heart in Christ) in which Paul states in a manner that pays respect to Philemon as an encourager of the apostle himself. Verse 21 has no imperative but states Paul's confidence in Philemon to do more than Paul even expects because as it is implied, Philemon is a very good and faithful man. Finally, the last imperative occurs in verse 22. This

Despite the broad application of politeness theory, it seems it can be of value even for this project of a more limited scope. The imperative is an important aspect of politeness. It is used and not used within this framework.

The work of Brown/Levinson and Leech (and others) is quite detailed. The use of politeness strategies will be simplified for three reasons. First, as mentioned above, politeness strategies are strategies employed in general communication, where the imperative is only one aspect of this concern. Second, most politeness theory is based on spoken communication situations.[38] Written communication is more limited in expression than spoken. Third, this work's corpus is very specific (religious discourse with rather fixed participant roles and ranks). Thus, it is a narrow example even among examples of written communication. Brown and Levinson attempt to account for many more types of situations than the database includes. Even the brief description of the three factors is really more complex than is necessary for the analysis here. For this work's purposes, *social distance* must be fixed within the culture of Jewish and Greco-Roman worlds of the New Testament. There are no relative situations like the Texans noted above in the New Testament. The closest possibility would occur during Paul's journeys recorded in Acts; however, even here his relationships are rather fixed. *Relative power* has more flexibility but again is rather fixed. In general, spiritual leaders (Jesus, Paul, John, etc.) are addressing (or in the case of some narrative passages, being addressed by) those who are their spiritual dependents or inferiors (for lack of a better term). In some minor areas it seems that the spiritual leaders are possibly portrayed as inferior. These

---

imperative seems rather strong. Paul is asking for a place to stay. However, in light of the cultural expectations of hospitality in the ancient world, this is probably not as bold of a request as it might seem today. For another brief example of "politeness" discussed within the context of biblical studies, see Willian Olhausen, "A 'Polite' Response to Anthony Thiselton," in *After Pentecost: Language and Biblical Interpretation.* Scripture and Hermeneutics Series, vol. 2, ed. Craig, Bartholomew, Colin Green, and Karl Möller (Grand Rapids: Zondervan Publishing House, 2001, 125-27).

[38]However, see Roger D. Cherry, "Politeness in Written Persuasion," *Journal of Pragmatics* 12 (1988): 63-81 and Greg Myers, "The Pragmatics of Politeness in Scientific Articles," *Applied Linguistics* 10 (1989): 1-35. Neither study directly applies to the type of written communication addressed in this work. Cherry examines communication directed towards a superior. The New Testament examples are primarily reversed. Myers approaches politeness basically like Brown and Levinson but modifies the approach for scientific writing. The modifications are intended to account for the lack of specific addressees and a difficulty in defining cultural variables. However, these are not issues with New Testament literature which is more explicit in these areas (especially the first which is the main problem; ibid., 3).

primarily occur in political situations in Acts (e.g., Paul before Roman officials). However, even here, there seems to be an overarching notion of God (and thus his people) in control.[39] Additionally, *absolute rank* can be seen in the corpus. Rabbis, teachers, etc., are of higher-rank than the common person.

Despite the simplified use of politeness theory, this work still must account for circumstances that may relativize rank. Some circumstances may cause a lower-ranked party to rise in rank in comparison to the addressee. Such circumstances include special (possibly damaging) knowledge about the higher-ranked individual and situations which make the higher-ranked individual's rank insecure (e.g., disfavor with his own superiors, recent errors made by the individual, etc.). Also, lower-ranked people in mass may feel more confident and be willing to exert themselves above their individual rank.[40] Finally, there are events which provoke communication situations where rank is irrelevant. Few would take the time to be indirect in matters of urgency such as fires or other events needing quick statements for the good of the recipients.

Essentially, contributions from politeness theories will be noted but the factors will be focused primarily upon social-rank. In general, those with higher social-rank have higher power and usually maintain positions of recognized authority. However, as the example from John 2:16 above revealed, the identification of social-rank is not always immediately evident. Therefore, following one of this work's guiding principles, that language presents the communicator's portrayal of reality, this chapter will suggest a distinction between *absolute rank* and *perceived rank*. *Absolute rank* was mentioned above and here will simply mean the rank of two individuals in a context without reference to personal beliefs. In some senses this is objective. A teacher is ranked higher than a student. Pilate is ranked higher than his subjects. This is helpful but less important for this work; *perceived rank* is the subjective belief of the communicator of his rank compared to the one he is addressing. A soldier may be absolutely ranked below his commander. However, if his commander is out of uniform and is not recognized by the soldier, the soldier may *perceive* the commander as a common citizen and speak to him as one of lower-rank. If

[39]This is most vividly seen when Jesus appears before Pilate. The Roman leader is officially the highest-ranking person in Jerusalem; however, Jesus acts as (and the writers present him as) the one with the real power (e.g., John 19:10-11).

[40]Additionally, a person representing a high-ranked individual may assume the rank of the one represented in the situation(s) in which he is representing the higher-ranked individual.

he uses an imperative, its usage will be as a superior to an inferior despite their respective absolute ranks.[41] Since the use of the imperative results from the communicator's *perceived rank*, this will be the primary concern here.

Observations about the initial sample have suggested the manner in which this work will proceed. Lesser-forced imperatives traditionally labeled *request* or *permission* include characteristics such as lower- to higher-rank, third person, and non-event-initiating actions. In addition, lexical items can be added which are clearly force-softening factors in other languages. The predetermined database will be used to determine whether these also apply in the New Testament. Lexical factors are of three types: there are polite words or phrases such as "please," "may I ask," etc., which may introduce an imperative in a non-threatening manner. Also, a lower-ranked communicator using an imperative may choose to use an honor term such as "sir" to address the higher-ranking participant serving to communicate respect to the addressee.[42] Finally, this work will explore whether the lexical choice for the imperative verb softens the force of the imperative.

Of the factors mentioned above, two are not structural characteristics. Event-sequence is a discourse feature but nevertheless can be clearly seen when clauses are examined. However, rank is not encoded in the structure at all. It may be obvious in most cases; however, as the distinction between *absolute* and *perceived* rank revealed, this is an issue of interpretation based on cultural expectations. Therefore, at this stage, a methodological decision will be made based on the principle of structural priority and the distribution of imperatives among speakers of rank as revealed by preliminary observations and those cited above from Boyer. The figures are rather lopsided. The vast majority (Boyer's

---

[41]An interesting example both literarily and historically of the complexity of this issue is Pilate's dealing with Jesus (see for example John 18:28-19:15). In the perspective of the ruling world power, Pilate is *absolutely* higher-ranked than Jesus and he deals with him accordingly. However, the perspective of Jesus and the reader is that Jesus is above the ruling power of the world and Pilate's only authority was given to him from God himself (John 19:11). Thus, in the larger picture, Jesus is *absolutely* higher-ranked than Pilate. It is from Jesus' ranking that he permits Pilate to do what he will do. Jesus never treats Pilate as of *absolute* higher-rank except in the sense that he is willfully submitting to him for his own purpose. The relationship between Pilate and the crowd is also an interesting study in this passage. Since it contains imperatives, it will be discussed below.

[42]Some languages have honorific systems to express honor. See S. Agesthialingom, "Imperative in Old Tamil," *Indian Linguistics: Journal of the Linguistic Society of India* 41 (1980): 102, 106.

figures suggest 87%) of imperatives are used by higher-ranking individuals to lower-ranking individuals or groups. In light of the observation in chapter 3 that the imperative is volitional-directive and thus rather strong, this observation is understandable.[43] This work's database overwhelmingly confirms this. The majority of imperatives are from higher- to lower-rank, event-initiating, and without any of the politeness features mentioned above. A variety of examples from the database will illustrate this point:

Matt 3:2   [καὶ] λέγων· **μετανοεῖτε**· ἤγγικεν γὰρ ἡ βασιλεία τῶν οὐρανῶν
               [and] he [John] said, "**Repent**, for the kingdom of heaven has drawn near"

Mark 14:34   καὶ λέγει αὐτοῖς· περίλυπός ἐστιν ἡ ψυχή μου ἕως θανάτου **μείνατε** ὧδε καὶ **γρηγορεῖτε**
               And he [Jesus] said to them, "my inner being is deeply distressed unto death **stay here** and **keep watch**

Luke 4:35   καὶ ἐπετίμησεν αὐτῷ ὁ 'Ιησοῦς λέγων· **φιμώθητι** καὶ **ἔξελθε** ἀπ' αὐτοῦ ...
               and Jesus ordered him saying, "**be quiet** and **come out** from him" ...

John 20:17   λέγει αὐτῇ 'Ιησοῦς· **μή** μου **ἅπτου**
               Jesus said to her, "**do not touch** me"

---

[43]The second-century grammarian Apollonius Dyscolus (*Syntax* III.105) made the following observation: "For every imperative is directed from a dominant person to a subordinate one." However, the translator and commentator of the edition (used here) observes that the grammarian fails to note that this is not always the case. Imperatives are directed from humans to gods and from slaves to masters (Fred W. Householder, *The Syntax of Apollonius Dyscolus: Translated, and with Commentary*, Amsterdam Studies in the Theory and History of Linguistic Science. Series 3—Studies in the History of Linguistics, ed. E. F. Konrad Koerner, vol. 23 [Amsterdam: John Benjamins, 1981], 192).

Acts 23:23   Καὶ προσκαλεσάμενος δύο [τινὰς] τῶν ἑκατονταρχῶν
                 εἶπεν· **ἑτοιμάσατε** στρατιώτας διακοσίους ...
                 and calling two of the centurions he [the tribune] said, "**Get**
                 two-hundred soldiers ...

Rom 6:11   οὕτως καὶ ὑμεῖς **λογίζεσθε** ἑαυτοὺς [εἶναι] νεκροὺς...
                 so also **consider** yourselves to be[44] dead to sin ...

1 Cor 5:7   **ἐκκαθάρατε** τὴν παλαιὰν ζύμην
                 clean out the old leaven

Phil 2:14   Πάντα **ποιεῖτε** χωρὶς γογγυσμῶν καὶ διαλογισμῶν
                 Do all things without grumbling and arguing

Heb 12:14   Εἰρήνην **διώκετε** μετὰ πάντων
                 Strive for peace with all men

1 John 2:15   **Μὴ ἀγαπᾶτε** τὸν κόσμον μηδὲ τὰ ἐν τῷ κόσμῳ ...
                 Do not love the world nor the things of the world ...

Rev 9:14   λέγοντα τῷ ἕκτῳ ἀγγέλῳ, ὁ ἔχων τὴν σάλπιγγα· **λῦσον**
                 τοὺς τέσσαρας ἀγγέλους τοὺς δεδεμένους ἐπὶ τῷ
                 ποταμῷ τῷ μεγάλῳ Εὐφράτῃ
                 the one saying to the sixth angel who has the trumpet,
                 "**Release** the four angels who are bound at the great river
                 Euphrates"

This type of passage could be multiplied.[45]

This sample demonstrates clearly the most common use of the imperative.[46]

---

[44]Even if the explicit infinitive is not original, it is implied.

[45]See for example: Matt 2:13, 20; 3:8; 5:24, 29; 10:17, 31; 11:4; Mark 13:7, 9, 33, 35; 14:13, 2; 16:6; Luke 1:13; 2:10; 3:11; John 1:43; 15:4, 9; Acts 3:4, 6; Rom 6:12, 13; 12:21; 1 Cor 14:1; Phil 1:27; 3:2, 17; 1 Thess 4:18; 5:11, 13; 1 Tim 4:11; Phlm 1:22; Heb 13:1, 2, 3; Jas 1:2; 5:7; 1 Pet 1:13, 15, 17; 2 Pet 3:17, 18; 1 John 2:28; 4:1 5:21; 2 John 1:8; 3 John 1:11; Jude 1:21, 22, 23; Rev 1:11, 17; 2:1; 3:3; etc.

[46]As has been the assumption of this project, the negative imperative will be considered in the same manner as the non-negative imperative.

In each case a superior-ranked individual uses the imperative to express his will to the recipients. There is no guarantee that the imperative will be fulfilled but the communicator expects and/or desires it to be followed. The imperative includes a rather strong force expressed by the expectation. Possibly the two examples which most vividly demonstrate the imperative in action are Acts 23:23 and Luke 4:35. In Acts 23:23, the imperative occurs within the context of military hierarchy. The military culture assures the fulfillment of the imperative. In Luke 4:35, Jesus uses imperatives to expels demons. Jesus' authority over the demons assures the fulfillment of the imperatives he utters. However, it must be remembered that fulfillment is not actually part of the imperative. Fulfillment of the imperative depends upon other factors. Nevertheless, the imperative expresses the desire of the speaker to direct the action of the recipients. Matthew 3:2 illustrates the difference between the presentation and the actual fulfillment. John's call to repentance expresses his desire to direct the action of the masses to repent. The force of John's command is no less strong than Jesus' or the Tribune's in Luke 4:35 and Acts 23:23. However, the fulfillment of the imperative is much less certain than in these passages. Finally, it is worth noting that the epistolary literature in the New Testament always proceeds from a higher-ranking individual to lower-ranked people. The relationship may differ between letter-writer and church,[47] but in every case this relationship rank (higher to lower) is the same.

Now this work is prepared to state the methodological point which this section has been building toward. Since rank is not encoded in structure and since the vast majority of imperatives occur in higher- to lower-ranked communication situations, I suggest that rank itself does not contribute to force. In other words, just because a lower-ranked individual uses an imperative, it does not follow that it is weakened. This is not the normal approach to rank. Normally, it assumes to weaken force. It will be demonstrated below that other factors contribute to the weakening of force. These are often present in lower to higher communication situations but are not required. It is these other factors, not rank, which weaken the force of the imperative. Nevertheless, rank is important for the use of the imperative. One's rank may influence whether to use the imperative at all. Generally, lower-ranked individuals do not use the

---

[47]For example, Paul's relationship to churches he has founded (e.g., in Philippi) will be somewhat different than those he had not (e.g., in Rome).

mood and/or lower-ranked individuals must employ certain strategies (e.g., politeness) in order to use the imperative. However, it does not weaken force itself. This approach has a number of benefits. First, the principle of structural priority is maintained. Second, it maintains a consistent view of the imperative (strong-forced unless context demands otherwise). Third, it permits lower-ranked individuals to use strong-forced imperatives. To summarize, rank does not affect the *force* of the imperative; rather, it affects the *choice* of whether or not to *use* the imperative. In rare situations where a lower-ranked party uses the imperative, the rank affects how the communicator will *use* the mood (politeness, etc.).

Therefore, I suggest that the imperative is strong-force unless there exists some feature to weaken the force. Rank does not itself affect force. Rather, rank may affect the choice of the imperative and/or the use of a politeness strategy. It will be demonstrated that in most cases of less-forced imperatives at least one of the above mentioned factors are present. Essentially, what these features do is deflect the *directness* of the imperative[48] and/or *softening* the impact in some way. In other words, they are politeness strategies. The exception to this is imperatives which do not initiate an action.[49] These imperatives are weakened because they are merely reacting in some way to an action already in process. Thus, as a working hypothesis, those imperatives with one or more of these features are weakened-force imperatives. These politeness features are primarily used to permit the lower-ranked individual/group to direct an imperative to a higher-ranked party without offense.

Features such as third person, lexical items, and non-event-initiation may be present in higher to lower-ranked communication situations. Purposes for these are related but nevertheless different than when used by lower-ranked individuals. They may be used in situations which are strained for some reason. Politeness strategies may be used by higher-ranked people who do not want to

---

[48]This strategy is most effectively used by departing from the imperative mood entirely (e.g., "could you open the window?" or "I am really hot" to communicate "open the window") (Brown and Levinson, *Politeness*, 132-45). A similar situation occurs in Greek when an infinitive is used in indirect discourse with a command nuance (e.g., John 4:40; Rom 12:1). Nevertheless, this strategy is also used within the imperative mood clauses themselves.

[49]The notion of non-event-initiation is quite different from politeness strategies. For one thing, they seem to be able to be used more equally among higher- to lower- and lower- to higher-ranked communication situations. This is one reason why this work will also discuss this feature separately.

use their rank[50] to get another to do something.[51] They may be used to show respect to the other party.[52] If the refusal of the imperative is still within the lower-ranked party's power to reject, politeness may be used to help secure the success of the imperative (if the fulfillment *benefits* the speaker)[53] or to encourage the addressee to succeed (if the fulfillment *benefits* the addressee).

One key to politeness strategies is *indirectness*. Whether third person, words of asking, etc., they all serve to deflect the directive impact. The strategies which will be explored here express indirectness in various way. They may serve to shift the focus from the recipient specifically to the recipient as part of a group. They may express a directive aimed at an individual in the form of a general precept.[54] Additionally, indirectness may be achieved through the choice of a subject related to the recipient (part of or something related to the

---

[50]Obedience of lower-ranked parties, especially those not under direct authority or those voluntarily submitting to authority, is not assured.

[51]See the discussion of both positive and negative effects of politeness strategies used by teachers with their students in Violetta Aeginitou, "The Power of Politeness in the Greek EFL Classroom," in *Themes in Greek Linguistics: Papers from the First International Conference on Greek Linguistics, Reading, September 1993*, ed. Irene Philippaki-Warburton, Katerina Nicolaidis, and Maria Sifianou (Amsterdam: John Benjamins Publishing Company, 1994), 297-303.

[52]This is also a significant factor in lower- to higher- (and equal-) ranked communication situations. In such situations it is more likely (essential?). Using politeness strategies seem to communicate recognition to the addressee (see René Dirven and Marjolijn Verspoor, *Cognitive Exploration of Language and Linguistics*, Cognitive Linguistics in Practice, ed. Günter Radden, vol. 1 [Amsterdam: John Benjamins Publishing Company, 1998], 180-84). The Gricean pragmatist Geoffrey Leech suggests that communicators observing the *politeness principle* will attempt to produce utterances that lean as far toward the polite as appropriate (*Pragmatics*, 82; for the *politeness principle*, see ibid., 79-84). However, RT is not as optimistic about the ability to predict this. Rather, it maintains that politeness is dictated by *relevance* (A. Jucker, "The Relevance of Politeness," *Multilingua* 7.4 [1988]: 380-381). Politeness is very relevant in lower- to higher-ranked communication. It may be so in higher to lower but it is not as certain nor is it likely.

[53]Brown and Levinson's notion of *social distance* may also be applied here (*Politeness*, 74-76). The further the social distance, the more likely politeness strategies will be utilized. This is due to two factors. First, the rank between socially distant communicators is not always known with certainty. Also, between socially distant participant, the likelihood of power for the higher-ranked party is less certain. However, as already mentioned, in this work's corpus there is little diversity of social distance.

[54]Whether a directive is expressed as specific or general does not necessarily correlate to limiting the directive to that classification in the real world. This is a matter of presentation. For a discussion of specific and general directives with the tenses, see chapter 2 and the literature cited there.

recipient).[55] This subject choice may be impersonal.[56]

It has been suggested above that rank itself is not a contributing factor to the pragmatic implicatures of the mood. Rather this work will address the imperative from two (rank perspective) points of view. First, since the vast majority of the imperatives are from higher to lower-ranked parties, why would a communicator use features that the third person or lexemes with weak inherent force? These features seem to weaken the force by making them somewhat indirect. Thus, the weakened-force is a *pragmatic implicature* resulting from the interaction of the semantic meaning and contextual elements.

Second, since the mood is rarely used by lower-ranked parties, under what circumstances is it used? How is the offense of the imperative which is implied by its distribution removed? Since there are few examples of equally-ranked communicators in our database, any imperatives which occur between equally-ranked parties will be treated as *non*-higher- to lower-ranked communication situations (i.e., as lower- to higher-ranked) and be so noted. This chapter will proceed by describing politeness strategies from both directions.

Another key strategy is to acknowledge the recipient in some way. This may include terms of honor in address (e.g., "sir") or even flattery.[57]

One further issue must be raised before preceding. The analysis here demands that a decision be made about the nature of force, politeness strategies, and the imperative. There are actually two ways that this could be approached. First, politeness strategies could be viewed as actually weakening the force of the imperative. Second, all imperatives could be assumed to have equal force (for their lexeme) and that politeness strategies are merely vehicles of making the imperative more acceptable. I suggest that both may adequately explain the data. The end result would be similar for exegesis.[58] Nevertheless, the first option will be assumed for three reasons. First, the main labels in traditional grammars are generally distinguished by force (command, request, permission, etc.). Second, this study is broader than politeness strategies. I have suggested

---

[55]A common use of the passive in all moods is to provide a means of indirectness.

[56]See the strategies presented by Brown and Levinson (*Politeness*, 129-227).

[57]See the strategies presented by Brown and Levinson (ibid., 101-29).

[58]Results may be similar but not necessarily identical. If force can be weakened, then a focus would be upon the imperative. If the imperative is constant and politeness strategies are a means for making the imperative acceptable, the focus of the study would be on the sociological factors contributing to the text. Whichever approach is taken, it is important to attempt to address both concerns.

that a fruitful study may result from focusing on politeness strategy alone. If this were the goal of this study, approaching the imperative as having a consistent force may be a preferable way to proceed. Third, and related to the second, imperatives are explicit in the text. In other words, the focus here on structure helps dictate the approach of this chapter. There are written imperatives available for analysis; however, exact details about cultural politeness strategies in the first century are not. Thus, there is less confidence about the politeness strategies of the ancient world. It is maintained that enough knowledge of this period is available to provide a valuable analysis but nevertheless, given the nature of this project, more confidence can be placed in
the approach taken here. Fourth, the resultant weakened-force is viewed in this project as a pragmatic implicature due to interaction between the semantic meaning and pragmatic contextual elements.

Higher- to Lower-Rank

There are a number of examples where politeness strategies are used among higher to lower parties. This seems to generally correspond with a weakening of the imperative force.

Lexemic Meaning of the Verb Itself

There are verbs which by their very nature seem rather weak. C. W. E. Miller has made the observation that in Attic oration mild imperatives such as ἐνθυμεῖσθαι, σκοπεῖν, σκέψασθαι, θεωρεῖν lack a sense of prescription (thus give no offense) and serve mainly to invoke the listeners to pay attention. They do not seem to be used in the argumentative section of a speech.[59]

In the New Testament only σκοπεῖν (2x) and θεωρεῖν (1x) occur in the imperative. Two occur in the database and a third in Luke 11:

---

[59]"The Limitation of the Imperative in the Attic Orators," *American Journal of Philology* 13 [1892]: 432-33.

Phil 3:17   Συμμιμηταί μου γίνεσθε, ἀδελφοί, καὶ **σκοπεῖτε** τοὺς
               οὕτω περιπατοῦντας καθὼς ἔχετε τύπον ἡμᾶς
               Become imitators of me, brothers, and **pay attention** to those
               who live just as you have an example in us

Heb 7:4   **Θεωρεῖτε** δὲ πηλίκος οὗτος, ᾧ [καὶ] δεκάτην 'Αβραὰμ
               ἔδωκεν ἐκ τῶν ἀκροθινίων ὁ πατριάρχης
               Now **notice** how great this one was to whom Abraham the
               patriarch gave him a tenth of the plunder

Luke 11:35   **σκόπει** οὖν μὴ τὸ φῶς τὸ ἐν σοὶ σκότος ἐστίν
               Therefore, **pay attention** that no light which is in you is
               darkness

Based on this limited database, it seems difficult to determine whether Miller's
thesis is applicable to the New Testament. The force of the imperatives at first
glance in these passages does not seem weaker than many imperatives used for
instruction. The LXX provides no help; the words occur only eight times and
never in the imperative.[60] However, at closer analysis, Miller's point may be
astute. The directive to observe or consider (pay attention) differs slightly from
commanding the action directly. In Phil 3:17 and Luke 11:35 the imperatives
act as an indirect means of commanding the action described in the following
clause. Philippians 3:17 seems to use the imperative to reiterate the preceding
imperative (Συμμιμηταί μου γίνεσθε). There is a strong force in the initial
clause and the second clause seems to approach the same order from a slightly
indirect manner. He could have commanded the Philippians to become imitators
of others. However, Paul is the primary example to imitate (or to be a co-
imitator with) and thus the second imperative is secondary.[61] Also, the Lukan
example could have been reworded in such a way as to command the light not
to be darkness. Luke's wording may simply be rhetorical or may be

---

[60]The verb ἐνθυμεῖσθαι occurs in Gen 6:6; Deut 21:11; Josh 6:18; 7:21 and θεωρεῖν
occurs in Josh 8:20; Judg 13:19, 20; 16:27.

[61]This observation would not hold if Gordon Fee's optional interpretation is accepted (which
Fee himself does not maintain). The translation "be on the lookout for" suggests a more active
nature to the imperative (*Paul's Letter to the Philippians*, New International Commentary on the
New Testament, ed. Gordon D. Fee [Grand Rapids: William B. Eerdmans Publishing Company,
1995], 366).

purposefully indirect. The Hebrews example does not fit Miller's Attic Greek thesis. There is an order "to notice" something. The statement about Abraham does not function as a command and thus made indirect. It clearly stands as the object of the imperative θεωρεῖτε.

What is being described however, really does not apply to this work's original inquiry. A verb may serve to weaken the imperative in the following clause but it does not necessarily affect the imperative nature of the verb itself. Lexical meaning varies among verbs. These may have different levels of subjective force based upon the lexical meaning. However, this work mainly concerns itself with the force of the imperative. A seemingly weak-forced lexeme such as *tap* does not have the forceful impact of the verb *smash*. The imperative morphology's job however is to make the verb into a *volitional-directive*. Therefore, "tap the glass" and "smash the glass" differ in the actual force of the statement (and in actual damage) but the force of the actual imperative is identical (with all else being equal).[62]

What can one conclude about Miller's thesis about classical Greek for the New Testament?[63] Once the issues are clarified and it is acknowledged that the lexical meaning of the verb does not affect the force of the morphology of the verb under consideration, there still remains the legitimate observation about the distribution of imperatives in a discourse. There simply is not a large enough database to evaluate its application in the New Testament with the words under consideration. However, the interaction of lexical meaning with the imperative morphology seems like a fruitful course to pursue.[64] However, such a project is beyond the scope of this work and cannot be pursued here. Therefore, at this stage this chapter will only note the potential for this area.

---

[62] A comparison could be made here with the aspect and *Aktionsart* relationship. The former is a grammatical category and the latter is a lexical category. They interact but are nevertheless distinct. Only the grammatical category is a matter of concern at this stage.

[63] It is worth recalling that another of Miller's observations about distribution was seen as helpful in establishing the semantic meaning of the mood (see chapter 3).

[64] Such a study would describe a different type of force than described here. This work concerns itself with grammatical force in which all imperatives are unmarked as strong. If this further study were to be pursued, the force in question would be relative among the lexical meaning of the verbs. In such a study, *tap* and *hit* and *smash* would have different forces.

Strategy 1: Words of Asking

A number of passages in the New Testament demonstrate the imperative is weakened by an introductory verb of *asking* (παρακαλέω, ἐρωτάω, δέομαι) preceding the imperative clause. For this study, the *asking* verb cannot be imperative because its purpose in the discourse includes the addition of a politeness feature which softens the directive nature of the imperative. This would not serve to weaken the forthcoming imperative but rather be a directive itself.[65] There are two possible types of examples.[66] First, there are imperatives where the asking verb is part of the speech itself. These are the most prominent examples in the epistles where the high-ranked writer is addressing lower-ranked addressees:[67]

1 Cor 4:16 <u>Παρακαλῶ</u> οὖν ὑμᾶς, μιμηταί μου **γίνεσθε**

     Therefore, I <u>exhort</u> you, **become** imitators of me

2 Cor 5:20 Ὑπὲρ Χριστοῦ οὖν πρεσβεύομεν ὡς τοῦ θεοῦ <u>παρακαλοῦντος</u> δι᾽ ἡμῶν· <u>δεόμεθα</u> ὑπὲρ Χριστοῦ, **καταλλάγητε** τῷ θεῷ[68]

     Therefore, on behalf of Christ we are ambassadors, as [if] God was <u>begging</u> through us. We <u>ask</u> on behalf of Christ, **be reconciled** to God

---

[65]See 2 Cor 13:11; 1 Thess 5:11; Titus 2:15.

[66]All New Testament examples will be discussed.

[67]Mark 11:29 and the parallel in Luke 20:3 fit the requirements for structural characteristics in the first type of examples (asking word within the speech itself). For example, Mark 11:29: ὁ δὲ Ἰησοῦς εἶπεν αὐτοῖς· <u>ἐπερωτήσω</u> ὑμᾶς ἕνα λόγον, καὶ **ἀποκρίθητέ** μοι καὶ ἐρῶ ὑμῖν ἐν ποίᾳ ἐξουσίᾳ ταῦτα ποιῶ· (and Jesus said to them, "I <u>will ask</u> you one thing, and **answer** me ..."); however, the verb of asking does not function in the same manner as the other examples. In other cases, the high-ranked person is asking for something to be done. Here the asking word does not function as a weakener of force. The imperative itself (and the next) is strong. The asking word's relationship to the imperative is not one of introduction (as the others) but one of information. It informs the addressees as to what Jesus requires.

[68]The primary weakening verb here is δεόμεθα; however παρακαλοῦντος also contributes to this nuance.

Phil 4:3   ναὶ <u>ἐρωτῶ</u> καὶ σέ, γνήσιε σύζυγε, **συλλαμβάνου** αὐταῖς...
Indeed I <u>ask</u> you true partner, **help** them ...

1 Thess 5:14   <u>Παρακαλοῦμεν</u> δὲ ὑμᾶς, ἀδελφοί, **νουθετεῖτε** τοὺς ἀτάκτους
And we <u>beg</u> you, brethren, **instruct** the lazy [undisciplined]

Heb 13:22   <u>Παρακαλῶ</u> δὲ ὑμᾶς, ἀδελφοί, **ἀνέχεσθε** τοῦ λόγου τῆς παρακλήσεως ...
And I <u>beg</u> you brethren, **be patient/bear with** this word of encouragement ...

The second type of example with asking words preceding an imperative occurs in narrative. In these cases, the asking verb functions as part of the introductory narration. For higher- to lower- rank, there are few examples of this type in the New Testament (for slightly more, see the discussion of lower- to higher-rank below). However, three examples fit the criteria but only one seems to weaken the imperative. The reason for this is clear.

Luke 22:64   καὶ περικαλύψαντες αὐτὸν <u>ἐπηρώτων</u> λέγοντες· **προφήτευσον**, τίς ἐστιν ὁ παίσας σε;
And blindfolding him [they were] <u>asking</u> [him] saying, "**Prophesy**, who is the one who hit you?"

John 5:12   <u>ἠρώτησαν</u> αὐτόν· τίς ἐστιν ὁ ἄνθρωπος ὁ εἰπών σοι· **ἆρον** καὶ περιπάτει;
They <u>asked</u> him. "Who is the man who said to you, '**take** up and walk?'"

Acts 2:40   ἑτέροις τε λόγοις πλείοσιν διεμαρτύρατο καὶ <u>παρεκάλει</u> αὐτοὺς λέγων· **σώθητε** ἀπὸ τῆς γενεᾶς τῆς σκολιᾶς ταύτης
And with many other words, he <u>urged</u> them saying "**Be saved** from this crooked generation"

In the first two examples, the narrator's introduction does not seem to affect the force of the following quoted imperative. I suggest that this occurs because the asking word is *describing* what transpires in the quotation. In other words, the quotation with the imperative contains an actual question. Thus, the asking word serves only to introduce the question. However, Acts 2:4 presents a different type of situation, the narrator is providing information about Peter's approach which seems to indicate a politeness strategy to make the following imperative more attractive. I am not suggesting that Luke's representation of Peter portrays him as desiring his hearers to respond. Rather, he desires for them to respond so strongly that he apparently *urges* his listeners to listen to him. This is recorded by Luke's introductory statement. It is important to keep in mind what is being argued here to avoid misunderstanding. It is not being suggested that Peter's imperative is weak in the actual speech, nor is it being suggested that Peter himself was less concerned about the fulfillment of the imperative. Rather, this work only states that the manner in which Luke presents this imperative (being introduced with a verb) suggests a politeness strategy on the part of the speaker.

One example certainly cannot provide enough evidence for a rule. As will be seen below, there are more examples with lower- to higher-ranked situations. However, I would suggest that this type of politeness strategy is less likely with higher to lower imperatives than with lower to higher for the simple reason that the narrator does not normally need to explain an imperative in these contexts.

Therefore, although the database is minimal, based on what has been demonstrated thus far, there does seem to be times that a higher-ranking person may wish to utilize a politeness strategy to soften his imperative.

Although most imperatives used by higher-ranking individuals addressing lower-ranking parties maintain a strong force, there are times when it is in the interest of the speaker to soften the force of the imperative. One means of accomplishing this is to introduce the imperative with an asking word, effectively downgrading the strong-forced imperative to a request.

Strategy 2: Indirect Third Person

The New Testament provides many examples of the third person imperative as a means of weakened imperative force. These will be explored below.[69] Most third person imperatives are used as second person directives. For the purpose here, this section is only concerned with its effect on the force of the imperative. The third person imperative has an inherent indirect nature. It is either indirect to the person/people being addressed (second person), indirect to a third person through an intermediary (which may be the only way to address them in the given communicative situation), or through a general directive to all parties in view including the addressee.

The third person is a natural politeness strategy. As noted already, it is a means of indirect address. A higher-ranked communicator may wish to employ this strategy to make his directive less *face* threatening. In this way he may be more successful in persuading the addressee to fulfill the imperative. The third person is not the only means of attempting this; however, it is an explicit way of doing so.[70]

Matt 9:30   καὶ ἠνεώχθησαν αὐτῶν οἱ ὀφθαλμοί. καὶ ἐνεβριμήθη αὐτοῖς ὁ ᾿Ιησοῦς λέγων· ὁρᾶτε μηδεὶς **γινωσκέτω**
and their eyes were opened and Jesus warned them, "See [here], do not **let** anyone **know** [about this]

Luke 9:23   ῎Ελεγεν δὲ πρὸς πάντας· εἴ τις θέλει ὀπίσω μου ἔρχεσθαι, **ἀρνησάσθω** ἑαυτὸν καὶ **ἀράτω** τὸν σταυρὸν αὐτοῦ καθ᾿ ἡμέραν καὶ **ἀκολουθείτω** μοι
And he was saying to them all, "If anyone wishes to come after me, **let** him **deny** himself, **take up** his cross daily, and **follow** me

---

[69]A section will be devoted to the third person later in this chapter. Therefore, some things discussed there will be assumed here. This is not ideal but seemed the best way to present the material.

[70]As already noted, a study of English teachers in a native Greek speaking classroom employed various strategies to encourage the students to learn English. This is despite the higher-rank of the teacher and certain motivational factors (benefits) for the student (Aeginitou, "Politeness," 297-304).

Eph 4:31 πᾶσα πικρία καὶ θυμὸς καὶ ὀργὴ καὶ κραυγὴ καὶ βλασφημία **ἀρθήτω** ἀφ᾽ ὑμῶν σὺν πάσῃ κακίᾳ
let all bitterness and anger and wrath and outcry and blasphemy **be removed** from you and all worry

1 Tim 4:12 Μηδείς σου τῆς νεότητος **καταφρονείτω**, ἀλλὰ τύπος γίνου τῶν πιστῶν ἐν λόγῳ, ἐν ἀναστροφῇ, ἐν ἀγάπῃ, ἐν πίστει, ἐν ἁγνείᾳ
Let no one **look down upon** your youthfulness; but be an example

These verses suggest that the third person can indeed be a means of making an imperative more attractive. Of course, one cannot suggest that every time a third person is used for a second person directive, its force is weakened. However, such a conclusion seems likely and the burden of proof should be on those who wish to view the force as strong to demonstrate otherwise.

These examples demonstrate a weakening of force with the imperative.[71] Matthew 9:30 seems to be an exception. Although the narrator uses a rather strong verb to describe Jesus' statement (ἐνεβριμήθη) and Jesus begins with a second person imperative, he concludes with a third person which may reveal Jesus' sensitivity to his hearers. By using the third person, he avoids being too harsh with those to whom he is addressing. Although the Lukan example is clearly a challenge, if these imperatives were in the second person the force would be much stronger. In each case, a choice must be made by the hearers; however, by Jesus' words as recorded here, the recipient is given an opportunity to consider these words without a significant threat to *face*.[72] In Eph 4:31, the intention of the author is not to make fulfillment of the directive less likely. On the contrary, the purpose is to present the imperative in its most attractive light. He does not highlight the recipients but the sin. *Face* is more likely to be saved and the imperative is more likely to be complied with.

Finally, although not the focus here, I will take a moment to look at a true third person imperative and the notion of force.

---

[71]The reader will not be able fully appreciate this statement until the section on the third person is read below.

[72]It may be possible that Jesus would prefer the response to be based on some measure of consideration rather than a direct challenge.

Gal 1:8-9   ἀνάθεμα ἔστω (2x)
                [if anyone preaches another gospel], **let** him **be** accursed

Although I will classify this as a true third person directive (see below), it may have second person implications. This is a very harsh warning and is emphasized by repetition. However, by using the third person he makes the statement less direct and gives any potential readers an opportunity to change without highlighting them specifically.[73]

One further point needs to be made about the weakening of force for third person imperatives directed toward the second person. The third person imperatives themselves may have strong force. It is the indirect nature which demands this work's interpretation. In other words, the force may be (and probably is) strong (normal imperative force) for its literary recipient (the third person); however, in the actual communication situation, the imperative is directed toward the second person. Thus to the second person, the imperative is indirect, and thus weakened. To an actual (rare) third person recipient, the use of the third person may be strong. A weakened-force must be accounted for from context (e.g., other indirect strategies, etc.).[74]

Finally, before concluding this section, some implications of the observation about force on the distribution of third person imperatives should be considered. These implications are only suggestions and may be of interest to some wishing to pursue this study in different directions.[75] First, two passages contain more concentrated third person imperatives than any other passages in

---

[73]One may argue that the opponents of Paul's message would not be reading this epistle. This may or may not be the case; however, some reading may certainly be considering the message of the opponents and even have made overtures in that direction. The third person maintains the warning to such individuals but its indirect nature permits some room for repentance without the loss of *face*. If the opponents would be assumed to not be reading this (which is probably more likely), the only way to be more direct would be to identify them specifically. However, this is only speculative because the main thesis proposes that when the third functions as a second person, the force is weakened.

[74]As already noted to some extent and to be developed further later in this chapter, the recipient identification of the third person is not as straightforward as the second. There may be a number of reasons for using a third person. If a purpose is indirectness, it is weakened. However, a reason for using the third person often must be pursued in order to determine whether it is weakened.

[75]Such projects could focus more specifically on politeness strategies and other sociological methods such as honor and shame. Such studies should go beyond the imperative moods and consider the entire communication situation.

the New Testament. First Corinthians has the most third person imperatives of any New Testament book (47). It is second only to 1 Timothy in the percentages of third person imperatives to total words.[76] However, 1 Corinthians chapters 7 and 14 have a very high frequency. First Corinthians 7 has 17 third person imperatives in 689 words (24.6/1000) and 1 Corinthians 14 has 13 in 608 (21.3/1000). These chapters have only five and eight second person imperatives respectively.

There are at least two or three possible reasons for the concentration of third persons in these passages. First, the intended recipients of the directives may be actual third persons. However, this is not likely because the recipient of the letter is a community of believers who seemed to ask Paul about these issues. The discussion of chapter 14 is clearly directed to the entire community. Chapter 7 is directed to a smaller group of the community but nevertheless they are part of the second person recipients of this letter. Second, the issues raised here are either especially important or delicate and Paul needs to proceed with caution. Therefore, he employs politeness strategies to make his advice more likely to be taken and applied. This is supported by the following politeness strategies: encouragement (7:35; 14:1), use of himself as an example and thus associating with the recipients (7:8; 14:18),[77] not evoking authority (7:6, 25, 40; and lack of mention of his position), and reasoned argument to support directives (14:2-4, 6-17).[78] Third, in 1 Corinthians 7, Paul's position is somewhat vulnerable since he presents his opinion rather than a command from God. It seems likely that both the second and third options are probable in this context.

In light of these observations, some comments can be made about a few books of the New Testament. Romans was written to a church which Paul neither founded nor visited. Paul does not use an imperative until 3:4 which is a third person and either directed to God or a general imperative with no particular recipient (idiomatic?). The next imperatives do not occur until 6:11-19 (5x); the second of which is a third person. Although Paul uses 62

---

[76]Gramcord reveals 1 Timothy has 8.2 third person imperatives for every 1000 words. 1 Corinthians has 6.9/1000. The next closest is Ephesians (3.3/1000) and Titus (3.0/1000). Gramcord for DOS was used for these figures because the Windows version is unable to produce these statistics. Gramcord only produced figures per book. The statistics following below for chapters are my own.

[77]Possibly related to the discussion in Brown and Levinson, *Politeness*, 117-24.

[78]Ibid., 128.

imperatives, sixteen of these are the concluding ἀσπάσασθε (greet) and eleven are third person. This late and reluctant use of the imperative confirms Paul's relationship with the Church at Rome as one of an outsider looking to present a positive and friendly image while still acknowledging his authority (he still is able to direct the church as a true Christian leader). Ephesians has a relatively high proportion of third person imperatives (3.3/1000 words; third highest). In contrast Philippians has very few (0.85/1000). This difference could support the circular nature of Ephesians in contrast to the personal and highly circumstantial nature of Philippians.

To summarize, the majority of imperatives are produced by higher-ranking people addressing lower-ranked parties. Most such imperatives are straightforward without any indirect features to explicitly weaken the force of the imperative. However, there are times when politeness strategies are used in this context. It seems that since even higher-ranked communicators cannot assure the fulfillment of their directives, the communicator may wish to utilize a politeness strategy to make the directive more attractive. However, despite the more attractive nature of politeness strategies, it must be noted that these do not necessarily assure the results intended better than a direct approach.[79] However, as with all communication situations, the participants must make educated guesses on strategies and take risks.[80]

Lower- to Higher-Rank

The vast majority of imperatives in the New Testament are uttered by higher-ranking individuals to subordinates.[81] As developed earlier, ranking may

---

[79] Aeginitou, "Politeness," 303-3.

[80] This is an interesting area but would be difficult to pursue with any accuracy and is beyond the scope of this study.

[81] Boyer's figure that 87% of imperatives are uttered by higher-ranked individuals in the New Testament has already been noted. The database (the entire New Testament) is not ideal for this task. I am not unaware of this problem. As religious literature written by apostles, those under the authority of (and probably under the instruction of) apostles, or other founding members of the community, there are no books written from lower-ranking individuals to higher. The examples must come from narrative but this literature focuses on Jesus and the apostles. Therefore, little potential exists for lower to higher-ranked communication situations in the database. Nevertheless, the examples that do exist will reveal some important observations.

be *absolute* (e.g., father to family[82]) or it may be *relative* (e.g., the people who fill the roles of employer to employee). Essential is the context in which the imperative is uttered.[83] In the specific context, the speaker uttering the imperative is usually superior. In *absolute* high-ranking communication situations, there is a consistent ranking of the parties. However, in *relative* ranking, the context is essential. For example, an employer may only be superior in work situations. Outside of this context, parties may be equal or the roles may be reversed. In addition, the notion of ranking is based upon the perception of the speaker. If the speaker believes himself to be superior, he will act accordingly. For example, a sergeant in the army sees an individual in a plain unadorned uniform and assumes he is a private and orders the individual to perform some action. In a rather unlikely scenario, the plainly dressed man could be a general. Nevertheless, the imperative was uttered as if he were a private. At this stage the general could choose not to reveal his rank and perform the action or he could reveal his rank with embarrassment to the sergeant who may even fear punishment for his insubordination. Military uniforms are used in part to make explicit the rank of individuals.

Since the overwhelming use of imperatives is by higher to lower-ranking individuals, this work must consider its use in rare instances by inferiors. Is there anything explicit in the text which makes the imperative more acceptable?[84] If such indicators are not present, can it be assumed that these imperatives have full force?

In order to justify the decision not to use rank itself as a factor contributing to the force of the imperative, it must be demonstrated that in cases of lower- to higher-ranked imperatives there is something other than rank itself demanding the weakened interpretation. It seems that there are two primary factors. First, there are words of asking used to introduce the imperative. Second, there are

---

[82]The example of father to family is based primarily on the role of the father in the biblical world. It generally applies today; however, there is much less emphasis placed on rank within the family in the modern western society.

[83]Also, it is possible to have contexts in which familiarity is so prevalent that rank is set aside altogether. However, such contexts do not occur in the New Testament.

[84]The database used here is comprised of only text. This is important because there is no opportunity for voice inflection or body language to possibly weaken the imperative. Any politeness (or other) strategy must be identifiable in the text itself. Of course, this is somewhat dependent upon knowing what to look for. Non-native speakers may need to study as much of the social and historical context as possible to identify these strategies.

terms of honor which the one using the imperative may use to acknowledge the higher status of the addressee. Third, the use of third person imperatives will be explored. Such factors of introducing the imperative and using an honor term function to make the imperative less direct and/or to avoid the affront to the higher-ranking addressee.

Strategy 1: Words of Asking

As with higher to lower-rank imperatives, non-imperative verbs of asking may precede the imperative clause and serve to weaken the directive force (three occur: παρακαλέω, ἐρωτάω, δέομαι). Although, also a politeness feature, in this context, the purpose is different than the higher to lower-ranked usages. In this case, the asking verb seems to be a strategy for the lower-ranked individual to get a hearing without offending the rank of the addressee. It is a form of acknowledging the higher-rank and noting that a strong-forced imperative is not intended. Unfortunately the database is restricted in this area. Ideally, one would be able to examine lower-ranked letters or correspondences to higher-ranked people.[85] However, these do not exist. This work depends upon narrative records of such speech. Of the eight examples in the entire New Testament to be considered, three include the asking verb in the speech itself: Luke 14:18-19 and Acts 21:39,

Luke 14:18   ... ὁ πρῶτος εἶπεν αὐτῷ· ἀγρὸν ἠγόρασα καὶ ἔχω ἀνάγκην ἐξελθὼν ἰδεῖν αὐτόν· <u>ἐρωτῶ</u> σε, **ἔχε** με παρῃτημένον. 19 καὶ ἕτερος εἶπεν· ζεύγη βοῶν ἠγόρασα πέντε καὶ πορεύομαι δοκιμάσαι αὐτά· <u>ἐρωτῶ</u> σε, **ἔχε** με παρῃτημένον

... the first one said to him, "I purchased a field and I have need to go and to see it. I <u>ask</u> you, **have** me excused [Please excuse me]," and another said "I purchased five yoke of oxen and I am going to test them. I <u>ask</u> you, **have** me excused [Please excuse me]"

---

[85]Such as the letters of the Younger Pliny written to the emperor Trajan.

Acts 21:39   εἶπεν δὲ ὁ Παῦλος· ἐγὼ ἄνθρωπος μέν εἰμι Ἰουδαῖος, Ταρσεὺς τῆς Κιλικίας, ... <u>δέομαι</u> δέ σου, **ἐπίτρεψόν** μοι λαλῆσαι πρὸς τὸν λαόν
              and Paul said to them, "I am a Jewish man of Tarsus of Cilicia ... I <u>ask</u> you, **allow** me to speak to the people

These examples occur within a story and are the closest parallels to the epistle examples in the section of higher to lower-rank listed above. The remaining New Testament examples are similar to one another,

Mark 5:12   καὶ <u>παρεκάλεσαν</u> αὐτὸν λέγοντες· **πέμψον** ἡμᾶς εἰς τοὺς χοίρους ...
              And they [demons] <u>begged</u> him saying, "**Send** us into the pigs ..."

|| Matt 8:31   οἱ δὲ δαίμονες <u>παρεκάλουν</u> αὐτὸν λέγοντες· εἰ ἐκβάλλεις ἡμᾶς, **ἀπόστειλον** ἡμᾶς εἰς τὴν ἀγέλην τῶν χοίρων
              And the demons <u>begged</u> him [Jesus] saying, "If you cast us out, **send** us into the heard of pigs"

Matt 15:23   ... καὶ προσελθόντες οἱ μαθηταὶ αὐτοῦ <u>ἠρώτουν</u> αὐτὸν λέγοντες· **ἀπόλυσον** αὐτήν ...
              ... and when his disciples came they <u>asked</u> him saying, "**Send** her **away** ..."

Matt 18:29   πεσὼν οὖν ὁ σύνδουλος αὐτοῦ <u>παρεκάλει</u> αὐτὸν λέγων· **μακροθύμησον** ἐπ᾽ ἐμοί, καὶ ἀποδώσω σοι
              Therefore, his fellow-slave falling down <u>begged</u> him saying, "**Be patient** with me, and I will repay you"

John 4:31   Ἐν τῷ μεταξὺ <u>ἠρώτων</u> αὐτὸν οἱ μαθηταὶ λέγοντες· ῥαββί, **φάγε**
              Meanwhile the disciples <u>were asking/requesting of</u> him saying, "Rabbi, **eat**

Acts 16:9   Καὶ ὅραμα διὰ [τῆς] νυκτὸς τῷ Παύλῳ ὤφθη, ἀνὴρ
              Μακεδών τις ἦν ἑστὼς καὶ <u>παρακαλῶν</u> αὐτὸν καὶ
              λέγων· διαβὰς εἰς Μακεδονίαν **βοήθησον** ἡμῖν
              And a vision was seen during the night by Paul, a Macedonian
              man who was standing and <u>begging</u> him and saying, "Come
              over to Macedonia, **help** us

In the first three passages, the asking verb seems to demand a weak force for
following imperative. The strategy appears clear. Also the five additional verses
clearly should be interpreted as weak. However, they may raise a problem for
the thesis that low-rank itself is not a weakening factor. The asking word does
not appear in the speech itself and one cannot expect the addressee to have been
aware of the introductory lines in the narration. In fact, it seems that the data
would better be explained by maintaining that the force of the imperative is
implicitly weakened by the low-rank and the narration is making this explicit
for the reader. Nevertheless, based on these five examples, the thesis will not
be abandoned for the following reasons. First, there are only five examples (four
if one consider the parallels [Mark 5:12 ‖ Matt 8:31]—albeit the imperatives in
these parallels are different lexemes). It has been noted that there may be
exceptions to the paradigm. Second, these occur in recorded events. It is
maintained that the authors are accurately recording the event; however, this
work is not claiming that they are recording the exact words. In fact, it is likely
in the case of the gospels, the event occurred in Aramaic. The different language
use may also make a difference. Third, and related to the previous, by noting the
asking word in the introductory material, the author does not need to include
any politeness features in the speech itself. The reader is already aware of the
weakened imperative (thus it is possibly omitted in the quotation).[86] Finally, the
vast majority of low-ranked imperatives possess an explicit politeness feature.
It would be imprudent to abandon the theory and potentially lose an important
observation about the imperative in the process. The imperative by low-ranked
communicators is rare. If the mere use by such individuals weakened the force
of the imperative, one would expect it to be more prevalent in these situations.

---

[86]Using narration, an author is able to include politeness (and other) pragmatic information
which may have been communicated in various ways in the actual event (both verbal and non-
verbal). Therefore, the use of the politeness indicator in the description may reflect a politeness
strategy in the actual discourse.

The lack of use among low-ranked individuals is best explained by the strong force being maintained and thus being avoided in most cases by these communicators.

Strategy 2: Terms of Honor

There are a number of possible imperatives uttered by lower-ranked individuals or groups to superiors in the New Testament. Some of these are questionable and this will be revealed as this work proceeds. A most obvious example involves Jesus' encounter with the Samaritan woman at the well (John 4). The context of this passage is well known. It was culturally inappropriate for women to speak to men, men were considered of higher-rank than women, etc. Also, it is possible that the woman was socially unacceptable.[87] Jesus uses the imperative freely in this exchange (4:7, 10, 16 [3x], 21). However, the woman uses the imperative only once: κύριε, δός μοι τοῦτο τὸ ὕδωρ ... ("**Sir, give** me this water ...") 4:15). There seems to have been opportunity for the woman to further probe Jesus with an imperative. In John 4:25 the woman subtly asks if Jesus is the Messiah. This is clearly the implicature of the woman's statement as is evident by Jesus' response (4:26). There is nothing in the woman's dealing with Jesus that would not be characterized by respect. She addresses Jesus with the title κύριε three times (4:11, 15, 19). She uses seemingly round-about statements to question or ask of Jesus (4:11, 25). With one exception, she avoids the volitional-directive and when she uses it, it is prefaced by addressing Jesus as κύριε. This is a politeness strategy to weaken (or prepares for) the coming imperative.

John 4 contributes two other passages for the purposes here (in addition to one discussed below). In John 4:31 the disciples tell Jesus, φάγε. However, ῥαββί, a term of honor, preceeds φάγε. Also, In John 4:49, a royal official petitions Jesus to save his child: κύριε, κατάβηθι πρὶν ἀποθανεῖν τὸ παιδίον μου. ("**Sir**, come down before my child dies"). To many, the official may seem of higher-rank than a traveling healer. However, the official seems to understand (at least partially) who Jesus is and addresses him as a superior

---

[87]In case the reader is unfamiliar with some of the issues in this passage, the author makes explicit comments to reveal them (4:9, 27).

(or presents is his imperative in such a way to be so perceived because of his need and his belief in Jesus' abilities–which is essentially the same thing).

A number of passages appear to be lower to higher communication situations which do not include any honor terms. First, in the passage discussed above, John 4, after the Samaritan woman leaves Jesus, she goes into the town and says to the town's people: δεῦτε ἴδετε ἄνθρωπον ὃς εἶπέν μοι πάντα ὅσα ἐποίησα, μήτι οὗτός ἐστιν ὁ χριστός; ("Come, see a man who told me all the things I did. He is not the Christ, is he?" 4:29). The imperative here is unmarked for a politeness strategy. However, the following question may reflect a desire to manipulate the response of the town by stating a question expecting a negative answer (through the use of μήτι). The imperative which is preceded by the idiomatic imperative form functioning as an interjection may maintain strong force in light of her desire to communicate her message (excitement, urgency?). The emphasis is on getting a response from the people through their disagreement with her statement. At this stage, she is unlikely to be concerned about politeness strategies because she carries a message of value to all. The following question is expected to get the people to respond to her imperative.[88]

In Luke 5:8, after witnessing a miracle during a fishing trip, Peter states, ἔξελθε ἀπ' ἐμοῦ, ὅτι ἀνὴρ ἁμαρτωλός εἰμι, **κύριε**. ("**depart** from me, because I am a sinful man, **Lord**"). One may argue that the entire exchange here is marked by reverence but nevertheless, Peter uses the honor term which contributes to a weakening force. Also, in Luke (13:8, 25 [|| Matt 7:22]) the imperative is used in a story where the lower-ranked person uses the honor term κύριε. The same honor term is used by Mary Magdalene for Jesus whom she assumes is a gardener (John 20:15).

In the database there are eight further imperatives in seven verses (plus two in synoptic parallels) which include an honor term near the imperative. These are all in examples of prayer. In Mark 14:36, Jesus prays to God while wrestling with his coming sacrifice: καὶ ἔλεγεν· **ἀββα ὁ πατήρ**, πάντα δυνατά σοι· **παρένεγκε** τὸ ποτήριον τοῦτο ἀπ' ἐμοῦ· ... (and he [Jesus] said, "**Abba Father**, you can do all things, **remove** this cup from me ..." (|| Matt 26:39 with third person imperative and πατήρ μου only || Luke 22:42 with πατήρ only).

---

[88]I owe the basis for these observations to the class lectures in Intermediate Greek 203 taught by Daniel Wallace at Dallas Theological Seminary, fall 1992.

The imperatives are introduced with the respectful [αββα ὁ] πατήρ.[89] In addition, between the honor term and imperative, a complementary phrase acknowledges God's abilities and rank.[90]

Jesus' prayer in John 17 includes four imperatives (17:1, 5, 11, 17). In John 17:1, the entire prayer and the first imperative is introduced by addressing God as πατήρ. The next imperative (v. 5) is also prefaced by πατήρ. The third imperative (v. 11) has an even more honorable address, πάτερ ἅγιε. There is no honor term introducing the final imperative (v. 17); however, the recent honor terms may still meet the politeness requirements. This prayer is very illustrative. Jesus is clearly presented both as God (e.g., 1:1) and subordinate to the Father (e.g., 14:28) in John's gospel. In this prayer he addresses God the Father with an honor term. Three of four imperatives are directly preceded by an honor term. The relationship between honor terms and imperatives in John 17:1-17 may be a coincidence but is nevertheless interesting and may be instructive. In this passage Jesus addresses God as πατήρ three times. There are only four imperatives in the passage. The three uses πατήρ occurs near the first three imperatives. There are three additional uses of πατήρ in the prayer later in the chapter (17:21, 24, 25; though no other imperatives occur in the chapter). This would not be unnatural since Jesus addresses God. Nevertheless, it is interesting that in the section of the prayer where the imperatives are used, the honor term is only *used* near the imperative (before in 17:1 and 11; after in 17:5; in all cases these are in close proximity to the imperatives).

Finally, in the Acts passages of the database, there are two other reported prayers with imperatives and in each case those praying address the prayers to κύριε (Acts 1:24; 4:29 [2x]).

Although honor terms are present in prayers and they will be noted as such at this stage, this work will develop (not overturn) this conclusion below in the addendum about prayer and the imperative.

Mark 13:4 is worth noting. The disciples question Jesus about the signs of the end of the times and say: **εἰπὸν** ἡμῖν, πότε ταῦτα ἔσται ... ("**Tell** us,

---

[89]Some have pointed out the personal and even familiar nature of this title, especially with αββα. This is not denied. However, the address of "father" in the ancient world was acknowledging a superior.

[90]Although Matthew and Luke's intermediate phrase differ slightly (εἰ δυνατόν ἐστιν and εἰ βούλει respectively; Matthew is very close), each acknowledges God's ability to fulfill the imperative.

when will these things be…"). Although Mark and its Matthean parallel (24:3 εἰπὲ) have the raw imperative, Luke does not. Luke instead omits the imperative altogether and uses an honor term: **διδάσκαλε, πότε οὖν ταῦτα ἔσται**. Although any conclusions about Luke's motives for change are speculative,[91] it is seems plausible that the raw imperative was uncomfortable for Luke and thus he omitted it. In addition, the implied directive is prefaced by the honor term. Therefore, this suggests that the disciples' raw imperative may have been understood as fully forced in Matthew and Luke. This supports the thesis that the imperative is strong and a politeness strategy is employed.

Two other passages demonstrate lower- to higher-ranked discourse. First, in Matt 13:36 the disciples are addressing Jesus for instruction. This very act may be acknowledging his role but nevertheless it lacks any honor term to weaken the imperative. Second, in Acts 23:17, Paul addresses a centurion. He states, τοῦτον ἀπάγαγε πρὸς τὸν χιλίαρχον, ἔχει γὰρ ἀπαγγεῖλαί τι αὐτῷ. ("**Lead** this young man to the [your] commander, he has something to tell to him"). There is no reason to assume that Paul's imperative was weak merely because he was not superior in rank.

There are other passages where lower-ranked people seem to be addressing higher-ranked parties where no honor words occur.[92] None of these passages probably fit the requirement that the speaker believes he is addressing a higher-ranking individual in the given circumstances. In any case, they are all likely to be full-forced imperatives. These include Acts 4:19 (Peter and John to the Jewish leaders),[93] Acts 16:9 (Paul's vision of a man asking him to come to Macedonia),[94] and Acts 24:20 (Paul before Felix).[95]

---

[91]It is assumed that Luke is using Mark here. The section quoted above is rather small. However even here there appears to be dependence (Luke adds the conjunction). The larger sections (the immediate passages: Mark 13:3-8 ‖ Matt 24:3-8 ‖ Luke 21:7-11; also the larger synoptic apocalypse) seem to support the dependency thesis.

[92]Not included is Luke 4:23. Here Jesus expresses what the crowd thinks. It is unlikely Jesus would use an honor term for himself even in this context. Also, it is doubtful whether this crowd would consider Jesus a superior.

[93]This is probably not a legitimate lower- to higher-communication situation. I suspect both parties felt they were superior. Peter and John speaking on God's behalf had no reason to weaken their imperative for their audience whom they probably felt were not superior to themselves.

[94]The vision may not represent an actual person. Also, since visions are from God in Acts, this command may be viewed as coming from God.

[95]This may be an example of a third person imperative directed to a third person. Therefore, Paul is probably addressing his opponents. However, if Felix is in some way the (or an) addressee, there is honorific discourse at the beginning of the speech which applies throughout

What can be made of this analysis? It seems rare for lower-ranked people to address superiors with the imperative. When they do, it is common to use an honor term as a politeness strategy. Fifteen imperatives are prefaced by an honor term. This includes eight in prayers (including John 17:17). There are only three likely lower- to higher-ranked communication situations which do not use these terms and another four that are debatable. One advantage to this work's analysis is that the determination of participant rank does not demand the conclusion of a specific force for an imperative. The raw imperatives are considered full-forced. Each case discussed above seems to be explainable in this respect. Rank itself does not weaken imperative force. Politeness strategies do. When lower to higher-ranked individuals choose not to use such strategies, one must question why.[96]

Strategy 3: Indirect Third Person

As noted, the third person has an inherent indirect nature. It is either indirect to the person/people being addressed [second person], indirect to a third person through an intermediary (which may be the only way to address them), or through a general directive to all parties in view including the addressee.

Interestingly, outside of prayer, the use of the third person is rare as a politeness strategy for lower-ranked individuals in the New Testament. The reason for the lack of examples may be due to a reluctance to use it because it might offend the higher-ranking individual by seemingly suggesting that he is not the one with whom the imperative's fulfillment is dependent. Therefore, although indirectness may be an important politeness strategy, in this case, the indirectness may suggest uncertainty of the ability of the higher-ranking individual.[97] I suspect that the third person may be employed as a strategy in

---

(24:10b). In addition, if this is second person directed, it may be weakened by the use of the third person. This work's position however, is that it is third person directed.

[96]For a somewhat related approach, see H. Paul Brown, "Addressing Agamemnon: A Pilot Study of Politeness and Pragmatics in the *Iliad*," *Transactions of the American Philological Association* 136 (2006): 1-46.

[97]This statement is purely speculative. It is merely an attempt to explain the lack of the use of the third person by lower-ranked communicators.

some cases;[98] however, the limited database suggests other strategies are preferred. Outside of examples of prayer there is really only one potential second person directed third person imperative:[99]

Luke 7:7   διὸ οὐδὲ ἐμαυτὸν ἠξίωσα πρὸς σὲ ἐλθεῖν· ἀλλὰ εἰπὲ λόγῳ, καὶ **ἰαθήτω** ὁ παῖς μου.

therefore, I did not consider myself worthy to come to you, but say [the] word and **let** my servant **be healed** [or, my servant will be healed]

This third person imperative seems to function like a future indicative here;[100]

---

[98]The discussion of the third person below does suggest that there are usages which may seem to enhance a lower- to higher-ranked imperative communication situation.

[99]The only other possible examples of lower-ranked individuals addressing superior-ranked people (or equal-ranking parties) with the third imperative are Matt 27:22-23 (2x); Mark 15:32 Matt 27:42-43 (2x) || Luke 23:35; Acts 16:37; 21:14; 24:20. However, none of these cases have unquestionable lower to higher-rank. First, in Matt 27:22:23 (σταυρωθήτω; 2x), the collective crowd realizes that it has Pilate in a vulnerable position (thus in relative situational rank, Pilate is lower). Also, there may be boldness in numbers which individuals do not possess. See also the section devoted to third person below. This passage is briefly discussed as the parallels in Mark and Luke have the second person. Second, Mark 15:32 and parallels seem somewhat rhetorical. At face value the crowd seems to be challenging Jesus in a conditional-like sentence; however, in reality, they really are speaking among themselves. They are postulating a hypothetical situation which they do not believe will happen and have no intention of fulfilling the subjunctive clause (ἵνα ... πιστεύσωμεν). After being illegally beaten in Philippi, Paul in Acts 16:37 uses a third person which is on the one hand a rejection of the official's action and on the other hand a challenge to an actual third party. The circumstances place Paul and his friends in a situationally higher-rank than those to whom he is speaking. In Acts 21:14 disciples attempt to persuade Paul not to go to Jerusalem. As a way of resigning themselves to the situation they state, τοῦ κυρίου τὸ θέλημα γινέσθω. This could be one (or more) of three options none of which is a directive to Paul. First, it could be a non-event-initiating imperative which already is quite weak (see below). Second, it may be a prayer-like address to God. Finally, it may almost be an idiomatic expression similar to the English use of the phrase. The final possibility seems quite anachronistic and would need further verification to prove (for which the New Testament does not provide data). In the last passage, Acts 24:20, Paul is not challenging Felix but addressing him (out of respect). Rather, he is challenging his opponents. Thus this may be an actual case of a third person imperative being aimed at a third person party.

[100]There is a textual variant here for the future, supported most importantly by ℵ, A, C, D. However, the imperative has stronger external support (most importantly P[75] and B) and is the more difficult reading. It is easy to see why one would change it from third imperative to future. The change to the imperative is not so easily explained. However, the observation that this is the only third person addressed from lower- to higher-rank outside of prayer in the New Testament may contribute to the argument for the future by suggesting that using an imperative is not the

however, as noted in chapter three, the volitional directive nature of the imperative seems to be more clearly present in the imperative.[101] In any case, if there is any anything in the third (such as avoidance) which may cause offense, there are a number of other politeness strategies already at play in this statement. First, Jesus is addressed with the honor term κύριε (v. 6); second, a second person has already been stated thus the question of avoidance with the third is muted;[102] finally, the entire speech is prefaced in humble and respectful language.[103]

The obvious examples of third person imperatives used by lower-ranked individuals in communication situations are in recorded prayers. Jesus instructs his disciples on prayer in the possible parallels Matt 6:9-13 and Luke 11:2-4. These passages contain five third person imperatives, two of which are parallel.

Matt 6:9-10   Οὕτως οὖν προσεύχεσθε ὑμεῖς· Πάτερ ἡμῶν ὁ ἐν τοῖς οὐρανοῖς· **ἁγιασθήτω** τὸ ὄνομά σου· 10 **ἐλθέτω** ἡ βασιλεία σου· **γενηθήτω** τὸ θέλημά σου, ὡς ἐν οὐρανῷ καὶ ἐπὶ γῆς ...

                 In this way then pray, "Our Father who is in the heavens, **make** your name **holy**, **let** your kingdom **come**, **let** your will **be done** as in heaven and on the earth ..."[104]

There are two reasons one may question the use of the third person as a politeness strategy here. First, the second person is also used throughout the prayer (Matthew 3x and Luke 2x: δός/δίδου (Matt 6:11 ‖ Luke 11:3); ἄφες

---

normal stylistic convention. Nevertheless, the argument that the imperative is the more difficult reading seems to outweigh this consideration and the imperative will still be considered the more likely reading. For further discussion see chapter 3 where this issue is also mentioned. For a similar situation, see the discussion of Luke 21:19 (with Mark 13:13 and Matt 24:13) above in chapter 3.

   [101]Again I refer the reader to the discussion of Luke 21:19 in chapter 3. However, the imperative there is second person and should have more force than the third person here. Thus, the imperative and future may be closer here than in the Luke 21:19 example.

   [102]This work will briefly explore the second person – third person imperative sequence below in the section devoted to the third person.

   [103]One further suggestion is worth noting. Because the speaker here is a leader, the use of a third person may be a common strategy

   [104]The two imperatives in Luke are parallel with the first two in Matthew.

(Matt 6:12 ∥ Luke 11:4); ῥῦσαι (Matt 6:13).[105] Also, the use of honor terms of address is present. The third person may simply serve to bring the subjects into focus. This may be the case but one significant observation may suggest that the third person is a politeness strategy.[106] The second person imperatives do not occur until late in the prayer, until after all of the third person imperatives have been expressed. Thus, it is possible that the third imperatives provide an indirect means of opening the prayer. As the prayer proceeds, the second person usages take over. There can be no doubt that these are second person directed.

Finally, there are three additional third person imperatives in prayer in the parallel passages: Matt 26:39, 42 ∥ Luke 22:42. Although the passages are parallel and the third person imperatives in Matt 26:42 and Luke 22:42 are identical, it does not seem that these are parallel verbs.[107] The prayer is highly emotional and somewhat urgent and before each imperative is an honor term.[108] Thus, the use of the third person is not necessary unless added politeness is desired. Indeed, Luke after an honor term and complementary phrase opens the prayer with a strong second person imperative. This makes it unlikely that Jesus would then use a third person imperative for a politeness strategy after the second person. Matthew however, may reflect a consistent politeness strategy.[109] First, he maintains the third person throughout the prayers even after the honor term and complementary phrase. Second, in the pericope in which these imperatives are found (Matt 26:36-46), Jesus switches from addressing the disciples (26:36-38, 40-41, 43, 45-46) to addressing God in prayer (26:39, 42, 44 [no words recorded]). In prayer to God, Jesus uses only the third person (26:39, 42 [as discussed above]); however, when addressing the disciples, Jesus

---

[105]The second person imperatives in Matt 6:9 and Luke 11:2 are addressed to the disciples and not part of the prayer.

[106]The use of the politeness strategy does not mean that focus is not also important.

[107]See the discussion in chapter 3. As noted there, although the Lukan imperative is not necessarily parallel with the second Matthew imperative, this could still be Luke's motivation for adding it here. However, certainty is impossible.

[108]See the section entitled "Strategy 2: Terms of Honor" above for a discussion of these verses with reference to honor terms.

[109]In contrasting Matthew and Luke I am not suggesting that there is a deep structure contradiction here. I am merely saying that Luke sees no need to use yet another politeness strategy since respect is already explicit. Jesus' words were unlikely to have been Greek and thus the authors are attempting to record what happened in a manner which is accurate. A recording of the *ipsissima verba* from the authors is not demanded. Rather, *ipsissima vox* is all that is necessary.

uses only the second person (6x: 26:36, 38 [2x], 42 [2x], 46). Thus to higher-ranking communication, Jesus uses the third person but when addressing inferiors, he uses the second person.

If the suggestion above is accurate, that the third person is avoided in lower to higher-ranking communication situations because it may imply by its indirectness that the addressee is unable to fulfill the imperative, how is its use in prayer explained? In addition to what has already been stated, I suggest that by the actual participation in prayer, the lower-ranked individual acknowledges the ability of God to accomplish the task. Thus, the negative implication is removed and it can function as a normal politeness strategy.

Addendum: Prayer and the Imperative

In the discussion of the imperative thus far, a number of politeness strategies used by both higher and lower-ranked individuals have been identified.[110] In this section, I briefly want to make some observations about the use of the imperative in the unquestionably lower to higher-ranked addressees of prayer. The New Testament database is rather small. Outside of the gospels and Acts there are at least five prayers in which Paul tells his readers what he prays for them (Eph 1:15-23; 3:14-21; Phil 1:9-11; Col 1:9-12; 2 Thess 1:11-12[111]). There are no imperatives in any of these. This is not the normal situation of prayer that has been seen (e.g., Matt 6:9-12; 26:36-46 [with parallels]; John 17). I suggest that the reason for the omission of imperatives in Paul's prayers is that he is merely explaining what he prays, not actually praying. Although Matt 6:9-12 (|| Luke 11:2-4) is also not an actual prayer event, it is instruction and an actual example. The imperatives, I suggest, are evidence that Jesus intended this prayer to be prayed.

In prayers there is always some type of politeness strategy employed. Honor terms always appear and the third person is common. Although the use of honor

---

[110]The purpose of this section is somewhat peripheral. There is no attempt to discuss tenses and other issues concerning prayer. For a detailed discussion of the uses of the aorist and present in prayer see Willem F. Bakker, *The Greek Imperative: An Investigation Into the Aspectual Differences Between the Present and Aorist Imperatives in Greek Prayer From Homer Up to the Present Day* (Amsterdam: Uitgeverij Adolf M. Hakkert, 1966), 98-127.

[111]See also, 1 Thess 1:2-5; 3:11-12 and 2 Thess 1:3, which seem like expressions of desire in the form of prayers but nevertheless can be seen as prayers.

terms was mentioned above in the appropriate section, here a slight modification to what was stated there will be made. The use of honor terms should be viewed as less of a politeness strategy in prayer than elsewhere. The reason for this is that the honor terms are also the *titles* for God. There is no way to address God without such terms. Therefore, this makes the choice of terms less optional and thus as a politeness strategy, less effective. However, when accompanied by a honor modifier (John 17:5: πατήρ ἅγιε) or a further complementary phrase (Mark 14:36: αββα ὁ πατήρ, πάντα δυνατά σοι· παρένεγκε τὸ ποτήριον τοῦτο ἀπ' ἐμοῦ· ...) ("Abba Father, you can do all things, remove this cup from me ..."), a politeness strategy is clear.[112]

The imperatives may be weakened by various politeness strategies; however, it is important to notice their presence. This work has been narrowly focusing on politeness strategies with explicit imperatives. One must remember that in the larger sociological context, politeness may demand that the imperative be avoided entirely. Therefore, in a broader sense one should consider their common existence significant. This may reveal the biblical author's view of his relationship with God. This relationship is such that although the one praying is significantly inferior, he has the confidence to address God and use the imperative mood frequently. This is not a relationship between a person and a distant, cruel, uncaring, or impotent deity. A personal relationship exists between a loving God and his imperfect and dependent creation (see also Rom 8:15 and Gal 4:6).

In the New Testament the presence of the imperative is mixed among verbs in the recorded prayer events which have been discussed. The percentage in Matt 26:36-46 is very high while John 17 is very low.[113] However, this is not a good representation of prayer. It is likely that the Matthew passage is only a very small percentage of Jesus' words and the prayer in John 17 has the dual

---

[112]This work is not suggesting that one avoid seeing honor in passages without modifiers. The point is merely that the speaker has little choice in selection of addresses. This makes the honor title almost obligatory. Nevertheless, it still is an honor term and should be treated as such noting the point made here.

[113]In Matt 26:36-46 (verses of prayer only: 26:39b, 42b) there are six finite verbs and one infinitive used verbally. Of these seven verbs, two are imperatives (28.6%). However, in the longest example of prayer, John 17:1b-26, there are only four imperatives in 93 finite verbs and four participles and two infinitives used verbally. Thus, only four of 99, 4%. This is well below the New Testament average of 8.5% of finite verbs (although this does not include verbal participles and infinitive which will lower this figure).

purpose of prayer to God and instruction for those present. Additionally, the authors' purposes will determine what is included in these passages.

It may be worthwhile to look briefly at the LXX for insight into the use of imperative in prayer.[114] The focus will only be on the Psalms and although the purposes of individual Psalms vary considerably and are often disputed, in general they serve as examples of expression of prayer to God (although he is not always the addressee). In the canonical Psalms there are 5910 verbs which include 842 imperatives (14%).[115] In some of the longer Psalms, a very high percentage of imperatives exist: LXX Ps 34 has 21/88 (23.9%); Ps 68 has 26/106 (24.5%); and Ps 118 has 65/363 (17.9%).[116] The very personal LXX Psalm 50 (Hebrew Ps 51) has 13 imperatives among 49 verb forms (26.5%).

These figures reveal that the imperative is not avoided in prayer, arguably the largest gap between participants in a lower to higher communication situation. Other politeness strategies are employed (e.g., third person and honor terms given the qualifications noted above). Nevertheless, the use of the imperative here is revealing. When one considers this with other personal devices (e.g., use of the address as πατήρ and especially αββα ὁ πατήρ[117]), one is impressed with this observation.[118]

---

[114]The use of the Septuagint is a complex matter for grammatical work in the New Testament. Although an example of *Koine*, it is translation Greek. However, it is clear that the authors of the New Testament were familiar with it. Its use with caution may be helpful in non-essential points of this work.

[115]I am being conservative here including all verbs. If non-verbal use of participles and infinitives used non-verbally are removed, this figure would be higher. Also, it must be noted that this average of imperatives is actually lower in the Psalms than in the entire LXX (6751 or 34,439 [19.6%]); however, this may be attributed to the actual type of literature in the LXX (especially prophetic). In any case, the use of the imperative for lower to higher parties is rare and the average is still more than the New Testament; thus, the Psalms seem helpful to the argument here.

[116]In addition, the use of the third person imperative is rather high: Twenty-two percent of all imperatives in the canonical LXX Psalms are third person (185/842; this is higher than the percentage in the entire LXX which is 15.7% (1059/6751). In the three passages listed, the percentage is even higher: LXX Ps 34 has 11/21 (53.4%); Ps 68 has 13/26 (50%); However, in Ps 118 there are only 9 of 65 (13.8%) which is still above the New Testament average but slightly below the LXX Psalms average. This supports the suggestion that the third person is a politeness strategy.

[117]The only prayer in which this occurs is quoted by Jesus (Mark 14:36); however, as alluded to above, it is clear that the Christian can also approach God with this personal address (see Rom 8:15; Gal 4:6).

[118]One may argue that the imperative is the best means to ask something of any deity. This is certainly true. However, one must not confuse the polytheistic, rather limited, deities with the all powerful God as described in the Old and New Testaments. In addition, it has already been

Other Observations about Force

Before concluding the discussion of force, it is worthwhile mentioning two further appropriate issues for consideration. First, the passive is a natural linguistic strategy for indirectness. If someone wishes to avoid a direct accusation, he might say, "The window was broken by Jim." Or, one can avoid naming the agent entirely. "The window was broken." There are many reasons one might use a passive. Such uses include maintaining a constant subject throughout a discourse, emphasizing the recipient, goal, or other usually object functioning entities. Therefore, one might suspect the passive to be a factor in the force of the imperative. However, this does not seem to be the case. Some of the most forceful imperatives are passive. For example, the passive is used in speech acts: καθαρίσθητι (be cleansed; Matt 8:3) cannot be considered weak. Jesus is the one using the imperative here. He has the power to accomplish the speech act. The recipient has no choice in the matter. Other examples demonstrate no lack of force by means of the passive only. In Romans 12:2 there are two passives: καὶ **μὴ συσχηματίζεσθε** τῷ αἰῶνι τούτῳ, ἀλλὰ **μεταμορφοῦσθε** τῇ ἀνακαινώσει τοῦ νοὸς (**do not be conformed** to this age but **be transformed** by the renewal of [your] mind). The imperatives here have full force. None of the features mentioned in previous sections which weaken force are present.[119] No other contextual reason suggests that these are weak-forced imperatives

Finally, the next section will discuss *event-initiation* and the imperative. On rare occasions the imperative does not intend to initiate an action. Rather it is a response and merely functions to keep the imperative action going. Although this has significance for force (and will contribute to the conclusions in this area), it seems to be an interesting phenomenon in its own right and thus will be considered distinct from force.

This observation further demonstrates the importance of *force* with the

---

noted that there are many techniques besides the imperative to get one's request fulfilled.

[119]Twenty-eight of 157 passive imperatives are φωβέω which only occurs in the passive form in the New Testament (95 times; however, two of these should be parsed imperfect middle: Mark 16:8; Acts 5:26). Of the 28 imperatives, twenty-two are negated and function as comfort sayings: Matt 10:28a; 10:31; 14:27; 17:7; 28:5; 28:10; Mark 5:36; 6:50; Luke 1:13; 1:30; 2:10; 5:10; 8:50; 12:7; 12:32; John 6:20; 12:15; Acts 18:9; 27:24; Rev 1:17; 2:10 (Matt 10:28b; Luke 12:5 [2x]; Rom 11:20; 13:4; 1 Pet 2:17; Rev 14:7 are not negated). For a succinct discussion of the passive imperative, see Boyer, "Imperatives," 49-50.

imperative. Using traditional terminology, a *command* has the most force of all imperatives, *permission/toleration* has the weakest force of examples thus far considered. Social rank among other things may contribute to the complexity of this usage. In contrast to *request*, one of high-rank with the ability to do something different may choose to permit action to continue on its course. Or, a lower-ranked individual may reluctantly allow an action he cannot change to continue. The force is so minimal that its directional and volitional nuances seem merely responsive and permissive. For whatever context-dependent reason, the speaker's presentation of the force behind the imperative is minimal.[120]

Guidelines for Determining the Force of an Imperative

Given the analysis presented in the preceding sections the following principles will be suggested to identify the force of a given imperative in context. As a preliminary matter, it is helpful to reiterate some general observations gleaned from this study thus far. First, force will be classified as either strong or weak. One could certainly provide more range here. For example, non-event-initiation imperatives have almost no force at all. However, it will be kept simple to avoid the propagation of excessive classifications. Also, a multidimensional paradigm will be provided elsewhere to indicate other factors such as non-event-initiation. In addition, the notions of strong and weak are relative. The unmarked imperative is strong despite lexemic intrinsic force. Therefore, both "tap the egg" and "smash the egg" are equally *strong*. The statements "please sir, tap the egg" and "please sir, smash the egg" are equally weak in comparison to the previous statements. It is irrelevant for this study that "smash" is a much stronger word than "tap."[121] Second, the vast majority of

---

[120]A further consideration beyond the scope of this work is whether force will differ between types of Greek writers. Due to the distance in time between us and the New Testament writers, it may be impossible to glean anything from this. For a modern study of a similar phenomenon, see Maria Economidou-Kogetsidis, "Greek Non-Native Speaker's Requests and Degree of Directness," in *Current Trends in Intercultual Cognitive and Social Pragmatics*, Intercultural Pragmatic Studies, ed. Pilar Garcés Conejos, Reyes Gómez Marón, Lucia Fernández Amaya, and Manuel Padilla Cruz (n.p.: University of Seville, n.d.,), 53-66.

[121]I ask the reader's pardon for making this point again. However, it is important to clarify the focus of this study at particular times in the work.

imperatives occur within communication situations where a higher-ranked party addresses a lower-ranked party without any explicit contextual element indicating a politeness strategy. These imperatives are assumed to be strong. Third, there is no guarantee that an imperative will be fulfilled when it is dependent upon a recipient's response. Some situations may be more likely to have the response desired by the speaker (e.g., military); however, there is no certainty. Therefore, politeness strategies may be employed by the speaker to maximize the fulfillment potential of the imperative. These politeness strategies may differ in both type and purpose depending upon whether the communication situation is initiated by a higher- or lower-ranked party. When a politeness strategy is used, the imperative will be considered weak. Fourth, in rare cases, the imperative is responsive and does not actually initiate a desired action. In these situations, the imperative is weak even without any explicit politeness strategy. Finally, no rules or principles can fully account for a complex linguistic and/or social phenomenon;[122] therefore, if there are significant contextual features which may lead the exegete to interpret the imperative outside this work's paradigm, it should be so interpreted and defended appropriately.

These principles can only be guidelines. Specific conclusions must be nuanced. Also, this is not meant merely to be a check list for classification; it is intended to be used with the preceding discussion in mind. Important discussion about the relative nature of determining rank, etc. must be considered but does not appear below. In addition, the usage of imperative morphology is only one aspect of the interpretation of the usage of the verb. The verb is only part of the clause which is part of the sentence, paragraph, etc. In other words, imperative usage is only a small part of the entire exegetical process. In addition to linguistic concerns, cultural factors must also be considered.[123]

1.   The majority of imperatives are from higher- to lower-rank, without any

---

[122]A balance must be struck between constructing guidelines and principles which are so specific that the number of exceptions become unmanageable and so general that they are unhelpful for exegesis.

[123]It seems that grammarians may ignore or minimize social, cultural, and historical issues in their exegesis. At the same time, some who focus on extra textual issues fail to include grammar as a significant part of exegesis. This may be because each of these areas are so large, one cannot explore both in any detail. However, it seems like balanced exegesis is dependent upon input from many diverse sources.

features to cause the interpretation of the imperative to be indirect, and event-initiating.

These are **strong-forced**.

2. If an imperative does not fit this description continue.

3. If the imperative is responsive and does not initiate an event, it is **weak**. However, it is worth considering whether politeness strategies are present for exegetical reasons and thus worth continuing.

4. If a higher-ranked party addresses a lower-ranked party but also includes indirect indicators, go to 5. If the producer and recipient are of equal-rank or the producer is of lower-rank, go to 6.

5. If in a higher- to lower-ranked communication situation the speaker or narrator apply one or more the following the politeness strategies, the force is considered **weak**.

    A. A non-imperative verb of asking (παρακαλέω, ἐρωτάω, δέομαι) in the narrative or discourse itself.

    B. Indirect third person used to address the hearer who would normally be addressed in the second person (unless closely preceded by a second person addressed to the same recipient[124]).

6. In communication situations where parties are of generally equal-rank or are from lower- to higher-rank are involved look for the following politeness strategies:

    A. A non-imperative verb of asking (παρακαλέω, ἐρωτάω, δέομαι) in the narrative or discourse itself.

    B. Terms of honor (e.g., κύριε, ῥαββί, etc.).

    C. Indirect third person used to address the hearer who would normally be addressed in the second person (unless closely preceded by a second person addressed to the same recipient[125]).

    If one of these occur, the force is considered **weak**. If none of these occur,

---

[124]This qualification will be discussed below.
[125]See previous note.

go to 7.

7. In communication situations where parties are of generally equal-rank or are of lower to higher-rank and no politeness strategy is employed, the imperative should be cautiously considered **strong**. Reasons for the strength of the imperative should be considered exegetically significant and thus should be pursued further in exegetical analysis.

Event-initiation and the Imperative

The imperative does not actually describe an action, event, or state; rather it is used to direct these verbal ideas. This is natural considering the observation that it is *volitional-directive*. This observation then suggests that an imperative would be used to *initiate* verbal content. The statement, "read the book" initiates a concept (in this case an action) which the speaker portrays as desiring to actually take place. However, although rare, there are times that the imperative is responsive. Thus, "I desire to read your book about grammar" may be responded to by, "read the book." The imperative, although certainly directive, only reveals volition in a responsive sense. This exchange alone cannot reveal whether the imperative expresses the actual desire of the communicator. However, it is portrayed with volition. The directive and volitional nature of the imperative is minimal. This is because the imperative is responsive; thus, a non-event-initiation imperative. Two examples using the second person imperative will vividly illustrate this point.

Luke 7:40   καὶ ἀποκριθεὶς ὁ ᾿Ιησοῦς εἶπεν πρὸς αὐτόν· Σίμων, ἔχω σοί τι εἰπεῖν. ὁ δέ· διδάσκαλε, **εἰπέ**, φησίν
and Jesus answered and said to him, "Simon, I have something to say to you." And he said, "Teacher, **speak**"

Matt 8:31-32   οἱ δὲ δαίμονες παρεκάλουν αὐτὸν λέγοντες· εἰ ἐκβάλλεις ἡμᾶς, ἀπόστειλον ἡμᾶς εἰς τὴν ἀγέλην τῶν χοίρων. 32 καὶ εἶπεν αὐτοῖς· **ὑπάγετε**
The demons were asking him, "If you cast us out, send us into the herd of swine" and he said to them, "**Go**"

In traditional terminology these are usually classified as *permission* or *toleration*.[126] The reason for this is clear. The imperative is used in what seems to be a response which merely confirms, permits, or tolerates an action/statement/question previously initiated or suggested. Whether or not the speaker of the imperative has the power to deny the previous statement determines whether it is permission (the speaker has the power) or confirmation of toleration (the speaker does not have the power).[127] Also, as discussed elsewhere, the imperative is a volitional-directive but does not necessarily mean that the speaker desires the imperative to be fulfilled. It is merely presented as such.

In Luke 7:40, Jesus announces that he wishes to speak to Simon Peter. In response, Simon Peter uses the imperative to signal to Jesus to communicate what he wishes. The announcement that Jesus desires to communicate a message prior to Simon Peter's responsive imperative removes the nuance of request (in traditional terminology) from the imperative. Thus, the volitional aspect of Simon's response is reactive (albeit still volitional). He did not necessarily desire for a specific message to be communicated to him at that time. In fact, he was unaware that such a message even existed. Once Jesus makes his intention known, Peter does have the option to exercise volition. His imperative expresses volition to confirm what Jesus introduced into the cognitive environment. In other words, Jesus' statement, in addition to causing other contextual implicatures,[128] introduced an element into the discourse.

---

[126]See chapter 3 where these are listed in a limited database from grammars in which they are so classified.

[127]These statements should not be considered absolute. I am not satisfied with this distinction. It is far too limiting. I acknowledge that toleration could be granted even if the communicator had sufficient authority to act. However, as a general principle it is helpful. One must remember that language only portrays reality. If language was rigid and categories precise, these statements would be objectively true. However, one can give permission for something that he has no power to stop or can tolerate something he can prevent but chooses not to.

[128]Jesus clearly announced his desire to communicate this message in order to stress the importance of what he was going to say. The preliminary statement adds an element of suspense to the situation. Simply giving the message may still have had a significant impact on his hearers by virtue of its importance. However, Jesus' decision to use the preliminary statement assured that Peter would understand what he meant to say was important. Other factors contribute to the importance of the statement. Jesus as teacher adds to the importance. For example, if an inferior made this statement, it only communicates (in the story) that the speaker himself thought what he was to say was important. There is no guarantee the superior-ranked listener would have concurred with this. Of course, one cannot guarantee that Simon would have given these words the importance Jesus would have liked. However, given the preliminary statement and the

Peter's reply functions as a sort of gateway to permit the already introduced concept (in this case an important message) to proceed.

In the second example (Matt 8:32), Jesus responds to a request made by the ones to whom he directs the imperative. It is true that Jesus has the power to grant the request and thus the imperative might seem rather strong. However, it is also true the verbal idea of "going" or "sending"[129] is already present. This seems to weaken the force in context.

One further characteristic of non-event-initiation imperatives will be noted before proceeding. The event-initiation is not introduced by the one using the imperative.[130] This makes it truly responsive. The one using the imperative has no control over the initiation. When the verbal action is initiated by the one who will use the imperative, the force does not seem to be affected by this element (e.g., Matt 7:12; 22:8-9; John 13:27; 20:27; Rom 6:13); however, the verbal action may be mentioned by the speaker of the imperative but in a way that clearly describes action not initiated by the speaker.[131] This is the only possible way for this to occur in any non-narrative discourse (e.g., epistles). See the examples below of 1 Cor 7:15, 36; 2 Cor 12:16.

Non-event-initiating imperatives depend upon previous contextual information beyond the immediate clause. Thus, analysis occurs at the sentence level. The use of this information must be defended here because further below sentence level information will be the reason for rejecting the classification of *conditional* as a legitimate label for the imperative. The main reason for this (as will be demonstrated) is that the pragmatic implicature created by non-event-initiation actually does affect the *force* of the imperative. It has already been determined that *force* will be an essential element for imperative classification. This is not the case with the conditional which seems to vary in force among examples. In any case, the sentence level nature of this analysis is why this work did not incorporate it entirely into the discussion of force but has dealt with it separately.

Non-event-initiating imperatives are rare; however, it is worth determining whether the observations about the previous two verses concerning the weak

---

relationship between speaker and hearer, the likelihood was greater.

[129]One need not be concerned that the exact verbs are not used in both clauses. Clearly the same thing is meant.

[130]This rules out passages like Matt 19:12.

[131]However, Matt 5:41 seems to be an exception. This seems to be a full-forced imperative.

force of such imperatives are valid consistently. First, this work will analyze the (remaining) verbs considered *permission/toleration* as discussed in chapter 3 to confirm whether they have the same relationship to the event-initiation.

John 19:6   Ὅτε οὖν εἶδον αὐτὸν οἱ ἀρχιερεῖς καὶ οἱ ὑπηρέται ἐκραύγασαν λέγοντες· σταύρωσον σταύρωσον. λέγει αὐτοῖς ὁ Πιλᾶτος· **λάβετε** αὐτὸν ὑμεῖς καὶ **σταυρώσατε** ...

Therefore, when the high priests and attendants saw him, they shouted, "Crucify! Crucify!" Pilate replied, "You **take** and **crucify** him ..."

1 Cor 7:15   εἰ δὲ ὁ ἄπιστος χωρίζεται, **χωριζέσθω**
               but if the unbelieving one departs, **let** him **depart**

1 Cor 7:36   Εἰ δέ τις ἀσχημονεῖν ἐπὶ τὴν παρθένον αὐτοῦ νομίζει, ἐὰν ᾖ ὑπέρακμος καὶ οὕτως ὀφείλει γίνεσθαι, ὃ θέλει **ποιείτω**, οὐχ ἁμαρτάνει, **γαμείτωσαν**
               But if anyone thinks he is acting improperly toward his virgin, if she be of age and it must be thus, **let** him **do** what he wants, he does not sin, **let** them **marry**

2 Cor 12:16   [15 ... ἧσσον ἀγαπῶμαι;] 16 **Ἔστω** δέ
               [15 ... am I to be loved less?] 16 then **let** it **be**

As with the first two examples, these cannot be classified in the traditional system as either *commands* or *requests*. The main reason for this is the placement of the imperative in the event-sequence (or chronology). Here the action or event (whether real or hypothetical) is initiated or suggested by another. The imperative is in essence a response. This is clear from the examples above. In John 19:6, Pilate suggests that the command or request[132]

---

[132]At first glance, this may seem like a *request* by the Jewish leaders because of Pilate's position. However, in light of their numbers (people take strength in groups), the serious accusations with which Jesus was accused (John 19:7-12), and (related) the possibility of a weak position of Pilate with the emperor Tiberius (assuming a date of this event after the treason conviction and execution of Pilate's probable patron Sejanus), the Jewish leaders may have felt

made by the Jewish officials be carried out by themselves. This may not be a good example of a non-event-initiation imperative because it could possibly be (better) viewed as a counter command to the Jewish leaders' demand.[133] Ultimately, Pilate did consent to the desire of the accusers; however, this is not realized by an imperative (John 19:16). The two examples from 1 Corinthians (7:15, 36) also display this pattern. In both cases, the author is simply directing action based on the actions and/or decisions of others. However, in light of Paul's authority, his imperatives in these instances will likely be heeded. In other words, his imperatives are not merely confirming the decisions of others. If he would have advised otherwise, it is likely that he would have expected his imperatives to be followed.[134] Nevertheless, such considerations go beyond this work's classification. In the final example, 2 Cor 12:16, Paul is acknowledging a hypothetical situation which if occurred, should be permitted. Again, the imperative is a response to a previously initiated (albeit hypothetical) activity.[135] The verb used in this passage, although not identical to the previous, can easily be interpreted as part of a sememic ellipsis implying the thought of the previous phrase.

Most of the initial samples of undisputed *permissive/tolerative* imperative are clearly non-event-initiation. However, in addition to the problems with John 19:6 already discussed, two do not fit this description:

Matt 10:13   καὶ ἐὰν μὲν ᾖ ἡ οἰκία ἀξία, **ἐλθάτω** ἡ εἰρήνη ὑμῶν ἐπ᾽ αὐτήν, ἐὰν δὲ μὴ ᾖ ἀξία, ἡ εἰρήνη ὑμῶν πρὸς ὑμᾶς **ἐπιστραφήτω**
                and if the house is worthy, **let** your peace **come** upon it, but if it is not worthy, **let** your peace **return** to you

Matt 23:32   καὶ ὑμεῖς **πληρώσατε** τὸ μέτρον τῶν πατέρων ὑμῶν
                complete then the measure [of guilt, sin] of your fathers

---

the leverage to demand Jesus' crucifixion. This is supported by Pilate's response (John 19:13-16).

[133]Therefore, this work also takes issue with the traditional classification of this imperative as *permission/toleration*.

[134]Given Paul's role in the Corinthian community, such counter imperatives to the actions/decisions of others would have probably been viewed as *command* (strong-forced) imperatives.

[135]Also, one cannot escape a possible rhetorical use of the imperative and its (previous) initiating statement.

In Matt 10:13 the coming or going of peace depends upon the worthiness of the recipient. Thus, it seems non-event-initiating; however, the notions of ἐλθάτω and ἐπιστραφήτω are initiated by Jesus in these directives. Nevertheless, the imperative seems to be weakened and this is probably due to the indirect nature of the third person.[136]

In Matt 23:32, in the midst of his somewhat historical sketch of his opponents wickedness, Jesus uses the imperative (πληρώσατε) to encourage the hearers to complete their wickedness. The hearers are not interested in Jesus' words nor would they change their actions one way or another. In fact, Jesus' words merely confirm them in the path which they are choosing.[137] At first glance this seems to fit the predetermined criteria. There seems to be little or no noticeable directive force in this imperative. However, I would argue this is not the case. It is the verbal idea "complete" which seems to communicate non-event-initiation. This is true of the larger issue. It encourages the hearers to continue on their present course. However, this work is concerned with the use of the imperative itself. Jesus initiates the directive "to continue" not "to sin." This may seem like a minor distinction and it must be admitted that the entire clause communicates this idea. However, this work is interested at this stage of analysis in the usage of the imperative alone, not the imperative clause. Therefore, based on the analysis in this section, these passages must be considered as having full-forced imperatives. The verbal ideas may seem quite weak; however, the imperative mood is utilized to its full potential with these

---

[136]At first glance these third person verbs look like actual third person directed imperatives (and thus not necessarily weakened by person). However, they seem to be the more common second person directed for two reasons. First, the second person pronoun is employed which often identifies that the second person is addressed. Second, the addressees appear to have power to enact the directives. This is probably due to the authority given to them by Jesus (see 10:1; Robert H. Gundry, *Matthew: A Commentary on His Handbook for a Mixed Church Under Persecution*, 2d ed. [Grand Rapids: William B. Eerdmans Publishing Company, 1994], 189). If a third person would be addressed, this passage might exclude the pronouns and would imply some type of divine power uncontrolled by the disciples. They would merely be mediators of the power without any real authority over its action. See also the discussion of the third person imperative below.

[137]Given a high Christology one could argue that Jesus could have prohibited his opponents from further wickedness by preventing them from killing him. In this case, the imperative would be more permissive; however, in addition to the obvious soteriological implications which demand the cross as both the will of God and the act of man, in the gospels Jesus is not presented as using his powers in this manner in the Gospels. The best understanding views Jesus' role here merely as confirmatory or tolerative.

lexically-weak verbs.

Two further observations are worth noting. First, the concept expressed by the imperative must not only have been previously introduced but have the same goal as the actual imperative. A number of cases demonstrate the imperative action has been introduced but not with the same purpose as the imperative under consideration. For example:

Matt 10:28   καὶ **μὴ φοβεῖσθε** ἀπὸ τῶν ἀποκτεννόντων τὸ σῶμα, τὴν
               δὲ ψυχὴν μὴ δυναμένων ἀποκτεῖναι· **φοβεῖσθε** δὲ μᾶλλον
               τὸν δυνάμενον καὶ ψυχὴν καὶ σῶμα ἀπολέσαι ἐν γεέννῃ
               and **do not fear** those who put to death the body but are not
               able to kill the soul. But **fear** the one able to destroy both the
               soul and body in Gehenna

Although the verbal action in this verse is the same, the objects of the verbal action (fear) are different. The first warns against human authority and the latter against God.

Second, many of the above examples occur within the apodosis of a conditional-type statement. Given the nature of such clauses, this seems natural. However, an imperative in the apodosis of a conditional statement usually initiates an event (Matt 4:3 ‖ Luke 4:3; Matt 5:29-30 [4x]). The verbal idea of the imperative must have been introduced earlier. It is quite common that the imperative initiates an event based on the conditional or conditional-like sentence (e.g., Mark 14:44).

In the cases surveyed in this section, since the imperative actually does not initiate the action or event, the force is minimal. Therefore, the place of the imperative within the event-sequence is an additional contextual element in the classification of imperative usage. If the imperative is not an event-initiator, the force is weak. In fact, due to their responsive nature, with the exception of idioms, non-event-initiating imperatives are the weakest of all imperatives.

There are a number of debatable examples in the New Testament. For example:

1 Cor 1:31   ὁ καυχώμενος ἐν κυρίῳ **καυχάσθω**[138]
let the one who boasts, **boast** in the Lord

Eph 4:28   ὁ κλέπτων μηκέτι **κλεπτέτω** ...
The one who steals **must** no longer **steal** ...

Rev 22:11   ὁ ἀδικῶν **ἀδικησάτω** ἔτι καὶ ὁ ῥυπαρὸς **ῥυπανθήτω** ἔτι,
καὶ ὁ δίκαιος δικαιοσύνην **ποιησάτω** ἔτι καὶ ὁ ἅγιος
ἁγιασθήτω ἔτι
Let the one who does wrong, still **do wrong**, and let the one
who is impure, remain **impure**, and let the righteous one, still
do righteousness, and let the one who is holy, still **be holy**

All of these examples seem to fit the criteria but yet seem somewhat unaffected
by the event-sequence. The force does not seem to be affected as the translation
of Eph 4:28 demonstrates. Indeed, Boyer even suggests that the four
imperatives of Rev 22:11 are permissive.[139] However, it seems best to view
these as event-initiating and attribute the apparent non-event-initiating attribute
to the description, not verbal action of the subject. Because in each of these
cases, the third person may truly be directed at third persons (or at least a
general principle), the force may not be weakened at all. The conclusion is that
these are full-forced imperatives. Boyer's classification of Rev 22:11 as
permission is not the best option. This is not a situation where
permission/toleration is being expressed. This is an example of the speaker
instructing the addressees to continue doing what they were doing. There may
be a touch of irony here; nevertheless, these are full-forced directives.

The Notion of Benefit and the Imperative

Although this chapter has focused on force and the imperative, the
classification of the mood must be expanded. In traditional grammar, categories
such as command, request, and permission/toleration may be compared and

---

[138]See also 2 Cor 10:17 which is identical with the exception of an added postpositive δέ.
[139]Boyer, "Imperatives," 37.

contrasted. However, categories such as warning, request, and command cannot. An imperative may be either a command, request, or permission/toleration. However, the same cannot be said of the second group. The statement "Do not eat that candy bar" may serve both as a command and a warning. To choose between the two may result in missing an important nuance about the usage. This seems to betray a further fault with the traditional system. One may argue that command is inherent in warning; however, this does not seem to be sustainable. A worker may say to his boss, "Sir, do not walk on the loose board." This is clearly not a command because its force appears weak. It may be better viewed as *request*. However, in any case, it is a warning.

Therefore, it seems necessary to add a factor to the imperative classification in addition to force, namely *benefit*.[140] In other words, imperatives will be classified not only as having strong or weak force but also as to which party benefits from fulfillment of the command. The statement "Give me a glass of water" is *speaker beneficial* and "Drink a glass of water" is *recipient beneficial*. One would expect most imperatives to be *speaker beneficial*; however, due to the strong instructive nature of the New Testament, this is not the case.

One could multiply the benefit categories (warning, instruction, order, etc). However, this work will limit the categories to two. An imperative either benefits the speaker or the hearer (or both). Further classification may be obvious.[141] The point is to realize the direction of *benefit* in the imperative.

This work will consider any imperative that is either a combination of benefits or more general in that it accomplishes a task, *speaker-benefit*. This is not a random position but is assumed because the speaker is the one using the imperative and has control over benefit choice. Supported also comes by the volitional nature of the imperative. Volition usually is something expressed by the speaker in a manner which he desires. Even if the benefit is not direct (as in acquiring something), it is a benefit if it fulfills the desire of the speaker. Of course this is also true of recipient beneficial imperatives; however, this work concerns itself with the overall thrust of the directive. If it is primarily for the

---

[140]See a similar discussion (although not in the context of imperative mood classification), in Diane Blakemore, *Understanding Utterances: An Introduction to Pragmatics* (Oxford: Blackwell Publishers, 1992), 112-13.

[141]For example, weak-force, speaker-benefit imperatives would normally be *requests* while strong force, recipient-benefit would be *warnings*.

good of the hearer, it will be so considered.[142] Ultimately, any directive that benefits the speaker in some way, will be so considered. The following imperatives are all speaker beneficial.

Luke 5:8   ἰδὼν δὲ Σίμων Πέτρος προσέπεσεν τοῖς γόνασιν Ἰησοῦ λέγων· **ἔξελθε** ἀπ᾽ ἐμοῦ, ὅτι ἀνὴρ ἁμαρτωλός εἰμι, κύριε
              when Simon Peter saw [this], he fell down at the knees of Jesus saying, "**Depart** from me because I am a sinful man, Lord"

John 4:7   ἔρχεται γυνὴ ἐκ τῆς Σαμαρείας ἀντλῆσαι ὕδωρ. λέγει αὐτῇ ὁ Ἰησοῦς· **δός** μοι πεῖν
              There came a woman from Samaria to draw water; Jesus said to her, "**give** me something to drink"

John 21:15   Ὅτε οὖν ἠρίστησαν λέγει τῷ Σίμωνι Πέτρῳ ὁ Ἰησοῦς· Σίμων Ἰωάννου, ἀγαπᾷς με πλέον τούτων; λέγει αὐτῷ· ναὶ κύριε, σὺ οἶδας ὅτι φιλῶ σε. λέγει αὐτῷ· **βόσκε** τὰ ἀρνία μου
              Therefore when they finished breakfast, Jesus said to Simon Peter, "Simon son of John, do you love me more than these?" "Yes, Lord you know that I love you." He said to him, "**Feed** my sheep"

Acts 3:4   ἀτενίσας δὲ Πέτρος εἰς αὐτὸν σὺν τῷ Ἰωάννῃ εἶπεν· **βλέψον** εἰς ἡμᾶς
              And Peter along with John was looking at him said, "**Look** at us"

1 Thess 5:25 Ἀδελφοί, **προσεύχεσθε** [καὶ] περὶ ἡμῶν
              Brethren, **pray** [also] for us

Phlm 22   ἅμα δὲ καὶ **ἐτοίμαζέ** μοι ξενίαν
              and in the same way also **prepare** for me a guest room

---

[142]It seems preferable to group what might be termed "middle-ground benefit imperatives" with speaker-directed benefit imperatives. A label such as "neutral-benefit" might incorrectly imply a lack of volition and reason for the imperative.

Heb 13:24   'Ασπάσασθε πάντας τοὺς ἡγουμένους ὑμῶν καὶ πάντας
τοὺς ἁγίους
Greet all your leaders and all the saints

With the exception of Acts 3:4, all these examples clearly demonstrate *speaker-benefit*.[143] The Acts passage will help clarify the classification discussion above. Although the man will ultimately benefit from Peter's interaction, the command to "look" at Peter and John itself does not benefit him. One further example will illustrate the nature of this classification:

Matt 10:6   **πορεύεσθε** δὲ μᾶλλον πρὸς τὰ πρόβατα τὰ ἀπολωλότα
οἴκου 'Ισραήλ. [7] πορευόμενοι δὲ **κηρύσσετε** λέγοντες
ὅτι ἤγγικεν ἡ βασιλεία τῶν οὐρανῶν. [8] ἀσθενοῦντας
θεραπεύετε, νεκροὺς **ἐγείρετε**, λεπροὺς **καθαρίζετε**,
δαιμόνια **ἐκβάλλετε**· δωρεὰν ἐλάβετε, δωρεὰν **δότε**
now **go** instead to the lost sheep of the house of Israel. [7] And
as you go, **preach** saying, the kingdom of heaven is near. [8]
Heal the sick, **raise** the dead, **cleanse** the lepers, **cast out**
demons, [as] you received gifts, **give** gifts

In this passage Jesus orders the disciples to preach and minister in the same manner as he had been doing. The notion of benefit is rather complex here. Essentially neither Jesus nor the disciples directly benefit. However, since this is the portrayed expressed *desire* of Jesus, it is classified as *speaker-benefit*. It may be argued that it is probably also the desire of the disciples; however, this is not explicit. Jesus utters the volitional directive; it is his will being expressed by the imperative.[144]

Because of the didactic purpose of much of Scripture, a strong presence of *recipient-benefit* imperatives remains. Promises, advice, instruction, comfort,

---

[143]There are many passages in which *speaker-benefit* is plainly evident. These include Matt 13:36; Mark 13:4; 14:36; 15:36; Luke 13:25; John 4:10, 49; 17:1, 5, 11; 20:15; Rom 16:3-16 (12x); Phil 4:21.

[144]There are many passages which would be classified as *speaker-benefit* which do not necessarily seem to benefit the speaker directly. Some of these are similar to the Matt 10:6-8 passage while others are more like orders to complete a task without any direct beneficial target. Matt 2:8; 3:15; 4:10; 10:11 (2x), 12, 13; 13:30 (4x); Mark 14:6, 13 (2x); 15:13; Luke 4:35 (2x); 5:4, 14 (2x); John 2:19 (challenge); 4:35; 20:17 (3x); 21:6, 10; Acts 1:24; 4:29 (2x); 16:9; 24:20.

certain types of warning, and probably preaching should be classified in this way.

Matt 3:2   [καὶ] λέγων· **μετανοεῖτε**· ἤγγικεν γὰρ ἡ βασιλεία τῶν οὐρανῶν
              [and] [John was] saying, "**Repent!** For the kingdom of heaven is near"

Luke 5:24   ... σοὶ λέγω, **ἔγειρε** καὶ ἄρας[145] τὸ κλινίδιόν σου **πορεύου** εἰς τὸν οἶκόν σου
              ... I say to you, "**Rise** and take up your bed and **go** to your house

Luke 13:31   Ἐν αὐτῇ τῇ ὥρᾳ προσῆλθάν τινες Φαρισαῖοι λέγοντες αὐτῷ· **ἔξελθε** καὶ **πορεύου** ἐντεῦθεν, ὅτι Ἡρῴδης θέλει σε ἀποκτεῖναι
              At that moment some Pharisees approached saying to him, "**Leave** and **go** from here because Herod desires to kill you

John 4:50   λέγει αὐτῷ ὁ Ἰησοῦς· **πορεύου**, ὁ υἱός σου ζῇ ...
              Jesus said to him, "**Go**, your son lives ..."

Acts 20:10   καταβὰς δὲ ὁ Παῦλος ἐπέπεσεν αὐτῷ καὶ συμπεριλαβὼν εἶπεν· **μὴ θορυβεῖσθε**, ἡ γὰρ ψυχὴ αὐτοῦ ἐν αὐτῷ ἐστιν
              and going down Paul fell on him and embracing [him] said, "**do not be worried**, for his life is in him

Acts 27:25   διὸ **εὐθυμεῖτε**, ἄνδρες· πιστεύω γὰρ τῷ θεῷ ὅτι οὕτως ἔσται καθ᾽ ὃν τρόπον λελάληταί μοι
              take courage men, for I believe God, that in this way it will be the way he has told me

---

[145]A participle (ἄρας) translated as an imperative ("take up"). Although it seems to take the force of the preceding imperative, it does not factor into our analysis.

John 20:22   καὶ τοῦτο εἰπὼν ἐνεφύσησεν καὶ λέγει αὐτοῖς· **λάβετε**
               πνεῦμα ἅγιον
               and when he said this, he breathed on them and said, "**Receive**
               the Holy Spirit"

Rom 13:1   Πᾶσα ψυχὴ ἐξουσίαις ὑπερεχούσαις **ὑποτασσέσθω**
               Let each of you **be subject** to the ruling authorities

1 Tim 6:11   Σὺ δέ, ὦ ἄνθρωπε θεοῦ, ταῦτα **φεῦγε· δίωκε** δὲ
               δικαιοσύνην εὐσέβειαν πίστιν, ἀγάπην ὑπομονὴν
               πραϋπαθίαν. [12] **ἀγωνίζου** τὸν καλὸν ἀγῶνα τῆς
               πίστεως, **ἐπιλαβοῦ** τῆς αἰωνίου ζωῆς, εἰς ἣν ἐκλήθης
               καὶ ὡμολόγησας τὴν καλὴν ὁμολογίαν ἐνώπιον πολλῶν
               μαρτύρων
               But you, O man of God, **flee** from these things, and **pursue**
               righteousness, godliness, faith, love, patience, gentleness, [12]
               fight the good fight of faith, **seize** eternal life to which you
               were called and you declared the good confession before many
               witnesses

These examples include preaching (Matt 3:2),[146] instruction (Luke 5:24;
Rom 13:1; 1 Tim 6:11-12),[147] warning (Luke 13:31), direct-benefit (John
4:50),[148] comfort (Acts 20:10),[149] encouragement (Acts 27:25),[150] and speech

---

[146]See also Matt 4:17; Luke 3:8, 11 (2x), 13, 14; John 1:23; Acts 2:14 (2x), 22, 38, 40; 3:19;
28:28.

[147]See also Matt 5:12, 24 (4x); Mark 13:5, 11b, 14 (2x); John 1:39; 15:4, 7; Acts 5:20; Rom
12:2; 1 Cor 3:18; Phil 2:5; 1 Tim 2:11; Heb 3:1; Jas 1:16; Jude 17; Rev 1:11; 3:2; etc. This is very
common both in the teaching passages of Jesus and in the epistles.

[148]See also Matt 4:3 ‖ Luke 4:3; Matt 4:6 ‖ Luke 4:9; Matt 12:13; Luke 4:23a; John 1:46 Acts
3:6; 16:5.

[149]The comfort nuance often occurs with the negated imperative of φοβέω: Rev 1:17: Καὶ
ὅτε εἶδον αὐτόν, ἔπεσα πρὸς τοὺς πόδας αὐτοῦ ὡς νεκρός, καὶ ἔθηκεν τὴν δεξιὰν
αὐτοῦ ἐπ᾽ ἐμὲ λέγων· **μὴ φοβοῦ·** ἐγώ εἰμι ὁ πρῶτος καὶ ὁ ἔσχατος (And when I saw him,
I fell to his feet as dead and he put his right hand on me saying, "**Do not be afraid,** I am the first
and the last"). This is the most common use of this lexeme in the imperative (which only occurs
in the passive in any mood). The imperative occurs 28 times and 20 are used for comfort (always
negated). In addition to Rev 1:17, this usage occurs in Matt 10:31; 14:27; 17:7; 28:5, 10; Mark
5:36; 6:50; Luke 1:13, 30, 2:10; 5:10; 8:50; 12:7, 32; John 6:20; 12:15; Acts 18:9; 27:24; Rev
2:10. All but one of the remaining imperatives of this verb are instruction (only one is negated):

acts (John 20:22). Specific usages within the *recipient-benefit* classification have been noted. These are only for illustrative purposes. This work only advocates classifying these imperatives as *recipient-benefit*. In practice, many specific verses are difficult to classify more specifically. For example, should Matt 3:2 be classified as preaching or warning? If the latter, it fails to be distinguished from Luke 13:31 which is clearly a warning. This is one reason why this work prefers to classify the imperative only with regard to the *direction* it is benefitting.

An objection may be raised that the approach presented is too general to be helpful. However, this objection may be responded to with four counterarguments. First, separating force from benefit is already a step forward. Usually, the benefit-receiver of the imperative is rarely discussed at all. Second, as has been seen above, very specific classification is often difficult and thus may result in two further problems: a failure to see the similarities among these imperatives and/or an excessive multiplication of categories.[151] Third, labels such as warning, instruction, advice, etc., may have slightly different semantic ranges among speakers and communities. There is overlap between the semantic ranges these terms cover. One group may see a directive as a warning, another may see it as advice.[152] Finally, these usages should not be limited to these nuances. This work did not mention any usages such as threats or advice in the *recipient-benefit examples*; however, it is likely such usages exist even in a

---

Matt 10:28 (2x, the first is negated); Luke 12:5 (2x); Rom 11:20; 13:4; 1 Pet 2:17. The final occurrence is a warning (Rev 14:7; not negated).

[150]See also John 4:29; Acts 18:9b.

[151]Although not making a separate category for force, one writer seems determined to be as specific as possible and includes eleven categories of the imperative (Perschbacher, *Greek Syntax*, 345-49; actually there are more but these eleven are similar to the specific labels used here). Some of these contain more than one classification (e.g., "challenge or dare"; "warning or caution"). This is a commendable attempt to be thorough. However, it seems preferable to distinguish between force and benefit eliminating the need for so many categories and permit the exegete to avoid the need to make difficult choices between very closely described categories. As mentioned above, this approach is criticized on a number of grounds, not least of which is the implied method of choosing one option and rejecting the rest.

[152]For example, one writer notes that the element of negation in imperatives is used for warning in Russian (A. Boguslawski, "The Problem of the Negated Imperative in Perfective Verbs Revisited," *Russian Linguistics* 9 [1985]: 237). However, the example labeled "warning" above in Luke 13:31 did not have negation. How would this be classified by Boguslawki if he were commenting upon it? He would not necessarily be wrong but he may conclude differently.

database as small as the New Testament.[153] For this reason, it seems that any specific nuance beyond the two choice classification be the responsibility of the exegete who knows the community (or himself) to whom he will be communicating the text.[154] Therefore, in addition to classifying an imperative with regard to force and event-initiation, it should also be classified with reference to whom the fulfillment of the imperative benefits.

Negation and the Classification of Imperatives

It has been mentioned throughout this work that the traditional label *prohibition* is misleading. This is because as it is presented it in a manner which suggests a choice between *prohibition* and *command*, *request*, etc. This implied choice fails to account for the notion of force. This has been stated throughout. The purpose of this brief section is to formally state the role of negation in the multidimensional paradigm developed above. With the exception of eight negated third person aorists, the imperative is negated by μή and only occurs with the second person present imperative. In the paradigm developed here, it is suggested that negation is merely a feature that is added to the paradigm. For example, an imperative that is strong-forced, event-initiating, and hearer-benefitting is either positive or negative. The later if it has the negated particle.[155]

The Third Person Imperative (Further Comments)

As with many portions of this work, one can only touch upon important areas of imperative usage demanding further attention. The third person

---

[153]For a discussion of some uses which may be relevant here from an RT theoretical perspective, see Wilson and Sperber, "Mood," 80-81.

[154]A possible solution to this would be to provide well defined categories; however, this may result in confusing terminology. If one classifies *warning* in such a way that it does not accurately reflect the semantic range of a community's use of the term, it will complicate matters unnecessarily.

[155]Much has been said about the negative imperative throughout this work, specifically when criticizing the traditional paradigm. Therefore, little is said in this section. This treatment reflects the belief that negation is not as significant as other features treated here.

imperative is such an area. Since the imperative is a directional mood, it seems natural for it to be primarily used in the second person. However, in ancient Greek the imperative also occurs in the third person.[156] The third person is not nearly as common as the second but nevertheless accounts for about 14% of imperatives in the New Testament.[157]

The third person imperative does not occur in every language. Indeed, some question whether it exists at all.[158] Some have preferred to use the term jussive to label such forms.[159] However, the term *jussive* often refers to a specific *use* of a form such as the imperative or subjunctive.[160] In *Koine* Greek there is clearly a morphologically specific third person imperative.

The third person imperative has been treated as a genuine imperative and the feature of person provides an option in Greek for the communicator to express himself.[161] It has been demonstrated that the third person may actually

---

[156]General linguistic inquiry also acknowledges that commands can be in the third person (Nicholas Rescher, *The Logic of Commands* [London: Routledge and Kegan Paul, 1966], 14-15). It is likely that morphology is not even considered by Rescher since his study seems philosophically based. Nevertheless, the observation is important.

[157]Gramcord reveals 234 third person imperatives in the New Testament. However, John 8:7 is within a passage of unlikely authenticity. Therefore, 233 third person imperatives are maintained. This form occurs in all books except 1 Thessalonians, Philemon, 2 John, 3 John and Jude. Only 32 third person imperatives are plural of which 25% (8) occur in 1 Timothy and almost as many in 1 Cor 7 and 14 (7x). In classical Greek literature, the third person imperative seems relatively common in Plato who ". . . uses more imperatives in the third person than all the other prose writers combined (hundreds in the *Laws* alone)" (J. E. Harry, "The Perfect Subjunctive, Optative and Imperative in Greek," *Classical Review* 19 [1905]: 353).

[158]John Lyons, *Semantics* (Cambridge: Cambridge University Press, 1977), 747. See also F. R. Palmer, *Mood and Modality*, Cambridge Textbooks in Linguistics, ed. B. Comrie et al. (Cambridge: University Press, 1986), 111. Palmer notes the third person in Greek (ibid., 109) but based on his definition of "imperative" concludes that "[i]t may be best to restrict the term 'Imperative' to 2nd person forms and to use 'Jussive' for the others" (ibid., 111).

[159]Ibid.

[160]J. Donovan, "Greek Jussives," *Classical Review* 9 (1895): 145; Nigel Turner, *Syntax*, vol. 3, *A Grammar of New Testament Greek*, ed. James Hope Moulton (Edinburgh: T. & T. Clark, 1963), 94 (under "subjunctive"). See also M. A. K. Halliday, *An Introduction to Functional Grammar*, 2d ed. (London: Edward Arnold, 1994), 87. Also of interest is J. Donovan, "German Opinion on Greek Jussives," *Classical Review* 9 (1895): 289-93, 342-46, 444-47.

[161]However, Ray Elliott states "Many occurrences of the [third person imperative] in Greek are not, in function, imperatives at all but have other semantic and/or discourse-related functions instead" ("Functions of the Third Person Imperative Verb Forms in the Greek New Testament," *Notes on Translation* 69 [1978]: 30 [underline in the original]). Elliott does not mention what these other functions are. He states that he is "in the process of analyzing and organizing these occurrences according to semantic function" (ibid.). I am unaware of whether or not this has been completed and published. A search of the indexes of *Notes on Translations*

contribute to the force of an imperative. This is most obvious when third person imperatives are used for second person directives. This weakening is due to the indirect nature (a politeness strategy) of the grammatical third person when addressing the immediate recipient of the imperative. This section will discuss the third person imperative in more detail. However, an in-depth analysis must await a project which can devote sufficient space to the task.

This section will consider four areas for inquiry. First, it will briefly review the classifications (i.e., identify the recipient of the directive) of the third person with some (albeit minimal) modification to the general usage of the third person imperative. Next, it will look at the few parallel passages in the synoptics which have a third person paralleled by a second person (or other form). The qualifications for this will be identical to this work's similar study of mood usage (imperative vs. other moods; see chapter 3) in the synoptics to try to determine why one would use the third person. Third, the rare negative third person aorist imperative will be mentioned. Fourth, this section will briefly exceed the morphological focus and look at some relationships between the third person and other clauses. In addition to these areas of inquiry, it will briefly consider whether this work's findings can contribute to the exegesis of Acts 2:38. This section will be completed with a brief summary.

Who is the Recipient of the Third Person Directive?

While discussing New Testament usages of the imperative mood in chapter 2, James Boyer's four classifications for the third person imperative were briefly introduced.[162] Boyer's work is helpful and generally endorsed here. First, Boyer suggests that the majority of third person imperatives are indirect commands to a second person. These can be of four types: 1. they may be addressed to "some part of you" (e.g., Matt 6:10; "your will be done"); 2. general commands including "you" (e.g., Mark 8:34); 3. the second person's responsibility to a third party (e.g., Luke 7:7); 4. the second person's permission

---

(http://www.sil.org/translation/Not-Ind.htm accessed last on 03 November, 2009) from 1970 through the first three issues of 2001 revealed nothing further on the subject by Elliott or anyone else. Although the index is not current, given that it covers over twenty years after the original article, it is unlikely further work was published by Elliott after this time.

[162]Boyer, "Imperatives," 47-48.

that someone do something (Col 3:16). Second, they are indirect commands to an actual third person which are addressed to the second person without any responsibility for the addressee to communicate the message or perform the directive (Jas 5:14). Third, Boyer suggests that three passages are third persons which reveal what is required of a third party (Matt 18:17; 1 Tim 3:12; 5:4). Fourth, usually with the verb γίνομαι or εἰμί, the third person may be used for promises or warnings of what might be (e.g., Rom 11:9).

Boyer's analysis reveals that less than 14% of third person imperatives in the New Testament are intended for third persons.[163] Additionally, 4% accounts for his final category of promise or warning.

In-depth analyses of the third person imperative in the New Testament are rare. Because of this, it is worthwhile to look cautiously elsewhere for studies of the phenomenon. A distinct analysis of the third person was produced by Judy Glaze and focused upon the Septuagint.[164] However, she believes that in a large number of cases, it does not function as an imperative at all[165] and her classification differs from Boyer's. Glaze concludes that the third person imperative in the Septuagint can be classified into three main groups. First, what Glaze labels the "true third person imperative" occurs when a command is directed to an actual third person.[166] This is divided into two categories. The third person may be commanded through an intermediary[167] or the third person may be commanded without an intermediary.[168] Second, the third person imperative is common in poetry. Her statistics suggest that one third of the third

---

[163]Indirect commands account for 12% and there are three examples of imperatives describing what is required of a third person.

[164]Judy Glaze, "The Septuagintal Use of the Third Person Imperative" (M.A. thesis, Harding Graduate School of Religion, 1979). I am not unaware of problems with the Septuagint and its language for my study. Although both are written in Greek during the *Koine* period, the Septuagint is primarily a (uneven) translation of the Hebrew and Aramaic Old Testament begun over two centuries before the first New Testament book was written. Nevertheless, the New Testament authors demonstrate significant familiarity with this work.

[165]Ibid., 12. This statement, like Ray Elliott's cited above, is puzzling. I suspect in context, Glaze means that third person imperatives are not true imperatives because they are not second person (see Lyons, *Semantics*, 747 and Palmer, *Mood*, 111 which have been noted above).

[166]Glaze, "Septuagintal Use," 12-17.

[167]Ibid., 12-15. Examples include Exodus 11:2 where God commands the Israelites through Moses and Judges 13:14 where a wife is commanded through her husband (Manoah).

[168]Ibid., 15-17. Glaze believes that in these cases the third person is used to soften the force of the imperative. Examples include Prov 31:4 where a king is instructed indirectly by pointing out proper and appropriate behavior for kings (in general).

person imperatives in the Septuagint are of this sort (about 300 of 900). She suggests that this form is used here for literary variation (especially within parallelism).[169] Finally, the third person imperative may be directed to the second person.[170]

Essentially, with the exception of Glaze's category of poetry which is not relevant for the data here, the two studies discussed above are generally in agreement with this work's findings. However, some adjustments will be made as all 233 third person imperatives are classified. It is this work's contention that the third person imperative in the New Testament is used in two, possibly three, ways. First, the third person imperative may be used as an indirect second person. Second, the third person may be directed to an actual third person. Finally, although rare and debatable, the third person imperative may be a general statement without any intended referent.

The vast majority of third person imperatives in the New Testament are directed toward the second person in one way or another. These examples can be divided into three. First, it is often used figuratively with the second person pronoun modifying either a part of the body (synecdoche) or something associated with the second person. Also, the pronoun may appear elsewhere in the clause. This use is rather common. There are 49 examples of this in the New Testament.[171]

Matt 5:16   οὕτως **λαμψάτω** τὸ φῶς <u>ὑμῶν</u> ἔμπροσθεν τῶν ἀνθρώπων
                   ...

                   thus, **let** <u>your</u> light **shine** before men ...

---

[169]Ibid., 18-23. Examples include Psalm 19:4 (Hebrew Masoretic text: 20:3); 101:2 (102:1); Sir 14:14. In the Sirach passage, the first half of the verse has a second person imperative and a third person occurs in the parallel half.

[170]Ibid., 24-38. Within this group Glaze discusses a number of issues and includes usages such as permission, decree, and dare. Examples respectively include Ruth 2:15 (Boaz tells his workers to permit Ruth to glean in his fields); Jonah 3:7 (decrees of the King of Nineveh after hearing of God's intent to destroy the city); Jer 17:15 (God quotes people who challenge him to let the word of the Lord come). There seems to be some overlap between this usage and the second sub-group of the first category mentioned above (a command to a third person without an intermediary).

[171]In addition to the four cited below, there are 45: Matt 5:37; 6:3, 9 (prayer), 10 (prayer; 2x), 8:13; 9:29; 10:13 (2x); 15:28; 18:17; 26:42 (prayer); Luke 11:2 (prayer; 2x); 12:35; 22:42 (prayer); John 14:27 (2x); Acts 2:14, 38; 13:38; 25:5; 28:28; Rom 14:16; 1 Cor 16:14; Eph 4:26, 29, 31; 5:3, 6, 33; Phil 4:5, 6; Col 2:16, 18; 3:15, 16; 1 Tim 4:12; Jas 4:9; 5:12; 1 Pet 3:3; 4:15; 2 Pet 3:8; 1 John 2:24; 3:7.

John 14:1 Μὴ **ταρασσέσθω** <u>ὑμῶν</u> ἡ καρδία· πιστεύετε εἰς τὸν θεὸν καὶ εἰς ἐμὲ πιστεύετε
Do not **let** <u>your</u> heart **be troubled**. Believe in God and believe in me

Acts 4:10 γνωστὸν **ἔστω** πᾶσιν <u>ὑμῖν</u> …
let it **be** known to all of <u>you</u> …

Rom 6:12 Μὴ οὖν **βασιλευέτω** ἡ ἁμαρτία ἐν τῷ θνητῷ <u>ὑμῶν</u> σώματι …
Do not **let** sin **rule** in <u>your</u> mortal body …

The second person pronoun is key here. This identifies the second person as the ultimate recipient of the directive. Initially I limited this to examples with the pronoun modifying the subject (e.g., Matt 5:16; John 14:1); however, the relationship of the pronoun to the subject elsewhere in the clause also identified the recipient and, therefore, this classification was open to other passages where the second person pronoun made this association (e.g., Acts 4:10; Rom 6:12).

Second, the third person imperative may also be used without the second person pronoun and without any structural ties to the second person but nevertheless be directed to the second person.[172] In these cases, the second person refers to the full recipient, whether one person or a community (compare with the following group):

Matt 27:22-23 λέγει αὐτοῖς ὁ Πιλᾶτος· τί οὖν ποιήσω Ἰησοῦν τὸν λεγόμενον χριστόν; λέγουσιν πάντες· **σταυρωθήτω**. [23] … **σταυρωθήτω**
Pilate said to them, "What therefore should I do with Jesus who is called "Christ"? They all replied, "**Let** him be **Crucified**." [23]… "**Let** him be **Crucified**"

---

[172]There are 31 imperatives that fit this subclassification. In addition to the 16 imperatives mentioned below, there are 15 other examples which fit in this category: Matt 9:30; 26:39 (prayer); Luke 7:7 (see the discussions on this passage concerning its textual problem and unique rank above and in chapter 3); 16:29; 1 Tim 2:11; 5:9, 16 (2x), 17; 6:1, 2 (2x); 2 Tim 2:19; Tit 2:15; 3:14.

Acts 2:36   ἀσφαλῶς οὖν **γινωσκέτω** πᾶς οἶκος 'Ισραὴλ ὅτι καὶ κύριον αὐτὸν καὶ χριστὸν ἐποίησεν ὁ θεός ...

therefore, **let** the entire house of Israel **know** for certain that God made him Lord and Christ ...

1 Tim 3:10   καὶ   οὗτοι   δὲ **δοκιμαζέσθωσαν** πρῶτον, εἶτα **διακονείτωσαν** ἀνέγκλητοι ὄντες

And **let** these first be **tested**, then being beyond reproach, **let** them **serve**

In each of these examples the role of the third person receives prominence; however, the directive is aimed at the addressee (second person) who is expected to fulfill the imperative. Matthew 27:22-23 records the crowd's instructions to Pilate. In Acts 2:26, the second person addressee is mentioned in the third person (the entire house of Israel). Nevertheless, the entire crowd belongs to this group (albeit the group is larger than the recipients). Finally, Paul directs his disciple Timothy on how to choose deacons to serve in his community.

Within this classification of usage of the third for second person, there are three other interesting sets of examples. First, two of Boyer's three examples of his third category called, "what is required of a third party,"[173] better fit as part of this group.

1 Tim 3:12   διάκονοι **ἔστωσαν** μιᾶς γυναικὸς ἄνδρες

let the deacons **be** husbands of one wife

1 Tim 5:4   εἰ δέ τις χήρα τέκνα ἢ ἔκγονα ἔχει, **μανθανέτωσαν** πρῶτον τὸν ἴδιον οἶκον εὐσεβεῖν ...

if a widow has children or grandchildren, **let** them first **learn** to take care of their own ...

---

[173]Boyer, "Imperatives," 48. The other example, Matt 18:17 is included in the first category mentioned above because of its second person pronoun: ἔστω <u>σοι</u> ὥσπερ ὁ ἐθνικὸς καὶ ὁ τελώνης. (... let him **be** to <u>you</u> as a Gentile and tax-collector). As with the examples from 1 Timothy here, although the requirement for a third person is prominent, the instruction is aimed at those responsible to carry out the directive. Boyer maintains that these are the only three examples of this classification.

In 1 Tim 3:12, Timothy receives instruction about the marital status of his deacons and in 5:4 he is instructed about the care of widows. Although the requirements (so Boyer's classification) are placed upon the third person, it is Timothy's role, as leader who is addressed, to deal with the people affected. This is clearer in the first passage since the context is one of the requirements for deacons. Timothy is responsible for their choice.[174] 1 Tim 5:4 is not as clear but in the context of the community, Timothy has the role as leader to assure these instructions are followed. Paul instructs him which widows should be given the limited resources of the church (5:1-16).

Next, there are 7 imperatives in four passages taken from the Old Testament.

Acts 1:20   γέγραπται γὰρ ἐν βίβλῳ ψαλμῶν· **γενηθήτω** ἡ ἔπαυλις
             αὐτοῦ ἔρημος καὶ μὴ **ἔστω** ὁ κατοικῶν ἐν αὐτῇ, καί·
             τὴν ἐπισκοπὴν αὐτοῦ **λαβέτω**[175] ἕτερος
             for it is written in the book of Psalms "**Let** his home **become**
             desolate and **do** not **let** anyone live in it, and **let** another **take**
             his position"

Rom 11:9-10 καὶ Δαυὶδ λέγει· **γενηθήτω** ἡ τράπεζα αὐτῶν εἰς παγίδα
             ... [10] **σκοτισθήτωσαν** οἱ ὀφθαλμοὶ αὐτῶν τοῦ μὴ
             βλέπειν ...
             and David said , "**let** their table **become** a snare, ... **let** their
             eyes **be darkened** and not see ..."

Rom 15:11   καὶ πάλιν· αἰνεῖτε, πάντα τὰ ἔθνη, τὸν κύριον καὶ
             ἐπαινεσάτωσαν αὐτὸν πάντες οἱ λαοί
             and again, praise all the Lord all the Gentiles and **let** all the
             peoples **praise** him

---

[174]Although the issue of choice is not explicit, it seems clear that Timothy is expected to have a significant role in the process. See 1 Tim 3:10 which instructs the young minister concerning the test for deacons. Someone needs to determine if one passes or fails. It seems likely that Timothy would be the main participant in this process.

[175]Psalm 108:8 (LXX) has the optative (λάβοι).

1 Cor 1:31   ἵνα   καθὼς   γέγραπται·   ὁ   καυχώμενος   ἐν   κυρίῳ
              καυχάσθω.
              that just as it is written, "**let** those who boast, **boast** in the
              Lord"

Acts 1:20 is a quotation from Ps 68:26 (LXX) and Ps 108:8 (LXX). Romans
11:9-10 is a quotation from Ps 68:23-24 (LXX). In the respective Old
Testament contexts these are prayers directed to God. They are indirect
directives asking God to punish their enemies. The contexts of Acts and
Romans use these passages in an illustrative manner and seem to maintain the
Old Testament intention (although the referent of the enemies is different). Ps
116:1 (LXX) is cited in Rom 15:11.[176] In this passage, Paul clearly applies it to
the readers of his letter. In 1 Cor 1:31, Paul uses wording from Jeremiah 9:24
as a directive for his readers.

Finally, there are two (parallel) passages that are parenthetical in nature and
are specifically directed to the reader. These words are those of the authors
(probably Mark) or the person responsible for the synoptic apocalypse which
Mark used.

Mark 13:14a ‖ Matt 24:15   ὁ ἀναγινώσκων **νοείτω**
                            Let the one who reads **understand**

The third type of third person for second is related to the previous. These
are directives without the structural pronoun and are general. The directives are
of such a nature that they should be heeded by all to whom they apply among
the recipients of the imperative. Some may apply to all hearers (Mark 8:34)
while others apply to only part of the recipient group (1 Cor 7:9 only applies to
unmarried including widows). In any case, all directives are aimed at some or
all of those to whom the utterances are given (thus second person). This is
probably a politeness strategy. A general principle is much more palatable than
a direct imperative. It is not insignificant that in the previous group there were
many examples from the pastoral epistles which are considered here as having
a single recipient. In the present group, there are many examples from letters
written to communities where there is a potential for diversity. The assumptions

---

[176]The verb in Ps 116:1 (LXX) is in second person.

of this work concerning the recipients of the letter affect classification. For example, if a passage such as 1 Cor 7:9 occurred in 1 Timothy, it would probably be classified as either the third imperative for second or a true third person imperative. However, since 1 Corinthians is written to a community and its message is meant to be communicated to all in the community, 7:9 is directed to those who fit the situation addressed. Such recipients are among of the direct recipients; thus they are second person. In addition, it is not uncommon for these types of imperatives to be preceded by a conditional-like statement which functions to introduce the context and circumstances for whom the directive is intended.[177]

Matt 5:31	Ἐρρέθη δέ· ὃς ἂν ἀπολύσῃ τὴν γυναῖκα αὐτοῦ, **δότω** αὐτῇ ἀποστάσιον But it was said, "Whoever sends away [divorces] his wife, **let him give** to her a divorce notice
John 7:37	... εἱστήκει ὁ Ἰησοῦς καὶ ἔκραξεν λέγων· ἐάν τις διψᾷ **ἐρχέσθω** πρός με καὶ **πινέτω** ... ... Jesus stood and cried out saying, "If anyone is thirsty, **let him come** to me and **drink** ..."
1 Cor 7:20	ἕκαστος ἐν τῇ κλήσει ᾗ ἐκλήθη, ἐν ταύτῃ **μενέτω** **let** each one **remain** in the calling [condition] in which he was called
Jas 1:9	**Καυχάσθω** δὲ ὁ ἀδελφὸς ὁ ταπεινὸς ἐν τῷ ὕψει αὐτοῦ But **let** the brother of humble circumstances **boast** in his high position

---

[177]In addition to the twenty examples mentioned explicitly, there are 121 third person imperatives which fit this classification (141 total): Matt 15:4; 16:24 (3x); 19:6, 12; 24:16, 17, 18; Mark 7:10; 8:34 (3x); 10:9; 13:14b, 15 (2x), 16; Luke 3:11 (2x); 9:23 (3x); 17:31 (2x); 21:1 (3x); 22:26, 36 (3x); John 12:26; Rom 13:1; 14:3 (2x), 5; 15:2; 1 Cor 3:10, 18 (2x), 21; 4:1; 7:2 (2x), 3, 9, 11 (2x), 12, 13, 15, 17, 18 (2x), 21, 24, 36 (2x); 10:12, 24; 11:6 (2x), 28 (3x), 34; 14:13, 26, 27, 28 (2x), 29 (2x), 30, 34 (2x), 35, 37, 40; 16:2, 22; 2 Cor 10:7, 11, 17; Gal 6:4, 6, 17; Eph 4:28 (2x); 2 Thess 3:10; Heb 13:1; Jas 1:4, 5, 6, 7, 13, 19; 3:13; 4:9; 5:13 (2x), 14 (2x), 20; 1 Pet 3:10, 11 (4x); 4:16 (2x), 19; Rev 13:18; 22:11 (4x), 17 (3x).

In addition there are two similar statements in which the speaker basically challenges his listeners to pay attention. Again, although third person, they are aimed at the second person recipient. First, ὁ ἔχων ὦτα ἀκουέτω (**let** the one who has ears **hear**) or similar occurs eight times (Matt 11:15; 13:9, 43; Mark 4:9, 23; Luke 8:8; 14:35; Rev 13:9).[178] Second, the similar statement Ὁ ἔχων οὖς ἀκουσάτω ... occurs 7 times (Rev 2:7, 11, 17, 29; 3:6, 13, 22).

It was suggested that the third person demands a weakened force. This may be the case; however, one other factor may also be important. The use of the third person may place an emphasis or focus upon its referent (i.e., the subject). Romans 6:12 seems to be a good example of this. The third person imperative is the second of four imperatives in the immediate context (6:11-13). There is no question what Paul expects from his readers. The third person may serve to emphasize the role of sin. This does not mean that the force is not weakened here also. The second person imperatives are generally mild verbs even if at full force (λογίζεσθε and παραστήσατε [2x]).

The third person imperative directed at the second person is clearly the primary use of this form. This is expected since the recipient of the imperative is necessarily grammatically the second person. The classification here has been sensitive to the nature of the genre in which the imperatives occur. The gospels present narratives which record communication situations.[179] The epistles are actual examples of communication situations. Thus, the recipients of the imperatives are the addressees themselves. For example, 1 Corinthians is addressed to a church and records many responses to questions that they asked of Paul. Therefore, third person imperatives which may seem to be aimed at third persons are actually second person directed because the recipients are all the intended hearers even though some directives will only apply to a minority of the congregation (see for example the specifics about marriage in chapter 7). The books addressed to Timothy are being assumed to be directed to one person primarily. Thus, books like 1 Corinthians and 1 Timothy have been viewed

---

[178]Mark 4:9 has ὃς ἔχει ὦτα ἀκούειν ἀκουέτω; Mark 4:23 has εἴ τις ἔχει ὦτα ἀκούειν ἀκουέτω; Luke 8:8 and 14:35 have ὁ ἔχων ὦτα ἀκούειν ἀκουέτω; Rev 13:9 has Εἴ τις ἔχει οὖς ἀκουσάτω (note the similarity to Mark 4:23).

[179]The Gospels themselves are also real examples of communication. However, they are more complex and involve an additional level of meaning. They record events and are meant to communicate to the readers of the book. Additionally, a message to a character in the book may or may not be the same as the intended message to the readers.

somewhat differently.

The second classification of third person imperatives is when the intended recipient of the third person imperative is an actual third person. This is also a pragmatically essential situation given the limitations on the use of writing for communication. If one writes to a specific audience and wants to direct another non-recipient with an imperative, the only means of this (short of writing another letter) is through the intermediary role of the recipient(s) of the letter. This is also an indirect means of directing; however, the reason for this is less certain. It may be indirect; however, it also may be because there is no other manner of reaching the third person.[180] Boyer's suggestion that there does not seem to be an implication for the recipient to communicate the directive to the third party may also suggest an essential indirectness to the form since the fulfillment of the imperative is even more dependent on the recipient and his ability, willingness, desire, etc., to pass on the directive.

There seem to be fewer third person imperatives for actual third persons than Boyer suggests. There are only six certain examples and possibly another four (which are in parallel passages).[181]

Acts 16:37　　… ἀλλὰ ἐλθόντες αὐτοὶ ἡμᾶς **ἐξαγαγέτωσαν**
[Paul to those who came to release him and his companions] … but **let** them come and release us

Acts 19:38　　εἰ μὲν οὖν Δημήτριος καὶ οἱ σὺν αὐτῷ τεχνῖται ἔχουσι πρός τινα λόγον, … **ἐγκαλείτωσαν** ἀλλήλοις
Therefore, if Demetrios and the workmen with him have a word (complaint) against him … **let** them **bring charges** against one another

---

[180]A number of reasons may be suggested for this. In some cases, the only way to reach the third party may be through the recipient. It also may be part of chain of command in which it is appropriate to address an inferior of another through his superior.

[181]Of Boyer's examples only one of three is considered by this work's analysis as a possible actual third person imperative to a third person (Luke 23:35). However, although accepting this passage, it can be conceded that this is somewhat debatable. His other passages, Luke 16:29 and Jas 5:14, were classified with second person intent.

Acts 24:20   ἢ αὐτοὶ οὗτοι **εἰπάτωσαν** τί εὗρον ἀδίκημα στάντος
            μου ἐπὶ τοῦ συνεδρίου
            or **let** these men **say** what bad works I am standing before the
            council

Gal 1:8-9   ἀνάθεμα **ἔστω** (2x)
            [if anyone preaches another gospel], **let** him **be** accursed

Heb 1:6   λέγει· καὶ **προσκυνησάτωσαν** αὐτῷ πάντες ἄγγελοι θεοῦ
            he said, "**Let** all the angels of God **worship** him"

Although each of these passages seems debatable, they seem to represent the best possibilities for a third person imperative being directed to an actual third person. In Acts 16:37, the directive seems to actually be filled by the third person to whom Paul is referring (Acts 16:39). In the other two Acts passages the court room and related situations seem to provide a setting where the third person imperative can be used for a third person. There are set rules of engagement in these types of settings and thus one may be addressing the required individual but communicating to another. The second passage (24:20) is a more convincing example.

It has been already noted that the imperatives in Gal 1:8-9 are probably not meant to be read by the opponents to whom Paul directs these strong words. However, they also will not apply directly to the readers. Finally, Heb 1:6 is a peculiar example. It is an Old Testament quotation and seems to be directed to angels, the third person subject of the saying.

There are four somewhat parallel passages in the synoptic passions which may be actual third persons (Matt 27: 42, 43; Mark 15:32; Luke 23:35). Jesus is on the cross and the bystanders are uttering third person imperatives with God (Matt 27:43) or Jesus (the other three e.g., **καταβάτω** νῦν ἀπὸ τοῦ σταυροῦ; **let** him now **come down** from the cross) as the subject. Although the discussion is really taking place among the spectators themselves, they also may be mocking challenges to Jesus. Therefore, although it was noted that it was unlikely that Jesus was being addressed (which seems to be the most likely conclusion), it is worthwhile considering the possibility that Jesus may be included as an intended addressee.

The third and final classification of the third person imperative is debatable.

The third person may be used without any specific addressee intended. They seem to function almost like a declarative statement or idiom with minimal force.[182] There are three passages that may be possible candidates for this classification,

Acts 21:14   τοῦ κυρίου τὸ θέλημα **γινέσθω**
                  Let the will of the Lord **be done**

Rom 3:4   **γινέσθω** δὲ ὁ θεὸς ἀληθής
                  let God **be** true

2 Cor 12:16   **Ἔστω** δέ …
                  But **be** that as it **may**

Both the Acts and Romans passages may be classified as third person directed imperatives aimed at God (especially Acts 21:14). However, they also may lack a real recipient. They seem to function as idiomatic expressions.

The use of the third person was important for the discussion of force. When used to direct a second person party, it has been observed that the third person is *indirect* and thus weaker than a direct second person imperative. It is possible that this claim cannot be sustained in every instance; however, it seems like a workable general principle.

---

[182]Interestingly, Boyer's fourth category is "promise or warning of what will be" ("Imperatives," 48). This would describe the classification here. However, this work would classify each of his examples differently which he uses to support this category (Boyer maintains 4% are so classified, it is possible that some of this work's choices would also be classified in this category). First, Matt 15:28, τότε ἀποκριθεὶς ὁ Ἰησοῦς εἶπεν αὐτῇ· ὦ γύναι, μεγάλη σου ἡ πίστις· **γενηθήτω** σοι ὡς θέλεις … (then Jesus answered and said to her, "O woman, your faith is great, **let** it **happen** to you as you desire …). This is a passive directive to the woman and thus has second person intention and may be non-event-initiating. This was included with second person directed imperatives identified by the second person pronoun. Second, Romans 11:9-10 has two third person imperatives, καὶ Δαυὶδ λέγει· **γενηθήτω** ἡ τράπεζα αὐτῶν εἰς παγίδα … [10] **σκοτισθήτωσαν** οἱ ὀφθαλμοὶ αὐτῶν τοῦ μὴ βλέπειν … (and David said, "**Let** their table **become** a snare, … **let** their eyes **be darkened** and not see …"). This is a quotation of LXX Ps 68:23-24 and is in the context of a prayer for David. The prayer is directed to God. It is an indirect directive asking God to punish his enemies. The context of Romans is illustrative maintaining the Old Testament intention. I am not suggesting that the Old Testament usage is to be read into the New; however, this passage seems to demand the Old Testament context to be understood.

Third versus Second Person: Clues to the Choice of Person

There are a limited number of imperatives in parallel passages in the synoptics in which one or more uses the second and another uses the third person.[183] First this work will list the four relevant groups of parallel passages and then draw some cautious conclusions.

This discussion will begin with a familiar group of parallel passages: Mark 14:36 ‖ Matt 26:39 ‖ Luke 22:42. There are two points of contrast in this passage. First, in Mark and Luke, the first imperative is second person but a third is in Matthew. Second, Luke has a third person imperative in contrast to a non-verbal clause; however, a second person indicative (θέλεις) is implied. Only the first contrast is relevant here (the second was discussed in chapter 3).

Mark 14:36   **παρένεγκε** τὸ ποτήριον τοῦτο ἀπ' ἐμοῦ· ἀλλ' οὐ τί ἐγὼ θέλω ἀλλὰ τί σύ
              remove this cup from me, but not what I desire but what you [desire]

Matt 26:39   **παρελθάτω** ἀπ' ἐμοῦ τὸ ποτήριον τοῦτο· πλὴν οὐχ ὡς ἐγὼ θέλω ἀλλ' ὡς σύ
              let this cup **pass** from me, yet not as I desire but as you [desire]

Luke 22:42   **παρένεγκε** τοῦτο τὸ ποτήριον ἀπ' ἐμοῦ· πλὴν μὴ τὸ θέλημά μου ἀλλὰ τὸ σὸν **γινέσθω**
              remove this cup from me; still not my desire but **let** yours **be done**

---

[183]There are a number of parallels where the third person imperative is used in two or more synoptics passages with no contrast. These are as follows: Mark 7:10 ‖ Matt 15:4; Mark 8:34 (3x) ‖ Matt 16:24 (3x) ‖ Luke 9:23 (3x; first imperative is a different lexeme); Mark 10:9 ‖ Matt 19:6; Mark 13:14 (2x) ‖ Matt 24:15-16 (2x) ‖ Luke 21:21 (3x; Luke's first imperative parallel's Matthew and Mark's second; Luke's final two imperatives are not paralleled); Mark 13:15-16 (3x; the second imperative is not paralleled) ‖ Matt 24:17-18 (2x) ‖ Luke 17:31 (2x)–these include seven of eight negative aorist imperatives and will be discussed briefly in a separate section below Mark 15:32 ‖ Matt 27:42 (plus an unparalleled third imperative in v. 43)–this passage with Luke 23:35 will be briefly noted below.

Note however, the unparalleled phrase[184] with a third person in Matt 26:42 from the same pericope:

Matt 26:42   πάτερ μου, εἰ οὐ δύναται τοῦτο παρελθεῖν ἐὰν μὴ αὐτὸ πίω, **γενηθήτω** τὸ θέλημά σου

               My Father, if this is not able to pass unless I drink it, <u>**let**</u> your will **be <u>done</u>**

This imperative is very similar to Luke 22:42. However, this prayer occurs after the initial prayer (as recorded in Mark 14:36 and parallels) and confrontation with his sleepy disciples. Matthew seems to be adding content to Mark's description (which is probably also implied in the addition of Luke 22:44,[185] although this version does not suggest any content to the prayer, only the emotional trauma of Jesus' prayer).

In Mark 15:13-14 ‖ Matt 27:22-23 ‖ Luke 23:21, 23 there are two imperatives in each gospel. Mark and Luke have the second person; however, Luke's second imperative is a repeat of the first and has an infinitive in contrast to the imperative. Matthew has two third person imperatives.

---

[184]The reason I suggest this is unparalleled is because the Lukan third person imperative is in contrast to the non-verbal phrase in Mark and Matthew.

[185]Against most English versions (e.g., NASB, NET), it seems unlikely that Luke 22:43-44 is original. They are omitted by P[75], ℵ[1], A, B, (and others). They are included by ℵ*, ℵ[2], D, the manuscripts represented by gothic M, many church fathers (and others). The external evidence favors the omission. Although there is no parallel to which one can identify a harmonization, Mark 14:39 seems to provide the motivation to add something here. Matthew chose to include similar wording from the first part of the prayer. It is possible that Luke did the same but instead of adding prayer content, he added further description of Jesus' emotional state at this difficult time. However, it is worth noting that Luke does not record a confrontation with the sleeping disciples between the two parts of the prayer. In any event, the addition does seem quite early and likely stems from the actual historical event. It certainly does seem to fit the situation. Nevertheless, only Luke is of concern here and these verse seem best to be considered an addition. The omission is supported by Bart D. Ehrman and Mark A. Plunkett who argue that in addition to the strong external evidence for the omission, there is important internal evidence as well. The passage is theologically intrusive in its context and structurally intrusive. They suggest that it is an anti-docetic polemic added early (before AD 160) ("The Angel and the Agony: The Textual Problem of Luke 22:43-44," *Catholic Biblical Quarterly* 45 [1983]: 401-16).

Mark 15:13-14   οἱ δὲ πάλιν ἔκραξαν· **σταύρωσον** αὐτόν ... 14 οἱ δὲ
περισσῶς ἔκραξαν· **σταύρωσον** αὐτόν
but they cried out back, "**Crucify** him!" ... 14 but all the more
they cried out, "**Crucify** him!"

Matt 27:22-23   λέγουσιν πάντες· **σταυρωθήτω** ... 23 οἱ δὲ περισσῶς
ἔκραζον λέγοντες· **σταυρωθήτω**
they all said, "<u>**Let**</u> him <u>**be crucified**</u>!" ... 23 but all the more
they were crying out saying, "<u>**Let**</u> him <u>**be crucified**</u>!"

Luke 23:21, 23   οἱ δὲ ἐπεφώνουν λέγοντες· **σταύρου σταύρου** αὐτόν ...
. 23 οἱ δὲ ἐπέκειντο φωναῖς μεγάλαις αἰτούμενοι αὐτὸν
σταυρωθῆναι
but they were shouting, saying, "**Crucify, crucify** him!" ... but
the crowds [were] asking with loud voices [that] he <u>be</u>
<u>crucified</u>

In the final two passages, the third person is again only in Matthew and
there are differences in lexemes among the verbs.

Mark 10:52   καὶ ὁ Ἰησοῦς εἶπεν αὐτῷ· **ὕπαγε**, ἡ πίστις σου σέσωκέν
σε. καὶ εὐθὺς ἀνέβλεψεν καὶ ἠκολούθει αὐτῷ ἐν τῇ ὁδῷ
and Jesus said to him, "**Go**, your faith has saved [healed] you
and immediately he regained his sight and followed him on the
road

Matt 9:29   τότε ἥψατο τῶν ὀφθαλμῶν αὐτῶν λέγων· κατὰ τὴν
πίστιν ὑμῶν **γενηθήτω** ὑμῖν
then he touched their eyes saying, "<u>**Let**</u> it <u>**be done**</u> to you
according to your faith

Luke 18:42   καὶ ὁ Ἰησοῦς εἶπεν αὐτῷ· **ἀνάβλεψον**· ἡ πίστις σου
σέσωκέν σε
and Jesus said to him, "**See** [or **regain your sight**], your faith
has saved [healed] you"

Mark 7:29   καὶ εἶπεν αὐτῇ· διὰ τοῦτον τὸν λόγον **ὕπαγε**,
             ἐξελήλυθεν ἐκ τῆς θυγατρός σου τὸ δαιμόνιον
             and he [Jesus] said to her, "Because of this word [answer], **go**
             the demon has left your daughter"

Matt 15:28   τότε ἀποκριθεὶς ὁ 'Ιησοῦς εἶπεν αὐτῇ· ὦ γύναι, μεγάλη
             σου ἡ πίστις· **γενηθήτω** σοι ὡς θέλεις ...
             then answering Jesus said to her, "O woman, your faith is
             great, **let** it **be done** to you as you wish ..."

What stands out about these examples is that it is always Matthew who makes the change to the third person. This is somewhat in line with the higher percentage of third person forms among imperative forms in Matthew. Of all imperatives, Matthew uses the third 11.5% (33/286) where Mark and Luke use it around 8% of the time.[186] However, this difference is not that great given that all four of the examples have Matthew making the change. One would expect that Matthew would use it more. Therefore, it seems likely that Matthew is using the third person for a particular reason in these examples. Of Matthew's 33 uses of the third person, 29 are words of Jesus. The majority are instructive (23),[187] but four aim at people to whom he grants healing and three use the same form of the verb γίνομαι.[188] Two occur in Jesus' agonizing prayer in the garden before his arrest.[189] The remaining four all occur at the cross and are uttered by those watching and ridiculing Jesus.[190]

The difficulty remains to determine why Matthew uses the third person in these instances. The instructional uses may be a strategy to make his imperatives more attractive (especially 16:24). The use in healing situations may be a means of emphasizing God's action and/or a means of comforting the

---

[186]Mark uses the third person 8.7% of the time (13/149–not including Mark 16:15) and Luke uses it 8.0% (23/284).

[187]Matt 5:16, 31, 37; 6:3, 9, 10 (2x; verses 9-10 are in the sample prayer for his disciples); 10:13 (2x); 11:15; 13:9, 43 (the three in chapters 11 and 13 are the concluding, ὁ ἔχων ὦτα ἀκουέτω); 15:4 (quotation); 16:24 (3x); 18:17; 19:6 (quotation), 12; 24:15, 16, 17, 18.

[188]Matt 8:13; 9:29, 30; 15:28. All with one exception use the singular aorist passive of γίνομαι; 9:30 uses the singular present passive of γινώσκω. The healing is granted to either the individual or someone associated with the individual who is coming to Jesus on his/her behalf.

[189]Matt 26:39, 42.

[190]Matt 27:22, 23, 42, 43.

listener. The use of the same lexeme may suggest a common saying of Jesus in these instances. I suggest that this is supported by Matthew's change to the third person in two of the four examples cited above (Matt 9:29; 15:28).

Matthew's use of the third person in the garden is complex. This passage has been discussed in other contexts and it seems using this passage to add to the debate at this stage may be more problematic than helpful. However, it is worth noting that the unparalleled third person imperative in 26:42 is the singular aorist passive of γίνομαι. The relationship to this verb is close in context with the third person in 26:39 which is one of four changes applied by Matthew. Two of the remaining three have been changed to this form. This may be significant but because of the common nature of this verb and a limited database, any conclusion must be tentative. This may again place the emphasis on the third person subject (God's will) or it may even function as a climax to God's activity of healing which is an answer to the sample prayer in Matt 6:10.[191] In other words, Jesus' example to his disciples is to pray for God's will (emphasis). In Matt 26:36-46 (esp. vv. 39, 42) Jesus models what this means in the context of his own life.[192] The healing may also be implied as Jesus' sacrifice ultimately is a means of healing.[193]

Finally there is little that can be learned from Matt 27:22-23 and parallels. In light of this study, it seems best to view these as both emphasis on the person to be crucified and the reluctance of the crowd to use a direct second person to the Roman magistrate.

Therefore, analysis of the few parallels available offers minimal help. Nevertheless, the parallels support the notion that the third person may be used as a politeness strategy and/or emphasis.[194]

---

[191]There are only five occurrences of this form in Matthew. Three are in the context of healing and have been already noted (8:13; 9:29; 15:28; the latter two were the Matthean changes). The first occurs in Matt 6:10, Jesus' sample prayer asking that God's will be done. The final one is the unparalleled third in Matt 26:42 which is related to the Matthean change immediately preceding in verse 39.

[192]It is likely that the actual change to third person in Matt 26:39 from Mark's second person is the politeness strategy which has been observed elsewhere.

[193]There may be other parallels between the prayers in Matthew 6 and Matthew 26 including acknowledging God's control. The submission to God's will is the explicit climatic aspect of the prayer.

[194]Although the contrast is not between second and third person imperatives, the parallel sections Mark 15:29-32 || Matt 27:39-43 || Luke 23:35 include a number of third person imperatives and it is worthwhile to discuss these albeit in the form of a note. Luke 23:35 (σωσάτω) seems to be in contrast with the infinitive in Mark 15:31 || Matt 27:42 (σῶσαι).

The Rare Negative Third Person Aorist Imperative

There are no examples of the negative second person aorist imperative in the New Testament. The subjunctive is used for all such directives. However, in the third person, a small number of negated aorist imperatives exists and their impact seems minimal.[195] The total number of occurrences of such forms is eight: Matt 6:3; 24:17, 18; Mark 13:15 (2x; the second aorist imperative occurrence is negated by μήδε); Luke 17:31 (2x). All eight of these third person aorist negative imperatives occur in direct speech of Jesus. The total of eight such forms is somewhat misleading. The actual count is much less. Other than the Matt 6:3 passage, all are in parallel passages. Assuming literary dependence (and a common original source–Jesus' synoptic apocalypse), the examples can be reduced to four: μὴ γνώτω (Matt 6:3); μὴ καταβάτω (Mark 13:15a; Matt 24:17; Luke 17:31a); μὴ ἐπιστρεψάτω (Mark 13:16; Matt 24:18; Luke 17:31b); μὴ εἰσελθάτω (Mark 13:15b). Even this may be somewhat misleading since three of these four are all in the same context. Therefore, there are only two contexts containing this form: Matt 6:3 and the others.

The uniqueness of this form may suggest that these passages go back to a non-Greek original (i.e., the actual teaching of Jesus) and thus may be attributed to translation. It is impossible to know whether Mark had the original and translated it, had the translation only, or had access to both the original and a

---

However, Mark 15:32 ‖ Matt 27:42 include a third person imperative (καταβάτω). One wonders whether Mark's use of the third person (unparalleled in Luke) was retained by Luke here with another lexeme (although a lexeme present in Mark). In other words, Luke, wishing to emphasize the challenge "to save" seems to raise the verb from the infinitive to finite status as an imperative. In doing so, with Mark's original before him, it is possible that Luke wished to maintain the third person morphology from the verb he omitted (καταβάτω) and included it with the main verb thus changing the infinitive (σῶσαι) to the third person imperative (σωσάτω). These examples were dismissed from serious consideration in chapter 3 because there may be larger redactional issues involved. The same will be done here. If what has been suggested is correct, there is no contrast of mood between the infinitive in Mark ‖ Matthew (σῶσαι) and the third person imperative in Luke (σωσάτω). Rather, there is a parallel use of the third person imperative with different lexemes (καταβάτω and σωσάτω). In addition this section includes a further unparalleled imperative which cannot contribute to the analysis (ῥυσάσθω).

[195]Moulton notes that the negated aorist imperative is used only in the third person but states, "we need not stay to ask why" (*Prolegomena*, 3d ed., vol. 1, *A Grammar of New Testament Greek*, ed. James Hope Moulton [Edinburgh: T. & T. Clark, 1908], 174-75). This seems to suggest he sees this phenomenon as relatively unimportant. In light of the immediate discussion, this evaluation will seem warranted for gleaning insight about the imperative. However, it may be of value for historical Jesus studies.

Greek translation. However, it seems clear that Luke and Matthew had access to at least the Greek Mark.

It is likely that Jesus taught in Aramaic (some or all of the time). An Aramaic original source for Jesus' own words is not an unwise position to maintain. Whatever the case, it is interesting that this form is preserved or translated in the gospel. For some reason Matthew and especially Luke (who seems to freely change his source[196] [assuming Mark and a sayings source]), did not feel free to change this to the subjunctive despite their apparent willingness to omit Mark's μὴ εἰσελθάτω. It is also interesting that although Mark's use of the third person imperative is strikingly minimal (thirteen occurrences in nine verses), more than one third of the occurrences of the third person imperatives are in the same immediate context (13:14-16: five: three negated aorist already mentioned and two present; Matthew's account also includes the two presents, thus four third imperatives together [24:15-18]; Luke has no parallel of the statement containing the earlier third person present imperatives).

Beyond noting the interesting nature of these passages, the minimal examples afforded by the New Testament do not provide one with enough data to make any specific claims about the imperative mood. However, there seems to be significant potential for the study of the historical Jesus. Most appropriately they may provide insight into the authenticity of the Sermon on the Mount and specifically the synoptic apocalypse. Further redactional work and its implications for the synoptic problem are beyond the scope of this work.

The Third Person and Some Clausal Relationships

Although this study focuses on the morphological imperative mood, it is worthwhile to briefly consider the higher clausal level relationships between some imperative verbs.[197] There are a number of passages where a second person imperative is followed by a third person imperative. In most cases the first imperative seems almost like an attention getting device and the third person gives more specific direction:

---

[196]See the synoptic analysis in chapter 3.

[197]We will again look at the clausal level in our discussion of conditional imperatives below. These two brief explorations into higher level analysis do not exhaust this area of study.

Matt 8:13   καὶ εἶπεν ὁ ᾽Ιησοῦς τῷ ἑκατοντάρχῃ· **ὕπαγε**, ὡς
              ἐπίστευσας **γενηθήτω** σοι ...
              And Jesus said to the centurion, "**Go**, as you have believed **let**
              it **be done** to you ..."

Matt 9:30   ὁρᾶτε μηδεὶς γινωσκέτω
              "**See!** **Let** no one **know** [about this]

The first imperative is strong and sets the tone of the utterance. I suggested this
functions as an attention getting device. This may be misleading. I do not intend
to minimize the force of the imperative with this description. It is a strong
directive. However, it is more general. More specific information is
forthcoming. In such cases it seems unlikely that the third person functions as
a force weakening politeness strategy because the second person has already
been expressed. If Glaze's LXX observations are correct and applicable to the
New Testament, when a second person plural imperative is followed by a third
person singular, an emphatic command results. She suggests that the two
imperatives "say essentially the same thing."[198] The use of multiple imperatives
suggests that the directive(s) is of utmost importance.[199] Therefore, in these
cases, it seems best to view the third person as a means of emphasis upon the
third person subject.[200]

Acts 2:38 and Our Study

Act 2:38 is one of the most difficult passages in the New Testament for the
modern church to understand:

---

[198]Glaze, "Septuagintal Use," 28. Glaze gives Exod 16:29; Josh 6:10; Jer 18:11; Ezek 20:7
as examples.

[199]This may be the case but one wonders whether or not any combination of parallel
imperative might have the same effect. In addition, other features may reveal the importance of
the directive(s).

[200]See Luke 11:2; Acts 2:38 (see below); Eph 4:26; Titus 2:15; Jas 1:19; 4:9. See also Matt
6:9; 18:17; Jas 5:12 which are debatable examples. These all have an intervening clause between
imperatives. Finally, Rev 22:17 has both second and third person imperatives but the relationship
between them is unique (e.g., the third precedes the second).

Acts 2:38   Πέτρος δὲ πρὸς αὐτούς· μετανοήσατε, [φησίν,] καὶ
βαπτισθήτω ἕκαστος ὑμῶν ἐπὶ τῷ ὀνόματι Ἰησοῦ
Χριστοῦ εἰς ἄφεσιν τῶν ἁμαρτιῶν ὑμῶν καὶ λήμψεσθε
τὴν δωρεὰν τοῦ ἁγίου πνεύματος
Now Peter [said] to them, "**Repent**, and <u>let</u> each of you <u>be</u>
<u>baptized</u> in the name of Jesus Christ from the forgiveness of
sin and you will receive the Holy Spirit

This passage contains many interpretive problems.[201] This work is only
interested in whether or not the imperatives can contribute to the debate. If the
observations above are correct, the second person plural followed by third
person singular imperative does not suggest a weakened force for the latter.
Most commentators do not seem to see much importance in the relationship
between the morphological person of the imperatives.[202] Some have suggested
that the third person makes it clear and emphatic. All the listeners are
addressed.[203] Another identifies the second person as referring to all Israel while

---

[201]Problems include the meaning of the preposition εἰς, the relationship and timing between
the imperatives and the future indicative, the actual role of baptism and its relationship to
repentance. The purpose here is only to reveal any grammatical insight which may be gleaned
from this work. See the commentaries on this passage for a discussion of the various problems
and options of interpretation. Concerning the preposition, it seems unwise to postulate rare or
awkward interpretations to avoid theological tension that may be caused by its normal usages.
Concerning the relationship between the imperatives and future indicative, Paul Elbert has been
examining the imperative + future indicative in Luke-Acts and in some Greco-Roman authors.
In one paper given at the 52d annual meeting of the Evangelical Theological Society (Nashville;
Nov 15-17, 2000) entitled "Acts 2:38c Reconsidered," Elbert argues that Luke is consistent in
his use of the imperative – future combination as a conditional construction in which the future
promise always occurs after (never simultaneously) with the imperative action. The implication
is clear. The reception of the Holy Spirit must occur after repentance has occurred. However, he
notes an inconsistency among other authors (both Greco-Roman and New Testament) and the
database is limited. In addition, even given his conclusions, in light of the dynamics of the
Pentecost experience recorded, how this should be understood in different contexts is still
debatable.
[202]See for example Darrell L. Bock, *Acts*, Baker Exegetical Commentary on the New
Testament (Grand Rapids: Baker Book House, 2007), 143-44; Hans Conzelmann, *Acts of the
Apostles: A Commentary on the Acts of the Apostles*, trans. James Limburg, A. Thomas Kraabel,
and Donald H. Juel, Hermeneia, ed. Eldon J. Epp with Christopher R. Matthews (Philadelphia:
Fortress Press, 1987), 22; Ben Witherington III, *The Acts of the Apostles: A Socio-Rhetorical
Commentary* (Grand Rapids: William B. Eerdmans Publishing Company, 1998), 153-55.
[203]Glaze, "Septuagintal Use," 28, n. 1; C. D. Osburn, "The Third Person Imperative in Acts
2:38," *Restoration Quarterly* 26 (1983): 81-84. Osburn follows Glaze on this point.

the third person individualizes the directive.[204] These observations are in line with the previous analysis. The imperatives are essentially directed to the same audience while the latter seems to express a more specific directive.[205] All of Peter's hearers, those directly responsible for Jesus' death and those who are not, must repent and be baptized (full force). This will result in the reception of the Holy Spirit.[206]

This passage also fits the *imperative + καί + future indicative* construction. It will be demonstrated below that at a sentence level this construction has a conditional nuance. However, Acts 2:38 is rather unique among examples of this structure. It is only one of three examples with a third person.[207] Also, although there are examples with multiple imperatives in the protasis with one future in the apodosis, this is the only one where the second imperative is a third person. The first unquestionably has a conditional nuance. However, if the second imperative is merely describing the previous imperative,[208] it is explanatory and not necessarily directly conditional.

However, beyond what has already been stated, grammar cannot provide answers. First, despite Elbert's claims, I am not convinced that this construction demands that the actions cannot be simultaneous. The database is simply too limited and the practice was not universal. In addition, even if there is a time gap between the imperatives and the future, this may be very small or reflect a particular situation. Second, the relationship between repentance and baptism is dubious. With the absence of prescriptive teaching on the necessity of baptism for conversion, Paul's teaching on the priority of faith, and 1 Pet 3:21 seemingly arguing against water baptism as salvific in itself, it is unwise to

---

[204]C. K. Barrett, *A Critical and Exegetical Commentary on the Acts of the Apostles*, vol. 1, International Critical Commentary, ed. J. A. Emerton, C. E. B. Cranfield, and G. N. Stanton (Edinburgh: T. & T. Clark, 1994), 153-54.

[205]Although not committing to the suggestion, Young goes too far in suggesting that a change of person may suggest the "soteriological necessity of the two actions" (*Intermediate New Testament Greek: A Linguistic and Exegetical Approach* [Nashville: Broadman and Holman Publishers, 1994], 143).

[206]It will be confirmed below that the imperative + future indicative combination adds the nuance of condition to the sentence.

[207]See also Matt 27:42 which has a clear conditional nuance at the sentence level and Acts 28:28 which is less obvious.

[208]The term parenthetical will be used below. This term should not be used to imply unimportance. Rather, it is parenthetical in reference to forwarding the argument.

demand this teaching from Acts 2:38.[209]

However, I have no intention of minimizing baptism. This appears to be a very important ritual for the early church (cf. Matt 28:19, etc.). There was an emphasis on this ritual that seems to have diminished in modern church practice. In fact, baptism in the early church may have been so closely associated with conversion that it was often used figuratively for the salvation commitment. Modern examples may exist in statements such as "I prayed to receive Christ, yesterday" or "I walked down the aisle at this church." Prayer and altar calls do not save people; however, contemporary evangelicals understand what is meant when they hear these statements.[210] Also, Rom 10:9 clearly associates outward confession with salvation and James 2:14-26 also stresses action. Although neither of these passages refer to baptism, they do reveal the importance of an outward and active faith.[211]

Summary

This section has probably raised more questions than it has answered. Nevertheless it has been worthwhile discussing the third person in some detail. Many issues relating to the third person are beyond the scope of this morphological study. Nevertheless, a few points may be reiterated here. The third person can be used as a directive to both third and second person recipients. The second person directed third person imperative is more common in the literature. The third may function as a politeness strategy especially by making a directive aimed a second person indirect. It may also place emphasis elsewhere (i.e., on a third person subject). These purposes need not be exclusive.

---

[209]I am aware that using passages outside of Luke to argue my point is not ideal. However, these books do reflect early teaching of the church.

[210]It is important to keep in mind that unlike praying to receive Christ and alter calls, baptism is commanded in Scripture (the call to salvation is commanded but not these expressions). One must be careful to avoid minimizing this command because one fears implications which seem contrary to the gospel.

[211]This work maintains that the position (option 4) which seems to be favored by Wallace is best (*Exegetical Syntax*, 370-71).

Conditional Imperative?: Problems and a Solution

The analysis thus far has avoided specific discussion of the imperative usage termed *conditional* by many New Testament grammars.[212] Indeed, it would seem that the analysis leaves little room for such a usage. This observation is not entirely incorrect.[213] The existence of a conditional usage in the *same manner*[214] as those discussed above is doubtful.[215] In other words, it will be argued that the traditional label *conditional* in contrast to other labels

---

[212]See for example BDF, 195 (within a broader usage labeled *concessive*); Boyer, "Imperatives," 38-40; James A. Brooks and Carlton L. Winbery, *Syntax of New Testament Greek* (Lanham, MD: University Press of America, 1979), 117; Wallace, *Exegetical Syntax*, 489-92; Young, *Intermediate*, 145. Concerning means of expressing condition, Boyer states that the conditional imperative "is more rare and less obvious." ("Other Conditional Elements in New Testament Greek," *Grace Theological Journal* 4 [1983]: 185).

[213]Although not using the same terminology, the position of Porter seems to be similar to what will be developed here (*Verbal Aspect in the Greek of the New Testament, with Reference to Tense and Mood*, Studies in Biblical Greek, ed. D. A. Carson, vol. 1 [New York: Peter Lang, 1989], 352-53).

[214]Up to this point pragmatic usages have primarily been classified within their own verbal clause (for a brief exception, see "The Third Person and Some Clausal Relationships" above). This does not mean other contextual information has not been considered. However, higher levels of discourse including the relationship between verbs in a sentence have not been explored in any detail. Therefore, the study has now moved to another level, namely, that of the sentence. This does not negate this work's more limited analysis; rather, it provides another level of meaning worth exploring. Both levels are important. Up until now, the analysis has generally not needed to go beyond this work's limited sphere. As will be seen below, failure to make this distinction may result in the eclipse of the imperative meaning of volitional–directive with a discourse pragmatic effect, namely, the conditional. These are not exclusive.

[215]It is not insignificant that many classical grammars do not include this usage. See William Watson Goodwin, *Syntax of the Moods and Tenses of the Greek Verb* (Boston: Ginn and Company, 1890), 86-89 (however, he does note that the imperative may be used to "express a mere assumption," 87, this seems close to a conditional in meaning); Raphael Kühner and Bernhard Gerth, *Ausführliche Grammatik der griechischen Sprache*, 4th ed., vol. 1 (Leverkusen: Gottschalksche, 1955), 236; Herbert Weir Smyth, *Greek Grammar*, rev. G. M. Messing ed. (Cambridge, MA: Harvard University Press, 1956), 409-11; John A. Thompson, *A Greek Grammar: Accidence and Syntax. For Schools and Colleges* (London: John Murray, 1902), 327-28). Schwyzer-Debrunner is an important exception, "Wie der Optativ . . . und der imperativische Infinitiv . . . so kann auch der Imperativsatz eine Voraussetzung ausdrücken, wodurch der Imp. einem Kondizional- oder Konzessivsatz gleichwertig wird" (Eduard Schwyzer, *Griechische Grammatik, ii. Syntax und syntaktische Stilistik*, ed. Albert Debrunner [Munich: C. H. Beck, 1950], 344). Also, one grammar suggests that the imperative may be used for "concession or supposition" which seems to include a conditional nuance ("ask me and I will tell you" = "if you ask me . . ."); A. Rijksbaron, *The Syntax and Semantics of the Verb in Classical Greek: An Introduction* (Amsterdam: J. C. Gieben, 1984), 42.

such as *command* and *request* is a misleading means of classification.[216]

The Problems with the Conditional Classification

There are two possible defenses for the traditional approach. First, it is possible that this usage merely has a very weak directive force which may be implied from those who classify it with permissive and/or concessive usages.[217] This is not satisfactory for two reasons. First, it obscures the fact that the directive force of these imperatives may vary. In other words, some conditional examples may be more forceful than others. In fact, it will be demonstrated below that these so-called *conditionals* exhibit the same general range of force for the moods as whole. Second, this classification fails to account for the larger structural context within which these all seem to occur.[218] Also, the seemingly distant usage of condition in contrast to the more directive force of other usages

---

[216]Concerning the conditional imperative in ancient Greek in general, see Gerry Wakker, *Conditions and Conditionals: An Investigation of Ancient Greek*. Amsterdam Studies in Classical Philology, ed. Albert Rijksbaron, Irene J. F. de Jong, and Harm Pinkster, vol. 3 (Amsterdam: J. C. Gieben, 1994), 255-56; 263-66. Wakker is discussing directives in general. For possible examples of conditionals in the apodosis in the papyri, see Basil G. Mandilaras, *The Verb in the Greek Non-Literary Papyri* (Athens: Hellenic Ministry of Culture and Sciences, 1973), 306-7. Mandilaras is primarily discussing the difference between the aorist and present here. For a discussion of conditional imperatives in English, see Eirlys E. Davies, "Some Restrictions of Conditional Imperatives," *Linguistics* 17 (1979): 1039-54. This article includes helpful discussion of the meaning and relationship of the related clauses. These three studies are of minimal value for the purposes here because the examples often involve a conditional particle, they are discussing sentence level imperatives, and/or their examples are minimal.

[217]See BDF 195, which seems to include within its category called *concessive* the usages often labeled *permissive, conditional*, and *concessive*; Friedrich Blass and Albert Debrunner, *Grammatik des neutestamentlichen Griechisch*, ed. Friedrich Rehkopf, 17th ed. (Göttingen: Vandenhoeck and Ruprecht, 1976), 313 (is similar to the English translation, BDF, [*Befehl, Bitte, Zugeständnis*]; however, the German edition acknowledges that the imperative may be used [I assume as sub-uses of *Zugeständnis*] as "Konditional oder Konzessivsatz"); Ernest DeWitt Burton, *Syntax of Moods and Tenses in New Testament Greek*, 3d ed. (Edinburgh: T. & T. Clark, 1898), 80-81 (*permission* is grouped with *conditional* and *concessive* and described as the mood which is "used to express consent, or merely propose an hypothesis"). As noted in chapter 2, the concessive usage is not widely accepted and those examples sometimes so considered can be otherwise classified without difficulty.

[218]Some acknowledge the structure. See Wallace, "Ephesians 4:26," 366-71; idem, *Exegetical Syntax*, 489-91; Boyer, "Imperatives," 38.

should make one question the legitimacy of this usage.[219]

It may also be possible to interpret the imperative in the protasis and its following verb (apodosis) as command followed by a promise.[220] This also is unsatisfactory because it fails to emphasize the connection between the two verbal ideas expressed by the imperative and following verb.[221]

Thus, the problems with the traditional approach are twofold. It implies (or in more extreme cases, it demands) the necessity of a choice: command or request or conditional, etc. Second, it fails to take seriously the relationship between verbs in consecutive clauses. Clausal relationships are not ignored. My point is merely that the stress on the label conditional is misplaced. The verb itself should be discussed with morphological level issues. Conditional is a clausal level nuance.

The Solution: Multilevel Analysis

The analysis of the imperative mood has shown that the essence of the imperative mood is volitional and directive. This should be maintained. Nevertheless, the directive force of a specific imperative verb will vary depending on its context. In other words, the pragmatic effects are determined by various factors, linguistic and otherwise, which *affect* the meaning in a given context. This section will look at one further context and the resulting pragmatic meaning of an imperative verb in this context. However, unlike previous discussions, due to the larger context of verb–to–verb relationships, the results

---

[219]This of course does not rule out the possibility of this usage; however, the linguistic system does seem to support consistency in its expression. For example, in phonological analysis, possible allophones for the phoneme /p/ are usually related bilabial phones such as [p], [pʰ], [b], [bʰ], [m], etc. It is not required that these be co-allophones and certainly many of these may be phonemic in certain languages. However, there is a pattern here. It is unlikely that one will consider the velar [g] as a possible allophone of the phoneme /p/. Pragmatic analysis is much more complex than phonological analysis and room must be made for more variety; however, the point is merely to question the possibility here.

[220]Boyer (ibid., 38) offers this as a possibility.

[221]However, Boyer gives a further, more complicated, option which does bring out a closer relationship between the verbal ideas, "it could be understood to imply that the promise is conditioned upon the doing of the thing commanded" (ibid.). However, the stronger label "promise" seems to add unnecessary meaning to the construction. *Promise* seems to demand that someone makes and ultimately assures the fulfillment of the promise; such an individual is not necessarily involved in these utterances.

will be *in addition* to the force of the usages already discussed. Wallace, building on the work of Boyer, provides a starting point. All undisputed conditional imperatives occur in the following structure: *imperative* + καί + *future indicative*.[222] The nature of the future indicative and the imperative when related in this way naturally seem to result in this interpretation. A command related to and followed by a future results in a condition in the former. Since the imperative is a volitional–directive mood which only expresses desire or intention, it fails to communicate whether the action will occur. Therefore, the realization of the future's expressed action is dependent upon the response of the party to which the imperative is directed. The imperative verbs in the statements, "eat and you will grow strong" and "eat and you will get fat" involve an implied condition. The future verbs' fulfillment demands a positive response to the imperative.[223] It should be added that although the imperative and future are closely related, neither is syntactically dependent on one another.

Boyer lists twenty-one examples of imperatives that may be considered conditional.[224] However, only nineteen fit the established structural criteria.[225] There are some differences in the sememic relationship between the protasis and

---

[222]Wallace, "Ephesians 4:26," 366-71; Wallace, *Exegetical Syntax*, 490; Boyer, "Imperatives," 38. Wallace also notes that disputed examples of the conditional usage have an imperative in the apodosis (where the future indicative occurs in undisputed examples). However, in legitimate examples, this second imperative functions like a future indicative. This will be discussed below.

[223]It is helpful to recall the discussion of reality and language here. Actual fulfillment of the verb is irrelevant to the use of language. The eater may or may not actually grow strong or get fat. However, the communicator presents the proposition in this manner.

[224]Matt 7:7 (3x); 27:42; Mark 11:29; Luke10:28; 11:9 (3x); John 7:42; 16:24; Acts 9:6 (2x), 16:31; Gal 6:2; Eph 5:14 (2x); Jas 4:7, 8, 10. Ibid., 39-40. However, he does not rule out the classification of *command* for these examples. In addition, Boyer lists three possible conditionals (John 2:19; 2 Cor 12:16; Eph 4:26). Only one of these will be considered conditional (John 2:19).

[225]John 7:52 fails to fit the conditional pattern of *imperative* + καί + *future*:

ἐραύνησον καὶ ἴδε ὅτι ἐκ τῆς Γαλιλαίας προφήτης οὐκ ἐγείρεται.
search and see that a prophet will not arise from Galilee

The future verb is actually in a dependent clause subordinate to a second imperative (which is often merely a fixed idiom [see chapter 3]). The structure of this sentence is: *imperative* + καί + *imperative*. Some translate the second imperative as the apodosis of the conditional statement: if you search, you will see ..." (see NIV, NRSV). Whether or not a conditional imperative occurs in this structure is controversial. A discussion will occur below. At this time this work is only concerned with the *imperative* + καί + *future* structure. Therefore, John 7:52 will be excluded.

apodosis. This is not identical between all examples;[226] nevertheless, they do share the conditional sense: the imperative verb (condition) must be realized for the action (etc.) of the future verb to occur.[227] Using these nineteen examples as a representative sample,[228] one may observe the structural elements of this construction.[229] These elements are:

1. Imperative + καί (clausal conjunction[230]) + future indicative structure.[231]

2. With the exception of parenthetical clauses,[232] there are no intervening finite verbs between the imperative(s) and the future.[233]

3. Neither verb is in a dependent clause (dependent upon one or the other or upon any verb).[234]

---

[226]A discussion of the various types of relationships between the protasis and apodosis within conditional sentences is beyond the scope of this study. For a detailed description these relationships within negative conditional sentences for ancient Greek (primarily Homeric and classical), see Bertha Theodora Koppers, *Negative Conditional Sentences in Greek and Some Other Indo-European Languages* (The Hague: N. V. Drij. Pier Westerbaan, 1959), 49-105. The various relationships seem also to apply to non-negative sentences. For a comprehensive treatment of conditionals in the New Testament, see Charles Edward Powell, "The Semantic Relationship Between the Protasis and the Apodosis of New Testament Conditional Constructions" (Ph.D. diss., Dallas Theological Seminary, 2000).

[227]This is true whether the conditional is hypothetical or actual.

[228]Matthew 7:7 and Luke 11:9 are identical (three examples in each verse). Therefore, there are sixteen different samples to be examined.

[229]For a remotely similar study of the English imperative, see Davies, "Some Restrictions," 1039-54. Davies determines the existence of two restrictions which demonstrate the independence of conditional imperatives from if–clauses. However, his study is much less focused on structure than the present.

[230]Conjunctions joining words or phrases within a clause are permitted (see Matt 6:33). In this section, καί will always refer to the clausal coordinating conjunction.

[231]More than one imperative can occur but both must be conditional and provide conditions for the same future verb in the apodosis (see Acts 9:6 and Eph 5:14).

[232]In both numbers two and four, parenthetical clauses provide an exception to the rule. This is because such clauses do not carry the argument further; rather, they are functionally inserted within the sentence.

[233]Participles can occur between the verbs (see Eph 5:14).

[234]However, the verbs in the clauses must have some sememic connection permitting a protasis/apodosis relationship. This non-structural element is not included in the requirements because it determines beforehand the meaning and relationship of the clauses (i.e., it is an observation about meaning and not structural). However, it is the contention of this work that when all structural elements are present, the sememic relationship will exist. In fact, the

4. With the exception of a post-positive conjunction in the first position after a clause initial imperative and conjunctions setting off parenthetical clauses, καί is the only clausal conjunction which can occur between the imperative and future verb(s). The conjunction is a required element.

5. Neither of the verbs are already embedded in a conditional clause.

All of the requirements can clearly be seen in the examples supplied by Boyer:

(3) Matt 7:7 ‖ (3) Luke 11:9   **Αἰτεῖτε** <u>καὶ</u> **δοθήσεται** ὑμῖν, **ζητεῖτε** <u>καὶ</u> **εὑρήσετε, κρούετε** <u>καὶ</u> **ἀνοιγήσεται** ὑμῖν
Ask <u>and</u> it will be given to you, **seek** <u>and</u> **you will find, knock** <u>and</u> **it will be opened** to you
(**If you ask** [and do so], it will be given to you, **if you seek** [and do so], you will find, **if you knock** [and do so], it **will be opened** to you)[235]

(2) Matt 11:29   **ἄρατε** τὸν ζυγόν μου ἐφ' ὑμᾶς καὶ **μάθετε** ἀπ' ἐμοῦ, ὅτι πραΰς εἰμι καὶ ταπεινὸς τῇ καρδίᾳ, <u>καὶ</u> **εὑρήσετε** ἀνάπαυσιν ταῖς ψυχαῖς ὑμῶν[236]
Take my yoke upon you and **learn** from me, because I am gentle and humble in heart, <u>and</u> **you will find** rest for your souls (yourselves) (**If you take** my yoke upon you [and do so] and **if you learn** [and do so] from me ...)

---

relationship will be demanded.

[235]The initial translation expresses the directive force of the imperative. The translation in parentheses makes the clausal level conditional nuance explicit ("if") and maintains the directive force in brackets (e.g., "[and do so]")

[236]Note the intervening explanatory ὅτι clause with finite verb. Since this clause is modifying principle elements and not furthering the discourse (thus parenthetical), it does not affect the structural requirements.

Matt 27:42b   καταβάτω νῦν ἀπὸ τοῦ σταυροῦ <u>καὶ</u> **πιστεύσομεν** ἐπ᾽ αὐτόν

let him now come down from the cross <u>and</u> **we will believe** in him (**if he comes down** from the cross [and we challenge him do so],[237] **we will believe** in him)

Mark 11:29   ... **ἀποκρίθητέ** μοι᾽<u>καὶ</u> ἐρῶ ὑμῖν ...

... **answer** me <u>and</u> **I will tell** you ...

(... **if you answer** me [and do so], **I will tell** you ...)

Luke 10:28b   τοῦτο **ποίει** <u>καὶ</u> **ζήσῃ**

do this <u>and</u> **you will live** (... **if you do** this [and do so], you will live)

John 16:24b   **αἰτεῖτε** <u>καὶ</u> **λήμψεσθε**

ask <u>and</u> **you will receive** (**if you ask** [and do so], **you will receive**)

(2) Acts 9:6   ἀλλὰ **ἀνάστηθι** καὶ **εἴσελθε** εἰς τὴν πόλιν <u>καὶ</u> **λαληθήσεταί** σοι ὅ τί σε δεῖ ποιεῖν

but **arise** and **enter** the city <u>and</u> **it will be told** to you what you should do (but **if you arise** [and do so] and **[if you] enter** [and do so] the city, you will be told what you should do)

Acts 16:31   ... **πίστευσον** ἐπὶ τὸν κύριον ᾽Ιησοῦν <u>καὶ</u> **σωθήσῃ** σὺ καὶ ὁ οἶκός σου

... **believe** in the Lord Jesus <u>and</u> **you will be saved**, you and your household (... **if you believe** [and do so] in the Lord Jesus, you will be saved, you and your household)

---

[237]The third person imperative has a weaker force than if this was directed to Jesus in the second person. Nevertheless, it seems to be a challenge to Jesus. However, it may not be limited to this. It could involve discussion between those watching at the cross as well.

Gal 6:2   Ἀλλήλων τὰ βάρη **βαστάζετε** <u>καὶ</u> οὕτως **ἀναπληρώσετε**
τὸν νόμον τοῦ Χριστοῦ
Bear the burdens of one another <u>and</u> in this way **you will meet**
the requirements of the law of Christ (**If you bear** one
another's burdens [and do so], in this you will meet the
requirements of the law of Christ)

(2) Eph 5:14   **ἔγειρε**, ὁ καθεύδων, καὶ **ἀνάστα** ἐκ τῶν νεκρῶν, <u>καὶ</u>
ἐπιφαύσει σοι ὁ Χριστός[238]
Arise, one who sleeps, and **awaken** from the dead <u>and</u> Christ
will shine on you (**If you arise** [and do so], sleeper, and **[if
you] awaken** [and do so] from the dead, Christ will shine on
you)

Jas 4:7b   **ἀντίστητε** δὲ τῷ διαβόλῳ <u>καὶ</u> **φεύξεται** ἀφ' ὑμῶν
but **resist** the devil <u>and</u> **he will run away** from you (but **if you
resist** the devil [and do so], he will run away from you)

Jas 4:8   **ἐγγίσατε** τῷ θεῷ <u>καὶ</u> **ἐγγιεῖ** ὑμῖν
draw near to God <u>and</u> **he will draw near** to you (**if you draw
near** to God [and do so], he will draw near to you)

Jas 4:10   **ταπεινώθητε** ἐνώπιον κυρίου <u>καὶ</u> **ὑψώσει** ὑμᾶς
be humble before the Lord <u>and</u> **he will exalt you** (**if you are
humble** before the Lord [and be so], he will exalt you)

Wallace includes three other passages not cited by Boyer as clear examples.
Each of these also follows the structural pattern described above:

Matt 8:8   ἀλλὰ μόνον **εἰπὲ** λόγῳ, <u>καὶ</u> **ἰαθήσεται** ὁ παῖς μου
But only **say** the word <u>and</u> my servant **will be healed** (but only
if you say the word [and do so], then my servant will be
healed)

---

[238]This passage is significant because it appears to be poetic and it still follows the proposed
structure.

John 1:39   ἔρχεσθε <u>καὶ</u> ὄψεσθε
              come and you will see (**if you come** [and do so], **you will see**)

John 2:19   **λύσατε** τὸν ναὸν τοῦτον <u>καὶ</u> ἐν τρισὶν ἡμέραις **ἐγερῶ**
              αὐτόν
              destroy this temple <u>and</u> in three days **I will raise** it **up** (**if you
              destroy** this temple [and do so], in three days I will raise it
              up)[239]

    Having determined a consistent structural pattern for those passages which are usually considered conditional, this section will pursue this structure further.[240] The analysis thus far proves little concerning the *imperative* + *καί* + *future indicative* construction. Although this work has only examined examples which were already considered conditional, this should be sufficient to serve as a starting point to analyze the construction further and place the burden of proof on any attempt to classify it otherwise. In order to determine with more certainty whether the meaning of this construction in the examples is consistent, all New Testament examples will be examined. It will be determined whether these should also be viewed as conditional sentences.

    In the New Testament there are 63 examples[241] of the *imperative* + *καί* + *future indicative* construction (including Boyer's examples already mentioned) which share all of the requirements listed above.[242] At this stage this work will

---

[239]Boyer ("Imperatives," 39-40) is noncommital on this as an example of a conditional. However, Wallace is correct to note Old Testament prophetic commands and the rhetorical nature of this statement in context. He also points out the value of the classification when he states, "if λύσατε follows the normal semantic pattern of conditional imperatives, the force is even stronger ..." (*Exegetical Syntax*, 490-91). By noting the structure in which this statement is constructed, he is able to consider a probable interpretive option that may be rejected otherwise.

[240]In addition to the structural requirements observed above, one non-structural observation can be made about these conditional statements: the imperative and future must be related in the sense that the former must potentially be able to cause the fulfillment of the later.

[241]Parallel synoptic examples are only counted once (Mark 10:21 (3) || Luke 18:22 (only 2); Mark 11:2 || Matt 21:2; Matt 6:33 || Luke 12:31; Matt 7:5 || Luke 6:42; Matt 7:7||Luke 11:9). Also, imperatives are being counted. Therefore, if more than one imperative occurs with only one future in the apodosis, these each will be counted (e.g., Matt 11:29 [2]; 2 Cor 13:11 [5]).

[242]In order to determine this figure, a broad search was constructed using Gramcord. The search deliberately cast a wide net; it simply looked for an imperative verb followed by a future indicative. Fifteen words and minor stops were permitted to intervene between the imperative and future indicative. The conjunction *καί* was not included as an element of the search in order to make available constructions with no or different conjunctions thus enabling one to observe

discuss some of these examples in light of the preceding analysis in this chapter. This analysis focused on the usage (force) of the imperative mood without reference to the higher level discourse relationships which will now be considered. This will help to demonstrate that the pragmatic *conditional* element is not necessarily related to force nor does its presence mean that the volitional–directive force is lacking.[243] In the majority of the 63 examples the conditional nuance is clearly evident. Admittedly, many are not normally considered conditional. This seems to be because the traditional model of imperative classification implies that one must choose between command, request, condition, etc. Thus, unless the conditional element is strong, it is likely that the interpreter would choose another classification. The approach in this work does not demand that one make a choice.

The stratified view of language provides a theoretical framework to maintain a consistent classification paradigm of volitional-directive usages and in addition account for a context in which an imperative can involve a *conditional* nuance. A choice does not need to be made.[244] This observation and

whether similar constructions permitted the nuance. In other words, this work wishes to determine whether καί is essential. Finite verbs were permitted at this stage in order to avoid overlooking multiple protases with more than one imperative and to confirm the second structural element. This search results in 149 examples in 163 verses. This provided the raw data for the analysis; many examples were rejected since they did not meet the structural requirements.

There are a number of examples which meet some but not all of the requirements. These do not include the conditional nuance. Some of these are worth mentioning to demonstrate the importance of the required elements. Luke 10:35; 13:25; 19:30 all fall short of the requirements and do not seem to contain the conditional nuance. These passages are briefly listed and commented on in appendix 5.

[243]The force of the imperative in these examples will again vary depending on the elements interacting with the verbs as discussed previously in the chapter. If a high-ranking individual such as a parent says to his child, "eat and you will grow strong," the imperative force may be very strong and the translation without "if" above may express this force best. However, if an adult child (lower-rank) says this to his aging parent, the force will be much weaker, "if you eat . . ." or more periphrastically, "you really should try to eat so you will gain strength."

[244]Another advantage to this approach is the avoidance of the appearance in some grammars that a choice needs to be made based on the list of usages (e.g., see the brief comment in Young, *Intermediate*, 145). Although not ideal, it is this work's opinion that it is preferable for an approach aimed at beginning and intermediate students to omit the conditional usage than to contrast it in an either-or manner with volitional usages (compare Young mentioned above with David Alan Black, *It's Still Greek to Me: An Easy-to-Understand Guide to Intermediate Greek* (Grand Rapids: Baker Books, 1998), 100-101). If a student concludes *condition* without reference to volition, his exegesis will be deficient. However, if the student classifies an imperative without the optional *conditional* usage, the volitional force will be maintained and in most cases, the *conditional* nuance will become obvious (although not necessarily consciously for the beginner)

the unique structure suggest that the conditional element is not an innate element of the imperative mood itself.[245]

All of the sixty-three passages (plus parallels) are listed and discussed where necessary in appendix 5. Only a few passages will be noted here to add to those passages already discussed above. Passages with specific illustrative potential will be chosen. These passages demonstrate both a conditional nuance and a range of force. Thus, there should not be a forced choice between conditional and any other traditional label.

Matt 6:33   ζητεῖτε δὲ πρῶτον τὴν βασιλείαν [τοῦ θεοῦ] καὶ τὴν δικαιοσύνην αὐτοῦ, καὶ ταῦτα πάντα προστεθήσεται ὑμῖν
But **seek** first the kingdom [of God] and his righteousness, and all this **will be given** to you (But **if you seek** first [and do so] the kingdom [of God] and his righteousness ...)

Matt 7:5   ὑποκριτά, ἔκβαλε πρῶτον ἐκ τοῦ ὀφθαλμοῦ σοῦ τὴν δοκόν, καὶ τότε διαβλέψεις ἐκβαλεῖν τὸ κάρφος ἐκ τοῦ ὀφθαλμοῦ τοῦ ἀδελφοῦ σου
Hypocrite, **take out** first the beam of wood from your eye, and then **you will see clearly** to take out the splinter out of the eye of your brother (Hypocrite, **if you take out** first [and do so] the beam of wood from your eye ...)

---

as the entire sentence is analyzed (e.g., "ask and it will be given to you" cannot escape some conditional nuance). As mentioned above, some astute grammarians explicitly state that the *conditional* nuance does not rule out the volitional force of the imperative (e.g., Wallace, *Exegetical Syntax*, 490; Porter, *Verbal Aspect*, 353; idem, *Idioms of the Greek New Testament*, 2d ed., Biblical Languages: Greek, vol. 2 [Sheffield: JSOT Press, 1994], 226).

[245]The analysis here is somewhat supported (but in no way contradicted) by the work of Billy Clark ("Relevance and 'Pseudo-Imperatives,'" *Linguistics and Philosophy* 16 [1993]: 79-121). Although discussing English, not making a sharp stratificational distinctions about language, nor focusing on the structural imperative (his work is looking at imperative statements in contrast to declarative, etc.), Clark attempts to account for "pseudo-imperatives" (primarily conditional statements which look like imperatives) within an RT framework. Most so-called conditional imperatives are not derived from conditional statements but are true imperatives. In a few cases which appear to be conditional (e.g., "Catch the flu and you can be ill for weeks"), Clark concludes that such statements are neither imperative nor conditional but a third class sharing characteristics of both.

Acts 28:28   γνωστὸν οὖν **ἔστω** ὑμῖν ὅτι τοῖς ἔθνεσιν ἀπεστάλη
τοῦτο τὸ σωτήριον τοῦ θεοῦ· αὐτοὶ <u>καὶ</u> **ἀκούσονται**
Therefore, **let it be known** to you that this salvation of God
was [has been] sent to the nations <u>and</u> **they will listen** (… **if it
be known** [and it should] …)
Here again we have a third person (see Matt 27:42 and Acts
28:28). Although the conditional nuance seems weak, there is
no reason to reject it here[246]

Rom 13:3b   … τὸ ἀγαθὸν **ποίει**, <u>καὶ</u> **ἕξεις** ἔπαινον ἐξ αὐτῆς
… **do good** <u>and</u> **you will have** approval from it [the authority]
(**if you do good** [and do so] …)

(3) 2 Cor 6:17   διὸ **ἐξέλθατε** ἐκ μέσου αὐτῶν καὶ **ἀφορίσθητε**, λέγει
κύριος, καὶ ἀκαθάρτου μὴ **ἅπτεσθε**· <u>κἀγὼ</u> **εἰσδέξομαι**
ὑμᾶς[247]
"Therefore, **come out** from their midst and **be separate**," says
the Lord, "and **do not touch** an unclean thing, <u>and</u> **I will
welcome you**"
(… **if you come out** from their midst [and do so] and **be
separate** [if you are separate–and do so]" says the Lord, "and
if you do not touch an unclean thing [and do not do so] …)

---

[246]This passage is the most questionable of all of the examples. However, because the other
fifty-nine examples do seem to have a conditional nuance it will be so considered here. The
burden of proof is upon those who wish to deny the nuance. Although the data is minimal the
third person does not seem to effect the nuance. The third person imperative in Acts 2:38 is
somewhat debatable but if it is not conditional, it may be explained as parenthetical. However,
Matt 27:42 clearly has the nuance. Acts 28:28 is closer to Matt 27:42 than it is to Acts 2:38.

[247]There are three imperatives in this verse. The intervening finite verb does not further the
argument so there is no violation of the requirements (thus parenthetical); however, the second
imperative is passive and it is difficult to determine whether this should be conditional.
Nevertheless, it may be better to leave it translated without the conditional clause because the
conditional nuance is still evident from the first imperative.

Rev 2:10   … γίνου πιστὸς ἄχρι θανάτου, <u>καὶ</u> **δώσω** σοι τὸν
στέφανον τῆς ζωῆς[248]
"… **be faithful** until death <u>and</u> **I will give** to you the crown of
life" ("**if you are faithful** until death [and do so] …")

The value of this work's approach is evident when looking at verses such
as Matt 6:33: ζητεῖτε δὲ πρῶτον τὴν βασιλείαν[249] καὶ τὴν δικαιοσύνην
αὐτοῦ, καὶ ταῦτα πάντα προστεθήσεται ὑμῖν (but seek first [if you seek
first, and do so] his kingdom and his righteousness, all these things will be
given to you). This passage is not normally considered conditional;[250] its
command nuance (strong force) is obvious. However, there is a clear "if-then"
relationship evident. The simple translation "seek first" does not make this
explicit. "All things" will not be given to the one who does not "seek first the
kingdom." The approach does not demand a choice between the nuances. This
strong force imperative is also part of a conditional clause. However, it is not
the same type of conditional found in the usual non-imperative constructions.
There is a strong volitional-directive nuance which implies the desire of the
speaker for the hearer to act on the instruction. The same observations may be
made about Matt 7:5; Rom 13:3b; 2 Cor 6:17; Rev 2:10.

Acts 28:28 provides further evidence to support the approach of this work.
This passage includes a third person imperative. The force of the imperative is
thus weak.[251] It is further weakened by an indirect subject. Although one may
view the conditional nuance as weak, it cannot be ignored. In order for the
nations to listen, the salvation of God must be made known to them.[252]

Therefore, it is possible to have various levels of force with conditional
constructions. Some are command-like and other weaker. This work suggests
that a preferable means of classifying these imperatives is first at the
morphological level as with all other imperatives (force, benefit, event-

[248]Note the present middle-passive imperative.
[249]The phrase τοῦ θεοῦ which is in brackets in NA[27] is omitted here based on strong external
evidence (including ℵ and B [although the order of surrounding words differ in these
manuscripts]) and the unlikelihood that a scribe would omit these words. The shorter reading is
preferred.
[250]See for example Gundry, *Matthew*, 118.
[251]See also Matt 8:8 cited above. This passage uses an honor term to weaken the imperative.
[252]Whether this passage is a promise or a general statement is beyond the scope of this study.
This needs to be discussed in the context of the semantics of conditional statements.

sequence) and then at the sentence level (conditional, etc.).

Thus far only the *imperative* + *καί* + *future* construction has been discussed. The conditional nuance seems likely in this structure. However, there are a number of passages that some consider conditional which include an imperative (e.g., John 1:46; 7:52) or a subjunctive (e.g., Luke 6:37), not a future indicative in the second clause. Concerning the imperative in the second clause, Wallace demonstrates that although there are 187 such constructions, there are only four probable and 17 potentially conditional imperatives among them. The former seem to function like a future indicative and the latter retain their injunctive force.[253] One example is worth pursuing for illustrative purposes:

John 1:46   λέγει αὐτῷ [ὁ] Φίλιππος· ἔρχου καὶ ἴδε
                 Philip said to him, "**Come** and **see**" (if you come, you will see)

This passage would normally not be considered in our study because the second imperative (ἴδε) is a common idiom. However, as noted in chapter three, some occurrences of this form may be legitimate imperatives. This is probably one of those examples. This discussion gives us an opportunity to look at this verse without considering it in our larger analysis (from which the major analysis of this chapter is drawn). In any case it serves as a good example here. If the first imperative has a conditional nuance, the second imperative functions as a future indicative.

This work is tempted to argue that none of these cases should be considered conditional. The imperatives interpreted without the conditional element seem to be understandable. However, conditional nuance in these cases will not be ruled out. Nevertheless, it is clear that the structure itself does not demand this interpretation. This then is left to more detailed clausal analysis. Therefore, only one passage will be looked at in detail in concluding this section.

Ephesians 4:26 and Our Study

There is one passage which demands some attention before leaving the

---

[253]"Ephesians 4:26," 367-71; idem, *Exegetical Syntax*, 489-92. See Wallace's detailed discussions in these works where he interacts with Boyer, Robertson and others.

study of conditional imperatives. Ephesians 4:26 has three imperatives. It is primarily the first two which are of interest.

Eph 4:26   ὀργίζεσθε καὶ μὴ ἁμαρτάνετε· ὁ ἥλιος μὴ ἐπιδυέτω ἐπὶ [τῷ] παροργισμῷ ὑμῶν
             be angry and **do not sin**; **do not let** the sun **set** on your anger

Because there is an obvious discomfort with the command to the readers to be angry, it is quite common for many to suggest that the first imperative is conditional or concessive, "if/although you are angry, then do not sin."[254] However, this method is problematic at the onset. The conditional or concessive label is an attempt to explain this imperative in this context when the most natural reading (for lack of a better description) seems to cause tension.

Wallace challenges this common interpretation.[255] Among his arguments

---

[254]See BDF, 195 (concessive; although this category includes conditional; translation reflects concessive); Boyer, "Imperatives," 39 (an option); A. T. Robertson, *A Grammar of the Greek New Testament in the Light of Historical Research*, 4th ed. (Nashville: Broadman Press, 1934), 949 (concessive); Porter, *Verbal Aspect*, 352-53 (the conditional element is a pragmatic effect). Commentators include: Markus Barth, *Ephesians: Translation and Commentary on Chapters 4–6*, Anchor Bible, ed. William Foxwell Albright and David Noel Freedman, vol. 34A (Garden City, NY: Doubleday, 1974), 513 (concessive); Ernest Best, *A Critical and Exegetical Commentary on Ephesians*, International Critical Commentary, ed. J. A. Emerton, C. E. B. Cranfield, and G. N. Stanton (Edinburgh: T. & T. Clark, 1998), 449; Andrew Lincoln, *Ephesians*, Word Biblical Commentary, ed. David A. Hubbard et al., vol. 42 (Dallas: Word, 1990), 292, 301 (concessive but "if" in the translation); Margaret Y. MacDonald, *Colossians and Ephesians*, Sacra Pagina 17 (Collegeville, MN: Liturgical Press, 2000; reprint with updated bibliography, 2008), 306 (conditional translation called "Semitic idiom"); Rudolf Schnackenburg, *Ephesians: A Commentary*, trans. Helen Heron (Edinburgh: T. & T. Clark, 1991): 207 ("semitic feel for the language" translation: "if you work yourself up into a rage, do not sin! Or better: do not sin by getting worked up in anger!"; the two translations here demonstrate that Schnackenburg, although noting the conditional nuance, understands the directive force); Ben Witherington III, *The Letters to Philemon, the Colossians, and the Ephesians: A Socio-Rhetorical Commentary on the Captivity Epistles* (Grand Rapids: William B. Eerdmans Publishing Company, 2007), 299 (concessive but "if" in the translation in the discussion). Also Charles Powell suggests that "Eph 4:26 could be seen as implying an unusual case concessive conditional. The sense would then be 'Even in the case that you are righteously angry, and should be, do not sin'" ("Conditional Constructions," 86-95, 135-41. Powell agrees with Wallace in a footnote that the imperative retains its injunctive force. Powell's solution is merely a suggestion. In his work he does not really cover implied conditionals, and he gives no parallel examples where this construction may be so interpreted.

[255]See especially Wallace, "Ephesians 4:26," 353-72. Also helpful is Wallace, *Exegetical Syntax*, 491-92.

favoring a command nuance here, Wallace suggests that undisputed conditionals occur only in the *imperative* + *καί* + *future indicative* construction. In addition, in any possible conditionals with either an imperative or subjunctive[256] in the apodosis, the verb functions like a future indicative. These are the arguments discussed above when these structures were considered. If the patterns observed by Wallace are to be applied here as they are in the rest of the New Testament, the conditional is unlikely. In addition to the unlikely structural argument, if conditional (as likely conditionals), the passage would have the meaning: "if you are angry (and I want you to be), then you will not sin."[257] This meaning is not what the verse intends. A straightforward *command* usage seems most probable.[258]

The purpose here is not to give a full blown exegesis of this passage. This work is only attempting to determine whether Wallace's (and this work's) analysis is superior to the conditional option.[259] Ernest Best considers Wallace's arguments in his commentary. He suggests that Eph 4:31 contradicts the command nuance and argues that Wallace's attempt to place this passage in a context of church discipline[260] should be rejected because it is without support.[261]

I commend Best for dealing with Wallace and his criticism about context may have some merit. However, Wallace is merely attempting to *explain* a possible context in which the command would make sense. This approach seems less objectionable than to ignore the consistent structural patterns for the conditional and suggest the nuance in other structures as a means to *explain* a difficult passage. Wallace's explanation is on more solid ground.

---

[256]The subjunctive is mentioned only in *Exegetical Syntax*, 489.

[257] Ibid., 491.

[258]See also, Harold W. Hoehner, Ephesians: A Exegetical Commentary. Grand Rapids: Baker Book House, 2002), 619-21 and Peter T. O'Brien, *The Letter to the Ephesians*, Pillar New Testament Commentary, ed. D. A. Carson (Grand Rapids: William B. Eerdmans Publishing Company, 1999], 337-38). Also, the command nuance seems to be assumed by Charles H. Talbert (*Ephesians and Colossians*. Paideia Commentaries on the New Testament [Grand Rapids: Baker Book House, 2007], 124).

[259]The approach here would permit both a command nuance at the morphological level and a conditional nuance at the sentence level (this is Porter's position where he describes the conditional nuance as pragmatic; Porter, *Verbal Aspect*, 353). However, unlike the *imperative* + *καί* + *future indicative* construction, the nuance is not demanded by the structure expressed in this verse.

[260]Thus, in such cases, the directive to *be angry* is justified.

[261]Best, *Ephesians*, 449.

Having defended Wallace's (and this work's) position on this passage, a few other observations are in order. Best never deals with Wallace's structural evidence. He states only, "The grammatical correctness of such a translation [conditional] has often been disputed."[262] Then instead of discussing this claim (or even stating the reasons for the charge), Best continues by explaining why such an interpretation is undesirable on contextual grounds alone. Such arguments should not be minimized, but the structural claims are strong and cannot be ignored. One would think that the weight of these claims should demand that the burden of proof be placed on the one attempting to find a rare meaning for this construction.[263] Second, Wallace does not rely on structure alone. Only about one-fourth of the article is devoted to structure (pages 366-71). Wallace is not arguing that one should blindly follow descriptive structural observations. Rather, he is pointing out what is probable on structural grounds and supporting this with contextual arguments.[264] It seems fair that those with other suggestions must demonstrate with detailed arguments why they depart from what seems to be the standard interpretation of a specific structure.

Summary

An analysis of the *imperative* + *καί* + *future indicative* construction has yielded two important results. First, one can be confident that imperatives in this construction include a conditional meaning at a clausal level in addition to the imperative force the verb brings to the sentence (also the factors of benefit and event-initiation). Second, since the imperative remains an imperative in essence, one can be confident that these conditional sentences are not identical to more traditional conditional sentences.[265] The imperative expresses the desire of the speaker/writer to fulfill the condition. To label these imperatives *conditional* in contrast to *command*, etc., the interpreter may miss the directive force of the

---

[262]Ibid.

[263]In arguing for a conditional here, one should also address the reason why the author did not use the normal conditional sentence (with particle).

[264]See the article for the contextual arguments.

[265]Sentences usually labeled first class conditionals, second class conditionals, third class conditionals, and fourth class conditionals.

imperative.[266] These are imperatives within a conditional construction. Both morphological and sentence level aspects of meaning must be considered.

This work has also explored briefly other constructions but found they did not assure a conditional element. A conditional nuance in all of these cases will be considered; however, interpretation must not eclipse the issues directly related to the morphology of the mood.

The Imperative and the People of God: Some Concluding Thoughts

This section could also be titled, "Stating the Obvious." This work has looked in some detail at communicative and linguistic theory. Among the many imperatives in the database, this work has focused on those which do not follow the normal pattern of higher to lower-ranked, strong-forced, event-initiating imperatives. This has been a methodological necessity since it is only through looking at these passages that one can understand the semantics and pragmatics of the mood. One needs to ask why the imperative is used in these different contexts.

In light of the emphasis of this work, it may be helpful to review some of the findings. The vast majority of imperatives are stated by higher to lower-ranking parties, are event-initiating in event time, and are strong in force. I know that this sounds redundant, but the implications of these facts are clear for the intended audiences of the New Testament. The one who states the imperative, whether a character in narrative or the author of a letter, willfully desires his imperative to be fulfilled. The choice of the imperative makes this observation certain.

This observation in itself is not profound or even important. However, given the absolute-rank of the one who utters the imperative, whether it be an apostle or other significant foundational figure, to their intended followers, it must be binding. Those (of us) who maintain divine authorship as unifying the holy Scripture, this challenge has even greater authority. It is essential that one

---

[266]Again, the astute analysis of Wallace notes that undisputed conditional imperatives maintain their "injunctive force" (Wallace, *Exegetical Syntax*, 490). What is being proposed here is not new; however, this work is attempting to refine and more precisely classify the linguistic elements involved.

understand the Scripture within its cultural context and attempt to understand its message on its own terms. However, those with a conviction of Scripture's divine importance must also attempt to understand its message to the church today. This cannot always be clearly established. Intensive exegetical study including familiarity with the language and culture of the recipients must be undertaken to discern how it is to be understood. But the fact remains, once exegetical work has established a probable meaning and account is taken for cultural peculiarities, the imperative is to be obeyed.[267]

In addition, the observation that imperatives are overwhelmingly used in higher to lower communication situations has a further interesting implication. The fact that they are common in prayer is not an unimportant observation. It is true that politeness strategies are common (especially the third person and the use of honor terms); nevertheless, their impressive presence should encourage the Christian. There is a certain boldness involved in a communication situation using the imperative. This echos the imperative's relatively common use in the Psalms where the authors approach God in ways that may make the modern reader uncomfortable. Nevertheless, it should cause us to approach our Lord with renewed excitement, boldness, and reverence. Thus, let us reflect upon the words of Heb 10:19-22a[268] in light of this study,

Ἔχοντες οὖν, ἀδελφοί,
παρρησίαν εἰς τὴν εἴσοδον τῶν ἁγίων ἐν τῷ αἵματι Ἰησοῦ,
ἣν ἐνεκαίνισεν ἡμῖν ὁδὸν πρόσφατον καὶ ζῶσαν
διὰ τοῦ καταπετάσματος, τοῦτ᾽ ἔστιν τῆς σαρκὸς αὐτοῦ,
καὶ ἱερέα μέγαν ἐπὶ τὸν οἶκον τοῦ θεοῦ,
προσερχώμεθα μετὰ ἀληθινῆς καρδίας ἐν πληροφορίᾳ πίστεως.

---

[267]The description of the exegetical and applicational method is necessarily simplified here. This work does not want to present this process as too simple which may result in distortions due to a failure of taking into account differences of time and culture. Nor does it wish to use cultural information to minimize the imperatives. This work also does not wish to present the process as too difficult and thus effectively make the Bible untouchable by the average believer. Understanding and applying Scripture is one of the most important tasks of the Christian. It must be undertaken with skill, wisdom, creativity, and dependence upon the Lord.

[268]This passage should be read through v. 25; however, the main point is made in v. 22.

Summary

This chapter has explored the imperative in context. It has been suggested that the traditional labels given to the imperative mood such as *command*, *request*, etc. are too limiting to explain the usage of the mood. Instead a three-pronged approach to the mood has been developed. Each occurrence of the mood may be classified by force, event-sequence, and benefit. These factors provide a more complete and satisfactory account of the mood. The new multidimensional paradigm did not consider negation a further factor for consideration. Rather, it was maintained that the three areas could be either positive or negative.

The first area of classification is force. It was demonstrated that force is an essential characteristic of the imperative mood. The use of the imperative itself is in some ways a bold communication strategy. The mood is considered strong-forced unless some type of contextual feature suggests otherwise. These features are generally politeness strategies that serve to make the directive somewhat indirect (e.g., the third person, words of asking) or they serve to acknowledge or pay respect the addressee (e.g., honor terms). It was maintained that social rank itself was not a factor in determining force but rather one's social rank may affect what type of politeness strategy may be used (or whether to use the imperative at all).

Second, related to force but also involving higher level factors is event-sequence. It was suggested that if an imperative did not initiate an action, it was responsive or reactive and thus weak in force.

Third, it was also maintained that it is helpful to consider who benefits from the fulfillment of the imperative. Speaker-benefit imperatives often were *orders* or other types of directives which benefit the speaker's purposes. Hearer-benefit imperatives included *instruction-* and *warning*-type communication which are ultimately meant to help the hearer.

In addition, the third person imperative and the conditional imperative have been explored. Usages and addressees for the third person imperative have been noted. This work has also demonstrated that the conditional nuance is not related to morphology but is something impacted by sentence level relationships.

Chapter 5

Conclusion

This study has attempted to meet a perceived need in the study of the Greek of the New Testament. It has been argued that there has been little attention paid to the imperative mood in a comprehensive manner. There have been valuable studies about specific aspects of the mood, most noticeably the use of the tenses. However, little has changed concerning the mood in over a hundred years (and probably longer). This is not necessarily negative. However, in light of the many advances in both method and access (e.g., computer searches, etc.) the *status quo* needed to be challenged. It was suggested that the traditional approach was found lacking because it did not (usually) provide a clear comprehensive definition of the imperative and its simplistic approach demanded an artificial choice between different types of usages.

A definition was proposed and a new system of classification for the imperative mood was presented. In order to accomplish this task, foundational matters about language and communication were discussed in detail. The linguistic theory called *neuro-cognitive stratificational linguistics* was utilized to help isolate the imperative mood from other aspects of the *linguistic system*. Postulating a relational stratified *linguistic system* permitted this work to focus on relevant issues relating to the mood itself. A communication theory called *relevance theory* was used to describe the communication process. Communication is more complex than the common code model can explain. Most importantly the notion that communication primarily involves inference and interpretation was suggested and defended. *Language expression* provides important input to be interpreted. However, the direct linguistic evidence is insufficient to provide an account for the meaning of the mood in various contexts. Other contextual features (both linguistic and non-linguistic) were also considered. These features included sociological factors such as the social rank of the parties in the communication situation and politeness. In addition, the use of *neuro-cognitive stratificational linguistics* and *relevance theory* provided a cognitive emphasis which served as a restraint on this work's conclusions.

After a survey of New Testament and select linguistic approaches to the imperative mood, this work suggested that the inherent, semantic meaning of the imperative mood was *volitional-directive*. Building on this meaning, it was suggested that the uses of the mood should be classified in a multidimensional manner. Each imperative should be classified according to *force*, which participant (speaker or hearer) *benefits* from the fulfillment of the imperative, and where the imperative falls within the *event sequence* of the utterance. Negation is an additional feature. An imperative is either positive or negative based on whether or not it is preceded by the negative particle μή. Finally, the third person imperative and the so-called *conditional* usage were discussed in some detail. The third person often serves to weaken the force of the imperative when directed at a second person and the *conditional* nuance is actually a sentence level phenomenon and thus is *in addition* to the morphological analysis of the mood.

This study has necessarily (with few exceptions) been focused on the morphological imperative mood. It seems that the method described here may be utilized with success for other aspects of Greek grammar, especially those with a multitude of usages in the traditional approach (e.g., genitive case, etc.). In addition, this study should serve as a basis for further study of the imperative mood and mood in general. The focus on the morphological level of the *language system* has provided data for studies wishing to focus on higher level verbal and discourse analysis. Only after thorough work on the morphological level of the Greek language has been undertaken can higher and more abstract analysis proceed with any authority.

Appendices

Appendix 1

Modern Linguistics:
Select History,
Use in New Testament Studies and in this Work,
Evaluation, and Proposals for Future Use

This brief appendix will discuss modern linguistics and its impact on and use in biblical studies. In addition, an evaluation of its use will be discussed. Concerns will be explained and suggestions for future work will be outlined. In addition, the history of the two theories used in this study will be more fully developed.

Brief History of Modern Linguistics

A comprehensive historical sketch of modern linguistics is far too complex for a work of this nature. However, because this work rests on a linguistic foundation, some discussion may be helpful to place this work and its linguistic influences within the diverse field of linguistics. It is generally considered that *modern linguistics* began with the posthumous publication of the class notes of Ferdinand de Saussure, *Cours de linguistique générale*.[1] Prior to Saussure, linguistics was primarily concerned with diachronic and historical matters (philology). Saussure contrasted the diachronic approach with his synchronic approach. Saussure states, "Depuis que linguistique moderne existe, on peut dire qu'elle s'est absorbée tout entière dans la diachronie. La grammaire comparée de l'indo-européen utilise les données qu'elle a en mains pour

---

[1]Ferdinand de Saussure, *Cours de linguistique générale*, ed. Charles Bally, Albert Sechehaye, and Albert Reidlinger (Lausanne: Librairie Payot and Cie, 1916); 3d ed., 1949; English translation: *Course in General Linguistics*, ed. Charles Bally, Albert Sechehaye, and Albert Reidlinger, trans. Wade Baskin (New York: McGraw-Hill Book Company, 1959). All citations in the appendix will be from the third French edition.

reconstruire hypothétiquement un type de langue antécédent."[2]

Influenced by Saussure, early in the twentieth century, American linguists focused on structural and descriptive approaches to language. In 1933, Leonard Bloomfield published his influential book entitled, *Language*.[3] This book and its descriptive and structural approach to language greatly influenced the course of American linguistics for more than twenty years. Bloomfield's views, although developed quite extensively by others, still maintain influence in some corners of the field. Bloomfield's *Language* may have been the most influential linguistic book in American linguistics until Noam Chomsky's revolutionary monograph, *Syntactic Structures*.[4] In this slim volume, Chomsky introduced concepts which departed from traditional descriptive approaches popular at the time. He approached syntax with a rule-based system which included both transformational and non-transformational rules from which utterances could be generated. Chomsky further refined and developed his generative-transformational approach with the publication of *Aspects of the Theory of Syntax* in 1965.[5] However, following the release of *Aspects*, various developments led to a number of different developing theories each with its own ontology and method. One such branch came from Chomsky himself which after considerable development was finally called "Government and Binding."[6] Despite major differences, all Chomskyan linguistic theories include a generative aspect which involve rules which can produce new utterances.[7] Edmondson and Burquest state that "the basics of [these Chomskyan developments] are nearly the same as for the *Aspects* model ..."[8] Chomsky himself states, "a generative grammar must be a system of rules that can iterate

---

[2]Ibid., *Cours*, 118. See also John Lyons, *Introduction to Theoretical Linguistics* (Cambridge: Cambridge University Press, 1968), 45-46. For a brief discussion of nineteenth century linguistics, see Geoffrey Sampson, *Schools of Linguistics* (Stanford, CA: Stanford University Press, 1980). For Saussure's contrast of synchrony with diachrony, see *Cours*, 124-29.

[3]Leonard Bloomfield, *Language* (New York: Holt, Rinehart and Winston, 1933; reprint, Chicago: University of Chicago Press, 1984).

[4]Noam Chomsky, *Syntactic Structures* (The Hague: Mouton, 1957).

[5]Noam Chomsky, *Aspects of the Theory of Syntax* (Cambridge, MA: MIT Press, 1965).

[6]See Noam Chomsky, *Lectures on Government and Binding* (Dordrecht, Holland: Foris Publications, 1981).

[7]For a discussion of various post-*Aspects* models see Jerold A. Edmondson and Donald A. Burquest, *A Survey of Linguistic Theories* (Dallas: Summer Institute of Linguistics, 1992), 119-46.

[8]Ibid., 120.

to generate an indefinitely large number of structures."[9] This generative approach is in contrast to the descriptive which is primarily concerned with describing language as it has occurred.

Although after the "Chomskyan revolution," the American linguistic landscape became primarily generative, a number of theories developed without significant input from Chomsky's ideas. The tagmemic models developed by Kenneth Pike and Robert Longacre maintained a descriptive emphasis and thus remained within the descriptivist tradition of Bloomfield.[10] Also, Sydney Lamb's stratificational model emphasized the relational nature of language with a descriptive method.[11] Although the dates of the works cited above may suggest that tagmemics and stratificational grammar reacted and/or rejected Chomsky's ideas, this assumption would be incorrect. Both theories were already being developed by the 1950's.[12] Nevertheless, these theories have remained relatively uninfluenced by Chomsky.[13]

In England (and in some of its commonwealth countries), linguistics has taken a somewhat different path. The influences of Bloomfield and Chomsky were/are not as strong as in the United States.[14] One important development is the functional theory developed by M. A. K. Halliday called systemics.[15] Halliday is in the tradition of the London School which included the influential linguist, J. R. Firth (1890-1960). Halliday's approach is less concerned with description and focuses on how language is used. Thus it is labeled *functional*.[16] Halliday's theory of linguistics is much closer to that of Lamb and Pike than to Chomsky. In fact there are strong similarities between theories such as tagmemics, stratificational linguistics, and systemics (and other structural,

---

[9]*Aspects*, 15-16

[10]Sampson, *Schools*, 79-80. See for example Kenneth L. Pike, *Language in Relation to a Unified Theory of the Structure of Human Behavior*, 2d rev. ed. (The Hague: Mouton and Co., 1967); idem, *Linguistic Concepts: An Introduction to Tagmemics* (Lincoln, NE: University of Nebraska Press, 1982); and Robert E. Longacre, *Grammar Discovery Procedures: A Field Manual* (The Hague: Mouton, 1964).

[11]*Outline of Stratificational Grammar* (Washington DC: Georgetown University Press, 1966).

[12]Edmondson and Burquest, *Survey*, 119.

[13]Chomsky could not be ignored; thus, in some sense these theories had to reject Chomsky's work as they chose to continue upon the path they began before Chomsky's *Syntactic Structures*.

[14]For an explanation of and some reasons for this, see Sampson, *Schools*, 212-35.

[15]*An Introduction to Functional Grammar*, 2d ed. (London: Edward Arnold, 1994).

[16]Ibid., xiii.

descriptive, and/or functional approaches). Christopher Butler acknowledges influence of Pike and Lamb (and others) on Halliday's systemics.[17] Also, there has been consistent interaction between these schools at conferences such as the annual Linguistic Association of Canada and the United States (LACUS).[18]

The brief survey here has been somewhat lopsided. It has generally focused on American linguistics with an emphasis on descriptive approaches. Systemics has been discussed because it shares much with these schools. The reason for this emphasis is twofold. First, and rather practically, this is my linguistic influence. Second, with some exceptions, these schools have had the most impact upon biblical studies.[19] It would be misleading to suggest that American descriptive schools have a large following even within America. Although many translation missionary groups (e.g., Wycliffe Bible Translators) would fall within this category (and thus include many linguists), the vast majority of scholarly linguistic work in the USA is primarily Chomskyan.

Having discussed various schools, a brief mention of emphasis can be stated. In general, until recently, modern linguistics has focused upon sentence level and below (clause, phrase, word, phonology, etc.).[20] In the 1990s, discourse analysis which analyzes larger chunks of texts became important. This became (and remains) an important topic in biblical studies.[21] In addition, although not ignored previously, the question of *meaning* (e.g., semantics and pragmatics) has become more central in the work of many linguists.

---

[17]*Systemic Linguistics: Theory and Applications* (London: Batsford Academic and Educational, 1985), 4.

[18]For further discussion of the developments within the different schools of linguistics mentioned above with the exception of systemics, see Edmondson and Burquest, *Survey*. For a discussion of the history and basic linguistic assumptions of systemics, see Butler, *Systemic Linguistics*, 1-13 and more broadly, concerning the London School, see Sampson, *School*, 212-35.

[19]For the above brief description of modern linguistics to be more thorough, a more extensive discussion of Chomskyan linguistics would need to be presented. Additionally, many philosophical, psychological, and specialized linguistic interests would need to be included. Philosophers have been asking linguistic questions for centuries; however, it seems best to exclude primarily philosophical approaches since they often are less concerned with language (and the pure data demanded by linguistic analysis) and interested in asking grander questions about *being, life, knowledge*, etc. Nevertheless, some philosophical ideas have been discussed in this book (e.g., speech act theory).

[20]As typified by the title of Chomsky's revolutionary book, *Syntactic Structures*.

[21]See the discussion in the following section.

Linguistics and Biblical Studies

The use of linguistics as a tool for biblical studies is not new. As early as 1960, H. A. Gleason Jr., in his inaugural address as professor of linguistics at Hartford Seminary stated: "Certainly for anyone who is to concentrate on Biblical studies, instruction in linguistics would seem today to be essential. I would venture to suggest that for all seminary students it could be most helpful."[22] Also, although not specifically linguistic studies in a formal sense (i.e., they are not by scholars in the field of linguistics), there have been influential works written by prominent biblical scholars such as James Barr and G. B. Caird utilized linguistic insights in their works.[23] Also, there have been a number of other works in biblical studies written from a linguistic perspective. These works are written by both New Testament scholars and linguists. First, there are general studies which suggest that linguistics can be a helpful tool for biblical studies and/or apply a specific linguistic theory to New Testament interpretation.[24] Other studies have attempted to apply linguistic methodology

---

[22]"Linguistics in the Service of the Church," *Hartford Quarterly* 1 (1960): 16-17.

[23]James Barr, *Semantics of Biblical Language* (Oxford: Oxford University Press, 1961); G. B. Caird, *The Language and Imagery of the Bible* (Philadelphia: Westminster Press, 1980).

[24]These works include: David Alan Black, *Linguistics for Students of New Testament Greek: A Survey of Basic Concepts and Applications*, 2d ed. (Grand Rapids: Baker Book House, 1995); S. Brown, "Biblical Philology, Linguistics and the Problem of Method," *Heythrop Journal* 20 (1979): 295-98; P. Cotterell and M. Turner, *Linguistics and Biblical Interpretation* (Downers Grove, IL: InterVarsity Press, 1989); Richard J. Erickson, "Linguistics and Biblical Language: A Wide-Open Field," *Journal of the Evangelical Theological Society* 26 (1983): 257-63; H. A. Gleason Jr., "Some Contributions of Linguistics to Biblical Studies," *Hartford Quarterly* 4 (1963): 47-56; Johannes P. Louw, "Linguistics and Hermeneutics," *Neotestamentica* 4 (1970): 8-18; Harold Leroy Metts, "Greek Sentence Structure: A Traditional, Descriptive Generative Study" (Th.D. diss., Southwestern Baptist Theological Seminary, 1977); Theodore H. Mueller, *New Testament Greek: A Case Grammar Approach* (Fort Wayne, IN: Concordia Theological Seminary Press, 1978); Idem, "Observations on Some New Testament Texts Based on Generative-Transformational Grammar," *The Bible Translator* 29 (1978): 117-20; Eugene A. Nida, "Implications of Contemporary Linguistics for Biblical Scholarship," *Journal of Biblical Literature* 91 (1972): 73-89; Stanley E. Porter, "Studying Ancient Languages from a Modern Linguistic Perspective: Essential Terms and Terminology," *Filología Neotestamentaria* 2 (1989): 147-72; Vern S. Poythress, "Analyzing a Biblical Text: Some Important Linguistic Distinctions," *Scottish Journal of Theology* 32 (1979): 113-37; D. D. Schmidt, "The Study of Hellenistic Greek Grammar in Light of Contemporary Linguistics," *Perspectives in Religious Studies* 11 (1984): 27-38; Moisés Silva, *God, Language, and Scripture: Reading the Bible in Light of General Linguistics*, Foundations of Contemporary Interpretation, ed. Moisés Silva, vol. 4 (Grand Rapids: Zondervan Publishing House, 1990); Charles R. Taber, "Exegesis and Linguistics," *The Bible Translator* 20 (1969): 150-53; Reinhard Wonneberger, "Greek Syntax: A New Approach,"

to Greek grammar in general[25] and to specific grammatical issues within the New Testament.[26] Possibly the earliest application of linguistics to biblical studies in any sustained manner was in the area of lexical semantics.[27] This is probably due to the influence of James Barr's work noted above. One area in which significant contributions seem probable is discourse analysis. In recent years a growing number of attempts to subject parts of the New Testament to discourse analysis have been attempted.[28] However, different underlying

---

Literary and Linguistic Computing 2 (1987): 71-79; and so on … See also the more specific study by Robert E. Longacre and Wilber B. Wallis, "Soteriology and Eschatology in Romans," *Journal of the Evangelical Theological Society* 41 (1998): 367-82.

[25]See for example the intermediate grammars: Stanley E. Porter, *Idioms of the Greek New Testament*, 2d ed., Biblical Languages: Greek, vol. 2 (Sheffield: JSOT Press, 1994); Richard A. Young, *Intermediate New Testament Greek: A Linguistic and Exegetical Approach* (Nashville: Broadman and Holman Publishers, 1994). However, despite the linguistic approach and the helpfulness of both of these grammars, one questions whether they make any significant improvement over more traditional grammars.

[26]Such works include: Rodney J. Decker, *Temporal Deixis of the Greek Verb in the Gospel of Mark with Reference to Verbal Aspect*, Studies in Biblical Greek, ed. D. A. Carson, vol. 4 (New York: Peter Lang, 2001); Mari Broman Olsen, *A Semantic and Pragmatic Model of Lexical and Grammatical Aspect* (New York and London: Garland Publishing, 1997); Micheal W. Palmer, *Levels of Constituent Structure in New Testament Greek*, Studies in Biblical Greek, ed. D. A. Carson, vol. 4 (New York: Peter Lang, 1995); Porter, *Verbal Aspect*; Stanley E. Porter, *Verbal Aspect in the Greek of the New Testament, with Reference to Tense and Mood*, Studies in Biblical Greek, ed. D. A. Carson, vol. 1 (New York: Peter Lang, 1989); D. D. Schmidt, *Hellenistic Greek Grammar and Noam Chomsky: Nominalizing Transformations* (Chico, CA: Scholars Press, 1981).

[27]See Richard J. Erickson, "Biblical Semantics, Semantic Structure, and Biblical Lexicology: A Study of Methods, with Special Reference to the Pauline Lexical Field of 'Cognition'" (Ph.D. diss., Fuller Theological Seminary, 1980); Johannes P. Louw, *Semantics of New Testament Greek* (Atlanta: Scholars Press, 1982); Johannes P. Louw and Eugene A. Nida, eds., *Greek-English Lexicon of the New Testament Based on Semantic Domains* (New York: United Bible Societies, 1988); Moisés Silva, *Biblical Words and Their Meaning: An Introduction to Lexical Semantics* (Grand Rapids: Zondervan Publishing House, 1983).

[28]David Alan Black, Katharine Barnwell, and Stephen Levinsohn, eds., *Linguistics and New Testament Interpretation: Essays on Discourse Analysis* (Nashville: Broadman Press, 1992); Stephen H. Levinsohn, *Discourse Features of New Testament Greek: A Coursebook*, 2d ed. (Dallas: Summer Institute of Linguistics, 2000); Stanley E. Porter and D. A. Carson, eds., *Discourse Analysis and Other Topics in Biblical Greek*, Journal for the Study of the New Testament Supplement Series, ed. Stanley E. Porter, vol. 113 (Sheffield: Sheffield Academic Press, 1995); Jeffrey T. Reed, *A Discourse Analysis of Philippians: Method and Rhetoric in the Debate Over Literary Integrity*, Journal for the Study of the New Testament Supplement Series, ed. Stanley E. Porter, vol. 136 (Sheffield: Sheffield Academic Press, 1997); Ralph Bruce Terry, *A Discourse Analysis of First Corinthians* (Dallas: Summer Institute of Linguistics, 1995). See also the essays in Walter R. Bodine, ed., *Discourse Analysis of Biblical Literature: What It Is and What It Offers* (Atlanta: Scholars Press, 1995).

methods and terminology have minimized the potential impact of this area of study.[29] Finally, the impact of linguistics and the likelihood of a sustained future within New Testament studies is evident by its presence at an important annual conference for biblical and theological studies.. Beginning in 1990, the annual meeting of the Society of Biblical Literature had a Consultation on Biblical Greek Language and Linguistics which in 1992 achieved the status of a Section.[30]

In the works cited above, the degree to which modern linguistics was used and the value of its results vary for New Testament studies. Nevertheless, formal calls for the use of modern linguistics in biblical studies appeared early in the second half of the twentieth century and application of linguistics for the study of the New Testament soon followed (of course, other linguistic applications for New Testament studies may have occurred earlier, especially with reference to missionary Bible translation).

In addition to works cited thus far, there is also a large body of literature devoted to Bible translation written by linguists (some works already cited also deal with translation).[31] Most of these works would not be considered "New Testament scholarship"; however, they include input from linguists on the Bible and its translation and thus are inherently related to New Testament Interpretation.[32]

---

[29]See further below.

[30]At these meetings, many important papers have been presented. Thus far, a number of volumes have appeared which include some of these papers: See for example, Stanley E. Porter and D. A. Carson, eds., *Biblical Greek Language and Linguistics: Open Questions in Current Research*, Journal for the Study of the New Testament Supplement Series, ed. Stanley E. Porter, vol. 80 (Sheffield: JSOT Press, 1993); idem, *Discourse Analysis and Other Topics*.

[31]See for example Eugene A. Nida, *Toward a Science of Translating* (Leiden: E. J. Brill, 1964); John Beekman and John Callow, *Translating the Word of God* (Grand Rapids: Zondervan Publishing House, 1974); Eugene A. Nida and Charles R. Taber, *The Theory and Practice of Translation*, Helps for Translators, vol. 8 (Leiden: E. J. Brill, 1969). Also, the Summer Institute of Linguistics (headquartered in Dallas) publishes many books and helps for translators including the journal, *Notes on Translation* (since 1962). The United Bible Society (New York) publishes a number of translation helps such as the journal entitled, *The Bible Translator* (since 1950) and the UBS Handbook Series which covers books in both the Old and New Testaments (e.g., B. M. Newman and Eugene A. Nida, *A Handbook on the Gospel of John*, UBS Handbook Series [New York: United Bible Societies, 1980]).

[32]Finally, it is worth noting the growing body of linguistic literature with specific reference to the Old Testament. See for example Walter R. Bodine, ed., *Linguistics and Biblical Hebrew* (Winona Lake, IN: Eisenbrauns, 1992); David Allen Dawson, *Text-Linguistics and Biblical Hebrew*, Journal for the Study of the Old Testament Supplement Series, ed. David A. J. Clines

Problems with the Use of Linguistics in Biblical Studies

Unfortunately, the rapid rise of linguistic theories which were not necessarily developed to analyze ancient languages has caused a number of problems for New Testament scholars. First, it cannot be maintained that the various linguistic theories are compatible with one another. At the most obvious level for outsiders, basic terminology is often used differently among linguists. Even within the same theoretical framework, terminology differences may occur. Between models, this is often a result of different theoretical preconceptions among the various theories. As has been discussed above, there are a number of linguistic models being developed and used. Familiarity with one theory does not assure an understanding of another (as mentioned above). For example, Butler early in his introductory systemics text warns the reader who may be trained in Chomskyan and other theories that he may need to "suspend certain preconceptions, and to approach language afresh, if he is to appreciate what Hallidayan linguistics has to offer."[33] The nature of this statement is alarming. Still more striking are Seok Choong Song's words at the beginning of a review of a popular-style Chomskyan based English syntax: "Like other scientific endeavors, theoretical linguistics has been advancing in all directions at such an unprecedented rate of speed that linguists of different theoretical persuasions find it difficult to assimilate the obscure and opaque jargons of other schools of thought. For ordinary mortals, the result of the latest research in the field of theoretical research is beyond their reach, and interpretation becomes not just desirable but necessary."[34] When scholars within the same broad field of linguistics need to "suspend certain preconceptions" to appreciate a theory or "find it difficult to assimilate the obscure and opaque jargons of other schools of thought," the New Testament scholar really needs to approach the field with caution and the willingness to invest the time to understand it.[35] To utilize a theory for advanced New Testament scholarly work,

---

and Philip R. Davies, vol. 177 (Sheffield: Sheffield Academic Press, 1994) and Robert E. Longacre, *Joseph: A Text Theoretical Textlinguistic Analysis of Genesis 37 and 39–40* (Winona Lake, IN: Eisenbrauns, 1989).

[33]*Systemic Linguistics*, 1.

[34]Review of *A Modern Course in English Syntax*, by Herman Wekker and Liliane Haegeman, *Word* 37 (1986): 219.

[35]Song's review was written in 1986. In light of further advances not only in theory but with analysis (using computers and other tools) his words are even more appropriate today.

one cannot rely on popular treatments or interpretations of the theory. He must deal with the theory in its primary form.

In additions to different preconceptions of language (and in some part because of them), there is strong disagreement between some theories, especially those influenced by Chomsky with approaches considered structural, descriptive, and/or functional. Such disagreements are often rooted in the cores of the theories themselves. At the 1988 LACUS conference held at Michigan State University, William J. Sullivan after examining four postulates of Chomsky's Government and Binding theory concludes,

> [this study] shows that these basic postulates of "the" theory are invalid logically, empirically, or both. As a result the theory derived from them has holes in it, holes of such a nature and of such a degree as to be devastating to the theory from both a logical and functional point of view. Moreover, it is clear that "the" theory is not a theory of language but a theory of some parts of the structure of language. Add these two shortcomings together and we may come up with the real mystery: why anybody attempts to apply this approach to linguistic theory to the description of language.[36]

Determining the legitimacy of Sullivan's claim is beyond the scope of this work. However, although not all disagreements are so strongly presented, this illustrates the serious differences between theories of linguistics. This makes the task of utilizing linguistics in the work of one primary trained in New Testament studies difficult. It also must be noted that even within the Chomskyan tradition itself, it may be difficult for one schooled in an earlier period to understand the later developed state of the tradition.[37] Thus, an unknowing New Testament scholar may read two linguistic books and have a difficult time seeing how they relate. It is possible that the scholar may come away from his reading more confused about linguistics than when he began.

It is important to understand why a theory was developed before determining whether it will be helpful to the New Testament scholar. For example, Kenneth Pike's *tagmemics* approach was partially developed as a tool for missionary translators.[38] Also, this theory views language as a part of a unified theory of

---

[36]William J. Sullivan, "Four Postulates of Government and Binding Theory," in *The Fifteenth LACUS Forum 1988*, ed. Ruth M. Brend and David G. Lockwood (Lake Bluff, IL: Linguistic Association of Canada and the United States, 1989), 66.

[37]Edmondson and Burquest, *Survey*, 119.

[38]See Kenneth Pike's motivation as discussed by his sister in Eunice V. Pike, *Ken Pike: Scholar and Christian* (Dallas: Summer Institute of Linguistics, 1981), 232-33.

human behavior.[39] It is very helpful that such presuppositions of the theory being utilized be understood by the New Testament scholar in order that he may understand how to effectively use a theory for his own purposes. It is possible that some portions of a theory will be more helpful than others.[40]

There seems to be little understanding of the differences between linguistic theories among biblical scholars. This is a matter of concern to the present writer. As linguistics become more and more entrenched within biblical studies, the number of differing theories seems to increase. Without proper knowledge of each theory, it becomes difficult if not impossible to combine them in application to New Testament exegesis. One major proponent of linguistics within New Testament studies seems to make a fundamental error about the basics of two linguistic approaches when he suggests that "all of the above communication principles [i.e., Grice's cooperative principle and maxims] may be summed up under Sperber and Wilson's single axiom of relevance."[41] This comment and the preceding discussion makes no distinction between Grice's theory and RT. It seems to infer that Sperber and Wilson merely use relevance as a means of summing up all Grice's maxims. This does not do justice to Grice's theory which claims more proponents than RT and would disagree with this statement. It also fails to do justice to RT which ultimately rejects Grice's maxims and states "that Grice's maxims can be replaced by the **principle of relevance**."[42] In fact, RT is not even mentioned as a separate theory in the discussion.[43] Sperber and Wilson make it clear that their theory is quite different from Grice's approach.[44] Such a

---

[39]See Pike, *Language in Relation*, 25-32.

[40]For a discussion of a number of linguistic theories contrasted, see Edmondson and Burquest, *Survey*.

[41]Jeffrey T. Reed, "Modern Linguistics and the New Testament: A Basic Guide to Theory, Terminology, and Literature," in *Approaches to New Testament Study*, ed. S. Porter and D. Tombs (Sheffield: Sheffield University Press, 1995), 242.

[42]Deirdre Wilson and Dan Sperber, "On Grice's Theory of Conversation," in *Conversation and Discourse: Structure and Interpretation*, ed. Paul Werth (New York: St. Martin's Press, 1981], 170. They also state concerning the maxims "that they may in fact be reduced to a single principle, which we call the principle of relevance" (ibid., 155-56). However, the precise nature of advanced linguistic discussion would consider Reed's "summed up" as quite different than Wilson and Sperber's "reduced to."

[43]Although sounding familiar, Grice's maxim *be relevant* is not the same as RT's *principle of relevance*. The difference may seem subtle (and the later may have been influenced by the former) but the distinction is important. N.B. This is a general observation and I am not accusing Reed of this misunderstanding.

[44]*Relevance*, 161-63.

misunderstanding of the difference between Grice's theory and RT is made more serious by the fact that the purpose of this article was to inform the New Testament discipline of basic linguistic issues.[45]

In addition to those theories already mentioned above used in published examples of biblical analysis/translation, I have seen/heard unpublished

---

[45]One would assume that the best approach for this type of article is to inform the reader of the most important theories and if he felt compelled to favor one, state his preference with a brief defense. This is especially important in this case where the statement seems to favor Wilson and Sperber whose theory is a minority theory of pragmatics. However, the discussion does not really favor one theory since it discusses Grice's work and mentions Sperber and Wilson without any suggestion of disagreement or even a switch in theoretical framework. One might see favor only if he already is aware that Grice and RT are competing theoretical frameworks. This neither seems to be assumed of the reader nor is there anything to indicate that the author is aware of this.

I do not want to be too critical of Reed here. I confess that I made the same error in preliminary work on this project (which was corrected after further consideration in a revision of chapter 1). Also it is possible that those only reading at a more popular level may infer this. For example, Blakemore states, ". . . Relevance Theory could be regarded as an attempt to develop Grice's basic insight [relevance]" (*Understanding Utterances: An Introduction to Pragmatics* [Oxford: Blackwell Publishers, 1992]); nevertheless, even here it is clear that RT is developing an insight of Grice, not summarizing Grice under one of his maxims.

In any case, this basic misunderstanding vividly illustrates at least three difficulties with cross-discipline study generally. First, it is difficult to master two fields of study in a way that does justice to both. New, diverse, and rapidly changing disciplines like linguistics are especially difficult to master as a secondary field. This of course depends on the secondary field. Although linguistics would seem to be closely related to New Testament studies, actually, although some goals are shared, the differences are great (note the goals of the theories mentioned elsewhere in this appendix). It may be easier to gain competence in secondary fields closer to New Testament studies such as Graeco-Roman or Jewish history (for select time periods). Second, when approaching a complex field of study, it is easy to overlook important aspects of the major works themselves. Reed's error would have been avoided had he noted a section in the very book he cited for his comment (Sperber and Wilson, *Relevance*, 161-63). Third, when approaching a secondary field (to one's primary), it is important to be current (as much as possible) on issues concerning and developments since seminal works. Because RT's most important work has been revised recently (Sperber and Wilson, *Relevance*, in 1995), this is less an issue; nevertheless, an appropriately titled older article by the major proponents of RT would have helped Reed to avoid the misunderstanding made evident by his statement (Wilson and Sperber, "On Grice's Theory of Conversation," 155-78).

It should also be noted that Reed's purpose was not to expound RT. However, by introducing Sperber and Wilson's work (and thus RT without mentioning it as a theory) in the last line of his section and then following it with a principle ("*the speaker tries to make the utterance as relevant as possible to the hearer*"), he has opened up significant methodological questions of which he seems unaware. In addition, his principle is limited to *relevance*; however, the section in which this discussion takes place has a broader purpose (Reed, "Modern Linguistics," 240-42). It may have been preferable for Reed not to introduce Sperber and Wilson's work and draw this principle from Grice's maxims in a new section.

applications of minimalist theory, cognitive grammar (not NCSL used here), and speech act theory applied to the text. Many of these theories have already been either radically modified or discarded. Certainly, others will suffer the same fate. At best, most these applications will remain unread and uninfluential. Possibly, methodological and presuppositional battles may occupy the time of biblical scholars. This can be positive or negative depending upon the results. At worst, theories already discarded by linguists may become important within biblical studies.[46]

Second, and related to the modern development and rapid advancement of the discipline, results once seemingly certain become obsolete and even wrong as the discipline advances. Gordon Messing, the editor of the reissued Greek grammar by H. W. Smyth, defends the re-publication of the work thirty-six years after its appearance because of its descriptive character. However, he notes there is a need for revision. He states, "Nevertheless, it is only fair to the reader to point out certain features of the original work which called for revision. Smyth spoke in his preface of having 'adopted many assured results of comparative linguistics'; inevitably, time has invalidated some of these supposedly assured results, and new discoveries have successively altered existing concepts or added to our fund of knowledge."[47] It may be argued that this could be said of all disciplines since advancements take place consistently. However, two points may be made here. First, Smyth was building upon "assured results" not upon debated or emerging points. This is the label a discipline gives to results upon which it can build. Second, the date of Messing's remarks appeared a year before Chomsky's revolutionary book, *Syntactic Structures*. The discipline really began changing after this. One need only note Chomsky's own modifications to his theory (see above)[48] to see the appropriateness of Messing's words to the state of the discipline today.

Third, the value of linguistic theories for New Testament studies still needs

---

[46]I must confess that after engaging in this process for a time, I am concerned that this work will contribute to the problem discussed here. Am I merely adding two more linguistic approaches to an already heavy burden of theory overload? Although depending upon two theories for this study, I have attempted to develop in some detail in chapter 1 what I believe to be sound linguistic principles gleaned from these theories. It is hopeful that despite further refinements in NCSL and RT, these principles themselves will be enduring.

[47]Herbert Weir Smyth, *Greek Grammar*, rev. G. M. Messing (Cambridge, MA: Harvard University Press, 1956), iii.

[48]In addition, his initial contribution caused much re-thinking of many aspects of the field.

to be determined. Many studies are attempting to apply a linguistic theory to one aspect of Greek grammar. For example, D. Schmidt applies Chomsky's *extended standard theory* to a study of nominalizing transformations in Greek (syntactic devices which embed sentences to function nominally [substantival] dependent clauses or nominal clauses),[49] and Stanley Porter applies a systemic analysis to verbal aspect.[50] Studies such as Porter's have contributed to an understanding of New Testament grammar, while studies like Schmidt's seem to primarily be an exercise of using a linguistic theory with the Greek text. This (latter) approach restates or confirms an aspect of Greek grammar already understood. However, a full blown linguistic analysis of Greek still needs to be developed. In light of the many linguistic theories available, there may be a number of such works produced. This should be beneficial for New Testament scholars because it should lead them to the more helpful theories for their purpose(s).

Fourth, to a number of New Testament scholars, it seems like some linguistic analyses yield few results for the effort exerted. This seems to be the case with Micheal Palmer's work on constituent structure.[51] The conclusions of this work do not seem to add much to the knowledge of Hellenistic Greek; rather, it primarily subjects Greek to an *extended standard theory* analysis. In some cases a work may simply put in linguistic terms results already known by traditional analysis. This seems to be the case with David Alan Black's little book, *Linguistics for Students of New Testament Greek*. In other cases, the study may primarily be of a theoretical nature.

It is important to consider a number of responses to this criticism. First, a work must be understood for its purpose. In the case of Black's book, the purpose is to introduce Greek students to linguistics and demonstrate how its findings can add to an understanding of the New Testament.[52] Its value must be judged on whether this is accomplished not whether it adds anything to current Greek studies. However, once this purpose is understood, a Greek scholar may or may not view such purposes as contributing to his specific needs. Also, Black's second edition includes a chapter on discourse analysis which does seem to be an emerging area in which linguistics is contributing to Greek studies. Second, when traditional results are verified by modern linguistic analysis, the

---

[49]Schmidt, *Hellenistic Greek Grammar*.
[50]Porter, *Verbal Aspect*.
[51]Palmer, *Levels of Constituent Structure*.
[52]Black, *Linguistics for the Students of New Testament Greek*, xii.

conclusions of the past are strengthened. Third, there is a need for purely theoretical works (albeit their value may vary for different scholars). Theory is not necessarily bad; theoretical works are needed. However, for a linguistic analysis to be adopted by New Testament scholars it must yield results which add to the knowledge of the language (and ultimately, exegesis).

A fourth response to this criticism is that some contributions of linguistics will be in areas other than Greek. For example, to the present writer, it seems that discourse analysis which focuses on higher-level aspects of the book (such as plot, theme, cohesion, etc.) may contribute in a broader way to exegesis (and hermeneutics[53]) and not specifically to Greek. In contrast, an approach which focuses on lower-level aspects of the text (conjunctions, particles etc.) may have more impact on Greek studies. Although these two approaches overlap to some extent, they do have different emphases and are attempting to answer different questions. Interestingly, these two approaches appear side by side in one volume. This volume which includes papers given on discourse analysis at the Society of Biblical Literature meeting in 1993, the higher-level approach is represented by Jeffrey T. Reed[54] and the lower-level approach, which may be more applicable to Greek study specifically, is represented by Stephen H. Levinsohn.[55] It seems that both approaches are valid and must be considered separately. Failure to do so will result in minimizing one approach in favor of another. To some extent, this seems to be what Porter does in his evaluation of Levinsohn in the same published volume.[56] Porter, in his introductory article, emphasizes higher-level

---

[53]Concerning RT and Hermeneutics, see Tim Meadowcroft, "Relevance as a Mediating Category in the Reading of Biblical Texts: Venturing beyond the Hermeneutic Circle," *Journal of the Evangelical Theological Society* 45 (2002): 611-27. See also, RT principles used in Jeannine K. Brown's *Scripture as Communication: Introducing Biblical Hermeneutics* (Grand Rapids: Baker Book House, 2007)

[54]"Identifying Theme in the New Testament: Insights from Discourse Analysis," in *Discourse Analysis and Other Topics in Biblical Greek*, ed. Stanley E. Porter and D. A. Carson (Sheffield: Sheffield Academic Press, 1995), 75-101. See also George H. Guthrie, *The Structure of Hebrews: A Text-Linguistic Analysis* (Grand Rapids: Baker Books, 1994); Hendrikus Boers, *The Justification of the Gentiles: Paul's Letters to the Galatians and Romans* (Peabody, MA: Hendrickson Publishers, 1994); and Reed, *Discourse Analysis*.

[55]"A Discourse Study of Constituent Order and the Article in Philippians," in *Discourse Analysis and Other Topics in Biblical Greek*, ed. Stanley E. Porter and D. A. Carson (Sheffield: Sheffield Academic Press, 1995), 60-74. See also Levinsohn, *Discourse Features*.

[56]"How Can Biblical Discourse Be Analyzed? A Response to Several Attempts," in *Discourse Analysis and Other Topics in Biblical Greek*, ed. Stanley E. Porter and D. A. Carson (Sheffield: Sheffield Academic Press, 1995), 107-108.

discourse as the more appropriate area of study;[57] however, one wonders why both of these areas are not considered valuable. Certainly all clause level analysis has not been completed and the discussion of the use of various conjunctions and particles do function at a level of discourse. Thus one wonders whether or not future studies in discourse analysis will be divided into lower-level approaches which apply more to Greek and higher-level approaches which apply more broadly. This would avoid the comparison of two different types of analyses. Thus, when considering the value of linguistics for biblical studies, one must not limit it to Greek. Fifth, there are and will be "bad" applications of linguistics to the New Testament. These will need to be identified and not allowed to influence Greek grammar.

Sixth, when reviewing the previous five points, it becomes clear that linguistic approaches to the New Testament will not be equally beneficial to all New Testament scholars. Those whose interests do not include highly theoretical studies will not utilize such studies in their work. Of course, the usefulness of linguistics to New Testament studies in general will be judged with reference to the value of specific works. Ultimately, it may be for the best that some linguistic analyses of Greek remain primarily in the domain of linguistics and not tools for New Testament studies.

Finally, more a potential attitude than a problem, there is a danger of viewing the use of linguistics in biblical studies as some type of magical key to unlocking the meaning of the biblical text. Or, more subdued, the use of linguistics gives one's interpretation more authority than another. To some extent, this is natural with many new approaches to Scripture. It is not that linguistics is not a valuable resource. However, it should not minimize the important grammatical tradition that New Testament scholars have inherited. Not accusing Porter of this attitude entirely (his work demonstrates a respect for past grammarians), it seems to be present in his critique of Fanning concerning verbal aspect.[58] There may be times to abandon past conclusions. However, it seems that Porter criticizes Fanning merely for maintaining a link with the past.[59] Additionally, Porter's view of the

---

[57]"Discourse Analysis and New Testament Studies: An Introductory Survey," in *Discourse Analysis and Other Topics in Biblical Greek*, ed. Stanley E. Porter and D. A. Carson (Sheffield: Sheffield Academic Press, 1995), 25-26.

[58]"In Defense of Verbal Aspect," in *Biblical Greek Language and Linguistics: Open Questions in Current Research*, ed. Stanley E. Porter and D. A. Carson (Sheffield: JSOT Press, 1993), 34-43.

[59]Ibid., 38. This is not Porter's only criticism.

developments based on modern linguistics seems to suggest that we have entered a new era of understanding in Greek grammar. This claim is not self evident. It may ultimately be proven true. However, Porter's presentation of linguistics is far too confident and it fails to recognize that even the theory to which he adheres is not accepted by the majority of linguists.

In addition to the seven problems raised above, a further area of concern must be mentioned before continuing. The present use of linguistics as a tool for biblical studies may minimize the enormous complexity of the field of linguistics. This has been alluded to above. Linguists train extensively in their field as New Testament scholars do in theirs. It is foolish to believe one can master both without enormous effort. This must be taken into consideration when a New Testament scholar writes in linguistics and a linguist writes in New Testament. I am not suggesting that such cross-specialty field work should not happen. In fact, others from outside a field may contribute fresh ideas that those immersed in a field have overlooked. Nevertheless, this must be considered when approaching (and producing) the cross-specialty work.

Linguistics seems to be an unavoidable aspect of the future of Greek grammar studies. Despite some of my concern above, I believe this is a good thing. Linguistics can bring much to New Testament studies not least of which is its extensive understanding of other languages and language in general. This is a positive and welcomed contribution to our field. However, one cannot approach the subject uninformed or without some plan for its use.[60] In the remainder of this section, I will conclude by drawing together some points already made and include others which may serve as some proposals for the use of linguistics within biblical studies.

First, understand that linguistics is a field of study in its own right. It is not merely a field developed for use in biblical studies. This may seem obvious but it must be remembered. Theories not necessarily developed for the purposes of biblical studies may need significant refinement.

Second, be aware of the significant differences among competing linguistic theories. Although an eclectic approach using aspects of different theories may be admirable and even helpful at times, one cannot ignore fundamental differences between theories. Eclecticism will be further discussed in proposal three immediately below.

---

[60]Of course any plan of action must be only tentative and flexible.

Many linguistic theories still need to be thoroughly tested in the field. Many may ultimately be rejected. This is an area which needs work and to which biblical scholars can contribute by testing theories and helping to publish results on positive and negative theories for use in biblical studies.[61] Until this type of work is done, any significant Greek work based extensively on a specific linguistic theory is in danger of being found useless to future generations.[62]

Third, survey linguistic work and attempt to understand one or two theories as a starting point. Once the biblical scholar understands that it is impossible to master all theories and can feel comfortable not knowing the entire field, he is free to focus on specific areas of method. With the diverse theories available, the temptation to be eclectic in one's approach is natural. However, one must consider this with caution. It is more important that one fully understands one or two specific theories and their implications than to have minimal understanding of many theories. An eclectic approach is still possible and may be beneficial.[63] However, it should not be approached lightly. Eclecticism must be limited and not attempt to encompass too many theories. It may be helpful to take from a number of theories, but one must attempt to remain consistent with the method and goals of one's primary theory. As discussed above, theories often have fundamental differences. Instead of a desired well balanced approach, an eclectic approach may result in the loss of a theoretical foundation all together. Knowing the strengths and weaknesses of a theory will enhance one's control over the method and provide more solid and defensible conclusions.

Focusing on one or two theories has a number of benefits. It allows one to stay abreast of developments within the theory given the limited amount of time available to the New Testament scholar. Solid knowledge of the theory will minimize the potential for misunderstanding and misappropriating the theory. The New Testament scholar can have credibility in the linguistic field if he

---

[61]This sounds easier than it actually is. Few people wish to invest time learning a theory and using it extensively only to discover it does not work well. Unfortunately, the tendency is to "make it work at all costs."

[62]In other words, basing a major reference grammar on a specific linguistic theory at this time would be premature. It may be wise for those considering such projects to avoid the temptation of using a revolutionary linguistic theory until it is tried and it can be determined if it remains valuable. On a more general note, a watchful approach to many linguistics theories is wise. After these theories are subjected to significant testing, one can focus on those theories which (if any) remain.

[63]This project utilized two different but compatible theories.

understands the theory sufficiently. Finally, he may be able to contribute not only to New Testament studies but to linguistics as well.

Fourth, as with any cross-speciality enterprise, beware of using outdated aspects of theories. The first major work on a theory may be of little more than historical value. In a young field such as linguistics things are moving very fast. Again, Chomsky's work is an excellent example. No one today would use *Syntactic Structures* (1957) or *Aspects* (1964) as their linguistic basis for analysis.[64] Once one has discovered a linguistic theory of interest, it is important to keep up on the latest discussion in the field. This may involve specific journal reading, conference attendance, etc. It is in these venues that theories take shape.

Fifth, in addition to work which tests existing theories of linguistics, I feel it necessary for biblical scholars and linguists with an interest in biblical studies to attempt to develop a theory of linguistics which has as its primary goal, *exegesis* of ancient languages, specifically Greek and Hebrew and Aramaic. Present linguistic theories could serve as a model but this is not necessary. An entirely new theory may need to be developed. Nevertheless, the experience of linguistics would be essential. Also, great body of learning inherited by New Testament scholars could be utilized instead of (as is sometimes the case) ignored. It must be kept in mind that linguists are often satisfied with analysis of a language which does not nearly approach the understand available for Greek through traditional methods. Therefore, a new theory would need to bring analysis to a new level in order for it to be useful to biblical studies.

In this section, I have been somewhat critical of the use of linguistic theories in New Testament studies. If this communicated a negative view of this process, I would be misunderstood. I wholeheartedly believe that a linguistic approach to New Testament Greek is the present way to approach the New Testament. I am confident this will result in further breakthroughs in our understanding. A solidly linguistic framework that respects our grammatical heritage and continues to focus on the text itself is crucial for further development. We cannot return to the pre-linguistic days. My critical comments are intended to be from the perspective of an insider, someone who is committed to this path and desires to make it as successful as possible. Further, critical comments about those scholars who are using linguistics in their New Testament grammatical research should

---

[64]Although not as drastic, Lamb's work could also serve as an example. If one presented a paper at a scholarly conference armed only with Lamb's *Outline* method (1966), the paper would receive severe criticism.

not be seen as disapproval. These comments apply to myself as well. This is a new game and we are all testing the waters. Some avenues will be fruitful, others may lead nowhere. The result will be a benefit to the discipline as a whole.

Neuro-Cognitive Linguistics and Relevance Theory: The Basis for This Work (Additional Comments)

Neuro-Cognitive Stratificational Linguistics (NCSL)

This work is based on two linguistic theories which maintain a cognitive emphasis in their approach to language and communication. In chapter 1 these theories were discussed in some detail; however, the focus at that time was on certain aspects of the theories and no discussion of their history was undertaken. The reason for this was to emphasize certain important contributions which irrespective of the theories' development or criticism, seemed to be sound linguistic principles. In other words, it was the structural nature of the language system and the inferential nature of communication, not the theories themselves which were important to this work.[65] In this brief section, further detail on the theories themselves will be presented.

Neuro-cognitive (stratificational) linguistics (NCSL) is primarily used in this work for its structural view of the language system. Relevance theory (RT) informs the understanding of the communication situation which is foundational. Although so classified, it is questionable whether the latter is a linguistic theory *per se*; rather, it may be better considered a (broader) communication theory. Nevertheless, both theories wish to account for the entire communication system within their own framework.[66]

In 1962 Sydney Lamb made available an outline of a linguistic theory for students at Berkeley with the label *stratificational linguistics*. In 1966, this brief work was revised and formally published under the title, *Outline of*

---

[65]This explains the lengthy development of these principles. These discussions were not meant as support for the theories *per se*; rather, their purpose was to demonstrate the feasibility and legitimacy of the linguistic principles on which this project was theoretically based.

[66]For the communication emphasis within neuro-cognitive linguistics, see Ilah Fleming, *Communication Analysis: A Stratificational Approach,* 2 vol. (Dallas: Summer Institute of Linguistics, 1988-1990). However, it is relevance theory's view of the communication situation which is assumed and developed in this work.

Stratificational Grammar.[67] Lamb and others have continued to develop the theory.[68] There are some minor differences in later approaches (see especially Fleming); however, unlike the state of affairs among the followers of Chomsky, the theory has not been significantly altered. In other words, although today one would not use Lamb's 1966 *Outline* as the sole theoretical basis for NCSL work, later theoretical developments do not make this work obsolete. Also, later forms of the theory are not unrecognizable to one who is only familiar with earlier works. Neuro-cognitive stratificational linguistics views language as a system of relationships (a network). In other words, various aspects of language such as morphology, syntax, etc., although separate in their own right, are related as different strata of a single network. Each stratum contributes to the language process as one produces and accounts for language. Viewing language as occurring in various sections or levels (to use NCSL's term, strata) is not unique. Most theories view distinct levels in language (e.g., semantics, syntax, phonology, etc.) and analyze each on its own terms.[69] Nevertheless, NCSL's emphasis is somewhat stronger (relatively speaking) within the theory itself. The stratal systems and relationship between each stratum is a dominant aspect of this theory's application. A stratified view of language was developed in the present work.

NCSL has an explicit goal to understand the way in which the brain functions. Thus, in a very simplified manner, proponents believe that the descriptive networks which describe language are analogous to the actual neurological connections in the brain. It is impossible to observe the brain (and

---

[67]Sydney Lamb, *Outline of Stratificational Grammar* (Washington DC: Georgetown University Press, 1966).

[68]See for example Lockwood, *Introduction to Stratificational Linguistics* (New York: Harcourt Brace Jovanovich, 1972); Ilah Fleming, *Communication Analysis,* 2 vols. Volume one of Fleming's work is unpublished and a third volume was planned but to my knowledge has either not materialized or is unavailable. Finally, see Lamb's latest description of his theory, *Pathways of the Brain: The Neurocognitive Basis of Language,* Amsterdam Studies in the Theory and History of Linguistic Science: Series 4 – Current Issues in Linguistic Theory, ed. E. F. Konrad Koerner (Amsterdam: John Benjamins Publishing Company, 1999).

[69]See for example the generative approach in Chomsky, *Aspects,* 15-18; for a systemic approach see Margaret Berry, *An Introduction to Systemic Linguistics,* vol. 2, *Levels and Links* (New York: St. Martin's Press, 1976), 1-3; for a tagmemic approach see Longacre, *Grammar,* 7-9 (and throughout the book) and Ruth M. Brend, "On Defining Grammatical Levels," in *Language in Context: Essays for Robert E. Longacre,* ed. Shin Ja J. Hwang and William R. Merrifield (Dallas: Summer Institute of Linguistics, 1992), 505-509 (highlighting Longacre's contribution).

mind) directly; however, language which is produced in the brain should provide a picture into at least one of its aspects. In Lamb's most recent description of the theory he has made the neurological aspect more explicit and thus renaming it, neuro-cognitive linguistics. Developments include insights gleaned from neurology as well as linguistic observation. These insights have lead to developments which refine the system to make it account for language better by attempting to observe how the brain actually produces and understands language.[70] Lamb insists that a linguist must examine four types of linguistic phenomena: 1. physical organs and the processes of speech production (articulatory phonetics); 2. ordinary people's linguistic productions (written texts and verbal utterances); 3. the actual processes of speaking and understanding, including language learning; 4. the neuro-cognitive basis of language (the brain/mind).[71] Lamb rightly observes that most linguistic analysis does not account for anything beyond the second type. Although the method of types three and four are beyond the scope of this work, the linguist who keeps these in mind as he analyzes data will be constrained both in his theory and analysis. This would seem to eliminate theories and analyses which are so complex one cannot understand how the mind could process data in such a manner. The stratified view of language as a network of relationships is very helpful for understanding the relationship between the meaning and usages of the Greek imperative mood. This was developed further in chapter 1 in the section entitled, "The Linguistic System as a Relational Network."[72]

Relevance Theory (RT)

The second theory used in this study is relevance theory (RT). Less needs to

---

[70]See Lamb, *Pathways to the Brain.*

[71]Sydney Lamb, "A Word from the Chair," *LACUS: The Linguistic Association of Canada and the United States Newsletter* 2, no. 1 (1996), 4.

[72]For a basic understanding NCSL see John Algeo, "Stratificational Grammar," in *Readings in Stratificational Linguistics*, ed. Adam Makkai and David G. Lockwood (University, AL: University of Alabama Press, 1973), 4-11; Geoffrey Sampson, *Schools of Linguistics* (Stanford, CA: Stanford University Press, 1980), 166-86; Pamela Cope, *Introductory Grammar: A Stratificational Approach* (Dallas: Summer Institute of Linguistics, 1994); Ilah Fleming, *Communication Analysis: A Stratificational Approach*, vol. 2 (Dallas: Summer Institute of Linguistics, 1988), 1-26; and Edmondson and Burquest, *Survey*, 97-118.

be stated here about this theory since it was developed more fully in chapter 1 than NCSL. Nevertheless, a few background issues are worth discussing that were not necessary to the argument there. RT was developed by Dan Sperber and Deirdre Wilson. Their foundational work is *Relevance: Communication and Cognition*.[73] Sperber and Wilson built on a fundamental observation that communication operates through *inference* as was suggested by the philosopher, H. Paul Grice.[74] However, RT ultimately views Grice's theory and its development by others as insufficient to account for the act of communication.[75]

Grice's theory has been and remains the dominant communication/pragmatic model. In chapter 1, some discussion of Sperber and Wilson's departure and development of Grice was noted. Here this will be pursued a little further. The brevity of this description is due to a number of factors. First, time and space do not permit a full exposition of the theory. Those interested in a basic understanding of the theory are encouraged to consult works noted when RT was introduced in chapter 1. Second, as with much of communication theory (and linguistic theories), RT seems primarily concerned with spoken communication. Any theory of communication must account for written communication. This is true for RT (but spoken is emphasized).[76] However, Keith Green points out that

[73]Dan Sperber and Deirdre Wilson, *Relevance: Communication and Cognition* (Cambridge, MA: Harvard University Press, 1986). A second edition appeared in 1995 that made only a few modifications based on further work in the area. In some places they added material to clear up possible misunderstandings and they added a chapter with some minor modifications and clarifications concerning the theory (*Relevance: Communication and Cognition*, 2d ed. [Oxford: Blackwell, 1995]). All citations are from the second edition.

[74]"Logic and Conversation," in *Syntax and Semantics, vol. 3: Speech Acts*, ed. P. Cole and J. Morgan (New York: Academic Press, 1975), 41-58. The importance of inference in the communication process is discussed and developed in chapter one in the subsection entitled, *The Nature of Communication*.

[75]For a brief introduction to RT, see Deirdre Wilson and Dan Sperber, "An Outline of Relevance Theory," *Notes on Linguistics* 39 (1987): 4-24; Ernst-August Gutt, "Unravelling Meaning: An Introduction to Relevance Theory," *Notes on Translation* 112 (1986): 10-20; idem, *Relevance Theory: A Guide to Successful Communication in Translation* (Dallas: Summer Institute of Linguistics, 1992); idem, *Translation and Relevance: Cognition and Context*, 2d ed. (Manchester: St Jerome Publishing, 2000), 24-46; Blakemore, *Understanding Utterances*. For examples of RT used in biblical exegesis, see Ernst-August Gutt, "Matthew 9:14-17 in the Light of Relevance Theory," *Notes on Translation* 113 (1986): 13-20; idem, *Relevance Theory*, 15-17. For a critique of the theories usefulness for Bible translation (especially as presented by Gutt), see Ernst R. Wendland, "On the Relevance of 'Relevance Theory' for Bible Translation," *The Bible Translator* 47 (1996): 126-37. Wendland sees value in the theory but feels that some modifications are necessary in order to use it successfully in Bible translation.

[76]For an RT approach to literary text, see Seiji Uchida, "Text and Relevance," in *Relevance*

literary texts and spoken utterances are not necessarily processed in the same way and that RT has not adequately accounted for written texts within its theory.[77] The New Testament is written document;[78] therefore, a full discussion of a complex theory of communication theory based on speech is unnecessary. Of course, there are similarities between both written and speech communication which justifies the use of the theory.[79] Third, in addition to placing this study within a sound communication theory, another important reason for the discussion of RT will involve questions of method. This was discussed in chapter 1 and throughout the work.

RT has not gained wide acceptance among pragmatists. Many still maintain

---

Theory: Applications and Implications, ed. Robyn Carston and Seiji Uchida (Amsterdam: John Benjamins Publishing Company, 1998), 162-78.

[77]"Relevance Theory and Literary Text: Some Problems and Perspectives," *Journal of Literary Semantics* 22 (1993): 207-17.

[78]In the case of the New Testament, economy due to writing material also may have influenced composition (a suggestion which cannot be explored here).

[79]Written communication by nature is often more carefully constructed than spoken. This is not always a rule. What is being compared here is communication between two parties for the purpose of propositional information exchange which occurs commonly in both speech and writing and is common in the New Testament. By its very nature, more consideration and effort is given to the production of written communication than oral (an exception is formal speeches; however, these are often based upon some form of written document). There are significant differences between spoken and written communication. The writer does not have verbal linguistic elements such as intonation and non-linguistics actions such as gestures to help communicate his message (see Wilhelm Egger, *How to Read the New Testament: An Introduction to Linguistic and Historical-Critical Methodology*, ed. Hendrikus Boers [Peabody, MA: Hendrickson Publishers, 1996], 129). Instead, the writer has punctuation and an endless supply of words to fulfill his communication needs. Speech is a more basic form of communication. All languages either have or had (in the case of extinct languages) speakers. However, a significant number of languages in the world even today do not have a written means of expression (John P. Hughes, "Languages and Writing," in *Language: Introductory Readings*, ed. Virginia P. Clark, Paul A. Eschholz, and Alfred F. Rosa [New York: St. Martin's Press, 1981], 436).

With reference to intentions, spoken communication can be much more complicated than written. Written language is not simple; however, intentions are often more explicit. The more formal the written communication, the more likely that intentions may be explicit or at least fall within very standard modes of expression. The more personal a written communication and the more the writer is familiar with the addressee(s), the more options the writer has to express his intentions. This generalization can be made based on the relational aspect of communication. The more the parties in the communication process share, the more implicit the communication can be. The New Testament includes written communication all along the relational spectrum from relatively formal (e.g., Luke) to very personal (e.g., Philemon). However, It would be an error to assume too much simplicity, an error hoped to be avoided here by insight gained from the theory's emphasis on spoken language. Nevertheless, the finer nuances of this theory will not be necessary for the this work.

Grice's original proposals in some fashion. This may be due to RT's emphasis upon cognition and psychology in contrast to the more philosophical approach of Grice and his followers.[80] There are a number of critical discussions of RT available.[81] Some criticism seems fair. For example, Mey[82] argues that Sperber and Wilson may be placing too much weight on *relevance* to explain communication. He argues that it is too much to maintain that by the act of communicating by a speaker "guarantees" relevance.[83] This charge may be warranted. RT may be too reductionalistic here. For one principle (or a set of two, namely, the *principle(s) of relevance*, see chapter 1) to accurately describe communication does not seem to do justice to the communication process. However, Sperber and Wilson acknowledge that such a *guarantee* from the speaker's point of view does not mean that "it will actually be optimally relevant to the hearer."[84] Also Sperber and Wilson are aware that there are some areas of communication where this does not apply.[85] At this point they are making fine distinctions concerning communication. Additionally, they acknowledge the need for (and inevitability of) further development.[86] For the purposes of this work, it is not necessary to delve into these fine issues of definition. Nevertheless, Mey's criticism does warn of oversimplification. Ernst R. Wendland, although somewhat favorable to RT, warns against simplification and other potential shortcomings which may result is an exclusive focus on RT in Bible translation.[87] Nevertheless, RT does seems like an improvement over Grice's cooperative principle and maxims which seem to be more assumed then empirically proven.[88]

Because this work is primarily concerned with a specific point of

---

[80]See Sperber and Wilson, *Relevance*, 31-32.

[81]Critical discussions of RT include Stephen C. Levinson, "Review of '*Relevance*,'" *Journal of Linguistics* 25 (1989): 455-72; Jacob L. Mey, *Pragmatics: An Introduction* (Oxford, MA: Blackwell Publishers, 1993), 80-82; and Lawrence D. Roberts, "Relevance as an Explanation of Communication," *Linguistics and Philosophy* 14 (1991): 453-72.

[82]*Pragmatics*, 81.

[83]See Wilson and Sperber, "Outline," 13-14 and Sperber and Wilson, *Relevance*, 155-61.

[84]Wilson and Sperber, "Outline," 14.

[85]See Sperber and Wilson, *Relevance*, 158-59.

[86]Ibid., 278-79. It is important to note that these pages are from the postface added to the second (1995) edition.

[87]"Relevance," 126-37.

[88]For a favorable review of Sperber and Wilson's work (and thus RT), see Alan M. Leslie, review of *Relevance: Communication and Cognition*, by Dan Sperber and Deirdre Wilson, *Mind & Language* 4 (1989): 147-50.

grammatical meaning, it will not be necessary to develop RT as fully as other projects might demand. Thus, in some ways, the presentation in chapter 1 is simplified. One specific area where the development of RT is simplified is in the use of the concept of *pragmatic implicatures*. Grice's basic notion has been developed further in RT into a more precise and possibly more accurate treatment utilizing both *explicatures* and *implicatures*. However, this terminology may be confusing because RT's implicatures are not identical to Grice's implicatures. Because the more precise terminology is not demanded for this work, my own definition of *implicature* introduced in chapter 1 is primarily Gricean.[89]

The weaknesses of Grice's work and RT must lead one to the conclusion that much work still needs to be done in communication theory and pragmatics. A consensus is still distant. The problem is complicated by the intricacies of the communication process, the creativity of human beings, and the complexities of the human brain. Understanding of these areas is just beginning. Also, the problems associated with using the communication process to describe itself cannot be underestimated. One is unable to get out from within to observe and describe the phenomenon of communication. This does not mean that one should abandon these theories. Rather, the infant state of knowledge should be acknowledged and one should be open to further discoveries.

This study is not dependent upon the complete accuracy of the linguistic and communication theories adopted. These theories are only utilized to present a basic foundation with which to analyze the text. The analysis itself should provide empirical evidence for the conclusions. The principles derived from these theories seem accurate even if the theories themselves do not ultimately prove to be the most efficient. However, based on the state of knowledge thus far, I believe these theories are the most promising options.

---

[89]For further development of RT's theory of *explicatures* and *implicatures*, see Sperber and Wilson, *Relevance*, 176-83 and Blakemore, *Understanding Utterances*, 57-64.

Appendix 2

General Comments on Grammatical Mood

Mood is a complex phenomenon and not unrelated to other aspects of grammar specifically and language generally.[1] Although the distinction is not always precise, some suggest a contrast between *mood* and *modality*, the former is an optional grammatically based category (analogous to tense), the latter refers to the broader obligatory experiential aspect of communication (analogous to time).[2] This work is only concerned with the former. Some have defined *mood* (or in older works, *mode*) simply as a vehicle to present reality or fact. It has been called "the *manner* of the *affirmation*."[3] Or, slightly more complex, it has been described as the speaker's perception of reality or factualness.[4] Although such grammarians acknowledge that mood may not be entirely objective, such a definition may be misleading because it fails to acknowledge the portrayal nature of language.[5] It is incorrect to assume that an indicative is used exclusively for certainty and fact while the subjunctive, optative, and imperative are used for less certain assertions respectively (the imperative being the least certain). Most lies and non-factual information are communicated in the indicative. For example, the following indicative statements, "a Ford Escort is smaller than a bread box" and "a tortoise runs fifty miles an hour," are not factual. Porter uses the term *attitude* for mood and

---

[1]For a full scale treatment of mood from a non-language specific linguistic perspective, see F. R. Palmer, *Mood and Modality*, Cambridge Textbooks in Linguistics, ed. B. Comrie et al. (Cambridge: University Press, 1986).

[2]Ibid., 21-23.

[3]A. T. Robertson and W. H. Davis, *A New Short Grammar of the Greek Testament for Students Familiar with the Elements of Greek*, 10th ed. (Grand Rapids: Baker, 1931), 306.

[4]See for example James A. Brooks and Carlton L. Winbery, *Syntax of New Testament Greek* (Lanham, MD: University Press of America, 1979), 103-104; H. E. Dana and Julius R. Mantey, *A Manual Grammar of the Greek New Testament* (New York: Macmillan, 1927), 165-68; Maximilian Zerwick, *Biblical Greek Illustrated by Examples*, trans. Joseph Smith, Scripta Pontificii Instituti Bibilici, vol. 114 (Rome: Editrice Pontificio Istituto Biblici, 1963), 100.

[5]Daniel B. Wallace, *Greek Grammar beyond the Basics: An Exegetical Syntax of the New Testament* (Grand Rapids: Zondervan Publishing House, 1996), 445.

acknowledges that the moods make no assertion about reality.[6]

Both the division of moods (or more accurately, sentence types) and the notion of factualness go back as least as far as the Stoics. Sextus Empiricus (late second-century AD) states,

> the Stoics maintained that truth and falsity exist in the "expression." And they say that "expression" is "that which subsists in conformity with a rational presentation," and that a rational presentation is one in which it is possible to establish by reason the presented object. And of expressions they term some "defective," others "self-complete"; the defective we may now pass over, but of the self-complete there are, as they assert, several varieties; for in fact they call some "jussive," ... others "declaratory," ... and others "interrogations," ... And some, too, are named by them "imprecatory," ... And they also term some of the self-complete expressions "propositions," in uttering which we either speak the truth or lie. ... (*Against the Logicians* 2.70-75).

Although mood is not the main concern of this work, it will need to be discussed indirectly in chapter 3 as this work seeks to discover the semantic meaning of the imperative mood. In order to understand the imperative one must understand it in relationship to the other moods. For the purposes here, a helpful definition of mood is as follows, "*Mood is the morphological feature of a verb that a speaker uses to **portray** his or her affirmation as to the certainty of the verbal action or state (whether an actuality or potentiality)*."[7]

---

[6]*Idioms of the Greek New Testament*, 2d ed. Biblical Languages: Greek, vol. 2, (Sheffield: JSOT, 1994), 50.

[7]Wallace, *Exegetical Syntax*, 445.

Appendix 3

Semantic and Pragmatic Distinction:
A Brief Evaluation
of a Recent Approach

In the mid-1990s, Mari Olsen completed a Ph.D. dissertation at Northwestern University on verbal aspect. She made a distinction between semantic and pragmatics similar to that which is followed here. However, certain significant differences are apparent. This dissertation was published as *A Semantic and Pragmatic Model of Lexical and Grammatical Aspect.*[1] This approach has value and has influenced others in their study of verbal aspect. Most recently, Constantine R. Campbell, in two volumes in same series in which the present volume appears, has used aspects of Olsen's work as an important part of his own.[2] Because our study is on the imperative mood, a grammatical topic, it is worthwhile to evaluate Olsen's theory. Olsen's distinction between semantics and pragmatics is based on the philosopher Paul Grice's notion of *cancelability* (and its contrasting or opposite principle, *redundancy*). This notion was briefly introduced by Paul Grice in his influential William James Lecture series given at Harvard University in1967.[3] For Olsen, semantic meaning "cannot be cancelable without contradiction nor reinforced without redundancy."[4] For a basic description of this principle, Olsen's own lexical example *plod* will be considered.[5] To determine whether the semantic

---

[1](New York and London: Garland Publishing, 1997).

[2]*Verbal Aspect, the Indicative Mood, and Narrative: Soundings in the Greek New Testament*, Studies in Biblical Greek, ed. D. A. Carson, vol. 13 (New York: Peter Lang, 2007) and *Verbal Aspect and Non-Indicative Verbs: Further Soundings in the Greek New Testament*, Studies in Biblical Greek, ed. D. A. Carson, vol. 15 (New York: Peter Lang, 2008).

[3]Published as "Logic and Conversation," in *Syntax and Semantics,* vol. 3, *Speech Acts*, ed. P. Cole and J. Morgan (New York: Academic Press, 1975), 57. It is explained further in another paper from the same lecture series, "Further Notes on Logic and Conversation," in *Syntax and Semantics,* vol. 9, *Pragmatics*, ed. P. Cole (New York: Academic Press, 1978), 115-18. It seems that only the former work was used by Olsen (see her bibliography).

[4]Olsen, *Semantic and Pragmatic Model*, 17.

[5]Ibid.

meaning of *plod* includes the meanings *slow* and *tired*, the following sentences may be considered:

Cancelable?:	Elsie plodded along, but not slowly
Reinforcement?:	Elsie plodded along, slowly
Cancelable?:	Elsie plodded along, although she wasn't tired
Reinforcement?:	Elsie plodded along; she was very tired

The meaning *slow* is part of Olsen's understanding of the semantic meaning of *plod*. The first sentence is nonsensical because the second clause contradicts or cancels the meaning of the first clause. However, concerning *tired*, both sentences are acceptable. Therefore, its presence in clause two neither cancels the first clause nor is redundant. However, since in a specific context the meaning of *plod* may include the notion of *tired*, this is a (pragmatic) conversational implicature of *slow*.

This procedure seems helpful for lexical semantic determination. However, can it effectively be used with grammatical structures? Olsen thinks so. First, however, Olsen describes the semantics and pragmatics of lexical aspect (often labeled *Aktionsart*) by assuming a privative system (in contrast to an equipollent system) and associating semantic uncancelable meaning with unmarkedness and cancelable (pragmatic) conversational implicatures with markedness.[6] For example, the verb *run* includes inherent features such as durative (+durative) and dynamic (+dynamic). These are semantic because they cannot be canceled without contradiction or reinforced without redundancy. However, the feature of telicity is a pragmatic implicature because it is cancelable and may be redundant. For example, "Carl Lewis ran" is a good sentence but does not comment on the end of the activity. However, the sentence, "Carl Lewis ran a mile" includes telicity but not in a cancelable or redundant manner. Therefore, the feature telicity is a pragmatic implicature (in this case, the goal of the verb) which is dependent upon the context.[7] Lexical aspect shares common properties with both lexical semantics and grammatical aspect. In addition to the study in lexical aspect in its own right, it seems to serve in a transitional manner to the

---

[6]Ibid., 19-22, 25-57.
[7]Ibid., 19-22.

study of grammatical aspect.

Once a description of lexical aspect is concluded, Olsen identifies distinguishing features of grammatical aspect.[8] Grammatical aspect is closely associated with lexical aspect and tense and is also part of a privative system with two possible grammatical aspects. Basically, the system maintains a two-part *event time* (the time when a situation holds or develops), nucleus and coda. Grammatical aspect presents the manner from which the situation is viewed. If the situation is viewed from the nucleus (i.e., event time intersects the time of reference at the nucleus; internal view), the imperfective is realized. If the situation is viewed from the coda (i.e., event time intersect the time of reference at the coda; external view), the perfective is realized.

This is not the place to critique the method of Olsen in any detail, and I am confident that the description here is insufficient to do her theory justice (there are many important aspects of her theory that have not been included). Her work should be consulted for a more thorough description. However, enough has been described to demonstrate the differences between her method and that described in this work. First, it is fair to say that Olsen has influenced this work and her approach provides a feasible explanation the data for verbal aspect. This is to be commended. However, an explicit goal of the present work is to maintain as much as possible a cognitive perspective. Although Olsen mentions and adheres to Grice's "cooperative principle," there are reasons to view her approach as *psychologically unreal*. First, as discussed in chapter 1, Grice's work, including the cooperative principle, was found lacking in describing the communication process. This should give one reason for caution. Second, just because something adequately explains the data does not mean it is the *best* explanation of the data. It is not my purpose here to determine whether Olsen's approach better accounts for the phenomenon of verbal aspect than others; however, it does not seem ideal for the purposes of this work. Third, the notions of cancelability and reinforcement seem to be too precise for grammatical work which examines data that has undergone significant change and is continually in this process. Also, various stylistic, dialectic, and other geographical and temporal influences seem to weaken certainty for such notions. It is difficult to prove whether a precise distinction such as cancelable and uncancelable can be made. However, given the process of language, such a contrast seems unlikely.

---

[8]Ibid., 59-116.

Fourth, although this method seems to work well for lexical analysis, the differences between lexical and grammatical work are significant. It seems much more difficult to examine and account for grammatical than lexical features. Nevertheless, Olsen's approach has accounted for her complex grammatical data.[9] However, even if this is proven to be the best manner in order to account for the data, its application to other areas of grammar cannot be assumed.

For these reasons this work has chosen not to utilize Olsen's method. The notion of semantic and pragmatic meanings in this work is not *uncancelable/redundant* and *cancelable/non-redundant*. In contrast, the less precise and more flexible terminology is preferred: *inherent* (semantic) and *non-inherent* (pragmatic) contextually derived meanings.[10] It seems that there may be pragmatic contextual effects which cancel out aspects of semantic meaning. It would be difficult to sustain the uncancelable distinction without constructing an artificial classification system.

Finally, some may not see a significant difference between Olsen and the method used in this study. They are similar. However, the constraint of this work's cognitive approach demands that one considers the likelihood of such an absolute distinction of meaning. The result of this emphasis demands that this approach not be adopted here.

---

[9]Ibid.

[10]See Stephen H. Levinsohn, *Discourse Features of New Testament Greek: A Coursebook on the Information Structure of New Testament Greek*, 2d ed. (Dallas: SIL International, 2000), ix. However, Levinsohn does not use the term *non-inherent*.

Appendix 4

Synoptic Mood Parallels

In chapter 3 of this work an analysis of synoptic parallels was undertaken in order to shed potential light upon the semantic meaning of the imperative mood. This work's interest was to look at parallel passages in the synoptics and to note differences in mood use. It was suggested that in this manner one might observe patterns of purpose for the use of imperative instead of other moods. The caution noted then is worth repeating: it is impossible to know with any certainty what was in the minds of the authors; therefore, any conclusions must be considered with this in mind. One cannot really expect to gain revolutionary insights from this process; however, this work was able to confirm and refine its previous observations about the mood's meaning.

The purpose of this appendix is to include a complete listing of the raw data from synoptic parallels. This appendix records the analysis not mentioned in the paper where parallel moods occurred. This data appears here because to some extent the choice of what sections, verses, and words are parallel is subjective. This appendix (with the discussion in chapter 3) gives the reader access to all data considered in the analysis. The only data duplicated are examples where two gospels agree with an imperative mood against another. The reason these are recorded is that although this work is only concerned with mood differences in the analysis, these examples also include a parallel imperative between two of the three. Therefore, they are included here in order to present the reader with all parallels. Any parallels which are between two gospels will be included in the section for those two gospels only.[1] In addition, a letter following a verse reference (e.g., Mark 6:10a; Luke 9:4b, etc.) refers to the imperative (or parallel) in the verse ("a" is the first, "b" is second, etc.).[2] Again, it must be

---

[1] For example, if Matthew and Mark agree against Luke, the example will be listed with Matthew and Mark parallel, not the section for all three.

[2] This is made explicit here because it may be confused with the normal convention of labeling the first part of a verse with "a," the second, "b," etc. In this work's description, the first imperative (or parallel) may appear late in a verse.

emphasized that this appendix lists parallels involving the imperative mood only. Thus, it will not include a comprehensive list of parallel passages.

The definition of "parallel" as described in chapter 3 is worth repeating. By "parallel" this work means verbs having the same mood in a parallel statement in a parallel section (the same pericope recorded in different gospels). Not every word or phrase in parallel passages must necessarily be exact. However, it must be clear that the clause in which the verb(s) occurs is conceptually parallel (compare the exact parallels in Mark 1:3 ‖ Matt 3:3 ‖ Luke 3:4 [however, note the slight difference at the end of these verses (αὐτοῦ) with Isa 40:3 (LXX) from which this is a quote: τοῦ θεοῦ ἡμῶν]) with conceptual parallels with significantly different wording in Mark 1:15 ‖ Matt 4:17 (although the imperative is the same [note Mark has an additional unparalleled imperative; however, it is related to the paralleled imperative by καί]). A different lexeme may occur for the parallel verbs on occasion. In the presentation below, for the sake for thoroughness, lexeme differences will be noted. However, a different lexical choice using the same mood does not contribute to the morphological analysis. In other words, this work is only concerned with mood choice, not lexeme choice. Parallels with identical moods are not important for the purposes here since it can determine little if anything from them beyond observing all appropriate authors felt this mood was best suited for the communicative purpose or that one or more author felt comfortable with the expression of source used.[3] The following symbols will be used to indicate parallel and contrasting moods between verses (in parallel sections) respectively, ‖ and ∦.

---

[3]This appendix could not have been undertaken without Kurt Aland, ed., *Synopsis of the Four Gospels: Greek-English Edition of the Synopsis Quattuor Evangeliorum*, 10th ed. (Stuttgart: German Bible Society, 1993). However, some passages presented as parallel (in the sense of pericopes, not verbs) by Aland were not so considered here. If the content of Aland's parallels clearly demonstrates that there was no literary dependence nor a common source, it was not treated as parallel. This is clearly the case with the infancy narratives and genealogies in Matthew (chapters 1–2) and Luke (chapters 1–2; 3:23-38) which are printed in parallel columns in Aland. However, if there was even a remote chance of a relationship, the passages are considered parallel (e.g., the Sermons in Matthew 5–7 and roughly Luke 6). In most cases, when the parallel is remote, little conceptual parallels with verbs (as defined above) occur.

Parallels between All Three Gospels:

Mark 1:3 || Matt 3:3 || Luke 3:4[4] (2 impvs; also in Isa 40:3 LXX of which this
  is a quote)

1:41 || 8:3 || 5:13

1:44 || 8:4 || 5:14 (2 impvs are parallel between all three; However four are
  parallel between Matthew and Mark; Luke has only the last two [final
  impv–variants of the same form: Mark and Luke: προσένεγκε; Matt:
  προσένεγκον]; the difference between Luke and the others is one of mood
  [see below])

2:9 || 9:5 || 5:3 (This is a complex example; Mark includes six imperative forms
  and Matthew and Luke include four imperatives and a participle. Thus, in
  places the three are parallel, in other places two agree against another; this
  example is discussed in chapter 3. To avoid unnecessary detail here, no
  attempt is made to label all the imperatives [e.g., a, b, c, etc.] as has been
  done elsewhere).

2:14 || 9:9 || 5:27

3:5 || 12:13 || 6:10

4:9 || 13:9 || 8:8

6:10a (present) || 10:11a (aorist) || Luke 9:4a (present)[5]

6:11 || 10:14 || 9:5 (Luke has a different lexeme)

6:36 || 14:15 || 9:12

6:37 || 14:16 || 9:13

8:15 || 16:6 || 12:1 (Mark and Matt have two impvs, the second are different
  lexemes (Mark: ὁρᾶτε, βλέπετε; Matt: ὁρᾶτε καὶ προσέχετε); Luke
  includes only one impv, identical to the second of Matthew, προσέχετε;
  there is no significance in the omission by Luke, the twin imperatives in the
  others are somewhat redundant)

8:34 || 16:24 || 9:23 (all have three identical imperatives)

9:7 || 17:5 || 9:35

9:19 || 17:17 || 9:41 (Luke uses a different lexeme)

10:14 || 19:14 || 18:16 (two impvs)

10:19 || 19:19 || 18:20

---

[4]The order of the gospels in the appendix is always as follows: Mark, Matthew, Luke.

[5]Luke 9:4b is an imperative which contrasts with the subjunctive in Mark 6:10b || Matt
10:11b

10:21 || 19:21 || 18:22 (Mark and Matthew have four impvs, Luke does not include the first and the third verb is a related cognate)

10:47-48 || 9:27 and 20:30-31 || 18:38-39 (2 impv; however, only one in Matt 9:27)

10:52 || 9:29 || 18:42 (different lexemes; Matthew has third person)

11:2 || 21:2 || 19:30 (Matthew has a different lexeme)

12:15 || 22:19 || 20:24 (different lexemes)

12:17 || 22:21 || 20:25

12:36 || 22:44 || 20:42 (LXX Ps 110:1)

13:5 || 24:4 || 21:8

13:14 || 24:15-16 || 21:21 (third person imperatives; Mark and Matthew have two parallels of which only one is paralleled in Luke; Luke adds two additional unparalleled imperatives; see further discussion on this passage in the section on the third person imperative in chapter 4)

13:15-16 || 24:17-18 || 17:31 (negative third person aorist imperatives; there are two paralleled by all three and one additional unparalleled in Mark; see further discussion on this passage in the section on the third person imperative in chapter 4)

13:28 || 24:32 || 21:29 (Luke has a different lexeme)

13:29 || 24:33 || 21:31

13:33 || 25:13 || 21:36 (different lexemes [Mark and Luke agree against Matthew]; Mark includes an extra imperative)

14:36 || 26:39 || 22:42a (Matthew has a different lexeme and is in the third person)

14:38b || 26:41b || 22:46

14:65 || 26:68 || 22:64

15:13 || 27:22 || 23:21 (Mark: 2 sg aor act impv; Matt: 3 sg aor pass impv; Luke: 2 sg pres act impv [2x]; for next parallel in context, see below under Mark and Matthew parallels: Mark 15:14 [same form] || Matt 27:23 [same form] ∥ Luke 23:23 [infinitive])

Parallels between Mark and Matthew:

Mark 1:15 || Matt 4:17 (Mark has an additional unparalleled imperative)

1:44 ‖ 8:4 ⫽ Luke 5:14 (4 impvs between Mark and Matthew;
Luke retains two)[6]

2:9 ‖ 9:5 ⫽ Luke 5:3[7]

5:12 ‖ 8:31 (different lexemes; also Luke's record does not include the saying)

6:50 ‖ 14:27 (2 impvs)

7:10 ‖ 15:4 (2 impvs)

7:14 ‖ 15:10 (2 impvs)

7:29 ‖ 15:28 (different person and different lexemes)

8:33 ‖ 16:23

9:22 ‖ 17:15 (different lexemes and different in the pericope)

9:43 ‖ 5:30 (different lexemes and an additional imperative in Matthew)

9:45 ‖ 18:8 (different but related lexemes and an additional imperative in Matthew)

9:47 ‖ 18:9 (same comments as previous)

10:9 ‖ 19:6

10:37 ‖ 20:21 (different lexemes)

11:23 ‖ 21:21b (2 impvs)

13:4 ‖ 24:3 ⫽ Luke 21:7 (different forms of the same parsing: 2 sg aor act impv (Mark: εἰπόν; Matt: εἰπὲ)

13:7 ‖ 24:6 (Matt has an additional imperative unparalleled) ⫽ Luke 21:9

13:9 ‖ 10:17 (different lexemes; Luke does not include this warning in his parallel, 21:12)

13:18 ‖ 24:20 (unparalleled in Luke 21:23)

13:35 ‖ 24:42 (unparalleled in Luke 17:36; the same impv is repeated [unparalleled] in Mark 13:37)

13:42 ‖ 26:46 (no parallel statement in Luke)

14:13a ‖ 26:18 ⫽ Luke 22:8 (Luke does include an imperative. However, this is an additional (unparalleled) imperative (ἐτοιμάσατε). Mark and Matthew's imperative ὑπάγετε is paralleled by Luke with a circumstantial participle of a related verb (πορευθέντες); this is discussed in chapter 3

14:14 ‖ 26:18b ⫽ Luke 22:10 (future, see chapter 3)

---

[6]These three passages are also listed as parallels for all three. This is because two of the imperatives are parallel among all three. However, the other two paralleled between Matthew and Mark are not paralleled in Luke who seems to have changed them.

[7]See the discussion of these verses in the section above, "Parallels between All Three Gospels."

14:22 || 26:26 (Matt has an additional impv; Luke 22:17 includes the parallel imperative (λάβετε) and an additional impv; however the context is different. In Matthew and Mark Jesus is discussing the bread and Luke Jesus is discussing the wine. Luke also includes an unparalleled imperative in 22:19)

14:32 || 26:36 (no parallel in Luke 22:40; however, Luke has an unparalleled imperative [προσεύχεσθε] although the verb occurs in the subjunctive in Matthew and Mark [προσεύξωμαι] in a different unparalleled statement)

14:34 || 26:38 (2 impvs; no parallel statement in Luke 22:40)

14:38a || 26:41a ⫽ Luke 22:46 (Luke has a circumstantial participle with a different lexeme; see chapter 3)

14:44 || 26:48 (Mark 14:44 has an additional unparalleled imperative; there is no parallel statement in Luke 22:47)

15:14 || 27:23 ⫽ Luke 23:23 (Luke has an infinitive, see chapter 3; for previous parallel to this, see above: Mark 15:13 || Matt 27:22 || Luke 23:21 [2x])

15:18 || 27:29 (the imperative form in these passages is the idiom, χαῖρε; it is included here for reasons of thoroughness)

15:30 || 27:40a (Luke 23:35 has no parallel; however, the same imperative occurs in a very similar context in Luke 23:37;[8] Matt 27:40b is contrasted with a participle; see chapter 3)

15:32 || 27:42 (third person; Matthew has an additional unparalleled third person imperative in 27:43; Also, although the third person imperative in Luke 23:35 [σωσάτω] seems best contrasted with the infinitives in Mark 15:31 || Matt 27:42 [σῶσαι]; however, it seem possible that there may be some relationship to the third person imperatives here [καταβάτω]; this may be supported by the parallel of the imperatives (σῶσον) and the imperative (κατάβηθι) ⫽ participle (καταβάς) in Matt 27:40 and Mark 15:30; note the verbal similarities; see chapter 3)

15:36 || 27:49 (Mark is plural; Matthew is singular; no parallel in Luke 23:45)

---

[8]It may be argued that this is a parallel; however, the placement of the imperatives within the chronology of the pericope is quite different (the spectators say it in Matthew and Mark but the soldiers say it in Luke) and thus will not be considered parallel here.

16:6 ‖ 28:5-6⁹ (2 imperatives; the first set of parallels is negated and has different lexemes; the second set involves recognized idioms: Mark: ἴδε [recognized idiom]; Matthew: δεῦτε ἴδετε [first is a recognized idiom; second is an imperative with the same root as the idiom in Mark])

16:7b ‖ 28:7b (16:7a is an imperative parallel with a participle. This passage was discussed in chapter 3.)

Parallels between Mark and Luke:

Mark 1:25 ‖ Luke 4:35

2:9 ‖ 5:3 ‖ Matt 9:5¹⁰

3:3 ‖ 6:8 (there is no parallel verb in the Matthew's pericope; also, Luke includes an additional imperative [στῆθι])

4:24 ‖ 8:18 (the second half of Matthew 7:2 seems parallel to the second half Mark 4:24; however, the first half of which contains the imperative in Mark is quite different and thus not a potential parallel [also the context of Matthew 7 is quite different than Mark 4:21-25])

5:19 ‖ 8:39 (different lexemes)

5:34, ‖ 8:48 (different lexemes; Mark includes an additional imperative without parallel clause in Luke)

5:36 ‖ 8:50 (2 impvs; the latter has different tense)

5:41 ‖ 8:54 (Mark includes an Aramaic transliterated imperative)

9:39 ‖ 9:50

11:29 ‖ 20:3 (different lexemes) ‖ Matt 21:24

12:38 ‖ 20:46 (different lexemes; although there is a somewhat parallel pericope in Matt 23:1-36; this statement does not seem paralleled; instead there is a lengthy discourse [23:2-5a which includes an unparalleled imperative in 23:3] before resuming where Mark and Luke pick up after the imperative)

---

⁹This and the following parallel is questionable. The resurrection accounts differ so much that one questions if any literary relationship exists. There seems like a possible connection between Matthew and Mark but Luke's material is so different it will not be considered. In addition, the imperative in Mark 16:15 is not considered since the passage is most likely not original.

¹⁰See these discussion of these verses in the section above, "Parallels between All Three Gospels."

13:11 ‖ 21:14 (different lexemes; although this seems parallel [conceptually], the verbal contexts are quite distinct)
14:13b ‖ 22:10 (no parallel statement in Matt 24:18)
14 15 ‖ 22:12 (no parallel statement in Matt 26:18)

Parallels between Matthew and Luke:

Matt 3:8 ‖ Luke 3:8 (3 impvs)
4:3 ‖ 4:3
4:6 ‖ 4:9
5:12 ‖ 6:23 (2 impvs–the second are different lexemes)
5:25 ‖ 12:58 (different lexemes)
5:42 (aorist) ‖ 6:30 (present)
5:44 ‖ 6:27 [and one of three impvs in 6:37] (2 impvs–second have different lexemes; also Luke 6:28 includes two imperatives, including προσεύχεσθε which occurs in Matt 5:44)
6:7-15 ‖ 11:1-4 (the Lord's prayer includes four parallel imperatives [one verb however, δίδωμι, occurs in the aorist in Matt and in the present in Luke–the present of this verb only occurs in Luke (6:30, 38; 11:3)] and there are two in Matthew without parallel clauses in Luke)
6:19-20 ‖ 12:33 (2 impvs with different lexemes but the parallel is weak)
6:25-34 ‖ 12:22-32 (4 impvs–two have different lexemes plus one in Luke is unparalleled in Matt; Matt 6:31, 34 ‖ Luke 12:29, 32 is noted in chapter 3)
7:1 ‖ 6:37 (Luke includes two unparalleled verbs)
7:4-5 ‖ 6:42 (2 impvs)
7:7 ‖ 11:9 (3 impvs)
7:12 ‖ 6:31
7:23 ‖ 13:27 (different lexemes)
8:9 ‖ 7:8 (3 impvs)
8:21-22 ‖ 9:59-60 (3 impvs; Luke includes one more in v. 60 and a repeated imperative in v. 61 in sayings not paralleled in Matt)
9:5 ‖ 5:3 ‖ Mark 2:9[11]

---

[11]See these discussion of these verses in the section above, "Parallels between All Three Gospels."

9:24 || 8:52 (different lexemes) ∦ Mark 5:39

9:38 || 10:2

10:7 || 10:11b (different lexemes)

10:8 || 10:9 (2 impvs, one with different lexemes; Matt has three additional impvs; the previous two examples are questionable parallels: Matthew's pericope is about the sending of the twelve and Luke's is about the sending of the seventy [also details are ordered differently]; nevertheless, it is possible, similar instructions were given to both groups; note in addition to those mentioned previously, two imperatives in Luke (10:7, 8) are in unparalleled statements in Matthew; see also discussions of 10:9-10a ∦ 10:4 and 10:14 ∦ 10:10-11a in chapter 3)

10:12 || 10:5 (different lexemes)

10:28 || 12:5 (different aspect; Luke repeats the imperative at the end of the clause)

10:31 || 12:7

11:4 || 7:22

14:18 || 9:14 ∦ Mark 6:36 (direct discourse; different lexemes; parallel in Mark 6:36 has the indicative in narrative; see discussion of direct speech and narrative in chapter 3)

17:20 || 17:6 (different lexemes; Luke has an additional imperative)

18:15 || 17:3 (this is a questionable parallel; Matthew includes two imperatives and Luke three: the first Lukan imperative is introductory and the statement is not paralleled in Matthew; the second Lukan imperative is paralleled by the two Matthean imperatives with no lexical agreement; the third Lukan imperative is paralleled by an indicative with a different lexeme; however, the two statements are very similar in function)

22:9 || 12:21 (two impvs, different lexemes; Luke 12:22 also includes a second similar double imperative construction)

23:26 || 11:41 (different lexemes; weak parallel–the context is similar but the clauses in question are quite different)

24:43 || 12:39 (Aland [section 295] also sees a potential parallel between Matt 24:43 and Luke 21:34; however content details are quite different [in addition, the verbs are also different])

24:44 || 12:40

25:28 ‖ 19:24 (2 impvs)[12]

26:52 ‖ 22:51 (this parallel is rather weak. Matthew's ἀπόστρεψον is within a detailed statement and Luke's ἐᾶτε is within a rather broad statement [ἐᾶτε ἕως τούτου, "no more of this"] which may or may not include the detail in Matthew. Nevertheless, it is included here as a possible parallel [as imperatives appearing in similar areas within two similar statements describing the same event])

---

[12]Although the accounts in Matt 25:14-30 and Luke 19:11-27 are very similar, there are significant differences. Luke 19:13 includes an imperative in an unparalleled saying. Also, The final verses of this pericope each contain imperatives (Matt 1; Luke 2x). However, Matt 25:30 and Luke 19:27 contain no parallel material. This may cause one to question whether the two accounts are parallel at all. However, the imperatives in Matt 25:28 and Luke 19:24 seem clearly parallel. Also, discussed in chapter 3 with a similar note, the imperatives in Luke 19:17, 19 seem paralleled with future indicatives in Matthew 25:21, 23. Imperatives in Matthew 25:21, 23 are in unparalleled statements.

Appendix 5

The Imperative + καί + Future Indicative Construction:
Examples in the New Testament

Chapter 4 of this work suggested that although the classification of *conditional* should not be used in contrast to labels like *command*, there are instances at the sentence level where the imperative is the main verb of the protasis of a conditional-like sentence. It was stressed that the imperative was important in its own right and is not merely a substitute for more explicit conditional sentences.[1]

It was suggested that when a sentence met the following conditions, it should be interpreted as conditional while taking into account its force as an imperative:

1. *Imperative + καί (clausal conjunction[2]) + future indicative* structure[3]
2. With the exception of parenthetical clauses,[4] there are no intervening finite verbs between the imperative(s) and the future[5]
3. Neither verb is in a dependent clause (dependent upon one or the other or upon any verb).[6]

---

[1]As was evident in chapter 4, the work of Daniel B. Wallace is foundational for this study of conditional imperatives, see " 'Οργίζεσθε in Ephesians 4:26: Command or Condition?" *Criswell Theological Review* 3 (1989): 353-72; and, *Greek Grammar beyond the Basics: An Exegetical Syntax of the New Testament* (Grand Rapids: Zondervan Publishing House, 1996), 489-92.

[2]Conjunctions joining words or phrases within a clause are permitted (see Matt 6:33). In this section, καί will always refer to the clausal coordinating conjunction.

[3]More than one imperative can occur but both must be conditional and provide conditions for the same future verb in the apodosis (see Acts 9:6 and Eph 5:14).

[4]In both numbers two and four, parenthetical clauses provide an exception to the rule. This is because such clauses do not carry the argument further; rather, they are functionally inserted within the sentence.

[5]Participles can occur between the verbs (see Eph 5:14).

[6]However, the verbs in the clauses must have some sememic connection permitting a protasis/apodosis relationship. This non-structural element is not included in the requirements

4   With the exception of a post-positive conjunction in the first position after a clause initial imperative and conjunctions setting off parenthetical clauses, *καί* is the only clausal conjunction which can occur between the imperative and future verb(s). The conjunction is a required element

5   Neither of the verbs are already embedded in a conditional clause.

Sixty-three instances have been identified (parallels are only counted once)[7] where these requirements are met. The purpose of this appendix is to list them all and offer brief comments where necessary. Below is a list of all those passages which fit the criteria.[8] The conditional nuance is clearly evident in the vast majority of these examples. Admittedly, many are not normally considered conditional. However, as noted in chapter 4, this is because the traditional model of imperative classification implies that one must choose between command, request, condition, etc. Thus, unless the conditional element is strong, it is likely the interpreter would choose another classification. The approach here does not demand that one make a choice.

Matt 6:33   **ζητεῖτε** δὲ πρῶτον τὴν βασιλείαν [τοῦ θεοῦ] καὶ τὴν δικαιοσύνην αὐτοῦ, <u>καὶ</u> ταῦτα πάντα **προστεθήσεται** ὑμῖν.

But **seek** first the kingdom [of God] and his righteousness, <u>and</u> all this **will be given** to you (But **if you seek** first [and do so] the kingdom [of God] and his righteousness ...)

‖ Luke 12:31   πλὴν **ζητεῖτε** τὴν βασιλείαν αὐτοῦ, <u>καὶ</u> ταῦτα **προστεθήσεται** ὑμῖν

---

because it determines beforehand the meaning and relationship of the clauses (i.e., it is an observation about meaning and not structural). However, it is this work's contention that when all structural elements are present, this sememic relationship will exist. In fact, the relationship will be demanded.

[7]Mark 10:21 (3) ‖ Luke 18:22 (only 2); Mark 11:2 ‖ Matt 21:2; Matt 6:33 ‖ Luke 12:31; Matt 7:5 ‖ Luke 6:42; Matt 7:7‖ Luke 11:9. Also, imperatives are being counted. Therefore, if more than one imperative occurs with only one future in the apodosis, these will each be counted (e.g., Matt 11:29 [2]; 2 Cor 13:11 [5]).

[8]Verses and/or comments in parentheses do not fit the criteria but are included to present a more complete picture.

| Matt 7:5 | ὑποκριτά, **ἔκβαλε** πρῶτον ἐκ τοῦ ὀφθαλμοῦ σοῦ τὴν δοκόν, <u>καὶ</u> τότε **διαβλέψεις** ἐκβαλεῖν τὸ κάρφος ἐκ τοῦ ὀφθαλμοῦ τοῦ ἀδελφοῦ σου |

Hypocrite, **take out** first the beam of wood from your eye, <u>and</u> then **you will see clearly** to take out the splinter out of the eye of your brother (Hypocrite, **if you take out** first [and do so] the beam of wood from your eye …)

|| Luke 6:42   ὑποκριτά, **ἔκβαλε** πρῶτον τὴν δοκὸν ἐκ τοῦ ὀφθαλμοῦ σου, <u>καὶ</u> τότε **διαβλέψεις** τὸ κάρφος τὸ ἐν τῷ ὀφθαλμῷ τοῦ ἀδελφοῦ σου ἐκβαλεῖν

(3) Matt 7:7   **Αἰτεῖτε** <u>καὶ</u> **δοθήσεται** ὑμῖν, **ζητεῖτε** <u>καὶ</u> **εὑρήσετε**, **κρούετε** <u>καὶ</u> **ἀνοιγήσεται** ὑμῖν

Ask <u>and</u> it **will be given** to you, **seek** <u>and</u> you **will find**, **knock** <u>and</u> it **will be opened** to you (**If you ask** [and do so], it will be given to you, **if you seek** [and do so], you will find, **if you knock** [and do so], it will be opened to you)

|| (3) Luke 11:9   Κἀγὼ ὑμῖν λέγω, **αἰτεῖτε** <u>καὶ</u> **δοθήσεται** ὑμῖν, **ζητεῖτε** <u>καὶ</u> **εὑρήσετε**, **κρούετε** <u>καὶ</u> **ἀνοιγήσεται** ὑμῖν

Matt 8:8   καὶ ἀποκριθεὶς ὁ ἑκατόνταρχος ἔφη· κύριε, οὐκ εἰμὶ ἱκανὸς ἵνα μου ὑπὸ τὴν στέγην εἰσέλθῃς, ἀλλὰ μόνον **εἰπὲ** λόγῳ, <u>καὶ</u> **ἰαθήσεται** ὁ παῖς μου

And the centurion answered [and] said, "Lord, I am not worthy that you might enter my home [lit. under my roof], but only **say** the word, <u>and</u> my servant **will be healed** (… , but **if you would** only **say** the word [and do so][9])

(|| in Luke 7:7 includes the third person imperative (ἰαθήτω) instead of the future.)[10]

---

[9]It would probably be better to include "please" (and please do so) to emphasize the lightened forced of the centurion's request.

[10]Verses and/or comments in parentheses do not fit the criteria but are included to present

Matt 9:18   ... ἰδοὺ ἄρχων εἷς ἐλθὼν προσεκύνει αὐτῷ λέγων ὅτι ἡ
              θυγάτηρ μου ἄρτι ἐτελεύτησεν· ἀλλὰ ἐλθὼν **ἐπίθες** τὴν
              χεῖρά σου ἐπ᾽ αὐτήν, <u>καὶ</u> **ζήσεται**

              ... behold a ruler came and bowed down before him saying,
              my daughter just died but come and **place** your hand on her
              <u>and</u> she **will be saved** (... **if you** come[11] and **place** your hand
              on her [and do so][12] ...)

(||s in Mark 5:23 there are two subjunctives [no imperative or future indicative]
and there is no request recorded by the official in Luke 8:40-42)

(2) Matt 11:29 **ἄρατε** τὸν ζυγόν μου ἐφ᾽ ὑμᾶς καὶ **μάθετε** ἀπ᾽ ἐμοῦ, ὅτι
              πραΰς εἰμι καὶ ταπεινὸς τῇ καρδίᾳ, <u>καὶ</u> **εὑρήσετε**
              ἀνάπαυσιν ταῖς ψυχαῖς ὑμῶν[13]
              Take my yoke upon you and **learn** from me, because I am
              gentle and humble in heart, <u>and</u> **you will find** rest for your
              souls (yourselves) (**If you take** my yoke upon you [and do so]
              and **if you learn** [and do so] from me ...)

(2) Matt 17:27 ἵνα δὲ μὴ σκανδαλίσωμεν αὐτούς, πορευθεὶς εἰς
              θάλασσαν **βάλε** ἄγκιστρον καὶ τὸν ἀναβάντα πρῶτον
              ἰχθὺν **ἆρον**, <u>καὶ</u> ἀνοίξας τὸ στόμα αὐτοῦ **εὑρήσεις**
              στατῆρα ...
              but lest we offend them, go to the sea and **cast** in a fishhook
              and **take up** the first fish, <u>and</u> when it opens [opening] its
              mouth, **you will find** a stater ...
              (... go to the sea and **if you cast** [and do so] in a fish hook and
              if you take up [and do so] the first fish ...)

---

a more complete picture of what is taking place.
    [11]The related attendant circumstance participle also seems to take the conditional nuance.
    [12]See the note on Matt 8:8.
    [13]Note the intervening explanatory ὅτι clause with finite verb. Since this clause is modifying
principal elements and not furthering the discourse (thus parenthetical), it does not affect
structural requirements.

Matt 18:26   πεσὼν οὖν ὁ δοῦλος προσεκύνει αὐτῷ λέγων·
μακροθύμησον ἐπ' ἐμοί, <u>καὶ</u> πάντα **ἀποδώσω** σοι
Therefore, falling down, the slave bowed down before him
saying, "**be patient** with me <u>and</u> **I will repay** everything to
you" (... "**if you are patient** [and do so][14] ...)

Matt 18:29   πεσὼν οὖν ὁ σύνδουλος αὐτοῦ παρεκάλει αὐτὸν λέγων·
μακροθύμησον ἐπ' ἐμοί, <u>καὶ</u> **ἀποδώσω** σοι
Therefore, falling down, the fellow-slave appealed to him
saying, "**be patient** with me <u>and</u> **I will repay you**" (... "**if you
are patient** [and do so][15] ...")

Matt 21:2 see ‖ Mark 11: 2 (Luke 19:30 is also ‖)

Matt 27:42   **καταβάτω** νῦν ἀπὸ τοῦ σταυροῦ <u>καὶ</u> **πιστεύσομεν** ἐπ'
αὐτόν
let him now come down from the cross <u>and</u> **we will believe** in
him (**if he comes down** from the cross [and do so],[16] we will
believe in him)[17]

Mark 6:22   ... εἶπεν ὁ βασιλεὺς τῷ κορασίῳ· **αἴτησόν** με ὃ ἐὰν
θέλῃς, <u>καὶ</u> **δώσω** σοι[18]
... the king said to the girl, "**ask** of me whatever you may
desire, wish, <u>and</u> **I will give** it to you" (... "**if you ask** [and do
so] ...")

---

[14]See note on Matt 8:8.

[15]See note on Matt 8:8.

[16]Possibly better: "we challenge him to do so." The third person imperative has a weaker
force than if this was directed to Jesus in the second person. Nevertheless, it seems to be a
challenge to Jesus. However, it may not be limited to this. In fact, it seems most probable as a
discussion between those watching at the cross.

[17]It must also be noted that it is likely that this is an insincere challenge—the speakers did
not expect Jesus to come down from the cross. Nevertheless, the rhetorical nature of this
imperative does not nullify the manner in which the speakers wished to express themselves.

[18]Note the intervening dependent clause with a finite verb. However, this clause is a
regression, giving detail about the imperative. It does not affect the structural rules.

(3) Mark 10:21 ὁ δὲ ᾿Ιησοῦς ... εἶπεν αὐτῷ· ἕν σε ὑστερεῖ· **ὕπαγε**, ὅσα ἔχεις **πώλησον** καὶ **δὸς** [τοῖς] πτωχοῖς, <u>καὶ</u> **ἕξεις** θησαυρὸν ἐν οὐρανῷ ...

But Jesus ... said to him, "there is one thing you lack, **go**, as much as you have **sell**, and **give** [it] to the poor, <u>and</u> **you will have** treasure in heaven ..." ("... **if you go** [and do so], ... **if you sell** [and do so], and **if you give** [and do so] to the poor ...")

|| Luke 18:22 ἀκούσας δὲ ὁ ᾿Ιησοῦς εἶπεν αὐτῷ· ἔτι ἕν σοι λείπει· πάντα ὅσα ἔχεις **πώλησον** καὶ **διάδος** πτωχοῖς, <u>καὶ</u> **ἕξεις** θησαυρὸν ἐν [τοῖς] οὐρανοῖς, καὶ δεῦρο ἀκολούθει μοι

Note Luke omits the first imperative from Mark and a related final imperative

(|| Matt 19:21 is within a conditional clause and thus does not meet the requirements).

Mark 11:2 καὶ λέγει αὐτοῖς· **ὑπάγετε** εἰς τὴν κώμην τὴν κατέναντι ὑμῶν, <u>καὶ</u> εὐθὺς εἰσπορευόμενοι εἰς αὐτὴν **εὑρήσετε** πῶλον δεδεμένον ...

and he said to them, "**go** into the village before you <u>and</u> immediately when you enter it, **you will find** a young donkey tied up [there]..."

(... "**if you go** into the village before you [and do so] ...")

|| Matt 21:2 λέγων αὐτοῖς· **πορεύεσθε** εἰς τὴν κώμην τὴν κατέναντι ὑμῶν, <u>καὶ</u> εὐθέως **εὑρήσετε** ὄνον δεδεμένην καὶ πῶλον μετ᾿ αὐτῆς· λύσαντες ἀγάγετέ μοι

(Note: there is a different imperative verb and no intervening participle as in Mark and Luke (below). It is interesting that the verb in Matthew is πορεύεσθε and the participle in the other two synoptics is the related term, εἰσπορευόμενοι

(‖ Luke 19:30 does not fit the criteria. It does not include καί. This will be discussed below).

Mark 11:24   διὰ τοῦτο λέγω ὑμῖν, πάντα ὅσα προσεύχεσθε καὶ αἰτεῖσθε, **πιστεύετε** ὅτι ἐλάβετε, <u>καὶ</u> **ἔσται** ὑμῖν
Therefore I say to you, "for whatever you pray and ask, **believe** that you have received it <u>and</u> **it will be [done]** for you" ("... **if you believe** [and do so]...")

Mark 11:29   ... **ἀποκρίθητέ** μοι **καὶ ἐρῶ** ὑμῖν ...
... **answer** me <u>and</u> **I will tell** you ... (... **if you answer** me [and do so] ...)

(‖s Matt 21:24 is in a conditional clause and Luke 20:3-4 is quite different with no question)

Mark 14:13   καὶ ἀποστέλλει δύο τῶν μαθητῶν αὐτοῦ καὶ λέγει αὐτοῖς· **ὑπάγετε** εἰς τὴν πόλιν, <u>καὶ</u> **ἀπαντήσει** ὑμῖν ἄνθρωπος κεράμιον ὕδατος βαστάζων ...
And he sent two of his disciples and said to them, "**go** into the city, <u>and</u> a man carrying a water jar **will meet you** ..." (... **if you go** into the city [and do so] ...)

(‖s Matt 26:18 has less detail and this clause is not included; Luke 22:10 does not have an imperative).

(3) Luke 6:35   πλὴν **ἀγαπᾶτε** τοὺς ἐχθροὺς ὑμῶν καὶ **ἀγαθοποιεῖτε** καὶ **δανίζετε** μηδὲν ἀπελπίζοντες· <u>καὶ</u> **ἔσται** ὁ μισθὸς ὑμῶν πολύς, καὶ **ἔσεσθε** υἱοὶ ὑψίστου
But **love** your enemies and **do good** and **lend** expecting in return nothing, <u>and</u> your reward **will be** great and **you will be** sons of the Most High (But **if you love** your enemies [and do so] and **if you do good** [and do so] and **if you lend** expecting in return nothing [and do so] ...)

(‖ Matt 5:44-45, has a different construction)

(2) Luke 6:37-38 Καὶ μὴ κρίνετε, καὶ οὐ μὴ κριθῆτε· καὶ μὴ καταδικάζετε, καὶ οὐ μὴ καταδικασθῆτε. ἀπολύετε, <u>καὶ</u> ἀπολυθήσεσθε· 38 δίδοτε, <u>καὶ</u> δοθήσεται ὑμῖν

And do not judge and do not be judged; and do not condemn and do not be condemned; **forgive <u>and</u> you will be forgiven; give <u>and</u> it will be given** to you... (... **if you forgive** [and do so] ... ; **if you give** [and do so] ...)

This passage begins with two *negative imperative* + *καί* + *negative aorist subjunctive* constructions. The aorist is usually translated as future in the English and it seems identical to the *negative imperative* + *καί* + *negative future indicative.*[19] This may be misleading. I suspect the reason for the subjunctive is to express the negative aorist directive which is very rare in the imperative (never in the second person in the New Testament). Thus, this functions like the imperative. Although some *imperative* + *καί* + *imperative* seem to have a conditional nuance, there are no undisputable examples.[20] Therefore, I suggest that Luke does not wish to imply any conditional element here. The aorists are passive directives. The conditional nuance only occurs with the final construction (as the translation suggests).[21]

---

[19]"And do not judge and you will not be judged; and do not condemn and you will not be condemned." If so translated, it has a conditional nuance (see comments below). This are commonly considered "emphatic negation subjunctives."

[20]Wallace, *Exegetical Syntax*, 489-92.

[21]The main concern of this work is not the subjunctive. The comments here may be uninformed (thus, possibly conditional). Nevertheless, in light of the double negatives, the subjunctives may best be classified as *emphatic negation* (Wallace, *Exegetical Syntax*, 468-69). Such a classification would demand a future-type translation. The problem with this is that with the preceding imperatives, the English suggests the conditional nuance which is being argued as unlikely here. It may be that the problem is with the English translation. It is unable to maintain the emphatic negation nuance without the conditional in this example. It is also possible that this could be a rare *prohibitive* subjunctive with the double negative (it usually is only negated with μή; ibid., 469). This appears to be possible but rare in classical Greek and it appears that there was a tendency for editors to change it to the future (Herbert Weir Smyth, *Greek Grammar*, rev. G. M. Messing [Cambridge, MA: Harvard University Press, 1956], 627). However, there does not appear to be any examples in the New Testament.

(‖Matt 7:1 has first imperative and subj with ἵνα but not the conjunction [Μὴ κρίνετε, ἵνα μὴ κριθῆτε·])

Luke 6:42 see ‖ Matt 7:5

Luke 8:50   ὁ δὲ ’Ιησοῦς ἀκούσας ἀπεκρίθη αὐτῷ· μὴ φοβοῦ,[22] μόνον **πίστευσον, καὶ σωθήσεται**
              But when Jesus heard this, he answered him, "do not be afraid, only **believe, and she will be restored**" (**if you only believe** [and do so] …)

Luke 10:28   εἶπεν δὲ αὐτῷ· ὀρθῶς ἀπεκρίθης· τοῦτο **ποίει καὶ ζήσῃ**
              and he said to him, "you have answered correctly, **do** this **and you will live**" ("… **if you do** this [and do so], you will live")

Luke 11:9 see ‖ Matt 7:7

Luke 12:31 see ‖ Matt 6:33

Luke 14:13-14 ἀλλ’ ὅταν δοχὴν ποιῇς, **κάλει** πτωχούς, ἀναπείρους, χωλούς, τυφλούς· [14] **καὶ** μακάριος **ἔσῃ**, ὅτι οὐκ ἔχουσιν ἀνταποδοῦναί σοι, ἀνταποδοθήσεται γάρ σοι ἐν τῇ ἀναστάσει τῶν δικαίων
              But when you provide a banquet, **ask** the poor, the cripple, the lame, the blind **and you will be** blessed (… **if you ask** the poor [and do so] …")

Luke 18:22 see ‖ Mark 10:21

John 1:39   … **ἔρχεσθε καὶ ὄψεσθε**
              "… **come and you will see**" (**if you come** [and do so] …)

---

[22] Note the first imperative is not part of this construction.

John 2:19   ἀπεκρίθη ᾿Ιησοῦς καὶ εἶπεν αὐτοῖς· **λύσατε** τὸν ναὸν
                τοῦτον <u>καὶ</u> ἐν τρισὶν ἡμέραις **ἐγερῶ** αὐτόν[23]
                Jesus answered and said to them, "**destroy** this temple <u>and</u> in
                three days **I will raise it up** (**if you destroy** this temple [and do
                so] ...)

John 16:24b   **αἰτεῖτε <u>καὶ</u> λήμψεσθε**
                ask <u>and</u> you will receive (**if you ask** [and do so] ...)

John 21:6a   ὁ δὲ εἶπεν αὐτοῖς· **βάλετε** εἰς τὰ δεξιὰ μέρη τοῦ πλοίου
                τὸ δίκτυον, <u>καὶ</u> **εὑρήσετε** ...
                But he said to them, "**throw** the fishing net to the right side of
                the boat <u>and</u> **you will find** [the fish]" (... "**if you throw** the
                fishing net [and do so]...")

(2) Acts 2:38   Πέτρος δὲ πρὸς αὐτούς· **μετανοήσατε,** [φησίν,] καὶ
                βαπτισθήτω ἕκαστος ὑμῶν ἐπὶ τῷ ὀνόματι ᾿Ιησοῦ
                Χριστοῦ εἰς ἄφεσιν τῶν ἁμαρτιῶν ὑμῶν <u>καὶ</u> **λήμψεσθε**
                τὴν δωρεὰν τοῦ ἁγίου πνεύματος
                But Peter [said] the them, "**repent** and [let] each of you **be
                baptized** in the name of Jesus Christ for the forgiveness of
                your sins <u>and</u> **you will receive** the gift of the Holy Spirit" (...
                "**if you repent** [and do so] and if each of you **are baptized** [and
                do so] ...")

---

[23]This passage is interesting on two levels. Jesus purposefully presents the imperative in a manner in which he is misunderstood. He really has no intention or expectation of physical temple destruction or construction which John makes explicit (2:21-22). However, it is unlikely that if those who misunderstood him did actually destroy the actual temple (an absurd and certainly impossible act) that there would be any fulfillment of physical temple reconstruction. Boyer ("A Classification of Imperatives: A Statistical Study," *Grace Theological Journal* 8 [1987]: 39-40) rejects this as an example of a conditional. However, Wallace is correct to note its similarity to Old Testament prophetic "ironic" commands which function as taunts or dares (e.g., Isa 8:9; Amos 4:4) and the rhetorical nature of this statement in context. He also points out the value of the classification when he states, "if λύσατε follows the normal semantic pattern of conditional imperatives, the force is even stronger..." (Wallace, *Exegetical Syntax*, 490-91). By noting the structure in which this statement is constructed, he is able to consider a probable interpretive option that may be rejected otherwise.

There is no reason to exclude this passage from a having one or two conditional elements. We are translating it here as if both imperatives have this nuance. However, it is possible to view the second imperative (βαπτισθήτω) as parenthetical. Although very rare, there seems no reason to view the third person as exempt from the structure (only also in Matt 27:42; Acts 28:28). See the further discussion on this passage in chapter 4.

(2) Acts 9:6   ἀλλὰ **ἀνάστηθι** καὶ **εἴσελθε** εἰς τὴν πόλιν <u>καὶ</u> **λαληθήσεταί** σοι ὅ τί σε δεῖ ποιεῖν
"but **arise** and **enter** the city <u>and</u> it **will be told** to you what you should do … "(but **if you arise** [and do so] and **[if you] enter** [and do so] the city …")

Acts 16:31   οἱ δὲ εἶπαν· **πίστευσον** ἐπὶ τὸν κύριον Ἰησοῦν <u>καὶ</u> **σωθήσῃ** σὺ καὶ ὁ οἶκός σου
And the said, "**believe** in the Lord Jesus <u>and</u> **you will be saved**, you and your household (… **if you believe** [and do so] in the Lord Jesus …")

Acts 22:10   … ὁ δὲ κύριος εἶπεν πρός με· ἀναστὰς **πορεύου** εἰς Δαμασκὸν <u>κἀκεῖ</u> σοι **λαληθήσεται** περὶ πάντων ὧν τέτακταί σοι ποιῆσαι
… and the Lord said to me, "arise and **go** to Damascus <u>and</u> there **it will be told** to you concerning all that was designated for you to do" ("… **if you go** [and do so] …")[24]

Acts 28:28   γνωστὸν οὖν **ἔστω** ὑμῖν ὅτι τοῖς ἔθνεσιν ἀπεστάλη τοῦτο τὸ σωτήριον τοῦ θεοῦ· αὐτοὶ <u>καὶ</u> **ἀκούσονται**
Therefore, **let it be known** to you that this salvation of God was [has been] sent to the nations <u>and</u> **they will listen** (… **if it be known** [and it should] …)

---

[24]Here is another attendant circumstance participle example.

Here again we have a third person (see Matt 27:42 and Acts 28:28). Although the conditional nuance seems weak, there is no reason to reject it here.[25]

Rom 13:3b   ... τὸ ἀγαθὸν **ποίει**, <u>καὶ</u> **ἕξεις** ἔπαινον ἐξ αὐτῆς
            ... **do good** <u>and</u> **you will have** approval from it [the authority]
            (**if you do good** [and do so] ...)

(3) 2 Cor 6:17   διὸ **ἐξέλθατε** ἐκ μέσου αὐτῶν καὶ **ἀφορίσθητε**, λέγει κύριος, καὶ ἀκαθάρτου μὴ **ἅπτεσθε**· <u>κἀγὼ</u> **εἰσδέξομαι** ὑμᾶς[26]
            "Therefore, **come out** from their midst and **be separate**," says the Lord, "and **do not touch** an unclean thing, <u>and</u> **I will welcome you**"
            (... **if you come out** from their midst [and do so] and **be separate** [if you are separate–and do so]" says the Lord, "and **if you do not touch** an unclean thing [and do not do so] ...)

---

[25]This passage is the most questionable of all of the examples. However, because the other 59 examples do seem to have a conditional nuance, it will be considered so here. The burden of proof is upon those who wish to deny the nuance. Although the data is minimal the third person does not seem to effect the nuance. The third person imperative in Acts 2:38 is somewhat debatable but if it is not conditional, it may be explained as parenthetical. However, Matt 27:42 clearly has the conditional nuance. Acts 28:28 is closer to Matt 27:42 than it is to Acts 2:38.

[26]There are three imperatives in this verse. The intervening finite verb does not further the argument so there is no violation of the requirements (thus parenthetical); however, the second imperative is passive and it is difficult to determine whether this should be conditional. Nevertheless, it may be better to leave it translated here without the conditional clause because the conditional nuance is still evident from the first imperative.

(5) 2 Cor 13:11

Λοιπόν, ἀδελφοί, **χαίρετε, καταρτίζεσθε, παρακαλεῖσθε,** τὸ αὐτὸ **φρονεῖτε, εἰρηνεύετε, καὶ** ὁ θεὸς τῆς ἀγάπης καὶ εἰρήνης **ἔσται** μεθ' ὑμῶν

Finally, brethren, **rejoice, be made complete, be comforted, be of one-mind, live peace,** and the God of love and peace **will be** with you (... if[27] you **rejoice, be made complete, be comforted, be of one-mind, live peace** ...)

Gal 6:2

᾿Αλλήλων τὰ βάρη **βαστάζετε** καὶ οὕτως **ἀναπληρώσετε** τὸν νόμον τοῦ Χριστοῦ

Bear one another's burdens and thus **you will fulfill** the law of Christ (**If you bear on another's burdens** [and do so] ...)

Gal 6:4

τὸ δὲ ἔργον ἑαυτοῦ **δοκιμαζέτω** ἕκαστος, καὶ τότε εἰς ἑαυτὸν μόνον τὸ καύχημα **ἕξει** καὶ οὐκ εἰς τὸν ἕτερον[28]

But **let each one examine** his own work, and then **he will have** [reason for] boasting for himself only and not for another (But **if each one examines** his own work [and do so] ...)

(2) Eph 5:14

... **ἔγειρε,** ὁ καθεύδων, καὶ **ἀνάστα** ἐκ τῶν νεκρῶν, καὶ **ἐπιφαύσει** σοι ὁ Χριστός[29]

... **Arise,** one who sleeps, and **awaken** from the dead and Christ **will shine** on you (**If you arise** [and do so], sleeper, and **[if you] awaken** [and do so] ...)

Phil 4:9

... ταῦτα **πράσσετε·** καὶ ὁ θεὸς τῆς εἰρήνης **ἔσται** μεθ' ὑμῶν

... **do/practice** these things and the God of peace **will be** with you (**If you do/practice** these things ...)

---

[27]The initial "if" governs all imperatives. Note again the passives as in 2 Cor 6:17. These may complicate the analysis.

[28]Note the third person imperative.

[29]This passage is significant because it seems to be poetic and it still follows the proposed structure.

Jas 2:18   'Αλλ' ἐρεῖ τις· σὺ πίστιν ἔχεις, κἀγὼ ἔργα ἔχω· **δεῖξόν**
               μοι τὴν πίστιν σου χωρὶς τῶν ἔργων, <u>**κἀγώ**</u> σοι **δείξω**
               ἐκ τῶν ἔργων μου τὴν πίστιν
               But someone will say, "you have faith, and I have works, **show**
               to me your faith without works <u>and</u> I **will show** to you my faith
               by my works" ("… **if you show** me your faith without works
               [and do so] …)[30]

Jas 4:7b   … **ἀντίστητε** δὲ τῷ διαβόλῳ <u>**καὶ**</u> **φεύξεται** ἀφ' ὑμῶν[31]
               … but **resist** the devil <u>and</u> **he will run away** from you (but **if
               you resist** the devil [and do so] …)

Jas 4:8   **ἐγγίσατε** τῷ θεῷ <u>**καὶ**</u> **ἐγγιεῖ** ὑμῖν
               draw near to God <u>and</u> **he will draw near** to you (**if you draw
               near** to God [and do so] …)

Jas 4:10   **ταπεινώθητε** ἐνώπιον κυρίου <u>**καὶ**</u> **ὑψώσει** ὑμᾶς
               be humble before the Lord <u>and</u> **he will exalt** you (**if you are
               humble** before the Lord [and be so] …)

Rev 2:10   … **γίνου** πιστὸς ἄχρι θανάτου, <u>**καὶ**</u> **δώσω** σοι τὸν
               στέφανον τῆς ζωῆς[32]
               "… **be faithful** until death <u>and</u> **I will give** to you the crown of
               life" (**if you are faithful** until death [and do so] …")

Rev 4:1   … **ἀνάβα** ὧδε, <u>**καὶ**</u> **δείξω** σοι ἃ δεῖ γενέσθαι μετὰ ταῦτα
               "… **come up** here, <u>and</u> **I will show** to you what must become
               after these things" ("… **if you come up** here [and do so] …")

---

[30]This one may be a candidate for further discussion. The structure suggests this is a challenge.

[31]Note the previous clause had an imperative (ὑποτάγητε) but this clearly is not related to the future indicative.

[32]Note the present middle/passive imperative.

(2) Rev 10:9   ... λάβε καὶ **κατάφαγε** αὐτό, <u>καὶ</u> **πικρανεῖ** σου τὴν
κοιλίαν, ἀλλ' ἐν τῷ στόματί σου ἔσται γλυκὺ ὡς μέλι
"... **take** and **devour** it, <u>and</u> **he will make it bitter** for you..."
(...**if you take** [it] [and do so] and [**if you**] **devour** it [and do
so] ...")

There are four examples worth noting that violate requirement 5. The
imperative is embedded within an explicit conditional clause. This has been
rejected because the conditional element is already present. Nevertheless, these
passages are worth noting because the conditional element of the imperative
almost seems independent from the clause.

John 15:7   ἐὰν μείνητε ἐν ἐμοὶ καὶ τὰ ῥήματά μου ἐν ὑμῖν μείνῃ,
ὃ ἐὰν θέλητε **αἰτήσασθε**, <u>καὶ</u> **γενήσεται** ὑμῖν
If you remain in me and my word remains in you, **ask**
whatever you desire <u>and</u> **it will done** for you (... **if you ask**
whatever you desire [and do so] ...)[33]

John 16:24   ἕως ἄρτι οὐκ ἠτήσατε οὐδὲν ἐν τῷ ὀνόματί μου·
αἰτεῖτε <u>καὶ</u> **λήμψεσθε**, ἵνα ἡ χαρὰ ὑμῶν ᾖ πεπληρωμένη
Until now you have asked for nothing in my name, **ask** <u>and</u>
you will receive ... (... **if you ask** [and do so] ...)

John 20:15   λέγει αὐτῇ ᾽Ιησοῦς· γύναι, τί κλαίεις; τίνα ζητεῖς;...
λέγει αὐτῷ· κύριε, εἰ σὺ ἐβάστασας αὐτόν, **εἰπέ** μοι ποῦ
ἔθηκας αὐτόν, <u>κἀγὼ</u> αὐτὸν **ἀρῶ**
Jesus said to her, "woman, why do you weep? Whom do you
seek?" ... she said, "sir, if you removed him, **tell** me where
you placed him <u>and</u> **I will take** him away" ("... **if you tell me**
[and do so] ...)[34]

---

[33]Note the subjunctive does not further move the narrative along but is the object of the
imperative. Therefore, this fits the structural requirements.
[34]Note the intervening participle.

Jas 1:5   Εἰ δέ τις ὑμῶν λείπεται σοφίας, **αἰτείτω** παρὰ τοῦ
                 διδόντος θεοῦ πᾶσιν ἁπλῶς καὶ μὴ ὀνειδίζοντος <u>καὶ</u>
                 δοθήσεται αὐτῷ
                 But if anyone lacks wisdom, **let this one ask** of God, the one
                 who gives to all generously and without reproach, <u>and</u> **it will
                 be given** to him (But if anyone lacks wisdom, **if he asks of
                 God** [and do so] …)

There are three passages worth noting which for various reasons besides an
explicit conditional marker do not meet the structural requirements.

Luke 10:35   … καὶ εἶπεν· **ἐπιμελήθητι** αὐτοῦ, <u>καὶ</u> ὅ τι ἂν
                 <u>προσδαπανήσῃς</u> ἐγὼ ἐν τῷ ἐπανέρχεσθαί με **ἀποδώσω**
                 σοι
                 … and he said "**take care** of him, <u>and</u> whatever additional <u>you
                 might spend</u>, when I return **I will repay** to you" (… "if you
                 take care of him [and do so] …")
                 The intervening subjunctive clause seems to carry the
                 argument further and thus this one might need to be removed
                 from the list.

Luke 13:25   "… κύριε, **ἄνοιξον** ἡμῖν, <u>καὶ</u> ἀποκριθεὶς **ἐρεῖ** ὑμῖν…"
                 "… lord, **open up** to us, <u>and</u> answering, **he will say** to you…"
                 ("… if you open up to us [and do so] …")
                 This passage does not fit the structural requirements. The
                 conjunction καί does not join the two imperatives and future.
                 Therefore, it does not include a conditional element.

Luke 19:30   λέγων· **ὑπάγετε** εἰς τὴν κατέναντι κώμην, ἐν ᾗ
                 εἰσπορευόμενοι **εὑρήσετε** πῶλον δεδεμένον, ἐφ' ὃν
                 οὐδεὶς πώποτε ἀνθρώπων ἐκάθισεν, καὶ λύσαντες αὐτὸν
                 ἀγάγετε
                 [he was] saying, "**Go** into the opposite village in which [upon]
                 entering **you will find** a colt ("If you go [and do so] …")

This passage is parallel to Mark 11:2 || Matt 21:2. However, Luke 19:30 does not have the conjunction. Therefore, Luke may be omitting the conditional nuance intentionally.

Bibliography

Aarts, Flor. "Imperative Sentences in English: Semantics and Pragmatics." *Studia Linguistica* 43 (1989): 119-34.

Abbott, Edwin A. *Johannine Grammar*. London: Adam and Charles Black, 1906.

Adams, Douglas Q. *Essential Modern Greek Grammar*. Mineola, NY: Dover Publications, 1987.

Adéwolé, L. O. "The Yorba Imperative." *African Languages and Cultures* 4 (1991): 103-12.

Aeginitou, Violetta. "The Power of Politeness in the Greek EFL Classroom." In *Themes in Greek Linguistics: Papers From the First International Conference on Greek Linguistics, Reading, September 1993*, ed. Irene Philippaki-Warburton, Katerina Nicolaidis, and Maria Sifianou, 297-304. Amsterdam: John Benjamins Publishing Company, 1994.

Agesthialingom, S. "Imperative in Old Tamil." *Indian Linguistics: Journal of the Linguistic Society of India* 41 (1980): 102-15.

Akmajian, Adrian, Richard A. Demers, and Robert M. Harnish. *Linguistics: An Introduction to Language and Communication*. 2d ed. Cambridge, MA: MIT Press, 1984.

Akmajian, Adrian, and Frank Heny. *An Introduction to the Principles of Transformation Syntax*. Cambridge, MA: MIT Press, 1975.

Aland, Kurt, ed. *Synopsis of the Four Gospels: Greek-English Edition of the Synopsis Quattuor Evangeliorum*. 10th ed. Stuttgart: German Bible Society, 1993.

Algeo, John. "Stratificational Grammar." In *Readings in Stratificational Linguistics*, ed. Adam Makkai and David G. Lockwood, 4-11. University, AL: University of Alabama Press, 1973.

Anzilotti, Gloria Italiano. "The Imperative—An Octopus Network." In *The Fifteenth LACUS Forum 1988*, ed. Ruth M. Brend and David G. Lockwood, 153-67. Lake Bluff, IL: Linguistic Association of Canada and the United States, 1989.

Aristotle. "de Interpretatione." In *The Complete Works of Aristotle: The Revised Oxford Translation*, ed. Jonathan Barnes, trans. J. L. Ackrill, vol. 1, 25-38. Princeton, NJ: Princeton University Press, 1984.

———. "Poetics." In *The Complete Works of Aristotle: The Revised Oxford Translation*, ed. Jonathan Barnes, trans. I. Bywater, vol. 2, 2316-40. Princeton, NJ: Princeton University Press, 1984.

Austin, J. L. *How to Do Things with Words*. Cambridge, MA: Harvard University Press, 1962.

Bach, K., and R. M. Harnish. *Linguistic Communication and Speech Acts*. Cambridge, MA: MIT Press, 1979.

Bakker, Willem F. *The Greek Imperative: An Investigation Into the Aspectual Differences Between the Present and Aorist Imperatives in Greek Prayer From Homer Up to the Present Day*. Amsterdam: Uitgeverij Adolf M. Hakkert, 1966.

Bango de la Campa, Flor M. "Aportaciones para un estudio del imperativo en frances moderno." *Verba* 11 (1984): 293-306.

Barker, Kit. "Divine Illocutions in Psalm 137." *Tyndale Bulletin* 60 (2009): 1-14.

Barnwell, Katharine. "Training of Mother-Tongue Translators." *Notes on Translation* 78 (1980): 26-29.

Barr, James. *Semantics of Biblical Language*. Oxford: Oxford University Press, 1961.

Barrett, C. K. *A Critical and Exegetical Commentary on the Acts of the Apostles*, vol. 1. International Critical Commentary, ed. J. A. Emerton, C. E. B. Cranfield, and G. N. Stanton. Edinburgh: T. & T. Clark, 1994.

Barrett, Walter C. "The Use of Tense in the Imperative Mood in First Corinthians." Th.M. thesis, Dallas Theological Seminary, 1973.

Barth, Markus. *Ephesians: Translation and Commentary on Chapters 4–6.* Anchor Bible, ed. William Foxwell Albright and David Noel Freedman, vol. 34A. Garden City, NY: Doubleday, 1974.

Bartholomew, Craig, Colin Green, and Karl Möller, eds., *After Pentecost: Language and Biblical Interpretation,* Scripture and Hermeneutics Series, vol. 2. Grand Rapids: Zondervan Publishing House, 2001.

Bauer, Walter. *A Greek-English Lexicon of the New Testament and Other Early Christian Literature.* Translated by William F. Arndt and F. Wilbur Gingrich; revised and augmented by F. Wilbur Gingrich and Frederick Danker, 2d ed. Chicago: University of Chicago Press, 1979.

Bauer, Walter. *A Greek-English Lexicon of the New Testament and Other Early Christian Literature.* Revised and edited by Frederick Danker, 3d ed. Chicago: University of Chicago, 2000.

Beekes, Robert S. P. "The Historical Grammar of Greek: A Case Study in the Results of Comparative Linguistics." In *Linguistic Change and Reconstruction Methodology,* ed. P. Baldi, 305-29. Berlin: Mouton de Gruyter, 1990.

Beekman, John. "Idiomatic Versus Literal Translations." *Notes on Translation* 18 (1965): 1-15.

———. "Missionary Translators, Committees, and Nationals." *Notes on Translation* 22 (1966): 17-18.

———, and John Callow. *Translating the Word of God.* Grand Rapids: Zondervan Publishing House, 1974.

Berry, Margaret. *An Introduction to Systemic Linguistics: 1. Structures and Systems ,* New York: St. Martin's Press, 1975.

———. *An Introduction to Systemic Linguistics: 2. Levels and Links.* New York: St. Martin's Press, 1976.

Bergh, Birger. "On Passive Imperatives." *Lingua Posnaniensis* 32-33 (1991): 31-38.

Bers, Victor. *Greek Poetic Syntax in the Classical Age.* New Haven, CT: Yale University Press, 1984.

Best, Ernest. *A Critical and Exegetical Commentary on Ephesians.* International Critical Commentary, ed. J. A. Emerton, C. E. B. Cranfield, and G. N. Stanton. Edinburgh: T. & T. Clark, 1998.

Bethin, Christina Y. "Syllable Structure and the Polish Imperative Desinence." *Slavic and East European Journal* 31 (1987): 76-89.

Beukema, Frits, and Peter Coopmans. "A Government-Binding Perspective on the Imperative in English." *Journal of Linguistics* 25 (1989): 417-36.

Black, David Alan. "Discourse Analysis, Synoptic Criticism, and Markan Grammar: Some Methodological Considerations." In *Linguistics and New Testament Interpretation,* ed. David Alan Black, Katharine Barnwell, and Stephen Levinsohn, 90-98. Nashville, TN: Broadman Press, 1992.

———. *It's Still Greek to Me: An Easy-to-Understand Guide to Intermediate Greek.* Grand Rapids: Baker Books, 1998.

———. *Linguistics for Students of New Testament Greek: A Survey of Basic Concepts and Applications.* 2d ed. Grand Rapids: Baker Book House, 1995.

———, Katharine Barnwell, and Stephen Levinsohn, eds. *Linguistics and New Testament Interpretation: Essays on Discourse Analysis.* Nashville, TN: Broadman Press, 1992.

Blakemore, Diane. *Semantic Constraints on Relevance.* Oxford: Basil Blackwell, 1987.

———. *Understanding Utterances: An Introduction to Pragmatics.* Oxford: Blackwell Publishers, 1992.

Blass, Friedrich, and Albert Debrunner. *Grammatik des neutestamentlichen Griechisch.* Ed. Friedrich Rehkopf. 17th ed. Göttingen: Vandenhoeck and Ruprecht, 1976.

———. *A Greek Grammar of the New Testament and Other Early Christian Literature.* Edited and translated by Robert W. Funk. Chicago: University of Chicago Press, 1961.

Bloomfield, Leonard. *Language.* New York: Holt, Rinehart and Winston, 1933. Reprint, Chicago: University of Chicago Press, 1984.

Bock, Darrell L. *Acts.* Baker Exegetical Commentary on the New Testament. Grand Rapids: Baker Book House, 2007.

———. "New Testament Word Analysis." In *Introducing New Testament Interpretation,* ed. Scot McKnight, 97-113. Grand Rapids: Baker Book House, 1989.

Bodine, Walter R., ed. *Discourse Analysis of Biblical Literature: What It Is and What It Offers.* Atlanta: Scholars Press, 1995.

———. ed. *Linguistics and Biblical Hebrew.* Winona Lake, IN: Eisenbrauns, 1992.

Boers, Hendrikus. *The Justification of the Gentiles: Paul's Letters to the Galatians and Romans.* Peabody, MA: Hendrickson Publishers, 1994.

Bogusławski, A. "The Problem of the Negated Imperative in Perfective Verbs Revisited." *Russian Linguistics* 9 (1985): 225-39.

Boulonnais, Dominique. Review of *Imperatives,* by C. L. Hamblin. *Journal of Pragmatics* 16 (1991): 280-87.

Boyer, James L. "A Classification of Imperatives: A Statistical Study." *Grace Theological Journal* 8 (1987): 35-54.

———. "Other Conditional Elements in New Testament Greek." *Grace Theological Journal* 4 (1983): 173-88.

Brend, Ruth M. "On Defining Grammatical Levels." In *Language in Context: Essays for Robert E. Longacre,* ed. Shin Ja J. Hwang and William R. Merrifield, 505-9. Dallas, TX: Summer Institute of Linguistics, 1992.

Brockway, Diane. "Semantic Constraints on Relevance." In *Possibilities and Limitations of Pragmatics: Proceedings of the Conference on Pragmatics, Urbino, July 8-14, 1979,* ed. Herman Parret, Marina Sbisà, and Jef Verschueren, 57-78. Amsterdam: John Benjamins, 1981.

Brook, G. L. *A History of the English Language.* London: Andre Deutsch, 1958.

Brooks, James A., and Carlton L. Winbery. *Syntax of New Testament Greek.* Lanham, MD: University Press of America, 1979.

Brown, H. Paul. "Addressing Agamemnon: A Pilot Study of Politeness and Pragmatics in the *Iliad.*" *Transactions of the American Philological Association* 136 (2006): 1-46.

Brown, Jeannine K. *Scripture as Communication: Introducing Biblical Hermeneutics.* Grand Rapids: Baker Book House, 2007.

Brown, Penelope, and Stephen C. Levinson, *Politeness: Some Universals in Language Usage.* Cambridge: Cambridge University Press, 1987.

Brown, S. "Biblical Philology, Linguistics and the Problem of Method." *Heythrop Journal* 20 (1979): 295-98.

Bullinger, E. W. *Figures of Speech Used in the Bible, Explained and Illustrated.* London: Eyre and Spottiswoode, 1898; Reprint, Grand Rapids: Baker Book House, 1968.

Burk, Denny. *Articular Infinitives in the Greek of the New Testament: On the Exegetical Benefit of Grammatical Precision.* New Testament Monographs, ed. Stanley E. Porter, vol. 14. Sheffield: Sheffield Phoenix Press, 2006.

Burton, Ernest DeWitt. *Syntax of Moods and Tenses in New Testament Greek.* 3d ed. Edinburgh: T. & T. Clark, 1898.

Butler, Christopher S. *Systemic Linguistics: Theory and Applications.* London: Batsford Academic and Educational, 1985.

Buttmann, Alexander. *A Grammar of the New Testament Greek*. Andover, MA: Warren F. Draper, 1873.

Caird, G. B. *The Language and Imagery of the Bible*. Philadelphia: Westminster Press, 1980.

Callary, Robert E. "Phonology." In *Language: Introductory Readings*, ed. Virginia P. Clark, Paul A. Eschholz, and Alfred F. Rosa, 279-307. New York: St. Martin's Press, 1981.

Campbell, Constantine R. *Verbal Aspect and Non-Indicative Verbs: Further Soundings in the Greek of the New Testament*. Studies in Biblical Greek, ed. D. A. Carson, vol. 15. New York: Peter Lang, 2008.

————. *Verbal Aspect, the Indicative Mood, and Narrative: Soundings in the Greek of the New Testament*. Studies in Biblical Greek, ed. D. A. Carson, vol. 13. New York: Peter Lang, 2007.

Canadian Consultation of the "Philosophy and Theology of Language and Biblical Interpretation." Meeting announcement for August 2000.

Carson, D. A. *Exegetical Fallacies*. 2d ed. Grand Rapids: Baker Book House, 1996.

————. *The Gospel According to John*. Pillar New Testament Commentary, ed. D. A. Carson. Grand Rapids: William B. Eerdmans Publishing Company, 1991.

————, and Douglas J. Moo. *An Introduction to the New Testament*. 2d ed. Grand Rapids: Zondervan Publishing House, 2005.

Cericola, Sandra A. "Communication Skills: The Art of Listening." *Plastic Surgical Nursing* 19 (1999): 41-42.

Chamberlain, William Douglas. *An Exegetical Grammar of the Greek New Testament*. New York: Macmillan, 1941. Reprint, Grand Rapids: Baker Book House, 1979.

Chaucer, Geoffrey. *The Canterbury Tales: Nine Tales and the General Prologue*. Ed. V. A. Kolve and Glending Olsen. New York: W. W. Norton and Company, 1989.

Cherry, Roger D. "Politeness in Written Persuasion." *Journal of Pragmatics* 12 (1988): 63-81.

Chomsky, Noam. *Aspects of the Theory of Syntax*. Cambridge, MA: MIT Press, 1965.

————. *Lectures on Government and Binding*. Dordrecht, Holland: Foris Publications, 1981.

————. *The Logical Structure of Linguistic Theory*. New York and London: Plenum Press, 1975.

————. *Syntactic Structures*. The Hague: Mouton, 1957.

Clark, Billy. "Relevance and 'Pseudo-Imperatives.'" *Linguistics and Philosophy* 16 (1993): 79-121.

Collinge, N. E. "Thoughts on the Pragmatics of Ancient Greek." *Proceedings of the Cambridge Philological Society* 214 [n.s. 34] (1988): 1-13.

Colwell, E. C. "A Definite Rule for the Use of the Article in the Greek New Testament." *Journal of Biblical Literature* 52 (1933): 12-21.

Comrie, Bernard. *Aspect*. Cambridge Textbooks in Linguistics, ed. B. Comrie et al. Cambridge: Cambridge University Press, 1976.

Conzelmann, Hans. *Acts of the Apostles: A Commentary on the Acts of the Apostles*. Trans. James Limburg, A. Thomas Kraabel, and Donald H. Juel. Hermeneia, ed. Eldon J. Epp with Christopher R. Matthews. Philadelphia: Fortress Press, 1987.

Cook, John G. *The Structure and Persuasive Power of Mark: A Linguistic Approach*. The Society of Biblical Literature Semeia Studies. Atlanta: Scholars Press, 1995.

Cook, Walter A. *Introduction to Tagmemic Analysis*. New York: Holt, Rinehart and Winston, 1969.

Cope, Pamela. *Introductory Grammar: A Stratificational Approach*. Dallas: Summer Institute of Linguistics, 1994.

Cotterell, P., and M. Turner. *Linguistics and Biblical Interpretation*. Downers Grove, IL: InterVarsity Press, 1989.

Cowie, A. P. "Phraseology." In *The Encyclopedia of Languages and Linguistics,* ed. R. E Asher and J. M. Y. Simpson, vol. 6, 3168-71. Oxford: Pergamon Press, 1994.

Dana, H. E., and Julius R. Mantey. *A Manual Grammar of the Greek New Testament.* New York: Macmillan Publishing Co., 1927.

Davidson, Donald. "Moods and Performances." In *In Meaning and Use: Papers Presented at the Second Jerusalem Philosophical Encounter April 1976,* ed. Avishai Margalit, 9-20. Dordrecht, Holland: D. Reidel Publishing Company, 1979.

Davies, Eirlys E. *The English Imperative.* Kent, England: Croom Helm., 1986.

———. "Some Restrictions of Conditional Imperatives." *Linguistics* 17 (1979): 1039-54.

Dawson, David Allen. *Text-Linguistics and Biblical Hebrew.* Journal for the Study of the Old Testament Supplement Series, ed. David J. A. Clines and Philip R. Davies, vol 177. Sheffield: Sheffield Academic Press, 1994.

Decker, Rodney J. *Temporal Deixis of the Greek Verb in the Gospel of Mark with Reference to Verbal Aspect,* Studies in Biblical Greek, ed. D. A. Carson, vol. 4. New York: Peter Lang, 2001.

Deibler, Ellis W., Jr. "National Involvement and Translation Checking." *Notes on Translation* 71 (1978): 2-16.

Dell, Gary S., and Peter A. Reich. "Slips of the Tongue: The Facts and a Stratificational Model." In *Rice University Studies: Papers in Cognitive-Stratificational Linguistics,* ed. James E. Copeland and Philip W. Davis, vol. 66, no. 2, 16-34. Houston: William Marsh Rice University, 1980.

deSilva, David Arthur. *Despising Shame: Honor Discourse and Community Maintenance in the Epistle to the Hebrews.* Society of Biblical Literature Dissertation Series, ed. Pheme Perkins, vol. 152. Atlanta: Scholars Press, 1995.

Dickinson, Frederick Walter Augustine. *The Use of the Optative Mood in the Works of John Chrysostom.* Catholic University of America Patristic Studies, vol. 11. Washington DC: Catholic University of America, 1926.

Dirven, René, and Marjolijn Verspoor. *Cognitive Exploration of Language and Linguistics.* Cognitive Linguistics in Practice, ed. Günter Radden, vol. 1. Amsterdam: John Benjamins Publishing Company, 1998.

Dodd, C. H. *Interpretation of the Fourth Gospel.* Cambridge: Cambridge University Press, 1953.

Donovan, J. "German Opinion on Greek Jussives." *Classical Review* 9 (1895): 289-93, 342-46, 444-47.

———. "Greek Jussives." *Classical Review* 9 (1895): 145-49.

Douglass, Scot R. "The Passive Imperative and Its Significance in Romans 12:1-2." Th.M. thesis, Dallas Theological Seminary, 1988.

Downes, William. "The Imperative and Pragmatics." *Journal of Linguistics* 13 (1977): 77-97.

Durst-Andersen, Per. "Imperative Frames and Modality: Direct vs. Indirect Speech Acts in Russian, Danish, and English." *Linguistics and Philosophy* 18 (1995): 611-53.

Economidou-Kogetsidis, Maria. "Greek Non-Native Speaker's Requests and Degree of Directness." In *Current Trends in Intercultual Cognitive and Social Pragmatics,* Intercultural Pragmatic Studies, ed. Pilar Garcés Conejos, Reyes Gómez Marón, Lucia Fernández Amaya, and Manuel Padilla Cruz, 53-66. N.p.: University of Seville, N.d.

Edmondson, Jerold A., and Donald A. Burquest. *A Survey of Linguistic Theories.* Dallas: Summer Institute of Linguistics, 1992.

Efird, James M. *A Grammar for New Testament Greek.* Nashville, TN: Abingdon Press, 1990.

Egger, Wilhelm. *How to Read the New Testament: An Introduction to Linguistic and Historical-Critical Methodology.* Ed. Hendrikus Boers. Peabody, MA: Hendrickson Publishers, 1996.

Ehrman, Bart D. and Mark A. Plunkett. "The Angel and the Agony: The Textual Problem of Luke 22:43-44." *Catholic Biblical Quarterly* 45 (1983): 401-16.

Elbert, Paul. *Acts 2:38c Reconsidered*. Evangelical Theological Society 52d Annual Meeting (Nashville, TN, Nov 15-17, 2002), audio cassette.

Elson, Benjamin, and Velma Pickett. *Beginning Morphology and Syntax*. Dallas: Summer Institute of Linguistics, 1983.

Elson, Mark J. "Present Tense and Imperative in Ukranian Conjugation." *Slavic and East European Journal* 32 (1988): 265-80.

Erickson, Rich. Review of *Greek Grammar Beyond the Basics*, by Daniel B. Wallace. *Journal of the Evangelical Theological Society* 42 (1999): 128-30.

Erickson, Richard J. "Biblical Semantics, Semantic Structure, and Biblical Lexicology: A Study of Methods, with Special Reference to the Pauline Lexical Field of 'Cognition.'" Ph.D. diss., Fuller Theological Seminary, 1980.

———. "Linguistics and Biblical Language: A Wide-Open Field." *Journal of the Evangelical Theological Society* 26 (1983): 257-63.

Eska, Joseph F. "The Third Person Imperative Desinences in Old Irish." *Historische Sprachforschung* 105 (1992): 265-72.

Falk, Julia S. "Semantics." In *Language: Introductory Readings*, ed. Virginia P. Clark, Paul A. Eschholz, and Alfred F. Rosa, 399-417. New York: St. Martin's Press, 1981.

Fanning, Buist M. *Verbal Aspect in New Testament Greek*. Oxford Theological Monographs, ed. J. Barton et al. Oxford: Clarendon Press, 1990.

Fantin, Joseph D. "The Lord of the Entire World: *Lord Jesus*, a Challenge to *Lord Caesar*?" Ph.D. thesis, University of Sheffield, 2007.

Farmer, William R. *The Synoptic Problem: A Critical Analysis*. New York: Macmillan, 1964.

Fee, Gordon D. *Paul's Letter to the Philippians*. New International Commentary on the New Testament, ed. Gordon D. Fee. Grand Rapids: William B. Eerdmans Publishing Company, 1995.

Fernando, A. P. "Translation of Questions and Prohibitions in Greek." *The Bible Translator* 27 (1976): 138-42.

Fitzmyer, Joseph A. *The Gospel According to Luke (X–XXIV)*. Anchor Bible, ed. William Foxwell Albright and David Noel Freedman, vol. 28A. Garden City, NY: Doubleday and Company, 1985.

Fleming, Ilah. "Communication Analysis: A Stratificational Approach," vol. 1, N.p.: Summer Institute of Linguistics, 1990 [unpublished].

———. *Communication Analysis: A Stratificational Approach*, vol. 2, Dallas: Summer Institute of Linguistics, 1988.

Franck, Dorothea. "Seven Sins of Pragmatics: Theses About Speech Act Theory, Conversational Analysis, Linguistics and Rhetoric." In *Possibilities and Limitations of Pragmatics: Proceedings of the Conference on Pragmatics, Urbino, July 8–14, 1979*, ed. Herman Parret, Marina Sbisà, and Jef Verschueren, 225-36. Amsterdam: John Benjamins, 1981.

Franklin, Karl J. "Speech Act Verbs and the Words of Jesus." In *Language in Context: Essays for Robert Longacre*, ed. Shin Ja J. Hwang and William R. Merrifield, 241-61. Dallas: Summer Institute of Linguistics, 1992.

Fries, Charles Carpenter. *American English Grammar: The Grammatical Structure of Present-Day American English with Especial Reference to Social Differences of Class Dialects*. New York: Appleton-Century-Crofts, 1940.

———. *The Structure of English: An Introduction to the Construction of English Sentences*. New York: Harcourt, Brace and World, 1952.

Funk, Robert W. *A Beginning-Intermediate Grammar of Hellenistic Greek*, vol. 2: *Syntax*. 2d ed. Missoula, MT: Society of Biblical Literature, 1973.

Gadazar, Gerald. "Speech Act Assignment." In *Elements of Discourse Understanding*, ed. A. K. Joshi, B. L. Webber, and I. A. Sag, 64-83. Cambridge: Cambridge University Press, 1981.

Gershevitch, Ilya. "The Ossetic 3rd Plural Imperative." *Transactions of the Philological Society* 89 (1991): 221-34.

Gildersleeve, Basil Lanneau, *Syntax of Classical Greek, From Homer to Demosthenes* . New York, 1900-11. Reprint, New York: American Book Company, 1980.

Gingiss, Peter. "Indirect Threats." *Word* 37 (1986): 153-58.

Glaze, Judy. "The Septuagintal Use of the Third Person Imperative." M.A. thesis, Harding Graduate School of Religion, 1979.

Gleason, H. A., Jr. *An Introduction to Descriptive Linguistics*. Rev. ed. New York: Holt, Rinehart and Winston, 1961.

————. "Linguistics in the Service of the Church." *Hartford Quarterly* 1 (1960): 7-27.

————. "Some Contributions of Linguistics to Biblical Studies." *Hartford Quarterly* 4 (1963): 47-56.

Glock, Naomi. "The Native Author—An Unexpected Goldmine." *Notes on Translation* 59 (1976): 33-34.

Gochet, Paul. "How to Combine Speech Act Theory with Formal Semantics: A New Account of Searle's Concept of Proposition." In *Possibilities and Limitations of Pragmatics: Proceedings of the Conference on Pragmatics, Urbino, July 8–14, 1979*, ed. Herman Parret, Marina Sbisà, and Jef Verschueren, 251-61. Amsterdam: John Benjamins, 1981.

Goetchius, Eugene Van Ness. *The Language of the New Testament*. New York: Charles Scribner's Sons, 1965.

Goodwin, William Watson. *An Elementary Greek Grammar*. Rev. and enl. ed. Boston: Ginn and Company, 1879.

————. *Syntax of the Moods and Tenses of the Greek Verb*. Boston: Ginn and Company, 1890.

GRAMCORD Greek New Testament for Windows 2.3bm [later 2.4cb] with Database 5.3. The Gramcord Institute, Vancouver, WA, 1998.

Grammenidis, Simos. "The Verbs Πηγαινω and Ερχομαι in Modern Greek." In *Themes in Greek Linguistics: Papers From the First International Conference on Greek Linguistics, Reading, September 1993*, ed. Irene Philippaki-Warburton, Katerina Nicolaidis, and Maria Sifianou, 193-99. Amsterdam: John Benjamins Publishing Company, 1994.

The Greek New Testament. Edited by Barbara Aland, Kurt Aland, Johannes Karavidopoulos, Carlo M Martini, and Bruce M. Metzger, 4th rev. ed. Stuttgart: Deutsche Bibelgesellschaft, 1993.

Green, Gene L. "Lexical Pragmatics and Biblical Interpretation," *Journal of the Evangelical Theological Society* 50 (2007): 799-812.

Green, Keith. "Relevance Theory and the Literary Text: Some Problems and Perspectives." *Journal of Literary Semantics* 22 (1993): 207-17.

Green, S. G. *Handbook to the Grammar of the Greek Testament*. Rev. ed. London: Religious Tract Society, 1907.

Greenlee, J. H. *A Concise Exegetical Grammar of New Testament Greek*. 5th rev. ed. Grand Rapids: William B. Eerdmans Publishing Company, 1986.

Grenfell, Bernard P., and Arthur S. Hunt, eds. *The Oxyrhynchus Papyri, Part IV: Edited with Translations and Notes*. London: Egypt Exploration Society, 1904.

Grice, H. Paul. "Further Notes on Logic and Conversation." In *Syntax and Semantics,* vol. 9, *Pragmatics*, ed. P. Cole, 113-27. New York: Academic Press, 1978.

————. "Logic and Conversation." In *Syntax and Semantics,* vol. 3, *Speech Acts*, ed. P. Cole and J. Morgan, 41-58. New York: Academic Press, 1975.

————. "Meaning." *Philosophical Review* 66 (1957): 377-88.

————. *Studies in the Way of Words*. Cambridge, MA: Harvard University Press, 1989.

Gundry, Robert H. *Matthew: A Commentary on His Handbook for a Mixed Church Under Persecution*. 2d ed. Grand Rapids: William B. Eerdmans Publishing Company, 1994.

Guthrie, George H. *The Structure of Hebrews: A Text-Linguistic Analysis*. Grand Rapids: Baker Books, 1994.

Gutt, Ernst-August. "Matthew 9:14-17 in the Light of Relevance Theory." *Notes on Translation*, 113 (1986): 13-20.

————. *Relevance Theory: A Guide to Successful Communication in Translation*. Dallas: Summer Institute of Linguistics, 1992.

————. *Translation and Relevance: Cognition and Context*. 2d ed. Manchester: St Jerome Publishing, 2000.

————. "Unravelling Meaning: An Introduction to Relevance Theory." *Notes on Translation* 112 (1986): 10-20.

Guy, Bernard and Jacques Marcoux. *Grec du nouveau testament*. N.p.: Editions Béthel, 1985.

Halliday, M. A. K. *An Introduction to Functional Grammar*. 2d ed. London: Edward Arnold, 1994.

Hamamoto, Hideki. "Irony From Cognative Perspective." In *Relevance Theory: Applications and Implications*, ed. Robyn Carston and Seiji Uchida, 257-70. Amsterdam: John Benjamins Publishing Company, 1998.

Hamblin, C. L. *Imperatives*. Oxford: Basil Blackwell, 1987.

Happé, Peter, ed. *English Mystery Plays: A Selection*. Harmondsworth, Middlesex, England: Penguin Books, 1975.

Hardy, David A. *Greek: Language and People. A BBC Television Course in Modern Greek for Beginners*. Edited by Terry Doyle. London: BBC Books, 1983.

Harmon, Henry M. "The Optative Mode in Hellenistic Greek." *Journal of the Society of Biblical Literature and Exegesis* 6 (1886): 3-12.

Harry, J. E. "The Perfect Subjunctive, Optative and Imperative in Greek." *Classical Review* 19 (1905): 347-54.

————. "The Perfect Subjunctive, Optative and Imperative in Greek Again." *Classical Review* 20 (1906): 100-03.

Hassman, Steven P. "Aspect Use in the Imperative: An Alternate View." *Russian Language Journal* 40 (1986): 25-32.

Headlam, W. "Greek Prohibitions." *Classical Review* 19 (1905): 30-36.

————. "Some Passages of Aeschylus and Others." *Classical Review* 17 (1903): 286-95.

Headland, Thomas N., Kenneth L. Pike, and Marvin Harris, eds. *Emics and Etics: The Insider/Outsider Debate*. Frontiers of Anthropology, vol. 7. Newbury Park, CA: Sage Publications, 1990.

Heatherington, Madelon E. "Pragmatics." In *Language: Introductory Readings*, ed. Virginia P. Clark, Paul A. Eschholz, and Alfred F. Rosa, 418-24. New York: St. Martin's Press, 1981.

Heckert, Jakob K. *Discourse Functions of Conjoiners in the Pastoral Epistles*. Dallas: Summer Institute of Linguistics, 1996.

Heidt, William. "Translating New Testament Imperatives." *Catholic Biblical Quarterly* 13 (1951): 253-56.

Hermann, Gottfried. *Opuscula*, vol. 1. Leipzig, 1827. Reprint, Hildesheim: Georg Olms Verlag, 1970.

Hewson, John, and Vit Bubenik. *Tense and Aspect in Indo-European Languages: Theory, Typology, Diachrony*. Series 4— Current Issues in Linguistic Theory, ed. E. F. Konrad Koerner, vol. 145. Amsterdam: John Benjamins Publishing Company, 1997.

Hjelmslev, Louis. *A Prolegomena to a Theory of Language*. Translated by Francis J. Whitfield, 2d ed. Madison, WI: University of Wisconsin Press, 1961.

Hockett, Charles F. *A Course in Modern Linguistics*. New York: Macmillan Company, 1958.

Hodges, John C., and Mary E. Whitten. *Harbrace College Handbook*. 9th ed. New York: Harcourt Brace Jovanovich, 1982.

Hoehner, Harold W. Ephesians: A Exegetical Commentary. Grand Rapids: Baker Book House, 2002.

Hoffmann, Ernst G., and Heinrich von Siebenthal. *Griechische Grammatik zum neuen Testament*. Riehen: Immanuel-Verlag, 1985.

Homer. *The Iliad*. Translated by A. T. Murray. 2 vols. Loeb Classical Library, ed. G. P. Goold. London: William Heinrmann, 1924-25.

Horrocks, Geoffrey. *Greek: A History of the Language and Its Speakers*. Longman Linguistic Library, ed. R. H. Robins, G. Horrocks, and D. Denison. London: Longman, 1997.

Horsley, Richard A. *Hidden Transcripts and the Arts of Resistance: Applying the Work of James C. Scott to Jesus and Paul*. Semeia Studies 48. Atlanta: Society of Biblical Literature, 2004..

Householder, Fred W. *The Syntax of Apollonius Dyscolus: Translated, and with Commentary*. Amsterdam Studies in the Theory and History of Linguistic Science. Series 3—Studies in the History of Linguistics, edited by E. F. Konrad Koerner, vol 23. Amsterdam: John Benjamins, 1981.

Huddleston, Rodney. "The Contrast Between Interrogatives and Questions." *Journal of Linguistics* 30 (1994): 411-40.

Hughes, John P. "Languages and Writing." In *Language: Introductory Readings*, ed. Virginia P. Clark, Paul A. Eschholz, and Alfred F. Rosa, 436-55. New York: St. Martin's Press, 1981.

Hugs, Jerome. "Relationship Between Naivete Checker and Translation Consultant: A Native Perspective." *Notes on Translation* 111 (1986): 22-24.

Humphreys, M. W. "On Negative Commands in Greek." *Transactions of the American Philological Association* 7 (1876): 46-49.

Huntley, Martin. "Propositions and the Imperative." *Synthese* 45 (1980): 281-310.

———. "The Semantics of English Imperatives." *Linguistics and Philosophy* 7 (1984): 103-33.

Jackson, Henry. "Prohibitions in Greek." *Classical Review* 18 (1904): 262-63.

Jakobson, Roman. "Closing Statement: Linguistics and Poetics." In *Style in Language*, ed. Thomas A. Sebeok, 350-77. Cambridge, MA: MIT Press, 1960.

Jannaris, A. N. *An Historical Greek Grammar Chiefly of the Attic Dialect*. London: Macmillan, 1897.

Jobes, Karen H. "Relevance Theory and the Translation of Scripture." *Journal of the Evangelical Theological Society* 50 (2007): 773-97.

Jucker, Andreas H. "The Relevance of Politeness." *Multilingua* 7-4 (1988): 375-84.

Kemble, John M., and Charles Hardwick, eds. *The Gospel According to Saint Matthew in Anglo-Saxon and Northumbrian Versions, Synoptically Arranged, with Collations of the Best Manuscripts*. Cambridge: Cambridge University Press, 1858.

Kieckers, E. "Zum Gebrauch des Imperativus Aoristi und Praesentis." *Indogermanische Forschungen* 24 (1909): 10-17.

King, David W. "Jesus' Use of the Imperative." Th.D. diss., Southwestern Baptist Theological Seminary, 1963.

Koppers, Bertha Theodora. *Negative Conditional Sentences in Greek and Some Other Indo-European Languages*. The Hague: N. V. Drij. Pier Westerbaan, 1959.

Kühner, Raphael. *Grammar of the Greek Language: For the Use of High Schools and Colleges*. Translated by B. B. Edwards and S. H. Taylor. Boston: B. B. Mussey and Co., 1849.

——— and Bernhard Gerth. *Ausführliche Grammatik der griechischen Sprache*. 4th ed. 2 vols. Leverkusen: Gottschalksche, 1955.

Kümmel, Werner Georg. *Introduction to the New Testament*. Translated by Howard Clark Kee. Rev. and enl. ed. Nashville, TN: Abingdon Press, 1975.

Kummer, Werner. "Formal Pragmatics." In *Pragmatik: Handbuch pragmatischen Denkens*, ed. Herbert Stachowiak, 104-22. Hamburg: Felix Meiner Verlag, 1993.

Kurzová, Helena. *Zur syntaktischen Struktur des Griechoschen /Infinitiv und Nebensatz.* Prague: Academia Verlag der Tschechoslowakischen Akademie der Wissenschaften, 1968.

Ladd, George Eldon. *A Theology of the New Testament.* Edited by Donald A. Hagner. Rev. ed. Grand Rapids: William B. Eerdmans Publishing Company, 1993.

Lamb, Sydney. "Language, Thought, and Mind: An Invitation to Neuro-Cognitive Linguistics." Unpublished course book. Rice University, 1996.

———. *Outline of Stratificational Grammar.* Washington DC: Georgetown University Press, 1966.

———. *Pathways of the Brain: The Neurocognitive Basis of Language.* Amsterdam Studies in the Theory and History of Linguistic Science: Series 4—Current Issues in Linguistic Theory, ed. E. F. Konrad Koerner. Amsterdam: John Benjamins Publishing Company, 1999.

———. "A Word From the Chair." *LACUS: The Linguistic Association of Canada and the United States Newsletter* 2, no. 1 (1996): 3-4.

Lee, J. A. L. "Some Features of the Speech of Jesus in Mark's Gospel." *Novum Testamentum* 27 (1985): 1-26.

Leech, Geoffrey N. *Principles of Pragmatics.* London: Longman, 1983.

Leeuwen, Raymond C. van. "On Bible Translation and Hermeneutics." In *After Pentecost: Language and Biblical Interpretation.* Scripture and Hermeneutics Series, vol. 2, ed. Craig, Bartholomew, Colin Green, and Karl Möller, 282-311. Grand Rapids: Zondervan Publishing House, 2001.

Leslie, Alan M. Review of *Relevance: Communication and Cognition,* by Dan Sperber and Deirdre Wilson. *Mind and Language* 4 (1989): 147-50.

Levinsohn, Stephen H. *Discourse Features of New Testament Greek: A Coursebook on the Information Structure of New Testament Greek.* 2d ed. Dallas: SIL International, 2000.

———. "A Discourse Study of Constituent Order and the Article in Philippians." In *Discourse Analysis and Other Topics in Biblical Greek,* ed. Stanley E. Porter and D. A. Carson, 60-74. Sheffield: Sheffield Academic Press, 1995.

Levinson, Stephen C. "The Essential Inadequacies of Speech Act Models of Dialogue." In *Possibilities and Limitations of Pragmatics: Proceedings of the Conference on Pragmatics, Urbino, July 8–14, 1979,* ed. Herman Parret, Marina Sbisà, and Jef Verschueren, 473-92. Amsterdam: John Benjamins, 1981.

———. *Pragmatics.* Cambridge Textbooks in Linguistics, ed. B. Comrie et al. Cambridge: Cambridge University Press, 1983.

———. "Review of '*Relevance.*'" *Journal of Linguistics* 25 (1989): 455-72.

Liddell, Henry George, and Robert Scott, comps. *A Greek-English Lexicon.* Revised and augmented by Henry Stuart Jones and Roderick McKenzie, 9th ed. with a revised supplement, 1996, ed. R. G. W. Glare and A. A. Thompson. Oxford: Clarendon Press, 1940.

Lightfoot, J. B., and J. R. Harmer, eds. and trans., *The Apostolic Fathers: Greek Texts and English Translations of Their Writings.* 2d ed., ed. and rev. Michael W. Holmes. Grand Rapids: Baker Book House, 1992.

Lincoln, Andrew. *Ephesians.* Word Biblical Commentary, ed. David A. Hubbard et al., vol. 42. Dallas: Word, 1990.

Lobel, E., C. H. Roberts, and E. P. Wegener, eds. *The Oxyrhynchus Papyri, Part XVIII Edited with Translations and Notes.* London: Egypt Exploration Society, 1941.

Lockwood, David G. *Introduction to Stratificational Linguistics.* New York: Harcourt Brace Jovanovich, 1972.

———. "Introduction to Stratificational Linguistics, rev. [unpublished] ed." Michigan State University, 1987.

————. "On Lexemic and Morphemic Case." In *Rice University Studies: Papers in Cognitive-Stratificational Linguistics,* ed. James E. Copeland and Philip W. Davis, vol. 66, no. 2, 35-58. Houston: William Marsh Rice University, 1980.

————. Verbal Class Lecture Notes Transcribed by the Author, LIN 831, Michigan State University, M.A. Program, Winter Term 1988.

Longacre, Robert E. *Grammar Discovery Procedures: A Field Manual.* The Hague: Mouton, 1964.

————. *Joseph: A Text Theoretical Textlinguistic Analysis of Genesis 37 and 39–40.* Winona Lake, IN: Eisenbrauns, 1989.

————, and Wilber B. Wallis. "Soteriology and Eschatology in Romans." *Journal of the Evangelical Theological Society* 41 (1998): 367-82.

Louw, Johannes P. "Linguistics and Hermeneutics." *Neotestamentica* 4 (1970): 8-18.

————. "On Greek Prohibitions." *Acta Classica* 2 (1959): 43-57.

————. *Semantics of New Testament Greek.* Atlanta: Scholars Press, 1982.

————, and Eugene A. Nida, eds. *Greek-English Lexicon of the New Testament Based on Semantic Domains.* New York: United Bible Societies, 1988.

Lyons, John. *Semantics,* 2 vols. Cambridge: Cambridge University Press, 1977.

————. *Introduction to Theoretical Linguistics.* Cambridge: Cambridge University Press, 1968.

————. *Language and Linguistics: An Introduction.* Cambridge: Cambridge University Press, 1981.

————. *Linguistic Semantics: An Introduction.* Cambridge: Cambridge University Press, 1995.

MacDonald, Margaret Y. *Colossians and Ephesians,* Sacra Pagina 17. Collegeville, MN: Liturgical Press, 2000; reprint with updated bibliography, 2008.

Malina, Bruce J. *The New Testament World: Insights From Cultural Anthropology.* 3d ed. Louisville, KY: Westminster John Knox Press, 2001.

Manabe, Takashi. "Speech Act Theory Based Interpretation Model for Written Texts." Ph.D. diss., University of Texas at Arlington, 1984.

Mandilaras, Basil G. *The Verb in the Greek Non-Literary Papyri.* Athens: Hellenic Ministry of Culture and Sciences, 1973.

Marmaridou, A. Sophia S. "Semantic and Pragmatic Parameters of Meaning." *Journal of Pragmatics* 11 (1987): 721-36.

Matthews, Peter. "Greek and Latin Linguistics." In *A History of Linguistics,* vol. 2, *Classical and Medieval Linguistics,* ed. Giulio Lepschy, 1-133. London and New York: Longman, 1994.

Mattina, Anthony. "Imperative Formations in Colville-Okanagan and in the Other Interior Salishan Languages." *Glossa* 14 (1980): 212-32.

McKay, K. L. "Aspect in Imperatival Constructions in New Testament Greek." *Novum Testamentum* 27 (1985): 201-26.

————. "Aspects of the Imperative in Ancient Greek." *Antichthon* 20 (1986): 41-58.

————. *A New Syntax of the Verb in New Testament Greek: An Aspectual Approach.* Studies in Biblical Greek, ed. D. A. Carson, vol. 5. New York: Peter Lang, 1994.

McQuilkin, J. Robertson. *Understanding and Applying the Bible.* Chicago: Moody Press, 1983.

Meadowcroft, Tim. "Relevance as a Mediating Category in the Reading of Biblical Texts: Venturing beyond the Hermeneutic Circle." *Journal of the Evangelical Theological Society* 45 (2002): 611-27.

Merin, Authur. "Imperatives: Linguistics vs. Philosophy." *Linguistics* 29 (1991): 669-702.

Metts, Harold Leroy. "Greek Sentence Structure: A Traditional, Descriptive Generative Study." Th.D. diss., Southwestern Baptist Theological Seminary, 1977.

Mey, Jacob L. *Pragmatics: An Introduction.* Oxford: Blackwell Publishers, 1993.

Miller, C. W. E. "The Limitation of the Imperative in the Attic Orators." *American Journal of Philology* 13 (1892): 399-436.

Montgomery, David A. "Directives in the New Testament: A Case Study of John 1:38." *Journal of the Evangelical Theological Society* 50 (2007): 275-88.

Moore, R. W. *Comparative Greek and Latin Syntax*. London: G. Bell and Sons, 1934.

Morrice, W. G. "Translating the Greek Imperative." *The Bible Translator* 24 (1973): 129-34.

Moule, C. F. D. *An Idiom Book of New Testament Greek*. 2d ed. Cambridge: Cambridge University Press, 1959.

Moulton, James Hope. *Prolegomena. A Grammar of New Testament Greek Based on W. F. Moulton's Edition of G. B. Winer's Grammar*, ed. James Hope Moulton, vol. 1. Edinburgh: T. & T. Clark, 1906.

————. *Prolegomena*. 3d ed. *A Grammar of New Testament Greek*, ed. James Hope Moulton, vol. 1. Edinburgh: T. & T. Clark, 1908.

————, and Wilbert Francis Howard. *Accidence and Word-Formation. A Grammar of New Testament Greek*, ed. James Hope Moulton, vol. 2. Edinburgh: T. & T. Clark, 1929.

————, and George Milligan. *The Vocabulary of the Greek Testament: Illustrated From the Papyri and Other Non-Literary Sources*. London: Hodder and Stoughton, 1930. Reprint, Grand Rapids: William B. Eerdmans Publishing Company, 1985.

Mounce, William D. *Basics of Biblical Greek: Grammar*. Grand Rapids: Zondervan Publishing House, 1993.

Mozley, F. W. "Notes on the Biblical Use of the Present and Aorist Imperative." *Journal of Theological Studies* 4 (1903): 279-82.

Mueller, Theodore H. *New Testament Greek: A Case Grammar Approach*. Fort Wayne, IN: Concordia Theological Seminary Press, 1978.

————. "Observations on Some New Testament Texts Based on Generative-Transformational Grammar." *The Bible Translator* 29 (1978): 117-20.

Myers, Greg. "The Pragmatics of Politeness in Scientific Articles." *Applied Linguistics* 10 (1989): 1-35.

Naylor, H. Darnley. "More Prohibitions in Greek." *Classical Review* 20 (1906): 348.

————. "Prohibitions in Greek." *Classical Review* 19 (1905): 26-30.

Neill, Stephen, and Tom Wright. *The Interpretation of the New Testament: 1861–1986*. 2d ed. Oxford: Oxford University Press, 1988.

New, David S. "The Injunctive Future and Existential Injunction in the New Testament." *Journal for the Study of the New Testament* 44 (1991): 113-27.

Newman, B. M., and Eugene A. Nida. *A Handbook on the Gospel of John*. UBS Handbook Series. New York: United Bible Societies, 1980.

Neyrey, Jerome H. *Honor and Shame in the Gospel of Matthew*. Louisville, KY: Westminster John Knox Press, 1998.

Nida, Eugene A. *Customs and Cultures: Anthropology for Christian Missions*. New York: Harper and Row, Publishers, 1954.

————. "Implications of Contemporary Linguistics for Biblical Scholarship." *Journal of Biblical Literature* 91 (1972): 73-89.

————. *Linguistic Interludes*. Glendale, CA: Summer Institute of Linguistics, 1947.

————. *Toward a Science of Translating*. Leiden: E. J. Brill, 1964.

————, and Charles R. Taber. *The Theory and Practice of Translation*. Helps for Translators, vol. 8. Leiden: E. J. Brill, 1969.

Noh, Eu-Ju. "A Relevance-Theoretical Account of Metarepresentative Uses in Conditionals." In *Current Issues in Relevance Theory*, ed. Villy Rouchota and Andreas H. Jucker, 271-304. Amsterdam: John Benjamins Publishing Company, 1998.

Novum Testamentum Graece. Edited by Barbara Aland, Kurt Aland, Matthew Black, Carlo M. Martini, Bruce M. Metzger, and Allen Wikgren. 26th rev. ed. Stuttgart: Deutsche Bibelgesellschaft, 1979.

Novum Testamentum Graece. Edited by Barbara Aland, Kurt Aland, Johannes Karavidopoulos, Carlo M. Martini and Bruce M. Metzger. 27th rev. ed. Stuttgart: Deutsche Bibelgesellschaft, 1993.

O'Brien, Peter T. *The Letter to the Ephesians.* Pillar New Testament Commentary, ed. D. A. Carson. Grand Rapids: William B. Eerdmans Publishing Company, 1999.

Olhausen, William. "A 'Polite' Response to Anthony Thiselton." In *After Pentecost: Language and Biblical Interpretation.* Scripture and Hermeneutics Series, vol. 2, ed. Craig, Bartholomew, Colin Green, and Karl Möller, 121-30. Grand Rapids: Zondervan Publishing House, 2001.

Olsen, Mari Broman. *A Semantic and Pragmatic Model of Lexical and Grammatical Aspect.* New York and London: Garland Publishing, 1997.

Osburn, C. D. "The Third Person Imperative in Acts 2:38." *Restoration Quarterly* 26 (1983): 81-84.

Palmer, F. R. *Mood and Modality.* Cambridge Textbooks in Linguistics, ed. B. Comrie et al. Cambridge: Cambridge University Press, 1986.

Palmer, Micheal W. *Levels of Constituent Structure in New Testament Greek.* Studies in Biblical Greek, ed. D. A. Carson, vol. 4. New York: Peter Lang, 1995.

Panther, Klaus-Uwe, and Linda Thornburg. "A Cognitive Approach to Inferencing in Conversation." *Journal of Pragmatics* 30 (1998): 755-69.

Pap, Leo. "Semantics–Syntactics–Pragmatics: A New Look at an Old Distinction." In *The Eleventh LACUS Forum 1984*, ed. Robert A. Hall, 303-13. Columbia, SC: Hornbeam Press, 1985.

Papafragou, Anna. "Modality and Semantic Underdeterminacy." In *Current Issues in Relevance Theory,* ed. Villy Rouchota and Andreas H. Jucker, 237-70. Amsterdam: John Benjamins Publishing Company, 1998.

Pattemore, Stephen. *The People of God in the Apocalypse: Discourse, Structure, and Exegesis.* Society of New Testament Studies Monograph Series 128. Cambridge: Cambridge University Press, 2004.

———. "The People of God in the Apocalypse: A Relevance-Theoretical Study." Ph.D. thesis, University of Otago [Dunedin, New Zealand], 2000.

Perschbacher, Wesley J. *New Testament Greek Syntax: An Illustrated Manual.* Chicago: Moody Press, 1995.

PHI Greek Documentary Texts [CD ROM #7. Software database]. Packard Humanities Institute, Los Altos, CA, 1991-1996.

Pike, Eunice V. *Ken Pike: Scholar and Christian.* Dallas: Summer Institute of Linguistics, 1981.

Pike, Kenneth L. *Language in Relation to a Unified Theory of the Structure of Human Behavior.* 2d rev. ed. The Hague: Mouton and Co., 1967.

———. *Language in Relation to a Unified Theory of the Structure of Human Behavior* (Part 1). Preliminary ed. Glendale, CA: Summer Institute of Linguistics, 1954.

———. *Linguistic Concepts: An Introduction to Tagmemics.* Lincoln, NE: University of Nebraska Press, 1982.

———. *Talk, Thought, and Thing: The Emic Road Toward Conscious Knowledge.* Dallas: Summer Institute of Linguistics, 1993.

———, and Evelyn G. Pike. *Grammatical Analysis.* 2d ed. Dallas: Summer Institute of Linguistics and the University of Texas at Arlington, 1982.

Porter, Stanley E. "Discourse Analysis and New Testament Studies: An Introductory Survey." In *Discourse Analysis and Other Topics in Biblical Greek,* ed. Stanley E. Porter and D. A. Carson, 14-35. Sheffield: Sheffield Academic Press, 1995.

————. "How Can Biblical Discourse Be Analyzed? A Response to Several Attempts." In *Discourse Analysis and Other Topics in Biblical Greek*, ed. Stanley E. Porter and D. A. Carson, 107-16. Sheffield: Sheffield Academic Press, 1995.

————. *Idioms of the Greek New Testament*. 2d ed. Biblical Languages: Greek, vol. 2. Sheffield: JSOT Press, 1994.

————. "In Defense of Verbal Aspect." In *Biblical Greek Language and Linguistics: Open Questions in Current Research*, ed. Stanley E. Porter and D. A. Carson, 26-45. Sheffield: JSOT Press, 1993.

————. "Studying Ancient Languages From a Modern Linguistic Perspective: Essential Terms and Terminology." *Filología Neotestamentaria* 2 (1989): 147-72.

————. *Verbal Aspect in the Greek of the New Testament, with Reference to Tense and Mood*. Studies in Biblical Greek, ed. D. A. Carson, vol. 1. New York: Peter Lang, 1989.

————, and D. A. Carson, eds. *Biblical Greek Language and Linguistics: Open Questions in Current Research*. Journal for the Study of the New Testament Supplement Series, ed. Stanley E. Porter, vol. 80. Sheffield: JSOT Press, 1993.

————, and D. A. Carson, eds. *Discourse Analysis and Other Topics in Biblical Greek*. Journal for the Study of the New Testament Supplement Series, ed. Stanley E. Porter, vol. 113. Sheffield: Sheffield Academic Press, 1995.

Powell, Charles Edward. "The Semantic Relationship Between the Protasis and the Apodosis of New Testament Conditional Constructions." Ph.D. diss., Dallas Theological Seminary, 2000.

Poythress, Vern S. "Analyzing a Biblical Text: Some Important Linguistic Distinctions." *Scottish Journal of Theology* 32 (1979): 113-37.

Pullum, Geoffrey K., and William A. Ladusaw. *Phonetic Symbol Guide*. 2d ed. Chicago: University of Chicago Press, 1996.

Radford, Andrew. *Transformational Syntax*. Cambridge: Cambridge University Press, 1981.

Ralli, Angela. "On the Morphological Status of Inflectional Features: Evidence From Modern Greek." In *Themes in Greek Linguistics II*, ed. Brian D. Joseph, Geoffrey C. Horrocks, and Irene Philippaki-Warburton, 51-74. Amsterdam: John Benjamins Publishing Company, 1998.

Reed, Jeffrey T. *A Discourse Analysis of Philippians: Method and Rhetoric in the Debate Over Literary Integrity*. Journal for the Study of the New Testament Supplement Series, ed. Stanley E. Porter, vol. 136. Sheffield: Sheffield Academic Press, 1997.

————. "Identifying Theme in the New Testament: Insights From Discourse Analysis." In *Discourse Analysis and Other Topics in Biblical Greek*, ed. Stanley E. Porter and D. A. Carson, 75-101. Sheffield: Sheffield Academic Press, 1995.

————. "Modern Linguistics and the New Testament: A Basic Guide to Theory, Terminology, and Literature." In *Approaches to New Testament Study*, ed. Stanley E. Porter and David Tombs, 222-65. Sheffield: Sheffield Academic Press, 1995.

Reich, Peter A. "Evidence for a Stratal Boundary from Slips of the Tongue." *Forum Linguisticum* 2 (1977): 119-32.

————. "Unintended Puns." In *The Eleventh LACUS Forum 1984*, ed. Robert A. Hall Jr., 314-22. Columbia, SC: Hornbeam Press, 1985.

Rescher, Nicholas. *The Logic of Commands*. London: Routledge and Kegan Paul, 1966.

Rijksbaron, A. *The Syntax and Semantics of the Verb in Classical Greek: An Introduction*. Amsterdam: J. C. Gieben, 1984.

Risselada, Rodie. *Imperatives and Other Directive Expressions in Latin: A Study in the Pragmatics of a Dead Language*. Amsterdam Studies in Classical Philology, ed. Albert Rijksbaron, Irene J. F. de Jong, and Harm Pinkster, vol. 2. Amsterdam: J. C. Gieben, 1993.

Rivero, Maria Luisa,, and Arhonto Terzi. "Imperatives, V-Movement and Logical Mood." *Journal of Linguistics* 31 (1995): 301-32.

Roberts, Lawrence D. "Relevance As an Explanation of Communication." *Linguistics and Philosophy* 14 (1991): 453-72.

Robertson, A. T. *A Grammar of the Greek New Testament in the Light of Historical Research.* 4th ed. Nashville, TN: Broadman Press, 1934.

———, and W. H. Davis. *A New Short Grammar of the Greek Testament for Students Familiar with the Elements of Greek.* 10th ed. New York: Harper, 1931. Reprint, Grand Rapids: Baker Book House, 1977.

Robertson, Stuart, and Frederic G. Cassidy. *The Development of Modern English.* 2d ed. Englewood Cliffs, NJ: Prentice-Hall, 1954.

Roby, H. J. "The Imperative in St. John 20:17." *Classical Review* 19 (1905): 229.

Rouchota, V. "The Subjunctive in Modern Greek: Dividing the Labour between Semantics and Pragmatics." *Journal of Modern Greek Studies* 12 (1994): 185-201.

Russell, Bertrand. *An Inquiry into Meaning and Truth.* London: George Allen and Unwin, 1940.

Rydbeck, Lars. "What Happened to Greek Grammar after Albert Debrunner?" *New Testament Studies* 21 (1974-75): 424-27.

Salom, A. P. "The Imperatival Use of the Participle in the New Testament." *Australian Biblical Review* 11 (1963): 41-49.

Sampson, Geoffrey. *Schools of Linguistics.* Stanford, CA: Stanford University Press, 1980.

Sanders, E. P. *Jesus and Judaism.* London: SCM Press, 1985

Saussure, Ferdinand de. *Cours de linguistique générale.* Edited by Charles Bally, Albert Sechehaye, and Albert Reidlinger. Lausanne: Librairie Payot and Cⁱᵉ, 1916.

———. *Cours de linguistique générale.* Edited by Charles Bally, Albert Sechehaye, and Albert Reidlinger, 3d ed. Paris: Payot, 1949.

———. *Course in General Linguistics.* Edited by Charles Bally, Albert Sechehaye, and Albert Reidlinger. Translated by Wade Baskin. New York: McGraw-Hill Book Company, 1959.

Schmidt, D. D. *Hellenistic Greek Grammar and Noam Chomsky: Nominalizing Transformations.* Chico, CA: Scholars Press, 1981.

———. "The Study of Hellenistic Greek Grammar in Light of Contemporary Linguistics." *Perspectives in Religious Studies* 11 (1984): 27-38.

Schnackenburg, Rudolf. *Ephesians: A Commentary.* Translated by Helen Heron. Edinburgh: T. & T. Clark, 1991.

Schweikert, H. C. *Early English Plays.* New York: Harcourt, Brace and Company, 1928.

Schwyzer, Eduard. *Griechische Grammatik, ii. Syntax und syntaktische Stilistik.* Edited by Albert Debrunner. Munich: C. H. Beck, 1950.

Scott, James C. *Domination and the Arts of Resistence: Hidden Transcripts.* New Haven, CN: Yale University Press, 1990.

Searle, J. R. *Expression and Meaning: Studies in the Theory of Speech Acts.* Cambridge: Cambridge University Press, 1979.

———. "Indirect Speech Acts." In *Syntax and Semantics,* vol. 3, *Speech Acts,* ed. P. Cole and J. Morgan, 59-82. New York: Academic Press, 1975.

———. *Intentionality: An Essay in the Philosophy of Mind.* Cambridge: Cambridge University Press, 1983.

———. *Speech Acts: An Essay in the Philosophy of Language.* London: Cambridge University Press, 1969.

———. "A Taxonomy of Illocutionary Acts." In *Language Mind and Knowledge,* ed. K. Gunderson, 344-69. Minneapolis: University of Minnesota Press, 1975.

Seaton, R. C. "Prohibition in Greek." *Classical Review* 20 (1906): 438.

Septuaginta. Edited by A. Rahlfs. Stuttgart: Deutsche Bibelgesellschaft, 1979.

Seto, Ken-Ichi. "On Non-Echoic Irony." In *Relevance Theory: Applications and Implications*, ed. Robyn Carston and Seiji Uchida, 239-55. Amsterdam: John Benjamins Publishing Company, 1998.

Sextus Empiricus. *Against the Logicians*. Trans. R. G. Bury. Loeb Classical Library, ed. T. E. Page et al. London: William Heinrmann, 1935.

Shakespeare, William. *The Complete Works of William Shakespeare*. New York: Avenel Books, 1975.

Shannon, Claude E., and Warren Weaver. *The Mathematical Theory of Communication*. Urbana, IL: University of Illinois Press, 1949.

Shields, Kenneth. "The Hittite First Person Singular Imperative Suffix *-lu*." *Journal of Indo European Studies* 11 (1983): 365-72.

Silva, Moisés. *Biblical Words and Their Meaning: An Introduction to Lexical Semantics*. Grand Rapids: Zondervan Publishing House, 1983.

———. *God, Language, and Scripture: Reading the Bible in Light of General Linguistics*. Foundations of Contemporary Interpretation, ed. Moisés Silva, vol. 4. Grand Rapids: Zondervan Publishing House, 1990.

Skeat, Walter W., ed. *The Gospel According to Saint John in Anglo-Saxon and Northumbrian Versions, Synoptically Arranged, with Collations Exhibiting All the Readings of All MSS.* Cambridge: Cambridge University Press, 1878.

Smith, Kevin Gary. "Bible Translation and Relevance Theory: The Translation of Titus." D.Litt. diss., University of Stellenbosch, South Africa, 2000.

Smyth, Herbert Weir. *Greek Grammar*. Revised by G. M. Messing. Cambridge, MA: Harvard University Press, 1956.

Song, Nam Sun. "Metaphor and Metonymy." In *Relevance Theory: Applications and Implications*, ed. Robyn Carston and Seiji Uchida, 87-104. Amsterdam: John Benjamins Publishing Company, 1998.

Song, Seok Choong. Review of *A Modern Course in English Syntax*, by Herman Wekker and Liliane Haegeman. *Word* 37 (1986): 219-26.

Sonnenschein, E. A. "The Perfect Subjunctive, Optative, and Imperative in Greek." *Classical Review* 20 (1906): 155-56.

———. "The Perfect Subjunctive, Optative, and Imperative in Greek—A Reply." *Classical Review* 19 (1905): 439-40.

Spears, Richard A. *NTC's American Idioms Dictionary*. 2d ed. Lincolnwood, IL: National Textbook Company, 1994.

Sperber, Dan, and Deirdre Wilson. "Irony and Relevance: A Reply to Seto, Hamamoto, and Yamanashi." In *Relevance Theory: Applications and Implications*, ed. Robyn Carston and Seiji Uchida, 283-93. Amsterdam: John Benjamins Publishing Company, 1998.

———. *Relevance: Communication and Cognition*. Cambridge, MA: Harvard University Press, 1986.

———. *Relevance: Communication and Cognition*. 2d ed. Oxford: Blackwell, 1995.

Stein, Robert H. *The Synoptic Problem: An Introduction*. Grand Rapids: Baker Book House, 1987.

Stephens, L. "The Origins of Homeric Peculiarity: MH Plus Aorist Imperative." *Transactions of the American Philological Association* 113 (1983): 69-78.

Sullivan, William J. "Four Postulates of Government and Binding Theory." In *The Fifteenth LACUS Forum 1988*, ed. Ruth M. Brend and David G. Lockwood, 57-67. Lake Bluff, IL: Linguistic Association of Canada and the United States, 1989.

Swan, Oscar E. "The Morphophonemics of the Russian Imperative." *Russian Linguistics* 8 (1984): 39-47.

Taber, Charles R. "Exegesis and Linguistics." *The Bible Translator* 20 (1969): 150-53.

Takahashi, Hidemitsu. "English Imperatives and Speaker Commitment." *Language Sciences* 16 (1994): 371-85.

Talbert, Charles H. *Ephesians and Colossians*. Paideia Commentaries on the New Testament. Grand Rapids: Baker, 2007.

Terry, Ralph Bruce. *A Discourse Analysis of First Corinthians*. Dallas: Summer Institute of Linguistics, 1995.

Thesaurus Lingua Graecae [CD ROM E. Software database]. Packard Humanities Institute, Los Altos, CA, 1999. [Initial work with CD ROM D]

Thiselton, Anthony C. *The First Epistle to the Corinthians: A Commentary on the Greek Text*. New International Greek Testament Commentary, ed. I Howard Marshall and Donald A. Hagner. Grand Rapids: William B. Eerdmans Publishing Company, 2000.

Thompson, John A. *A Greek Grammar: Accidence and Syntax. For Schools and Colleges*. London: John Murray, 1902.

Thomson, George. *A Manual of Modern Greek*. London: Collet's (Publishers), 1967.

Thumb, Albert. *Handbook of the Modern Greek Vernacular: Grammar, Texts, Glossary*. Translated by S. Angus. Edinburgh: T. & T. Clark, 1912.

Traugott, Elizabeth Closs, and Mary Louise Pratt. *Linguistics for Students of Literature*. New York: Harcourt Brace Jovanovich, 1980.

Turner, Nigel. *Syntax*. Vol 3, *A Grammar of New Testament Greek*, ed. James Hope Moulton. Edinburgh: T. & T. Clark, 1963.

Uchida, Seiji. "Text and Relevance." In *Relevance Theory: Applications and Implications*, ed. Robyn Carston and Seiji Uchida, 162-78. Amsterdam: John Benjamins Publishing Company, 1998.

Vanhoozer, Kevin J. "From Speech Acts to Scripture Acts: The Covenant of Discourse and the Discourse of Covenant." In *After Pentecost: Language and Biblical Interpretation*. Scripture and Hermeneutics Series, vol. 2, ed. Craig, Bartholomew, Colin Green, and Karl Möller, 1-49. Grand Rapids: Zondervan Publishing House, 2001.

Voelz, James W. *Fundamental Greek Grammar*. St. Louis, MO: Concordia Publishing House, 1986.

———. "The Use of the Present and Aorist Imperatives and Prohibitions in the New Testament." Ph.D. diss., University of Cambridge, 1977.

Wakker, Gerry. *Conditions and Conditionals: An Investigation of Ancient Greek*. Amsterdam Studies in Classical Philology, ed. Albert Rijksbaron, Irene J. F. de Jong, and Harm Pinkster, vol. 3. Amsterdam: J. C. Gieben, 1994.

Wallace, Daniel B. "The Article with Multiple Substantives Connected by Kaí in the New Testament: Semantics and Significance." Ph.D. diss., Dallas Theological Seminary, 1995.

———. *Granville Sharp's Canon and Its Kin: Semantics and Significance*. Studies in Biblical Greek, ed. D. A. Carson, vol. 14. New York: Peter Lang, 2009.

———. *Greek Grammar beyond the Basics: An Exegetical Syntax of the New Testament*. Grand Rapids: Zondervan Publishing House, 1996.

———. " 'Οργίζεσθε in Ephesians 4:26: Command or Condition?" *Criswell Theological Review* 3 (1989): 353-72.

Warfel, Harry R. *Who Killed Grammar?* Gainesville, FL: University of Florida Press, 1952.

Wendland, Ernst R. "On the Relevance of 'Relevance Theory' for Bible Translation." *The Bible Translator* 47 (1996): 126-37.

Werth, Paul. "The Concept of 'Relevance' in Conversational Analysis." In *Conversation and Discourse: Structure and Interpretation*, ed. Paul Werth, 129-54. New York: St. Martin's Press, 1981.

White, Hugh C., ed. *Semeia* 41 (1988): 1-178 [all articles within the issues; volume entitled: *Speech Act Theory and Biblical Criticism*].

Whitelaw, R. "On Μή Prohibitive with Future Indicative." *Classical Review* 2 (1888): 322-23.

Williams, Kenneth. "Extending the Usefulness of Informants." *Notes on Translation* 22 (1966): 18.

Wilson, Andrew. "The Pragmatics of Politeness and Pauline Epistolography: A Case Study of the Letter to Philemon." *Journal for the Study of the New Testament* 48 (1992): 107-19.

Wilson, Deirdre, and Dan Sperber. "Mood and the Analysis of Non-Declarative Sentences." In *Human Agency: Language, Duty and Value*, ed. J. Dancy, J. Moravcsik, and C. Taylor, 77-101. Stanford, CA: Stanford University Press, 1988.

————. "On Grice's Theory of Conversation." In *Conversation and Discourse: Structure and Interpretation*, ed. Paul Werth, 155-78. New York: St. Martin's Press, 1981.

————. "An Outline of Relevance Theory." *Notes on Linguistics* 39 (1987): 5-24.

Winer, G. B. *A Treatise on the Grammar of New Testament Greek*. Translated by W. F. Moulton. 3d rev. ed. Edinburgh: T. & T. Clark: 1882. Reprint, Eugene, OR: Wipf and Stock Publishers, 1997.

Witherington, Ben, III. *The Acts of the Apostles: A Socio-Rhetorical Commentary*. Grand Rapids: William B. Eerdmans Publishing Company, 1998.

————. *The Letters to Philemon, the Colossians, and the Ephesians: A Socio-Rhetorical Commentary on the Captivity Epistles*. Grand Rapids: William B. Eerdmans Publishing Company, 2007.

Wonneberger, Reinhard. "Greek Syntax: A New Approach." *Literary and Linguistic Computing* 2 (1987): 71-79.

Wright, Joseph. *Comparative Grammar of the Greek Language*. London: Henry Frowde, 1912.

Yamanashi, Masa-Aki. "Some Issues in the Treatment of Irony and Related Tropes." In *Relevance Theory: Applications and Implications*, ed. Robyn Carston and Seiji Uchida, 271-81. Amsterdam: John Benjamins Publishing Company, 1998.

Young, Richard A. "A Classification of Conditional Sentences Based on Speech Act Theory." *Grace Theological Journal* 10 (1989): 29-49.

————. *Intermediate New Testament Greek: A Linguistic and Exegetical Approach*. Nashville, TN: Broadman and Holman Publishers, 1994.

Zerwick, Maximilian. *Biblical Greek Illustrated by Examples*. Translated by Joseph Smith. Scripta Pontificii Instituti Bibilici, vol. 114. Rome: Editrice Pontificio Istituto Biblico, 1963.

Zhang, Shi. "The Status of Imperatives in Theories of Grammar." Ph.D. diss., University of Arizona, 1990.

Zuber, Richard. *Non-Declarative Sentences*. Pragmatics and Beyond, ed. Hubert Cuyckens, Herman Parret, and Jef Verschueren, vol 4:2. Amsterdam: John Benjamins Publishing Company, 1983.

Ancient Reference Index

Scripture

Jonah
   3:7   269

Zephaniah
   3:16   90

Tobit
   4:14   90

Sirach
   14:14   269

Susanna
   1:60   90

1 Maccabees
   10:43   90

2 Maccabees
   6:17   90
   7:42   90
   9:20   90
   11:21   90
   11:28   90
   11:33   90

3 Maccabees
   7:9   90

4 Maccabees
   1:35   90

New Testament

Matthew
   1–2   159
   1–5   68
   1:8   261
   2:13   156
   2:16   220
   2:20   77, 216
   3:2   215, 217, 262, 263, 264
   3:3   158, 349
   3:8   216, 354
   3:15   261
   4:3   161, 257, 263, 354
   4:6   161, 263, 354
   4:10   157, 261

Matthew (continued)
   4:17   158, 192, 263, 350
   5–7   159
   5:12   91, 133, 136, 139, 263, 354
   5:16   269, 270, 282
   5:17   9, 164
   5:20   165
   5:24   216, 263
   5:25   354
   5:26   165
   5:29-30 257
   5:29   216
   5:30   351
   5:31   274, 282
   5:37   269, 282
   5:40   162
   5:41   253
   5:42   136, 140, 145, 354
   5:44-45 363
   5:44   137, 354
   5:48   9
   6   283
   6:3   76, 152, 153, 155, 269, 282, 284, 298
   6:5   9
   6:7-15   354
   6:9-10   242, 282
   6:9-12   244
   6:9-13   78, 141, 145, 208, 242
   6:9   169, 185 243, 269, 282
   6:10   267, 269, 282, 283
   6:11   145, 242
   6:12   243
   6:13   243
   6:14   167
   6:18   165
   6:19-20 354
   6:25-34 354
   6:31   162, 354
   6:33   294, 300, 302, 357, 358, 365
   6:34   162
   7   353
   7:1   354, 365
   7:2   353
   7:4-5   354
   7:5   298, 300, 302, 358, 359, 365

Matthew (continued)

7:6	76
7:7	80, 151, 152, 293, 294, 295, 298, 354, 358, 359, 365
7:12	252, 354
7:13	185
7:17	182
7:22	237
7:23	354
8:3	247, 349
8:4	191, 349, 351
8:8	151, 152, 172, 297, 302, 359, 361
8:9	84, 137, 354
8:13	269, 282, 283, 286
8:21-22	354
8:26	161
8:31-32	141, 144, 145, 148, 149, 181, 201, 251
8:31	234, 235, 351
8:32	78, 181, 184, 253
9:5-6	189
9:5	189, 349, 351, 353, 354
9:9	349
9:18	166, 360
9:24	178, 355
9:29	269, 281, 282, 283
9:30	227, 228, 270, 282, 286
9:38	355
10–13	68
10:6-8	261
10:6	261
10:7-8	188
10:7	355
10:8	355
10:9-10	163
10:11	165, 166, 261, 349
10:12	261, 355
10:13	148, 208, 255, 256, 261, 269
10:14	184, 349
10:17	216, 351
10:27	156, 172, 173
10:28	163, 247, 257, 355
10:31	247, 263, 355
11:2-4	242
11:4	161, 216, 355
11:15	275
11:29	295, 298, 358, 360

Matthew (continued)

12:13	263, 349
13:9	275, 349
13:18	179
13:30	261
13:36	239, 261
13:43	275
14:7	167, 171
14:13	181
14:15	349
14:16	349
14:18	182, 184, 355
14:23	182
14:27	27, 247, 263, 351
14:36	245
15:4	274, 279, 282, 351
15:10	351
15:15	183
15:22-24	183
15:23	234
15:25	183
15:28	269, 278, 282, 283, 351
16:6	349
16:23	351
16:24	274, 279, 282, 349
17:5	349
17:7	161, 247, 263
17:15	351
17:17	349
17:18	161
17:20	355
17:27	360
18:8	351
18:9	351
18:15-18	180
18:15	180, 355
18:17	268, 269, 271, 282
18:26	361
18:29	234, 361
19:6	274, 279, 282, 351
19:12	253, 274, 282
19:14	349
19:18	9
19:19	349
19:21	350, 362
19:27	350
19:29	350
20:21	351
20:26	186

Matthew (continued)

20:30-31	350
20:32	182, 184
21:2	298, 350, 358, 361, 362, 373
21:3	175
21:6	177
21:21	167, 351
21:23	159
21:24	168, 353, 363
21:33	189
22:3	188
22:5	188
22:8-9	253
22:9	355
22:12	90
22:17	159
22:19	350
22:21	350
22:34-35	181
22:34	90
22:44	350
23:1-36	353
23:2-5	353
23:3	353
23:23	255
23:26	355
23:32	148, 180, 256
24:3	239, 351
24:4	81, 350
24:6	164, 351
24:13	172, 175
24:15-16	279
24:15-18	285
24:15	273, 282
24:16	274, 282
24:17-18	279, 350
24:17	76, 155, 274, 282, 284
24:18	155, 274, 282, 284, 354
24:20	351
24:23	165
24:32	350
24:33	350
24:42	351
24:43	355
24:44	355
25:13	350
25:14-30	355
25:14	30, 174
25:20	132

Matthew (continued)

25:21-23	173
25:21	174, 355
25:22	132
25:23	173, 355
25:25	132
25:28	174, 355
25:30	174, 355
26	283
26:10	161
26:18	175, 190, 351, 354, 363
26:26	352
26:27	182
26:35	132
26:36-38	243
26:36-46	243, 244, 245, 283
26:36	352
26:38	352
26:39	141, 145, 180, 208, 237, 243, 245, 270, 279, 282, 283, 350
26:41	190, 350, 352
26:42	142, 145, 180, 208, 2243, 245, 269, 280, 282, 283, 284
26:43	243
26:44	243
26:45-46	243
26:45	179
26:46	351
26:28	352
26:49	81, 133
26:52	355
26:63	168, 177
26:68	350
27:20	170
27:22-23	84, 241, 270, 271, 280, 281, 283
27:22	283, 350
27:23	188, 282, 350, 352
27:29	81, 133, 352
27:39-43	187, 283
27:40	187, 191, 352
27:42-43	241
27:42	186, 277, 279, 282, 283, 284, 288, 293, 296, 301, 368, 352, 361, 367, 368
27:43	277, 279, 282, 352
27:49	352
28:5-6	353

‌‌‌

Acts (continued)		1 Corinthians (continued)	
25:5	269	7:3	274
27:24	247, 263	7:6	230
27:25	262, 263	7:8	230
28:28	263, 269, 301, 302, 367, 368	7:9	273, 274
		7:11	274
		7:12	274
Romans	68	7:15	83, 149, 208, 254, 255, 274
3:4	194, 230, 278	7:17	274
4:8	164	7:18	274
6:1	108	7:20	274
6:11-13	275	7:21	274
6:11-19	230	7:24	274
6:11	194, 216	7:25	230
6:12	79, 216, 270, 275	7:35	230
6:13	76, 138, 216, 253	7:36	78, 148, 149, 254, 255, 274
7	46	7:40	230
7:7	9	8:9	81
8:15	245, 246	10:7	76
11:9-10	272, 273, 278	10:10	76
11:9	268	10:12	274
11:20	264	10:18	81
11:22	132	10:24	274
12:1	218	11:2-16	24
12:2	84, 153, 247, 263	11:6	274
12:14	98	11:20	247
12:15	9, 81, 185	11:28	274
12:21	216	11:34	274
13:1	263, 274	12–16	
13:3	301, 302, 368	13:4	247
13:4	264	14	230
14:3	274	14:1	156, 216, 230
14:5	274	14:2-4	230
14:16	269	14:6-17	230
15:2	274	14:14	274
15:11	272, 273	14:18	230
16:3-16	261	14:26	274
		14:27	274
1 Corinthians		14:28	274
1–7	68	14:29	274
1:31	138, 207, 258, 273	14:30	274
3:10	274	14:34	274
3:18	263, 274	14:35	274
3:21	274	14:37	274
4:1	274	14:40	274
4:16	224	16:2	274
5:7	216	16:10	81
6:9	153	16:11	164
7	230		
7:2	274		

1 Corinthians (continued)
  16:14   269
  16:22   274

2 Corinthians
  1–8   194
  2:3   81
  5:20   143, 145, 156, 194, 224
  6:9   153
  6:17   301, 302, 368, 369
  9–13   194
  10:7   138, 207, 274
  10:11   274
  10:17   258, 274
  12:13   143
  12:16   149, 208, 254, 255, 278,
           293
  13:5   138
  13:11   81, 133, 224, 298, 358,
           369

Galatians
  1–3   194
  1:8-9   194, 229, 277
  4–6   194
  4:6   245, 246
  5:2   133
  5:15   81
  5:16   165
  6:1   139
  6:2   293, 297, 369
  6:4   274, 369
  6:6   274
  6:17   274

Ephesians
  1–3   194
  1:15-23 244
  2:11   194
  3:14-21 244
  4:26   2, 80, 269, 274, 286,
           293, 303-306
  4:27   76
  4:28   258
  4:29   269
  4:31   228, 269
  5:3   269
  5:5   89
  5:6   269

Ephesians (continued)
  5:14   151, 293, 294, 297, 357,
           369
  5:15   81
  5:18   79
  5:33   9, 269

Philippians 68
  1:9-11   244
  1:27   216
  2:5   263
  2:14   216
  2:18   81, 133
  3:1   81, 133
  3:2   81, 201, 216
  3:16   185
  3:17   216, 222
  4:3   225
  4:4   81, 133
  4:5   269
  4:6   269
  4:9   369
  4:21   261

Colossians
  1–2   194
  1:9-12   244
  2:6   194
  2:8   81
  2:16   269
  2:18   269
  2:21   76
  3:12   84
  3:15   269
  3:16   268, 269

1 Thessalonians 68, 211
  1:2-5   244
  3:11-12 244
  4   194
  4:18   216
  5   195
  5:11   216, 224
  5:13   216
  5:14   225
  5:16   81, 133, 139
  5:19   154
  5:25   260

Other Ancient References

Apollonius Dyscolus
3.16	86
3.19	85
3.31	85
3.72	85
3.90	85
3.140	85
4.48	85

Aristotle
Politics
18	85

Hermogenes
Concerning Types of Style
1.7.100	85

Homer
Iliad
4.410	164, 165
5.684	165
9.33	165
9.552	165
15.115	165
18.134	164, 165
23.407	165
24.568	165
24.779	165

Odyssey
3..55	165
11.251	165
15.263	165
24.248	164, 165

Ignatius
Ephesians
21.2	89

Magnesians
15	89

Philadelphians
11.2	89

Polycarp
8.3	89

Oxyrhynchus Papyri
744.4	154
2195.2.6	90

Plato
Apology
20E	92
21A	92

Studies in Biblical Greek

This series of monographs is designed to promote and publish the latest research into biblical Greek (Old and New Testaments). The series does not assume that biblical Greek is a distinct dialect within the larger world of *koine*, but focuses on these corpora because it recognizes the particular interest they generate. Research into the broader evidence of the period, including epigraphical and inscriptional materials, is welcome in the series, provided the results are cast in terms of their bearing on biblical Greek. Primarily, however, the series is devoted to fresh philological, syntactical, text-critical, and linguistic study of the Greek of the biblical books, with the subsidiary aim of displaying the contribution of such study to accurate exegesis.

For additional information about this series or for the submission of manuscripts, please contact:

Peter Lang Publishing, Inc.
P.O. Box 1246
Bel Air, MD 21014-1246

To order other books in this series, please contact our Customer Service Department:

(800) 770-LANG (within the U.S.)
(212) 647-7706 (outside the U.S.)
(212) 647-7707 FAX

Or browse online by series at:

www.peterlang.com